THE STATE OF THE ART OF
ENTREPRENEURSHIP

THE STATE OF THE ART OF
ENTREPRENEURSHIP

Edited by

Donald L. Sexton
The Ohio State University

John D. Kasarda
University of North Carolina, Chapel Hill

PWS-KENT PUBLISHING COMPANY
Boston

PWS–KENT
Publishing Company

Sponsoring Editor: Rolf A. Janke
Production Editor: Pam Rockwell
Production Service: Hockett Editorial Service
Manufacturing Coordinator: Lisa Flanagan
Interior Designer: Rita Naughton
Cover Designer: Pam Rockwell
Typesetter: Graphic Sciences Corporation
Printer/Binder: Maple-Vail Book Manufacturing Group

PWS-KENT Publishing Company is a division of Wadsworth, Inc.

Printed in the United States of America
1 2 3 4 5 6 7 8 9 — 96 95 94 93 92

Library of Congress Cataloging-in-Publication Data

The State of the art of Entrepreneurship / edited by Donald L. Sexton and John D. Kasarda.
    p.   cm.
  Includes bibliographical references and index.
  ISBN 0-534-92868-4
  1. Entrepreneurship. 2. New business enterprises — Management.
  3. Venture capital. I. Sexton, Donald L. II. Kasarda, John D.
  HB615.S725 1991
  658.4'21 — dc20   91-39075
                                               CIP

This book is dedicated
to our benefactors,
Frank Hawkins Kenan and William H. Davis ;
to our wives,
Mary Ann Kasarda and Carol Ann Sexton ;
and in the memory of
William C. Davis, 1929–1991.

Contents

Figures and Tables   x

Forewords   xiii

Preface   xvii

About the Contributors, Sponsors, and Editors   xxii

   1   INTRODUCTION *John D. Kasarda*   1

Part 1   ENTREPRENEURSHIP EDUCATION

   2   ENTREPRENEURSHIP EDUCATION RESEARCH :
EXPERIENCE AND CHALLENGE *Zenas Block
and Stephen A. Stumpf*   17

Part 2   ENTREPRENEURSHIP AND ECONOMIC DEVELOPMENT

   3   THE SOCIAL AND ECONOMIC IMPACT OF ENTREPRENEURSHIP
Zoltan J. Acs and David B. Audretsch   45

4   THE GOVERNMENT AS ENTREPRENEUR : INDUSTRIAL DEVELOPMENT
    AND THE CREATION OF NEW VENTURES   *Jon P. Goodman,*
    James W. Meany, and Larry E. Pate   68

Part 3   ENTREPRENEURSHIP RESEARCH :
LINKAGES AND METHODOLOGY

5   ENTREPRENEURSHIP THROUGH AN ETHICAL LENS : DILEMMAS AND ISSUES
    FOR RESEARCH AND PRACTICE   *J. Gregory Dees*
    and Jennifer A. Starr   89

6   RESEARCH LINKAGES BETWEEN ENTREPRENEURSHIP AND STRATEGIC
    MANAGEMENT OR GENERAL MANAGEMENT   *Diana L. Day*   117

7   MARKETING AND ENTREPRENEURSHIP : THE STATE OF THE ART
    Gerald E. Hills and Raymond W. LaForge   164

8   METHODS IN OUR MADNESS ? TRENDS IN ENTREPRENEURSHIP RESEARCH
    Howard E. Aldrich   191

9   LONGITUDINAL METHODS FOR STUDYING THE PROCESS
    OF ENTREPRENEURSHIP   *Andrew H. Van de Ven*   214

10   RESEARCH APPLICATIONS OF THE SMALL BUSINESS DATA BASE
    OF THE U.S. SMALL BUSINESS ADMINISTRATION   *Bruce A. Kirchhoff*
    and Bruce D. Phillips   243

11   PREDICTING NEW-FIRM BIRTHS : INTERACTIONS OF ORGANIZATIONAL
    AND HUMAN POPULATIONS   *Paul D. Reynolds*   268

Part 4   ENTREPRENEURIAL FIRM GROWTH AND FINANCING

12   ENTREPRENEURS, PROCESSES OF FOUNDING, AND NEW-FIRM
    PERFORMANCE   *Arnold C. Cooper and F. Javier Gimeno Gascón*   301

13   STRATEGIES AND ENVIRONMENTS OF HIGH-GROWTH FIRMS   *Frank Hoy,*
    Patricia P. McDougall, and Derrick E. Dsouza   341

14   CREATING AND MAINTAINING HIGH-PERFORMANCE TEAMS
    Dennis P. Slevin and Jeffrey G. Covin   358

15   FINANCING THE NEW VENTURE : A REPORT ON RECENT RESEARCH
    David J. Brophy   387

16   VENTURE CAPITAL : THE DECADE AHEAD   *Jeffry A. Timmons*
    and Harry J. Sapienza   402

17   VENTURE CAPITAL RETURNS IN THE 1980s   *William D. Bygrave*   438

18   THE INFORMAL VENTURE CAPITAL MARKET IN THE 1990s   *John Freear*
    and William E. Wetzel, Jr.   462

19 PROGRESS IN RESEARCH ON CORPORATE VENTURING *S. Venkataraman, Ian C. MacMillan, and Rita Gunther McGrath* 487

Part 5 **INTERNATIONAL ENTREPRENEURSHIP AND RESEARCH NEEDS FOR THE 1990s**

20 JOINT VENTURES : RESEARCH BASE AND USE IN INTERNATIONAL MARKETS *Robert D. Hisrich* 520

21 ENTREPRENEURSHIP EDUCATION AND RESEARCH IN EUROPE *Robert H. Brockhaus, Sr.* 560

22 RESEARCH ISSUES IN ENTREPRENEURSHIP *Neil C. Churchill* 579

INDEX 597

Figures and Tables

FIGURES

2–1   Criteria for Evaluating the Effectiveness of Entrepreneurship Education

2–2   Relative Size of Entrepreneurship Audiences

3–1   Percent of Sales Contributed by Small Manufacturing Firms, 1976–1986

3–2   Sales Distribution of Firms in Czechoslovakian Manufacturing

3–3   Composition Percent of the National Income in Czechoslovakia, 1948–1985

5–1   Four Dimensions of Ethics Research

6–1   Framework for Identifying Research Linkages between Entrepreneurship and Strategic and General Management

7–1   Marketing Management and Entrepreneurship

7–2   Marketing Strategy Conceptualization

9–1   Minnesota Innovation Research Program

9–2   Graphs of Monthly Expanding-Contracting Actions with Positive-Negative Outcomes in Three Innovations

13–1   Proposed Conceptual Framework for High-Growth Strategies

14–1   The Environment Is Changing

14–2   A Research Model of Project Team Performance

16–1   USA Venture Capital : Number of Venture Capital Firms and Average Size of Firm, 1980–1989

16–2 USA Venture Capital : Annual Capital Commitments and Annual Disbursements, 1980–1989

16–3 USA Venture Capital Source Distribution, 1978 and 1989

16–4 Worldwide Venture Capital : Growth in VC Pool and Annual Capital Commitments

16–5 Worldwide Venture Capital : Number of VC Firms and Average Size of VC Firm

16–6 Sources of VC Funding : Europe 1989 and JAFCO 1988

16–7 U.S. Capital under Management by Firm Type, 1978 and 1989

16–8 Largest 95 VC Firms Control the Majority of Capital

16–9 Smallest 205 VC Firms Control Less than 3 Percent of Capital

16–10 U.S. Investment by Industry Sector, 1978–1980 and 1987–1989

16–11 Investment by Industry Sector, Europe 1989 and Canada 1989

16–12 Determinants of Venture Capital Profitability

16–13 Worldwide Average Investment Size, Early Stage vs. LBO

16–14 U.S. Investment by Stage, 1980 and 1989

16–15 Investment by Stage, Europe 1989 and Australia 1988

16–16 U.S. Proportion of Number of Investments, New vs. Follow-on, 1979 and 1989

16–17 Europe & Canada Proportion of Number of Investments : New vs. Follow-on, 1989

17–1 Overall Rates of Return

17–2 Median Rates of Return by Calendar Year

17–3 Median Rates of Return by Age of Fund

17–4 Distribution of Returns : All 3- and 5-Year-Old Funds

17–5 Venture Capital Industry : A Resource Exchange Model

17–6 Number of IPOs and Acquisitions : Venture-Capital-Backed Companies

17–7 Difference between 5-Year Returns on Small Company and S&P 500 Stocks

17–8 Factors Influencing the Flows of Venture Capital

■ ■ ■ ■ ■ ■ ■

TABLES

2–1 Sample Questions to Assess Aspects of Entrepreneurial Education

2–2 Objectives and the Audiences for Entrepreneurship Education

2–3 Objectives and Pedagogical Preferences for Entrepreneurship Education

3–1 The Percentage Share of Employees in Small Manufacturing Firms

3–2 The Share of Manufacturing Establishments by Firm Size

5–1 Illustrative Ethical Virtues and Values

5–2 Selected Ethical Dilemmas of Entrepreneurial Management

7–1 Market Acceptance Testing : Extent of Applicability to New Small Business Ventures

7–2 Entry Strategy Propositions

7–3 Growth Strategy Propositions

7–4 Marketing Mix Propositions

8–1 Description of Research Methodologies Used by Churchill and Lewis (1986)

8–2 Research Methods Used in Entrepreneurship Articles, 1981–1990

8–3 Scope of Research : All 1985–1990 Articles

8–4 Research Design and Analytic Methods Used for Survey and Public Data Base Studies, 1985–1990

9–1 Research Assumptions in Theories of Change and Equilibrium

9–2 A Comparison of the Conventional Wisdom and MIRP Observations

9–3 Example of Innovation Incidents in Qualitative Data File for One MIRP Study

9–4   Illustration of Coding Tracks on Core MIRP Dimensions
9–5   Partial Bit-Map of Innovation Incidents in One MIRP Study
10–1 A Comparison of Comparative Static and Dynamic Methodologies Net Change In Employment Attributable to Each Size Class : 1976–1980
10–2 Percentage of Jobs Created in the United States by Firms with Fewer than 100 Employees, 1969–1986
10–3 Employment Dynamics by Firm Size, 1976–1984
10–4 Small- and Large-Business-Dominated and Indeterminate Industries' Share of Total Employment, 1981–1987 (Percent)
11–1 Estimate of Number of U.S. Businesses : 1986
11–2 U.S. Business/Population Ratios : 1976–1986
11–3 U.S. Establishment and Small-Firm Birth and Death Rates : 1976–1986
11–4 Regression Model Prediction of New-Firm Births : 1982–1984
17–1 Venture Capital : Compound Annual Rates of Return
18–1 Rounds Invested in NTBFs
18–2 Total Private Investments Raised per Stage of Financing
19–1 Framework for the Study of Corporate Venturing
20–1 Strategic Alternatives
20–2 Significant Mergers and Acquisitions in 1989
20–3 Business Enterprise — Mergers and Acquisitions
20–4 U.S. Imports and Exports by Country or Region (in millions of dollars)
20–5 Number of Soviet and East European Investments in the West by Country, October 1987
20–6 Rules Governing the Establishment of Joint Ventures in Eastern Europe
20–7 Hungarian/U.S. Joint Ventures Operating in June 1989

Forewords

There is an economic revolution going on in America that is more profound than the Industrial Revolution and that will have a greater impact on our children's children than the Industrial Revolution had several generations ago — namely, the entrepreneurial revolution.

The entrepreneurial movement is more important than most Americans realize. During the 1980–1988 period, 17 million new jobs were created in the United States. Yet during the same period the Fortune 500 firms lost 3.5 million jobs. The trend continues today. The number of new jobs last year was only 2 million, and these jobs were created by a few fast growing firms. Clearly, if we ever put a damper on entrepreneurial activity in the United States, we will be in real trouble. If it weren't for the entrepreneurs, we would be in a depression that would make 1929 seem like a "boom." If we had continued to depend on large corporations as the source of new jobs the black Monday of a couple of years ago would have become a black Tuesday and Wednesday and Thursday and would still be going on. It is only the entrepreneurs who are running these new, fast-growing businesses who have made the difference between "Boom" and "Bust."

In the United States there are only 1.4 million firms that have grown and are expected to continue to grow 15 percent per year. Furthermore, these companies are purchasing 44 percent of all business products. The 8,000 large companies purchase another 48 percent, leaving the remaining nearly 18 million small companies in America purchasing only 8 percent of the business gross national product. A relatively small number of firms are growing and creating jobs.

Entrepreneurs are not the norm. They are a different breed of people, with unique likes and dislikes. At a recent *Inc.* 500 conference, an entrepreneur said there were three things entrepreneurs did not like: people making passes at their spouses, people trying to steal their companies, and people calling them small businesses.

It's hard to believe that fast-growing companies were ever small, since they are founded by people of great vision. The entrepreneur's characteristics are more like those of large company founders than small business owners. Perhaps because of this, they live in an economic no man's land: they are too large to be called "small," and too small to be called "large." Government programs have tended to treat all new businesses as a homogeneous group. However, politicians must realize that entrepreneurs and small businesses are not necessarily the same entities, and that they need different forms of assistance. Money spent to help small businesses does not necessarily address the problems of rapid-growth firms.

Why do people become entrepreneurs? Why do they do what they do? Why do they live under the stress and pressures of rapid growth, and do so for so many hours each day, week-in and week-out. The real reason is that these individuals want the freedom to explore, to discover, to be their own person. They want to relish the feeling of freedom.

There is great hope for the entrepreneurial movement. Yet as educators, we must ask ourselves, are we really doing the right things? Are we preparing students to live in the world today or in the world that was — the world of corporate America? Unfortunately, too many colleges teach *that which was* and *not even that which is*, let alone *what will be*.

The entrepreneurial revolution, both in business and in academia, is inaugurating an era of dynamic changes. Long live the revolution!

Wilson L. Harrell
Former Publisher of *Inc.* Magazine

The two major types of criticism of management education in American colleges, according to the Porter and McKibbin report on management education and development, are related to insufficient emphasis on generating vision in students and insufficient emphasis on integration across functional areas. Entrepreneurship encompasses vision and integration. Entrepreneurs (the self-employed) need a vision of their ventures and an understanding of all functional business areas. The vision of the entrepreneur involves controlling one's destiny, enjoying self-direction, being able to speak out, being able to establish your ethics, and not being beholden to the politics within the corporation or the government. And, while an understanding of the functional aspects of business is important, it is not enough. Only practice provides the opportunity to become self-reliant and independent. We see the Porter-McKibbin report as an important document, long awaited but well worth the wait.

Entrepreneurship has been the wave of the past, is certainly the wave of the present, and will continue to be the wave of the future. Universities and teachers, if they are to be part of the thrust into the 20th century, must broaden their vision from public corporate America to the rapid-growing emerging private businesses that are the major contributors to growth in jobs and economic development in the United States.

Students must be made aware that life does not begin at an entry-level job in a large publicly owned organization. There is another alternative, and students need to be exposed to the benefits as well as the problems of self-employment. At the same time, they must also learn that while being an entrepreneur is not easy, it is not "too tough" to do. Finally, entrepreneurship should be incorporated into each class within the business curriculum. Why can't new product introductions or market expansions be included in marketing classes, or financing growth be stressed in finance classes ? And shouldn't the management of growth be just as important as managing the status quo ? Must all management look and be the same ? Can initiative and structuring, and making the right decisions and implementing them, be taught under the guise of management education and development ? We believe the answer is *yes*, but that this is not how subjects are currently being presented. The Porter-McKibbin report seems to agree.

Research should be directed to the profession, including educators, students and practitioners. The impact of business school research on the practice of business has not "been much," according to Porter and McKibbin. Perhaps it is time to recognize that entrepreneurship depends on the movement of information from academics to entrepreneurs and vice versa. As entrepreneurs who are both receivers and transmitters of information, we have a responsibility to do our part to make sure that, as Sexton and Kasarda assert, entrepreneurship education thrusts, rather than drifts, into the 21st century.

The Coleman Foundation and the Fannie May Candies Corporation have embarked on a set of actions designed to increase the awareness of entrepreneurship as a vocational choice. Others are doing the same thing, but as Mae West once stated, "Too much of a good thing can be wonderful." Towards this end, Jean D. Thorne, Chairman of Fannie May Candies, and I have spoken to entrepreneurship classes at numerous colleges and high schools, and the Coleman Foundation has endowed chairs in entrepreneurship at five universities. A number of other entrepreneurship initiatives have been supported at other institutions. The Coleman Foundation, through its $12.5 million in endowments and funding for entrepreneurship programs, has demonstrated its support to this very important area. Their message to students is : control your own destiny, take the risk, and receive the reward.

We do not believe that entrepreneurship awareness education is a passing phenomenon. Our concerns are that too few among us are aware of the rewards and benefits of entrepreneurship. We look to our scholars to communicate entrepreneurship beyond the academy, while entrepreneurs communicate it beyond the business world. The partnership will indeed be intriguing.

John E. Hughes

Vice-Chairman (former CEO) of Fannie May Candies
President of the Coleman Foundation, Inc.

Preface

The entrepreneurial revolution that is currently under way will have a greater impact on the future economic growth of the United States than any other event in our nation's history. As we learn more about the relatively small number of emerging firms that are contributing to the growth in jobs and economic development, the importance and enormity of the field are becoming more and more apparent. Academicians and practitioners alike need to recognize the breadth and nature of the research which will guide us as we seek to promote the awareness, the teaching, and the understanding of the field of entrepreneurship. This was the consensus of a state-of-the-art research conference at the Center for Private Enterprise and Entrepreneurship at Baylor University in 1981; a second conference five years later at the Institute for Constructive Capitalism at the University of Texas; and a third conference, from which this book was developed, at the Kenan Institute of Private Enterprise at the University of North Carolina in 1990.

In 1980, the concerns of researchers in the field were: What do we know about entrepreneurs and the process of venture initiation? What issues should we clarify in order to develop curricula and public policy? What directions should we pursue in future academic inquiry about entrepreneurship? What are the gaps in our knowledge, and what types of research will be most effective and useful in the future ? The conclusions at that initial meeting in 1981 were that the study of entrepreneurship had more important underpinnings than just the satisfaction of intellectual curiosity, that little was known about the process, and that much of the putative knowledge of the field could not pass the test of serious inquiry. Other conclusions were that the environment for entrepreneurship should occupy a position of importance in public policy, and that innovation and venture initiation were not limited to small businesses. The general consensus was that we lacked a clear educational agenda, and that research and education in entrepreneurship were in the early stages of development.

The second conference in 1985 showed that while academic interest in the field had undergone explosive growth, much more work needed to be done. The concerns at this conference were related to whether or not our ability to analyze, synthesize, and explain causal relationships would stymie the growth of the field ; the uneven progress of research ; the need for convergent theories to provide a broader understanding of the field ; and the need to link theory with practice by developing research that could lead to practical applications in both the private and public sectors.

The third conference in 1991, and the one on which this book is based, provided an opportunity to look back over the previous 5- and 10-year periods to examine the current status of the field, to gauge how much it had progressed, and more importantly, to determine how we are to face the new and dynamic challenges of the 1990s. The researchers represented in this volume agree that the field of entrepreneurship is an area of study much larger than had been previously envisioned. They reflect a recognition that broad-based research methodologies are applicable and available, and they offer a clearer vision of what research can accomplish in the decade ahead.

The field has matured greatly in the last 10 years. Tremendous strides have been made, and yet many more steps need to be taken. Some of the research topics deemed to be important over the last 10 years are either not as significant as they once were, or they are now included as part of a broader perspective. For example, topics such as the psychological characteristics of entrepreneurs, the social dimensions of entrepreneurship, high-tech businesses, and technology transfer have been incorporated into growth orientations. The small business/entrepreneurship interface has also been more clearly defined. Further, definitional problems have been recognized as being important only for research replication purposes, and *why* an action was taken has replaced concern about *what* was done. Data access continues to be a problem, but large data bases have been developed and are now available, and more are being generated as we recognize that entrepreneurship research must be accessible to the profession — including educators, students, and practitioners.

Trends have emerged which will provide a more focused approach to research in the future. It is now clear that the economic impact of entrepreneurship occurs as the result of a small number of rapidly growing firms. The consensus is that entrepreneurship is broader than the first step of initiating a venture; it is a process of opportunity recognition and pursuit that leads to growth — an event which has become a distinguishing factor between *entrepreneurship* and *small business*. This awareness, combined with the idea that growth is vocational choice, is expected to lead to better developed theories at the strategic management/entrepreneurship interface for thinking about entrepreneurship in a broader context. In addition, the burgeoning approach to entrepreneurship in an international context has created new opportunities for expanding entrepreneurship research beyond national boundaries.

The field has certainly grown, yet some research is done not to expand the body of knowledge nor to add to the development of concepts but to contribute to spurious research only done for promotion and tenure. As Churchill points out in his chapter on research issues, such actions risk alienating the subjects of our research, and expose us to potential ridicule by knowledgeable people in the industry and by researchers in other fields. The study of entrepreneurship has grown to the point where we must accept responsibility for the fact that our efforts not only affect our students and our colleagues but also entrepreneurs and public policy makers.

The entrepreneurial revolution — recent though it is — is not a passing phenomenon but a permanent change in the economic landscape. As academic practitioners we cannot sit idly by and passively observe it, nor can we exert ourselves only halfheartedly. We must, as our research subjects do, fully immerse ourselves in the "flow," with nothing less than a total commitment and a total acceptance of the attendant risks. Anything less is a disservice to our constituents and to ourselves and will contribute to our field drifting, rather than thrusting, into the 21st century.

ACKNOWLEDGMENTS

Books, like entrepreneurial growth, do not just happen. They are the result of a vision combined with the resources to make a dream come true. In this book, the vision was provided by Frank H. Kenan, Jr. and William H. Davis when they endowed the Frank Hawkins Kenan Institute of Private Enterprise at the University of North Carolina and the William H. Davis Chair in the Free Enterprise System at The Ohio State University. Their goals were to enhance the understanding of the private enterprise system and the role of the entrepreneur in economic development. Such is also the purpose of this book — namely, to enhance our understanding of the phenomenon called entrepreneurship by examining the state of the art in order to determine what we know, what we don't know, and what we need to know.

Like a growing new venture, a book takes its nourishment from a team of individuals dedicated to its success. This book started with senior researchers in the field identifying current research needs as well as scholars who were contributing significant solutions to our collective research problems. Many of the senior researchers who began this effort have contributed chapters to this book. Two that have contributed significantly to the field but could not participate in this endeavor due to other commitments are Karl H. Vesper of the University of Washington, who was extolling the virtues of entrepreneurship education before it became popular to do so, and Howard H. Stevenson of Harvard University, who introduced the field to the idea that growth could occur via opportunity recognition and pursuit regardless of the available resources.

The key to the success of an emerging firm is the implementation of plans to achieve the desired objectives. So it is with this volume. Through the tireless efforts of the staff at the Kenan Institute, especially Jean Elia and Pat Zigas, and Kathy Hutton at The Ohio State University, the findings of our contributors were gathered and edited into this volume.

Others were also involved in the opportunity recognition and pursuit process. Dick Thiel, a former adjunct professor of entrepreneurship, now Field Editor with PWS-KENT and Rolf A. Janke, Managing Editor of PWS-KENT Publishing, recognized the benefit of a state-of-the-art book on entrepreneurship and made the preparation and publication of the text an efficient and effective process.

John E. Hughes and Jean Thorne of the Coleman Foundation, in an effort to increase entrepreneurship awareness, enhanced the publication of the text by ensuring that a number of copies will be made available to readers as part of the foundation's entrepreneurship awareness program.

Entrepreneurship recognizes no national boundaries. Brockhaus's chapter on entrepreneurship education and research in Europe was made possible through the cooperation of research scholars throughout the world, particularly:

David B. Audretsch, Wissenschaftszentrum Berlin für Sozialforschung, Germany

Sue Birley, Management School, Imperial College, United Kingdom

Tobie De Coning, University of Stellenbosch, South Africa

Rik Donckels, Universitaire Faculteiten, Sint-Aloysius, Belgium

J. J. D. Havenga, Potchefstroom University, South Africa

Sang-Nyung Huh, Korea Federation of Small Business, Korea

David A. Kirby, Durham University Business School, United Kingdom

Heinz Klandt, Förderkreis Gründungsforschung, Germany

Josef Mugler, Dietmar Roessl, and Hermann Frank, Wirtschaftsuniversität Wien, Institut für Klein-und Mittelbetriebe, Austria

Phillip A. Neck, International Labour Organization, Thailand

Jean-Jacques Obrecht, Gestion Université Lou, France

Barra O'Cinneide, University of Limerick, Ireland

Hans Jobst Pleitner, Schweizerisches Inst. f. gewerbliche, Wirtschaft an der Hochschule St., Switzerland

Yoshio Sato, Keio University, Japan

Krishna Sharma, Punjab University, India

Peter Szermai, National Association of Entrepreneurs, Hungary

Jose M. Veciana, Universitat Autonoma de Barcelona, Spain

Alan J. Williams, The University of Newcastle, Australia

Finally, each of us wishes to thank his co-editor for making this, our first joint venture, an exciting and rewarding effort.

D.L.S.
J.D.K.

About the Contributors, Sponsors, and Editors

THE CONTRIBUTORS

Zoltan J. Acs is Associate Professor of Economics at the University of Baltimore.

Howard E. Aldrich is Professor of Sociology at the University of North Carolina.

David B. Audretsch is a Research Associate at the Wissenschaftszentrum für Sozialforschung, Berlin, Germany.

Zenas Block is Clinical Professor of Management at New York University.

Robert H. Brockhaus, Sr. holds the Coleman/Fannie May Candies Chair in Entrepreneurship at St. Louis University.

David J. Brophy is Associate Professor of Finance at The University of Michigan.

William D. Bygrave is Associate Professor of Entrepreneurship at Babson College.

Neil C. Churchill is the Paul T. Babson Professor of Entrepreneurship at Babson College.

Arnold C. Cooper is the Louis A. Weil Professor of Management at Purdue University.

Jeffrey G. Covin is Associate Professor of Management at Georgia State University.

Diana L. Day is the Ehrenkranz/Greenwall Assistant Professor of Management at the Wharton School, University of Pennsylvania.

J. Gregory Dees is Assistant Professor of Management at Harvard University, Graduate School of Business Administration.

Derrick E. Dsouza is Assistant Professor of Management at North Texas State University.

John Freear is Professor of Accounting and Finance at the University of New Hampshire.

F. Javier Gimeno Gascón is a graduate student at Purdue University.

Jon P. Goodman is Director of the Entrepreneur Program at the University of Southern California.

Gerald E. Hills holds the Denton Thorne Chair in Entrepreneurship at the University of Illinois at Chicago.

Robert D. Hisrich holds the Bovaird Chair of Entrepreneurial Studies at the University of Tulsa.

Frank Hoy is Dean, College of Business Administration, University of Texas at El Paso State University.

Bruce A. Kirchhoff is Director of the Center for Entrepreneurship and Public Policy of the George Rothman Institute for Entrepreneurial Studies at Fairleigh Dickinson University.

Raymond W. LaForge is the Brown Forman Professor of Marketing at the University of Louisville.

Ian C. MacMillan is Director of the Snider Entrepreneurial Center at the Wharton School, University of Pennsylvania.

Patricia P. McDougall is Assistant Professor of Management at Georgia State University.

Rita Gunther McGrath is a doctoral student at the Wharton School, University of Pennsylvania and a Senior Research Associate at its Snider Entrepreneurial Center.

James W. Meany is a graduate student at the University of Southern California.

Larry E. Pate is Research Director of the Entrepreneur Program at the University of Southern California.

Bruce D. Phillips is Director of Data Base Development, Office of Advocacy, U.S. Small Business Administration.

Paul D. Reynolds is Coleman/Fannie May Professor in Entrepreneurship at Marquette University.

Harry J. Sapienza is Assistant Professor of Management at the University of South Carolina.

Dennis P. Slevin is Professor of Business Administration at the University of Pittsburgh.

Jennifer A. Starr is Assistant Professor of Management at Babson College.

Stephen A. Stumpf is Professor of Management at New York University.

Jeffry A. Timmons is the Frederick Hamilton Professor of Free Enterprise at Babson College and also the Class of 1954 Professor at the Harvard Business School.

Andrew H. Van de Ven is the 3M Professor of Human Systems Management in the Carlson School of Management, and Director of the Minnesota Innovation Research Program in the Strategic Management Research Center of the University of Minnesota.

S. Venkataraman is the Nelson Peltz Term Assistant Professor of Management at the Wharton School, University of Pennsylvania.

William E. Wetzel, Jr. is the Forbes Professor of Management at the University of New Hampshire.

━━ ━━ ━━ ━━ ━━ ━━ ━━

THE SPONSORS

William H. Davis Chair in the American Free Enterprise System

The William H. Davis Chair in the American Free Enterprise System was established at The Ohio State University by the late William H. Davis in 1976. Mr. Davis believed that faculty leadership in the College of Business could provide increased understanding of free private enterprise in the American economy, an activity that is the essence of American capitalism. The general activities of the Chair focus on past, present, and future challenges to economic progress in our society. The goal is to make American corporations, both large and small, more understandable, especially to the young people who will ultimately lead these companies, and to others who will assume varied responsibilities in the business community and in our society.

The specific activities of the Chair holder are directed towards research promoting an understanding of the role of the entrepreneur and the process of entrepreneurship in the American economy. The dissemination of this information to both business and nonbusiness students will assist in their awareness of the problems faced, the various roles played, and the process of generating growth in the emerging firm. The Chair holder is also responsible for conducting applied research designed to enhance the effectiveness of growth-oriented emerging firms, which contribute to the economic development of the American economy through the generation of new markets, products, and jobs. In addition, the Chair holder is charged with conducting research to assist policy makers in developing programs designed to promote entrepreneurship and economic development.

The Kenan Institute of Private Enterprise

The Kenan Institute of Private Enterprise, a part of the Business School at the University of North Carolina, Chapel Hill, fosters mutual understanding among people working in business, academia, and government, and encourages cooperative efforts among these communities to strengthen the private enterprise system in the United States and worldwide. The Institute achieves its objectives through research and analysis; education and training; managerial assistance and dissemination of information about private enterprise; and a wide variety of publications, conferences, and workshops.

Six research centers operate within the Kenan Institute, providing research and ongoing forums for interaction: The Center for Competitiveness and Employment Growth; The Center for International Trade and Investment Promotion; The Center for Management Studies; The Center for Manufacturing Excellence; The Financial Services Research Center; and the International Private Enterprise Development Research Center.

The Kenan Institute recently developed a comprehensive set of international initiatives that focus on eastern Europe and southeast Asia, two regions with immense private sector growth potential and of strategic economic and competitive significance for U.S. businesses. In addition to the two international research centers mentioned above, these initiatives include an MBA Enterprise Corps, which places recent MBA graduates from leading U.S. business schools in private enterprises in eastern Europe and southeast Asia to assist in management, production, finance, marketing, and technology transfer.

The Coleman/Fannie May Candies Foundation

Since its formation in 1951 by Mr. and Mrs. J. D. Stetson Coleman, then owners of Fannie May Candies, The Coleman/Fannie May Candies Foundation has sought to improve the quality of life for everyone. As the foundation grew to its maturity in the early 1980s, its members advanced that mission in part through entrepreneurship (self-employment) awareness education. To further this aim, the foundation has given more than $12.5 million, including individual grants of $1 million, to endow Chairs in Entrepreneurship at Beloit College, De Paul University, Marquette University, St. Louis University, and the University of Illinois at Chicago.

In addition, the foundation's funds have supported entrepreneurship initiatives related to elementary and secondary school students, low-income people, minorities, the handicapped, and the incarcerated by teaching self-employment throughout Chicago and midwest schools and centers.

To promote entrepreneurship awareness education, the foundation has also formed and funded the Campus Entrepreneurship Learning Program (CELP) at over 50 schools, and sponsors the Collegiate Entrepreneurs of the Midwest (CEM) and the Association of Collegiate Entrepreneurs (ACE). Jean D. Thorne, Executive Director of the foundation, and John E. Hughes, President, have spoken at over 60 universities, colleges, high schools, and conferences.

The foundation has, to the best of our knowledge, been the single largest contributor to entrepreneurship awareness education in the United States.

The foundation's message is intended to support entrepreneurship in all its facets; the message is: take charge of your own destiny — you take the risk, have the control, and receive the reward.

THE EDITORS

Donald L. Sexton

Dr. Donald L. Sexton is the William H. Davis Professor of American Free Enterprise System in the College of Business at The Ohio State University. Prior to going to Ohio State, he was the Director of the Center for Entrepreneurship and the Caruth Professor of Entrepreneurship in the Hankamer School of Business at Baylor University. While at Baylor, he established entrepreneurship majors at both the undergraduate and graduate level, an Innovation Evaluation Program, and a Venture Assistance Program. He is the senior Entrepreneurship Chair holder in the United States.

Dr. Sexton holds a B.S. in Math and Physics from Wilmington College, and an M.B.A. and Ph.D. from The Ohio State University. Prior to joining academia, he spent 18 years in industry, including 6 years in operations research and 8 years as a turnaround specialist. He managed 4 firms from losses to profitable operations.

He has co-authored or co-edited seven books in entrepreneurship, two of which are related to the state of the art in entrepreneurship research. They are the *Encyclopedia of Entrepreneurship* (1981), co-edited by Calvin A. Kent and Karl H. Vesper, and the *Art and Science of Entrepreneurship* (1986), co-edited by Raymond W. Smilor.

Dr. Sexton has received numerous awards, including the Freedoms Foundation's Leavey Award in 1985 and the Association of Collegiate Entrepreneurs Outstanding Entrepreneurship Educators Award in 1991. He is listed in *Who's Who in Finance and Industry* and *Who's Who in America.*

John D. Kasarda

Dr. John D. Kasarda is Kenan Professor of Business Administration and Sociology and Director of the Kenan Institute of Private Enterprise at the Business School of the University of North Carolina, Chapel Hill. His research specialties include urban economic development, job creation, and business demographics.

Dr. Kasarda has produced more than 50 scholarly articles and 7 books on urban development, demographics, and employment issues, including *Jobs, Earnings and Employment Growth Policies in the United States* (Kluwer, 1990). He is frequently quoted in the major news media and serves on the editorial boards of a variety of professional journals. He has also served as a consultant on national urban policy to both the Carter and Reagan administrations and has testified numerous times before U.S. congressional committees on urban and employment issues.

Dr. Kasarda received his B.A. and M.B.A. from Cornell University and his Ph.D. from the University of North Carolina. He has been the recipient of many research grants and awards from such organizations as the National Science Foundation, the National Academy of Sciences, the U.S. Department of State, the Agency for International Development (AID), and the Urban Land Institute.

Chapter

1

Introduction

John D. Kasarda

●

The United States (and much of the western world) is experiencing a dramatic transformation from a corporate-bureaucratic to an entrepreneurial-driven economy. While Fortune 500 firms eliminated over 4 million workers during the 1980s, total U.S. employment expanded by more than 20 million. By the end of the 1980s, 1.3 million enterprises were being started in the United States each year, including the newly self-employed who averaged 500,000 start-ups per year (Birch 1990). This new wave of business development is multifaceted, complex, and incompletely understood. It has as much to do with changes in values, perception, attitudes, and demographics as it does with economic and technological events (Drucker 1985). Growing numbers of scholars from a variety of disciplines are thus being attracted to entrepreneurial research, in order to understand: 1) macrostructural factors shaping the new economy; 2) the nature of firms in the new economy; 3) innovation and technology transfer; 4) the process of venturing; and 5) the growth strategies of the entrepreneurs who are the driving force of the new economy.

An impetus for entrepreneurship study has also come from within academic institutions themselves. On most campuses, students are demanding practical as well as classroom education in entrepreneurship. Colleges and universities are responding with a variety of courses, practica, and programs to prepare these students for entrepreneurial pursuits; but underlying even this academic interest are the practical implications of entrepreneurship — job creation and wealth. As the large corporation continues to loom as a restrictive, less-than-secure employment opportunity, assertive, ambitious men and women are seeking to create their own limitless opportunities through entrepreneurship.

Interest in entrepreneurship has moved across our borders and around the world as well. Up until now, entrepreneurship has been treated primarily as an American phenomenon, but that is quickly changing. The political upheaval in central and eastern Europe is opening the door to private sector development and entrepreneurial activity in major world regions where such activity was unthinkable just a few years ago. And in other parts of the world where developed and developing economies are working to establish themselves as globally competitive (Southeast Asia comes particularly to mind) public services and previously government-owned sectors are privatizing. These changing political and economic environments no doubt will provide the impetus to spawning entrepreneurship globally. Indeed, entrepreneurship is already taking place in some countries around the world, with significant support from their governments (Rondinelli and Kasarda 1991).

Apropos the above, Donald Sexton, writing in the preface to a 1982 book on the state of the art in entrepreneurship research, commented, "Knowledge about the entrepreneur should lead to understanding and out of this understanding should come both public and private policy designed to strengthen and hasten the process of change. [But] ignorance about entrepreneurship has led to policies that discourage rather than enhance the environment for venture initiation. This, in turn, has resulted in a lower standard of living throughout the world." Perhaps emerging support from governments around the globe for private sector development in general, and entrepreneurship in particular, will unleash heretofore stifled initiative that will stimulate new economic growth.

If there is one primary objective that our continuing research into entrepreneurship should achieve, it is to effectively communicate to public policy makers the profound benefits of entrepreneurship. By doing so, we will promote public policy reform that will encourage entrepreneurial efforts worldwide to create jobs and improve the economic well-being of all social strata.

The chapters in this book provide substantial support for the importance of the entrepreneur and the value of entrepreneurship. To fully appreciate how entrepreneurship research has progressed since we first began to formally assess its content and contributions, it may be helpful to revisit briefly the state of the art 10 years ago and the progress made between 1980 and 1985.

Ten years ago the leading scholars in the field seemed to be in consensus that:

● Entrepreneurship is an important economic activity.
● Little is known about the process of entrepreneurship.

● The climate for entrepreneurship in the United States is becoming increasingly negative, particularly as compared to other industrial nations.
● There is evidence of entrepreneurship in larger corporations.
● There is some question as to the extent to which entrepreneurship can be taught.
● Research and education in entrepreneurship are in the early stages.

The field had expanded, but research was fragmented and more of an exploratory, descriptive nature. The greatest abundance of research 10 years ago dealt with the psychology of the entrepreneur, the sociology of entrepreneurship, and the issue of venture capital. Other important areas were lean : for example, innovation from entrepreneurship, the environment for entrepreneurship, and the technology of entrepreneurship (how to do it well). Furthermore, the number of published pieces on entrepreneurship education was minimal. The overarching conclusion one could draw in 1980 was that the field of entrepreneurship, while fertile territory for research and scholarship, lay largely uncharted.

The need for further research was evident in many areas : for example, women entrepreneurs ; the economic and social contributions of new and growing firms ; the effects of public policy and resource allocation on new ventures ; the characteristics that enable entrepreneurs to adjust management styles to the more formal organization of a growing firm ; and how to make the public sector a positive force in entrepreneurship. The research needs in new venture creation were described as overwhelming, and venture capital research was described as lacking reliable data for systematic, longitudinal studies of smaller firms, or of the link between small firms and organized financial markets.

Finally, as an academic discipline, entrepreneurship in 1980 was still in its infancy. Nothing was known about the types of instruction that stimulate potential entrepreneurs or assist practicing ones. The hope was that more advanced research and scholarship would establish entrepreneurship not only as a significant area of inquiry but also as a legitimate academic discipline.

Five years later, however, it became clear that the 1980s were shaping up as the most entrepreneurial decade in U.S. history — the golden age of entrepreneurship — and the entrepreneurial explosion was predicted to continue. By 1985 research results began demonstrating that the process of entrepreneurship was both an art and a science. Great strides were made in scholarship concerning the sociological aspects of venture initiation, the woman entrepreneur, corporate venturing, venture and informal risk capital, and new venture creation. (New venture creation, in fact, was described as having moved beyond describing the steps and stages to the development of models depicting interrelationships between founders, the opportunity, and the necessary resources.) At the same time, the importance of entrepreneurship as an academic endeavor increased substantially.

Nonetheless, in the mid-1980s there were still strategic challenges that needed to be addressed in entrepreneurship research. Methodologies for testing hypotheses required further development as the body of knowledge expanded and became more complex; specifically cited was the need for applying more sophisticated statistical techniques and longitudinal analyses. Two research issues of major concern were the development of models that illuminate the interrelationships of various components of entrepreneurship, and the development of more comprehensive theoretical frameworks.

The predominant conclusion from the 1985 vantage point, however, was that entrepreneurship was a dynamic and creative process that had clearly become a vibrant and important arena for scholarly inquiry. Since 1985, the truth of this conclusion has been manifested in the mushrooming opportunities for researchers of entrepreneurship to present papers at a wide variety of professional conferences and to publish in numerous well-regarded academic journals and monograph series. This, together with the expansion of college curricula in entrepreneurship and growing use of entrepreneurship research by public sector officials, lends support to the claim that entrepreneurship has been legitimized as a field for scholarly discourse with four distinct audiences: students, academic colleagues, practitioners, and public policy makers.

Certainly the chapters presented in this volume further substantiate that contention. The writings fall into six categories: 1) entrepreneurship education; 2) entrepreneurship and economic development; 3) entrepreneurship research linkages and methodologies; 4) entrepreneurial firm growth and financing; 5) international entrepreneurship; and 6) research needs and issues for the 1990s. With overlapping appeal to the audiences mentioned earlier, the work certainly reflects the maturation that entrepreneurship research has achieved. Models and methodologies have been refined; micro data bases to facilitate longitudinal studies are more prevalent; the relationships between small business, entrepreneurial activity, and corporations are being explored; the investigation of international entrepreneurial activity has begun; the body of information on entrepreneurship technology issues has been significantly enhanced; and the establishment of entrepreneurship as an academic discipline has been further cemented.

■■ ■■ ■■ ■■ ■■ ■■ ■■ ■■
ENTREPRENEURSHIP
EDUCATION

Block and Stumpf propose a number of challenges to entrepreneurship education research: in the development of research methodologies for measuring entrepreneurship education effectiveness; in the content and approaches of entrepreneurship education; in the qualities of entrepreneurship educators; in the acceptance of entrepreneurship education in schools other than business; in the existence or development of a common body of knowledge in the field; in the effectiveness of pedagogical alternatives; and in the learning requirements of practicing entrepreneurs as they move through the venture life cycle. In addition, the authors spell out what they perceive to be the objectives of entrepreneurship education : namely, to acquire understanding of the concepts germane to entrepreneurship; to integrate business knowledge across functional areas and synthesize action plans; to identify and stimulate entrepreneurial drive, talent, and skill; to undo the risk-averse bias of many analytical techniques; to develop empathy and support for the unique aspects of entrepreneurship; and to change attitudes towards growth and development.

ENTREPRENEURSHIP AND ECONOMIC DEVELOPMENT

Acs and Audretsch provide a brief discussion of the role of entrepreneurship in job creation, relying on Birch's findings to reiterate the importance of small business in providing jobs. The authors then move on to discuss several stylized facts regarding the economic role of small firms, exploring the social and economic consequences of entrepreneurship, and providing a discussion of industrial restructuring in eastern Europe. Among their conclusions regarding the economic role of entrepreneurship, Acs and Audretsch emphasize that firm size has shifted from larger to smaller; small firms are as innovative as large firms; small firms face binding liquidity constraints; firm survival is positively related to firm size and age ; most new manufacturing enters on the small scale ; and small firms produce at least a proportionate share of new jobs. As for the social and economic consequences of entrepreneurship, the authors emphasize the crucial contribution to job creation and to innovative activity. They point out that small firms in eastern Europe were systematically eliminated in the years following World War II, but that a recent countertrend is developing as democratization in eastern Europe takes hold. Acs and Audretsch conclude by pointing out that a fundamental change has occurred worldwide in social and political institutions that in this century have supported mass production but that in the future will benefit the entrepreneur.

Authors Goodman, Meany, and Pate examine the entrepreneurial actions of governments (such as locating opportunity, accumulating resources, building the organization, and producing and marketing the product) and classify various forms and strategies of governmental entrepreneurial activity occurring within and across different national and cultural boundaries. Among the industrial development strategies identified are the following: reviving depressed economies and promoting growth (both regional and national); changing the economic focus, i.e., from a less developed country to a developed one ; providing new sources of hard currency ; supporting strategic national interests such as defense or space exploration ; developing an essential industry that is too risky or too expensive for the private sector (for example, space technology or the French computer industry); creating jobs as a cure for unemployment; supporting one industry by subsidizing a second interrelated industry ; reducing dependence on foreign suppliers for goods and services (such as oil) ;

and supporting or retarding foreign investment as a method for economic development. The chapter continues with a discussion of the types of industrial promotion and development used by governments and concludes by raising questions for future research.

━━ ━━ ━━ ━━ ━━ ━━ ━━
ENTREPRENEURSHIP
RESEARCH LINKAGES
AND METHODOLOGIES

Dees and Starr point out a conspicuous absence of research on the ethics of entrepreneurship and propose a need for such study based on the historical association of entrepreneurs with ethically questionable techniques such as trickery and deception. The authors believe the greatest value will be created through a study of the ethical dilemmas most likely to arise in the process of entrepreneurial management. They go on to suggest three general questions for researchers to address: 1) What are the ethical dilemmas most characteristic of entrepreneurial management? 2) How do entrepreneurs manage these dilemmas? 3) How might they develop greater skill in managing these dilemmas? Using the definition of entrepreneurial management as "the process of uncovering or developing an opportunity to create value through some innovation, and seizing that opportunity, despite initially possessing insufficient resources," Dees and Starr delineate several ethical dilemmas and propose ways in which to research them.

Because the success of an entrepreneur depends on negotiating strategically advantageous relationships and managing the objections and expectations of key resource controllers, this need poses ethical dilemmas for the entrepreneur as promoter when juxtaposed against the ethical importance of honesty and of respecting the autonomy of others. Network relationships are key to the success of the entrepreneur, but they present ethical dilemmas as well in terms of tactics, techniques, conflicts of interest, pre-venture and post-venture role changes, and the like. Innovation can also pose ethical dilemmas because it can have unwanted side effects, force social reconsideration of norms and values, and raise unanticipated ethical questions. Using these dilemmas, Dees and Starr then propose four interrelated dimensions of ethics research: 1) specifying the relevant ethical consideration; 2) framing the dilemma; 3) creating categories for analyzing responses to the dilemma; and 4) constructing the rules and ideals to guide practice.

Based on the premise that entrepreneurs share many of the challenges of managers of existing firms, Day extracts some of the knowledge from strategic management that can be applied to entrepreneurial studies. She traces the links between three streams of management research: entrepreneurial management, strategic management, and general management. Her survey indicates numerous cross-connections and shows that entrepreneurial researchers can learn from the approaches and findings of strategic management and general management research.

Market opportunities and marketing *may* be the two most important elements underpinning successful business creation, according to Hills and LaForge. The study of new ventures and entrepreneurship as a *process* and the study of the early stages of the business life cycle belong as much to marketing as to any other business function. Market opportunity analysis, new product development, the diffusion of innovation, and marketing strategies are at the heart of both marketing and entrepreneurship. These also represent the most relevant, existing marketing literature bases. After comparing definitions of marketing and entrepreneurship and defining the research interface, the authors review the literature at the interface of entrepreneurship and marketing management in the context of four main issues. First, they examine company mission. They note that the impact of the entrepreneur's personal goals on the mission (and marketing goals), as well as the role of the marketing concept, are unique to the marketing/entrepreneurship interface as compared to large, mature firms. Second, they look at market opportunity analysis, finding that a key part of new venture planning is feasibility assessment and sales forecasting. Third, they explore market strategy. They show that for independent new ventures marketing a single product to a well-defined target market, there are few differences in the market strategies also used for corporate, business, and product marketing. Finally, they explore implementation and control. Implementation and execution under great uncertainty and severe resource constraints probably make this subject even more important than in large, mature, and relatively stable firms. Concluding the chapter is a look to the future in marketing/entrepreneurship research, described as still in its infancy. Very little mainstream marketing literature explicitly addresses the area of entrepreneurship, despite the importance of the interface.

Aldrich reviews the research on entrepreneurship over the years, specifically the work done for the 1981 and 1985 State of the Art Conferences, to draw conclusions regarding changes through the years and to determine the progress that has been made in entrepreneurship research over the decade. He devotes careful attention to a discussion of implicit norms governing entrepreneurship research: 1) comparisons with an ideal based upon a model of normal science; 2) multiple paradigms perspectives; and 3) methods chosen to match researchers' purposes. Aldrich concludes by stating that, "Current social, economic, and political considerations will govern what issues are researched, and changing conditions will drive research practice, not abstract methodological concerns."

Believing that the entrepreneur needs a *process theory* that explains innovation development, and that the process theory is fundamental to entrepreneurship management, Van de Ven takes a developmental view of the entrepreneurial process. He asks the how's and why's of the process over time, and proposes a set of longitudinal research methods for studying entrepreneurial ventures based on the work of the Minnesota Innovation Research Program. Specific longitudinal research design issues include sample selection, real-time process observations, the selection and evolution of core concepts, the comparison of alternative process models, and problems of measurement and sequence analysis. He indicates that this process theory should include statements that explain innovation as "1) a dynamic evolutionary process 2) in which many actors (including entrepreneurs) undertake time-dependent sequences of activities and events, 3) which produce cycles of discontinuity and continuity, that 4) both create and are constrained by different hierarchical levels of the social system."

Kirchhoff and Phillips propose that the most useful source of data for examining the population of small businesses is the Small Business Data Base, the creation of which grew out of David Birch's work using Dun & Bradstreet data. The authors show the ways in which the SBDB is useful: 1) in the analysis of job creation by small firms; 2) in financial applications; 3) in defining macroindicators of the economy; 4) in studies of specific policy areas; and 5) in studies of industry restructuring. They state that the greatest value provided by the SBDB is in longitudinal studies. For instance, research using the data base's short-run analyses prepared biennially supports the thesis that small business's job creation share is larger than its share of employment in the economy. Nevertheless, small businesses do create the majority of new jobs; and this has also been confirmed for other countries using similar micro data sources.

Reynolds examines the interaction of organizational and human populations that result in new firm births, stating that the presence of two variables — an economic opportunity for a new endeavor and a person predisposed to entrepreneurial behavior — will result in a new firm being founded. The social condition and the personal predisposition may be affected by many factors, but these two variables are critical to new firm birth. After a discussion of the ideal research setting, Reynolds discusses the research to date for four population types: 1) all firms in all industries in a single nation; 2) all firms of one type or in a single industry; 3) firms within a single subnational region; and 4) the source of entrepreneurs — the human population.

━ ━ ━ ━ ━ ━ ━ ━
ENTREPRENEURIAL FIRM GROWTH AND FINANCING

Cooper and Gascon focus on formal, empirical research which considers independent start-ups and factors that bear upon their performance. Research to date directs attention to the experience, education, and psychological makeup of individual entrepreneurs; how decisions are made; how entrepreneurs start and manage firms; and how environmental and industry conditions shape opportunities. Research problems reflect a lack of well-developed theories of causal relationships, as well as variation in samples, variety in performance measure, and differences in analytical methods. The authors argue that future research should direct more attention to theory, place more emphasis on contingency relationships, and give careful consideration to the performance measures chosen and to the implications of particular samples. Results should be communicated in scholarly journals, as well as through conference presentations. While research on entrepreneurs, the processes of founding, and new firm performance has progressed greatly in recent years, the mixed patterns of findings, as well as the opportunities to strengthen research approaches, suggest that much work remains to be done.

According to Hoy, McDougall, and Dsouza, economic development strategies that encompass job creation and venture growth have implications for public policy formulation. These implications are likely to either encourage or discourage firm creation, and to lead to the development of public sector programs to advocate and support venture creation and growth. Understanding how firms plot their courses for growth within this broader economic environment requires studying venture strategy formulation and implementation. Strategic planning is important for firms, particularly if it addresses resource acquisition to sustain growth. Research is incomplete regarding how the strategies of high-growth companies differ from those with slower growth. In order to sustain high growth, companies should ensure that they are quickly acquiring and using relevant data about market growth and the velocity within their competitive environments. Because of the inordinate demands growth places on organizational resources, they must also monitor the broader, general environment, which could act both as a constraint on and a source of resources to achieve growth. Research on high-growth firms is increasing both in quantity and quality. Advances in designs and methodologies are enhancing the results of case studies, while new technologies are improving our ability to analyze data. Researchers are also benefitting from more comprehensive and more accurate data bases.

Research by Slevin and Covin reveals that firms in the 1990s must become much more entrepreneurial and adaptable to survive and grow in a rapidly changing world. Environmental pressures have altered the basic nature of the business enterprise, and the challenges these pressures bring to business will continue to increase both in diversity and intensity. Because today's economy is more global, the entire organization must respond adaptively and collectively to environmental change. Since products and markets are likely to change rapidly, entrepreneurial behavior must respond to these shorter competitive half-lives at the organizational level. In support of this strategic orientation, entrepreneurial firms characteristically emphasize technological leadership and research and development. Successful organizations of the future need to create and maintain high-performance teams for the accomplishment of both process and product innovation. Studying the creation and maintenance of such high-performance teams will be an important task for entrepreneurship researchers over the next several decades.

In his report on new venture financing research, Brophy reveals that empirical studies done through surveys and personal interviews have provided an understanding of the structural arrangements and processes through which venture capital investors go about finding, evaluating, choosing, and managing their investments. Similar studies done through the use of established data bases have allowed researchers to perform quantitative analysis using "hard data" that were previously unavailable. The compilation and analysis of the appropriate information has permitted institutional investors, venture capital fund managers, and the founders and managers of emerging growth companies to develop a common view of the economics of the venture capital investment market. Continued analysis of this data will provide the ability to track capital costs and performance over time, perhaps making more efficient the acquisition of growth capital by emerging firms at all stages of their lives. The increase in precision, consistency, and continuity through the kinds of research mentioned here offers promise for those who have worked for years with only "hearsay" evidence, and may quickly enrich our understanding of the longer-term development and growth patterns of entrepreneurially-generated firms.

Timmons and Sapienza suggest that the 1990s hold great challenges for the venture capital industry. Competition will continue to intensify. Venture capital firms will be challenged to earn attractive returns while seeking ways of differentiating themselves from the growing pack of U.S. and foreign-based competitors. Successful venture capital firms will be those which counter the growing threat of substitutes by learning how to add value to the entrepreneurial process and to communicate that value to the increasingly wary and sophisticated suppliers and users of capital. Domestic venture capital firms will also have to contend with federal and state policies which dampen their incentive to provide early stage investments and put them at a competitive disadvantage relative to foreign competitors. In addition, venture capital firms will be faced with an increasingly complex legal environment. The array of research opportunities in the venture capital arena in the 1990s will continue to be vast and of direct interest to the suppliers of capital (limited partners), the users of capital (entrepreneurs), the investors (venture capitalists), and public policy makers. These opportunities will be realized only if researchers seek methods and issues which bring them in close contact with industry as it exists in the real world.

Historically, investment fund portfolio managers have had an abundance of information on rates of return when they invest in stocks, bonds, and debt instruments. According to Bygrave, that situation is reversed when these managers have invested in venture capital partnerships. From the venture capital industry's beginnings in 1946, reliable rates of return on venture capital have been hard to come by. Because many of the venture capital firms are private, data on rates of return is hard to find, although there is no shortage of anecdotal accounts. Most studies of venture capital returns have used small samples of publicly-held firms, primarily small business investment companies (SBICs). However, such studies are limited by a lack of an industry-wide standard for computing the financial returns of these funds. Bygrave looks at venture capital returns from 1975 through 1989 and proposes a model for the factors that influence them. A critical factor in that model is venture-capital-backed IPOs. With more reliable measures of performance for venture capital funds available for the 1990s, researchers will be better able to systematically understand their behavior, what influences it, and how those things are related to outcomes.

According to Freear and Wetzel, the informal venture capital market is an invisible and inefficient market made up of a diverse and dispersed population of high net worth individual investors ("business angels"). These investors often provide know-how and capital to the ventures they back. Most of the information about informal venture capital is derived from U.S. data, although research is actively taking place in Canada and in Europe. In the United States there are about 2 million investors with individual net worths of more than $1 million. Equity investments in ventures in which investors have no management interest exceed $100 billion and may approach $300 billion. Individual investors invest over $30 billion per year in more than 100,000 ventures. By the year 2000, informal venture capital will be a more visible and efficient segment of the general venture capital market and active source of funds in the United States and abroad. The amount of information about the market that is available to potential and actual participants will have increased substantially.

Venkataraman, MacMillan, and McGrath state that the key concepts of corporate venturing are to investigate how market and firm conditions influence the creation of new businesses within existing firms. Venturing activities include business founding, managing the hierarchical process, and managing the institutional context in which founding and fostering take place. Such management challenges do not remain constant over time, but evolve with idea development, start-up, growth, maturity, and, perhaps, decline. Remaining consistent with such research, the authors divide the total venturing process into four conditions — definition, penetration, contagion, and institutionalization — to address the research questions that arise with each stage of development. The basic idea underlying these conditions is that the nature of the venturing problem faced by managers of a firm changes with each condition. Using the four conditions as an analytical framework, discrete outcomes of venturing activity can be identified as new organizational units, vestiges, and spin-offs. This chapter comprehensively identifies areas where there is some understanding of the process, as well as those territories where there is little understanding. The authors reveal that the main roadblock facing the field of corporate venturing will remain the challenge of obtaining access to cross-sectional data from large corporations.

INTERNATIONAL ENTREPRENEURSHIP

Business risks, competition, and market volatility make joint ventures an important strategy option, Hisrich states in his opening remarks. Through joint ventures, firms undertake activities that could not be undertaken alone. Such activities include acquiring process or product technology, diversifying by entering new markets or introducing new products, expanding production capacity, and vertically integrating the firm's efforts. The most frequent reason for forming joint ventures is to share the costs and risks of uncertain projects. Other reasons include synergy between firms (this could apply to people, inventory, plants, or equipment), and market leverage (allowing companies to access new customers by expanding their market base). Seen as a strategy to enter foreign markets, joint ventures have become an effective means for businesses to accelerate technological development, enhance productivity, and lower investment risks. Particularly in eastern Europe, joint ventures provide a mechanism for market entrance that would be difficult, if not impossible, to obtain otherwise, while at the same time establishing a vehicle for accessing the European Economic Community in 1992. Because international joint ventures play such a key role in global enterprise competitiveness, the development of a systematic, conceptual framework for data collection and analysis is an important research objective for the future.

The importance of small business to the economy is now widely recognized not only by the western industrialized world, but also by many countries which formally had socialistic forms of government. Brockhaus, with the help of colleagues from around the world, surveys the research and education efforts in the study of entrepreneurship. He reviews the work by country and discusses the range of work done in each. The conclusions reveal that the United States and Europe are not the only places in the world where entrepreneurship is recognized as a major "player" in economic development. Former Communist countries as well as less developed countries that are working to fuel their economies are expending considerable effort to foster entrepreneurship. With governmental support, many of these nations' colleges offer courses and are conducting research in entrepreneurship. Brockhaus proposes that as entrepreneurship and small business research conferences become more international in scope, the lines drawn in the research agenda will become blurred as regional differences become less distinct. Rather than exhausting the international research available on entrepreneurship, Brockhaus demonstrates how extensive the potential research activities are, calling his work in this chapter the "tip of the iceberg."

RESEARCH NEEDS AND ISSUES IN THE 1990S

The state of the art in entrepreneurship research has changed dramatically since 1980. As Churchill points out, in 1980 the atmosphere of entrepreneurship research was one of relatively unguided exploration; in 1985 the attitude was one of excitement, proselytizing and a few breakthroughs; and in 1990 it was optimism and a maturing understanding of the size and complexity of the subject at hand.

Churchill, in assessing the current state of the art, holds that the overall challenge to entrepreneurship research is understanding. He states, "We have done exploratory studies, most of which are probing in nature; and we have begun to understand the breadth of the field. What is now called for is more attention to constructing more fully developed theoretical frameworks for predicting, explaining cause and effect relationships, and guiding empirical testing." The key to research is that it adds to the intellectual capital in the field in such a way that it enhances both theory and practice and can be used in the classroom in ways that enhance curriculum and learning.

As researchers, we still face a number of problems related to access and relevance. We must recognize that like other professional academic areas our research must be applicable both to students and to practitioners. Our field seems to contain more than its share of voluminous and meaningless research more directed to personal gain than to expansion of the body of knowledge. According to Churchill, the consequences of this are a risk of alienating the practitioners, a risk of ridicule by knowledgeable people in the industry, and a risk of ridicule by researchers in other fields.

Taken together, the chapters in this volume provide a window to the diversity of entrepreneurship research and enlarge our understanding of the process, character, and contributions of entrepreneurship. The authors provide an informative look at where the field stands at present and anticipate research directions for the 1990s.

REFERENCES

Birch, D. L. 1990 Sources of job growth — and some implications. In *Jobs, earnings, and employment growth policies in the United States,* ed. J. D. Kasarda, 71–76. Norwell, Mass.: Kluwer Academic Publishers.

Drucker, P. F. 1985 *Innovation and entrepreneurship: Practice and principles.* New York: Harper & Row.

Rondinelli, D. A., and J. D. Kasarda 1991 Privatizing public services in the developing countries: What do we know? *Business in the Contemporary World,* ed. D. A. Rondinelli and J. D. Kasarda, 3 (2): 102–113.

Sexton, D. L. 1982 Preface. In *Encyclopedia of Entrepreneurship,* ed. C. A. Kent, D. L. Sexton, and K. H. Vesper. Englewood Cliffs, NJ: Prentice-Hall.

Part

1

ENTREPRENEURSHIP
EDUCATION

Chapter

2

Entrepreneurship Education Research: Experience and Challenge

Zenas Block
and
Stephen A. Stumpf

●

INTRODUCTION

In this chapter, the newly evolving field of entrepreneurship education research is examined. We offer a hierarchy of criteria for the evaluation of educational effectiveness as a potential framework for research, and we review the literature since 1985 for current research interests in the context of those criteria. We go on to discuss the special challenges of entrepreneurship education research, and then relate this area of research to the state of education research in general. Finally, we examine the numerous and diverse audiences for such education, identify research questions, and discuss the potential applications of research findings.

THE HISTORY OF ENTREPRENEURSHIP EDUCATION RESEARCH

Entrepreneurship education research has evolved in ways that are typical, necessary, and totally appropriate for a new research field. As in other emerging disciplines, observations are made and reported, and case situations are studied. New course designs and educational innovations have preceded the development of a scientific theoretical framework. In general, entrepreneurship education research cannot be viewed out of the context of entrepreneurship research itself. After all, it is only in the past few years that models, paradigms, and emerging theories have been formulated for entrepreneurship. The research in the past five years in education has begun to look more fundamentally at the education issue, but still is very sparse overall.

With just a 20-year history to work from, one should not expect there to be hundreds of research studies reported on the development of knowledge in entrepreneurship education. Yet, interesting findings have been reported regarding the value of entrepreneurship education in the formation of new ventures (Clark, Davis, and Harnish 1984), in the value added by university-based new venture outreach programs (McMullan, Long, and Graham 1986), and in the benefits of using ill-structured approaches to teaching entrepreneurship courses (Sexton and Bowman-Upton 1987, 1988).

As with the field of business education in general (e.g., Freedman and Stumpf 1982; Freedman, Cooper, and Stumpf 1982), the focus of research during the early stage of the development of a discipline tends to be on the appropriateness of course content (e.g., Cullen and Dick 1989; Hills 1988; Vesper 1986), the selection and usefulness of course concepts (e.g., Sexton and Bowman 1984; Vesper 1988), and the efficacy of different techniques for improving teaching performance and student learning within specific educational settings (e.g., Leepson 1988; McMullan and Long 1983; Sexton and Bowman-Upton 1987, 1988).

Many of the research questions addressed tend to be germane to a faculty member's particular course, or to a school's program. While useful to the specific program or course, the results are limited in generalizability to the emerging field. For example, research tends to be conducted that addresses such questions as: "What material should be taught in an entrepreneurship course within the curriculum of this school?" "Which methods are feasible and applicable to teach this material?"

The primary outcome measures used in such research tend to be student satisfaction with a specific course and instructor, student performance, and student attitudes about the course content and activities.

Such research is useful and appropriate for the development of courses and instructors in an emerging discipline (Lundberg and Westacott 1982). It provides the researcher with feedback on his or her classroom activities with respect to various short-term criteria that can be used to redesign a course, alter a teaching style, and/or target a course to students with learning objectives that parallel those of the instructor. To the extent that many such studies are conducted — each with reasonable rigor — they can collectively contribute to our knowledge about entrepreneurship education. Yet each study alone is more of an empirically examined case study than a hypothesis-testing research study. It is these latter studies, when linked to theories of how people learn via different teaching methods (e.g., House 1982), or how they learn a particular content area (e.g., Cooper 1982), that most often lead to useful inferences and generalizations which contribute to the body of knowledge in a field. Similarly, it is the theory-based, hypothesis-testing research studies that tend to meet scholarly journal standards for publication, which is so important to academic faculty for tenure and promotion.

The Audience for Entrepreneurship Education

The underlying assumption of entrepreneurship education appears to have been that its purpose is to educate students who wish to start new businesses — either independently, or more recently, in a corporate framework. This is considerably broader than the earlier focus on small businesses.

If the definition of entrepreneurship used is the pursuit of opportunity without regard to currently available resources (Stevenson and Gumpert 1985), the audience (or potential market) for entrepreneurship education broadens considerably beyond potential new business starters. In addition to the self-employed, the small business starter, the starter of high-growth potential businesses, business acquirers who use acquisition as a base for high growth, and the pure "deal makers," this definition would include : those who manage entrepreneurs in organizations ; top managers who must provide vision and leadership for corporations which must innovate in order to survive ; potential resource people (accountants, lawyers, consultants) used by entrepreneurs ; and possibly those who wish to be supportive of people who actually pursue opportunities.

The Relationship of Research to Purpose

Two goals of most business education are to prepare people for career success and to increase their capacity for future learning. Equally important are the learner's personal fulfillment and contribution to society. The ultimate measure of entrepreneurship education is how well it fosters all these aspirations.

Virtually every career in business involves some combination of knowledge, technique, and people skills, but few involve the integration and combination of all functional knowledge and skills to the extent that entrepreneurial activity does. For example, it is possible to provide an examination to test whether the accountant has the requisite knowledge to practice his/her profession, and thus should be graduated ; or whether a marketing major is suitable for entry-level employment in marketing ; and certainly whether the finance major knows enough about finance facts and theory to be able to work in that field.

In entrepreneurship, however, while there is good deal of fundamental business knowledge required which can be taught in a classroom, there is not yet a guiding theory to assist the would-be entrepreneur in dealing with the uncertainties which surround any new business creation. And even if there were, the real test is performance under actual conditions with all the real-world pressures, over a period of several years.

If entrepreneurship education is to be effective, it must be so not only through the factual knowledge and limited skills acquirable in the classroom, but also through the stimulation of new enterprise, the success of that enterprise, and the increasing capacity of the entrepreneur to pursue ever-greater successes. A second objective, if entrepreneurship education is to develop fully, is to educate people who choose an academic/research career in entrepreneurship and innovation-related areas.

Porter and McKibbin (1988), in a study funded by the American Assembly of Collegiate Schools of Business (AACSB), provide a comprehensive study of management education from 1960 to 1985. This study, the result of a number of years of preparation initiated informally in 1975, includes input from U.S. and European educators through a series of conferences spanning the decade between 1975 and 1985. The data for the final report, using interviews and surveys, were obtained from business school deans, faculty, placement directors, executive education directors, provosts, advisory councils, students, and alumni; and from CEO's, vice presidents of human resources, directors of management development, recruiting directors, and operating managers of corporations and businesses.

In the Porter and McKibbin study, perceptions of the quality of management school education were gathered from those who employed graduates. Since business/management students enter the work force at junior levels, reporting to people senior to them, judgement of performance is directly obtainable from those who employ and evaluate their performance. Any weaknesses in educational preparation are apparent on the job, the knowledge and skill requirements for specific jobs are well known, and the relative performance of different people in the same job classification can be fairly easily observed. From data obtained in this manner, conclusions were reached regarding the effectiveness of business education, and recommendations for improvement were offered. One of the deficiencies noted in the survey was insufficient attention given to entrepreneurship. The final conclusions suggested that business schools should build their educational efforts around four main themes, each of which has direct application to the needs of entrepreneurship education:

1. Continuous quality assessment.
2. Continuous attention to theory/practice linkages.
3. Continuous adaptability to change.
4. Continuous innovation.

Evaluation Criteria

Given these themes, it seems appropriate to the purposes of entrepreneurship and management education to suggest criteria for education effectiveness as a basis for evaluating past and ongoing research efforts, as well as for identifying factors to be considered in designing future research.

Those criteria, which reflect our view of education objectives, are shown in Figure 2–1. These objectives overlap but in some respects differ from those reported by Hills (1988). We certainly agree that the objectives identified by Hills are desirable — for example, increasing awareness and understanding of the process of initiating a new business enterprise ; developing career options ; understanding the interrelationships among disciplines ; and appreciating entrepreneurial qualities. But other criteria can also be imagined, such as the reputation of a course or program among peers and administrators.

It is clear from an examination of Figure 2–1 that the selection of appropriate control groups is crucial to our emerging understanding of the benefits of entrepreneurship education. Only then will we be able to relate many of the longer time frame outputs to educational input. Appropriate control groups might be people who have had no entrepreneurial education at all, no business education at all, or non-MBA students.

In reflecting on the entrepreneurship education research published since 1985, the following studies can be recommended :

On teaching approaches : Sexton and Bowman-Upton (1988).

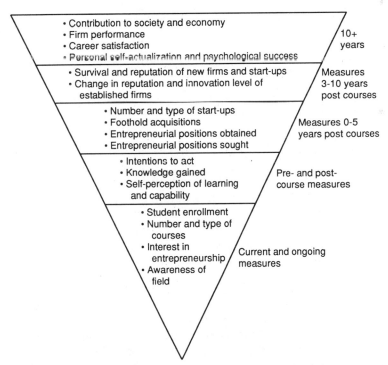

FIGURE 2–1 Criteria for Evaluating the Effectiveness of Entrepreneurship Education

On student characteristics, and on approaches to and popularity of courses: Hills and Welsch (1986); Robinson and Hunt (1989)

On the relationship of education to new venture formation, survival, failure, and exit: Clark, Davis, and Harnish (1984); Scott (1989).

On the relationship of education to entrepreneurs (career choice, perception of needs, benefits, and educational history): Cooper and Dunkelberg (1987); Shuman, Seeger, and Teebagy (1987); McMullan, Long, and Graham (1986); Brown, Christy, and Banowitz (1987).

On the economic benefits of education: McMullan et al. (1986).

On entrepreneurship education, including objectives, course content, programs: Hills (1988).

However, while these papers do address the different criteria of interest to entrepreneurship education, their usefulness is limited to ideas around course design and/or content.

AREAS OF CURRENT RESEARCH INTEREST

In September of 1989, the Center for Entrepreneurial Studies at the Stern School of Business at New York University issued a call for research proposals in entrepreneurship education. Their intention was to stimulate research in this area by offering funding. The research questions suggested in the call included:

1. What is/should be taught? To whom? Where? With what objectives?
2. How effective is present educational activity?
3. What are the teaching methods in use, and how successful are they?
4. Can nonentrepreneurs teach entrepreneurship effectively? With what training?
5. What do prospective entrepreneurs need to learn?
6. What do existing entrepreneurs perceive as their learning needs?
7. How does entrepreneurship education differ from general management education?

Over 2,500 announcements were sent to: the deans of every accredited engineering school, all entrepreneurship centers, all Babson Conference participants, and a sample of Academy of Management members. But only 77 proposals were received in response, as noted below. The low response rate might be explained by a number of factors, such as the relatively small amount of funding offered, the normal "fatality rate" of mail received by faculty, or the low level of interest in the area itself. The virtual absence of return from the engineering school sample is interesting in light of the need for venture management know-how by innovative engineers who start new firms.

It is interesting to note that with some 300 universities reporting courses in entrepreneurship, the predominant area of interest is in learning what it is that entrepreneurs need to learn! Implied or stated in this area of interest is the objective of learning how to start and manage a new enterprise. Interest in pedagogy is reflected in proposals for course design, i.e., for product development. It should be noted that the purpose of the call for proposals was to *stimulate* research and not to prove where research interests lay. The results shown below, however, do provide an indirect indication of those interests. Here is the breakout of responses received, by area of interest:

Learning needs	27
Needs vs. need fulfillment	11
Course development	7
Learning process	2
Country comparisons	3
Education and economic development	3
Pedagogy	1
Education needs by business life cycle stage	3
Surveys of courses taught	6
MBA demand for courses	1
Faculty training	1
Non-education-focused proposal	12

The five studies which have received funding based on their research focus and rigor were shorter-term projects related to the identification of various needs:

1. Educational needs at different stages of the business life cycle.
2. Comparative needs of entrepreneurs and intrapreneurs.
3. Skill inventories required at different stages of a firm's life cycle related to firm performance.
4. Organizational development skill requirements for entrepreneurs.
5. The understanding of prospective and retrospective learning needs of entrepreneurs.

No direct comparative studies of people who take entrepreneurship courses and those who don't were among the proposals received. This suggests a number of research challenges.

Challenge 1: Develop research methodologies for measuring entrepreneurship education effectiveness.

Without such methodologies, we can suspect, conjecture, and have faith, but we cannot supply data and conclusions which can be generalized. "Effectiveness" might be defined as the extent to which objectives are met. Those objectives may differ for each of the audiences that have interests in entrepreneurship.

There is no question that student acceptance is a necessary measure of effectiveness, but it is hardly sufficient. The fundamental measures of effectiveness are the number of new business formations when coupled with the survival and level of success record, with the contribution to the economy in terms of employment, and with the degree of satisfaction of the student with career — *when compared to others who have not had any formal entrepreneurial education experience.* The remaining issue to be considered is the possibility that those who choose some form of entrepreneurial career are already self-selected, and that factors other than education (such as strength of motivation) may confound results. Result measures for each of the audiences require specific design. In the case of entrepreneurial managers, the judgment of peers, superiors, and subordinates might be useful when conducting research to evaluate the effectiveness of management education.

To measure student satisfaction and impact on student knowledge and attitudes, a uniform method of evaluation which permits comparisons between students, faculty, pedagogical method, course content, and other variables is needed. A sampling of items that might be used to construct and validate such a tool is shown in Table 2–1.

The problems to be solved in measuring effectiveness are not only to determine the appropriate measures, but actually to obtain the necessary information over the time period of interest. Perhaps the most significant obstacle is the tenure and promotion system operative at major universities. What junior faculty member is going to do a five- to ten-year research project, given the rate of publications required to achieve tenure and promotion? A possible solution might be to get funding to subsidize senior faculty to organize, guide, coordinate, and carry out research projects which involve long-term tracking of subjects.

Challenge 2: What are the educational needs of different audiences? What should be taught?

This question includes what different target audiences think should be taught, as well as what instructors think should be taught. When 100 students enrolled in two sections of the same entrepreneurship course, they were asked what they wanted to get out of the course and to write their response. The vast majority said, "To learn how to convert an idea into a successful business." One hundred percent of the students indicated that they wanted to start a business someday and stated that this was the reason for taking the course. Many also identified the desire to learn about the factors that are responsible for business success and failure.

TABLE 2–1 — Sample Questions to Assess Aspects of Entrepreneurial Education

Please rate yourself on each of the following items, based on a 5-point scale ranging from 1 = none to 5 = a great amount :

1. Desire to start a business someday.
2. Desire to buy a business someday or to start an entrepreneurial career.
3. Confidence in your ability to start and run a business.
4. Confidence in your ability to buy / run a business.
5. Your knowledge level to become a successful entrepreneur.
6. Your skill level to become a successful entrepreneur.
7. How much more do you think you need to learn to become a successful entrepreneur ?
8. Present ability to find information and learn more about starting / buying / running your own business.
9. Ability to evaluate yourself as a potential entrepreneur.
10. Ability to find / identify business opportunities.
11. Ability to evaluate new opportunities.
12. Ability to provide services to entrepreneurs.
13. When do you think you will start a business after graduation ?_____years after graduation.

Our challenge as researchers and scholars is to develop a framework and set of hypotheses for the study of successes and failures, and to find people who are willing to supply the information about their business. Such people are the link we need to bridge the gap between actuality and such perceptions as, "I had a terrible lawyer, my accountant gave me the figures too late, I was undercapitalized, my partner and I couldn't agree, I couldn't get the labor I needed, the cost of ingredients climbed out of sight, my competition undercut me right out of business, I just couldn't get enough business to survive, and it was the wrong location." As we learn more about the effectiveness of what we do and the reasons for failure, it will contribute to content formulation for the courses we teach or should teach. In short, it will help us determine what people *need* to learn and *want* to learn.

Challenge 3 : Who should teach entrepreneurship courses ? Can people without entrepreneurial experience be effective teachers ? What are the qualifications required ? What kind of training is required ? What are the characteristics of the outstanding teachers in this field, and how can we obtain this information ?

The opinion of prominent educators reported by Hills (1988) indicates that a majority of respondents believe that adjunct professors should be used to teach entrepreneurship courses. A minority (about 26 percent) believe that the use of adjuncts should be minimized. Why ? In courses which have a theoretical foundation, it is common for nonpractitioners to teach effectively. If we use student satisfaction as a sole criterion, we can find ample evidence to justify many views. The use of a commonly accepted evaluation tool which also measures knowledge acquired would help to provide a more reliable answer to this question, as well as facilitate improvement of course design, content, and pedagogy to enhance student satisfaction.

Challenge 4 :   What is the need, feasibility, and possibility for acceptance of entrepreneurship education in professional schools other than business schools ?

This is not a new question, since it was previously raised by Vesper, McMullan, and Ray (1988). A study of the needs perceived by students and administrators would be a start towards answering that question.

Challenge 5 :   What are the learning requirements of practicing entrepreneurs at each stage of their venture life cycle ? What is now being done, and what can we learn about the effectiveness of existing programs ?

Challenge 6 :   Is there a common body of knowledge in the field ? What is it ? If not, what should it be ?

There are certainly many textbooks available, and lots of people teaching. How much commonality is there to the knowledge component of courses now taught ? Is it possible to identify what those components should be ? One of the major steps forward between 1965 and 1985 in business school program standards promulgated by the AACSB cited by Porter and McKibbin (1988) is the inclusion of "a common body of knowledge" requirement. This is probably a minimum requirement for our field in order to achieve and retain respectability.

Challenge 7 :   What is the relative effectiveness of pedagogical alternatives ? What pedagogies are now used, and with what results, however measured ? What new pedagogical possibilities exist ?

In this area, we need to look at other fields which require a high degree of creativity, resourcefulness, flexibility, and adaptability. This repeats a proposal made earlier by Vesper, McMullan, and Ray (1988). That challenge might best be faced by people who are principally interested in pedagogical methods to see what works for entrepreneurship. Inherent in this area is the need to know more about how different kinds of people learn, and whether learning style preferences by entrepreneurs are any different than those of nonentrepreneurs. Valid learning style inventory tests based on different learning theories are available.

EDUCATIONAL RESEARCH

An examination of research on education in other disciplines (e.g., business education) suggests directions for the design of future research on entrepreneurship education. Journals such as the *Journal of Educational Psychology,*

Research in Higher Education, and *Educational and Psychological Measurement* have adjusted their publication standards for research to reflect the evolution of the field of education in general. Today they require the use of more rigorous research designs than in the past. Sample sizes need to be larger, often representing a greater number of course sections and colleges, and less often being "convenience samples." Studies that generate and test hypotheses, explore multiple conditions, use well-validated pre- and post-course measures, and have control groups are more readily published than those studies that do not have these design attributes (Stone 1982). Longitudinal research studies, particularly those that employ criteria that are of great relevance to the field or to society in general, are actively sought by the editors of such journals.

With the current interest in entrepreneurship education, and the lack of an accepted paradigm or theories of entrepreneurship education (Hills 1988; McMullan and Long 1990; Vesper 1988), we are at an exciting juncture for mapping out possible questions that entrepreneurship education research might address in the coming years. As an approach to this, our discussion now turns to potential audiences for entrepreneurship education, along with the probable objectives of primary interest to these audiences (Block 1985; Hills 1988). The objectives of entrepreneurship education are discussed in greater detail, exploring possible teacher and learner roles in the educational process. This is followed by a series of propositions which seem to merit further research, and the exploration of the possible applications of hypothetical research findings.

━━ ━━ ━━ ━━ ━━ ━━ ━━ ━━
AUDIENCES FOR ENTREPRENEURIAL EDUCATION

As noted earlier, the existing and potential audiences for entrepreneurship education go beyond the potential individual new business starter. The evolving entrepreneurial concept is considerably broader (for a review of the history of entrepreneurial thought see Herbert and Link 1982; McMullan and Long 1990, 57–69). As suggested in Figure 2–2, the target audiences for entrepreneurship education to be discussed include: entrepreneurs; managers of entrepreneurs; and those who support, encourage, and assist entrepreneurs, whom we call entrepreneurial sympathizers. In addition some students simply wish to develop an entrepreneurial style or to cultivate an entrepreneurial spirit. Some people may be in more than one of these audiences, particularly at different points in time. Also, at a particular point in time many individuals who would want an educational experience involving entrepreneurship are likely to have learning goals that more closely parallel individuals in only one of the four audiences than the other three. This leads to our first research question.

Research Question 1: Do sufficiently discrete audiences for entrepreneurship education exist (as suggested in Figure 2–2), so as to warrant the development

FIGURE 2–2 Relative Size of Entrepreneurship Audiences

of specific courses and course delivery systems tailored to each audience's learning objectives ?

Most entrepreneurship educational programs have diverse objectives — from the specific and immediately measurable objectives of student knowledge acquisition (e.g., test performance) and student satisfaction with the course or instructor, to more general objectives of skill acquisition in the use of various techniques and analyses that promote mature judgment as an entrepreneur. Presumably these learning objectives can be linked to the ultimate objective of entrepreneurial success and career satisfaction. As we discuss each audience for entrepreneurship education below, we have tried to identify the probable learning objectives of each audience.

Entrepreneurs

Several different kinds of entrepreneurs can be identified (see Vesper 1980):

1. Independent, high-potential business starters, often an innovator or inventor.
2. New business starters within corporations, sometimes called intrapreneurs.
3. Those who are self-employed, including professionals such as physicians, lawyers, accountants.
4. Acquirers and operators.
5. Deal makers and brokers.
6. Turnaround specialists.

People perform these tasks as entrepreneurs when their career goals reflect an ongoing search for new opportunities, responding to select opportunities, and exploiting them (Drucker 1985). They need to exhibit creative opportunism, managerial competence, and tolerance of uncertainty and risk. Some who attend entrepreneurship courses will have started one or more new ventures and plan to continue to do so. Others intend to start a new venture in the future. The new venture may involve an independent start-up from scratch, or an internal corporate venture. It could be a for-profit activity, or a venture to earn a profit in order to support a nonprofit activity. All will require application of business and management knowledge to some activity involving change or innovation, as well as specific knowledge of what it takes to launch a new business successfully.

It is likely that the knowledge and skill requirements for each type of entrepreneur will differ in some ways. For example, the negotiating and valuation skills needed by a deal maker would be different than the planning, interpersonal, and managerial skills needed by an accountant or dentist. Certainly there are specific bodies of knowledge and skills needed by different professions. But there are also aspects of entrepreneurship that can be generalized across professions, with respect to both content and motivational support. Such learning includes acquiring knowledge and understanding concepts about business management, including how to find opportunities and how to acquire resources; gaining skill in the use of analytical and management techniques, including the ability to analyze a business situation and synthesize an action plan; and identifying and stimulating existing entrepreneurial drive, talent, and skills.

Managers of Entrepreneurs

These are the senior managers who foster opportunity identification and exploitation, or middle managers who are involved in the identification of opportunities and allocating resources to them. They tend to foster an entrepreneurial spirit among those whom they manage. The primary learning objectives relevant to these managers include acquiring knowledge and understanding concepts which will enhance their ability to foster innovation, minimize barriers to innovation, train people for entrepreneurial activities, and undo risk-averse bias.

Entrepreneurial Sympathizers

Individuals who wish to support either entrepreneurs or entrepreneurial managers can be thought of an entrepreneurial sympathizers. They do not actively search for opportunities, nor do they get actively involved in the analysis or management of new ventures. But once a venture is identified and approved, they seek an understanding of the venture and its challenges and are often important supporters. They can be influential with their views even if not directly linked to the venture.

The primary learning objectives germane to entrepreneurial sympathizers include developing empathy and support for the unique aspects of entrepreneurship, and developing greater understanding and support for mechanisms of change.

Those with Entrepreneurial Spirit

A fourth possible target group for entrepreneurship education is individuals who have or wish to kindle an entrepreneurial spirit within themselves. They have a willingness to try new things or do things differently just because things can be done differently. They do not necessarily have a desire to start a business, nor do they wish to have an entrepreneurial career. Yet, they want to be able to embrace change, experiment with ideas, and be open and flexible in their actions.

Learning objectives that are consistent with a target audience of people with an entrepreneurial spirit might include: identifying and stimulating entrepreneurial drive, talent, and skill; undoing the risk-averse bias of many analytical techniques; and developing empathy and support for the unique aspects of entrepreneurship.

These audiences and their primary and secondary objectives are summarized in Table 2–2.

OBJECTIVES OF ENTREPRENEURSHIP EDUCATION

By identifying the various audiences and objectives of entrepreneurship education, we should be better able to understand the sum total of our educational needs. Such an understanding should affect how we choose evaluative criteria and pedagogical techniques in our research studies, so we can successfully address our research questions.

Research Question 2: Are different entrepreneurship education learning objectives best accomplished (as measured by different criteria) through different instructor and student roles?

We discuss various objectives for entrepreneurship education below, beginning with those objectives that are measurable either during or immediately after a course, and concluding with the more distal objectives that are more usefully measured months or years later. Following a definition of each objective, we identify roles for the instructor and students that management educational theory suggests would facilitate the accomplishment of the objective, and we propose research measures that might be used to assess the utility of the education provided.

TABLE 2-2 — Objectives and Audiences for Entrepreneurship Education

	AUDIENCE			
OBJECTIVES	Entrepreneurs	Managers of Entrepreneurs	Entrepreneurial Sympathizers	Those with Entrepreneurial Spirit
Acquire knowledge germane to entrepreneurship	Primary	Primary		
Acquire skill in the use of techniques, in the analysis of business situations, and in the synthesis of action plans	Primary	Secondary		
Identify and stimulate entrepreneurial drive, talent, and skill	Primary			Primary
Undo the risk-averse bias of many analytical techniques	Secondary	Primary		Primary
Develop empathy and support for the unique aspects of entrepreneurship		Primary	Primary	Primary
Revise attitudes toward change		Secondary	Primary	Secondary

Acquire Knowledge and Understand Concepts Germane to Entrepreneurship

The thrust of many college courses is to provide content knowledge about some specific area or discipline. Within the field of entrepreneurship, such knowledge often takes the form of increasing awareness and understanding of the processes involved in initiating and managing a new business enterprise. For example, content areas covered in many entrepreneurship courses include:

1. The nature and unique demands of start-up ventures.
2. Alternative ways of identifying business opportunities.
3. Techniques for analyzing and evaluating opportunities.
4. Frameworks for identifying resources (capital, materials, labor, advisors, mentors) and constraints (licenses, laws, taxes).
5. How to facilitate the maturation of new ventures into growing businesses.
6. The role of new and smaller firms within the economy.

Knowledge, concepts, and techniques are typically taught through lectures, class discussions, expositions of business practices, sample problems, and structured cases, and often through developing a business plan for a new venture.

For these learning objectives, Dooley and Skinner (1977) propose that the instructor's role is to narrate, expose, enlighten, provide expertise, and explain taxonomies, techniques, and interrelationships among concepts. The student's role is to listen, question, and work through problems and examples. Success can be measured by the level of student interest, knowledge retention, playback accuracy, and ability to work through problems correctly.

Acquire Skill in the Use of Techniques, in the Analysis of Business Situations, and in the Synthesis of Action Plans

Entrepreneurship involves the use of the knowledge acquired in many different business school courses such as accounting, financial analysis, marketing, information systems, leadership, and general management. The ability to integrate the functional knowledge of business into a holistic activity requires exercising the skills of analysis and synthesis. For example, confronting realistic business situations or complex, ill-structured cases that emphasize taking action forces students to go beyond the knowledge they have acquired to using that information in constructive ways. Developing a business plan for a new venture or product requires the integration of separate functional skills into a single document and presentation. By grappling with the ambiguity and conflicts within such activities, students have the opportunity to move from concepts to practice.

In contrast to the instructor's role noted above for the knowledge acquisition objective, Dooley and Skinner (1977) propose that the instructor's role is to challenge, question, and encourage students to develop greater realism. The use of role-plays in addition to complex cases and projects can be used for this purpose. The student's role is to develop skill in applying techniques, evolve an understanding of cause-effect relationships based on the analysis of facts and logical inferences, and establish priorities for action based on probable outcomes and implications. Success can be measured by the thoroughness, variety, and completeness of analyses, and the creativity, realism, and practicality of recommendations.

Identify and Stimulate Entrepreneurial Drive, Talent, and Skill

The willingness and ability to lead a venture under conditions of relatively high uncertainty varies among individuals, and possibly within individuals depending on the situation and their life experiences. A third objective of entrepreneurship courses is to increase student awareness of new venture/smaller company career possibilities and to help individuals develop an awareness of their entrepreneurial interests, capability, and potential. What does it mean to be an entrepreneur? How well does one function under conditions of ambiguity, adversity, and personal or professional risk? Does one have the ability to champion an idea, yet remain flexible in approach and have the resilience to bounce back after setbacks?

Developing an awareness of what it feels like to manage under such conditions may be as important to developing successful entrepreneurial careers as are the knowledge, concepts, and skills acquired. Our ability to help individuals assess their entrepreneurial drive, talent, and skills may be somewhat constrained within the classroom. Peer and self-appraisals are one way to stimulate self-understanding and insight. Entrepreneurial activities outside of the traditional classroom might also be relevant to this objective. For example, the use of assessment center techniques, business simulations, and management games can stimulate awareness of and interest in one's entrepreneurial potential (Stumpf 1988).

The role of the instructor in identifying and stimulating entrepreneurial drive, talent, and skill is that of a counselor or coach. The majority of time is spent listening, observing, and sharing constructive feedback. The student's role involves active diagnosis and reflection, sharing one's insights, and seeking additional viewpoints and experiences to validate the insights. Entrepreneurial actions, in contrast to analyses and attitudes, are likely to be the most meaningful indices of success.

Undo the Risk-Averse Bias of Many Analytical Techniques

Business school courses, particularly those in finance and accounting, have done an exceptional job of training people how to measure and avoid financial risk in work organizations. Frequently, behavioral science courses reinforce this risk-averse value by discouraging personal and interpersonal risk taking. Students who generate creative answers that differ from the norm in case or critical incident analysis are often given negative feedback. Rarely do business schools place sufficient emphasis on developing creativity, on finding many right answers to situations, or on exploring the ethical aspects of entrepreneurial issues (Porter and McKibbin 1988). The result has been a bias towards quantitative analysis and an emphasis on postponing action until all the desired data are available for review. Since there is rarely a single, obvious answer to the more interesting business situations, this academic tendency prizes analysis over intuition, visioning, or other, less analytical ways of thinking.

A fourth objective of some entrepreneurial education has been to undo this bias for analysis and of finding the "analytically right solution." Undoing the bias means education on how to manage risks through actions that spread risk across a wider group of stakeholders, and how to cut losses and stretch gains well beyond what textbooks tend to suggest. The extent to which the bias for risk aversion is reduced is currently difficult to assess through testing. In contrast, it is potentially observable in student actions, either in actual entrepreneurial activities or through their presentations of entrepreneurial analyses — both in terms of the presentation process and its content.

The instructor's role in helping individuals to convert from risk aversion to risk management is first a deconstructive role, followed by reconstructive role. Through the examination of issues from many different perspectives, a variety of possible courses of action can be articulated. By denying the more risk-averse possibilities, attention can be directed towards those actions that balance risk with precautions and rewards. The student's role in this is to debate outcomes while remaining open to many viable courses of action. Success may be indexed by changes in attitudes, increased confidence in actions that are not as analytically precise, and the development of a sense of personal responsibility for making one's recommendations work.

Develop Empathy and Support for the Unique Aspects of Entrepreneurship

Not all individuals who take a course in entrepreneurship wish to be entrepreneurs. Some may wish to explore entrepreneurship on an intellectual level. Others may recognize the need for entrepreneurship in society, and attend a program so as to better understand this discipline. A learning objective for this latter group is to have them develop an understanding of the distinct characteristics of a business in evolution from the seed of an idea to a stable, ongoing enterprise. Similarly, it may be useful for such learners to understand more fully the distinct characteristics of individuals as entrepreneurs.

The value of such an objective is similar to individuals taking courses in any field outside of their major area of study. They are interested in content knowledge, but not for its direct application to their immediate career. Rather, they are trying to broaden their understanding of their life or work environment so as to be more effective in working with and through other people. Developing effectiveness measures of the cognitive aspect of this learning objective could be done through tests and other graded assignments. However, the more important objective is with respect to the development of empathy and support for entrepreneurial activities. Are people who attend entrepreneurial courses more supportive of entrepreneurship in their work organizations ? Are they more inclined to permit new ventures to start, provide emotional and political support to the more promising ventures, and mitigate some of the resistance that routinely emerges around most new initiatives ?

The instructor's role in developing empathy and support for entrepreneurship is to raise the issue of a manager's attitudes towards entrepreneurship and stimulate excitement about entrepreneurial activities. The student's role is to develop a meaningful place for entrepreneurship within their work lives. In some ways this is equivalent to art appreciation for nonartists. Success in attaining this objective may be evaluated in the same ways that art appreciation programs are judged as successful — through attendance and interest, through financial and personal contributions, and through communicating positive attitudes towards the field.

Revise Attitudes Towards Change

A sixth objective of entrepreneurship courses may be to educate people, particularly corporate managers, on how to encourage and embrace the desire to innovate within their subordinates. As with the objectives of reducing risk aversion and developing empathy and support for entrepreneurship, creating a positive attitude towards change involves more emotional learning than cognitive learning.

The role of the instructor is to assist individuals in developing more open attitudes towards change. The student's role is to tolerate the ambiguity created, accept the uncomfortable feelings that initially emerge, and trust their intuition that changes can be managed productively. To measure the effectiveness of such education, we need to track the actions of people over time within their work organizations. Our focus becomes, do people with managers that embrace change and innovation actually champion ideas and develop successful entrepreneurial ventures more often than people who have managers that resist change ?

A summary of these six objectives for entrepreneurship education and the proposed teacher role, student role, and measures of effectiveness for each objective are provided in Table 2–3.

--- --- --- --- --- --- --- ---

POSSIBLE RESEARCH STUDIES AND IMPLICATIONS FOR ENTREPRENEURSHIP EDUCATION

We began with a discussion of the challenges in entrepreneurship education research. It seems fitting to close with a discussion of some possible research approaches that may enable us to meet some of those challenges.

TABLE 2–3 — Objectives and Pedagogical Preferences for Entrepreneurship Education

OBJECTIVES	PEDAGOGICAL PREFERENCES		Measures
	Instructor Role	Student Role	
Acquire knowledge germane to entrepreneurship.	Narrate, expose, enlighten, and explain various techniques, concepts, etc.	Listen, question, work problems, and gain content knowledge.	Level of interest, knowledge retention, playback accuracy, work problems correctly.
Acquire skill in the use of techniques, in the analysis of business situations, and in the synthesis of action plans.	Challenge, question, and probe students to develop greater realism.	Develop skill in applying techniques, evolve understandings, establish real-world priorities.	Evaluation of the thoroughness, variety, and completeness of analyses and recommendations.
Identify and stimulate entrepreneurial drive, talent, and skill.	Be a counselor or coach — listen, observe, and share feedback.	Active diagnosis and reflection, share insights, seek many viewpoints and experiences.	Entrepreneurial actions, searching for change opportunities.
Undo the risk-averse bias of many analytical techniques.	Deconstruction of past perspectives, reconstructive attitudes.	Debate outcomes, remain open to alternatives.	Attitude change, confidence in ambiguous actions, personal responsibility for results.
Develop empathy and support for the unique aspects of entrepreneurship.	Raise questions about attitudes, stimulate excitement.	Develop a sense of the role for entrepreneurship in their work lives.	Attendance, financial and personal interest, positive attitudes.
Revise attitudes toward change.	Assist people to develop more positive attitudes towards change.	Tolerate ambiguity, accept uncomfortable feelings, trust intuition.	Track actions of people over time, embrace change, support champions.

The Question of Criteria

One of the easier research questions to answer is that of customer or student satisfaction with courses taken. One method, generally used throughout the NYU Stern School of Business, is a uniform instrument which students fill in at the end of the semester before their grades are reported. This instrument measures students' views of course content, subject interest, course usefulness, instructor appeal, and the like. The ratings are made on a Likert-like scale of 1–7. Generally courses and instructors with higher ratings get higher enrollment, and it is alleged that faculty who give higher grades also get higher ratings. It is a reasonable measure of satisfaction. The problem is that the instrument does not reveal directly whether the student learned anything.

An important question is what value is added by a specific course. In an effort to answer this question, a pre- and post-course questionnaire (see Table 2–1) was given to students which measures their self-perception of their knowledge and ability to start and run a business, and their desire and expectation as to when they will do so. This questionnaire was used by two faculty members each teaching a different section of the same course. The "before" and "after" course results were tabulated and analyzed for significance. In both sections, students' perception of their capability increased significantly, and the results in each section were remarkably similar.

These results were compared with two sections of a course offered at another university which used the same questionnaire. There were significant differences between instructors in that case, and significant differences between schools as well. In addition, the "before" responses were compared with the responses of a sample of students who did not take the course and did not intend to take any entrepreneurship courses. While 60 percent of those students expressed an intention to start or own a business someday, compared with 90 percent of the course takers, and the time by which they expected this to happen was 2 to 3 years later than the course takers, almost all other self-perceptions were similar to those of the course takers' pre-course responses.

The point of this is merely to suggest that an instrument which can be widely used among many schools is possible, reliability can be established, and we can learn a great deal more about this type of evaluation as a potential source of information for general use.

Further, if such investigation is added to the recognition of a common body of knowledge for which examinations can be designed, significant progress in early measures of effectiveness will be made. We will also have better instruments for measuring the results of experimentation.

The above study exemplifies the complexity of evaluating the effectiveness of entrepreneurship education. We briefly explored various other evaluative criteria in Figure 2–1. Most of the research done to date focuses on the more immediate measures of effectiveness (student interest and affect, student knowledge acquisition, etc.). Longitudinal research designs using control groups to compare participants with individuals who did *not* have entrepreneurial educational experience are needed to examine the lasting effects of the education. In other words, true experiments are needed. The systematic tracking of participants and nonparticipants with similar interests ought to become one of the research agendas for many entrepreneurial studies centers. Without such research, the efficacy and survival of entrepreneurship education is limited to the local power base of interested faculty and the generosity of the funding sources. To change a culture, an economy, and indeed a society, many more stakeholders will need to be convinced that entrepreneurship education makes a difference over the life span of an entrepreneur.

The Pursuers of Opportunity

Survey research should be conducted to understand more fully the number and relative interests of people who are inclined to actively pursue entrepreneurial opportunities as a main thrust in their careers. Do the dimensions suggested earlier in conjunction with Table 2–2 actually reflect the preferences of people who are predisposed to participate in entrepreneurship education? What percentage of MBA students and other adult education students fit each category of opportunity seeker? Are there sufficiently large and distinguishable target audiences to warrant offering courses tailored to their specific interests?

Longitudinal survey research should be conducted to explore how peoples' intentions to pursue opportunity change over time. What effect does a start-up failure have on future entrepreneurial activities — does it stimulate or inhibit future activities?

The Objectives of Entrepreneurship Education

Hills' (1988) survey research of 15 highly regarded entrepreneurship educators' views of entrepreneurship education objectives is an interesting point of departure. Having identified possible objectives, are these objectives equally shared by participants in our educational programs? Do people that fall into different entrepreneurship audiences have different objectives in mind when they attend an educational program?

Table 2–3 proposes that people who are or intend to become entrepreneurs or entrepreneurial managers will have objectives for their education that focus on acquiring knowledge germane to entrepreneurship and acquiring the related entrepreneurial skills and techniques. In contrast, people who might see themselves as entrepreneurial sympathizers or having entrepreneurial spirit would have objectives that focus on skill development, attitude change, and developing empathy for the unique aspects of entrepreneurship. Can these propositions be empirically supported?

Content and Pedagogical Preferences

The most difficult and costly research on entrepreneurship education will involve the examination of different program content and pedagogical methods used to accomplish educational objectives. Dozens of possible hypotheses are implicitly suggested by Table 2–3. For example, the use of lectures and discussions to present course concepts is suggested as being appropriate to convey knowledge germane to entrepreneurship, but is not suggested for the stimulation of entrepreneurial drive, talent, and skill. Can such a proposition be empirically supported?

For meaningful results to be obtained, different program content/pedagogical method combinations need to be examined across a number of institutions, classes, and instructors. Through the design of critical experiments, it would be possible to address the relative value of the education provided. A critical experiment would contrast two or more content/method combinations across multiple sections of courses taught by comparable instructors.

A separate research thrust could explore whether or not individuals interested in entrepreneurship have different learning styles from those not interested in entrepreneurship. Are educational approaches that include concrete experiences and active experimentation preferred by entrepreneurs over reflective observation and abstract conceptualization approaches? Do those interested in entrepreneurship learn in ways that are different from people in general?

Some Propositions which Warrant Investigation

1. Graduates with MBA's who have had entrepreneurship courses and who follow an entreprencurial career will build significantly larger, more profitable businesses, and will employ more workers than people without a graduate business education. They will start more businesses, and survive better than MBA's who have not had such courses.
2. An MBA education without entrepreneurship courses will reduce the desire of graduates to become entrepreneurs. Graduates without a business education will start more businesses than those with a business education.
3. Entrepreneurs' learning needs as perceived by them will not coincide with needs identified by objective observers who study the companies of the entrepreneurs.
4. Understanding the anatomy of failures is crucial to achieving success. Entrepreneurs who have experienced a failure build better (larger, more innovative, more successful) businesses than those who have not.
5. The distribution of learning style preferences of entrepreneurs is not significantly different than the learning style preferences of high achievers in any field, and probably no different than low achievers.

6. There are no distinguishable personality differences between entrepreneurs who have failed and those who have succeeded.
7. Successful entrepreneurs who have failed and later succeed tend to blame their failure on themselves and their own deficiency; failure repeaters tend to blame their failure on either others or uncontrollable conditions.
8. There is a high degree of commonality of knowledge taught in entrepreneurship courses, much of it without a verifiable research basis.
9. Students with entrepreneurial objectives who do not take courses fail to do so because they believe they are not necessary, or because other courses have higher priorities within the constraints imposed by the institution.
10. Entrepreneurship students tend to be poorer students than nonentrepreneurship students (i.e., have a lower GPA).
11. Retrospective studies of perceived learning needs by entrepreneurs will differ markedly from perceived learning needs by entrepreneurship students.
12. With respect to starting a new venture, learning needs perceived by entrepreneurship students will not differ from perceived learning needs by students in general.

Implications for Entrepreneurship Education

Rigorous research is clearly needed to understand the target audiences for entrepreneurship education, their unique educational objectives and learning styles, and the types of content to be covered for each audience, and which specific pedagogical methods will most effectively meet their educational goals. Such research must look at both the proximal criteria of student interest and immediate feedback as well as the more distal criteria of actual behavior over 10 or more years.

As entrepreneurship researchers, we can begin to build a data base, founded on valid sampling and sound research methodology. For maximum value, we should consider the use of a common language, criteria for evaluation, and other appropriate standards for material to be included in a collaborative and cumulative data base. Centers of entrepreneurship can be useful mechanisms for raising funds to support the needed research. The data can serve as a basis for research by others, including untenured faculty who must meet requirements for publication volume and quality in order to achieve tenure. Experimentation with audiences, pedagogy, and content can simultaneously produce innovation in education while adding to cumulative knowledge, with appropriate attention to experimental design.

If we can learn how to match up audiences, objectives, content, and pedagogies, we should be able to get a greater return on our educational effort. But we'd better be careful. If we are too successful, we may find that there will be educational institutions devoted to entrepreneurship which also teach business!

━━━━━━━━
REFERENCES

Block, Z. 1985 The management of entrepreneurship : Educational and research needs. In *Entrepreneurship : What it is and how to teach it*, eds. J. Kao and H. Stevenson. Cambridge, Mass. : Harvard Business School.

Brockhaus, R. H. 1987 Entrepreneurial folklore. *Journal of Small Business Management* 25 (3) : 1–6.

1988 Entrepreneurial research : Are we playing the correct game ? *American Journal of Small Business* 12 (3) : 55–62.

Brown, I. E., R. L. Christy, and A. F. Banowitz 1987 Perceptions of success in business start-up and the impact of entrepreneurial education. In *Frontiers of Entrepreneurship Research*, eds. N. C. Churchill, J. A. Hornaday, B. A. Kirchhoff, O. J. Krasner, and K. H. Vesper, 600–602. Wellesley, Mass. : Babson College.

Clark, B. W., C. H. Davis, and V. C. Harnish 1984 Do courses in entrepreneurship aid in new venture creation ? *Journal of Small Business Management* 22 (2) : 26–31.

Cooper, A. C., and W. C. Dunkelberg 1987 Entrepreneurial research : Old questions, new answers, and methodological issues. *American Journal of Small Business* 11 (3) : 11–23.

Cooper, C. L. 1982 A theory of management learning : Its implications for management education. In *Management education : Issues in theory, research, and practice*, eds. R. D. Freedman, C. L. Cooper, and S. A. Stumpf, 45–55. N.Y. : John Wiley & Sons.

Cullen, T. P., and T. J. Dick 1989 Tomorrow's entrepreneur and today's hospitality curriculum. *Cornell Hotel and Restaurant Administration Quarterly* 30 (2) : 54–57.

Dooley, A. R., and W. Skinner 1977 Casing casemethod methods. *Academy of Management Review* 2 : 277–289.

Drucker, P. 1985 *Innovation and entrepreneurship*. N.Y. : Harper & Row.

Freedman, R. D., and S. A. Stumpf 1982 Management education : Its theory, research, and practice. In *Management education : Issues in theory, research, and practice*, eds. R. D. Freedman, C. L. Cooper, and S. A. Stumpf, 3–20. N.Y. : John Wiley & Sons.

Freedman, R. D., C. L. Cooper, and S. A. Stumpf, eds. 1982 *Management education : Issues in theory, research, and practice*. N.Y. : John Wiley & Sons.

Herbert, R. F., and A. N. Link 1982 *The entrepreneur*. N.Y. : Praeger.

Hills, G. E. 1988 Variations in university entrepreneurship education : An empirical study of an evolving field. *Journal of Business Venturing* 3 : 109–122.

Hills, G. E., and H. Welsch 1986 Entrepreneurship behaviour intentions and student independence : Characteristics and experiences. In *Frontiers of entrepreneurship research*, eds. R. Ronstadt, J. A. Hornaday, R. Peterson, and K. H. Vesper, 173–186. Wellesley, Mass. : Babson College.

House, R. J. 1982 Experiential learning : A social learning theory analysis. In *Management education : Issues in theory, research, and practice*, eds. R. D. Freedman, C. L. Cooper, and S. A. Stumpf, 23–44. N.Y. : John Wiley & Sons.

Leepson, M. 1988 Building a business : A matter of course. *Nation's Business* 76 (4) : 42–43.

Lundberg, C. C., and G. Westacott 1982 Enhancing instructional practice : Toward a model for self-research. In *Management education : Issues in theory, research, and practice*, eds. R. D. Freedman, C. L. Cooper, and S. A. Stumpf, 59–83. N.Y. : John Wiley & Sons.

McMullan, W. E., and W. A. Long 1983 An approach to educating entrepreneurs. *The Canadian Journal of Small Business* 1 (2) : 32–36.

1990 *Developing new ventures : The entrepreneurial option.* N.Y. : Harcourt Brace Jovanovich.

McMullan, W. E., W. A. Long, and J. B. Graham 1986 Assessing economic value added by university-based new-venture outreach programs. *Journal of Business Venturing* 1 : 225–240.

Porter, L. W., and L. E. McKibbin 1988 *Management education and development : Drift or thrust into the 21st century ?* N.Y. : McGraw-Hill.

Robinson, P. B., and H. K. Hunt 1989 Entrepreneurial research on students may not generalize to real entrepreneurs. In *Frontiers of entrepreneurship research*, eds. R. Brockhaus, N. Churchill, J. Katz, B. Kirchhoff, K. Vesper, and W. Wetzel, Jr., 491–492. Wellesley, Mass. : Babson College.

Scott, M. G. 1989 The survival, failure, and exit of a five year cohort of graduate entrepreneurs. In *Frontiers of entrepreneurship research*, eds. R. Brockhaus, N. Churchill, J. Katz, B. Kirchhoff, K. Vesper, and W. Wetzel, Jr., 110–112. Wellesley, Mass. : Babson College.

Sexton, D. L., and N. B. Bowman 1984 Entrepreneurship education : Suggestions for increasing effectiveness. *Journal of Small Business Management* 22 (1) : 18–25.

1987 Evaluation of an innovative approach to teaching entrepreneurship. *Journal of Small Business Management* 25 (1) : 35–43.

1988 Validation of an innovative teaching approach for entrepreneurship courses. *American Journal of Small Business* 12 (3) : 11–18.

Shuman, J. C., J. A. Seeger, and N. C. Teebagy 1987 Entrepreneurial activity and educational background. In *Frontiers of entrepreneurship research*, eds. N. C. Churchill, J. A. Hornaday, B. A. Kirchhoff, O. J. Krasner, and K. H. Vesper, 590–599. Wellesley, Mass. : Babson College.

Stevenson, H. H., and D. E. Gumpert 1985 The heart of entrepreneurship. *Harvard Business Review* 63 (2) : 85–94.

Stone, E. F. 1982 Research design : Issues in studies assessing the effects of management education. In *Management education : Issues in theory, research, and practice*, eds. R. D. Freedman, C. L. Cooper, and S. A. Stumpf, 87–132. N.Y. : John Wiley & Sons.

Stumpf, S. A. 1988 Business simulations for skill diagnosis and development. In *The HR professional and employee career development*, eds. M. London and E. Mone, 195–206. Westport, Conn. : Greenwood Press.

Vesper, K. H. 1980 *New venture strategies.* Englewood Cliffs, N.J. : Prentice-Hall, Inc.

1986 New development in entrepreneurship education. In *The art and science of entrepreneurship*, eds. D. L. Sexton and R. Smilor, 379–387, N.Y. : Ballinger.

1988 Entrepreneurial academics — How can we tell when the field is getting somewhere ? *Journal of Business Venturing* 3 : 1–10.

Vesper, K. H., W. E. McMullan, and D. M. Ray 1988 Designing an entrepreneurship program : What can we learn from other fields ? *Revista Economica de Catalunya* 9 (2) : 77–82.

Part

2

ENTREPRENEURSHIP AND ECONOMIC DEVELOPMENT

Chapter

3

The Social and Economic
Impact of Entrepreneurship

Zoltan J. Acs
and
David B. Audretsch

INTRODUCTION

Our story begins in the United States. It was in the area of job generation that the recent emergence of small firms was first identified. One decade ago David Birch revealed the startling findings from his long-term study of American job generation. Despite the prevailing conventional wisdom, Birch reported that, " . . . whatever else they are doing large firms are no longer the major providers of new jobs for Americans" (1981, 8). Rather, Birch discovered that most new jobs originated in small firms.

Birch's findings met resistance for at least three reasons. First, at that time the literature in industrial economics, the field most directly associated with studying markets, was preoccupied with identifying the extent of concentration in markets and its effects on economic performance. Given the existing state of knowledge about the source of economic activity, this preoccupation was not surprising. The long-term trend had been clearly identified by the early 1970s as an increased concentration in economic activity both at the aggregate as well as at the market level. For example, the percentage of total U.S. manufacturing assets accounted for by the largest one hundred corporations increased from about 36 percent in 1924 and 39 percent after the second World

War to over 50 percent by the end of the 1960s, causing F. M. Scherer to conclude in the 1970 edition of *Industrial Market Structure and Economic Performance*, "Despite the [statistical] uncertainties, one thing is clear. The increasing domestic dominance of the 100 largest manufacturing firms since 1947 is not a statistical illusion" (44). Thus, it was not readily apparent how to reconcile Birch's claim that 80 percent of new jobs were created in small firms with the stylized facts which emerged in the industrial economics literature. These facts indicated an ever-increasing tendency towards concentrated economic activity, both in individual markets as well as the overall economy.

A second point of contention was raised regarding the exact methodology and application of the underlying data (Armington and Odle 1982; Storey and Johnson 1987; and FitzRoy 1989). As Evans (1991) points out, reconciliation between the enterprise (firm) and establishment (plant) records in the Dun and Bradstreet data files leads to substantially different results than those reached by Birch. As Evans also emphasizes, both the publication of and reaction to *Employers Large and Small* by Brown, Hamilton, and Medoff (1990) serve as a barometer of the ongoing debate that still rages over the statistical validity of Birch's claims.

The third major challenge raised against Birch's finding is the relevance in examining the numbers of newly created jobs. As Brown et al. (1990) point out, many of these newly generated jobs subsequently disappear. Focusing solely on the number of new jobs created by small firms, without considering the number of job disappearances, leads to an overstatement of the amount of economic activity actually stemming from small firms (Storey 1990).

Despite these well-founded challenges to Birch's claims, a number of independent studies based on different statistical methodologies have converged towards a singular conclusion: namely, between the mid-1970s and the early 1990s, a substantial shift has occurred in American economic activity. Small firms are apparently playing a relatively more important role in the economy. For example, Brock and Evans (1989) report that the number of new-firm start-ups in the United States has increased dramatically over time. While 376,000 new firms were established in 1976, 703,000 new businesses were incorporated in 1986. This 87 percent increase in the number of new-firm start-ups was more than twice as great as the 39 percent increase in real gross national product which occurred over the same period. Equally striking is the reversal in the steady increase in average firm size that has taken place throughout the post-war period. While the average real GNP-per-firm rose by nearly two-thirds between 1947 and 1980, from $150,000 to $250,000, it subsequently declined by about 14 percent during the subsequent six years to $210,000.

This shift in U.S. economic activity away from large firms and towards smaller firms has not escaped the attention of the popular press. For example, *The Economist* reports:

> Despite ever-larger and noisier mergers, the biggest change coming over the world of business is that firms are getting smaller. The trend of a century is being re-

versed. Until the mid-1970s, the size of firms everywhere grew ; the number of self-employed fell. Ford and General Motors replaced the carriage-maker's atelier ; McDonald's, Safeway and W. H. Smith supplanted the corner shop. No longer. Now it is the big firms that are shrinking and small ones that are on the rise. The trend is unmistakable — and businessmen and policy-makers will ignore it at their peril. ("The Rise and Rise of America's Small Firms," 21 January 1989)

Of course, as Thomas Gray (1991) points out, there is a temptation to attribute the relative increase in the number of small firms and in small-firm employment to the obvious long-term transition of employment into the service sector and out of manufacturing. Between 1960 and 1990 the employment share of manufacturing fell from 40 percent to about 25 percent. However, as Figure 3–1 shows, a substantial shift in the share of manufacturing sales accounted for by small firms occurred between 1976 and 1986. While firms with fewer than 500 employees accounted for about 21 percent of manufacturing employment in 1976, the small-firm sales share had risen to approximately 25 percent by 1986.

In the next section of this chapter we present the stylized facts on the economic role of small firms in market economies. Subsequent sections examine the larger socioeconomic "picture" for the shift toward small firms and plants, and discuss the impending industrial restructuring in eastern Europe and the Soviet Union. In the final section we conclude that the planned economies must completely abandon the administrative system, and reinstitute a technologically progressive small-firm sector.

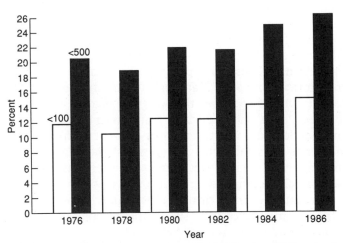

FIGURE 3–1 Percent of Sales Contributed by Small Manufacturing Firms, 1976–1986. For each year listed there are two columns. Column one (< **100**) represents small firms with fewer than 100 employees. Column two (< **500**) represents small firms with fewer than 500 employees. (*Source :* U.S. Establishment and Enterprise Microdata File (Small Business Administration, Washington, D.C., April 1988).)

THE ECONOMIC ROLE
OF SMALL FIRMS :
THE STYLIZED FACTS

While the small-firm sector has remained an enigma for years, a series of empirical studies have recently enabled researchers to assemble a far better understanding of the economic role of small firms and entrepreneurship.

Stylized fact 1 :

A shift in the size distribution of firms has occurred away from larger firms towards smaller ones.

The shift in the firm size distribution found in the United States can be found in other industrialized countries at both the enterprise and establishment level (Loveman and Sengenberger 1991). In general, the increase has been at the expense of large enterprises and establishments. While the magnitude of the increase varies considerably from country to country and across sectors, its significance rests primarily on the fact that it signals the reversal of a substantial downward trend in the employment shares of small firms that had prevailed for many decades. For example, the small- and medium-firm share of employment in Japanese manufacturing industries declined from 83 percent in 1935 to 63 percent in 1972 but then increased to 67 percent in 1983 (Sato 1989 ; Yokokara 1988). A similar trend can be observed in the other developed countries, although in the socialist countries no such trend can be observed.

While there has been a shift in the size distribution of firms in most countries during the past two decades, Table 3–1 shows that the share of small- and medium-sized firms (SME) differs across countries. While the small- and medium-firm sector accounted for almost 50 percent of employment in 1985 in Belgium, 70 percent in Switzerland, and 31 percent in the United States, it accounted for a very low share of employment in Czechoslovakia and the former German Democratic Republic. As Loveman and Sengenberger (1991, 5) point out, the actual size distribution of firms at any particular point in time depends on the institutional or historical context : "Major criteria for structuring SME sectors are the legal status (such as in France), the ownership status (as in Hungary), the distinction between 'craft' and 'industrial' firms (as in the Federal Republic of Germany), independent and subordinate firms (as in Japan), or small firms in small-firm industries vs. small firms in industries where large enterprises dominate or where there is a mixed size composition." In other words, while there appears to be no predetermined optimal size distribution of firms, the shift toward a larger percentage of small firms in most countries is even more remarkable given that these firms started from such different points.

Stylized fact 2 :

The firm growth rate decreases with firm size and firm age.

Recent studies have considerably expanded the state of knowledge about the relationship between firm size and growth. Hall (1987) identified a four

**TABLE 3-1 — The Percentage Share of Employees
in Small Manufacturing Firms**

Country	Fewer than 100 Employees	Fewer than 500 Employees
Italy (1981)	58.9	80.2
Japan (1980)	57.8	73.4[a]
Ireland (1980)	38.1	79.6
Portugal (1985)	43.8	77.5
Denmark (1982)	39.8	74.4
France (1980)	44.1	72.9
Switzerland (1985)	41.2	70.5
Spain (1978)	43.4	65.2
Austria (1976)	39.0	62.7
Netherlands (1980)	38.8	—
Belgium (1985)	32.8	58.7
Luxembourg (1980)	19.2	45.0
Finland (1984)[b]	25.5	43.8
F.R.G. (1983)[c]	16.0	40.8
U.K. (1983)	22.0	36.4
U.S. (1986)	23.7	37.4
Hungary (1987)[d]	23.0	34.0
Czechoslovakia (1985)	.5	0.7
GDR (1986)	.4	1.1

[a] Enterprises with fewer than 300 employees : 78 percent
[b] Industry
[c] Only enterprises with more than 20 employees : 22 percent and 47 percent, respectively
[d] State and cooperative sector
Sources : For EEC countries : S. Johnson and D. J. Storey, *Small and Medium Sized Enterprises and Employment Creation in the EEC Countries,* Summary Report (1988), 7.
Japan : Small Business Agency, *Small Business in Japan 1984* (Ministry for International Trade and Industry, 1984), 92.
Austria : A. Aiginger and S. Tichy, *Die Größe der Kleinen* (Signum Verlag, 1985), 43.
Finland : *Statistik arsbok for Finland* (1987), 195.
United States : *The State of Small Business : A Report of the President* (Washington, D.C. : GPO, 1988), 49.

percentage point difference in the annual growth rates between firms in the 25th and 75th percentiles within publicly traded firms. Smaller firms were found to grow faster than their larger counterparts. Hall argued that differences in investment and R&D outlays explained the truly superior job creation performance of smaller firms. Building on the work of Jovanovic (1982), Evans (1987a, 1987b) also cast considerable doubt on Gibrat's Law of the relationship between firm size and firm growth. In his 1987a paper, Evans selected 100 four-digit Standard Industrial Classification industries and calculated individual firm growth rates between 1976 and 1980. He found that Gibrat's Law did not hold in 89 percent of the industries. In both of Evans' papers the same conclusion was reached. The firm growth rate is found to decrease with both firm size and firm age. These results have been confirmed for Italy (Contini and Revelli, 1990).

Stylized fact 3 :
Small firms are at least as innovative as large firms on a per employee basis and generally have the innovative advantage in high-technology industries.

The most convincing evidence in support of the innovative advantage of small firms (Scherer, 1991 ; Cohen and Klepper, forthcoming) comes from the U.S. Small Business Innovation Data Base, and is analyzed in our 1987 and 1988 papers and 1990 book. We found that in 1982, large firms in manufacturing introduced 2,608 innovations. Small firms contributed 1,923 innovations. However, small-firm employment was only about one-half as great as large-firm employment, so that the mean small-firm innovation rate was 322 innovations per million employees. By contrast, the large-firm innovation rate was 225 innovations per million employees. The small-firm innovation rate is relatively higher in the high-technology industries, such as instruments, chemicals, non-electrical machinery, and computers.

Similar results have been found in the United Kingdom using the Science Policy Research Unit (SPRU) Innovation Data Base at the University of Sussex (Pavitt, Robson, and Townsend 1987). The SPRU data also revealed that the relatively high innovative activity rate of small firms is a new phenomenon that did not emerge until around 1970 (Rothwell 1989).

Stylized fact 4 :
Small firms face binding liquidity constraints.

It has long been suspected that small firms face liquidity constraints because of imperfect capital markets. Recently Evans and Jovanovic (1989) concluded that imperfect credit markets do indeed constrain entrepreneurs. They based their judgement on econometric tests in which wealthier people are shown to be more likely, *ceteris paribus,* to switch from paid employment into self-employment. Fazzari, Hubbard, and Peterson (1988) found that for a sample of publicly traded companies, financing was more difficult than for larger firms. Finally, Blanchflower and Oswald (1990), using British data, found that the probability of self-employment depends upon whether the individual ever received a gift or inheritance. Those who were given or inherited 5,000 pounds, for example, were approximately twice as likely, *ceteris paribus,* to establish a business. These results are consistent with the U.S. results stressing the importance of capital and liquidity constraints.

Stylized fact 5 :
The small-firm share of employment is growing faster in the goods-producing sectors than for the economy as a whole.

In the United States the small-firm share of employment declined in every major sector between 1958 and 1977. However, between 1977 and 1986 the small-firm share of employment increased in the goods-producing sectors and decreased in the non-goods-producing sectors. Small-firm employment increased by 7.8 percent in mining, 3.5 percent in construction, and 1.8 percent in manufacturing. During the same time period, small-firm employment decreased by 0.8 percent in wholesale trade, 7.5 percent in retail trade, and 3.2 percent in services (Brown, Hamilton, and Medoff 1990, 26). Of course we should remember that even though firms in the non-goods-producing sector are getting relatively larger, they are only about one-third the size of firms in the goods-producing sector. A similar trend can be found in other OECD countries. Even after taking into account sectoral shifts, the small-firm share of employment in manufacturing has increased (Loveman and Sengenberger 1991).

Stylized fact 6 :
Firm survival is positively related to firm size and firm age.

New-firm start-ups, as well as new plants, tend to have a lower rate of survival than established firms. These results were substantiated with different data sets in the United States by Dunne, Roberts, and Samuelson (1989), Evans (1987a, 1987b), and Hall (1987). Industries experiencing substantial entry in the form of entrepreneurial start-ups are more likely also to experience a high rate of firm failure. Such industries can be characterized by a high degree of what Invernizzi and Revelli (1991) call "turbulence" — the simultaneous entry of new firms and exit of incumbents.

While it is well known that new firms fail at a higher rate than established firms, exactly how many firms survive for a "long" time, and therefore make a meaningful contribution to the economy, is unclear. Recently Phillips and Kirchhoff (1989), using the U.S. Small Business Data Base, developed an estimate for the whole economy between the years 1976 and 1986. They found that 39.9 percent of the new entrants survived at least six years. Even more striking was the finding that the survival rate was highest in manufacturing (46.9 percent) and the lowest in construction (35.3 percent).

Evans and Leighton (1988), using the U.S. current population survey, show that about three-fifths of those entering self-employment are still in business after 10 years. Moreover, Evans and Leighton (1990) also find that the failure rate for those entering self-employment from unemployment is twice as high as for those who were not previously unemployed. These issues have been further examined by David Storey (1991) for the United Kingdom, and by Michael Fritsch (1991). Fritsch points out that new-firm start-ups in (former) West Germany face a lower rate of survival than do established firms.

Stylized fact 7 :
Most new manufacturing plants enter on a small scale.

The increase in the number of U.S. manufacturing establishments by 32,000 over a six-year period (from 448,000 in 1980 to 480,000 in 1986) does not suggest a particularly important role for the entry of new manufacturing plants. On average, there was an increase of just slightly more than one percentage point in the number of establishments each year. However, when the amount of *gross* rather than *net* entry is examined, a considerably different picture emerges. In fact, 205,000 new manufacturing establishments entered between 1980 and 1986, representing a gross entry rate of 45.8 percent. At the same time, 173,000 manufacturing establishments exited from manufacturing, resulting in an exit rate of 38.6 percent (Acs and Audretsch 1990). Using a different data set over a longer time period, Dunne, Roberts, and Samuelson (1989) confirmed these results. Dunne et al. found that in each census year, plants with fewer than five employees accounted for 36 percent of the total number of plants.

Data on entry and exit for European industry has been compiled by Geroski (1990). He concluded that gross entry rates of around 5 percent seem to be something of a norm in manufacturing, with a shift towards smaller plants during the 1970s and 1980s. When comparing the entry and exit of new plants in Yugoslavia with those in the United States, the entry and exit process that we observe in the West is nonexistent (Estrin and Petrin 1990).

Stylized fact 8 :
Small firms produce at least a proportionate share of new jobs.

It is in the area of job generation where the greatest amount of international research has been done. These studies are summarized in Sengenberger, Loveman, and Piore (1990), Storey and Johnson (1987), and OECD (1985). The results from these international studies broadly suggest that the trend in the United States observed by Birch (1981) has similar counterparts in other countries. However, there are two points that must be kept in mind. First, in Europe substantial job losses by large firms dominated the employment statistics and offset the employment gains of smaller firms. Second, the net new jobs result from a very dynamic process of expansion and contraction — births and deaths — within the small-firm sector. Alan Hughes (1991) observes that there has been an increase in the share of small-firm employment in the U.K. manufacturing sector ; however, it has not been as large as previously suggested, and the trend can be traced back to the 1970s.

▬ ▬ ▬ ▬ ▬ ▬ ▬ ▬

THE SOCIAL AND ECONOMIC CONSEQUENCES OF ENTREPRENEURSHIP

The ability of the U.S. economy to maintain full employment while providing international leadership in high-technology markets during the latter part of the 1980s has not gone unnoticed in Europe. In this section we show that the main consequences of entrepreneurship have been crucial contributions in job generation as well as innovative activity. Not only have small firms been the major driving force behind job generation, but as a result, they are playing a more important role in the economy.

While Europeans have become increasingly aware of American success, few question the "conventional wisdom" that the source of this success is greater efficiency enjoyed by the giant corporations. The "European Challenge" is perhaps best summed up by FitzRoy (1990, 22), who suggests that Europeans should " . . . abandon their cherished but unrealistic faith in economies of scale, and institute a thoroughgoing reversal of current policy towards large firms, preferably coupled with support for venture capital for new start-up and small firms." It could be argued that the United Kingdom has had a decade of policies that reflect this view. Unfortunately, there is no way to demonstrate if these policies have been responsible for Britain's economic revival in the 1980s. We believe that, despite the unevenness of the recovery, the United Kingdom has experienced a renaissance in this decade.

Small Firms, New Entry, and Employment

The vast literature on labor market change and small firms has been recently surveyed by Storey and Johnson (1987) and FitzRoy (1989). One of the most remarkable findings in the growing literature on small firms is that their share of employment in U.S. *manufacturing* has increased substantially in recent years, while shares have remained constant in the former Federal Republic of Germany (Acs and Audretsch 1990). We suggest that rapid employment growth in the United States and the decline of stagnation in the main European economies (with the exception of Italy) may be related to the more dynamic small-firm sector in the United States, with its generally lower barriers to new entry (Audretsch and Acs, forthcoming). It should be pointed out that small firms are relatively more important in Europe and Japan than in the United States (Roman 1990). However, the rate of change in the relative presence of small firms has been greater in the United States than in Europe.

The main sources of these differences can be traced to misguided government policies in Europe supporting large firms, as well as to a much larger venture capital market in the United States, and the willingness of scientists and experienced managers in Europe to leave secure jobs and share the entrepreneurial risks in new enterprises. For example, the venture capital market has expanded rapidly recently in the United Kingdom, while it is still of modest importance in the Federal Republic of Germany.

In the United States small high-tech firms are responsible for much of the innovation which has compensated for the decline of traditional industries. In general, unions are weak in the firms that innovate, while profit sharing and work sharing are most prevalent there (Acs and Audretsch 1988). Of course, small high-tech firms account for perhaps no more than 5 percent of the new jobs. Most of the jobs are in lower paid services and manufacturing, and this has led to several critiques of job creation in the small-firm sector as a solution to unemployment problems.

It is perceived that workers with the same skills and other personal characteristics may sometimes be paid more in large firms than in small firms. In the Federal Republic of Germany, even if there is an earnings gap between large and small firms, compared with other countries such as the United States or Japan, this gap is relatively narrow. Average earnings in small firms in the Federal Republic of Germany are 90 percent of those in firms with more than 500 employees. The figures for Japan and the United States are only 77 percent and 57 percent respectively. A fundamental cause of this relatively small gap, in international terms, lies in the German system of central, sector-wide collective bargaining (OECD 1985). At the same time, the more bureaucratic and regimented working conditions of large organizations lead to greater worker dissatisfaction, and workers in large firms are much more prone to strike. Higher pay in large firms may include a compensating differential for difficult working conditions. Thus a low-paying job may be preferred to no job at all, especially by those not receiving generous unemployment benefits. From the point of experience, even a low-paying job will provide intangible benefits in the form of work experience and work references. It is also quite conceivable that a job that is unacceptable to some workers is preferable to lengthy unemployment for others. There is convincing evidence that long bouts of unemployment erode human capital and motivation, and over time lead to exclusion from the labor market. There is little evidence that being unemployed facilitates the search for employment, while the lack of contact in the workplace may handicap search by the unemployed.

Job creation and small- and new-firm entry in Europe have been severely discouraged by decades of government policy in support of large corporations and quasi-monopolistic suppliers of state industries (Geroski and Jacquemin 1985). New-firm entry would be encouraged by labor market flexibility and deregulation as well as by access to the R&D infrastructure. Existing state subsidies and other support for large corporations should be reduced. Indeed, if they are so efficient, why the subsidies in the first place? Enlargement of the small- and medium-firm sector, in turn, would increase competition, enhance the overall rate of return on capital, and most important, expand employment, as we have seen in the United States. Even in "centrally planned economies" like Hungary, where decades of policies have favored large firms over small ones, strengthening and expanding the small-firm sector is considered a prerequisite to the revitalization of the economy.

As FitzRoy (1989a) explains, the European experience of the 1980s poses a profound challenge to standard Keynesian and classical theories of economic fluctuations. Focusing employment policy exclusively on aggregate demand, or on wages and the labor market, will thus miss important channels through which employment, competition, and economic welfare can all be influenced simultaneously without additional public expenditure.

Innovation, Strategy, and Flexibility

Throughout most of this century, industrial technology favored mass production, or the application of special-purpose machines to produce standardized products. Inherent in this technology was inflexibility and a bias towards large firms and plants over smaller ones. However, more recently manufacturing technology " . . . has been revolutionized by the cost reduction of small-scale production relative to large-scale and the degree of flexibility offered by the technology" (Carlsson 1984, 91). Indeed, the new breed of "flexible" capital equipment is considered to be especially well suited to a small-firm strategy favoring small batch customized production (Dosi 1988). Between 1972 and 1982 the mean establishment size in U.S. engineering industries declined by 12.7 percent, and the average plant size declined in 79 out of the 106 four-digit industries. The trend was verified for both the employment and value-of-shipments measure (Carlsson 1989; Carlsson, Audretsch, and Acs 1990; Audretsch and Acs 1990).

While the small-firm sector could be "easily" expanded by entrepreneurial activity to accommodate new flexibility, in larger firms radical reorganization is needed to create smaller, more horizontally coordinated organizational units that behave more like independent small firms within the corporation. This decentralization in terms of both employment and production is a strategy for large firms to restructure mass production enterprises by combining the dynamism of small entities with the labor standards, compensation, financial resources, and R&D of large enterprises.

Flexible specialization requires an institutional structure that is radically different from that associated with mass production. We would like to argue that the existence of a sizeable small-firm sector in the industrialized West gave it a critical advantage in relation to their eastern European and Soviet counterparts. The most important institutional characteristics of flexible specialization are: technological dynamism, the combination of extensive cooperation and vigorous competition, and location within a community or social structure.

Small high-technology firms in the United States provide a dramatic example of the new system. First, small firms derive their technological dynamism from their ability to innovate at least as much as large firms. Second, these firms have been able while competing vigorously in the market (some would claim too vigorously) to exhibit significant amounts of cooperation in R&D, marketing, and technology transfer. Third, these small high-tech firms have survived by being closely linked to U.S. universities (Link and Rees 1990) and by forming production networks in areas such as Silicon Valley (Carlsson and Acs 1990). Such U.S. technological agglomerations are the counterparts of the Japanese subcontracting system, and the industrial districts of the "Third Italy" which have provided the social structure for small firms to survive and prosper in those countries. The "Third Italy" refers to the region around Emilia-Romagna, where small entrepreneurial firms have been very successful (Contini and Revelli 1990).

Dodgson's (1990) research represents more than a decade of study at the Science Policy Research Unit (SPRU) at the University of Sussex. Dodgson has shown that small firms in the United Kingdom are also significant innovators. However, he takes this research a step forward by suggesting that technology *strategy* is important for small firms, as well as for large ones, in the innovation process. Advanced technologies are enormously complex. Complexity results from the convergence of technologies between, for example, electronics and mechanics to create "mechatronics." Few firms possess internally the range of skills required to merge previously discrete technologies. Given the high cost of R&D investment, and the potentially long-term scale before returns are forthcoming from such investments, technology needs to be considered strategically. Firms often have to collaborate in their technological activities. Dodgson offers the following hypotheses for a technology strategy: 1) small firms must dedicate considerable resources to the R&D effort; and 2) there must be a high level of integration among a firm's internal functions, and between its activities and the activities of other firms in complementary areas. The key to innovativeness is not so much the *creation* of knowledge as the *commercialization* of knowledge.

Carlsson (1989a) has also considered the issues of strategy by analyzing the metalworking industry. His comparative analysis of the role of small firms in the machine tool industry shows how the Japanese followed strategies that allowed them to increase their share of the market at the expense of U.S. firms. Among the strategies pursued by Japanese firms was collaboration with other firms in their technological activities. While U.S. and European machine tool manufacturers were building complex and sophisticated Numerical Control (NC) machines, the Japanese, realizing the limits of this market, began to make more general-purpose machines. The potential number of customers then increased dramatically for the first time, allowing machine tool firms to take advantage of scale economies in production. However, the Japanese were simply the first to reap the benefits. Up to the mid-1970s, the industry consisted almost entirely of small firms. Since the Japanese machine tool makers are basically assemblers, whereas Western firms tend to be more vertically integrated, the size differences in terms of employment between Japanese and Western firms underestimate the true differences.

Several factors besides exploitation of scale economies put the Japanese ahead. The introduction and integration of electronics into an industry previously dominated by mechanical technologies required new technological skills that the small firms did not have. But the Japanese had special links to larger industry groups. Of the ten largest machine tool firms in Japan, at least four belonged to such a group. One suspects that belonging to such a group helped develop new technologies. While there were few such examples of technological cooperation in Europe, there were none in the United States. Many U.S. firms have been taken over by large firms (conglomerates), but these acquisitions appear to be motivated more by financial gain rather than vertical integration. In many instances these takeovers have resulted in U.S. machine tool makers having their overhead cut, and engineering staffs reduced, further weakening their competitiveness in relation to the Japanese. The Japanese strategy of closer integration between suppliers of technology and machine builders has resulted in a substantial lead over their U.S. and European counterparts (Yokokara 1988; FitzRoy and Acs 1989).

Several key studies have indeed found that innovative activity is a key mechanism by which new entrepreneurial start-ups attempt to enter an industry (Geroski 1990; Acs and Audretsch 1989a, 1989b; Florida and Kenny 1988). Brunner (1991) shows that the role of small firms — as represented by innovative entry — is not restricted only to the developed western nations. He finds that entrepreneurial start-ups provided a significant share of the innovative activity in the Indian computer industry. :

The extent to which new firms in an industry are able to serve as agents of change is implied to some extent by two quite different literatures. Winter (1984) and Gort and Klepper (1982) argue that the technological conditions determine the relative ease with which firms outside of the industry are able to innovate and therefore enter. The models of "learning by doing" introduced by Jovanovic (1982) and Pakes and Ericson (1987) suggest that firms may enter an industry at suboptimal scale, in order to obtain the opportunity to learn and subsequently expand if successful.

In fact, the technological regime characterizing the industry, along with the role which learning by doing plays, may explain a considerable amount of industry turbulence — the extent of firm movement into, within, and out of an industry (Acs and Audretsch 1990).

■ ■ ■ ■ ■ ■ ■ ■

INDUSTRIAL
RESTRUCTURING IN
EASTERN EUROPE

While western economies have been restructuring their industries to smaller production units, the average establishment size for most countries in eastern Europe has increased dramatically. As McDermit and Mestrik (1991) and Grachev et al. (1991) emphasize, countries in eastern Europe, as well as the Soviet Union, chose to push the mass production paradigm to its logical and perhaps fatal limits. However, the division of labor is not as developed in the Soviet economy as in western countries. Soviet firms are not specialized, and they produce almost everything they need due to shortages and supply uncertainties. This is one of the reasons the USSR has mostly large firms. But in comparison with big western firms, many Soviet production units have not reached the upper limits of effective mass production. The number of cars produced in the USSR can be compared with that of a single Japanese corporation.

Stylized fact 9 :
Small firms in eastern Europe were systematically eliminated.

For example, in his study of former East Germany, Hans-Gerd Bannasch (1991) finds a drastic concentration of economic assets has taken place. While there were 11,253 establishments in East Germany in 1971, this number had been reduced through the Kombinate system to 349 by 1987. Similarly, the share of employment accounted for by small firms in Czechoslovakian manufacturing fell from 13 percent in 1956 to 1.4 percent in 1986 (Figure 3–2). It should, however, be pointed out that this took place all at once and not gradually. The mean number of employees per establishment tripled from 1,121 in 1956 to 3,102 by 1988. As McDermit and Mastrik (1991) suggest, the current monopolistic situation in the Czechoslovakian economy has no historical precedent. This shift in the firm size distribution towards extreme concentration was a conscious policy decision that had more to do with state ownership and political control by the party than economics.

One can interpret this industrial concentration as an admission of the failure of centralized planning. The centralization into large production units was an admission that you could not plan a decentralized economy. Figure 3–3 illustrates that in 1948, 33.4 percent of the Czechoslovakian economy was in the private sector and an additional 1.1 percent was individually owned. But by 1985 the share of firms in the private sector had decreased to 0.6 percent of the total economy. By this time, the socialist sector accounted for 97.2 percent of

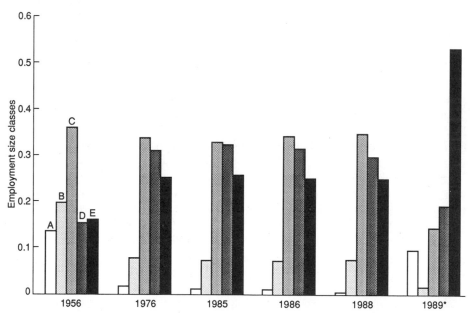

FIGURE 3–2   Sales Distribution of Firms in Czechoslovakian Manufacturing.
Column A represents firms with fewer than 500 employees ; **column B** represents firms with 501 to 1000 ; **column C** represents firms with 1001 to 2500 ; **column D** represents firms with 2500 to 5000 ; and **column E** represents firms with 5000 or more. Figures for 1989 refer to state enterprises as of 1 April 1989. (*Source : Statisticka rocenka Czech and Slovak Socialist Republic* (CSSR Statistical Abstract for the respective years) and the Federal Office of Statistics (1989).)

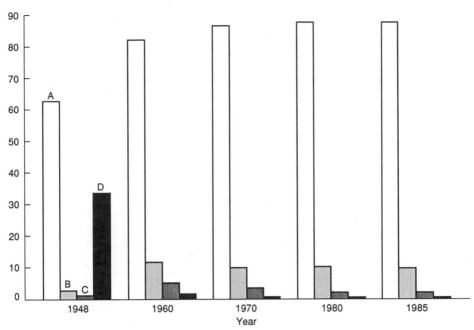

FIGURE 3–3 **Composition Percent of the National Income in Czechoslovakia, 1948–1985.**
Column A represents national income (NI) produced in the socialist state-owned firms ; **column B** represents NI produced in socialist co-operatives ; **column C** represents NI produced in individual- or family-owned firms : **column D** represents NI produced in the private sector. (*Source : Tschechoslowakei in Zahlen und Fakten* (Prague Praha : Presseagentur Orbis, 1988).)

output, with state-owned firms comprising 87.5 percent, and the co-operatives comprising 9.7 percent.

Similar trends can be observed in all of the eastern European economies, as well as in the Soviet Union. During the same period, the percentage of employment in enterprises employing more than 5,000 increased by 74 percent. This trend toward industrial concentration appears to be continuing. By 1989 the share of employment in the largest firm size category increased to 53 percent of total manufacturing employment.

Table 3–2 illustrates the extent of the presence of large establishments in the manufacturing industries of the former German Democratic Republic (GDR), the Federal Republic of Germany (FRG), and the United States. The share of manufacturing establishments (plants) with more than 500 employees was almost 10 times as great in the GDR as in the FRG. While only 10 percent of U.S. plants have over 500 employees, 40 percent of the plants in the GDR have over 500 employees. Similarly, in the United States and the FRG about 88 percent of the plants have fewer than 100 employees ; but only 18 percent do in the GDR. The employment figures are even more revealing. While the

TABLE 3–2 — The Share of Manufacturing Establishments by Firm Size

	SHARE OF ESTABLISHMENTS (%)			SHARE OF EMPLOYMENT (%)		
	GDR (1987)	FRG (1986)	U.S. (1982)	GDR (1987)	FRG (1986)	U.S. (1982)
Fewer than 500 employees	60	97	90	20	50	30
Fewer than 100 employees	18	86	88	11	20	27

Source : GDR : *Statistisches Jahrbuch der GDR* (1988)
FRG : *Statistisches Bundesamt*, Fachserie 4, Reihe 4.1.2 (1986)
U.S. : U.S. Department of Commerce, Bureau of the Census, *Census of Manufacturing* (Washington, D.C., 1982)

United States has 70 percent of employment in plants with more than 500 employees, the GDR has 80 percent, and the FRG only 50 percent. The almost complete lack of employment in small firms in the GDR (11 percent) is in stark contrast to the United States, where 27 percent of employees work in plants with fewer than 100 employees.

A recent counterexample to this trend in industrial concentration can be found in Hungary. Between 1950 and 1980 the number of state-owned enterprises declined from 1,425 to 700. Since then the number has increased by 50 percent. In 1987, 1,043 state-owned enterprises employed 1,258,000 workers and produced 80.3 percent of industrial output. There are also 1,392 industrial co-operatives accounting for 6.1 percent of industrial output. The majority of their 3,973 establishments have fewer than 500 employees accounting for 95.7 percent of employment. Nonindustrial organizations employ 218,000 workers and operate 16,667 establishments. Although these organizations are only semi-autonomous, under the special Hungarian circumstances they function like small businesses. On the basis of these figures, 34 percent of manufacturing employment can be considered as taking place in small establishments (Roman 1989). However, this still puts the share of small-firm establishments below countries like the United Kingdom and France.

In Poland, where reforms were instituted during the 1980s, the presence of private manufacturing firms has increased significantly. Between 1985 and 1988 the number of small manufacturing firms increased by 11 percent from 207,000 to 231,000. For the economy as a whole, there were 1,287,000 new small firms in 1988. The entry and exit of small firms in Poland also exhibits a high rate of turbulence. In January 1990, 22,321 new firms were established and 18,090 exited. In other words, about 2.7 percent of the total number of firms are replaced each month (Gwiazda 1990).

The Soviet Union may have one of the most concentrated economies in the world, according to the *Economist* (August 1990, 63): "Many of what are the most basic goods in any economy — polypropylene, stainless-steel pipes, concrete mixers — are produced entirely or almost entirely not merely by a single organization but by a single factory. Between 30 percent and 40 percent of the value of Soviet goods are produced on single sites." However, with the economic reforms under *perestroika* a new entrepreneurial sector, called co-operatives, has been introduced into the economy. According to Grachev et al. (1991), in 1990 there were 250,000 co-operatives registered employing 5.5 million people (4 percent of the labor force), and producing 40 billion rubles worth of goods and services. On average these co-operatives are small firms with 23 employees and can be found in almost all sectors of the economy, including the high-tech sector.

The best example of high-technology development is the DOKA-Center organized in May 1987. The DOKA-Center is an "independent," self-supporting R&D facility in Zolenograd, near Moscow. The Center has 32 full-time employees and more than 2,500 skilled professionals from 17 cities working on a contract basis. It is also a profit center with 52 percent of profits channeled back into R&D. DOKA-Center is an attempt to create a technological agglomeration similar to that in western countries. In the spring of 1990, the Soviet Government identified small, high-technology business development as an integral ingredient shifting the size distribution of businesses. While in market economies, especially in the United States, small firms have access to new technology, in the USSR small firms do not.

Given the fact that eastern European economies are in the process of changing the ownership structure and political administration of the economy, the floodgates are open to redirect the size distribution of firms towards smaller businesses. The restructuring of these economies away from large firms towards smaller ones has two objectives. The first is to downsize the already large-firm sector in order to facilitate smaller establishments. The second is to create an economic environment that is conducive to entrepreneurial activity, by instituting a network that will provide the infrastructure for promoting and financing new-firm entry. As we have noticed in Poland, where the majority of political and administrative barriers hindering the development of small firms have been removed, new problems arise. These could have been predicted from the experiences in the United States — liquidity constraints (*stylized fact 8*), a lack of management skills, and a shortage of consultants and other institutional support. Perhaps one of the most important lessons that we can learn from the Anglo-Saxon countries is that deregulation and wage cutting in the labor market alone will not lead to a healthy small-firm sector.

The small-firm sector in eastern Europe faces three choices. First, small firms can ask for support and protection from the state. Second, they can join with large firms as subcontractors (Kooij 1991). Third, small firms can build a joint support system with other small businesses. By forming communities or agglomerations, small firms can overcome the kinds of deficiencies which they face as individual market agents acting entirely on their own. As previously noted, there is a wide variety of historical and modern communal support systems, ranging from co-operatives to industrial districts, employee ownership, science parks, craft combines, and *ad hoc* cooperation. What makes these supportive institutions especially interesting is that they have been spreading in the West in recent years. For example, effective forms of communal organizations that exhibit strong forms of cooperation and competition can be found in the garment district in New York City. In these support systems, while long-run competition is intense, short-run competition is replaced with cooperation.

The most promising form of small-firm communal support system in eastern Europe appears to be the co-operative. Indeed, we have seen this form of support already working in Hungary (Roman 1989) and the USSR (Grachev 1991). This form of organization can accommodate both traditional small firms and high-technology development. In the USSR a new form of organization is growing: "Butec," the association of firms that are not under central control and that have bought out their assets from the state. Moreover, the co-operatives are already an existing form of organization and new systems are difficult to implement.

The virtual obliteration of small firms and entrepreneurship has deprived eastern European countries of a key element to industrial restructuring and technological progress (Roman 1989). Therefore, a crucial ingredient of restructuring in the eastern European economies involves generating a vital base of entrepreneurial activity. While the exact mechanism by which entrepreneurship in eastern Europe can be promoted is the topic of considerable debate, this chapter makes clear the consequences of its absence.

━ ━ ━ ━ ━ ━ ━ ━
CONCLUSION

The industrial restructuring that has taken place in Japan and the United States, the ongoing restructuring in western Europe, and the emerging restructuring in eastern Europe (*perestroika*), suggest that nothing less than a fundamental change in the social and political institutions that have supported mass production in this century is transpiring. While these changes were accommodated in the West at great cost, i.e., 30 million unemployed in OECD countries for the better part of a decade (FitzRoy 1990), the impact that restructuring will have in eastern Europe is unknown. The re-emergence of small units of production in general, and of small firms in particular, in the world economy has left eastern European economies with a new, and as of yet untried, social experiment. We believe that only by completely abandoning the existing social and political structure will these economies be able to restructure. In fact, this has been started with the elimination of the Communist party monopoly in Czechoslovakia, Hungary, and Poland; the unification of the two Germanies; and *perestroika* in the Soviet Union.

While the United States, Japan, and western Europe all faced a difficult task of restructuring, the challenges facing eastern Europe are even more complex. First, their economies must regenerate a small-firm sector. Second, they must create smaller establishments in their large-firm sector by : 1) encouraging entrepreneurship (Puchev 1990) ; and 2) breaking up the existing combines to create smaller units. Third, they must institute a system of private property. Fourth, and perhaps most important, *they must have very liberal bankruptcy laws.* (You should be allowed to fail at least 50 times !) Learning should be encouraged above all. The situation is complicated by the fact that eastern European countries lack both the entrepreneurial talent to create small firms and the managerial skills to create decentralized large enterprises.

Thus with the beginning of the elimination of internal barriers, new-firm entry has begun to play an important role in the rejuvenation of markets in eastern Europe. It is worthwhile noting that entrants need not be large or long-lived, and that they need not unduly disrupt the position of those market leaders that adapt quickly to the changes initiated by such entrants. What occurs in response to entry is a fundamental restructuring of product and production processes (Geroski 1990). Our conclusion, then, is that entry is a highly specific tool of industrial restructuring.

Finally, one of the most striking findings from the U.S. experience is that small-firm turbulence (simultaneous entry and exit) is more than one-third greater under the entrepreneurial regime then under mass production. While much attention has been directed in the popular press and by policy makers on both sides of the Atlantic to the desirability of fostering a vital sector of highly innovative small firms in new high-technology industries, the results of this chapter strongly suggest that a high rate of turbulence is associated with such markets. That is, any policy maker advocating programs designed to encourage small entrepreneurial firms in new high-technology industries should also recognize the accompanying firm failure and at least temporary job displacement and unemployment. The experience of the United States suggests that while such industries may generate innovative activity and perhaps ultimately employment growth, extensive turbulence is apparently intricately entwined with industries under the entrepreneurial regime.

REFERENCES

Acs, Z. J., and D. B. Audretsch 1987 Innovation, market structure, and firm size. *Review of Economics and Statistics* 69 (4) : 567–575.

1988 Innovation in small and large firms : An empirical analysis. *American Economic Review* 78 (4) : 678–690.

1989a Births and firm size. *Southern Economic Journal* 56 (2) : 467–475.

1989b Small-firm entry in U.S. manufacturing. *Economica* 56 (2) : 255–256.

1989c Job creation and firm size in the U.S. and West Germany. *International Small Business Journal* 7 (4) : 9–22.

1990 *Innovation and small firms.* (Cambridge, Mass. : MIT Press).

Aiginger, K., and G. Tichy 1991 Small firms and the merger mania. *Small Business Economics.*

Armington, C., and M. Odle 1982 Small business — How many jobs? *The Brookings Review* 1 : 14–17.

Audretsch, D. B., and Z. J. Acs Forthcoming Technological regimes, learning and industry turbulence. In *Innovation and technological change: An evolutionary approach*, ed. Mark Perlman. Ann Arbor: Univ. of Michigan Press.

Baldwin, J. R., and P. K. Gorecki 1987 Plant creation versus plant acquisition: The entry process in Canadian manufacturing. *International Journal of Industrial Organization* 5 : 21–42.

Bannasch, H.-G. 1991 The evolution of small business in the Soviet economy. In *Small firms and entrepreneurship: A global perspective*, eds. Z. J. Acs and D. B. Audretsch. Cambridge: Cambridge Univ. Press.

Beesley, M. E., and R. T. Hamilton 1984 Small firm's seedbed role and the concept of turbulence. *Journal of Industrial Economics* 33 : 217–232.

Birch, D. L. 1981 Who creates jobs? *The Public Interest*: 3–14.

Blanchflower, D. G., and A. Oswald 1990 What makes a young entrepreneur? Cambridge, Mass.: National Bureau of Economic Research, Rept. No. 3252.

Bond, R. S. 1975 Mergers and mobility among the largest manufacturing corporations. *The Antitrust Bulletin* 20 : 505–519.

Brock, W. A., and D. S. Evans 1989 Small business economics. *Small Business Economics* 1 (1): 7–20.

Brown, C., J. Hamilton, and J. Medoff 1990 *Employers large and small*. Cambridge, Mass.: Harvard Univ. Press.

Brunner, H.-P. 1991 The development experience and government politics in Southeast Asia with respect to small firms: Lessons for eastern Europe. In *Small firms and entrepreneurship: A global perspective*, eds. Z. J. Acs and D. B. Audretsch. Cambridge: Cambridge Univ. Press.

Cable, J., and J. Schwalbach 1990 International comparisons of entry and exit. In *Entry and market contestability: An international comparison*, eds. P. Geroski and J. Schwalbach. Oxford: Basil Blackwell.

Carlsson, B. 1984 The development and use of machine tools in historical perspective. *Journal of Economic Behaviour and Organization* 5 : 91–114.

1989a The evolution of manufacturing technology and its impact on industrial structure: An international study. *Small Business Economics* 1 (1): 21–38.

1989b Small-scale industry at a crossroads: U.S. machine tools in a global perspective. *Small Business Economics* 1 (4): 245–262.

Carlsson, B., D. B. Audretsch, and Z. J. Acs 1990 Flexible technologies and plant size: U.S. manufacturing and metalworking industries. Working paper, Case Western Reserve Univ.

Cohen, W. M., and S. Klepper Forthcoming Firm size versus diversity in the achievement of technological advance. In *Innovation and technological change: An international comparison*, eds. Z. J. Acs and D. B. Audretsch. Ann Arbor: Univ. of Michigan Press.

Collins, N. R., and L. E. Preston 1961 The size structure of the largest industrial firms. *American Economic Review* 51 : 986–1011.

Contini, B., and R. Revelli 1990 The relationship between firm growth and labor demand. In *The economics of small firms: A European challenge*, eds. Z. J. Acs and D. B. Audretsch, 53–60. Boston: Kluwer Academic Publishers.

Dodgson, M. 1990 Technology strategy in small and medium-sized firms. In *The economics of small firms: A European challenge*, eds. Z. J. Acs and D. B. Audretsch, 157–167. Boston: Kluwer Academic Publishers.

Dosi, G. 1988 Sources, procedures, and microeconomic effects of innovation. *Journal of Economic Literature* 26 (3): 1120–1171.

Dunne, T., M. J. Roberts, and L. Samuelson 1989 The growth and failure of U.S. manufacturing plants. *Quarterly Journal of Economics* 104 (4): 671–698.

Estrin, S., and T. Petrin 1990 Patterns of entry, exit and merger in Yugoslavia. In *Entry and market dynamics*, eds. P. Geroski and J. Schwalbach. Oxford: Basil Blackwell.

Evans, D. 1987a The relationship between firm growth, size, and age: Estimates for 100 manufacturing industries. *Journal of Industrial Economics* 35: 567–581.

1987b Test of alternative theories of firm growth. *Journal of Political Economy* 95: 657–674.

1991 Are small businesses bad for American national health? In *Small firms and entrepreneurship: A global perspective*, eds. Z. J. Acs and D. B. Audretsch. Cambridge: Cambridge Univ. Press.

Evans, D., and B. Jovanovic 1989 Estimates of a model of entrepreneurial choice under liquidity constraints. *Journal of Political Economy* 97 (4): 808–827.

Evans, D., and L. S. Leighton 1988 Some empirical aspects of entrepreneurship. *American Economic Review* 78 (3): 519–535.

1990 Small business formation by unemployed and employed workers. *Small Business Economics* 2 (4).

Fazzari, S., R. Hubbard, and B. Peterson 1988 Financing constraints and corporate investment. *Brookings Papers on Economic Activity*: 141–207.

FitzRoy, F. R. 1989 Firm size, efficiency and employment: A review article. *Small Business Economics* 1 (1): 75–80.

1990 Employment, entrepreneurship and 1992: Microeconomic policy and European problems. *Small Business Economics* 2 (1): 11–24.

FitzRoy, F. R., and Z. J. Acs 1989 The new institutional economics of the firm and lessons from Japan. Working paper, Wissenschaftszentrum Berlin, FS-4 89-16 (January).

Florida, R. L., and M. Kenney 1988 Venture capital-financed innovation and technological change in the U.S. *Research Policy* 17: 119–137.

Fritsch, M. 1991 The role of small firms in West Germany. In *Small firms and entrepreneurship: A global perspective*, eds. Z. J. Acs and D. B. Audretsch. Cambridge: Cambridge Univ. Press.

Geroski, P. A. 1990 Entry, exit and structural adjustment in European industry. London Business School.

Geroski, P. A., and A. Jacquemin 1985 Industrial change, barriers to mobility and European industrial policy. *Economic Policy* 1 (November): 172–217.

Geroski, P. A., and J. Schwalbach, eds. 1990 *Entry and market contestability: An international comparison.* Oxford: Basil Blackwell.

Gort, M., and S. Klepper 1982 Time paths in the diffusion of product innovations. *Economic Journal* 92: 650–653.

Grachev, M. V., and A. A. Ageev 1991 Entrepreneurship and small business in the Soviet economy. In *Small firms and entrepreneurship: A global perspective*, eds. Z. J. Acs and D. B. Audretsch. Cambridge: Cambridge Univ. Press.

Gray, T. A. Forthcoming U.S. government policy toward small firms in the 1990s. In *Small firms and entrepreneurship: A global perspective*, eds. Z. J. Acs and D. B. Audretsch. Cambridge: Cambridge Univ. Press.

Gwiazda, A. 1990 The new environment and options for small firms in Poland. (September). Warsaw, Poland. Mimeo.

Hall, B. H. 1987 The relationship between firm size and firm growth in the U.S. manufacturing sector. *Journal of Industrial Economics* 35 : 583–605.

Hughes, A. Forthcoming Concentration and the small business sector in the U.K. : The 1980s in historical perspective. In *Small firms and entrepreneurship : A global perspective*, eds. Z. J. Acs and D. B. Audretsch. Cambridge : Cambridge Univ. Press.

Invernizzi, B., and R. Revelli Forthcoming Small firms in the Italian economy : Structural changes and evidence of turbulence. In *Small firms and entrepreneurship : A global perspective*, eds. Z. J. Acs and D. B. Audretsch. Cambridge : Cambridge Univ. Press.

Johnson, P. 1989 Employment change in the small business sector : Evidence from five manufacturing industries. *Small Business Economics* 1 (4) : 315–324.

Jovanovic, B. 1982 Selection and evolution of industry. *Econometrica* 50 : 649–670.

Kaplan, A. D. H. 1954 *Big enterprise in a competitive system.* Washington, D.C. : The Brookings Institution.

Khemani, R. S., and D. M. Shapiro 1986 The determinants of new plant entry in Canada. *Applied Economics* 18 : 1243–1257.

Kooij, E. van 1991 Japanese subcontracting at a crossroad. *Small Business Economics.*

Link, A. N., and J. Rees 1990 Firm size, university based research, and the returns to R&D. *Small Business Economics* 2 (1) : 25–32.

Loveman, G., and S. Johnson Forthcoming Small business development in Gdansk during the Polish economic reform. In *Small firms and entrepreneurship : A global perspective*, eds. Z. J. Acs and D. B. Audretsch. Cambridge : Cambridge Univ. Press.

Loveman, G., and W. Sengenberger 1991 The re-emergence of small-scale production : An international perspective. *Small Business Economics* 3 (1).

McDermit, G. A., and M. Mejstrik Forthcoming Czechoslovak competitiveness and the role of small firms. In *Small firms and entrepreneurship : A global perspective*, eds. Z. J. Acs and D. B. Audretsch. Cambridge : Cambridge Univ. Press.

Mills, D. E., and L. Schumann 1985 Industry structure with fluctuating demand. *American Economic Review* 75 : 758–767.

OECD 1985 Employment in small and large firms : Where have the jobs come from ? *Employment Outlook* (September). Paris.

Orr, D. 1974 The determinants of entry : A study of the Canadian manufacturing industries. *Review of Economics and Statistics* 56 : 58–66.

Pakes, A., and R. Ericson 1987 Empirical implications of alternative models of firm dynamics. Manuscript, Department of Economics, University of Wisconsin-Madison.

Pavitt, K., M. Robson, and J. Townsend 1987 The size distribution of innovating firms in the U.K. : 1945–1983. *The Journal of Industrial Economics* 55 : 291–316.

Phillips, B. D., and B. A. Kirchhoff 1989 Formation, growth and survival : Small firm dynamics in the U.S. economy. *Small Business Economics* 1 (1) : 65–74.

Piore, M. J., and C. F. Sabel 1984 *The second industrial divide : Possibilities for prosperity.* New York : Basic Books.

Puchev, P. 1990 A note on government policy and the new "entrepreneurship" in Bulgaria. *Small Business Economics* 2 (1) : 73–76.

Roman, Z. 1989 The size of the small-firm sector in Hungary. *Small Business Economics* 1 (4) : 303–308.

Rothwell, R. 1989 Small firms, innovation and industrial change. *Small Business Economics* 1 (1) : 51–64.

Sato, Yoshio 1989 Small business in Japan. *Small Business Economics* 1 (2) : 121–128.

Scherer, F. M. 1970 *Industrial market structure and economic performance.* Chicago : Rand McNally.

Scherer, F. M. 1991 Changing perspectives on the firm size problem. In *Innovation and technological change: An international comparison,* eds. Z. J. Acs and D. B. Audretsch, 24–38. Ann Arbor : Univ. of Michigan Press.

Schwalbach, J. 1989 Small business economics in German manufacturing. *Small Business Economics* 1 (2) : 136–139.

Sengenberger, W., G. Loveman, and M. Piore 1990 *The re-emergence of small enterprises: Industrial restructuring of industrialized countries.* Geneva : International Labor Organization.

Storey, D. J. 1990 Firm performance and size : Explanations from the small firm sectors. In *The economics of small firms: A European challenge,* eds. Z. J. Acs and D. B. Audretsch, 43–50. Boston : Kluwer Academic Publishers.

Storey, D. J. 1991 The birth of new firms : Does unemployment matter ? In *Small firms and entrepreneurship: A global perspective,* eds. Z. J. Acs and D. B. Audretsch. Cambridge : Cambridge Univ. Press.

Storey, D. J., and S. Johnson 1987 *Job generation and labour market changes.* London : Macmillan.

Thurik, R. Forthcoming Recent developments in the Dutch firm-size distribution and the question of decreasing economies of scale over time. In *Small firms and entrepreneurship: A global perspective,* eds. Z. J. Acs and D. B. Audretsch. Cambridge : Cambridge Univ. Press.

White, L. J. 1982 The determinants of the relative importance of small business. *Review of Economics and Statistics* 64 : 42–49.

Winter, S. G. 1984 Schumpeterian competition in alternative technological regimes. *Journal of Economic Behavior and Organization* 5 (September-December) : 287–320.

Yokokara, T. 1988 Small and medium enterprises. In *Industrial policy of Japan,* eds. R. Komiya, M. Okuno, and K. Sazumura. New York : Academic Press.

Chapter

4

The Government as
Entrepreneur: Industrial
Development and the
Creation of New Ventures

Jon P. Goodman, James W. Meany,
and
Larry E. Pate
●

Industrial development, particularly actions that supply direct funding or
government grants-in-aid for the development of specific industries or technologies, has become an increasingly common tool for the expansion of national economies in the latter half of the twentieth century. In many cases, governmental intervention closely resembles the entrepreneurial process variable
described by Gartner (1985) in that the government (as opposed to the individual) locates an opportunity, accumulates resources, builds the organization,
and produces and markets the product. Thus, the intent of this chapter is to examine the entrepreneurial actions of governments and to classify the various
forms and strategies of governmental entrepreneurial activity occurring within
and across different national and cultural boundaries.

In some cases, a governmental entity retains a significant ownership in the
company that results. In other cases this is not so. Government funding for the
development of specific technologies often results in the establishment of spin-
off companies, all of which can be said to have been created (however indirectly) by government support.

In the United States, programs for economic expansion have been, for the
most part, designed to assist individual businesses or categories of individuals,
such as women or minorities. The most familiar of these, such as the U.S.

Small Business Administration's 7a loan program, 504 loan program, the Energy Related Inventions Program of the National Institute of Standards and Technology, the Small Business Innovation Research (SBIR) Program, and other similar loan, grant, or credit enhancement programs, have all provided assistance to individual businesses or individuals, independent of specific industry.

Direct funding to private industry in the United States has taken the form of support of basic science consortia such as MCC (Microelectronics) and Sematech (computer industry/government consortia). Although there are obvious exceptions to this in the government "bailouts" of Lockheed and Chrysler, as well as support to the U.S. steel industry, these examples are uncommon.

U.S. universities and government agencies have a considerable history of joint ventures, but the emphasis has been on basic scientific research. Direct government funding to aid in the development of an industry (as opposed to the support of individual businesses) has been extremely limited in this country, except in times of war.

When a government causes businesses to be created through direct actions, it can be said that the government has acted entrepreneurially. Some of the more interesting issues in government-sponsored industrial development are related to the underlying reasons why particular actions are taken and particular industries or technologies are chosen for development.

Industrial development tactics fall into a reasonably ordered taxonomy among developed nations. Other than in the United States, there seem to be significant, commonly shared reasons for promoting certain industries to the exclusion of others and for the establishment of national industrial policies.

Regardless of the motivation, policy involves a government's assuming an entrepreneurial role in the establishment and promotion of various industries. Governmental policies, when successful, result in the creation of new ventures or the retention of older companies through umbrella support to particular technologies or industries. The following sections describe the more common industrial development strategies employed in developed nations, presents tentative results of these strategies, and provides recommendations for further research.

▬ ▬ ▬ ▬ ▬ ▬ ▬ ▬

INDUSTRIAL
DEVELOPMENT
STRATEGIES

Policies for industrial development arise from different ideological or political perspectives. One of the more common perspectives is derived from the belief that job creation is a primary responsibility of government and that government should be the employer of first as well as last resort. Seeking a cure for unemployment can be related to or independent of trying to establish a competitive presence in world markets. A more sophisticated industrial development strategy is the creation of a captive market for one of the country's industries. The discussion below attempts to order the existing literature on this subject into categories.

Reviving Depressed Economies

A main reason for government intervention in the creation of new ventures is the need to invigorate a depressed economy and to promote economic growth. This was most apparent after World War II, when Germany and Japan sought to rebuild their devastated economies with considerable assistance from the United States. After the war, Japan's Ministry of International Trade and Industry (MITI) was a potent force in contributing to that country's development into an economic powerhouse (Schlesinger 1990). Although there is dispute today as to MITI's current impact (Porter 1990b), there is little disagreement over its historical role in Japan's industrial development.

Government intervention involves regional as well as national development. Government organizations have attempted industrial reorganizations in steel- and coal-producing regions in the United States, France, Germany, and Scotland (Singh and Borzutzky 1988). These reorganizations were directed at revitalizing severely depressed local economies.

Changing Economic Focus

Intervention can also be designed to effect a fundamental change in a region's economy, not just to invigorate it. For instance, governments intervene to promote the evolution from a less developed country to a developed country.

Tanzania's promotion of the building of a massive ammonia plant in the early 1980s serves as one example (Barrett 1986). Ireland's courting of the drug industry is another (Richards 1983). The privatization of Soviet co-operatives is one example of the most striking restructuring of an economy in the last century (*Business Week* 1990b), as the integration of capitalism into much of eastern Europe takes place.

New Sources of Hard Currency

Government strategies for the creation and promotion of new ventures frequently focus on the effects those ventures can have on foreign exchange and balance of payments (van Liemt 1984). This holds true even when discussing non–trade-barrier intervention.

In 1989, the Soviets earned roughly 40 percent of their hard currency ($17.6 billion) from oil exports (Maremont and Brandy 1990). With so much at stake in a country starved for hard currency, it is easy to see why the Soviet government is restructuring its oil industry to allow joint ventures with western partners to enhance and expand production.

Similarly, the Tanzanian government stood to realize a 40 percent return on its investment and $800 million in foreign exchange over 25 years from the previously mentioned ammonia plant.

Strategic National Interests

Governments often cite strategic importance as justification for subsidizing certain industries (van Liemt 1984). Witness the United States' expenditures of hundreds of billions of dollars in the aerospace, shipbuilding (including submarines), and weapons industries on projects such as the Strategic Defense Initiative, the Stealth Bomber, linear accelerators, and others (ibid.).

Governments may also consider certain industries too important to their countries' destinies to be left in the hands of the private sector. This then results in government ownership of those industries.

Some researchers claim that there are disadvantages a country can suffer when it does not possess or control a critical factor of production of strategic materials (as with the United States' reliance on South Africa for nickel to make high-strength steel alloys). Policies that support a particular industry are often framed in an argument in support of strategic national defense (van Liemt 1984).

Many times governments find it advantageous to encourage or control those industries which possess or comprise key factors of production (Mazzolini 1979). This is a particularly compelling reason when those factors of production are of strategic importance. Members of OPEC recognized the leverage their abundant reserves of oil conferred upon them. To protect these strategic factors of production, certain governments have nationalized all refining facilities.

The French government-supported Groupe Bull acquired Honeywell's computer operations when it realized that a major portion (70 percent) of the sale of Groupe Bull came from products for which it did not control the technology (Mazzolini 1979). The French government has long regarded the computer industry as a strategic one for the country, with Groupe Bull being the linchpin. For this reason, technological control has been regarded as a critical issue (ibid.). The government had long sought a national computer champion for strategic as well as nationalistic reasons. In support of that industry, the French government has contributed more than $1 billion in capital to Groupe Bull since 1983 (Levine and McWilliams 1990).

National Pride

National pride often shapes a government's industrial development policy (van Liemt 1984). Ever since the Russians beat the United States into space with *Sputnik,* the United States has poured funds into NASA and ancillary space programs. While it cannot be said that national pride was the driving force behind the establishment and subsequent support of the U.S. space effort, certainly competitive urgency and a sense of "national ego" have been involved in the continuation of that support.

In the case of Quebec, strong government-business cooperation has helped fuel a drive toward independence (Peterson and Holstein 1990). This cooperation has resulted in a two-edged sword : the economy of Quebec has been measurably strengthened and has shown a rise in disposable income and standard of living, but the province's success has also caused a greater Canadian sensitivity to Quebec's economic importance to the rest of the country.

Economic nationalism has also been cited as at least partly underlying U.S. efforts to rise to the challenge of Japan (Lehner and Murray 1990). It is unlikely that the reader of any current American newspaper or periodical can escape the conclusion that competition with Japan is a major concern in this country.

Even when not an issue of pride, government intervention often follows lines of national priority. The Chinese government tends to fund those industries and research activities that have practical, readily commercial application (Curry and Freundlich 1990). Although stated goals of Chinese industrial policy emphasize industrial infrastructure more than extremely advanced technology, the Chinese are active in the satellite-launching market, presumably as this provides communications infrastructure support as well as hard currency revenues.

Perceived Barriers to Private Development

Government intervention often grows out of a need or desire to develop an industry that is either too expensive or too risky for the private sector to undertake. Examples include the French computer industry previously discussed as well as the European aviation industry.

In some respects, government assumes the role of venture capitalist in the economic arena. It provides incentives and support for fledgling ventures in order for those ventures to establish a foothold in the marketplace. Several examples of this can be seen in France, with government venture capital providing seed and second-stage funding.

While much of the European airline consortium has undergone privatization in a move toward self-sufficiency, Airbus began as a make-work program dedicated to reclaiming a portion of the jet airliner business from U.S. manufacturers (Banks 1990). Its initial capital funding was entirely derived from government subsidies (ibid.). The combination of capital requirements beyond the means of the private sector and the national priority the French government assigned the establishment of an airline industry contributed to its subsidizing Airbus.

NASA's space program exists as a result of government backing. Originally, only science fiction writers conceived of the financial rewards that would accrue from the risk of space exploration. Even now that the potential returns of commercial space travel have become more apparent, no private, nonsubsidized space exploration company has yet demonstrated sustained viability, although many are trying to penetrate the satellite-launching market.

Job Creation

Perhaps the most often-used and least-questioned reason for government intervention is as a cure for unemployment (van Liemt 1984). It is a reason that is cited in a number of different circumstances. When a government steps in to save a company from bankruptcy, much of the argument used in support of the action is that it will save jobs (*Wall Street Journal* 1990). When it steps in to create an industry in a depressed area, the reason used in support of the action is that it will create jobs that displaced workers can fill (Singh and Borzutzky 1988). And when job creation requires new investment, the government is usually seen as the only capable and appropriate source of capital.

When government solicits industry to relocate to depressed areas, the relocation costs to the government are most frequently in terms of foregone tax revenue, loan subsidies, job training, and credit enhancements. Examples include South African government loans and interest concessions extended to East Rand Proprietary Mines Ltd., to prevent closure of its Johannesburg gold mine and the accompanying loss of 10,000 jobs (*Wall Street Journal* 1990).

The rescue of a failing company or a failing industry and the resulting jobs saved, motivate governments to act entrepreneurially in creating newly viable ventures. Classic examples include not only the loans the U.S. government made to Chrysler Corporation to aid its turnaround but also the more recent bailout of the failed savings and loan industry.

FDIC payments to depositors in failed thrifts may, on the surface, constitute nothing more than an insurer's conducting business as usual — the discharge of a contractual obligation. However, when one considers the impact on employment as well as on new job creation from *not* providing support to the economies of those states hit hardest (Texas, for example), government actions are clearly perceived as providing more than merely contractual relief.

Leveraging One Industry Against Another

Considering the interrelatedness of many industries as a result of vertical integration and supplier-purchaser relationships, governments can at times support one industry by subsidizing a second industry that buys the output of the first. That is, the government provides a captive market for a national industry.

The European semiconductor industry, particularly in France, provides an example of this. Semiconductors are electronic components that are used in many products including computers, military hardware, and consumer electronics. As all three of these industries grew in Europe, a national semiconductor industry became more critical. The United States and Japan have led Europe in semiconductor technology. In order to be globally competitive in markets requiring these components, European governments found it necessary to develop an advanced semiconductor industry. One strategy employed was that of supporting the supplier industry by supporting the end user industry. Therefore, whether intentionally or not, European governments supported the growth and development of the semiconductor industry through their support of the computer industry by establishing a market for semiconductors. Direct purchases of semiconductors by government contractors have the same effect; only in supporting the computer industry, the government is now one step removed from direct support of the semiconductor industry (Dosi 1983).

In the same way, Japan encouraged the development of its mainframe and semiconductor industries by establishing research projects in these fields with Japanese electronics companies that were restricted to buying only domestic products. As a result, it created a market for these industries as they were developing (Schlesinger 1990).

Reducing Foreign Dependence

While industries and national economies must, of necessity, assume a more global perspective, reliance on foreign suppliers of critical goods still causes concern. Oil may be the best example (apart from a purely strategic industry such as weapons) of a critical good whose supply is always a concern.

Oil is critical as an energy source and as a raw material for a vast number of products. With the world's major oil-producing region, the Middle East, constantly embroiled in war and politically volatile standoffs, any country lacking considerable reserves of its own is at the mercy of the ruling factions of the supplier countries. Therefore it is to an oil-dependent country's advantage to develop alternative sources of energy.

As a result, the United States developed a national energy policy which naturally led to a window of subsidized opportunity for the solar industry. Investment tax credits and legislation mandating solar technology on new construction (such as that passed by the city of Palo Alto, California) subsidized and promoted the industry.

With the easing of the energy crunch in the 1980s, alternative energy development became less of a national priority. However, with the recent conflict in Kuwait, and the United States importing approximately 50 percent of its oil, it may be likely that alternative energy development will again receive favorable consideration from the U.S. government.

A newer example is Taiwan's establishment of science parks to encourage innovation and development of new products, particularly those which are imported into that country in significant quantities (Yang and Quek 1990). Korea's $670 million commitment to its microchip industry is directed at making it competitive not with the United States but with its own neighbor, Japan, the source of virtually all microchip imports into Korea.

Supporting or Retarding Foreign Investment

Some countries, such as Ireland, actively solicit and encourage foreign investment in their industries as a method of economic development. Others want domestic industries to stay domestic and do not want foreign ownership or control.

Governments will erect barriers to foreign inward investment to prevent foreign ownership of domestic industries. They also will subsidize native industries to prevent foreign control. Japan again provides an example in its requirement (at one time) that IBM license Japanese competitors for use of IBM technology as a prerequisite for doing business in Japan.

■ ■■ ■■ ■■ ■■ ■■ ■

TYPES OF INDUSTRIAL PROMOTION/ DEVELOPMENT

Governments have at their disposal many ways of promoting and subsidizing specific industries. The methods fall into financial and nonfinancial assistance categories. This section addresses types of financial support governments are known to give to new ventures, but does not cover other nonfinancial supports such as tariff barriers and nontariff barriers (quotas, etc.), management assistance, and educational/vocational training.

Direct Grants and Subsidies

One method of support utilized by governments is that of investment grants and subsidies to business. European countries, in particular, stress the importance of nurturing small-company ventures such as robotics in Norway and West Germany (Port 1990b).

Both Japan and Europe subsidize operations that generate specific new technology — technology that, according to Porter (1990a), translates directly into competitive advantage. Porter suggested that any notion of industrial development which confers an advantage to a particular industry falls under the guise of developing "generic technologies" (ibid.).

Small business development centers, grants, credit enhancement programs, and subsidized loans are tools for business development in the United States, but they are not guided by an overall industrial planning policy determining eligibility.

In Korea, the government utilizes grants and subsidies to promote R&D efforts aimed at developing innovative products and technologies (Neff and Nakarmi 1990a). France has utilized equity investments or direct subsidies to establish the two major industries it champions — the airline and computer industries.

Many governments own portions of certain industries outright. Quebec uses its provincial pension fund, the Caisse de Depot et Placement, to fund private companies' strategic acquisitions (Neff and Nakarmi 1990b). Governments also give outright grants to companies to encourage new venture development. These grants very often go to research projects aimed at innovation.

In 1989, Israel's Industry and Trade Ministry awarded over $100 million in matching funds to 640 research projects mostly in high-technology fields. The specific aim was to spur commercial innovation. Most of the funds went to kibbutzim that operate microindustries, to start-ups, and to incubation centers. Already, a few extraordinarily successful companies have arisen in such traditionally entrepreneurial fields as computer imaging and advanced electronics (Sandler 1990).

Grants have facilitated the transformation of a region from a base of declining industry to a new center of economic and political power in areas such as the Nord-Pas-de-Calais in France. These grants have encouraged the development of more competitive and viable manufacturing firms where previously steel firms languished (Singh and Borzutzky 1988). Significant creation of jobs accompanied the revitalization of the region. This particular strategy of direct grants has been employed throughout France, and is particularly associated with the establishment of Société Developmente Regionales (SDR's), regional research organizations that focus on particular technologies and industries, the aim of which is to establish a strong industrial base with competitive advantage in one particular section of the country.

Ireland is noted for the significant variety of cash grants it has offered companies to relocate to the country (Richards 1983). Among them are grants of up to 50 percent to cover R&D and the construction of permanent R&D facilities. Also available are grants for covering fixed assets, training, travel, and even for the creation of new jobs (ibid.).

Low-Cost or Subsidized Loans

Government actions such as manipulating credit policy, extending credit, and providing low-interest and subsidized loans combine to create a climate that can be either conducive or detrimental to the development of new or small ventures. The strategy of credit enhancement and subsidization has been used in virtually every developed economy, and was the major tool used by Japan's MITI in providing support for industrial development.

In Korea, the government has established a $400 million fund for long-term, low-cost financing for new chipmaking facilities (Neff and Nakarmi 1990a). Chipmaking is an example of an industry that the Korean government has chosen to develop into a source of national pride. Korea has chosen Japan's chipmaking industry as the target of its efforts and the standard by which to measure its progress.

Japan's MITI has helped redefine Japan's industrial mission many times since MITI's inception. It has implemented those changes with the help of, among other things, its financial leverage in terms of loans. In the 1970s, it targeted clean technologies such as mainframe computers and semiconductors for development. These industries received low-cost loans while MITI used trade curbs to maintain Japan's advantage in the previously targeted strategic sector of heavy machinery (Schlesinger 1990).

Ireland has used loan power to encourage the growth of *small* industry as a support structure for its large, foreign-based corporations. The government helps Irish nationals and those with at least one Irish grandparent to obtain financing for the establishment of small enterprises, and then guarantees up to 50 percent of the loans (Richards 1983).

In another case, the United States and German governments have proposed government-backed loan packages to domestic companies that would create enormous industrial opportunities, such as providing the Soviet food industry with redevelopment and overhaul (Borrus, Schares, and Templeman 1990).

Government Procurement Policies

Government procurement policies are also industrial development tools in many parts of the world. One can look at government purchases from two perspectives: that of industry promoter and that of industry sustainer. Government can opt to buy industry output, even when foreign technology is superior, in order to support and promote a fledgling or struggling industry (Schlesinger 1990).

Japan again provides an example. In the 1970s, Japan bought only domestic products in the semiconductor and mainframe market (ibid.). This action facilitated the development of these industries because by guaranteeing them a market for their output, Japan removed one of the biggest hurdles for a new venture.

France's computer industry supplies another example. Groupe Bull began life as a captive supplier to the French government (Levine and McWilliams 1990). A guaranteed market for their products combined with over $1 billion in capital from the French government provided a strong competitive advantage.

It is possible that the development of the innovative supercomputer in the United States would not have proceeded had national laboratories and intelligence agencies not provided markets for products from companies such as Cray Computers.

Government buys industry output to *sustain* an industry as well. Often, it is perceived as advantageous for a particular government to maintain an industry in a healthy state (van Liemt 1984). An example is the U.S. weapons and aerospace industries. Some maintain that strategic advantage mandates the continued viability of those industries. The argument is that in times of conflict the United States must control the factors of production within its defense system (ibid.).

Government-Sponsored Research

Government-sponsored research, a less direct method of promoting certain industries than the actual purchase of industry output, is a major determinant in the direction of a country's industrial development (Yang, Hutcheon, and Quek 1990). Research priorities vary by country. The United States tends to emphasize basic research, while Japan promotes research in products with commercial application.

Research is a potent force in establishing national agendas at different times. With the more than $25 billion the United States has spent since 1983 on research projects such as the Strategic Defense Initiative, the space station, the National Aerospace Plane, the Human Genome Project, and the Superconducting Supercollider (Davis 1990), it becomes more clear where our administration's priorities lie.

Carey (1990) has written that smaller projects and more research in emerging technologies would encourage more new product development and innovation. However, Merrifield (ibid.) counters that the United States spends more, at $15 billion per year, in basic research than any other nation and has the greatest capacity ever for innovation. The approximately $300 million committed to the Sematech consortium might well lead to more computer innovation. The special legislation guaranteeing protection from antitrust prosecution that made this multicorporate consortium possible is further evidence of the government's commitment to the computer industry.

Some other government-sponsored research projects of interest include MITI's targeting the development of an advanced jet engine for supersonic travel (Schlesinger 1990). Taiwan, Korea, and Singapore have established high-tech research parks with government funds. Funding of the basic research into recombinant DNA technology has made the biotechnology industry a U.S. strength in the world market.

So important is the role of government research that debate exists among experts as to which direction (toward basic or applied research) the efforts should take. There is also concern that directed research can be detrimental, in that concentrated research in one field comes at the expense of other, unsupported fields (Murray and Lehner 1990; Murray and Mossberg 1990).

Direct Tax Incentives

Tax incentives often form the basis for research spending. They are also a form of government intervention in industrial development in their own right.

While France utilizes tax incentives to encourage R&D spending (Peterson and Holstein 1990), Ireland uses them to encourage company relocation (Richards 1983). Overhaul of the federal tax system in the United States changed the nature of business during the 1980s. We have also seen favored tax status granted to industries ranging from alternative energy development to the construction of low-income housing.

Tax incentives seem to be a fairly universal tool of government intervention: every country mentioned in this section has some form of tax incentive for research, job creation, relocation, or new investment.

Structural Changes

Some feel government can drive the creation of new ventures by actually changing the structure of a region's economy (Singh and Borzutzky 1988).

Structural change often entails discarding the economic development model on which a country or region's economy has operated (Walsh 1986). Old patterns of capital investment, labor utilization, and population concentration are changed as the economic development model changes.

Maintaining an industry in obvious terminal decline can be counterproductive to revitalization. Often, the more rational approach is to restructure the region to promote more profitable and sustainable industries. Such is the case with the steel-producing regions of the United States.

Concentration on producing more exotic alloys or on custom manufacturing is often more profitable than producing commodity steel products, which are better left to low-cost offshore producers. Education policies, research priorities, and incentives to attract a work force that is highly skilled in specific disciplines are ways in which government effects structural change, allowing a fundamental change in the types of ventures a region develops. The government itself can restructure in order to accommodate the revitalization of an area. In France, there has been, since 1982, a decentralization of political power to the règions that has facilitated development of new ventures appropriate for a region's human and capital resources (Singh and Borzutzky 1988).

While we have been discussing fairly specific ways in which the government intervenes in the creation of new ventures, most intervention falls under the umbrella of the government's changing the environment in which commerce transpires. Deregulation of the trucking and airline industries in the United States changed the basic way in which companies in these industries operate. The breakup of AT&T allowed a new form of competition and enabled new competitors to enter the communications market. Companies that were unheard of 15 years ago are now multibillion-dollar concerns, all as a result of the government's changing the regulatory environment of long distance communication.

On the other hand, we have seen instances (as with the semiconductor industry in France) where the government has actually *encouraged* mergers within industries. Both environmental changes and mergers are cases in which the government creates an environment particularly conducive to the growth of one or another industry.

In Mexico, it is the divestiture of government-controlled enterprises and the promise of free trade that have attracted outside capital. In the Soviet Union, it is the promise of joint ventures that is encouraging foreign investment in the oil industry.

Brazil's drastic opening of its state-controlled economy will usher in a new style of competition and pave the way for entrepreneurial start-ups (*Business Week* 1990a). Robert A. Mosbacher, U.S. Secretary of Commerce, focuses on the importance of an improved climate for doing business when describing methods of assistance offered by the Department of Commerce to U.S. businesses wanting to export (ibid.). Meanwhile, European nations are making an explicit commitment to *innovation,* not just to economic development. The European Economic Community is promoting cooperative research and

"Europe-first" technology standards, as well as trying to foster venture capital (Peterson and Holstein 1990).

The evidence seems to indicate that government, with its power to regulate, deregulate, and legislate, can have a major role in shaping the environment in which business operates.

■■ ■■ ■■ ■■ ■■ ■■
RESULTS OF EMPIRICAL
RESEARCH

There is a lack of empirical research which can yield quantifiable results on the role of government in the creation of new ventures. Much work has been done on economic development in general in such dynamic areas as Asia (Wu and Wu 1980; Kosai and Harada 1985), and economic development is becoming an emerging research area with a small but growing number of scholarly outlets. Since the era of mercantilism, researchers have looked at how nations gain and maintain competitive advantage and the role of government in that process. But there is a paucity of results-oriented research, and an almost total absence of empirical work relating an industrial development strategy to the actual numbers of companies (and jobs) created by that strategy.

Many of the findings in existing research studies are conceptual or qualitative. Figures on employment statistics, GNP, and per capita income trends supply the only real hard data.

Van Liemt (1984) points to the need for detailed and reliable statistics on factors such as last month's national output and productivity. These statistics would presumably provide feedback on the effectiveness of various government intervention policies.

Kindleberger (1987) has looked to western Europe for precedents in trying to understand the explosive reactions that have followed deregulation in Latin America. His is a purely historical and qualitative approach, however, with no hard numbers on new business development following deregulation.

Singh and Borzutzky (1988) cited employment and population growth (decline) figures for various distressed steel and manufacturing areas in western Europe and North America and discussed potential strategies for reversing the trends. However, no data were provided that would illuminate the magnitude of the effect government policy can have on new venture development.

Van Liemt (1984) gives reasons for and strategies of government intervention in adjusting economies but takes a strictly qualitative, instructive approach.

Uppal (1986) quantifies the amount of public financial assistance given to industrial enterprises in India by recipient, during the period from 1969 to 1982. He concludes that "large houses" received preferential treatment, an action that continued to result in economic concentration contrary to India's avowed economic policy. Uppal does not discuss how that public assistance changed the structure or output of the economy.

While there are good data sources available on government-sponsored research budgets and other government inputs, there is a lack of information on how those inputs have affected the numbers of new businesses or products created.

Systematic research into the job creation effects, technological advances, and competitive advantages of industrial development policies of the kind described above has not been pursued. The actual long-term effects of pursuing a nationwide industrial development policy, as opposed to the business-by-business assistance programs in the United States, has not been addressed other than in conceptual or anecdotal commentaries.

━━ ━━ ━━ ━━ ━━ ━━ ━━

CONCLUSION

Throughout this chapter we have examined the various forms and major causes of governmental entrepreneurial activity, particularly in relationship to industrial development. Government intervention occurs for a variety of reasons, including to revive depressed economies, change economic focus, create jobs and new sources of hard currency, leverage industries, reduce foreign dependence, foster national pride, and affect strategic national interests. The particular reason for promoting industrial development influences the government's subsequent selection of solution strategies. These strategies for promotion include investment grants and subsidies, cash grants, credit policy and loans, government purchases, tax incentives, and both structural and environmental interventions.

However, even with an examination of the taxonomy of relationships between reasons and strategies for industrial development, many questions remain due to a lack of available empirical research evidence on the effectiveness and efficiency of these various factors. Perhaps even more disturbing is that many of the essential research questions that would facilitate the healthy development of governmental entrepreneurial activity have apparently not even been raised. Both quantitative and qualitative empirical research is needed into a variety of related research questions, such as:

1. How effective have the various solution strategies been within and across national and cultural boundaries?
2. What cultural factors encourage or discourage the use and effectiveness of the various solution strategies?
3. What is the relationship between reasons and strategies, and how do the mix of reasons affect both the selection and effectiveness of chosen strategies?
4. What optimal fits exist between governmental problems, cultural constraints, and available solutions?
5. What strategies work well within some cultural contexts that could readily be applied to different cultures?

6. What problems exist in the application of various solution strategies that are exaggerated or diminished by national or political governmental variables?
7. What new strategies need to be developed for evolving governmental problems, and are means available to generate these strategies?
8. What effects will major global change, such as the unification of Germany and the improved relationship between the United States and the Soviet Union, have upon the available solution strategies of various governmental bodies?
9. When does it best serve a government to retain ownership in a company it has created, and when does it not?
10. What is the most efficient balance between direct and indirect funding to private industry for a variety of circumstances?
11. What factors encourage and restrict policy makers to behave in a more entrepreneurial manner when considering the various solution strategies?
12. To what extent do tradition and the past practices of various types of governments limit their effective use of alternative solutions?

The above research questions are representative of the kinds of issues deserving attention if we are truly to understand the uncertain balance between governments as simultaneously the guardians of the status quo and the innovators/creators of change. Just as Fritz Kapfra observed in *The Tao of Physics,* situations and circumstances normally thought to represent the epitome of structure and rules (such as physics) also contain the essential elements opposed to that structure and to those rules. Certainly the stereotype of governmental bureaucracies as the staunch supporters of maintaining order through the status quo is based in reality. But there is another side to government that has been ignored and that we have addressed in this chapter. Namely, the necessary manner in which governments foster the healthy movement of a body from one set of evolving circumstances to another. As governments and governmental problems change, so must the methods and solutions for creation of new ventures change. As new technology develops and becomes an accepted tool for a governmental body, that technology carries with it the seed of change in the launch of new ventures, creation of jobs, and innovation in various forms.

■ ■ ■ ■ ■ ■ ■ ■ ■
REFERENCES

Banks, H. 1990 Talking tough. *Forbes.* July 23, 41–44.

Barrett, M. 1986 Project finance develops new risks. *Euromoney.* October, 73–81.

Borrus, A., G. Schares, and J. Templeman 1990 Suddenly the unthinkable is almost certain. *Business Week.* July 16, 29.

Business Week 1990a Managing global expansion. June 15, 12 ff.

1990b The right kind of aid for the Soviets. July 19, 178.

Bygrave, W. 1989a The entrepreneurship paradigm (I): A philosophical look at its research methodologies. *Entrepreneurship Theory and Practice* 14 (1, Fall): 7–26.

1989b The entrepreneurship paradigm (II): Chaos and catastrophes among quantum jumps? *Entrepreneurship Theory and Practice* 14 (2, Winter): 7–29.

Carey, J. 1990 The myth that America can't compete. *Business Week.* June 15, 44–48.

Corden, W. M. 1976 Conclusions on the logic of government intervention. In *Public assistance to industry*, eds. W. M. Corden and G. Fels. Boulder, Col.: Westview Press.

Cunningham, W. 1925 *The growth of English industry and commerce in modern times.* Cambridge: The University Press.

Curry, L., and N. Freundlich 1990 China: Science feels the crackdown. *Business Week.* June 15, 162–166.

Darlin, D. 1990 Taiwan, long noted for cheap imitations, becomes an innovator. *Wall Street Journal.* June 1, 1.

Davis, B. 1990 Star wars. *Wall Street Journal.* July 9, 1.

Denton, G. 1976 Financial assistance to British industry. In *Public assistance to industry*, eds. W. M. Corden and G. Fels. Boulder, Col.: Westview Press.

Dosi, G. 1983 Semiconductors: Europe's precarious survival in high technology. In *Europe's industries: Public and private strategies for change*, eds. G. Shepherd, F. Duchene, and C. Saunders. Ithaca, N.Y.: Cornell Univ. Press.

Emshwiller, J. 1990 Militant small-business coalition. *Wall Street Journal.* June 25, B2.

Fels, G. 1976 Overall assistance to German industry. In *Public assistance to industry*, eds. W. M. Corden and G. Fels. Boulder, Col.: Westview Press.

Ford, R. 1983 Revitalizing the distressed community: GSOC and ESOP alternatives to enterprise zones. *Growth and Change* 14 (4): 22–31.

Gartner, W. 1985 A conceptual framework for describing the phenomenon of new venture creation. *The Academy of Management Review* 10 (4). 696–706.

Goldman, D. 1990 A revolution you can invest in. *Forbes.* July 9, 48–54.

Gross, N., and O. Port 1990 Hustling to catch up in science. *Business Week.* June 15, 74–82.

Hanseanne, M. 1990 31 million reasons to fight unemployment. *OCED Observor.* January, 12–15.

Heuer, H. 1989 Local initiatives for the promotion of innovation in the Federal Republic of Germany. In *Regional development in Europe: Recent initiatives and experiences*, ed. J. Allesch. Berlin: Walter de Gruyter.

Hoadley, W. 1985 Role of government in resource development. *Journal of Commerce and Commercial.* August 3, 4A.

Hoerr, J. 1990 Making high school diplomas tickets to the workplace. *Business Week.* July 9, 76.

Johnson, C. 1985 Political institutions and economic performance: The government-business relationship in Japan, South Korea, and Taiwan. In *Asian economic development — present and future*, eds. R. Scalapino, S. Sato, and J. Wanandi. Berkeley, Cal.: Institute of Asian Studies.

Kikkawa, M. 1983 Shipbuilding, motor cars and semiconductors: The diminishing role of industrial policy in Japan. In *Europe's industries: Public and private strategies for change*, eds. G. Shepherd, F. Duchene, and C. Saunders. Ithaca, N.Y.: Cornell Univ. Press.

Kindleberger, C. 1987 Financial deregulation and economic performance. *Journal of Development Economics* 27: 339–351.

Kosai, Y., and Harada, Y. 1985 Economic development in Japan : A reconsideration. In *Asian economic development — present and future*, eds. R. Scalapino, S. Sato, and J. Wanandi. Berkeley, Cal. : Institute of Asian Studies.

Lee, D. 1990a China may find it hard to cash in on Fang's freedom. *Business Week*. July 19, 43.

1990b Too early for a party. *Forbes*. July 23, 36–39.

Lehner, U., and A. Murray 1990 Strained alliance. *Wall Street Journal*. July 2, 1.

Levine, J. 1990 Suddenly, high tech is a three-way race. *Business Week*. June 15, 118–123.

Levine, J., and McWilliams, G. 1990 Francis Lorentz' scheme to get Bull charging. *Business Week*. July 16, 154–156.

Maremont, M., and Brandy, R. 1990 Fields of dreams : The west gets a crack at Soviet oil. *Business Week*. June 11, 36–38.

Mazzolini, R. 1979 *Government controlled enterprises : International strategic and policy decisions*. Chichester, Eng. : John Wiley & Sons.

Melcher, R., and G. McWilliams 1990 Shakeup on the factory floor. *Business Week*. July 9, 34.

Moffett, M. 1990 Free-trade talk puts Mexico in spotlight. *Wall Street Journal*. July 9, A8.

Murray, A., and Lehner, U. 1990 What U.S. scientists discover, the Japanese convert — into profit. *Wall Street Journal*. June 25, A1.

Murray, A., and Mossberg, W. 1990 Can aid to Soviets help a sick economy ? *Wall Street Journal*. June 25, A1.

Neff, R., and Nakarmi, L. 1990a Will an r&d scramble get Korea's edge back ? *Business Week*. June 15, 156–158.

1990b In Korea, all circuits are go. *Business Week*. July 9, 59–60.

Oulton, N. 1976 Effective protection of British industry. In *Public assistance to industry*, eds. W. M. Corden and G. Fels. Boulder, Col. : Westview Press.

Peterson, T., and Holstein, W. 1990 How a freer Quebec could reshape the continent. *Business Week*. July 9, 40–41.

Port, O. 1990a Why the U.S. is losing the lead. *Business Week*. June 15, 35–39.

1990b Developments to watch. *Science and Technology*. July 9, 73K.

Porter, M. 1990a *The competitive advantage of nations*. New York : The Free Press.

1990b Japan isn't playing by different rules. *The New York Times*. July 22, f13.

Reichlin, I. 1990 From two Germanys, one dynamo ? *Business Week*. June 15, 124–126.

Richards, R. 1983 Ireland remains a haven for overseas drug firms. *Drug and Cosmetic Industry* 133 (5, November) : 62–64, 104.

Ruell, P. 1990 The outlook : A helping hand for U.S. exports. *Wall Street Journal*. July 9, A1.

Sandler, N. 1990 The brains keep draining in. *Business Week*. June 15, 160.

Schares, G. 1990 Hunting pay dirt in eastern Europe. *Business Week*. June 15, 132–133.

Schlesinger, J. 1990 A new Nippon ? *Wall Street Journal*. July 3, A1.

Shepherd, G., and F. Duchene 1983 Introduction : Industrial change and intervention in western Europe. In *Europe's industries : Public and private strategies for change*, eds. G. Shepherd, F. Duchene, and C. Saunders. Ithaca, N.Y. : Cornell Univ. Press.

Singh, V., and S. Borzutzky 1988 The state of the mature industrial regions in western Europe and North America. *Urban Studies* 25 : 212–227.

Stewart, M. 1983 No longer quiet on the western front. *Inc*. April, 138–140.

Stout, H. 1990 Thrift bailout to transfer wealth to few states with most s&l woes. *Wall Street Journal.* June 25, A2.

Trebat, T. 1983 *Brazil's state-owned enterprises.* Cambridge : Cambridge Univ. Press.

Uppal, J. 1986 Public financial institutions and economic concentration in India. *Journal of Development Economics* 20 : 135–144.

van Liemt, G. 1984 Adjusting to change. *International Labour Review* 123 (6, November/December) : 693–703.

Wall Street Journal 1982 Steps taken to find aid for Mexico. August 19, 1A.

1990 South Africa to give troubled gold mine, East Rand, more aid. July 9, A4.

Williams, M. W. 1986 A steel plant shows how U.S. and Mexico differ on development. *Wall Street Journal.* May 2, 1.

Wu, Y., and C. Wu 1980 *Economic development in Southeast Asia : The Chinese dimension.* Stanford : Hoover Institution Press.

Yang, D., S. Hutcheon, and J. Quek 1990 Is Asia breeding a whole pack of tigers ? *Business Week.* June 15, 152–155.

Part

3

ENTREPRENEURSHIP RESEARCH: LINKAGES AND METHODOLOGY

Chapter

5

Entrepreneurship through an Ethical Lens: Dilemmas and Issues for Research and Practice[1]

J. Gregory Dees
and
Jennifer A. Starr

●

Thirty years ago, in his landmark study, *The Achieving Society,* David McClelland issued a call for research: "We do not know at the present time what makes an entrepreneur more or less ethical in his dealings, but obviously there are *few problems of greater importance* for future research" (McClelland 1961, 331, emphasis added). The fields of entrepreneurship and business ethics have since emerged as vital and growing areas of interest and inquiry for business researchers, educators, and practitioners. Yet McClelland's call remains virtually unanswered.

The phenomenon of entrepreneurship has been examined under a number of disciplinary and subdisciplinary microscopes. This volume and its predecessors provide a good overview of the various approaches, issues, and developments in the field of entrepreneurship (Kent, Sexton, and Vesper 1982; Sexton and Smilor 1986). Much of this work has been suggestive of ethical themes, but rarely are these themes openly or critically discussed. There are but a handful of papers that explicitly address ethical questions in the context of entrepre-

[1] The authors gratefully acknowledge the support of the Sol C. Snider Entrepreneurial Center and helpful comments from Joe Badaracco, Amar Bhide, George Lodge, Ian MacMillan, Scotty McLennan, Howard Stevenson, and Jeff Timmons.

neurial management (Ackoff 1987; Longenecker, McKinney, and Moore 1988) and small business management (Wilson 1980; Brown and King 1982; Chrisman and Fry 1982; Longenecker, McKinney, and Moore 1989). Research produced in the field of business ethics has focused almost exclusively on moral issues in large, publicly held corporations, overlooking the ethical dilemmas, moral judgements, and moral imagination that might be distinctive to entrepreneurial management (Beauchamp and Bowie 1983; Iannone 1989). The primary objective of this chapter is to propose a research agenda to bridge these two literatures.

▬▬▬▬▬▬▬▬▬
THE NEED FOR ETHICS
RESEARCH

Is the conspicuous absence of research on this topic a problem? A case can be made that solid research in this area could have both academic and practical benefits. A number of compelling questions remain unanswered. How do the ethical issues facing entrepreneurs differ from those facing other businesspeople? What sorts of ethical dilemmas do entrepreneurs lose sleep over? What sorts of dilemmas, from a societal point of view, do we wish they *would* lose sleep over? How do they resolve the dilemmas they face? Do entrepreneurs have a different set of ethical obligations because of the distinctive role they play in the economy? In what ways do ethical standards contribute to or hamper entrepreneurial success?

These are not simply idle academic queries. When Timmons and Stevenson (1983) asked the owner/presidents of small to mid-sized companies what should be taught in business schools, 72 percent responded that ethics both can and should be taught. "The most prominently cited reason was that ethical behavior is at the core of long-term business success, because it provides the glue that binds enduring successful business and personal relationships together" (117). In another survey, CEOs of highly successful entrepreneurial firms cited integrity and honesty as the second most important success factor, just behind product and service quality (Hills and Narayana 1989). These surveys indicate that ethics is viewed as an essential aspect of entrepreneurial management.

The Timmons and Stevenson survey also suggests that entrepreneurs are looking for assistance. Difficult ethical decisions are part and parcel of the entrepreneur's life. Our own conversations with entrepreneurs confirm this. The ability to anticipate ethical difficulties, to prevent them when possible, and to manage them effectively when they arise seem to be important ingredients in the mix of skills needed for entrepreneurial management. The desire for practical ethical guidance has been recognized by several authors of entrepreneurship texts (e.g., Ronstadt 1985; Timmons, Smollen and Dingee 1985; Bird 1989; Sexton and Bowman-Upton 1991). Each offers useful suggestions, but surely their advice would be stronger if it could be grounded in a solid base of research. In our current ignorance, it is difficult to see how we as teachers and consultants, as well as scholars, might help entrepreneurs.

Entrepreneurs have often been regarded with both admiration and suspicion. The suspicion derives from an age-old image of the entrepreneur as willing to engage in ethically questionable business practices in order to succeed against the odds. The association of entrepreneurs with trickery and deception dates back to the role of Hermes, a devious god, as the patron of merchants in ancient Athens (McClelland 1961, 329–331). An important issue to be addressed in any entrepreneurial ethics research program is the tension between the claim often made by entrepreneurs that honesty and integrity are essential to long-term success, and the image of entrepreneurs as self-serving tricksters. Brenner (1987), in his recent work on rivalry, has highlighted this tension by arguing that crime and entrepreneurship have common motivational roots stemming from the perceived loss of relative standing in society. The image of the devious entrepreneur is also reinforced in the popular business press. This happens not only through reports of scandals, such as the collapse of ZZZZ Best (Akst 1987), but also when entrepreneurs candidly discuss the tactics used to keep their businesses alive.

For example, a recent interview with Philippe Kahn, founder of Borland International, begins by describing the elaborate deception that he set up in order to get *Byte* magazine to run his first advertisement on favorable credit terms (Lyons and Mamis 1989). This deception proved crucial to the success of the firm. Kahn exemplifies the classic entrepreneurial "trickster." Is honesty truly a requirement of entrepreneurial success, or does every entrepreneur have to be a bit of a snake-oil promoter? To what extent is the negative image of entrepreneurs just a by-product of general business bashing? To what extent are the ethical concerns of entrepreneurs distinctive from those of their corporate counterparts? Research is needed to help us understand the complex reality behind this tension.

Even if ethical standards do not prove to be the determining factor in individual entrepreneurial success, they may be important in distinguishing socially productive forms of entrepreneurship from unproductive forms. McClelland found that the greatest rates of economic development have occurred in societies that are characterized by a combination of a high need for achievement and a high level of "other-directedness," a characteristic that he associated with the establishment of a "market morality" (McClelland 1961, 201–203). Market morality apparently channels achievement motivation into more socially productive activities. He concluded that dishonest entrepreneurs "have by and large not been the ones responsible in a major way for economic development" (330). Though one may question McClelland's analysis, it raises a number of intriguing questions about the role of moral norms in promoting a productive, developing economy. Research that provides a better understanding of the relationship between specific ethical norms and social and economic outcomes could have far-reaching implications.

━━ ━━ ━━ ━━ ━━
FRAMING A RESEARCH
AGENDA

Given the richness and complexity of this topic, there is a need to encourage exploration and discussion among a diverse audience of social scientists, entrepreneurship and management scholars, philosophers and ethicists, and practicing individual and corporate entrepreneurs. All of these parties have something to contribute and learn from a conversation about ethics in entrepreneurship. In order to engage this heterogeneous group, one potentially productive approach is to study the ethical dilemmas most likely to arise in the process of entrepreneurial management. The research agenda should focus on three general questions:

1. What are the ethical dilemmas most characteristic of entrepreneurial management?
2. How do entrepreneurs manage these dilemmas?
3. How might they develop greater skills in managing these dilemmas?

Why Entrepreneurial Management?

Entrepreneurship research is marked by tremendous diversity. This diversity may be partially attributed to the fact that there is no consensus definition of entrepreneurship. Entrepreneurship may be distinguished by innovation, by growth, by uncertainty, by risk bearing, by ownership, by smallness, or by newness (Gartner 1990). Some scholars think of entrepreneurship only in terms of independent ventures, while others allow for entrepreneurial enterprise in both independent and corporate settings (Maidique 1980; Stevenson and Jarillo 1990).

To complicate matters further, increasing interest in the field of entrepreneurship has been accompanied by the development of a strong multidisciplinary research tradition. The multidisciplinary nature of entrepreneurship research enriches the field but also makes it difficult to define the boundaries. Driven by different disciplinary backgrounds, some researchers concentrate their work at the level of the individual entrepreneur, e.g., identifying personality characteristics of entrepreneurs; others direct their efforts at the venture level, e.g., focusing on new venture strategies; and still others are more concerned with the macrolevel, exploring the social and economic environments within which entrepreneurs and their ventures operate. To examine all of the ways in which ethics might be integrated into this vast literature would be a task too great for one chapter.

Our strategy has been to craft a research agenda that is grounded in theory but is also likely to have an immediate and direct return for practitioners as well as researchers. A promising avenue is to follow the lead of researchers who have chosen to concentrate on entrepreneurial management: the behaviors, processes, and skills developed in actual entrepreneurial practice (Stevenson and Jarillo 1990). The objective of this line of research is to better understand the distinctive characteristics and skills related to *entrepreneurial management* (in contrast to administrative management), defined as follows:

> Entrepreneurial management is the process of uncovering or developing an opportunity to create value through innovation, and pursuing that opportunity, despite initially possessing insufficient resources. (Modified from Stevenson, Roberts, and Grousbeck 1989)

Innovations are conceptualized in Schumpeterian terms, including improvements in products, processes, or forms of organization. As defined here, the entrepreneurial management process may play itself out through an independent venture, or within a large corporation. Typically, there will be a leader in this effort who can be identified as the entrepreneur. The process is likely to be characterized by uncertainty, initial small scale, high growth potential, high failure risk, extensive use of social assets, and the initiation of some new organizational entity. These and other distinguishing characteristics of entrepreneurial management are likely to lead to a distinctive set of ethical issues for research.

Why Ethical Dilemmas ?

Before discussing the ethical dilemmas inherent in entrepreneurial management, something should be said about the nature of ethics and ethical dilemmas. The first step in laying a foundation for ethics research is providing a credible account of ethics and how it might be studied.

Ethics is essentially normative and other-regarding. Ethics is commonly defined as the answer to Socrates' question, "How ought one to live ?" However, this question masks the essentially social aspects of ethics. The central questions of ethics might be better framed in more social terms: "How ought we to live together ?" and "What should we expect of one another ?" Ethics is about standards for determining right and wrong conduct, but it is also about values, about what makes for a good person, a good life, and a good society. It is useful to think of it as encompassing both rules and ideals (Hennessey and Gert 1985). The rules set the minimal standards for how we ought to treat one another, and the ideals establish admirable targets toward which we should aspire.

At this time, and for the foreseeable future, it is safe to say that humankind has achieved no complete consensus on these matters. It is not uncommon for different individuals, especially in modern pluralistic societies, to hold different ethical beliefs. This leads many to conclude that ethics is simply subjective, that no one's beliefs are better than any other's. However, this is to lose sight of the social dimension of ethics. If people are to live successfully together, they need to have some common ground rules, and it helps if they share some ultimate goals. Trust, confidence, and legitimacy are the foundations of social and economic life. They must be maintained through a system of laws and informal norms. One person's willingness to be dishonest when it serves his or her interests is not just that person's business. It is the business of everyone with whom he or she attempts to transact business. Some ethical beliefs are more conducive to social life than others.

Since social scientists and ethicists both use the notion of a value, it might be helpful to illustrate the difference between a personal psychological value and a personal ethical value. For instance, psychologists have found that entrepreneurs value autonomy (Brockhaus and Horwitz 1986). This generally means that the entrepreneur values his or her own independence — freedom from control by others. This is quite distinct from the entrepreneur having autonomy as an ethical value. To hold autonomy as an ethical value is to believe that it is important to respect *everyone's* autonomy, that a good society is one in which people enjoy a high degree of autonomy. Entrepreneurs who have autonomy as an ethical value would presumably structure their own organizations so as to promote autonomy for their employees as well as themselves. Entrepreneurs who value autonomy for themselves (psychologically) need not see it as an ethical value. They may be quite authoritarian and controlling in their treatment of employees. Values, as psychologists typically discuss them, are like preferences or tastes and are essentially self-regarding ("I value this for me"). In contrast, values, as ethicists talk about them, are essentially other-regarding. Accordingly, research on ethics would focus on these other-regarding values or principles, rather than on the personal preferences of the entrepreneur.

Despite differences in ethical views, some shared values and some consensus (however tentative) on social obligations are necessary for a productive, fulfilling life together. Otherwise, we might find ourselves in the lawless anarchy that constitutes a Hobbesian state of nature, an aggressive, individualistic competition with no rules in which life is "solitary, poor, nasty, brutish, and short." In liberal societies, we try to tolerate a wide range of views on ethics, but we still need shared values and norms in order to realize the benefits of social association. Any social ethics is likely to include commitment to a minimal set of what might be called the "social lubrication" virtues, as well as to some generally defined core social values (Table 5–1). The specific interpretations of

TABLE 5–1 — Illustrative Ethical Virtues and Values

Social Lubrication Virtues	Core Social Values
Honesty	Survival
Promise keeping	Prosperity
Respect for personal property	Justice
Trustworthiness	Economy
Sense of fairness	Liberty
Concern for others' welfare	Individual self-respect
Refusal to free ride	Preservation of public goods

these virtues and values evolve and change over time and across societies (Lodge 1975).

At any given point in time, details of the social consensus on values and principles will be somewhat ill-defined. It is also likely to include principles that come into conflict with one another. There will be gray areas that call for a judgement. Situations will inevitably arise that are not anticipated in the current ethical scheme of things. Social ethics change to reflect uncertainty, changing technology, new social arrangements, the growth of knowledge, shifting political power, and the rise and fall of religious systems. Each change is an experiment testing and refining ethical principles.

Even in the richest, most developed ethical traditions, ethical dilemmas are inevitable. They arise in a number of ways. For convenience, they may be grouped into four categories. In cases of *moral conflict*, individuals must sort out apparently conflicting moral commitments (obligations, values, or loyalties). These conflicts can arise out of general obligations, role obligations, or commitments voluntarily made. In cases of *moral ambiguity*, individuals face moral choices for which they have no clear answer. Important facts may be unknown. Relevant moral principles or values may be too vague, with no precedents to guide the decision. In cases of *prudential tension*, morality demands that the individual take an action contrary to his own self-interest. The sacrifice of self-interest may range from missing an attractive opportunity to risking one's life or livelihood. In cases of *personal-social conflict*, the individual's moral values conflict with the moral values (or common practices) of the social context in which he or she is operating. This may happen in the individual's native society, or more commonly, in a foreign culture. Often a personal decision will involve a mixture of these dilemma-creating characteristics. From a practical point of view, the greatest ethical challenge an individual faces is in recognizing and responding to these sorts of ethical dilemmas. Since this is where people need the most help, it is a logical focus for research.

▬ ▬ ▬ ▬ ▬ ▬ ▬ ▬
ETHICAL DILEMMAS OF ENTREPRENEURIAL MANAGEMENT

Though this agenda poses, rather than answers, questions, it might be useful at this point to illustrate the kinds of dilemmas that entrepreneurs are likely to face. Using the previously mentioned definition of entrepreneurial management, various research findings and theories, as well as anecdotal case reports in the entrepreneurship literature, one can characterize a few of the ethical dilemmas that appear to be particularly salient for the individual engaged in the entrepreneurial management process. These fall into three general categories: promoter dilemmas, relationship dilemmas, and innovator dilemmas (Table 5-2).

TABLE 5–2 — Selected Ethical Dilemmas of Entrepreneurial Management

DILEMMA	Elements
Promoter dilemmas	Entrepreneurial euphoria Impression management Pragmatic vs. moral considerations
Relationship dilemmas	Conflicts of interest and roles Transactional ethics Guerilla tactics
Innovator dilemmas	"Frankenstein's problem" New types of ethical problems Ethic of change
Other dilemmas	Finders-keepers ethic Conflict between personal values and business goals Unsavory industry practices

Promoter Dilemmas

The entrepreneur's celebrated promoter mentality is driven by the uncertainty associated with innovation, the pursuit of possibilities and prospects, and the lack of currently controlled resources. His or her unique skills and abilities — foresight, imagination, and judgement — provide a vision of the future at odds with the conservative majority (Casson 1982). Yet, the entrepreneur's success depends on negotiating strategically advantageous relationships and managing the objections and expectations of key resource controllers (MacMillan 1983). Others have to be drawn into this risky venture, and be induced to commit their resources or their time, to forego other opportunities, and to accept some of the risk. Due to generic internal and external obstacles which threaten the venture's survival — the "liabilities of newness and small size" — start-up conditions are often precarious (Stinchcombe 1965; Aldrich and Auster 1986). Thus, to achieve his or her goal, the entrepreneur must engineer consent, using powers of persuasion and influence to overcome the skepticism and resistance of guardians of the status quo. This requirement for strong persuasive skills seems to hold for both independent and corporate entrepreneurs (Howell and Higgins 1990).

When juxtaposed against the ethical importance of honesty (Bok 1978) and of respecting the autonomy of others, this need to promote poses ethical dilemmas. What does honesty mean when promoting an innovation? Does it require complete disclosure of the risks and uncertainties? Does it require a dispassionate analysis of the situation, with equal time given to the downside as well as the upside? What sorts of influence tactics cross the line from encouragement and inducement to manipulation and coercion? What does it mean for resource controllers to make autonomous choices? If the goal is to promote fully informed, rational choice on the part of the resource-controlling parties, entrepreneurs may be constrained in the persuasion and influence tactics they can ethically use. Certainly the elaborate deception that Philippe Kahn used to get ad space in *Byte* on favorable credit terms would be disallowed on this informed-choice interpretation of the ethical requirements of honesty. But what about simply playing down some of the less obvious risks in a venture? What about leading a potential investor to believe that others are ready to commit substantial sums to the venture, when in fact they have only expressed interest? Entrepreneurs must draw the line somewhere.

This dilemma is complicated by the fact that the exhilaration we call *entrepreneurial euphoria* can be a self-fulfilling prophecy that inspires action and achievement. "Can-do" optimism and enthusiasm are characteristic of the entrepreneurial psychological profile, i.e., moderate risk-taking propensity, and high internal locus of control and need for achievement (Brockhaus and Horwitz 1986). One study found that entrepreneurs are extremely optimistic about potential economic and social benefits and their likelihood of success (Cooper, Woo, and Dunkelberg 1988). This belief is bound to influence their presentation of the venture to others. Although intoxicating, entrepreneurial overconfidence can lead to a perception of invincibility and a refusal to examine problems critically. We must rely on the resource controllers's due diligence to provide a reality check on unwarranted hyperbole and exaggeration. However, in many cases, such as the Kahn case, this does not work out, either because of information asymmetries, or because the resource controller is too trusting or just too careless.

As champions of innovation and change, entrepreneurs are often in a position where they must manage the perception of risk, uncertainty, and novelty for others. The Minnesota Innovation Research Program's longitudinal studies of 16 innovations in a variety of organizational settings observed differences in the concerns and performance expectations of innovation managers and resource controllers (Dornblaser, Lin, and Van de Ven 1989). Although expectations changed over time, the differences between the two parties remained. To maintain appearances of control and progress, innovation managers camouflaged negative information, surprises, and setbacks with "sugar-coated" assurances and slick presentations. But investors often viewed these projections and promises as actual commitments, and intervened when ventures failed to live up to their promised potential, perhaps to the detriment of the venture.

Thus, entrepreneurs use *impression management* to project appearances and promote images of themselves and their organizations to others. They understand that judgement of value is often based on appearances, not actual content. To counteract the "liabilities of newness and smallness," elaborate scripts may be used to "stage" interpersonal encounters which convey an image of stability and certainty that is essential to survival (Goffman 1959). Thus, the "vice-president of strategic planning and marketing" is actually a one-man show operating out of his basement. This interpretive sociological framework is supported by recent findings in decision theory that suggest that choices can be manipulated by framing alternatives, beliefs, agendas, and decision out-comes (Kahneman and Tversky 1984). Entrepreneurs may have an instinct for taking advantage of the cognitive biases of their audiences.

The essential question raised by the promoter dilemma is what criteria are used to distinguish harmless puffery, customary influence, and bargaining tac-tics, and effective salesmanship (Carr 1967) from immoral distortion and de-ceptive practices. Future research needs to discover whether entrepreneurs perceive this as a dilemma, how they respond to it, and how resource control-lers deal with it. A recent study of business practice suggests that practitioners, including entrepreneurs, are more honest than would be expected from purely rational, self-interested decision makers (Bhide and Stevenson 1990). This finding highlights the distinction between a purely *pragmatic perspective* that weighs the probabilities and risks of truth telling and lying, and a moral per-spective that gives greater priority to moral concerns and values (Etzioni 1988).

Fundamentally, the dilemma raises a serious normative question about whether entrepreneurs play such a valuable social role that we should allow them a wider range of discretion in allowing euphoria to color their judge-ments. What would be the consequences of convincing entrepreneurs to be fully honest and candid, or to make themselves more objective ? Would it stifle innovation ?

Relationship Dilemmas

New venture development is both a social and an economic enterprise, charac-terized by face-to-face relationships and informal interpersonal exchange. This arises largely because of the entrepreneur's need for resources, trust, and credi-bility. It is more difficult to get these from strangers than it is from those with whom one has closer ties (Johannisson 1987b). Previous working relation-ships, voluntary connections, kinship, and community ties lay the groundwork for independent new ventures (Birley 1985; Aldrich and Zimmer 1986). By using social relationships, entrepreneurs "cash in" on the patterns of expecta-tions, norms, governance structures, and social resources built into these pre-vious interactions (Ben-Porath 1980; Granovetter 1985; Johannisson 1987a; Starr and MacMillan 1990). The costs and the risks of start-ups can be reduced by using social assets such as friendship, trust, gratitude, and obligation (Starr and MacMillan 1990). And where innovation and access are a priority, net-work relationships offer many benefits to entrepreneurial ventures, including: know-how and technology transfer, speed and richness of communication, and cooperation and mutual exchange (Jarillo 1988; Powell 1990).

While the advantages of network relationships have been emphasized in the literature, they pose certain ethical dilemmas, as well. One type of dilemma has to do with conflicts that might arise as roles and relationships change from their pre-venture to their post-venture status. Another type concerns, more broadly, the nature of tactics and techniques used by the entrepreneur to achieve his or her goals in managing these relationships. Behind both sorts of dilemmas lies the tension between an image of business using arms-length transactions in which all parties are largely free to look out for their own interests, and the moral expectations arising from prior (and perhaps, continuing) relationships. Perceived obligations to the venture may lead the entrepreneur to treat others in ways that violate obligations arising out of an ongoing relationship. How do entrepreneurs balance these two forces?

Family, friends, and business colleagues are generally the first line of support in new ventures. The transformation of social and kinship networks into instrumental business relationships raises possibilities for *conflicts of interests* due to conflicting roles. As soon as an entrepreneur has persuaded someone with whom he has had a prior relationship to join in a new business relationship, roles and expectations change. There is the potential for conflict with the former roles and embedded expectations which may continue. Personal interests may be in opposition to organizational interests, challenging the priorities and loyalties of the entrepreneur. Decisions may be influenced by affiliative rather than task-based concerns. Because different individuals involved in the new venture will have different types of prior relationships with the entrepreneur, concerns about favoritism might be raised and must be managed. Multifaceted expectations and obligations can affect independent business judgement that could be potentially detrimental to the firm.

In addition, these relationships are often built upon unspecified and unchallenged assumptions. Perhaps the most dramatic example of the strain that can be created when very different roles are mixed occurs when a parent becomes an investor in an independent entrepreneurial venture (Hyatt 1990). Similar problems can arise when a former boss is brought onto the new venture team. Nonhierarchical friendships can also pose problems when they are converted into organization-based relationships. Previously unspecified roles and authority structures in interpersonal relationships are forced into new organizational structures. Since these relationships were initially built on trust, it may be difficult to impose standard organizational control mechanisms, or to take courses of action that serve business objectives but harm established relationships. These lax monitoring conditions are also ripe for various forms of advantage-taking on the part of those with prior close relationships. In the extreme, this could mean embezzlement or misappropriation of funds. Furthermore, preexisting personal relationships make it hard to confirm suspicions. This line of inquiry has received most attention in the family business literature, but it becomes an issue among nonkinship business relationships as well.

According to Collins, Moore, and Unwalla (1964), the "transactional mode of interpersonal relationships" of entrepreneurs is based on instrumentality and the norms of reciprocity. Entrepreneurs engage in relationships so long as they are advantageous, and are able to sever ties when they lose their value or become threatening. They also learn the important skill of how to keep other people in such relationships as long as the relationship is advantageous to the entrepreneur. Derived from this view is a notion of *transactional ethics,* which views individuals as a means to an economic end, subject to *guerilla tactics*, manipulation, and exploitation (Webster 1976). This idea is in direct conflict with one central tenet of ethics — namely, that we should never treat others as mere means to our ends, but respect them as ends in themselves. It also conflicts with morally valuable emotions such as empathy and care. In addition, this instrumental, transactional ethic conflicts with the often close-knit nature of entrepreneurial ventures.

Is this instrumental view an accurate depiction of entrepreneurial management? Does it contribute to entrepreneurial success? Surely it allows for more managerial flexibility as the entrepreneur responds to the changing needs of the venture as it moves through different stages, or to the unanticipated events characteristic of an entrepreneurial venture. A transactional entrepreneur is not bound by the values inherent in enduring, caring social relationships. This may be why some advise that one should "never do business with friends." Transactional entrepreneurs do not allow themselves to become personally attached. But are there feasible alternatives? Could entrepreneurs effectively use a more transformational style of leadership, with an ethic that focuses on the development of others, cooperation, genuine caring, and even a touch of altruism?

Innovator's Dilemmas

Entrepreneurs are the shock troops of innovation. In response to changing environmental and societal conditions, they create new technological, administrative, and social innovations that challenge the status quo (Etzioni 1986). In the process of organizing for the future, they provide an adaptive social function. Their new ideas and organizations forge new institutional infrastructures and values (Van de Ven 1986). Viewed historically, their cumulative impact on our community is clear. In an age where banking practices are international in scale, it is difficult to imagine that 15th century Europe considered money lending to be immoral. Nonetheless, in the midst of adjustment and transition, entrepreneurs betting on new ideas are viewed as deviants, renegades, and revolutionaries (Brenner 1987). Ethical dilemmas arise out of the risks and costs inherent in innovation. Innovation can have unwanted side effects, negative externalities. It can also force a social reconsideration of norms and values. Overall, innovation can raise unanticipated ethical questions.

Winner (1977) identifies what he calls "*Frankenstein's problem.*" In Mary Shelley's novel, Dr. Frankenstein makes several attempts to avoid the responsibility of his creations, to run away, but he cannot. No doubt many entrepreneurs have the same desires occasionally, when they recognize the potential problems raised by the innovations that they are developing. While technological innovations seem to draw the most attention to the Frankenstein problem, other entrepreneurial inventions raise similar concerns about the future impact of unknown harms. An example of an administrative and social innovation that may disturb community values is the development of an AIDS hospice in a residential neighborhood.

There are many complex, ambiguous situations that entrepreneurs have chosen to ignore. For instance, early 20th century prognosticators of the telephone anticipated its broad economic benefits, but there were fears and suspicions of possible side effects, such as hearing loss, the spread of tuberculosis, the depletion of natural resources, and invasion of privacy (de Sola Pool 1983). On other occasions, we wish entrepreneurs were more sensitive to the potential side effects of their innovations. An example of this sort, also in the early years of this century, was the sale of radium medicines as cure-alls (Winslow 1990). How is an entrepreneur to know, for instance, whether or not recent debates about the impact of information technology and biotechnology, will turn out to be unfounded ? To what extent do we want resource-constrained entrepreneurs to accept responsibility for the uncertainties surrounding the potential social costs of their innovations for future generations, or the uses of their innovations by others to promote their own questionable ends ? Or is this a job for the government ? Or for the markets ?

In our view, the assessment of the risk of new harms must be balanced against the potential value of improved goods and services that address existing or new needs. The dilemma poses a need to act and choose, keeping in mind all the existing data, novel questions, and uncertain answers about what the future will hold. This is made more difficult when nearly any challenge to the status quo will raise some concerns. Innovation generally requires some at least temporary dislocation and disruption. It is likely to be threatening to someone. It may take a certain moral courage to proceed despite alleged risks.

The problem is not limited to the potential for untoward by-products of innovation. Innovation can create *new types of ethical problems* to which there are not ready answers. As information technology creates new capabilities for access to information, questions about property rights to that information arise. Genetic engineering also poses new questions and risks. Furthermore, entrepreneurs may test the ethical limits of market mechanisms. A dramatic case of value-challenging entrepreneurial activities arises with the international entrepreneurs who have attempted to establish a market for purchasing human organs that might be used in transplants. Should the world's poor be allowed (induced) to sell their kidneys ? Along similar lines, consider the potential medical and scientific markets for aborted fetal tissue. Any entrepreneur who attempts to exploit that opportunity will face a host of complex ethical questions. Whom should he pay for the tissue — the doctor who performed the abortion or the woman who had it ? Will this business induce women who would not have had an abortion to seek one ? To take a more mundane example, should an entrepreneur produce and promote radar detectors if he or she knows that they will be used to assist in breaking the law ? They may lead to more speeding, and possibly to more accidents. Surely there are businesses that present opportunities to make money, but which raise ethical issues so troubling that one should forego them. How do entrepreneurs make the decisions not to pursue certain possibilities for ethical reasons? What considerations drive their choices?

More than 20 years ago, Schon described the need for an "*ethic of change*" — a set of principles for change and norms for prizing the process of discovery for society as a whole. This ethic runs counter to the traditional value placed on stability in social arrangements. Individuals and institutions tend to support the myth of stability and illusion of security maintained by incremental transitions from stable state to stable state (Schon 1967). But change, not stability, is the status quo. Thus, an ethic of change would accept that norms and objectives will continuously evolve, accompanying changes in technology, institutions, and objectives (Rubin 1982). Such an ethic would help entrepreneurs to cope with some of the ethical stresses associated with innovation. In a society guided by this ethic, an adaptive problem-solving approach that values experimentation would compensate for the loss of permanence and threats due to the deterioration of individual identity, existing roles, and skills. By breaking with the past and creating new traditions, individuals would have the freedom to change. Unfortunately, in the nearly 25 years since Schon's writing such an ethic has yet to emerge. Perhaps some attention to the innovation dilemmas of entrepreneurs will help us structure and promote such an ethic. However, even with an ethic of change, individual entrepreneurs will still face troubling questions about responsibility for their innovations, the by-products, and the new ethical questions created.

Other Dilemmas

These are but a few of the potential ethical dilemmas that arise out of our definition of entrepreneurial management and the literature of entrepreneurship. Several could be added to this list. For instance, if the venture is a success and value is created, the entrepreneur often plays a key role (at least in independent ventures) of distributing the gains. What is a fair way of dividing the profits when they are the result of a collective, cooperative effort? Does Kirzner's (1989) "*finders-keepers ethic*" prevail, with the entrepreneur taking all gains that he or she did not explicitly contract away?

Additionally, both independent founders and corporate product champions take a significant leadership role in creating the organizational culture of an emerging new business. The personal values and assumptions of the founders and key leaders are explicitly and implicitly embedded in the new firm's structure (Schein 1983; Kets de Vries 1985; Manz et al. 1989). Do entrepreneurs recognize the creative and destructive potential of this intimate connection between their *personal values* and *business goals*? How do they manage situations where there are conflicts between their personal preferences and professional requirements?

In some industries, *unsavory practices* (such as bribery) are typical or may become common practice over time. A new entrant into one of these industries may be under pressure to engage in these practices simply to get established. An entrepreneur with honest principles may be compelled to conform. How do entrepreneurs cope with these ethical pressures? Are there any creative response strategies? No doubt readers can think of many more problematic questions. Whether entrepreneurs recognize our hypothesized moral conflicts and ambiguities as dilemmas is a question for empirical research. Perhaps discussions with entrepreneurs about the ethical issues that trouble them would reveal a very different list. By identifying some potential sources of ethical quandaries which emerge in entrepreneurial decision making, this chapter begins to map the terrain for future exploration of the ethical aspects of entrepreneurial decisions.

━━ ━━ ━━ ━━ ━━ ━━ ━━
FOUR DIMENSIONS OF ETHICS RESEARCH

Beyond characterizing them, what can be done with these dilemmas? How can they be researched? At this point, it probably makes sense to provide an overview, a road map of ethics research. Ethics research can be described as having four interrelated dimensions. Any given piece of research will fit into at least one, and may cut across several of these dimensions. The four dimensions become the basis for a model for interdisciplinary ethics research (Figure 5–1).

This model borrows part of its structure from recent work in the decision sciences in that it draws a distinction between normative and prescriptive work (Bell, Raiffa, and Tversky 1988). The term "normative" is used to capture the abstract theoretical analysis that determines the ideals against which practice might be evaluated. This is the philosophical contribution to ethics research. It parallels probability theory and its assumption of fully rational actors with infinite information processing capabilities. The term "prescriptive" is reserved for analysis aimed at producing practical guidance for real people. The model is intended to keep us focused on the ultimate theoretical and practical question: "So what?" The research is driven by two considerations, one theoretical, the other applied. The ultimate objectives are to generate a theory of entrepreneurial ethics-in-practice, and to produce some concrete recommendations for improving practice, where this is both desirable and feasible. The theory of ethics-in-practice serves as a bridge from philosophical ethics to practical advice. The model (Figure 5–1) also serves as a map for understanding where individual pieces of research fit into the overall research process.

Normative Dimension

This is the one dimension most likely to be unfamiliar (and uncomfortable) to researchers trained in the social sciences or management disciplines. Accord-

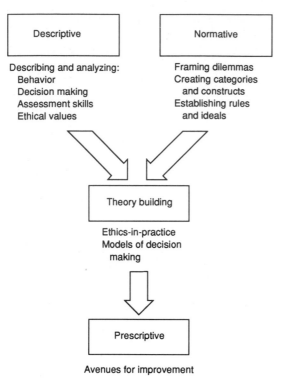

FIGURE 5–1   Four Dimensions of Ethics Research

ingly, a disproportionate amount of space in this section is devoted to explaining the work that must take place in this research dimension. The sort of normative ethical analysis that is needed is typically the bailiwick of philosophers specializing in applied ethics. To be most effective, the philosophers generally need to work closely with someone familiar with the field of application, or to draw heavily on existing descriptive literature about the field.

Ethical analysis contributes to our proposed research project on three levels, two of which are relatively straightforward. Since each requires slightly different work, let us discuss them in turn.

Framing the dilemmas.

A basic understanding of ethical considerations is needed simply to characterize the ethical dilemmas that entrepreneurs face. This level of ethical analysis was illustrated modestly in the previous section of this chapter. It can begin at the highly general level of the values and virtues expressed in Table 5–1, the level of common sense morality. For instance, the promoter dilemma is framed around the norm of being honest, since this norm might clash with the pressures and tendencies of being a promoter for a new idea. The innovator dilemma is framed around the duty not to harm innocent people. Philosophers may be helpful in drawing out the subtleties in a given dilemma, but social scientists, armed with a basic understanding of ethical norms and values, can do a reasonably good job at this level of ethical analysis.

Creating categories for responses to the dilemmas.

Ethical analysis and theory can also provide a basis for categorizing the reasoning and response processes of entrepreneurs faced with dilemmas. Philosophers are able to draw upon a rich heritage of ethical thought that can be used to construct possible categories for research in the descriptive dimension of ethics research (the second dimension in our model, discussed below). For instance, the notion of egoism that was adduced by Longenecker, Mckinney, and Moore (1988) to explain entrepreneurs' responses to a survey about ethics, is a notion with a rich history in ethical thought. It might be useful to look at this attribution in light of the theory of ethical egoism. One caveat is in order : while philosophers are likely to recognize patterns of thought that mimic standard philosophical theories of ethics, there is no assurance that practitioners think in ways that consistently match philosophical theories and categories. Nonetheless, philosophical categories might provide a useful starting point, even if the final categories are likely to deviate from pure philosophical definitions. (A model of this process of category refinement can be found in Victor and Cullen's (1988) analysis of ethical types of organizational work climates.) In any case, researchers should feel free to move beyond existing philosophical categories, to draw on useful social science categories, or to be entrepreneurial in devising their own.

Constructing the rules and ideals to guide practice.

Finally, normative analysis can be used to establish (to the extent possible) the ethical principles that should ideally govern practice. An example along these lines is the principle that guides Ackoff's (1987) proposal for a consensus-based ethical management process. He proposes that decisions should be made by consensus of all who are directly affected.

With regard to entrepreneurship, this level of analysis ultimately includes answering the following questions : What are the minimum standards to which we as a society want to hold entrepreneurs ? What are the values that we would like to see reflected in their practices ? What are the ideals toward which we would like them to strive ? How does entrepreneurship fit into our vision of the good society ? Do entrepreneurs play a special role that deserves its own set of ethical principles ? Answering these questions is clearly a much harder job than that at either of the other two levels of ethical analysis. The objective is to determine what kind of behavior we want to promote and what kind we want to discourage in our society, our moral community. The question is how we are to make such a determination.

Currently, ethical principles are characterized by and derive from the core values in our fragile, dynamic social ethic. Ultimately, they are grounded in what philosophers call the "moral point of view." The moral point of view is generally taken to be a benevolent and impartial perspective, from which one respects the dignity and cares about the interests of each person equally. It should be apparent how Ackoff's principle about consent and many of the values and virtues previously discussed (Table 5–1) might be drawn from this perspective.

This abstract notion is not without some controversy regarding interpretation. Much of the controversy focuses on the meaning of impartiality and the role of the emotions in moral judgement. The dominant philosophical school of thought on this matter emphasizes impartiality and interprets the moral point of view as primarily rational (Baier 1958 ; Nagel 1970). This interpretation leads to an ethics of rationally derived duties. The fundamental concern in this camp is to make sure that ethical judgement is not clouded by personal biases or emotion. An opposing interpretation of the moral point of view emphasizes benevolence over impartiality and explicitly includes moral emotions such as empathy and caring. The ethics of caring has received a boost in recent years from the work of Carol Gilligan (1982) on the moral psychology of young women, and from philosophical attention to the role of friendship and altruistic emotions in moral life (Blum 1980). No consensus interpretation of the moral point of view has emerged. To incorporate both perspectives, Goodpaster (1982) has suggested that the moral point of view is a mental and emotional standpoint from which all persons have a special dignity or worth. Common moral tests, such as the golden rule, are devices that move one closer to this distinctive point of view in order to break out of one's own narrow perspective on the world and provide a vantage point on the perspective of others.

Rarely, however, does applied normative analysis start at ground zero in this abstract moral point of view. The process is a bit more complex. It generally takes place as an attempt to resolve questions in an ongoing conversation about ethical standards and ideals. Faced with the assessment of a type of behavior or practice, ethicists will typically begin by drawing on some widely accepted moral principles (e.g., do not lie ; do not steal ; treat people fairly ; etc.). Facts will be gathered to determine which principles might apply. If there is no conflict among the principles and no ambiguity, a conclusion may be drawn straight away. However, in difficult cases, such as the ones that most interest us, principles will conflict, or there will be some ambiguity about how a given principle is to be applied, in which case the initial principles must be revised to cope with the new situation. A philosopher will propose a new specification of the principle as it applies to the issues at hand. For instance, the overly general principle "Do not withhold information" might be revised to read "Do not withhold information from the naive or innocent." The revised principle must then pass certain tests. Beyond checking the reasoning for internal consistency and for factual accuracy and completeness, proposed principles are typically tested in one or more of the following ways :

Coherence :   How well does it fit with other deeply held principles or values ?

Robustness :   Does it stand up to the considered judgements of un-biased judges, based on a review of a wide range of relevant examples ?

Generalization :   Are we prepared to make the principle into a univer-sal law, applicable to everyone ?

Consequences :   Are the consequences of adopting the principle bet-ter for all concerned than the consequences of re-jecting it ?

These are the major touchstones of normative ethical methodology. Individual philosophers may favor one test over the others, depending on their school of thought. For instance, utilitarians focus exclusively on consequences. (Accessible introductions to different philosophical theories of ethics can be found in Downie 1971 and Mackie 1977.) Many applied ethicists use all these tests in one form or another. These tests do not guarantee a unique outcome, but they do narrow the field considerably. Proposing and revising specific principles that should govern practice from a moral point of view provide the foundation for developing some (at least tentative) guidelines for assessing the ethics of entrepreneurs facing these dilemmas.

Descriptive Dimension

The second dimension of ethics research — the descriptive dimension — should be quite familiar to most of our readers. This is the home territory of the social sciences. Normative analysis alone is not all that useful. It must be informed by the complex realities of practice. Furthermore, ethicists are generally not equipped with the skills of systematic data gathering and analysis, or with the theoretical concepts that might explain actual responses to ethical dilemmas. Over the years, social scientists have developed a variety of methodologies for describing, characterizing, and explaining beliefs, attitudes, values, decision-making processes, and behavior. These methods range from casual observation, to soliciting responses to a survey, to generating the "thick descriptions" of actual practices that characterize ethnography. For the purposes of ethics research, our bias is that the thicker the descriptions, the better.

Descriptive research on entrepreneurial responses to ethical dilemmas is an essential element in ethics research. The kinds of questions that need to be addressed include the following :

What dilemmas do entrepreneurs feel most acutely ? Are there any dilemmas that they encounter which they do not see as dilemmas ?

How do they assess ethical risks ? Do they have strategies for preventing dilemmas from arising ? Do they exhibit any biases or blind spots ?

What values, standards, and ideals come into play in their management of the ethical dilemmas ? Are there rules of thumb or heuristics that entrepreneurs use ?

Can the entrepreneurial population be meaningfully segmented with regard to how they see or respond to these dilemmas?

How do entrepreneurs assess their own handling of these dilemmas?

What skills seem to underlie effective handling of ethical dilemmas? How do entrepreneurs develop the skills to deal with ethical dilemmas effectively?

Interaction between ethical analysis and descriptive research is likely to be frequent and intense, especially in the early stages of this ethics research project. This give-and-take between social science and ethics should lead to the generation of some descriptive models of practice, which feeds into our next dimension.

Theory-Building Dimension

The central goal of the research effort discussed in this chapter is to develop a theory of ethics in the practice of entrepreneurship. From our current vantage point it is difficult to describe what such a theory might look like. It is possible that the descriptive and normative steps will leave us with a number of tensions, contradictions, and paradoxes. Even so, it should be possible to use these in a theoretically constructive way (Poole and Van de Ven 1989). Theorists may be able to build on recent efforts to model ethical decision making in business contexts (Trevino 1986; Hunt and Vitell 1986; Bommer et al. 1987) but should not be constrained by these frameworks. The theory may emerge gradually, as various insights are gleaned and limited models are developed, refined, and generalized. The end result might well resemble some of the recent theory development in the decision sciences (see Bell, Raiffa, and Tversky 1988) by highlighting the heuristics and biases reflected in actual judgement and conduct. Baron (1988, chapters 19–20) has already begun to do this with regard to moral thinking in general. Such a theory will likely encompass the role of emotion and imagination as well as moral reason.

Whatever the theory is, it will require a mix of input from practitioners, ethicists, and social scientists. It will be directed to answering three central questions: 1) What accounts for the gaps that exist between ethical ideals and actual entrepreneurial practice? 2) What factors come into play in determining the entrepreneur's sensitivity to ethical dilemmas and his or her ability to anticipate, prevent, or respond to them? 3) What accounts for the behavioral differences that are observed in practice? The result of this research effort should be a model (or several competing models) of how ethical considerations enter into the practice of entrepreneurial management.

Prescriptive Dimension

One of the greatest challenges facing ethics research is to determine whether, to what extent, and in what ways common practice can feasibly be improved, both from the entrepreneur's perspective and from society's perspective. Presumably, based on the Timmons and Stevenson survey (1983), practitioners believe there is room for improvement in practice. As scholars develop greater understanding of the challenges inherent in the attempt to integrate ethics into entrepreneurial practice, they may be able to offer some meaningful assistance. Moral exhortation has its role, but simply preaching moral ideals is likely to have a limited effect. The academic community needs to be able to offer more practical advice — advice that is sensitive to the moral point of view but that also reflects considerations of prudence and feasibility. This calls for entrepreneurial and managerial thinking that draws on the research dimensions previously discussed, and that crosses disciplinary boundaries. It requires both analytic thinking and creativity. Possible contributions that might be offered include : providing examples of "best" practice ; highlighting potential blind spots and biases ; developing exercises to build ethical assessment skills ; and sketching generic (and entrepreneurial) strategies for handling some of the more common dilemmas. No doubt much of the initial efforts will be trial-and-error experimentation. The quality of help should improve over time.

The questions to be addressed in this final dimension of ethics research are : What (if anything) can be done to improve the ethical conduct of entrepreneurs ? What can entrepreneurs do themselves, as individual decision makers ? What can they do in shaping their organizations (e.g., establishing ethics codes, consensus decision making) ? What can educational institutions do ? What sorts of public policies or social practices will provide guidance ?

In outlining this research model, there is no intent to imply a strict sequential structure. Though the dimensions are logically related and presented in a logical order, research probably will and should proceed in its usual chaotic way, as an iterative, interactive process. Ackoff, for example, is prepared to move to the final dimension, prescribing a consensus-style organizational structure to safeguard ethics in entrepreneurial firms (Ackoff 1987). He does this based on an ethical ideal and his own extensive experience with a number of organizations. The model does not imply that such a leap is illogical, but it does raise questions, such as : To which problems in practice is this prescription a solution ? Are there ethical dilemmas not addressed by this approach ? Are there new dilemmas created ? In what ways will group decision making be superior (or inferior) to more typical models of single-decision-maker management ? How well suited is Ackoff's consensus-style management to the entrepreneurial management process, in which flexibility and quick response may be crucial ? What is the implicit theory of ethics-in-practice behind Ackoff's recommendations ? Even with such bold and exciting effort, much work remains to be done.

CONCLUSION

Proposing a specific research agenda has required the intentional omission of a number of topics that would naturally arise in a broader discussion of ethics in entrepreneurial management. These topics include : how ethical dilemmas and responses fit into the organizational life cycle ; the similarities and differences between the ethical dilemmas of independent and corporate entrepreneurs ; the relationship between ethics and the law ; international or cross-cultural differences ; the moral foundations of the free enterprise system as compared to other systems of social organization ; and the role of government through regulation and public policy. No doubt the attentive reader can name several more interesting and relevant issues. Our research focus has not meant to imply that these issues should be neglected ; rather, it represents a choice to explore in depth one potentially fruitful track.

Our presentation of that track and the issues involved in it has purposefully highlighted the ethical complexities associated with entrepreneurial management, in order to pose a challenge that encourages research and fosters debate in this previously untapped area of the field. The themes in the entrepreneurship literature caution against a simplified account of entrepreneurship viewed through an ethical lens. It would be misguided to accept either of the two common but oversimplified views about the subject : namely, that it all can be reduced to a morality play between the forces of greed and those of goodness, or that single-minded devotion to ethics is just good business. Rather, business judgements may be complicated by the conflicting values, ambiguity, lack of precedent, and high degree of managerial discretion inherent in the entrepreneurial function. Assessment of the ethical aspects of entrepreneurial decisions incorporates self-interest, relationship and role morality, as well as more general moral values. These considerations have implications for practice, research, and education.

Implications for Practice

The ethical dilemmas inherent in entrepreneurial management may be some of the most challenging decisions that entrepreneurs face. Ethical risks and ethical opportunities call upon entrepreneurial moral imagination and courage. However, this imagination cannot benefit from the common language and the generally accepted tools that characterize the more traditional dimensions of the entrepreneur's business life, such as finance, marketing, strategy, or accounting. Ethical theories were developed for philosophical purposes and seem less well suited to direct practical application than some of the frameworks offered by other disciplines. Applied ethicists have not yet produced the kinds of tools nor instilled the common language for addressing these issues. For these and other reasons, ethical decisions are rarely discussed. Businesspeople in general tend to suffer from "moral muteness" (Bird and Waters 1989). As a result, entrepreneurs may have difficulty finding individuals in whom they can confide about these traditionally undiscussed issues. In addition, given the demands of their roles, entrepreneurs often seem to follow their own norms and principles, perhaps at odds with generally accepted standards. These norms may be viewed suspiciously by onlookers and unknowing participants, supporting the negative stereotype of the entrepreneur as trickster.

The performance implications are as yet unclear, but the end result may be moral stress in the form of harbored resentments, deep disappointments, underlying feelings of guilt or shame, and unexpected regrets that hinder action. The Timmons and Stevenson (1983) survey suggests that ethics is considered an important topic by entrepreneurs, but it is unclear what contributions and benefits could be offered by ethics education. A sound basis of research and theory in which to ground any attempts at improvement is needed.

Implications for Research

As scholars begin to explore the ethical aspects of entrepreneurial management, they will face their own set of challenges and dilemmas. While the multidisciplinary tradition of the entrepreneurship literature can be further enhanced by drawing upon the discipline of philosophy, at first glance it may be difficult for nonphilosophers to gain access to its vocabulary and methodology. This sort of cross-disciplinary work, from humanities to the social sciences, may prove more difficult than work across various social science disciplines (Hirschman 1981). But it is essential for quality research in this area. Philosophy is not just a body of knowledge of "thou shalt nots," but a way of reasoning, of drawing distinctions, of constructing normative theories that will provide social scientists with a new perspective. Discourse and collaborative research between social scientists and philosophers is one avenue for transferring knowledge. To promote this end, this chapter has presented basic terminology and modes of ethical inquiry, with references to key literature and specific applications to entrepreneurial decision making.

As co-authors with different disciplinary backgrounds, we have tried to set an example in the development of this chapter. As a philosopher and a social scientist, we have struggled with targeting the material for a hybrid audience. This affected the tone, choice of vocabulary, and decisions where to begin and conclude. Our process has been to educate each other first through shared readings; then to challenge each other in discussion. We were pleased to discover some valuable similarities of perspective, but we still approach the topic from somewhat different angles. Some compromise in styles and approaches is inevitable in this sort of collaboration. This chapter is a unique product of our particular interdisciplinary relationship, and others would no doubt do it differently. We encourage the effort.

Researching ethical issues poses dilemmas for researchers much like the ones sketched for entrepreneurs. There are both practical and ethical considerations in the conduct and reporting of research in this area. The general ethical issues of social science research (Mirvis and Seashore 1979) are magnified in ethics research, for our questions ask entrepreneurs to discuss the undiscussible. Consequently, the sensitive nature of this topic heightens the importance of gaining access and earning the trust of entrepreneurs. This creates the potential for subtle deception of the subjects, for role conflicts (e.g., independent researcher versus confidante), and for the researcher bringing his own ethical views into the research. (Researchers must be particularly sensitive to the views that they bring into the research.) In addition, some of the methodological difficulties of decision analysis research certainly apply in the case of ethics research, e.g., the accuracy of *ex post facto* explanations of reasoning or behavior, the potential for self-justifying rationalizations, and the difficulties of capturing real-time self-reports (Nisbett and Wilson 1977). Beyond gathering the data, the researcher must make difficult decisions about how to analyze and present it. This requires respect for and sensitivity to the ramifications of reporting results to the research and business community. To what extent do researchers want to reinforce stereotypes? The investigator must balance the promise of confidentiality with other research obligations, such as the obligations to report findings with some degree of independence and completeness, and to facilitate the reproducibility of results.

Our research model recognizes the multiple purposes of ethics research. Actual business practice encompasses great diversity. Thus, a research program should explore meaningful and subtle differences rather than attempting to construct an average ethics among entrepreneurs or a simple set of ethical tests for entrepreneurial management (Gartner 1985; Stevenson and Harmeling 1990). Further, academics need to be cautious not to preach or sermonize. Since at this point our knowledge base is so preliminary, we are in a position where we want to listen and learn from entrepreneurs, as well as to provide them with assistance. Our objective in creating new knowledge is to inform and instruct, perhaps ultimately to change or "improve" behavior. Accordingly, there is a need to be sensitive to the methods used in the effort to improve what we may not yet understand.

Implications for Education

At this stage, educators can provide a forum so that students may learn, listen, and discuss this aspect of entrepreneurial practice. Some important considerations in doing this include: a nonjudgemental environment that acknowledges variation in assumptions, skills, and behaviors; and a format which identifies multiple forms of ethical reasoning. Open discussion and multidimensional thinking should be encouraged in order to understand the dilemmas more fully and to encourage creative, ethically sensitive solutions. This should lead to the enrichment of ethical assessment skills. However, this research project may pose a dilemma for educators. What if educators discover that successful entrepreneurship is often linked to moral flexibility, a willingness to "cross over the line" when the situation calls for it. Do they convey this message in the classroom? How is it likely to affect student behavior? As this work proceeds, it is important to chart a course between naive moralism and cynical Machiavellianism.

━━ ━━ ━━ ━━ ━━ ━━ ━━

REFERENCES

Ackoff, R. 1987 Business ethics and the entrepreneur. *Journal of Business Venturing* 2 : 185–191.

Akst, D. 1987 How whiz-kid chief of ZZZZ Best had, and lost, it all. *Wall Street Journal.* July 9 : 1&18.

Aldrich, H., and E. Auster 1986 Even dwarfs started small : Liabilities of age and size and their strategic implications. *Research in Organizational Behavior* 8 : 165–198.

Aldrich, H., and C. Zimmer 1986 Entrepreneurship through social networks. In *The art and science of entrepreneurship*, eds. D. Sexton and R. Smilor, 3–24. Cambridge, Mass. : Ballinger Publishing Co.

Baier, K. 1958 *The moral point of view : A rational basis of ethics.* Cornell, N.Y. : Cornell Univ. Press.

Baron, J. 1988 *Thinking and deciding.* Cambridge : Cambridge Univ. Press.

Beauchamp, T., and N. Bowie 1983 *Ethical theory and business.* 2d ed. Englewood Cliffs, N.J. : Prentice-Hall, Inc.

Bell, D., H. Raiffa, and A. Tversky 1988 *Decision making : Descriptive, normative, and prescriptive interactions.* Cambridge, Eng. : Cambridge Univ. Press.

Ben-Porath, Y. 1980 The F-connection : Families, friends and firms and the organization of exchange. *Population and Development Review* 6 (March) : 1–30.

Bhide, A., and H. Stevenson 1990 Why be honest if honesty doesn't pay ? *Harvard Business Review* 68 (5) : 121–129.

Bird, B. 1989 *Entrepreneurial behavior.* Glenview, Ill. : Scott, Foresman and Co.

Bird, F., and J. Waters 1989 The moral muteness of managers. *California Management Review* 32 (1, Fall) : 73–88.

Birley, S. 1985 The role of networks in the entrepreneurial process. *Journal of Business Venturing* 1 : 107–117.

Blum, L. A. 1980 *Friendship, altruism and morality.* London : Routledge & Kegan Paul.

Bok, S. 1978 *Lying : Moral choice in public and private life.* New York : Vintage Books.

Brenner R. 1987 *Rivalry : In business, science, among nations.* Cambridge, Eng. : Cambridge Univ. Press.

Brockhaus, R., and P. Horwitz 1986 The psychology of the entrepreneur. In *Encyclopedia of entrepreneurship*, eds. C. Kent, D. Sexton, and K. Vesper, 39–57. Englewood Cliffs, N.J. : Prentice-Hall, Inc.

Brommer, M., C. Gratto, J. Gravander, and M. Tuttle 1987 A behavioral model of ethical and unethical decision making. *Journal of Business Ethics* 6 : 265–280.

Brown, D. J., and J. B. King 1982 Small business ethics : Influences and perceptions. *Journal of Small Business Management* 20 : 11–18.

Carr, A. 1967 Is business bluffing ethical ? *Harvard Business Review* 46 (1) : 143–150.

Casson, M. 1982 *The entrepreneur.* Totowa, N.J. : Barnes & Noble Books.

Chrisman, J. J., and F. L. Fry 1982 Public versus business expectations : Two views on social responsibility for small business. *Journal of Small Business Management* 20 : 19–26.

Collins, O., D. Moore, and D. Unwalla 1964 *The enterprising man.* East Lansing, Mich. : MSU Business Studies.

Cooper, A., C. Woo, and W. Dunkelberg 1988 Entrepreneur's perceived chances for success. *Journal of Business Venturing* 3 (2) : 97–108.

de Sola Pool, I. 1983 *Forecasting the telephone : A retrospective technology assessment.* Norwood, N.J. : Ablex Publishing Corp.

Dornblaster, B., T. Lin, and A. Van de Ven 1989 Innovation outcomes, learning and action loops. In *Research on the management of the innovation*, eds. A. Van de Ven, H. Angle, and R. S. Poole, 193–217. Cambridge, Mass. : Ballinger Publishing Co.

Downie, R. 1971 *Roles and values.* London : Methuen & Co.

Etzioni, A. 1987 Entrepreneurship, adaptation and legitimation. *Journal of Economic Behavior and Organization* 8 : 175–189.

1988 *The moral dimension : Toward a new economics.* New York : The Free Press.

Gartner, W. 1985 A conceptual framework for describing the phenomenon of new venture creation. *Academy of Management Review* 10 (4) : 696–706.

1990 What are we talking about when we talk about entrepreneurship ? *Journal of Business Venturing* 5 (1) : 15–28.

Gilligan, C. 1982 *In a different voice.* Cambridge, Mass. : Harvard Univ. Press.

Goffman, E. 1959 *The presentation of self in everyday life.* Garden City, N.Y. : Doubleday.

Goodpaster, K. 1982 Some avenues for ethical analysis in general management. Harvard Business School. Case 383–007.

Granovetter, M. 1985 Economic action and social structure : The problem of embeddedness. *American Journal of Sociology* 91 (3) : 481–510.

Hennessey, J. W., Jr., and B. Gert 1985 Moral rules and moral ideals : A useful distinction in business and professional practice. *Journal of Business Ethics* 4 : 105–115.

Hills, G. E., and C. L. Narayana 1989 Profile characteristics, success factors, and marketing in highly successful firms. In *Frontiers of entrepreneurship research*, eds. R. H. Brockhaus, Sr., et al. Wellesley, Mass. : Babson College Center for Entrepreneurial Studies.

Hirschman, A. 1981 Morality and the social sciences. In *Essays in trespassing : Economics to politics and beyond*, 294–306. Cambridge, Eng. : Cambridge Univ. Press.

Howell, J., and C. Higgins 1990 Champions of technological innovation. *Administration Science Quarterly* 35 : 317–341.

Hunt, S., and S. Vitell 1986 A general theory of marketing ethics. *Journal of Macromarketing* 6 (1) : 5–16.

Hyatt, J. 1990 The parent trap. *Inc.* October, 49 ff.

Iannone, A. P. 1989 *Contemporary moral controversies in business.* New York : Oxford Univ. Press.

Jarillo, J. C. 1988 On strategic networks. *Strategic Management Journal* 9 : 31–41.

Johannisson, B. 1987a. Beyond process and structure : social exchange networks. *International Studies of Management and Organization* 17 : 3–23.

1987b Anarchists and organizers : Entrepreneurs in a network perspective. *International Studies of Management and Organization* 17 : 49–63.

Kahneman, D., and A. Tversky 1984 Choices, values, and frames. *American Psychologist* 39 (4) : 341–350.

Kent, C., D. Sexton, and K. Vesper 1982 *Encyclopedia of entrepreneurship.* Englewood Cliffs, N.J. : Prentice-Hall, Inc.

Kets de Vries, M. 1985 The dark side of entrepreneurship. *Harvard Business Review* 63(6) : 160–167.

Kirzner, I. 1989 Some ethical implications for capitalism of the socialist calculation debate. In *Capitalism*, eds. E. Paul, et al. Oxford : Basil Blackwell.

Lodge, G. 1975 *The new American ideology.* New York : Knopf.

Longenecker, J., J. Mckinney, and C. Moore 1988 Egoism and independence : Entrepreneurial ethics. *Organizational Dynamics* 16(3) : 64–72.

1989 Ethics in small business. *Journal of Small Business Management* 27 : 27–31.

Lyons, N., and R. Mamis 1989 Management by necessity : How Philippe Kahn built an $80 million growth company without even knowing how to write a business plan. *Inc.* March, 33 ff.

Mackie, J. *Ethics : Inventing right and wrong.* New York : Penguin Books.

MacMillan, I. 1983 The politics of new venture management. *Harvard Business Review* 61(6) : 4–8.

Maidique, M. Entrepreneurs, champions and technological innovation. *Sloan Management Review* 21 (2, Winter) : 59–76.

Manz, C., D. Bastien, T. Hostager, and G. Shapiro 1989 Leadership and innovation : A longitudinal process view. In *Research on the management of innovation*, eds. A. Van de Ven, H. Angle, and R. S. Poole, 613–636. Cambridge, Mass. : Ballinger Publishing Co.

McClelland, D. 1961 *The achieving society.* New York : Van Nostrand.

Mirvis, P., and S. Seashore 1979 Being ethical in organization research. *American Psychologist* 34 : 766–780.

Nagel, T. 1970 *The possibility of altruism.* Princeton, N.J. : Princeton Univ. Press.

Nisbett, R., and T. Wilson 1977 Telling more than we can know : Verbal reports on mental processes. *Psychology Review* 84 (3) : 231–259.

Poole, M., and A. Van de Ven 1989 Using paradox to build management and organization theories. *Academy of Management Review* 14 (4) : 562–578.

Powell, W. 1990 Neither market nor hierarchy : Network forms of organization. *Research in Organizational Behavior* 12 : 295–336.

Ronstadt, R. 1985 *Entrepreneurship.* Natick, Mass. : Lord Publishing.

Rubin, P. 1982 Evolved ethics and efficient ethics. *Journal of Economic Behavior and Organization* 3 : 161–174.

Schein, E. 1983 The role of the founder in creating organizational culture. *Organization Dynamics.* 12(1) : 13–28

Schon, D. 1967 *Technology and change : The new Heraclitus.* New York : Delacorte Press.

Sexton, D., and N. Bowman-Upton 1991 *Entrepreneurship : Creativity and growth.* New York : Macmillan.

Starr, J., and I. MacMillan 1990 Resource cooptation via social contracting : Resource acquisition strategies for new ventures. *Strategic Management Journal* 11 : 79–92.

Stevenson, H., and S. Harmeling 1990 Entrepreneurial management's need for a more "chaotic" theory. *Journal of Business Venturing* 5 (1) : 1–14.

Stevenson, H., and J. C. Jarillo 1990 A paradigm of entrepreneurship : Entrepreneurial management. *Strategic Management Journal* 11 : 17–27.

Stevenson, H., M. Roberts, and H. Grousbeck 1989 *New business ventures and the entrepreneur.* 3d ed. Homewood, Ill. : Irwin.

Stinchcombe, A. 1965 Social structure and organizations. In *Handbook of organizations*, ed. J. March, 142–193. Chicago : Rand McNally.

Timmons, J. A., L. Smollen, and A. Dingee 1985 *New venture creation.* Homewood, Ill. : Irwin.

Timmons, J. A., and H. S. Stevenson 1983 Entrepreneurship education in the 1980s : What entrepreneurs say. In *Entrepreneurship : What it is and how to teach it*, eds. J. J. Kao and H. H. Stevenson, 45–134. Boston : Harvard Business School.

Trevino, L. K. 1986 Ethical decision making in organizations : A person-situation interactionist model. *Academy of Management Review* 2 (3) : 601–617.

Van de Ven, A. 1986 Central problems in the management of innovation. *Management Science* 32 : 590–607.

Victor, B., and J. Cullen 1988 The organizational bases of ethical work climates. *Administrative Science Quarterly* 33 : 101–125.

Webster, F. 1976 A model for new venture initiation : A disclosure on rapacity and the independent entrepreneur. *Academy of Management Review* 1 (1) : 26–37.

Wilson, E. 1980 Social responsibility of business : What are the small business perspectives ? *Journal of Small Business Management* 18 : 17–24.

Winner, L. 1977 *Autonomous technology.* Cambridge, Mass. : The MIT Press.

Winslow, R. 1990 The radium water worked fine until his jaw came off. *Wall Street Journal.* August 1 : A1, A5.

Chapter

6

Research Linkages between Entrepreneurship and Strategic Management or General Management[1]

Diana L. Day

●

INTRODUCTION

Most researchers seeking to define entrepreneurial management would readily agree that entrepreneurship issues include the creation of new businesses. Most would also include intimately linked activities such as the development of innovations. Schumpeter (1950) has described entrepreneurship as the combining of *existing* resources but in new ways (mainly within larger, established firms). More recently, Stevenson et al. (1989) describe entrepreneurship as the pursuit of an opportunity without concern for current resources or capabilities; hence, entrepreneurship may require the development of *new* resources or capabilities. This chapter combines these ideas, and defines entrepreneurial management as follows:

> Entrepreneurial management entails all management actions and decisions concerning the creation of new businesses and the related development of innovations from new or reconfigured resources, regardless of the scope of such development efforts (i.e., from start-ups to large, established firms).

[1] Funding for this study was provided by the Sol C. Snider Entrepreneurial Center of the Wharton School through a grant from Citibank, N.A.

If we use this definition to examine issues with potential relevance to entrepreneurial, strategic, and general management, numerous linkages are readily apparent. In fact, many strategy or general management researchers would argue that entrepreneurship is, in fact, a subset of strategic or general management. Clearly, a large pool of research in strategic or general management is related to entrepreneurship, making an exhaustive study of research linkages virtually impossible. Instead, this review plunges into the heart of the matter and draws together one possible configuration of some of the complex interrelations between these areas. As might be expected, some linkages are given substantially less coverage than others. However, it is hoped that significant linkages receive the attention they deserve. Given the multidisciplinary nature of our subject, this review draws on all relevant research, regardless of where such studies were published.

At the outset of this discussion, a framework drawn from strategic/general management theory is presented as a roadmap for the reader. The topics relevant to entrepreneurial management are placed within that framework, as diagrammed in Figure 6–1. This simple framework is one way of organizing a wide body of research in a useful format. Because of its simplicity, however, this framework forces one to arbitrarily separate multifaceted issues which in the real world are much more intimately linked. For example, it is very difficult to separate decision making and the decision makers from the actual decisions that result. As a consequence, some research could logically be placed in any of several locations.

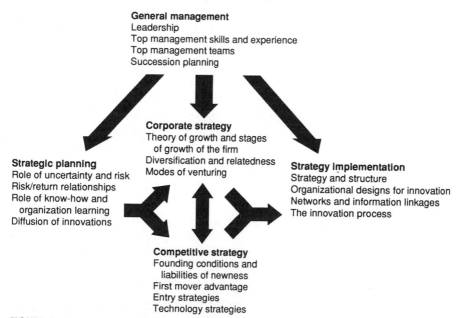

General management
Leadership
Top management skills and experience
Top management teams
Succession planning

Corporate strategy
Theory of growth and stages
 of growth of the firm
Diversification and relatedness
Modes of venturing

Strategic planning
Role of uncertainty and risk
Risk/return relationships
Role of know-how and
 organization learning
Diffusion of innovations

Strategy implementation
Strategy and structure
Organizational designs for innovation
Networks and information linkages
The innovation process

Competitive strategy
Founding conditions and
 liabilities of newness
First mover advantage
Entry strategies
Technology strategies

FIGURE 6–1 Framework for Identifying Research Linkages between Entrepreneurship and Strategic and General Management

A brief note on methodology : since the first goal of this discussion is to reveal linkages between entrepreneurship and the broader fields of strategic or general management, and since a preliminary review of the literature (without delving into the traditional entrepreneurship journals) yielded approximately 347 articles, a decision was made to focus largely on journals not directly concerned with entrepreneurship. Therefore, while some of the research published in entrepreneurship journals may have occasionally been included, it was decided not to focus on research from these journals.

Strategic management involves the set of decisions and actions that leads to the creation and implementation of strategies that will achieve the objectives of the organization. Strategic management research can be divided into two broad categories : strategy content, which addresses the issue of *what* strategy to employ, and strategic process, which is concerned with *how* firms decide upon and implement that strategy. Strategy content research can be further divided into topics that address competitive or corporate strategy (Hofer and Schendel 1978). Competitive strategy involves business-level decisions, asking questions such as, "How should the firm compete in this business ?" On the other hand, corporate strategy addresses firm-level issues of growth and survival, considering such questions as, "What businesses should the firm pursue ?"

Similarly, we divide strategic process research into two broad areas : strategic planning and strategy implementation. Strategic planning is concerned with how the firm arrives at its strategy, and draws largely from the literature on decision making. Strategy implementation is concerned with how the firms will actually carry out these strategic plans, and draws largely from organization design literature.

General management concerns both the internal structure of the firm and its external posture. The final section of this chapter focuses on the role of the general manager of the organization, both as an organization builder and a strategist. More specifically, this final section includes the issues of leadership, top management skills and experience, top management teams, and succession planning.

▬ ▬ ▬ ▬ ▬ ▬ ▬ ▬ ▬

STRATEGY CONTENT

Strategy content issues include both competitive strategy — i.e., determining how to compete within an individual product market or industry, and corporate strategy — i.e., determining which product markets or industries the firm should pursue.

Competitive Strategy

This section reviews the literature related to entrepreneurship, both in terms of the competitive environment and competitive choices of the business. More specifically, strategy literature is examined in regard to founding conditions ; entry timing, order of entry, and other entry strategy decisions ; and technology strategies to enhance competitiveness. However, this research barely scratches the surface, particularly with regard to competitive strategies for independent start-ups. For further information on independent start-ups, see Chapter 12.

Founding conditions.

Creating competitive advantage requires matching the strengths and weaknesses of the firm to the key factors for success in the competitive or product market environment.

In determining the competitive strategy for new firms, entrepreneurs must first understand the nature of the initial competitive environment or the "founding conditions." The founding conditions also leave an "imprint" on the firm (Stinchcombe 1965). Many researchers have studied founding conditions (such as environmental munificence, density, etc.) as well as imprinting, thus the studies reviewed here provide only a small sample but a good place to start.

Carroll and Hannan (1989) find that the density of firms in the industry at the time of a venture's founding has a significant positive effect on the mortality rates of those ventures. However, Romanelli (1989) shows that under most environmental conditions, both niche and aggressive strategies increased a venture's chances for early survival.

Eisenhardt and Schoonhoven (1990), in reviewing past research, find several studies that link the founding conditions of firms to organizational growth. Specifically, they find that characteristics of the top management team and market stage influence a firm's ability to grow. Boeker (1989) finds that founding conditions, both in terms of the developmental stage of the industry and the functional experience of the entrepreneur, affect subsequent subunit importance and power. Lambkin (1988) also examines the issues of founding conditions and corporate venture strategies in terms of the relationship between the parent and the venture.

Turbulent environments create unique challenges for firms, particularly start-ups. Venkataraman, et al. (1990) have developed a model which shows that the probability of transaction failures is a product of the failure rate at the level of the organizational population, as well as the kinds of transactions in which individual firms engage. They conclude that the very strategies which assist in overcoming liabilities of newness and small size are also the driving forces behind failure.

---

[2] It is important to differentiate between this perspective on innovation and others common in sociology and economics. For example, Tornatzky et al. (1983) focus on innovation in terms of its newness not only to the product/market but also to the firm. Nelson and Winter (1977) argue that differentiating between innovator and imitator is not particularly useful. In addition, Cohen and Levin (1989) provide a review of the extensive work on innovativeness and performance in the field of economics. These studies do not, however, use measures of innovativeness that correspond to entry positions. Instead, most of these studies measure innovativeness using firm-level inputs (e.g., R&D expenditures or personnel) or outputs (e.g., patents).

Entry timing or order of entry.

Schumpeter's (1934) early work led to a widely held belief that innovators (also called pioneers or first movers)[2] enjoy substantially higher returns compared with imitators or later entrants. In its more current form, this belief has been translated and expanded to suggest that innovators not only have superior profits (typically labeled *Schumpeterian rents*) but also market share advantages compared with those who follow.

In recent years, researchers have begun challenging this assumption. Empirical tests from a number of studies, however, tend to support Schumpeter. For example, Lambkin (1988) reported higher long-term profits and larger market shares for pioneers compared with subsequent entrants. Pioneers outperformed followers in market shares according to other studies as well (Robinson and Fornell 1985; Urban et al. 1986; Robinson 1988). More specifically, while entry order accounted for only 8 percent of the variance in industrial markets' shares (Robinson 1988), it explained 18 percent of the variance in consumer markets' shares (Robinson and Fornell 1985). In consumer markets, in fact, the very next entrant (i.e., number two) averaged only about 75 percent of the pioneer's market share (Urban et al. 1986).

According to some research, consumer market pioneers can frequently sustain those market share leads over significant periods of time. For example, 12 out of 18 grocery product categories introduced since 1945 in the United Kingdom still had first place in the mid-1970s. Even more striking, after almost 60 years, 80 percent of the 25 brand leaders from 1923 still held leading positions (Ries and Trout 1986). However, Lilien and Yoon's (1990) study of new industrial products found a *lower* likelihood of long-term success for first and second (as well as fifth and sixth) entrants compared with those entering third and fourth.

Clearly, these empirical studies have not truly resolved timing or order-of-entry issues, but, taken together, they could provide some valuable insights into requirements for further theoretical, conceptual, or empirical work. For example, the later studies seem to indicate significant variations in the rewards for innovation, depending on the type of buyer (i.e., consumer versus industrial). Lieberman and Montgomery (1988) identify several empirical issues which future research needs to examine — such as the manner in which "first movers" are defined and identified; the endogenous nature of pioneering opportunities and the potential for sample selection bias; and economic profits as a criterion in analysis.

More importantly, Lieberman and Montgomery provide this essential synthesis of the recent theoretical and empirical literature, developing a framework for the mechanisms underlying first movers' advantages (and disadvantages). They identify three approaches (each with several specific mechanisms) that may provide pioneers with larger and/or more enduring economic profits: leading technologically, preempting scarce resources, and developing buyer-switching costs. They also describe four ways that a pioneer's economic benefits can be threatened: free riders, delays in resolving uncertainty, technological or market discontinuities, and various types of organizational inertia.

Since Lieberman and Montgomery's review and synthesis is well organized and quite comprehensive, we will now concentrate on research which further elaborates specific mechanisms or extends reviewed research (with a few exceptions — e.g., frequently sighted or particularly important research where separate attention might prove beneficial). Before proceeding, it is important to note that many specific mechanisms have been identified, dating back to the initial barriers to entry identified by Bain (1956). However, more recent, expanded lists such as the key one by Rumelt (1987) include *isolating mechanism* as much more relevant for strategy and entrepreneurship. Rumelt has also developed a framework for determining where entrepreneurial activity is likely to occur and finds that this activity will be encouraged where appropriability is low and isolating mechanisms are high.

Technological (as well as market) discontinuities are one of the major threats to pioneers (Lieberman and Montgomery 1988). Implicitly elaborating this mechanism, Tushman and Anderson (1986) identify two very different types of technological shifts: those which are knowledge- or competence-destroying and those which are competence-enhancing. While they find that most competence-destroying shifts come from new entrants and have significant deleterious effects on incumbents, they find the *opposite* occurs with most competence-enhancing ones — i.e., these shifts come from within incumbents and strengthen their positions.

Providing further elaboration for this mechanism, Abernathy and Clark (1985) and Clark (1987) develop a framework which maps both technological and market innovators along intersecting continuums. They also introduce a new type of innovation — architectural innovation. Architectural innovations change the relationships between or among various components or subsystems of a product's "architecture" (Henderson and Clark 1990).

Henderson and Clark (1990) find that, like competence-destroying shifts, architectural shifts can also significantly disadvantage or even totally displace incumbents. Using a behavioral framework, they argue that such displacements are largely caused by incumbents' reduced capacities to learn. Insights about this type of shift suggest a potentially valuable alternative for less endowed, entrepreneurial firms (e.g., smaller/newer firms). More specifically, since these innovations do not necessarily involve changes in the basic knowledge or "science" embedded in the product, compared with radical technical innovations, they may be less costly to develop (yet they should still have the same effect on the redistribution of market shares and profits). If future research provides support for these propositions, architectural innovations could potentially provide a powerful approach for entrepreneurial firms. Despite the number of years since architectural innovations were first identified, however, little research exists on them or the types of firms that typically pursue them.

Based on an individual (rather than an organizational) behavioral perspective, Carpenter and Nakamoto's 1989 and 1990 studies of entry issues in consumer markets hypothesize pioneering advantages (as well as alternative positioning strategies for subsequent entrants) and test these using laboratory experiments. The authors find that a pioneer can favorably bias consumers' perceptions about preferred attributes, establishing itself as the prototype against which all subsequent entrants are judged (assuming it generates sufficient trial). Consequently, the pioneer becomes the dominant brand, achieving both substantial and persistent advantages based on its envied and also highly insulated position as the preferred brand. They also identify preference asymmetries (i.e., differential responses to similar products due largely to the product's source — the pioneer versus later entrants) which make a differentiated late-entry strategy optimal, even if preferences would appear to dictate otherwise. Finally, they determine that "me-too" strategies are not equilibrium late-entry strategies.

According to Lieberman and Montgomery (1988), first movers also face potentially significant problems because followers are often able to "free ride" off their initial investments (e.g., technical, market, and infrastructure development). More specifically, Mansfield, Schwartz, and Wagner's 1981 study of patented pharmaceutical, chemical, and electrical products found that imitators' costs were 35 percent lower than pioneers', with 60 percent of the pioneers constrained within four years. In fact, Mansfield (1985) found that information concerning development decisions diffuses to rivals within about 12 to 18 months, and information concerning the detailed nature and operation of a new product or process generally leaks out within a year. Fershtman, Mahajan, and Muller (1990) present a theoretical model that shows the decline of innovator or first mover advantages over time because of this diffusion of information. Finally, in a broad-based study, Levin et al. (1984) reported that imitators' ability to benefit from the pioneer's investments varies widely across industries in terms of imitators' time and costs to follow and the nature of appropriability mechanisms.

The diffusion of important strategic information (such as when R&D leaks as a result of licensing or imitation) should affect firms' strategies regarding the nature and timing of innovation. Recent evidence suggests it does. For example, Katz and Shapiro (1987) find that industry leaders will tend to pursue radical innovations only if imitation is difficult, choosing incremental improvements otherwise. However, further theoretical and empirical linkages between free riders and specific strategic decisions are needed.

In just that vein, Teece (1986)[3] provides a pivotal contribution to our understanding of timing strategies and the related distribution of profits between innovators and imitators/suppliers. He identifies, and then conceptually connects, three key factors to explain why innovators may often reap substantially fewer economic benefits from their own innovations than imitators and/or suppliers. To explain the distribution of profits, his conceptual framework links the following three factors: 1) the innovation's appropriability or the extent of protection from imitators/suppliers (high or low); 2) the industry's evolutionary stage (pre- or post-dominant design); and 3) the innovation's essential complementary assets (generic, specialized, or cospecialized). Equally

[3] Also see Teece (1986) for additional insights.

important, however, are the normative implications concerning licensing, collaboration, and integration that Teece derives from his framework.

Building on Teece (1986), Mitchell (1989) provides further elaboration of the role that complementary, specialized assets play not only in timing but also in the probability of entry. Based on data concerning entry into subfields of the medical diagnostic imaging industry, Mitchell finds that specialized assets are positively associated with the probability of entry into industry subfields. Concerning timing considerations, he finds that when significant potential rivalry exists, specialized assets are positively correlated with early entry; otherwise, such assets are negatively correlated. He also finds that incumbents will be early entrants to emerging subfields that threaten to cannibalize the firm's core products.

Conner (1988) derives an analytical model of optimal R&D and entry timing for subsequent new products introduced by industry leaders. She concludes that the leading firm should invest more in new product development than should competitors. However, the firm should then wait to introduce the product until the rival's product comes to market. Conner argues that this fast follower strategy allows the leader to avoid cannibalizing its own rent stream but also to quickly protect its dominant position after the competitor enters the market. In contrast, Wilson and Norton (1989) conclude that a firm should introduce a line extension early in the life cycle of the original product or not at all. They also find that the optimal entry time, to maximize total profits from the original product and the line extension, depends on the product pair's substitutability. Finally, while some strategists advise established firms to be second but better, Crawford (1988) concludes that even nondominant innovators can counter this strategy by bringing on their own stream of subsequent innovations.

In conclusion, Lieberman and Montgomery (1988) argue that different order strategies are appropriate for different firms depending on each firm's resource base. Lilien and Yoon (1990) contend that scant attention has been given to the risks associated with various order positions and recommend balancing the risks of premature entry against the missed opportunity of late entry in dynamic, competitive environments. In other words, potential entrants each have different *strategic windows* (Abell 1978) for entry which open for limited time periods only. However, more theoretical/conceptual work is needed before we can begin to say exactly when those windows are likely to be open for a given firm.

Other entry strategy decisions.

Biggadike's (1976) study of new entrants shows that rapid, large-scale entry and market share building is highly correlated with subsequent profits. MacMillan and Day's (1987) study further explores strategies of aggressive entry (but limited to corporate ventures entering industrial markets). They find three main sets of results: 1) a significant correlation between the market attractiveness of the target industry and the initial share objective; 2) a significant correlation between the share objective, set at the launch of the venture, and key initial marketing and capacity investments; and 3) significant correlations between aggressive entry variables and both higher market share *and* ROI. Interestingly, Robinson (1988) finds that incumbents' reactions to new entrants are relatively rare during the first two years, but when the entrants pursue aggressive strategies or the incumbent's core products are threatened, reactions can be substantial.

Based on previous research, Schoonhoven, Eisenhardt, and Lyman (1990) contend that the speedy introduction of a start-up's first product can be an important indicator of survival potential as well as long-term success (especially in the semiconductor industry, their study's focus). They hypothesize that technological innovation, as well as environmental, organizational, and entrepreneurial characteristics, can affect the venture's ability to launch quickly. In a longitudinal study of semiconductor start-ups, they test these hypotheses and find that speedy entry is negatively associated with monthly expenditures and technological innovativeness, but (surprisingly) positively associated with the number of competitors in Silicon Valley, and with organizations that have both manufacturing and marketing positions. Interestingly, they find no relationship with characteristics of the founding entrepreneurs, mimetic isomorphism, venture capital ownership, and outside investors on the board of directors. Their study should provide stimulus for many extensions using other industries, multiple industries, and other key events as variables.

In a study of market share and product innovation characteristics, the most significant correlation with market share was a product's advantage relative to its competitors (Robinson 1990). On the other hand, proprietary products were negatively correlated with market share. Surprisingly, the product's incompatibility with customers' current approach was not associated with market share. Using an analysis of software piracy issues, Conner and Rumelt (1991) show that in some circumstances, even with significant piracy, not protecting one's product can be the best entry strategy both in terms of higher profits and lower selling prices. Conner's analysis hinges on the presence of a network externality and the fact that piracy increases the total number of program uses. She argues that the externality exists because consumers have an incentive to economize on postpurchase learning as well as potential customization costs. Conner (1990) models generic industries characterized by network externalities and shows that in such industries, an innovator's optimal strategy is to encourage "clones" of its product.

Mason (1990) offers a more general model of the effect of new product entries on overall demand for a product class as well as the resulting distribution of market shares. Such a model should prove useful in subsequent empirical work on entry timing and market shares. In addition, Potter (1989) argues that by taking a "customer's eye view" of product innovation, firms can be first with new products and preempt competitors' new offerings. Furthermore, he states that by understanding the customer's cost of adopting the innovation, the firm can decide whether to focus on service or features and can more clearly identify its target market.

Technology / innovation strategy.

While the importance of technology to competitive advantage was recognized by Schumpeter as early as 1934, only recently have firms begun to focus on developing technology strategies to achieve strategic objectives. Porter (1983) was among the early strategy researchers to note the lack of research linking technological change and competitive strategy. His article proceeds to relate technology strategy to his three generic competitive strategies: overall cost leadership, overall differentiation, and a narrow business segment focus. Abernathy and Clark (1985) and Clark (1987) provide an excellent integration of some of the key issues in competitive strategy with the pursuit of various types of innovations.

Hambrick, MacMillan, and Barbosa (1983) provide an early empirical study linking R&D to competitive strategy. They find that R&D decisions in growth businesses are responsive to competition, evolving strategies, and intra-firm resource flows, while in mature businesses there is a pattern of stability and R&D equilibrium. In addition, Hambrick and MacMillan (1985) find that the link between R&D and new product sales is related to the technological opportunities of the firm, scale and experience, market linkages, and manufacturing suitability. Gort and Wall (1986) also find that declining technological opportunities over the industry life cycle contribute to a decline in overall investment in innovative activity.

Horwitch and Thietart (1987) argue that one of the major decisions that firms face in R&D-intensive businesses is the appropriate level of internal strategic interdependency within and among business units. They find that the interdependencies required to achieve high performance are contingent upon the nature of the business and its environmental characteristics. They conclude that effective competition for a firm with diverse R&D-intensive businesses may often require the ability to support and shift multiple levels of internal interdependencies.

A company's relationships with its suppliers and customers can be an integral part of its overall R&D strategy. Schill (1986) concludes that this strategy should contain elements such as: using technological change and R&D to raise the entry costs facing potential new rivals; preventing or anticipating the entry of substitutes; and raising exit costs to customers and suppliers, perhaps by involving them in technological development.

Zirger and Maidique (1990) find several key factors that affect the success of high-technology product innovation and outcome — most notably, that managerial superiority is crucial to new product success. Other important factors are: 1) the quality of the R&D organization, 2) the technical performance of the product, 3) the product's value to the customer, 4) the synergy of the new product with the firm's existing competencies, and 5) management support during the product development and introduction process.

Friar and Horwitch (1985) argue that, until recently, technological innovation has been treated largely as separate from the firm's strategy and overall management. They found that firms had begun to experiment with multiple methods for technological acquisition and development. However, few articles, with some notable exceptions (Hamilton 1986), explicitly link technology and firm strategies. For example, the costs and structure of R&D within the firm are clearly important elements of technology strategy. In this light, Low and Silver (1986) conclude that the firm can respond to fluctuations in demand for R&D by contracting out technology, licensing, collaboration, or mergers. But their article does not address how such activities may impact the overall competitive or corporate strategy.

Pelc (1986) finds that when a firm's technology is outdistanced by competitors, the firm can use three R&D strategies to regain its technological lead : it can 1) rapidly improve product performance in the current generation of products to become competitive with the leader, 2) enter the next generation before the leader, or 3) skip the next generation and direct efforts to entering the third generation before the competitor. Rothwell and Gardiner (1989) point out that firms can plan for the "reinvention" of their products through two strategies : 1) by combining the existing product with the new product, and 2) by creating an original product with a "robust design" that has enough flexibility to allow evolution into a family of variants.

These and other exceptions aside, as yet little research exists which explicitly incorporates technology strategy in strategic management studies. However, McGee and Thomas (1989) note a *growing* interest among strategic management researchers in the interface between technology and strategic management.

From the technology side, Allen and George (1989), in a recent survey of technology management research, find that the most popular areas of interest include organizational issues, the interface between R&D and production, and the impact of information technology. More specifically, these include : integrating R&D into corporate strategy ; defining the new role of basic R&D in technology ; organizing for technological assessment/flexibility and speed in the R&D process ; and measuring the impact of new information technology.

Using the argument that R&D management is very different from strategic technology management, Lauglaug (1987) develops a process model that views the strategic management of technologies as *techno-business management,* in which technology, business strategy, planning, and implementation are facilitated by portfolio frameworks and technology-forecasting techniques.

Despite the repeated acknowledgements by both strategy and technology researchers, little work is available that explicitly links these two key areas. Given that this linkage is also crucial in entrepreneurship research, perhaps greater strides will be made if scholars from all three fields focus research in this area or come together to co-author research.

Corporate Strategy

Corporate strategy addresses *firm-level* issues of survival and growth. However, as Aldrich and Auster (1986) have noted, small, new organizations' strengths are often large, old organizations' weaknesses, and vice versa. Hence, research on critical issues, including potential solutions related to survival and growth, is likely to reveal different, sometimes even directly opposite, results for these two types of firms. Consequently, after examining research on growth issues, the following discussion explores issues largely concerning smaller, new firms — and more specifically, liabilities of newness. This section then addresses large-firm issues concerning diversification and relatedness, and modes of venturing.

Research on growth issues.[4]

Past research has identified many different motives for firm growth. The main motive driving new firms to strive for growth is to overcome liabilities of smallness which can threaten their survival. Among older, more established firms, however, motives for growth more frequently spring from : 1) the desire to employ excess capacity or underutilized capabilities (Penrose 1959); 2) agency problems which arise in larger firms because of the tendency to separate ownership and management; 3) the desire for Schumpeterian or entrepreneurial rents as the margins in their more mature markets get tighter over time; and 4) avoiding the other liabilities of age.

To grow, firms need to develop distinctive competencies which allow them to gain competitive advantages in specific product markets. In established firms, they must maintain some balance between exploiting the firm's existing resources and building new capabilities upon which its future may one day depend.

Several authors have proposed stages of growth models; however, Kazanjian and Drazin's (1989) recent study provides a rare empirical test of their model. Their growth model for technology-based start-ups includes four discrete states: conception and development, commercialization, growth, and stability. Although they note some variation of interstate transition patterns, their longitudinal study of 71 technology start-ups provides ample empirical support for their four stages of growth.

Achieving an optimal growth rate requires maintaining a delicate balance between the exploitation of existing resources and the development of new ones (Penrose 1959; Rubin 1973; Wernerfelt 1984). However, little research exists on the optimal growth rates of firms, the duration times for "Penrose effects" — cycles of growth and stability (Richardson 1964; Uzawa 1969; Shen 1970) — or the limits of growth rates of firms. However, organization design research challenges Penrose's position that there are no limits on the ultimate size of the firm. Future research should focus not only on strategies for and stages of growth, but also on the limits of growth, optimal growth rates, and duration times of Penrose effects.

---

[4] This section provides a limited discussion of research on issues related to firm growth (mostly from sources not often encountered in entrepreneurship research). For a fuller discussion of current research agendas related to growth strategies, see Chapter 13 in this volume.

Liabilities of newness.

Stinchcombe (1965) was the first to propose a *liability of newness* partly as an explanation for why so many start-ups die. One of the key problems faced by start-ups is that they lack legitimacy. Singh, House, and Tucker (1986a), in a study of voluntary social services organizations, found that the strategies used to acquire legitimacy and overcome the liabilities of newness have an impact on organization survival; that is, organization legitimacy helps the group overcome the liabilities of newness and survive. Those groups without legitimacy tend to die out over time.

At the firm level, Schoonhoven and Eisenhardt (1985) and Venkataraman (1990) find that establishing a relationship with a key dominant player can lead to early success for new ventures. However, Venkataraman also finds that the exact same strategy can be the source of demise for the new venture because the venture's very survival depends on the success of that one relationship.

Fichman and Levinthal (1991) identify two important periods within the adolescent stage of the firm. In the honeymoon period, start-ups have an initial pool of resources to support them; hence, death rates are relatively low. However, in the subsequent period, the start-up becomes subject to all the liabilities of newness recognized in the population ecology literature; the probability of failure is high at this stage, but it decreases monotonically over time. Bruderl and Schussler (1990) also find evidence for a period of adolescence with a similar pattern of age-dependent, monotonically declining hazard rates for start-ups due to *liabilities of adolescence* for new firms. They find that, depending on the original resources of the firm, mortality peaks between 1 and 15 years after founding.

Diversification and relatedness moves.

Historically, firms have found that every product, market, and technology has limits and eventually faces decline. Therefore, if companies are to grow or even survive, ultimately they must move into new products, markets, and/or technologies. These moves, called *diversification moves,*[5] are also essentially corporate ventures.[6]

Interestingly, while the broad topic of diversification is perhaps the most extensively researched area in the strategy field, very little research addresses diversification moves[7] or its corollary, corporate venturing (with the exception

---

[5] Diversification moves are any entry into a new product market that requires a substantial increase in the knowledge or skill of the firm (Rumelt 1974).

[6] Corporate ventures can be defined as any business that is new to the firm on at least two of three dimensions of products, markets, and/or technologies, and demands significant investments to achieve results beyond the year of investment (Biggadike 1979).

[7] In an extensive review and synthesis of diversification research, Ramanujam and Varadarajan (1989) also note, albeit indirectly, the lack of research on diversification moves and related issues and call for a shift in level of analysis. Drawn mainly from strategic management research, Ramanujam and Varadarajan's article provides a useful compilation and critique of diversification studies for those interested in more information about this line of inquiry.

of the extensive research on mergers and acquisitions, e.g., Singh and Montgomery 1987). However, it is useful to know that Rumelt's (1974) now classic study of diversification, as well as the majority of others on this topic, basically found that related firms outperformed unrelated firms. Hence, the results from the firm level on relatedness and diversification would suggest that diversification moves should not be totally unrelated to the capabilities or resources of the firm.

Day (1986) argues that learning *how* firms can survive and grow profitably requires understanding how relatedness between the firm and each diversification move improves the venture's chances for success in its new product markets, because it is these ventures or diversification moves which provide the engines (Penrose 1959) of ultimate growth and profits. Day proposes a framework which links the opportunity for positive synergies as well as negative or dis-synergies (Ansoff 1965) to specific resources and the mechanisms that underlie each, depending on the nature of the competitive environment. More recently, Day (1990) suggests that a better way of studying relatedness would be to define and measure it on the basis of the related individual resources or cospecialized assets utilized in each diversification move. In a study of internal corporate ventures, Day (1989a) argues that the value of sharing certain resources varies by the stage of development of the product market at the time the venture enters. She finds that ventures launched at different stages do, in fact, have significantly different payoffs and costs of sharing specific resources with other operating businesses in the firm.

In another empirical study, Day (1989b) suggests that the value to the new venture of sharing plant and equipment with another business within the firm depends on whether the competitive market for that product is commodity-like or differentiated. Her results show that ventures in differentiated markets which shared plant and equipment with another business within the firm had *poorer* performance than those that did not. Conversely, in commodity-like markets, ventures which shared plant and equipment had performance that was *superior* to those that did not.

Additionally, Day (1989c) examines the relationship between the type of market (i.e., consumer versus industrial) and the sharing of marketing assets in launching internal corporate ventures. Her results show that consumer ventures which shared distribution channels and marketing programs had superior performance to those that did not, but just the opposite was true in industrial markets.

Cooper (1989) finds that the most advantageous corporate strategy is diversification into a high-profit area based on a market-related perspective that uses R&D to develop new products with competitive advantages, rather than new processes. On the other hand, in a study of diversification in small, emerging firms, Mosakowski (1990) finds that organizational slack is positively related to diversification and that unsuccessful firms have greater rates of diversification into new businesses.

Modes of venturing.

Corporate venturing for growth and development can be achieved using various alternative governance structures (Roberts 1980; Williamson 1985). Selecting the appropriate governance structure or venturing mode is a key theoretical issue in organizational economics (Williamson 1985); however, more linkages are needed between the theoretical literature on governance and such issues as: 1) the characteristics of the venture's environment, 2) the goals of the firm in a given diversification move, and 3) the firm's related or complementary resources/capabilities and its degree of specialization (i.e., generic, specialized, or cospecialized).

Teece's (1986) framework for entry strategy suggests some key issues to consider in determining the appropriate mode of venturing, particularly between internal (i.e., internal development or acquisition) versus external strategies (i.e., contracting, licensing, or collaboration). More specifically, his work suggests normative implications concerning licensing, collaboration, and integration. He argues persuasively that the boundaries of the firm, and its complementary assets, are important strategic variables for the innovating firm to consider in determining whether to use an internal strategy versus an external one, or one somewhere between the two — such as collaboration.

The venturing modes span a broad spectrum from making the new capabilities internally — for example, internal development (Burgelman 1983a, 1983b; Fast 1977), to buying capabilities on the market — for example, external acquisition (Salter and Weinhold 1979; Singh and Montgomery 1987). In addition, combining capabilities or collaborative strategies such as joint ventures (Harrigan 1985; Kogut 1988) are also common venturing modes. Aldrich and Auster (1986) recommend that large firms emulate smaller firms or exploit them through subcontracting or franchising.

Recent strategy research has begun to examine less common, newer, and "hybrid" modes of venturing which can achieve some or all of the goals of more traditional governance structures and are increasingly found in practice. These alternative modes include ICJVs (internal corporate joint ventures), strategic alliances, franchises, corporate venture capital, venture nurturing, research grants, and minority investments, to name a few.

Shortell and Zajac (1988) examine the structuring, development, and performance of internal corporate joint ventures — that is, a hybrid of both traditional joint ventures and internal corporate ventures. They find that both resource scarcity and prior experience play a role in the development and performance of ICJVs.

Strategic alliances involving hybrids and networks are also newly evolving organizational forms for moving into new product markets and/or developing new capabilities, according to Borys and Jemison (1989). Lorenzoni and Ornati (1988) examine *constellations* of cooperative relationships between a given firm and various external start-ups. They find that such alliances allow the firm to grow without significant direct investments. Shaw (1988) argues that cooperative strategies — including the transfer, exchange, and pooling of existing technologies — can help firms make the best use of their technological resources. He finds that such alliances restructure and revitalize industries, create interdependence, increase flexibility and risk sharing, and force top management to determine a balanced product development portfolio.

Norton (1988) argues that through franchising, larger-scale retail outlets can achieve quasi-vertical integration without integration's frequently encountered higher coordination and monitoring costs. He notes that the broad dispersion of outlets and the importance of brand name capital which are prerequisites for successful, large-scale retailing also exacerbate the problem of entrepreneurial capacity. On the other hand, franchising offsets these pressures and can even accommodate slightly larger local outlets than nonfranchised operations, according to Norton.

With a few exceptions, however (e.g., Lamont and Anderson 1985; Roberts and Berry 1985), little strategy research exists which compares different modes of venturing in terms of their performance or even their adoption rates.[8] In contrast, the appropriate mode for entering new country markets is one of the central issues in international business research. While this research will be somewhat biased because the market is the major new area for new ventures in all international business research, it is still a valuable source of extensive empirical data. In addition, direct foreign investment theory[9] may provide some useful theoretical perspectives for entrepreneurship researchers interested in this issue.

Kogut (1988) argues that joint ventures provide firms with *real* options to expand when technological or market uncertainties become clearer. His asymmetric results offer strong support for this contention. Hamilton (1986) recommends research contracts as another method for establishing future options in specific, emerging technologies or markets. In a study of organizational boundaries and economic performance, Mosakowski (1991) examines the relationship between contracting activities of entrepreneurial computer firms and their economic performance. She finds the contracting activities are correlated with performance and, furthermore, that the firms' product market strategies moderated their contracting-performance relationships.

Others (Hamilton 1986; Roberts and Berry 1985) suggest that research grants, minority investments, corporate venture capital, and venture nurturing (both capital investments and managerial assistance to external start-ups) can all provide established firms with windows on emerging technologies and/or

[8] For further discussion, see Ramanujam and Varadarajan's (1989, 526–527) review of the mode as one of the seven areas of diversification. Note, however, that this review does not cover research on modes of diversification from either the entrepreneurship or functional literatures nor from international business research. However, given the enormity of the task they undertook, this oversight seems quite understandable.

[9] For example, see Root's (1987) managerially oriented book for a discourse on issues of multinational entry strategies.

markets. More importantly, they do so without forcing firms to make extensive commitments and hence lock themselves in at premature stages when significant uncertainties still exist. While such activities do not allow the firm to obtain a clear position or even necessarily an option in the new technology or market, they do provide the firm with increased awareness, knowledge, and flexibility, which are all crucial in early developmental stages. Also, the limited resources required for such activities allow large firms to invest in and monitor a broad spectrum of technologies or markets simultaneously.

Another form of venturing is the spin-off (Roberts 1980). Venture spin-offs are strategic misfits which may arise out of R&D, mergers and acquisitions (M&A), or other corporate venturing activities, or because of corporate downsizing or corporate strategy shifts. In this form of venturing, internal businesses or technologies are spun off as separate, independent companies with the parent company typically maintaining a minority stake in the new venture. This action allows the parent to reduce its risk exposure yet still reap some of the rewards of the investments it made. On the other hand, the venture's new, independent status should provide it with substantially more latitude and flexibility than could be achieved within the corporate framework, while providing the venture's management team with challenges and potential rewards largely comparable with other independent entrepreneurs. Although venture spin-offs offer many interesting research issues, to date they have gone largely unnoticed.

Furthermore, the theoretical and empirical work that exists needs to be synthesized (much like Liebermand and Montgomery 1988) to begin building a normative theory with clear insights about where the gaps are.

STRATEGIC PROCESSES

While strategy content research is concerned with selecting the right strategy, strategic process research is concerned with *how* the firm arrives at and implements that strategy. Strategic process research covers two broad areas: strategic planning and strategy implementation. Strategic planning, drawing in part from the literature on decision making, is concerned with how the firm arrives at its strategy; while strategy implementation, drawing largely from organization theory and design, is concerned with how that strategy is carried out.

Although the numbers may be changing, comparatively little research has been done on strategic processes to date. This may be partially due to the fact that no readily available data on strategic processes exists. In contrast, extensive data relevant to content research is available from the government (e.g., the FTC's lines of business or M&A data sets) as well as private sources (e.g., PIMS, Compustat, CRSP, Rumelt's data base, etc.). Additionally, many process issues often require time- and labor-intensive methodologies.

Given the small number of process studies in general, many crucial, generic issues still remain unexplored. Furthermore, the extensive unmet agenda in process research suggests that studies specifying whether and how entrepreneurial processes differ are even fewer. All this being said, many strategic process studies contain subtle but potentially important implications for entrepreneurship research. The discussion that follows will illustrate some of these ideas. The studies discussed below should also provide fruitful theoretical perspectives or methodological approaches for entrepreneurship research; however, given the limits imposed here such insights will be left largely for each reader to discover.

Strategic Planning

The goal of strategic planning is to identify the best strategy for obtaining specific objective(s) (also determined as part of the planning process). Two theoretical perspectives on decision making borrowed from different underlying disciplines are potentially relevant to research on the planning process. From economics, the normative approach treats decision making as a rational process for determining the optimal strategy to achieve the firm's goal (normally economic rents or excess returns). Past research using this perspective has not been particularly useful to strategy, because highly restrictive assumptions, employed to make optimization possible (i.e., mathematically tractable and hence analytically solvable), require situations that are strategically uninteresting. More recently, some of the more restrictive and unrealistic assumptions are being relaxed, promising more potentially useful models from this perspective in the future.

The second perspective, drawn from psychology, takes a behavioral view of decision making (building on work by March and Simon 1958; and Marris 1964). In this approach, managers face constraints in their cognitive abilities to process information (both in attention and memory), which results in limitations on their ability to optimize. In most strategic situations, optimal strategies cannot be derived, because of the complexity and uncertainty inherent in them. As a result, managers develop "heuristics" — i.e., simpler rules of thumb or decision models for decision making. These heuristics have inherent biases. Furthermore, managers use cognitive schemata to organize and interpret their perceptions of reality (Tversky and Kahneman 1981; Schwenk 1984). Finally, they also employ personal schemas to deal with their own cognitive limitations (Tversky and Kahneman 1974, 1981; Barnes 1984; Schwenk 1984, 1986, 1988). Prospect theory (Tversky and Kahneman 1974, 1981), which originated this latest, most innovative stream of research, leads one to question the utility of the normative rational model for strategic decision making. Issues of decision making under uncertainty and organizational learning which are critical to entrepreneurial management draw on this research.

In the following discussion, we first examine the strategic planning literature. Beyond the broader strategic planning literature, however, this section also explores topic-specific, strategically related process research concerning issues highly relevant to entrepreneurship. These issues include the role of uncertainty and risk in planning, the organizational learning process, and the diffusion of innovations.

Strategic planning literature.

Dess (1987) finds that in planning strategy, top management consensus is positively related to organizational performance. Given his results and others which indicate that politics is negatively associated with performance, findings from Eisenhardt and Bourgeois (1988) are particularly curious. They find that senior executives participate in and even instigate political behavior among subordinates when planning strategy. Similarly, Frederickson's (1985) findings suggest that the motive behind the decision and current performance may influence how strategic decisions are made. Furthermore, Thomas and McDaniel (1990) show that the structure used by top management to process information, as well as the firm's strategy, affect how the CEO interprets strategic issues. Jackson and Dutton (1988) find that management may be better at perceiving threats than opportunities. Finally, contrary to the popular belief that speedy decisions are often carelessly made, Eisenhardt (1989) finds, in a study of high-velocity environments, that fast decision makers typically use more information and develop more alternatives than slow ones. She also shows that resolving conflict and integrating strategic decisions with tactical plans both play critical roles in the process. She concludes from her study that fast decisions employing these principles lead to superior performance.

As noted earlier, few studies in the field of strategy/management explicitly examine how entrepreneurial processes differ from those in more predictable situations. Jennings and Lumpkin (1989) provide one of the few exceptions. According to their results, the entrepreneurial decision-making process is participative and relies on specialized personnel. They find that entrepreneurial organizations do not penalize managers if risky products fail, and they arrive at performance objectives based on shared participation.

Jelinek and Schoonhoven (1990) provide some useful insights into how strategic planning is managed in high-technology firms. They find that such firms have formal planning systems and do strategic planning; however, these firms also incorporate other elements to help them cope with the requirements of competing in such difficult environments.

The studies mentioned here could have relevance for a number of areas in entrepreneurship research. For example, some of the key decisions entrepreneurs must face are those surrounding entry. These studies highlight some variables which potentially could affect the process or the outcome of entrepreneurs' initial entry decisions. On the incumbents' side, they also suggest process variables which could affect the probability, nature, and timing of incumbents' reactions to entry. To date, however, scant research on entry decision processes exists.

The role of risk and uncertainty in planning.

Strategic planning during entry into untested markets is like flying on radar; many of the standard landmarks that indicate success for the product are not on the screen. As such, firms must often make decisions without the type of market research that they prefer to rely on in more typical situations. If, in fact, they do rely on market research or other such standard practice, they may well take the wrong actions. For example, market research on the calculators for Hewlett Packard indicated that this was not a good business to enter. Lotus's sales figures for its first year of operation were off by a factor of 10. Dougherty (1990) considers why corporate entrepreneurs tend to do a poor job assessing new markets, and suggests that organizational factors affect market knowledge creation at the departmental, project, and project-to-firm levels. While firms should try to improve these factors, there is no way of really knowing all that would be useful in making decisions in these situations because the markets, technologies, and other factors are uncertain.

Uncertainty exists when one cannot ascertain, through either a priori reasoning or statistical inference, the probabilities of a wide range of outcomes (Casson 1982, 371). In contrast, risk relates to the knowledge of the likely distribution of possible outcomes (Alchian 1950). The consideration of risk does not result in entrepreneurial profits (Knight 1921; Schumpeter 1934). Theoretically, the return for undertaking risk is directly proportional to the degree of risk taken. Thus, actions bearing risk are distinguished from pure entrepreneurial profits. Entrepreneurial profits relate to individuals taking advantage of unique opportunities when the outcome cannot be determined a priori.

Smithson's (1989) seminal work on the concept of uncertainty and its relation to the broader category of ignorance makes useful reading. He points out that within the social sciences there are errors in decision making due to ignorance, not only due to the incompleteness of information but also to the distortion of information. He argues further that researchers tend to treat the whole area of incompleteness as uncertainty, when in fact incompleteness has two components: uncertainty and absence.

Krickx (1990) reviews the theoretical treatment and empirical measures of uncertainty and their impact on vertical interpretation. He proposes a broader typology of uncertainty which allows one to interpret the impact of product, process, and governance innovations, and concludes that different types of uncertainty have been found to have different implications for the make-or-buy decision.

Schoemaker (1990) focuses on two approaches to decision making: the normative approach, with its rational view of decision making, and the descriptive approach (Kahneman and Tversky 1982). Schoemaker proposes that strategy, at its nucleus, concerns itself with the development and testing of heuristics for high-stakes decisions in environments unlikely to be optimized because of instability and complexity.

Schoemaker relates corporate strategy to views about the creation, exploitation, and protection of economic rents. He advocates a temporary rent view, which he links to recent developments in microeconomics and behavioral decision theory. He notes that future theories of strategy must address important friction forces, including technological and environmental ones, while concentrating on the most important ones, which he argues are psychological.

In terms of risk assessment, several theories suggest that people replace probabilities with decision weights when evaluating risky outcomes. Hogarth and Einhorn (1990) propose a model, called venture theory, of how people assess decision weights. It is assumed that people first anchor on a stated probability and then adjust this by simulating other possibilities. The net effect of the adjustment is a function of both individual and situational variables, and in particular, the sign and size of payoffs.

Organizational learning.

The concepts and mechanisms related to organizational learning are still not totally defined ; however, what is clear is that all organizations must be able to learn if they are to move into new businesses. In fact, virtually every aspect of organizational learning has relevance either directly or indirectly for entrepreneurial management.[10] Huber (1991) uses four constructs — knowledge acquisition, information distribution, information interpretation, and organizational memory — in his analysis of this subject. Despite this lack of clarity, however, several researchers have examined how organizations accumulate and use knowledge. Their research is examined as it relates to capacities for learning ; strategies for learning ; sources of learning ; time required to learn ; and the manner in which time varies by strategy.

However, any discussion of organization learning must start by examining its most basic assumption : do organizations possess the necessary factors to be able to change ("adapt") over time ? Levinthal (1991) has tried to answer this question by simulating the effects of different assumptions regarding the ability of organizations to learn and adapt. He defines learning assumptions that lead to different kinds of population level outcomes. Similarly, Lounamaa and March (1987) outline some rules for using organizational learning to improve performance.

Although selection and adaptation are often seen as conflicting theories of organizational change and learning, Singh, Tucker, and House (1986b) find that they may actually be complementary. They claim that theories of the ecological, adaptation, and random organizational action perspectives depend on the location of the changes in the organization, whether in the core or at the periphery.

Their findings suggest another important issue : does an organization's capacity to learn diminish over time or vary by industry ? In that regard, an early work by Frankel (1955) examines technological change in a maturing economy

---

[10] For an excellent overview of the issues and status of work on organizational learning, *Organization Science* (1991), eds. M. D. Cohen and L. S. Sproull, provides a valuable starting point.

and finds that mature firms are sometimes unable to assimilate technological change, which may indicate a reduced capacity to learn. Furthermore, in a study of the failures of early American telephone companies, Barnett (1990) finds that technological changes do not favor advanced organizations. The findings strongly support an ecological approach to technological interdependence. Pisano (1990), however, argues that the effects of competence-destroying technological change on a firm's R&D boundary depend on the organization's history and experience, as well as small-numbers-bargaining problems.

Looking at learning capacity in a slightly different way, Cohen and Levinthal (1990) argue that R&D not only creates specific innovations, it also increases a firm's absorptive (learning) capacity. Even if the knowledge spills over into the environment, the firm gains an enhanced ability to absorb and learn as the product class evolves. Many years ago, Arrow (1962) addressed this question and concluded that competition does not lead to a perfect allocation of resources because of indivisibilities, inappropriabilities, and uncertainty. He concludes that because of uncertainty, in particular, optimal allocation to research requires the involvement of governments or universities.

At a much more detailed level, Dougherty (1990) examines why innovators in large firms have difficulty collaborating across departmental boundaries. Her study describes two interpretive schemes or cultures in a firm that inhibit the kind of working relationships necessary for innovation and, hence, organizational learning — departmental thought worlds and organizational routines. People in each department operate with qualitatively different understandings of new product development, which seriously limits their ability to synthesize their expertise; rather than help overcome them, organizational routines reinforce these separations. The main implication is that product innovation requires that these interpretive barriers be overcome directly, and suggestions for doing so are offered.

Various *strategies for learning* include formal search procedures and knowledge acquisition, as well as informal environmental scanning and knowledge acquisition modes, including relationships and networks as sources of learning, learning by experience or "learning-by-doing," and trial-and-error learning.

The conventional industrial organization research has used different kinds of learning models, out of which the cumulative output-cost curve approach is most popular. Epple, Argote, and Devadas (1991) have tried to show how a learning curve model can be generalized to investigate potential explanations of organizational learning. Their results simply point to the problem of codependencies in a firm's abilities to exploit new technologies.

Argote, Beckman, and Epple (1990) examine the persistence of learning within organizations and the transfers of learning across organizations. Their results indicate that knowledge acquired through production depreciates rapidly, and that the conventional measure of learning, cumulative output, significantly overstates the persistence of learning.

Successes and failures in the Maidique and Zirger (1985) sample were strongly interrelated. They found that knowledge gained from failures was often instrumental in achieving subsequent successes, while success often resulted in unlearning the very process that led to the original success. On this basis, they postulate a new product *learning cycle model,* in which commercial successes and failures alternate in an irregular pattern of learning and unlearning.

Another issue is the *sources of learning,* both internal and external. In terms of the new product innovation process, repeated evidence exists that external sources are often the best sources for learning. Von Hippel (1981) discovered that most new product ideas are driven by interactions with customers. Know-how is also brought in from outside the organization, sometimes even from direct rivals (von Hippel 1987). More specifically, Utterback (1971) finds that almost 75 percent of the ideas used to develop product innovations came from outside the organization. However, differences seem to exist in the nature of those product innovations. Utterback (1974) argues that customer- or market-driven innovations are usually based on old technologies applied in new ways, whereas new technologies are likely to be derived from other sources and require a lengthy search to find appropriate applications and markets.

Clark (1985) develops a conceptual framework for analyzing the sequence of technological changes that underlie the development of industries. This framework examines the interaction between design decisions and the choices of customers. The author argues that the logic of problem solving in design and the formation of concepts that underlie choice in the marketplace impose a hierarchical structure on the evolution of technology. The nature of the evolutionary process has implications for the dynamics of competition and the management of innovation.

Another critical aspect of learning is the time dimension, both with regard to modes (e.g., experiential) and sources of learning (e.g., customers, competitors). March (1991) explores complications in resource allocation decisions between the *exploration* of new possibilities and the *exploitation* of old certainties when considered in terms of the distribution of costs and benefits over time and space. He argues that adaptation through refining exploitation is more rapid than exploration. However, while exploitation is beneficial in the short run, it is self-destructive in the long run. Interestingly, Johne and Snelson (1988) find that leading product innovators engage in both old and new product development. Top managers, they argue, are responsible for strategy, shared values, style, and structure, while middle managers tend to focus on skills, staff, and system. They find that less successful firms view product development as a necessary evil and focus their efforts on old product development.

In a somewhat different manner, Roberts and Berry (1985) present a venture matrix which indicates the appropriate mode of venturing based on the degree of learning involved, and recommend different modes of learning from internal development to *educational acquisitions.* In addition, Kogut (1988) argues that firms undertake joint ventures to learn or retain their capabilities. Kazanjian and Drazin (1987) explore internal diversification as an organizational learning process. Finally, an important problem in entrepreneurship is that the very nature of entrepreneurship and innovation focuses on uniqueness and one-time occurrences.

Other issues in organizational learning include structures and processes which encourage learning, differences in learning across the levels of the organization and based on the focus of learning, the role of networks and teams in learning, and transfer mechanisms and learning.

Diffusion of Innovations.

Advances in technology are widely regarded as major sources of improvements in the competitive positions of firms and industries, as well as increases in national economic growth rates and standards of living (Gold 1981). Quirmbach (1986) relates the diffusion of new technology to the market structure of the industry and the firm. He finds that joint ventures adopt innovations at a rate that is slower than socially optimal, compared with other corporate governance structures. A monopoly supplier, on the other hand, adopts at a rate that is faster than socially optimal.

Gatignon and Robertson (1985) point out that the interdisciplinary roots of diffusion theory can be traced to rural sociology, geography, medical sociology, cultural anthropology, and industrial economics. Gatignon and Robertson (1986) also extend as well as integrate the diverse studies in behavioral and modeling literatures on diffusion. They identify the basic constructs of diffusion as : the innovation, the adopter categories, the adoption process, personal influence, and the patterns of diffusion. In addition, they find that consumer diffusion theory has considerable further potential as a theory of communications and as an important framework for new product marketing. However, they note that assumptions underlying diffusion models have not been adequately tested by consumer behavior literature. In a later study (1989), they extend the paradigm for studying innovation diffusion to include competitive factors.

Mahajan, Muller, and Bass (1990) examine a broad range of research on modelling the diffusion of innovations. For example, the Bass model (1969) for the timing of new product adoption has been successfully applied and extended in studies across the United States. Mansfield (1963) examines the rate of intra-firm diffusion of innovations. Bass, Russell, and Horsky (1980) later added the experience-curve theory to Mansfield's model in order to reflect the impact of econometric forces such as price. Gatignon, Eliashberg, and Robertson (1989) create a new econometric model of international diffusion patterns that can be used to predict expected diffusion patterns prior to market entry.

Finally, Mahajan, Muller, and Bass (1990) stress the need for further refinement of diffusion models. There is a need for further empirical research which will consider the industry level as well as the firm level as the unit of analysis. Although almost all diffusion research has utilized survey methods, Gatignon and Robertson recommend extending the research base to experimental approaches that utilize experimental designs in which respondents make adoption decisions facing different competitive environments as described in various scenarios.

Strategy Implementation

Strategy implementation is concerned with studying how firms actually carry out their strategic plans. It includes issues such as organizational designs for innovation, and the innovation process.

Organizational designs for innovation.

In an effort to encourage innovation within the firm, corporations have tried a variety of approaches, including varying their processes, control mechanisms, and organizational structures. For example, Foxall and Minkes (1980) argue that the development of firms has to be explained in terms of a complex of internal and external processes : these are organizational in light of decision processes, and environmental in light of interactions of the firm with its market. They argue that entrepreneurship is simultaneously an intra- and interorganizational feat which still includes the individual as an entrepreneurial influence in creating and exploiting innovative ideas. The process of innovation within the firm causes tensions with existing operations or mainstreams of the firm. Burgelman (1983a) develops a framework for examining entrepreneurial management in complex organizations, and finds that new managerial approaches and innovative administrative arrangements that provide diversity are required to encourage entrepreneurship.

Furthermore, as Kanter (1989) describes, these *newstreams* of innovation are characterized by intense and highly uncertain environments, and by the need for a great deal of autonomy. With an increasing emphasis on entrepreneurship within the corporation, there will be increasing opportunities for conflict and tension between newstreams and mainstreams.

Innovations within the firm can be managed as a *self-renewal* process for the organization, according to Nonaka and Yamanouchi (1989). They find that developing new products forces members of an organization to create innovative approaches to problems which may lead to shifts in the thinking of the firm. Gummer (1986) outlines a range of research on organizational innovation and entrepreneurship that indicates how organizations adopt innovations to respond to change, including the creation of an entrepreneurial atmosphere and vision, the tying of the vision to the market, keeping organizations small and flat, taking multiple approaches, structuring developmental shoot-outs, and using *skunkworks*. Further, Kanter (1988) finds that while structural isolation is an asset in the early idea generation stage, it becomes a liability to innovative production.

The drive to optimize innovation has spurred interest in an emerging organizational form — the new corporate venture (Fast 1979; Fast and Pratt 1981), as well as its underlying process — corporate entrepreneurship (see Schollhammer 1982 and MacMillan 1986 for reviews of this literature). Organizations have increasingly turned to alternative forms, such as joint and internal corporate ventures, as well as a similar, newly developing organizational form — the internal corporate joint venture (ICJV). Corporate ventures often consist of operating groups which are external to existing operating units, directed by a person labelled a corporate entrepreneur or intrapreneur (Pinchot 1985). This form contrasts with internalized revitalization strategies, which focus on developing a more entrepreneurial or innovative bent in managers within the existing divisionalized structure of large firms using *changemasters* (Kanter 1983), and new task groups within the division, referred to as *adhocracies* (Mintzberg 1979), *new product teams* (Kidder 1981), or *skunkworks* (Peters and Waterman 1982).

Kanter (1985) concludes that established corporations may be unable to develop and manage new ventures successfully, perhaps because they do not differentiate between the requirements of administrative and entrepreneurial management. Weiss (1981) provides some empirical support for Kanter's position. He finds that it is difficult for intrapreneurs in large firms to match the performance of start-ups by individual entrepreneurs, and argues that large corporations may perform better if new market entries are treated from the start as "stand-alone" businesses.

Several researchers have examined the challenges of setting up ventures in a corporation and studied the effectiveness of various corporate structures. The structure-based idea regarding new venture units underlies much of the important earlier thought on optimizing invention and innovation in firms (Ansoff and Brandenburg 1971; Hanan 1976; Hutchinson 1976). Autonomous new corporate venture designs or divisions were believed to overcome the ills of bureaucracy better than the traditional operating division design. Most importantly, this belief led managers to invent and invest in new organizational units, structures, and personnel rather than revitalizing existing ones. This idea underlies much of the literature on new corporate units (Ansoff and Brandenburg 1971; Hanan 1976; Hutchinson 1976; Fast 1979; Galbraith 1982; Burgelman 1985). It is perhaps one of the most important ideas in corporate entrepreneurship research, but to date little empirical research has explicitly examined this notion. However, Burgelman (1985) found that the new venture division, which was designed to facilitate corporate entrepreneurship, may create problems in the interface between the new venture division and the rest of the corporation.

Fast (1979) also points out that organizational and structural issues of a new venture department may actually overshadow the effectiveness of the new venture division in determining its survival. He concludes that the primary reasons for the "failure" of new venture departments were 1) changes in the firm's strategy or 2) a loss of power by the new venture division in the political structure of the firm.

Dougherty and Heller (1990) identify nine organizational problems encountered by innovators in large firms: two concerning how the product itself is developed; three concerning lateral relationships; and four concerning project-to-firm or strategic difficulties.

Day (1990) shows how dramatically different innovation and invention are, given that those organization design characteristics which enhance inventiveness do not necessarily enhance innovativeness (with the single exception of top management support), and vice versa. Her findings call into question previous research which treats the innovation process as a single phenomenon. The primary implication of her work is that large firms have difficulty with innovativeness because their people do not *collectively* know how to be innovative. Dougherty and Heller (1990) conclude that improving innovativeness requires developing the means to solve these problems, not merely redesigning the firm or improving its strategy. Hence, innovations cannot be separated from the organization unless there remains a strong interaction with the firm's ongoing definition of its business and configuration of its resources.

The literature on organization design provides some interesting insights as theoretical starting points regarding autonomy. Historically, organization research has shown that too close a tie between operating units and corporate structure in large firms can produce poor performance, including low degrees of invention/innovation (e.g., Burns and Stalker 1961). This tendency is sufficiently pronounced to have been described as an organizational pathology (Merton 1957). These arguments stem from theoretical notions about the negative effects of bureaucracy in general (Merton 1957; Thompson 1961; Downs 1967), the inertial properties of large bureaucratic organizations (Crozier 1964; Hannan and Freeman 1977, 1984), and the problems of communication/information and power when there are many levels between a particular unit and top management (Kierulff 1979; Friedlander and Scott 1981; Kanter 1988). Williamson (1975, 206) states that separating new product processes and the management of proven resources may be more efficient. Furthermore, Kazanjian and Drazin (1987) argue that successful implementation of internal diversification strategies is dependent on contingency factors in terms of organization design choices.

In contrast, however, Dougherty, Corse, and Heller (1990) find that the root cause of difficulties with innovation lie in the way people organize their thinking and action — what they call their "organizing scheme." They argue that an organizing scheme of instrumental rationality seems central to the efficient operation of their established businesses, but it is an anathema to innovation. In addition, they argue that it is not the bureaucratic structure per se which is the problem, but rather the organizing scheme of instrumental rationality and the concomitant capacities it cultivates. Also in contrast to bureaucratic arguments, Galbraith (1982) implies that the need for autonomy may partially derive from the political problems innovation engenders. As he notes, innovative ideas are destructive not only in terms of tangible assets but also in terms of people's careers, and as such, the management of innovation is a political process.

While much of the previous literature has supported autonomy as a key ingredient in organizing for innovation as well as invention (Mansfield 1963; Burns and Stalker 1961; Shapero 1984; Hill and Hlavacek 1972; Roberts and Frohman 1972; Roberts 1980), Hisrich and Peters (1984) found no significant difference in sales between new products (i.e., innovation) of firms with autonomous venture units and those without such units. Furthermore, Dunn (1977) found that one of the key features of a number of failed ventures was that they were given too much autonomy.

In addition, while Kanter (1988, 191) insists that autonomy is an essential ingredient for invention, she, along with others (Ansoff 1965; Lawrence and Lorsch 1967; Galbraith 1982; Harrigan 1985), recommends integration with an operating division at the innovation stage so that the appropriate strategic and structural linkages can be made to commercialize the invention (i.e., innovation). Much of the previous research in support of autonomy (Shapero 1984; Hill and Hlavacek 1972; Roberts and Frohman 1972; Roberts 1980) has been based mainly on relatively large Fortune 500 firms; hence, such arguments have yet to be tested.

Day (1990) finds that structural autonomy is positively associated with innovation in the largest firms, but there is no association between new venture divisions or autonomous ventures and invention. Her results run contrary, however, to arguments for integration at the innovation stage (Ansoff 1965; Lawrence and Lorsch 1967; Galbraith 1982; Harrigan 1985; Kanter 1988). Interestingly, technology that is developed within corporations slips through the cracks of the organization. Ehretsmann et al. (1989) examine stagnant technologies which a corporation develops but fails to bring to market — not because of the innovation but because of the structure of the organization. They suggest that a catalyst firm could be formed to identify stagnant technologies, find suitable partners, and assist in the management of the partnership to commercialization.

Zajac, Golden, and Shortell (1991) examine the degree of innovativeness in a newly developing organizational form, the internal corporate joint venture (ICJV), and identify factors most strongly associated with the degree of innovativeness in these new organizations. They suggest that greater attention be devoted to studying *nested innovation* — that is, innovation within a new organizational form that is itself an administrative innovation.

A number of other potentially important structural factors explaining invention/innovation are found in the literature. While these factors have not been the focus of this review, any attempt to build a comprehensive model that has significant explanatory power should include such variables as the firm's culture, the size of the innovating venture within the firm, the size of the venture team, both the internal and external interconnectedness of the venture, the diversity of the firm (per se), and issues of geographical space and distance, organization slack, rewards and incentives, reporting relationships, and so forth. Finally, Venkataraman, MacMillan, and McGrath's chapter on corporate venturing in this volume (Chapter 19) provides another important discussion of this topic.

The international transfer of technology poses problems for individual firms and national policy makers. Teece (1981) finds that the internalization of the exchange process within multinational firms serves to bypass many of these difficulties, and that regulations appear unlikely to eliminate inefficiencies.

Models of the innovation process range from serial or assembly line to parallel or simultaneous models. Teece (1989) points out that the process of innovation requires complex interaction and integration among a multiplicity of organizational units, as well as linkages to external institutions. Tushman (1977) points out the important boundary roles in the innovative process, and finds that innovation from external areas enters innovating units in an indirect, two-step process.

The Innovation process.

The first theories of technological innovation date back to Schumpeter (1934). He theorized that economic development was dependent on innovation, and that successful innovation required sufficient organizational scale. Since then much organization research has been done on the process of innovation (see Tornatzky et al. 1983 for a review of this literature).

How are innovations generated ? There have been a wide variety of models created to describe and analyze the entrepreneurial process. In a review of studies on the process of generating innovations, Dosi (1988) concludes that progress has been made in the last 20 years in the conceptualization and empirical analysis of the process of generation of innovations and their effects. However, the innovation process is, by nature, hard to define and describe. Nelson and Winter (1977) find that the problem is the prevailing theories of innovation, which are not useful because they are fragmented and neglect uncertainty and the impact of the institutional structure. In contrast, Baumol (1982) argues that the main reason entrepreneurial activity has eluded economic analysis is that this activity by nature cannot be standardized. He outlines factors in the environment, such as rewards and institutionalized constraints, and high taxes and antitrust programs, which encourage or constrain entrepreneurs.

Drawing from the Minnesota Innovation Research Program, Van de Ven, Angle, and Poole (1989) published a collection of studies on the evolution of ventures and their innovations. They conclude by presenting a framework for analyzing innovations. This collection of studies is an excellent source for those who want to understand the process better. Earlier, Schroeder et al. (1986) described a fluid process of innovation that includes an initial shock in which it is created, a period of proliferation of the original idea, numerous stacks and surprises which result in both learning and failure, and, ultimately, a blending of the old with the new to launch the innovation.

Aldrich and Zimmer (1986) were among the first to examine the linkages or relations between key components of the innovation process in entrepreneurship. They note that entrepreneurs must establish connections to resources and niches in an opportunity structure, and at some point they must have been affected by relations with socializing agents who motivated them. Hutt, Reingen, and Ronchetto (1988) suggest that autonomous strategic initiatives can be aided by encouraging the exchange of information among the firm's functional areas and business units. Barley (1990) shows that the structures of organizations and occupations are related to the technologies that they employ, but argues that microsocial dynamics occasioned by new technologies, rather than contingency theory, best explain the impact of technology on the structure of an organization's social networks.

Imai, Nonaka, and Takeuchi (1985) comment that Japanese firms see product development as a trial-and-error process, rather than the systematic process of U.S. firms. In the United States new product development is handled by specialists, while in Japan it is undertaken by generalists. In the United States the process is an important strategic tool, while in Japan it serves more as a "change agent" in the firm.

Utterback and Abernathy (1975) suggest that the kind of innovation activity most suitable to a firm will depend on the firm's growth strategies, environment, and competition. Calantone, di Benedetto, and Meloche (1988) confirm the Utterback and Abernathy model through applying a log-linear regression to a data base of about 1,600 innovations, and find that in a new field, successful innovations tend to be focused on products, while in mature markets, innovations tend to be focused on improvements to process technologies.

GENERAL MANAGEMENT

Entrepreneurs share many of the challenges of managers of existing businesses or firms. Hence, research on general management should offer insights for entrepreneurial research. More specifically, this section examines the role of the general manager, including research on leadership, top management skills, top management teams, and succession planning. The critical examination of the role of the general manager largely originated with the publication of Hambrick and Mason's (1984) seminal article on upper echelons. Prior to that time, most research had found that managers had very little strategic control over the direction or ultimate success of the firms they managed; hence, their only function was as an integrator of the various businesses (at the corporate level) or functions (at the business or competitive level) they managed. Since then, a stream of research has emerged, culminating most recently in a special issue on top management teams in the *Strategic Management Journal.* The following research is incorporated here because it either directly addresses the role of the entrepreneur as top manager or has implications for future research on the role of the top manager, either as an entrepreneur or in establishing an entrepreneurial organization.

Leadership.

As Steve Jobs found out at Apple, the leadership needed to launch an entrepreneurial firm is very different from the leadership needed for a large corporation. Covin and Slevin (1988) suggest that the utility of an entrepreneurial top management style depends on the structure of the organization. In addition, Shrivastava and Nachman (1989) identify four strategic leadership patterns: entrepreneurial, bureaucratic, political, and professional. They challenge the assumption that only chief executives provide leadership in organizations, and point out that strategic research on leadership in organizations remains an underresearched topic predominantly focused on the upper echelons of organizations.

Interestingly, Day's (1990) study of venture sponsorship indicates support for Shrivastava and Nachman's position. While her results clearly show that top management can play an important sponsorship role throughout the innovation process, they also show that during the innovation stage, the value of middle management sponsors may be even greater for some ventures. Her findings give further support to those who argue that invention/innovation is often best propagated by managers in the very top positions who can organize the energies, resources, and symbols of the entire firm (Pfeffer 1978; Kimberly 1979; Kanter 1983; following Katz and Kahn 1978), yet her findings also lend empirical support to those like Burgelman (1983b) and Galbraith (1982) who argue that middle managers have important leadership roles in the innovation process as well.

Furthermore, according to Guth and MacMillan (1986), even the best competitive strategy will fall flat if it is not implemented effectively. More specifically, they find that middle managers can not only redirect a strategy or reduce the quality of its implementation, they can completely sabotage it. Burgelman (1985) further elaborates that top management's most important contribution is strategic recognition rather than planning, and that new managerial approaches and innovative administrative arrangements are required to encourage entrepreneurship.

On the other hand, in a paired comparison of successful and unsuccessful innovations, Rothwell et al. (1974) find that successful innovators place more senior-level people in charge of the project. However, Sathe (1989) concludes that if entrepreneurship is to flourish in an organization, lower-level managers need to be free to identify and pursue promising opportunities.

Van de Ven (1986) identifies four basic factors general managers must consider in innovation: new ideas, people, transactions, and institutional context. In addition, managers must deal with human, process, structural, and strategic problems: the human problem of managing attention, the process problem of transforming new ideas into good currency, the structural problem of managing part-whole relationships, and the strategic problem of the organization's leadership.

Howell and Higgins (1990) find that champions used transformational leadership behaviors to a significantly greater extent than did nonchampions; they exhibit higher risk taking and innovativeness, initiate more influence attempts, and use a greater variety of influence tactics. Westley and Mintzberg (1989) present a model of visionary leadership as drama, an interaction of repetition, representation, and assistance. In addition, considering the experiences of a number of visionary leaders in terms of style, process, content, and context, their article describes various types of visionary leadership — the creator, the proselytizer, the idealist, the *bricoleur,* and the diviner. In addition, MacMillan (1987) analyzed the difference in behavior of CEOs of major divisions of corporations who are successful at new business development and those who are not. He finds that transformational leadership is the fundamental difference between the success or failure of a new business development program.

Noel (1989) shows how obsessions establish causality between intention and action. Following one month of continuous, direct observation of CEOs at work, strategies were revealed to be intentional. By their activities, the CEOs generated a strategic core consistent with their preoccupations. The "magnificent obsession" latent in their preoccupations appeared as a common element in all their activities and served as a key to understanding their compulsion to address certain issues over others.

Top management skills and experience.

Low and MacMillan (1988) point out that early entrepreneurship research focused primarily on the individual entrepreneur rather than the social context in which the entrepreneur operates. There has been a series of studies on the style, personality, psychology, and family and career backgrounds of entrepreneurs. Several characteristics attributed to entrepreneurs, but not supported by research, are internal locus of control and high risk-taking propensity. One characteristic that *does* distinguish entrepreneurs is tolerance for ambiguity.

However, in a comparison of successful and failing corporate ventures, Von Hippel (1977) finds that the venture team's prior experience and the venture manager's previous organizational experience were key factors in the venture's success. In contrast, he finds that corporate venturing, far from requiring very precise conditions within a corporation, can succeed in a wide range of industries, on a wide range of scales, in a variety of organizational structures, and can be led by a wide variety of managers.

Boeker (1989) finds that the functional experience of the entrepreneur affects subsequent subunit importance and power in the semiconductor industry. In this study, the entrepreneur's functional experience was measured as: 1) research, design, and development; 2) manufacturing and production; or 3) marketing, sales, and customer service.

Keeley and Roure (1990) developed and tested a structural model to analyze the impact of management characteristics, business strategy, and industry structure on the performance of new, technology-based firms. Their findings suggest that, because all three factors are important, researchers should include all three in empirical studies whenever possible. Sandberg and Hofer (1987) find that the interactive effect of industry, strategy, and the entrepreneur have a greater impact than any of the three factors in isolation. After the combined effects, industry structure has the greatest impact, and differentiated strategies outperform focused strategies.

Several articles have recently been published which stress the importance of matching managerial talent with organizational strategy. These have generally relied on selection in order to "fit" the manager to the strategy. Kerr and Jackofsky (1989) propose the use of management development as an alternate means of achieving manager-strategy alignment, contrasted with the costs, benefits, and strategic role of selection. They suggest that choice of alignment method (i.e., management development versus selection) is contingent upon particular strategic, structural, and cultural factors.

Top management teams.

Increasingly, the makeup of the top management group is believed to affect the identification, development, and exploitation of strategic as well as entrepreneurial opportunities. Eisenhardt and Schoonhoven (1990) find that characteristics of the top management team influence firm growth. Zajac, Golden, and Shortell (1991) identify age similarity among team members as one of the three factors most strongly associated with the degree of innovativeness in internal corporate joint ventures. In contrast, Bantel and Jackson (1989) examine the relationship between top management team composition and innovation adoptions. Their results indicate that more innovative firms are managed by more educated teams who are diverse with respect to their functional areas of expertise.

Lumsden and Singh (1990) examine the budding of corporate cultures from those of preexisting firms, relating it to entrepreneurial thinking in the firm. Hurst, Rush, and White (1989), focusing on the need for firm renewal, explain a creative management model which goes beyond conventional strategic management and identifies the behaviors of top managers needed for such ongoing renewal. They suggest that these behaviors cluster and can be aligned with different and distinct cognitive styles or types, and that such diversity can yield great strength if the differences can be focused and unified.

Murray (1989) expected that homogeneous top management groups would interact more efficiently and therefore be preferable when competition is intense, but that heterogeneous groups would facilitate adaptation and therefore be preferable under conditions of environmental change. Partial support for these hypotheses was found; yet, the pattern of results indicate numerous difficulties in untangling and identifying the determinants of firm performance.

Virany and Tushman (1986) find that while high-performing firms recruit new top management with new skills that are appropriate to the evolving environment, lower-performing firms tend to make wrong executive recruitment decisions. In addition, commitment of the top management team to the entrepreneurial strategies of the firm, such as active venturing or organizational renewal, is important to success. Dess (1987) finds a positive relationship between the consensus of the top management team and organizational performance. Furthermore, Thomas and McDaniel (1990) find that the strategy and information processing structure of the top management team affects the interpretation of strategic issues by the CEO.

However, Eisenhardt and Bourgeois (1988) find that politics plays an important role in top management planning. Although politics is associated with poor firm performance, they find that senior executives participate in politics and create political behavior among subordinates. Most important for entrepreneurship in the large firm, they find that coalitions are *not* organized around issues, but rather around demographic characteristics such as office locations and age of employees.

Finally, Adler and Ferdows (1990) focus on a new addition to the top management team — the chief technology officer (CTO), concluding that they are likely to become increasingly common figures in top management teams. Their responsibilities included coordinating business units' technological efforts to ensure synergy and economies of scale, and supervising new technological development.

Succession planning.

Succession in leadership is a critical factor in the management and long-term performance of any firm. In entrepreneurship, where start-ups clearly go through stages of growth which require different skills and abilities, the need to understand and manage succession is essential. Theories regarding managerial succession fall into two broad categories: performance-based and development-based. Marino and Dollinger (1987) find that top management succession is a common and important phenomenon in entrepreneurial firms, and that existing theories provide a useful, but incomplete, understanding of management changes in these firms.

Growing evidence in the executive succession literature and the business press makes clear that new CEOs often attempt to introduce strategic change upon entering their jobs. Yet strategy researchers have generally neglected to document the internal dynamics of these interventions, and many scholars remain pessimistic about the likelihood of success. Greiner and Bhambri (1989) present an empirical case study in which a new CEO succeeds at strategic change, using an intervention approach they call *comprehensive/collaborative.*

Finally, Tushman, Virany, and Romanelli (1987) suggest that performance shortfalls drive executive succession for low performers, while strategic reorientations prompt succession for high-performing firms. The effects of succession depend on whether strategic reorientation accompanies executive change. Only when executive succession occurs with reorientations does future organizational performance increase; otherwise, there is no association between executive succession and subsequent organizational performance.

■ ■ ■ ■ ■ ■ ■ ■

CONCLUSION: DIRECTIONS FOR FUTURE RESEARCH

As this review of the literature indicates, there is a rich array of research in strategic and general management with implications for entrepreneurship research. As noted at the outset, however, this chapter is only an initial attempt to draw parallels between these diverse fields of research. Future researchers will surely be able to find even more connections between these fields, perhaps by identifying additional topics or developing new links between topics. Furthermore, many of the studies cited in this review present agendas for further research, which may also suggest some new topics or linkages.

The studies also suggest that the areas of strategic management, general management, and entrepreneurship are, at a minimum, intertwined, if not part of a general concept that includes all three areas. The close relationship seems to suggest a higher research productivity by combining the research into broader issues rather than separating it into different streams.

A comprehensive and detailed list of the studies mentioned in this chapter may be obtained from the author.

■ ■ ■ ■ ■ ■ ■ ■

REFERENCES

Abell, D. F. 1978 Strategic windows. *Journal of Marketing* 42 : 21–26.

Abernathy, W. J., and K. B. Clark 1985 Innovation: Mapping the winds of creative destruction. *Research Policy* 14 : 3–22.

Adler, P. S., and K. Ferdows 1990 The chief technological officer. *California Management Review* 32 (3, Spring): 55–62.

Alchian, A. A. 1950 Uncertainty, evolution and economic theory. *Journal of Political Economy* 58 (3, June): 211–221.

Aldrich, H., and E. R. Auster 1986 Even dwarfs started small: Liabilities of age and size and their strategic implications. *Research in Organizational Behavior* 8 : 165–198.

Aldrich, H., and C. Zimmer 1986 Entrepreneurship through social networks. In *The art and science of entrepreneurship*, eds. D. L. Sexton and R. W. Smilor, 2–23. Cambridge, Mass.: Ballinger.

Allen, T., and V. George 1989 Changes in the field of R&D management over the past 20 years. *R&D Management* 19 (2): 102–113.

Amit, R., L. Glosten, and E. Muller 1990 Entrepreneurial ability, venture investments, and risk sharing. *Management Science* 36(10): 1232–1245.

Ansoff, I. H. 1965 *Corporate strategy: An analytical approach to business policy for growth and expansion.* N.Y.: McGraw-Hill.

Ansoff, I. H., and R. G. Brandenburg 1971 A language for organization design : Part 2. *Management Science* 17(12): B717–B731.

Argote, L., S. Beckman, and D. Epple 1990 Persistence and transfer of learning in industrial settings. *Management Science* 36(2): 140–154.

Arrow, K. J. 1962 Economic welfare and the allocation of resources for invention. In *The rate and direction of inventive activity*, ed. R. R. Nelson, 609–626. Princeton, N.J.: Princeton Univ. Press.

Bain, J. S. 1956 *Barriers to new competition.* Cambridge, Mass.: Harvard Univ. Press.

Bantel, K. A., and S. E. Jackson 1989 Top management and innovations in banking : Does the composition of the top team make a difference ? *Strategic Management Journal* 10: 107–124.

Barley, S. R. 1990 The alignment of technology and structure through roles and networks. *Administrative Science Quarterly* 35: 61–103.

Barnes, J. H. 1984 Cognitive biases and their impact on strategic planning. *Strategic Management Journal* 5: 129–137.

Barnett, W. P. 1990 The organizational ecology of a technological system. *Administrative Science Quarterly* 35: 31–60.

Bass, F. M. 1969 A new product growth model for consumer durables. *Management Science* 15 (5): 215–227.

Bass, F. M., T. Russell, and D. Horsky 1980 The relationship between diffusion rates, experience curves, and demand elasticities for consumer durable technological innovations/comments. *Journal of Business* 53 (3): s51–s78.

Baumol, W. J. 1982 Toward operational models of entrepreneurship. In *Entrepreneurship*, ed. J. Ronen. Lexington, Mass.: Lexington Books.

Bettis, R., and D. Weeks 1987 Financial returns and strategic interaction : The case of instant photography. *Strategic Management Journal* 8 (November-December): 549–563.

Biggadike, R. 1976 Entry, strategy, and performance. Unpublished Ph.D. diss., Harvard University.

1979 The risky business of diversification. *Harvard Business Review* 57(3): 103–111.

Birley, S., and D. Norburn 1987 Owners and managers : The Venture 100 vs. the Fortune 500. *Journal of Business Venturing* 2 (4, Fall): 277–382.

Boeker, W. 1989 The development and institutionalization of subunit power in organizations. *Administrative Science Quarterly* 34: 388–410.

Borys, B., and D. B. Jemison 1989 Hybrid arrangements as strategic alliances : Theoretical issues in organizational combinations. *Academy of Management Review* 14: 234–249.

Bruderl, J., and R. Schussler 1990 Organization mortality : The liabilities of newness and adolescence. *Administrative Science Quarterly* 35: 530–547.

Burgelman, R. A. 1983a A process model of internal corporate venturing in the diversified major firm. *Administrative Science Quarterly* 28: 223–244.

1983b Corporate entrepreneurship and strategic management : Insights from a process study. *Management Science* 29 (12): 1349–1364.

1985 Managing the new venture division : Research findings and implications for strategic management. *Strategic Management Journal* 6: 39–54.

Burkhardt, M. E., and D. J. Brass 1990 Changing patterns and patterns of change : The effects of a change in technology on social network structure and power. *Administrative Science Quarterly* 35: 104–127.

Burns, T., and G. M. Stalker 1961 *The management of innovation*. London : Tavistock.

Bygrave, W., N. Fast, R. Khoylian, L. Vincent, and W. Yue 1988 Rates of return on venture capital investing : A study of 131 funds. In *Frontiers of entrepreneurship research*, eds. B. A. Kirchhoff, W. A. Long, K. H. Vesper, and W. E. Wetzel, Jr., 275–289.

Calantone, R. J., C. A. di Benedetto, and M. S. Meloche 1988 Strategies of product and process innovation : A loglinear analysis. *R&D Management* 18 (1) : 13–21.

Carpenter, G., and K. Nakamoto 1989 Consumer preference formation and pioneering advantage. *Journal of Marketing Research* 26 (August) : 285–298.

1990 Competitive strategies for late entry into a market with a dominant brand. *Management Science* 36 (October) : 1268–1279.

Carroll, G., and M. T. Hannan 1989 Density in organizational populations : A model and five empirical tests. *American Science Quarterly* 34 (3) : 411–430.

Casson, M. 1982 *The entrepreneur : An economic theory*. Totowa, N.J. : Barnes & Noble Books.

Chakrabarti, A. K. 1974 The role of champion in product innovation. *California Management Review* 17 : 58–62.

Chandler, A. D., Jr. 1962 *Strategy and structure : Chapters in the history of American industrial enterprise*. Cambridge, Mass. : MIT Press.

Chatterjee, S., and B. Wernerfelt 1988 Related or unrelated diversification : A resource-based approach. *Academy of Management Proceedings* : 7–16.

Clark, K. B. 1985 The interaction of design hierarchies and market concepts in technological evolution. *Research Policy* 14 : 235–251.

1987 The investment in new technology and competitive advantage. *The competitive challenge*, ed. D. Teece, 59–82. N.Y. : Ballinger.

Cohen, M. D., and L. S. Sproull 1991 Organizational learning : Papers in honor of (and by) James G. March. *Organizational Science* 2 (1) Introduction.

Cohen, W. M., and R. C. Levin 1989 Empirical studies of innovation and market structure. *Handbook of Industrial Organization*, eds. R. Schmalensee and R. D. Willig, Vol. 2. N.Y. : Elsevier Science Publishing Co.

Cohen, W. M., and D. A. Levinthal 1990 Absorptive capacity : A new perspective on learning and innovation. *Administrative Science Quarterly* 35 : 128–152.

Conner, K. R. 1988 Strategies for product cannibalism. *Strategic Management Journal* 9 : 9–26.

1990 Obtaining strategic advantage from being imitated : When can encouraging "clones" pay ? Jones Center Working paper, Wharton School, University of Pennsylvania.

Conner, K. R., and R. R. Rumelt 1991 Software piracy : Analysis of protection strategies. *Management Science* 37 (2) : 125–139.

Cooper, A. C. 1989 Research findings in strategic management with implications for R&D management. *R&D Management (UK)* 19 (2) : 115–125.

Covin, J. G., and D. P. Slevin 1988 The influence of organization structure on the utility of an entrepreneurial top management style. *Journal of Management Studies* 25 (3, May) : 217–234.

Crawford, C. M. 1988 How product innovation can foreclose the options of adaptive followers. *Journal of Consumer Marketing* 5 (4) : 17–24.

Crozier, M. 1964 *The bureaucratic phenomenon*. Chicago : Univ. of Chicago Press.

Day, D. L. 1986 A contingency theory of relatedness in corporate venturing and venture performance. Unpublished Ph.D. diss., Columbia University.

1989a A contingent analysis of product life cycle, relatedness and resulting synergies in corporate venturing. Working paper, Management Department, Wharton School, University of Pennsylvania.

1989b The value of sharing plant and equipment in commodity versus differentiated environments. Working paper, Management Department, Wharton School, University of Pennsylvania.

1989c The value of sharing marketing assets in consumer versus industrial markets. Working paper, Management Department, Wharton School, University of Pennsylvania.

1990 Technological innovation and organization design in internal corporate venturing. Working paper, Sol C. Snider Entrepreneurial Center, Wharton School, University of Pennsylvania.

Day, D. L., and D. Parkinson 1990 Diversification and firm resources : Toward direct measurement of relatedness. Working paper, Management Department, Wharton School, University of Pennsylvania.

Dess, G. G. 1987 Consensus on strategy formulation and organizational performance. *Strategic Management Journal* 8 (3, May-June) : 259–277.

Dosi, G. 1988 Sources, procedure, and microeconomic effects of innovation. *Journal of Economic Literature* 26 (September) : 1120–1171.

Dougherty, D. 1990 Understanding new markets for new products. *Strategic Management Journal* 11 : 59–78.

1992 Interpretive barriers to new product development in large firms. *Organizational Science.* Forthcoming.

Dougherty, D., and S. Corse, 1991 The limits of instrument rationality : Inculturating innovation. Working paper, Management Department, Wharton School, University of Pennsylvania.

Dougherty, D., and T. Heller 1991 The illegitimacy of product innovation in large firms. Working paper, Department of Management, Wharton School, University of Pennsylvania.

Downs, A. 1967 *Inside bureaucracy.* Boston : Little, Brown.

Dunn, D. T. 1977 The rise and fall of ten new venture groups. *Business Horizons* (October) : 32–41.

Dunne, T., M. J. Roberts, and L. Samuelson 1988 Patterns of firm entry and exit in U.S. manufacturing industries. *RAND Journal of Economics* 19 (4) : 495–515.

Ehretsmann, J., A. Hinkly, A. Minty, and A. W. Pearson 1989 The commercialization of stagnant technologies. *R&D Management* 19 (3) : 231–242.

Eisenhardt, K. M. 1989 Making fast strategic decisions in high-velocity environments. *Academy of Management Journal* 32 (3) : 543–576.

Eisenhardt, K. M., and L. J. Bourgeois, III 1988 Politics of strategic decision making in high-velocity environments : Toward a midrange theory. *Academy of Management Journal* 31 (4) : 737–770.

Eisenhardt, K. M., and C. B. Schoonhoven 1990 Organizational growth : Linking founding team, strategy, environment, and growth among U.S. semiconductor ventures (1978–1988). *Administrative Science Quarterly* 35 (3) : 504–529.

Epple, D., L. Argote, and R. Devadas 1991 Organizational learning curves : A method for investigation inter-plant transfer of knowledge of learning by doing. *Organizational Science* 2(1) : 58–70.

Fast, N. D. 1977 The evolution of corporate new venture divisions. Unpublished Ph.D. diss., Harvard Business School.

1979 The future of industrial new venture departments. *Industrial Marketing Management* 8 : 264–273.

Fast, N. D., and S. E. Pratt 1981 Individual entrepreneurship and the large corporation. In *Frontiers of Entrepreneurship Research*, ed. K. Vesper, 443–450. Wellesley, Mass. : Babson College.

Fershtman, C., V. Mahajan, and E. Muller 1990 Market share pioneering advantage : A theoretical approach. *Management Science* 36 : 900–918.

Fichman, M. A., and D. A. Levinthal 1991 Honeymoons and the liability of adolescence : A new perspective on duration dependence in social and organizational relationships. *Academy of Management Review* 16(2) : 442–468.

Foxall, G. R., and A. L. Minkes 1980 Entrepreneurship, strategy, and organization : Individual and organization in the behavior of the firm. *Strategic Management Journal* 1 : 295–301.

Frankel, M. 1955 Obsolescence and technological change in a maturing economy. *American Economic Review* 45 (June) : 296–319.

Frederickson, J. W. 1985 Effects of decision motive and organizational performance level on strategic decision process. *Academy of Management Journal* 28 (4, December) : 821–843.

Friar, J., and M. Horwitch 1985 The emergence of technology strategy : A new dimension of strategic management. *Technology in Society* 7 : 143–178.

Friedlander, F., and B. Scott 1981 The use of task forces in organizational change. In *Groups at work*, eds. C. Cooper and R. Payne. N.Y. : John Wiley & Sons.

Gabrowski, H., and J. Vernon 1990 Returns and risks to pharmaceutical R&D. *Management Science* 36 : 804–821.

Galbraith, J. 1982 Designing the innovating organization. *Organizational Dynamics* 10 : 5–25.

Gatignon, H., and T. S. Robertson 1985 A propositional inventory for new diffusion research. *Journal of Consumer Research* 11 (4) : 859–867.

1986 Integration of consumer diffusion theory and diffusion models : New research directions. In *Innovation diffusion models of new product acceptance*, eds. V. Mahajan and Y. Wind, 37–60. Cambridge, Mass. : Ballinger Publishing Co.

1989 Technology diffusion : An empirical test of competitive effects. *Journal of Marketing* 53 (1) : 35–49.

1990 Innovative decision process. In *Handbook of consumer behavior theory and research*, eds. H. Kassarjian and T. S. Robertson, 316–348. Englewood Cliffs, N.J. : Prentice-Hall, Inc.

Gatignon, H., J. Eliashberg, and T. Robertson 1989 Modeling multinational diffusion patterns : An efficient methodology. *Marketing Science* 8 (3) : 231–247.

Gold, B. 1981 Technological diffusion in industry : Research needs and shortcomings. *Journal of Industrial Economics* 29 (3) : 247–169.

Gort, M., and R. A. Wall 1986 The evolution of technologies and investment in innovation. *Economics Journal* 96 (383) : 741–757.

Govindarajan, V. 1989 Implementing competitive strategies at the business unit level : Implications of matching managers to strategies. *Strategic Management Journal* 10 : 251–269.

Grabowski, H., and J. Vernon 1990 A new look at the returns and risks to pharmaceutical research and development. *Management Science* 36 (7) : 804–821.

Greiner, L. E., and A. Bhambri 1989 New CEO intervention and dynamics of deliberate strategic change. *Strategic Management Journal* 10 (Summer) : 67–86.

Gummer, B. 1986 So what's new ? : Organizational innovation and entrepreneurship. *Administration in Social Work* 10 (2) : 91–105.

Guth, W. D., and I. C. MacMillan 1986 Strategy implementation versus middle management self-interest. *Strategic Management Journal* 7 (4, July-August) : 313–327.

Guth, W., and A. Ginsberg 1990 Guest editor's introduction : Corporate entrepreneurship. *Strategic Management Journal* 11(2) : 5–16.

Hambrick, D. C., and I. C. MacMillan 1985 Efficiency of product R&D in business units : The role of strategic context. *Academy of Management Journal* 28 (3, September) : 527–547.

Hambrick, D. C., I. C. MacMillan, and R. R. Barbosa 1983 Business unit strategy and changes in the product R&D budget. *Management Science* 29 (7, July) : 757–769.

Hambrick, D. C., and P. A. Mason 1984 Upper echelons : The organization as reflection of its top managers. *Academy of Management Review* 9 : 193–206.

Hamilton, W. F. 1986 Corporate strategies for managing emerging technologies. *Technology in Society* 7 : 197–212.

Hanan, M. 1976 *New venture management.* N.Y. : McGraw-Hill.

Hannan, M. T., and J. Freeman 1977 The population ecology of organizations. *American Journal of Sociology* 82 : 929–964.

1984 Structural inertia and organizational change. *American Sociological Review* 49 : 149–164.

Harrigan, K. R. 1983 *Strategies for vertical integration.* Lexington, Mass. : Heath.

1985 *Strategies for joint ventures.* Lexington, Mass. : Lexington Books.

Haspeslaugh, P., and D. B. Jemison 1987 Acquisitions — myths and reality. *Sloan Management Review* 29 (2) : 53–58.

Henderson, R. M., and K. B. Clark 1990 Architectural innovations : The reconfiguration of existing product technologies and the failure of established firms. *Administrative Science Quarterly* 35 : 9–30.

Hill, R. M., and J. D. Hlavacek 1972 The venture team : A new concept in marketing organization. *Journal of Marketing* 36 : 44–50.

Hisrich, R. D., and M. P. Peters 1984 Internal venturing in large corporation : The new business venture unit. In *Frontiers of entrepreneurship research*, eds. J. Hornaday, F. Tarpley, Jr., J. Timmons, and K. Vesper, 321–342. Wellesley, Mass. : Babson College.

Hofer, C. W., and Schendel, D. 1978 *Strategy formulation : Analytical concepts.* St. Paul, Minn. : West.

Hogarth, C. W., and H. J. Einhorn 1990 Venture theory : A model of decision weights. *Management Science* 36 : 780–803.

Horwitch, M., and R. A. Thietart 1987 The effect of business interdependencies on product R&D-intensive business performance. *Management Science* 33 (2, February) : 178–197.

Howell, J. M., and C. A. Higgins 1990 Champions of technological innovation. *Administrative Science Quarterly* 35 : 317–341.

Huber, G. O. 1991 Organizational learning : The contributing processes and the literatures. *Organizational Science* 2(1) : 88–115.

Hurst, D. K., J. C. Rush, and R. E. White 1989 Top management teams and organizational renewal. *Strategic Management Journal* 10 (Summer) : 87–105.

Hutchinson, J. 1976 Evolving organizational forms. *Columbia Journal of World Business* 11 : 48–58.

Hutt, M. D., P. H. Reingen, and J. R. Ronchetto, Jr. 1988 Tracing emergent processes in marketing strategy formation. *Journal of Marketing* 52 (1, January): 4–19.

Imai, K., I. Nonaka, and H. Takeuchi 1985 Managing the new product development process: How Japanese companies learn and unlearn. In *The uneasy alliance: Managing the productivity-technology dilemma*, eds. K. Clarke, R. Hayes, and C. Lorenz, 337–381. Boston: Harvard Business School Press.

Jackson, S. E., and J. E. Dutton 1988 Discerning threats and opportunities. *Administrative Science Quarterly* 33: 370–387.

Jelinek, M., and C. B. Schoonhoven 1990 *Innovation marathon.* N.Y.: Basil Blackwell.

Jennings, D. F., and J. R. Lumpkin 1989 Functioning modeling corporate entrepreneurship: An empirical integrative analysis. *Journal of Management* 15 (3): 485–502.

Johne, A., and P. Snelson 1988 Auditing product innovation activities in manufacturing firms. *R&D Management* 18 (3, July): 227–233.

Kahneman, D., P. Slovic, and A. Tversky, eds. 1982 *Judgement under uncertainty: Heuristics and biases.* Cambridge, Mass.: Cambridge Press.

Kanter, R. M. 1983 *The change masters.* N.Y.: Simon and Schuster.

1985 Supporting innovation and venture development in established companies. *Journal of Business Venturing* 1 (1, Winter): 47–60.

1988 When a thousand flowers bloom: Structural, collective, and social conditions for innovation in organization. *Research in Organizational Behavior* 10: 169–211.

1989 Swimming in newstreams: Mastering innovation dilemmas. *California Management Review* 31(4): 45–69.

Katz, D., and R. L. Kahn 1978 *Social psychology of organizations.* N.Y.: John Wiley & Sons.

Katz, M. L., and C. Shapiro 1987 R&D rivalry with licensing or imitation. *American Economic Review* 77 (3, June): 402–420.

Kazanjian, R. K., and R. Drazin 1987 Implementing internal diversification: Contingency factors for organization design choices. *Academy of Management Review* 12: 342–354.

1989 An empirical test of a stage of growth progression model. *Management Science* 35 (12): 1490–1503.

Keeley, R. H., and J. B. Roure 1990 Management, strategy and industry structure as influences on the success of new firms: A structural model. *Management Science* 36(10): 1256–1268.

Kerr, J. L., and E. F. Jackofsky 1989 Aligning managers with strategies: Management development versus selection. *Strategic Management Journal* 10 (Summer): 157–170.

Kidder, T. 1981 *The soul of a new machine.* Boston: Little, Brown.

Kierulff, H. E. 1979 Finding and keeping corporate entrepreneurs. *Business Horizons* 22(1): 6–15.

Kimberly, J. 1979 Issues in the creation of organizations: Initiation, innovation and institutionalization. *Academy of Management Journal* 22: 437–457.

Klein, G., H. Moskowitz, and A. Ravidram 1990 Interactive multiobjective optimization under uncertainty. *Management Science* 36: 58–75.

Knight, F. H. 1921 *Risk, uncertainty and profits* (reprinted). Chicago, Ill.: Univ. of Chicago Press.

Kogut, B. 1988 Joint ventures: Theoretical and empirical perspectives. *Strategic Management Journal* 9: 319–332.

Krickx, G. A. 1990 Uncertainty, transaction costs and vertical integration : Theory and evidence. Working paper WP #013, The Wharton School, October.

Lambkin, M. 1988 Order of entry and performance in new markets. *Strategic Management Journal* 9 : 127–140.

Lamont, T., and C. R. Anderson 1985 Mode of corporate diversification and economic performance. *Academy of Management Journal* 28 : 926–934.

Lauglaug, A. S. 1987 A framework for the strategic management of future tyre technology. *Long Range Planning* 20 (5) : 21–41.

Lawrence, P., and J. Lorsch 1967 *Organization and environment.* Boston : Graduate School of Business Administration, Harvard University.

Lemelin, A. 1982 Relatedness in the patterns of interindustry diversification. *The Review of Economics and Statistics* 64 : 646–647.

Levin, R., A. Klevorick, R. Nelson, and S. G. Winter 1984 Survey research on R&D appropriability and technical opportunity — Part I : Appropriability. Working paper, Yale University.

Levinthal, D. 1991 Organizational adaptation and environmental selection — Interrelated processes of change. *Organizational Science* 2(1) : 140–145.

Lieberman, M. B., and D. B. Montgomery 1988 First-mover advantages. *Strategic Management Journal* 9 (Special Issue) : 41–58.

Lilien, G. L., and E. Yoon 1990 Timing of competitive market entry. *Management Science* 36 : 568–585.

Lorenzoni, G., and O. A. Ornati 1988 Constellations of firms and new ventures. *Journal of Business Venturing* 3 (1) : 41–57.

Lounamaa, P. H., and J. G. March 1988 Adaptive coordination of a learning team. *Management Science* 33 : 107–123.

Low, J., and M. Silver 1986 R&D strategies and variable demand. *R&D Management* 16 (4) : 325–333.

Low, M., and I. C. MacMillan 1988 Entrepreneurship : Past research and future challenges. *Journal of Management* 14(10) : 139–161.

Lumsden, C. J., and J. Singh 1990 The dynamics of organizational speciation. *Organizational Evolution* : 145–163.

MacMillan, I. C. 1983 Preemptive strategies. *Journal of Business Strategy* 4 (2) : 16–26.

1986 Progress in research on corporate venturing. In *The art and science of entrepreneurship*, eds. D. L. Sexton and R. W. Smilor, 241–264. Cambridge, Mass. : Ballinger Publishing Co.

1987 New business development : Challenge for transformational leadership. *Human Resource Management* 26 (4) : 439–454.

MacMillan, I. C., and D. L. Day 1987 Corporate ventures into industrial markets : Dynamics of aggressive entry. *Journal of Business Venturing* 2 : 29–39.

MacMillan, I. C., and R. George 1985 Corporate venturing : Challenges for senior managers. *Journal of Business Strategy* 5 (3) : 34–44.

Mahajan, V., E. Muller, and F. Bass 1990 New product diffusion models in marketing : A review and directions for research. *Journal of Marketing* 54 : 1–26.

Maidique, M. A., and B. J. Zirger 1985 The new product learning cycle. *Research Policy* 14 : 299–313.

Mansfield, E. 1961 Technical change and the rate of imitation. *Econometrica* 29 : 741–766.

1963 Intrafirm rates of diffusion of an innovation. *Review of Economics and Statistics* 45 : 348–359.

1968 *Economics of technological change.* N.Y. : Norton.

1985 How rapidly does new industrial technology leak out ? *Journal of Industrial Economics* 34 (2) : 217–223.

Mansfield, E., M. Schwartz, and S. Wagner 1981 Imitation costs and patents : An empirical study. *Economic Journal* 91 : 907–918.

March, J. G. 1991 Exploration and exploitation in organizational learning. *Organizational Science* 2(1) : 71–87.

March, J. G., and A. Simon, II 1958 *Organization.* New York : John Wiley & Sons.

Marino, K. E., and M. J. Dollinger 1987 Top management succession in entrepreneurial firms : Cases from the computer industry. *Journal of Management Case Studies* 3 (1, Spring) : 70–79.

Marris, R. 1964 *The Economic theory of managerial capitalism.* Glencoe, Ill. : Free Press.

McGee, J., and H. Thomas 1989 Technology and strategic management progress and future directions. *R&D Management* 19 (3) : 205–213.

Merton, R. K. 1957 *Social theory and social structure.* 2d ed. Glencoe, Ill. : Free Press.

Miles, R. H. 1982 *Coffin nails and corporate strategies.* Englewood Cliffs, N.J. : Prentice-Hall, Inc.

Mintzberg, H. 1979 *The structuring of organizations.* Englewood Cliffs, N.J. : Prentice-Hall, Inc.

Mitchell, W. 1989 Whether and when ? Probability and timing of incumbents' entry into emerging industrial subfields. *Administrative Science Quarterly* 34 : 208–230.

Mosakowski, E. 1990 Entrepreneurial diversification and causal ambiguity : A dynamic analysis of entrepreneurial computer firms. *Academy of Management Proceedings* x : 64–68.

1991 Organizational boundaries and economic performance : An empirical study of entrepreneurial computer firms. *Strategic Management Journal* 12 · 115–133.

Murray, A. I. 1989 Top management group heterogeneity and firm performance. *Strategic Management Journal* 10 (Summer) : 125–142.

Nathanson, D. 1980 The relationship between situation factors, organizational characteristics, and financial performance. Ph.D. diss., Wharton School, University of Pennsylvania.

Nelson, R. R., and S. G. Winter 1977 In search of useful theory of innovation. *Research Policy* 6 : 36–76.

Noel, A. 1989 Strategic cores and magnificent obsessions : Discovering strategy formation through daily activities of CEOs. *Strategic Management Journal* 10 : 33–49.

Nonaka, I., and T. Yamanouchi 1989 Managing innovation as a self-renewing process. *Journal of Business Venturing* 4 : 299–315.

Norton, J. A., and F. M. Bass 1987 A diffusion theory model of adoption and substitution for successive generations of high-technology products. *Management Science* 33 (9) : 1069–1097.

Norton, S. W. 1988 Franchising, brand name capital, and the entrepreneurial capacity problem. *Strategic Management Journal* 9 : 105–114.

Pelc, K. I. 1986 Management of R&D for reduction of technological delay : A strategic viewpoint. *R&D Management* 16 (2) : 97–102.

Penrose, E. 1959 *The theory of the growth of the firm.* Oxford : Basil Blackwell.

Peters, T. J., and R. H. Waterman, Jr. 1982 *In search of excellence.* N.Y. : Harper & Row.

Pfeffer, J. 1978 *Organizational design.* Arlington Heights, Ill. : AHM Publishing Co.

Pinchot, G., III 1985 *Intrapreneuring.* N.Y. : Harper & Row.

Pisano, G. 1990 R&D boundaries of the firm : An empirical analysis. *Administrative Science Quarterly* 35 : 153–176.

Porter, M. E. 1983 The technological dimension of competitive strategy. *Research on Technological Innovation, Management and Policy* 1 : 1–33.

Potter, D. V. 1989 From experience : The customer's eye view of innovation. *Journal of Product Innovation Management* 16 (1) : 35–42.

Quirmbach, H. C. 1986 The diffusion of new technology and the market for an innovation. *Rand Journal of Economics* 17 (1) : 33–47.

Ramanujam, V., and P. Varadarajan 1989 Research on corporate diversification : A synthesis. *Strategic Management Journal* 10 : 523–551.

Richardson, G. B. 1964 The limits to a firm's rate of growth. *Oxford Economic Papers* 16 : 9–23.

Ries, A., and J. Trout 1986 *Marketing warfare.* New York : McGraw-Hill.

Roberts, E. B. 1980 New ventures for corporate growth. *Harvard Business Review* (July-August) : 134–142.

Roberts, E. B., and C. A. Berry 1985 Entering new businesses : Selecting strategies for success. *Sloan Management Review* 26(3) : 3–17.

Roberts, E. B., and A. L. Frohman 1972 Internal entrepreneurship : Strategy for growth. *The Business Quarterly* (Spring) : 71–78.

Robinson, W. T. 1988a Sources of market pioneer advantages : The case of industrial goods industries. *Journal of Market Research* 25 : 87–94.

1988b Marketing mix reactions to entry. *Marketing Science* 7 (Fall) : 368–385.

1990 Product innovation and start-up business market share performance. *Management Science* 36 (10) : 1279–1289.

Robinson, W. T., and C. Fornell 1985 The sources of market pioneer advantages in consumer goods industries. *Journal of Market Research* 22 : 297–304.

Rogers, E. M. 1983 *Diffusion of innovations.* 3d ed. N.Y. : Free Press.

Romanelli, E. 1989 Environments and strategy of organization start-up : Effects on early survival. *Administrative Science Quarterly* 34 : 369–387.

Root, F. R. 1987 *Entry strategies for international markets.* Lexington, Mass. : Heath.

Rothwell, R., C. Freeman, A. Horlsey, V. T. P. Jervis, A. B. Robertson, and J. Townsend 1974 SAPPHO updated : Project SAPPHO phase II. *Research Policy* 3 : 258–291.

Rothwell, R., and P. Gardiner 1989 The strategic management of re-innovation. *R&D Management* 19 (2) : 147–160.

Rubin, P. H. 1973 The expansion of firms. *Journal of Political Economy* 81 : 936–949.

Ruefli, T. W. 1990 Mean-variance approaches to risk-return relationships in strategy : Paradox lost. *Management Science* 36 : 368–380.

Rumelt, R. P. 1974 Strategy, structure, and economic performance. Ph.D. diss., Graduate School of Business Administration, Harvard University.

1987 Theory, strategy, and entrepreneurship. In *The competitive challenge,* ed. D. J. Teece, 137–158. Cambridge, Mass. : Ballinger.

Salter, M. S., and W. S. Weinhold 1979 *Diversification through acquisition.* New York : Free Press.

Sandberg, W. R., and C. W. Hofer 1987 Improving new venture performance : The role of strategy, industry, structure, and the entrepreneur. *Journal of Business Venturing* 2 : 5–28.

Sathe, V. 1989 Fostering entrepreneurship in the large, diversified firm. *Organizational Dynamics* 18 (1, Summer) : 20–32.

Schendel, D. 1990 Introduction to the special issue on corporate entrepreneurship. *Strategic Management Journal* 11(2) : 1–4.

Schill, R. L. 1986 Managing technology for competitive advantage in interindustry markets. *R&D Management* 16 (2) : 103–116.

Schoemaker, P. 1990 Strategy, complexity and economic rent. *Management Science* 36(10) : 1178–1192.

Schollhammer, H. 1981 Internal corporate entrepreneurship. In *Encyclopedia of entrepreneurship*, eds. C. Kent, D. Sexton, and K. Vesper, 209–229. Englewood Cliffs, N.J. : Prentice-Hall.

Schoonhoven, C. B., and K. M. Eisenhardt 1985 Influence of organizational, entrepreneurial, and environmental factors on the growth and development of technology-based start-up firms : A research proposal. Economic Development Administration, U.S. Department of Commerce.

Schoonhoven, C. B., K. M. Eisenhardt, and K. Lyman 1990 Speeding products to market : Waiting time to first product introduction in new firms. *Administrative Science Quarterly* 35 : 177–207.

Schroeder, R., A. Van de Ven, G. Scudder, and D. Polley 1986 Managing innovation and change processes : Findings from the Minnesota Innovation Research Program. *Agribusiness* 2 (4) : 501–523.

Schumpeter, J. A. 1934 *The theory of economic development.* Cambridge, Mass. : Harvard Univ. Press.

1950 *Capitalism, socialism and democracy.* 3d ed. N.Y. : Harper & Row.

Schwenk, C. R. 1984 Cognitive simplification processes in strategic decision-making. *Strategic Management Journal* 5 : 111–128.

1986 Information, cognitive biases, and commitment to a course of action. *Academy of Management Review* 11 : 289–310.

1988 *The essence of strategic decision making.* Lexington, Mass. : Heath.

Shaw, B. 1988 Gaining added value from centres for excellence in the UK medical equipment industry. *R&D Management* 18 (2) : 123–130.

Shapero, A. 1984 Intracorporate entrepreneuring : A clash of cultures. Working paper, Ohio State University.

Shen, T. Y. 1970 Economies of scale, Penrose-effect, growth of plants and their size distribution. *Journal of Political Economy* 78 : 702–716.

Shortell, S. M., and E. J. Zajac 1988 Internal corporate joint ventures : Development processes and performance outcomes. *Strategic Management Journal* 9 : 527–542.

Shrivastava, P., and S. A. Nachman 1989 Strategic leadership patterns. *Strategic Management Journal* 10 (Summer) : 377–386.

Singh, H., and C. A. Montgomery 1987 Corporate acquisition strategies and economic performance. *Strategic Management Journal* 8 : 377–386.

Singh, J. V., R. J. House, and D. J. Tucker 1986a Organizational change and organizational mortality. *Administrative Science Quarterly* 31 : 587–611.

Singh, J. V., D. J. Tucker, and R. J. House 1986b Organizational legitimacy and the liability of newness. *Administrative Science Quarterly* 31 : 171–193.

Smithson, M. 1989 *Ignorance and uncertainty.* N.Y. : Springer Verlag.

Stevenson, H. H., M. J. Roberts, and I. H. Grousbeck 1989 *New business ventures and the entrepreneur.* Boston : Irwin.

Stinchcombe, A. L. 1965 Social structure and organizations. In *Handbook of organizations,* ed. J. G. March, 142–193. Chicago : Rand McNally.

Sykes, H. B., and Z. Block 1989 Corporate venturing obstacles: Sources and solutions. *Journal of Business Venturing* 4 (3): 159–167.

Teece, D. J. 1980 Economies of scope and the scope of the enterprise. *Journal of Economic Behavior and Organization* 1: 223–247.

1981 The market for know-how and the efficient international transfer of technology. *ANNALS, AAPSS* 458 (November): 81–96. (American Academy of Political and Social Science)

1982 Towards an economic theory of the multiproduct firm. *Journal of Economic Behavior and Organization* 3: 39–63.

1986 Profiting from technological innovation: Implications for integration, collaboration, licensing, and public policy. *Research Policy* 15(6): 285–305.

1989 Inter-organizational requirements of the innovation process. *Managerial and Decision Economics* (Special Issue): 35–42.

Teece, D. J., G. Pisano, and A. Shuen 1990 Firm capabilities, resources and the concept of strategy. Working paper, University of California, Berkeley.

Thomas, J. B., and R. R. McDaniel, Jr. 1990 Interpreting strategic issues: Effects of strategy and the information-processing structure of top management teams. *Academy of Management Journal* 33 (2): 286–306.

Thompson, J. D. 1961 *The science of administration.* N.Y.: John Wiley & Sons.

Tornatzky, G., J. D. Eveland, M. Boylan, W. Hetzner, E. Johnson, D. Roitman, and J. Schneider 1983 *The process of technological innovation: Reviewing the literature.* Washington, D.C.: National Science Foundation.

Tushman, M. L. 1977 Special boundary roles in the innovation process. *Administrative Science Quarterly* 22: 587–605.

Tushman, M. L., and P. Anderson 1986 Technological discontinuities and organizational environments. *Administrative Science Quarterly* 31: 439–465.

Tushman, M. L., and E. Romanelli 1985 Organizational evolution: A metamorphosis model of convergence and reorientation. In *Research in organizational behavior,* eds. B. Staw and L. Cummings, Vol. 7, 171–222.

Tushman, M., V. Virany, and E. Romanelli 1987 Effects of CEO and executive team succession: a longitudinal analysis. Working paper, Columbia University.

Tversky, A., and D. Kahneman 1974 Judgement under uncertainty: Heuristics and biases. *Science* 185: 1124–1131.

1981 The framing of decision and the psychology of choice. *Science* 211: 453–458.

Urban, Glen, R. Carter, S. Gaskin, and Z. Mucha 1986 Market share rewards to pioneering brands: An empirical analysis and strategic implications. *Management Science* 6 (June): 645–659.

Utterback, J. 1974 Innovation in industry and the diffusion of technology. *Science* 183: 620–626.

1971 The process of technological innovation within the firm. *Academy of Management Journal* 14: 75–88.

Utterback, J. M., and W. J. Abernathy 1975 A dynamic model of product and process innovation. *OMEGA, The International Journal of Management Science* 3 (6): 639–655.

Uzawa, H. 1969 Time preference and the Penrose effect in a two-class model of economic growth. *Journal of Political Economy* 77: 628–652.

Van de Ven, A. H. 1986 Central problems in the management of innovation. *Management Science* 32 (5): 590–607.

Van De Ven, A. H., H. L. Angle, and M. S. Poole 1989 *Research on the management of innovation: The Minnesota studies.* Grand Rapids, Mich.: Harper & Row.

Venkataraman, S. 1990 Liabilities of newness, transaction set and new venture development. Working paper, Management Department, Wharton School, University of Pennsylvania.

Venkataraman, S., A. H. Van de Ven, J. Buckeye, and R. Hudson 1990 Starting up in a turbulent environment: A process model of failure among firms with high customer dependence. *Journal of Business Strategy* 5 (5): 277–295.

Virany, B., and M. L. Tushman 1986 Top management teams and corporate success in an emerging industry. *Journal of Business Venturing* 1(3): 261–274.

Von Hippel, E. 1977 Successful and failing internal corporate ventures: An empirical analysis. *Industrial Marketing Management* 6: 163–174.

Von Hippel, E. 1981 Users as innovators. In *Corporate strategy and product innovation,* ed. R. R. Rothberg, 239–252. New York: Free Press.

1987 Cooperation between rivals: Informal know-how trading. *Research Policy* 16: 291–302.

Weiss, L. A. 1981 Start-up businesses: A comparison of performances. *Sloan Management Review* (Fall): 37–53.

Wernerfelt, B. 1984 A resource-based view of the firm. *Strategic Management Journal* 5: 171–180.

Westley, F., and H. Mintzberg 1989 Visionary leadership and strategic management. *Strategic Management Journal* 10 (Summer): 17–32.

Williamson, O. E. 1975 *Markets and hierarchies.* N.Y.: Free Press.

1985 *The economic institutions of capitalism: Firms, markets, relational contracting.* N.Y.: Free Press.

Wilson, L. O., and J. A. Norton 1989 Optimal entry timing for a product line extension. *Marketing Science* 8 (Winter): 1–17.

Zajac, E. J., B. R. Golden, and S. M. Shortell 1991 New organizational forms for enhancing innovation: The case of internal corporate joint ventures. *Management Science* 37 (2): 170–184.

Zirger, B. J., and M. A. Maidique 1990 A model of new product development: An empirical test. *Management Science* 36 (7): 867–883.

Chapter

7

Marketing and Entrepreneurship: The State of the Art

Gerald E. Hills
and
Raymond W. LaForge

●

Market opportunities and marketing *may* be the two most important elements underpinning successful business creation, but scholarly attention to this interface has occurred only in recent years. This chapter attempts to define and conceptualize this interface, assess the status of the subject in the marketing discipline, and review relevant knowledge concerning a firm's mission, marketing opportunity analysis, marketing strategy development, and control. Finally, attention is given to directions for future research.

DEFINING THE DOMAIN

There is growing evidence that entrepreneurship should be treated as a major conceptual dimension within the marketing discipline. Marketing journals, programs, and associations are structured around: 1) different marketing functions such as product development and advertising; and 2) types of markets and firms such as consumer and industrial, services, health care marketing, and retailing. The time has come also to study firms at their inception and in the early stages of the business life cycle.

To illustrate the potential, following are four conclusions drawn from Gerald Hills' in-depth, exploratory survey of expert opinion. Hisrich (1989) and Wortman, Spann, and Adams (1989) each cited this study as the first to examine the marketing/entrepreneurship interface. Although the study results are based on interviews with only fourteen venture capitalists, the venture capitalists had dealt with hundreds of sophisticated entrepreneurs and collectively financed and guided more than 200 new ventures (Hills 1984):

1. Venture capitalists rated marketing management at 6.7 on a 7.0 scale as important to the success of new ventures.
2. Venture capitalists overwhelmingly agreed that venture failure rates could be reduced, perhaps as much as 60 percent, through better pre-venture market analysis.
3. Three-quarters of the venture capitalists felt that entrepreneurs tend to be biased toward their venture idea, ignore negative market information, and resist obtaining in-depth market information due to their prior commitment to the venture idea.
4. Venture capitalists agreed on several unique marketing-related challenges that face entrepreneurs, such as the inability to spread advertising costs, poor access to good quality distributors, and lack of access to retail shelf space.

It was clear that these new venture observers perceived marketing as a critically important part of entrepreneurship and, importantly, as different in some significant ways from marketing in mature firms. Further, Hisrich (1989) and a number of others have observed that surveys of entrepreneurs in the United States as well as throughout the world reveal that the two biggest problem areas are marketing and finance.

Marketing

In order to study the marketing/entrepreneurship interface, it is important to make definitional issues explicit. Marketing may be defined in a variety of ways and, in general the proper domain and boundaries of marketing are not fully known (Sheth, Gardner, and Garrett 1988). Historically, there have been several schools of thought in the marketing discipline such as the commodity, functional, institutional, buyer behavior, macromarketing, and managerial perspectives. But the implicit focus in all of them is on exchange and transactions.

The managerial perspective was adopted by Kotler (1972) when he proposed a generic concept of marketing concerned with how transactions are created, stimulated, facilitated, and valued. More recently it was noted that the main purpose of marketing is to create and distribute values among the market parties through the process of transactions and market relationships (Sheth, Gardner, and Garrett 1988). It is rather striking that substitution of the word

"entrepreneurship" for the word "marketing" could yield a defensible definition as well! In both cases, there is win-win market behavior.

To move to a more operational level, the American Marketing Association
has defined marketing as the process of planning and executing the conception,
pricing, promotion, and distribution of ideas, goods, and services to create exchanges that satisfy individual and organizational objectives. Marketing management is the process of scanning the environment, analyzing market opportunities, designing marketing strategies, and then effectively implementing
and controlling marketing practices (Cravens, Hills, and Woodruff 1987). In
this chapter, we are addressing research at the *interface* of marketing and entrepreneurship, and we will primarily use the latter definition.

Entrepreneurship

The study of new venture development and entrepreneurship *as a process,* and
the study of the early stages of the business life cycle, belong as much or more
to marketing than to any other business function. Indeed, some argue that the
very term "management" may be somewhat in definitional conflict with the
term "entrepreneurship." Further, if we address the entrepreneurial *spirit,* it
may be hypothesized that marketing is the organizational function most dominated by boundary agents, by open, interactive systems, and by truly entrepreneurial activity. Market opportunity analysis, new product development, the
diffusion of innovation, and marketing strategies to create growing firms are at
the heart of both marketing and entrepreneurship. These also represent the
most relevant, existing marketing literature bases.

Entrepreneurship as defined by Stevenson and Jarillo-Mossi (1986) focuses on opportunity and is therefore particularly relevant to the marketing interface; that is, the process of creating value by combining resources to exploit
an opportunity.

Finally, what is the role of small business in entrepreneurship research? In
academic research, "small business" is quite simply the *size* variable, with
focus on the lower end of the scale. Although the very term "small business"
often conjures forth images of mediocre research and stagnant, nongrowth
firms, this prejudice can make potentially exciting research issues seem unim-
portant. The research issue is quite clear: should we incorporate the size variable, business life cycle, and other related variables when we do organizational
research on marketing?

The Interface

Marketing definitions vary greatly. Yet the relationship to several innovation,
growth, and uniqueness attributes is clear, as well as to organization creation
and the creation of value. In an earlier essay, Hunt, Voegele, and Robinson
(1987) defined marketing as a social process and entrepreneurship as wealth
creation, and expressed skepticism that marketing is any different for entrepre-

neurs than for anyone else. From a managerial viewpoint, Figure 7–1 illustrates the relationship between marketing management and entrepreneurship. Although the exact placement of some of the entrepreneurship descriptors is arbitrary, others fit logically. Venture idea identification, innovation, and exploiting opportunities seem to fit naturally between environmental scanning and market opportunity analysis. Team building becomes critical as the implementation stage is approached and the venture is launched. The business plan is partially comprised of market feasibility analysis and marketing strategy. Following the initial sales generation, managing growth becomes relevant, and creating value ultimately depends on customer feedback and a constant reappraisal of customer needs relative to the product or service offered. Risk taking and creativity permeate the entire process, but most fundamentally at the business mission level. It is readily evident that the interface between marketing and entrepreneurship is extensive.

In defining the research interface, it may be important to look beyond narrow definitions of entrepreneurship, and seek to evaluate the importance of other factors or variables. Related variables often include few, if any, economies of scale, severe resource constraints, a limited geographic market presence, a limited market image, little brand loyalty or market share, little specialized management expertise, decision making under even more imperfect information conditions than in larger firms, a marked scarcity of time per major management task, a scarcity of professional managers, and a mixture of personal, nonmaximizing financial goals. Just as a child is not a little adult, a new venture or smaller firm is not a little Fortune 100 firm. In firms where sev-

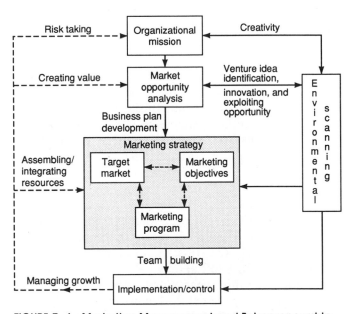

FIGURE 7–1 Marketing Management and Entrepreneurship

eral of these conditions exist, one could expect that the marketing function would both be *viewed* differently and *performed* differently than in mature firms. Although the basic definition of marketing remains intact, new venture marketing should join the ranks of other specialized areas such as international marketing, industrial marketing, and services marketing. A study of the inherent definitional and conceptual similarity between marketing and entrepreneurship supports the hypothesis that more entrepreneurial firms should also be more marketing oriented (Morris and Paul 1987). Perhaps marketing *is* the home for entrepreneurship.

▬▬▬▬▬▬▬▬▬

THE MARKETING DISCIPLINE AND ENTREPRENEURSHIP

In the mid-1980s it was observed that because the importance of new ventures was well documented, one might expect marketing scholars to commonly enter "stage of the business life cycle" and "firm size" variables into marketing studies (Davis, Hills, and LaForge 1985). The evidence, however, suggests that marketing academicians have almost entirely neglected such investigations. A review of the *Journal of Marketing* from 1936 to the present failed to identify any titles directed wholly toward marketing and new ventures or firm size. Rarely did any of the articles even include these subjects as a secondary focus. A similar review of the *Journal of Retailing* since 1927 identified only four articles dealing with these subjects, the most recent published in 1952.

A review of the sources of entrepreneurship literature over more recent years identified four articles (2 percent of the total number of articles) in which marketing was the major field of orientation. Articles "mentioning" marketing totaled 17 (Hisrich 1989).

In 1983, proceedings were published as the result of a research meeting on marketing and entrepreneurship, cosponsored by the American Marketing Association and the International Council for Small Business (Hills, Barnaby, and Duffus 1983). The primary value of this publication was the identification of important research issues, although it was clear at that time that few in the marketing discipline were interested. Four years later a second symposium was held, and this time it met with a new level of interest among established researchers in the marketing discipline (Hills 1987). Subsequent meetings have provided an outlet for research and an AMA Task Force on Marketing and Entrepreneurship has been created. As of this writing, a total of four Symposia on Marketing and Entrepreneurship have been held, resulting in published proceedings including 115 articles (Hills 1987; Hills, LaForge, and Parker 1989; Hills, LaForge, and Welsch 1990; Hills and LaForge 1991).

The AMA Task Force is now in its third year of existence and has accumulated growing evidence of the importance of entrepreneurship to AMA educators as well as to business members. The Task Force has been given AMA line item budget status, serves an Interest Group of more than 200 professors, distributes a quarterly newsletter, and is working on several projects.

In 1989, entrepreneurship session tracks were included at the Academy of Marketing Science World Congress in Singapore. In 1990 and in 1991, entrepreneurship tracks were included in the AMA Educators Conference. Leaders of the discipline are recognizing the value of the subject, and a growing number of scholars are devoting attention to it. Yet the subject is still not institutionalized and, compared to the management discipline, the subject is still at the early growth stage (Hoy 1987). However, interest is growing rapidly. David Gardner (1991) has observed that the next major school of thought in the marketing discipline may well develop from the interface with entrepreneurship.

We now discuss important literature at the interface of entrepreneurship and marketing management (see Figure 7–1) in the context of the organizational mission, market opportunity analysis, and marketing strategy and control.

━━━━━━━━
COMPANY MISSION

The mission of new ventures is based, in part, on the markets and marketing strategies the firm pursues. In determining the mission, there are at least two factors that are unique to the marketing/entrepreneurship interface as compared to large, mature firms. One is the impact of the entrepreneur's personal goals on the mission (and marketing objectives), and the second is the role of the marketing concept.

Sexton and Bowman-Upton (1987) noted that the personal goals of business founders can have a direct impact on both the rate of sales growth as well as the ultimate size of the firm. "Lifestyle firms" may contribute an adequate, stable income over many years but, depending on the nature of the product/market and/or the personal goals of the entrepreneur, the business may not generate a high sales level or substantial personal wealth for the owner. This type of business mission has a direct impact on marketing goals and, therefore, on marketing opportunity analysis and marketing strategy (see Figure 7–1). In contrast, a business financed by venture capital will have aggressive, competitive marketing strategies with high return on investment objectives.

The "marketing concept," first articulated in the 1950s, also has special relevance to new and growing firms. The marketing concept is a partial philosophy for starting and operating a business with the primary focus on a customer orientation, integrating that orientation throughout the organization, and thereby achieving goals that transcend just sales (most notably profit). In a study of nearly 100 entrepreneurial, small and mid-size growing firms, the CEOs rated product/service quality and a passionate responsiveness to customers among the most important factors (out of 26) underpinning success (Hills and Narayana 1989). Although several studies have measured the adoption of the marketing concept in large mature firms, there has been limited research regarding the use of the marketing concept in new ventures. Gardner (1983) researched 15 existing entrepreneurial firms ($1 million–$30 million in sales) in the first study to qualitatively examine the marketing concept/new venture issue, and found that distribution firms were typically deficient in understanding the needs and wants of their customers, but that manufacturing firms typically knew each customer intimately, often in a close cooperative effort. Peter (1989), in a study of small businesses (very small, including firms of marginal success), asked the owners to indicate whether descriptions of a marketing, sales, production, or societal orientation best described their business philosophy. Marketing was selected as the leading orientation only by retailers (50 percent), with a sales philosophy leading in service firms (42 percent) and wholesale firms (57 percent), and a production philosophy leading in manufacturing firms (58 percent). Unfortunately, respondents had to select one orientation (as opposed to rating them all), and the results were not analyzed by the level of success or business age. Yet these studies provide an important beginning for studying the potentially unique relevance of customer orientation to new ventures.

MARKET OPPORTUNITY ANALYSIS

A key part of new venture planning is market opportunity analysis, where the feasibility of the venture is assessed and a sales forecast is derived. Major components of a market opportunity analysis typically include macroenvironmental analysis, industry analysis, competitor analysis, and customer analysis (Woodruff and Cadotte 1987). This detailed study of the market provides the basis for both the sales forecast and the formulation of marketing strategy. Most entrepreneurship textbooks treat market analysis superficially, with sometimes only a few paragraphs devoted to this section of the business plan.

Venture Idea Identification

The market analysis literature, however, presumes an existing business concept or product/service idea. Although there are volumes of literature regarding evaluating business/product ideas, there is a knowledge void regarding how potentially viable business ideas may first be identified. Entrepreneurship and product management textbooks typically identify the most obvious general sources of ideas, list new product data bases, and may also include a section on human creativity. Drucker (1985) cited industry and market conditions that tend to create opportunities, a significant contribution to the literature.

Christensen and Peterson (1990) effectively defined the subject and its importance and also reported on the sources of venture ideas in electronics companies in Denmark. An in-depth study of 15 ventures found that half of the ideas were an outgrowth of internal problems, and the remainder were evenly divided into customer problems and imitation as the source. A subsequent survey of 76 companies found that 74 percent of the respondents agreed with "specific problem solutions" and 79 percent with "informal contacts" as sources of opportunities. Creative exploration of this subject area will certainly result in major contributions to new knowledge.

Venture Idea Evaluation

New venture failures are often the result of inadequate advance testing of market acceptance. Many potential entrepreneurs instead dwell on obtaining financial backing without equivalent attention to assessing market feasibility. Those who attempt to conduct market studies also often lack the prerequisite understanding and training. The typical sophistication level is best described by the often-cited decision to "do a market survey." Such a statement often reflects just enough knowledge to generate considerable self-inflicted harm.

Methodologies for testing new *product* acceptance have long been used by major consumer product companies, and they also offer merit for testing new *venture* ideas. Concept testing, product use testing, and/or market testing may be used (Tauber 1977).

Concept testing may occur early in the new product or venture planning process, before the venture concept has been completely developed. Potential customers are asked to evaluate a product or venture concept *description* rather than the actual product or venture. Respondents are given a pictorial and verbal description of the product (venture) and asked to visualize their actual use and indicate (in an interview) their likelihood of purchase.

Product use testing involves having respondents actually use a new product (venture) prior to being interviewed. Depending on the nature of the product, the respondents may use it for a few minutes, or more likely, over several days in their homes. Product use tests are less abstract than concept tests and contribute to higher test reliability. However, product use testing is not possible if product or venture prototypes are too expensive or too time-consuming to produce in advance of full-scale marketing. Also, the use of this approach for new ventures requires that the venture be structured around a single product or service (or a small number) rather than a wide assortment of merchandise.

A third methodology for measuring market acceptance — market testing — is the most expensive and complex approach, but also the most realistic for potential customers. Market testing involves presenting the full marketing strategy to customers (products, prices, advertising, distribution, etc.) and duplicates the actual market situation on a small scale — often in a limited geographic area. Because new business ventures are by definition often oriented to a small geographic area, market testing could in effect require that the full venture be launched. The practical usefulness of market testing for new ventures is therefore limited, although small manufacturing ventures seeking widespread geographic distribution provide an important exception. It may be argued that new, but potentially multi-unit retail ventures often begin by "market testing" at one location. Nonetheless, the disadvantages of market testing include the possibility of alerting competition to future plans and the related prospect of competitors sabotaging test market results by making immediate competitive responses.

It is apparent that concept testing, product use testing, and market testing are not equally applicable to new venture market acceptance testing, as shown in Table 7–1. A single product venture facilitates the transferability of new product market testing methods to new ventures (column 1 indicates high applicability for all three testing methods). Ventures involving large assortments of products (column 2) do not lend themselves to product use tests but may allow for the use of market testing if the ultimate objective is to serve a large geographic market. The complexity of a multiproduct market test is high, however, so only "moderate" applicability is noted. Concept testing of multiproduct assortment ventures is possible, although the complexity of the concept description must be limited (thus "moderate/low" applicability is noted in column 2).

A venture strategy with heavy reliance on the product itself (and price) for successful market penetration has a high potential fit with all three market acceptance methods (column 3). Ventures that place considerable importance on distribution and/or promotion strategy elements by definition fit less well (column 4). Product use tests, again by definition, fare poorly in applicability to the distribution/promotion dominated venture strategy, whereas market testing, because of its attention to all the marketing strategy elements, demonstrates moderate to high applicability. Concept testing, through incorporating distribution and promotional elements, has moderate to high applicability to ventures that place considerable emphasis on those elements.

A third dimension for evaluating the relevance of the three methodologies to new ventures is whether or not the venture is continuous or discontinuous with respect to customer use (Tauber 1977). Continuous innovations are products that are similar enough to existing items to require little or no change in the consumer's behavior to be adopted. Discontinuous innovations, at the other extreme, require significant changes in consumption patterns and/or consumer usage behavior. As shown in Table 7–1 (column 5), the methods for testing the market acceptance of ventures that represent continuous innovations are all highly applicable. Concept testing has a poor record in forecasting the acceptance of discontinuous innovations. The more actual involvement the respondent has with the new product or venture, however, the higher the likelihood of a valid forecast (column 6). To conclude, concept testing, despite less realism for potential customers, is the most applicable of the three methods to new ventures, due in part to its more moderate cost.

Entrepreneurs and Marketing Research/Plans

The normative academic literature places considerable emphasis on the development of detailed marketing and business plans, as well as on the conduct of market research (Robinson and Pearce 1984). There is increasing evidence,

TABLE 7–1 — Market Acceptance Testing : Extent of Applicability to New Small Business Ventures

TYPE OF NEW VENTURE

Alternative Methodologies	(1) Single Product Venture	(2) Multiproduct Venture	(3) Product / Price Dominance	(4) Promotion / Distribution Dominance	(5) Continuous Innovation Ventures	(6) Discontinuous Innovation Ventures
Concept testing	High	Moderate / low	High	Moderate / high	High	Low
Product use testing	High	Low	High	Low	High	Moderate
Market testing (objective is a large geographic market)	High	Moderate	High	Moderate / high	High	High

however, that many new ventures do not have detailed marketing plans and that marketing research is, at best, viewed in a "lukewarm" way by entrepreneurs (Andrus et al. 1987; Spitzer, Hills, and Alpar 1989).

In a study of 362 technology entrepreneurs, 47 percent had a written marketing plan when they started, and 42 percent had a written business plan. The mean responses of these entrepreneurs to negative statements about marketing research hovered around the midpoint of the scale (agree/disagree). Yet in comparing the venture capitalists to the entrepreneurs, it was found that the entrepreneurs attached more value to marketing research than the venture capitalists thought they would.

As noted earlier, venture capitalists believe that venture failure rates can be greatly reduced through advance marketing research and they also perceive many entrepreneurs as even actively avoiding negative market information (Hills 1984). In consideration of the vast resources that are lost in new business failures each year, academic research that better explains the gap between the perceptions of professionals as compared to entrepreneurs is extremely important. Which is closest to reality? What is the *actual* value of formal marketing research at the start-up stage, and what are the implications for entrepreneurs, market researchers, and the financial community? If market research has a more valuable role to play, which interventionist strategies could effectively encourage new business owners to utilize it more? These are critical issues.

MARKETING STRATEGY

The marketing literature concerning the marketing concept and market opportunity analysis has much to offer the entrepreneurship field. This is also true for the marketing strategy literature, but the mainstream research has typically been limited to examining marketing strategy relationships for brands offered by large, mature firms (Wind and Robertson 1983). There is a small but growing literature on marketing strategies for new ventures and smaller, growth-oriented firms in the published proceedings from the four University of Illinois at Chicago/American Marketing Association Research Symposia on Marketing and Entrepreneurship (Hills 1987; Hills, LaForge, and Parker 1989; Hills, LaForge, and Welsch 1990; Hills and LaForge 1991). Yet the mainstream marketing strategy research needs to encompass marketing strategy relationships for new ventures and smaller, growth-oriented firms.

Marketing Strategy Conceptualization

A conceptualization of the marketing strategy area is presented in Figure 7–2. Marketing strategy researchers are typically interested in examining relationships between marketing strategy and firm performance. There is, however, general agreement that a number of contingencies affect these relationships. The contingencies are classified as either market factors or company factors.

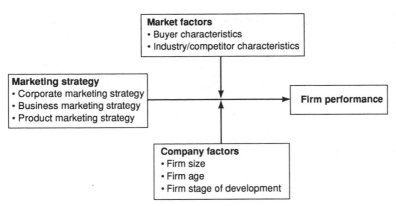

FIGURE 7-2 Marketing Strategy Conceptualization

Although the marketing strategy construct can be defined in a number of ways, our conceptualization defines marketing strategy in terms of three levels within a firm (Jain 1985; Lunsford and LaForge 1987). Corporate marketing strategy refers to strategic decisions that determine the product scope of the firm: for example, the timing of entry into new business areas and the degree of product diversification. Business marketing strategy decisions determine the relative importance of specific marketing elements in achieving competitive advantage for a business unit. Product marketing strategy refers to the selection of target markets and the development and implementation of marketing mixes for specific products. For independent new ventures marketing a single product to a well-defined target market, there are few differences in the three strategy levels. However, once a venture has been established, the different marketing strategy levels become important, since management must determine whether or not to enter new business areas as well as how to compete in each business area, and must determine marketing strategies for all of the firm's products.

Market factors refer to both the demand side and the supply side of the exchange relationship (Lambkin and Day 1989). The demand side is captured by buyer characteristics (e.g., number of buyers, types of buyers, growth rate of the buyer market), while the supply side is captured by industry/competitor characteristics (e.g., intensity of competition, industry size, industry concentration). The mixture of buyer and industry/competitor characteristics in a given situation influences the relationship between marketing strategy and firm performance.

Company factors refer to firm characteristics (firm size, firm age, firm stage of the life cycle) that affect the relationship between marketing strategy and firm performance. These characteristics are directly relevant to the marketing/entrepreneurship interface, since it is being recognized that marketing strategy relationships are likely to be different for new ventures versus existing firms, for small businesses versus larger firms, and for firms with other different characteristics. Yet little research has been directed toward new ventures or independent, growth-oriented firms.

Firm performance in the marketing strategy literature has most often been defined in terms of financial performance using measures such as sales, sales growth, return on sales, and return on equity. Occasionally, firms are placed into performance categories such as high- and low-performing firms or successful and unsuccessful firms. Although these financial performance measures are typically appropriate for large, mature firms, they may not be appropriate measures for new ventures and smaller, growth-oriented firms where entrepreneurs are likely to have personal goals that extend beyond financial considerations.

The conceptualization in Figure 7–1 provides a framework for organizing the recent marketing strategy literature and suggesting how specific research results might be relevant to new ventures.

Corporate Marketing Strategies

Corporate marketing strategies have received limited research attention, and what has appeared has been focused on large, mature firms. Thus, the marketing strategy literature on corporate marketing strategy is more relevant to corporate venturing than to independent ventures.

Assessing new venture risk.

Marketers have typically used the risk-return financial portfolio model based on the capital asset pricing model as the basis for assessing the risk of new ventures. This approach defines risk as the variance of an investment's return on investment. Dickson and Giglierano (1986) view this perspective of risk as "*sinking*-the-boat" risk and argue that it produces a short-sighted orientation to assessing new venture risk. They suggest the need to incorporate the perspective of "*missing*-the-boat" risk into the new venture assessment process. Missing-the-boat risk is defined as the risk of not identifying promising new venture opportunities and not acting on new venture opportunities once identified. The missing-the-boat risk orientation provides a longer term perspective for assessing new venture risk. It is recommended to balance the sinking-the-boat and missing-the-boat risk orientations.

Market entry strategies for new ventures.

In the purest sense, "entrepreneurial" ventures are those where the new venture introduces a new product class to a new market. However, being the market pioneer is not always possible and may not even be desirable. Thus the timing of market entry is an important consideration for new ventures.

Robinson and Fornell (1985) and Robinson (1988) investigated the sources of market pioneer advantages for corporate ventures in both consumer goods and industrial goods industries. Their results suggest that market pioneers tend to achieve higher market shares than later entrants by developing important and sustainable competitive advantages. In fact, these studies found a consistent association between order of entry and market share. The sources of pioneer advantages were similar across consumer and industrial goods industries and were typically based on higher product quality in the short run and broader product lines in the long run. Because the PIMS data base was used for both studies, the ability to generalize these results is limited. However, independent new ventures have the potential to develop strong market positions and sustainable competitive advantages by being market pioneers.

Independent ventures might employ different strategies for achieving market pioneer advantages. Farquhar (1989) suggested the use of a bypass strategy by first starting small and not attracting attention from competitors until it is too late for them to respond. Alternatively, product preannouncements can sometimes be used to start to capture the market before the product is ready. Product preannouncement strategies include a preemptive strategy, defensive strategy, or signalling strategy.

When it is not possible or desirable to be the market pioneer, entrepreneurs must determine whether or not to enter a new market, and how to protect their market position once a market is entered. Karakaya and Stahl (1989) studied the barriers to entry and market entry decisions of large consumer and industrial goods firms. The cost advantages of established firms, product differentiation capital requirements, access to distribution channels, customer switching costs, and government policy restrictions were found to be the most important barriers to entry. Because of limited resources and limited market presence, entrepreneurial ventures are likely to find it more difficult to overcome entry barriers due to competitors' cost advantages, capital requirements, or access to distribution channels. For the same reasons, once an entrepreneurial venture has entered a new market, it is more likely to be able to erect effective barriers to entry for potential competitors if they are based on product differentiation, customer switching costs, or government policy restrictions.

Product diversification strategies.

Once a new venture has been established, the desired product scope of the firm must be determined. The three basic strategic options are intensive growth within the current product domain, diversification into related product areas, and diversification into unrelated product areas.

Varadarajan (1989) studied the product diversification strategies of the 10 largest firms in the 24 largest industries in the United States. The study indicates that firms employing related product diversification strategies typically performed better than firms performing unrelated product diversification strategies. Lunsford, LaForge, and Miller (1989) and Lunsford (1990) replicated and extended Varadarajan's study by examining product diversification relationships for firms of different sizes in the Disclosure Database and *Inc.* 500 firms respectively. Both studies found that many ventures diversify into unrelated product areas within their first 10 years of existence. In addition, the relationships between product diversification strategy and firm performance were different for these smaller firms as compared to the larger firms. The smaller firms tended to achieve better growth performance, but poorer profit performance, using unrelated product diversification strategies.

These findings illustrate the potential problems when the results of studies employing large, mature firms are generalized to independent, new ventures and growth-oriented firms. Marketing strategy research conducted with large, mature firms must be interpreted with caution for new ventures.

Business Marketing Strategies

Business marketing strategy research (see Figure 7–2) has also received limited attention in the marketing discipline. Most researchers have investigated the importance of marketing strategy elements in achieving competitive advantage for a business unit (Jacobson and Aaker 1987; Walker and Ruekert 1987; McDaniel and Kolari 1987; LaForge and Miller 1987). For example, Walker and Ruekert (1987) developed propositions concerning the relative importance of marketing strategy elements for business units employing prospector, low-cost defender, and differentiated defender business strategies. McDaniel and Kolari (1987) tested similar relationships empirically. This study included firms of various sizes. The overall research findings were that 12 of the 16 marketing strategy elements investigated differed in importance depending upon whether a defender, prospector, or analyzer business strategy was employed. However, when firm size was controlled, only 10 significant relationships were found. Unfortunately, the researchers did not investigate the two situations where firm size affected the relationship between marketing strategy elements and business strategy, and this is typical of much of the marketing strategy literature.

One exception to this void was a study by LaForge and Miller (1987). They employed hierarchical regression and subgroup analysis to test both the form and the strength of the relationships between market characteristics, firm size, and the importance of marketing strategy elements for a sample of independent manufacturing firms of varying sizes. Company size was found to have a moderating effect in 8 of their 13 models. Firm size affected the form of the marketing strategy relationships in 2 models and affected the strength of these relationships in 6 models.

The results of the McDaniel and Kolari (1987) and LaForge and Miller (1987) studies provide strong evidence that the importance of marketing strategy elements in business strategy differs for firms of different sizes. Unfortunately, very little research has investigated firm size relationships or relationships in new ventures.

Product Marketing Strategies

Product marketing strategies refer to the selection of target markets and the development and implementation of marketing mixes to serve the selected target markets. Marketing strategies are typically developed for complete product lines and for individual brands within a product line. Most of the marketing strategy literature focuses on the product level, and researchers tend to focus on only one or two elements of the marketing mix in their studies. Therefore, we will now examine the product level marketing strategy literature in the product, price, promotion, and distribution strategy areas.

Product strategies.

One of the critical decisions facing new ventures is the introduction of new products. These decisions are often particularly difficult when the firm markets high-technology products. Recent marketing strategy research has addressed both the new product introduction and high-technology product marketing areas.

Giglierano, Haughey, and Kallis (1989) suggest the use of Porter's value chain as a basis for developing marketing strategies to introduce new products. In essence, their propositions indicate that new product introductions are more likely to be successful when the firm has a competitive advantage in one or more areas of the value chain. The value chain approach can be applied to new ventures, but it is more appropriate for existing firms since their value chains are more established.

After new ventures are established, future growth is largely dependent on the introduction of new products. The second product for a new venture seems to be especially critical. Giglierano and Kallis (1990) found that the four motivating factors for a second product are financial, technological, customer-education, and internal needs. Successful second product introductions tended to include "experimental marketing planning" and a substantial information flow from customers throughout the new product development process.

Aaker and Keller (1990) examined the use of brand extensions as a way to introduce a stream of new products. Brand extensions provide a way to reduce the risk of new product failure by taking advantage of an existing brand's image.

Their results suggest that brand extension strategies are more likely to be successful when the initial brand is perceived as high quality and when there is a perceived "fit" by customers between the initial brand and the brand extension.

The introduction and marketing of high-technology products places additional demands upon entrepreneurial firms. Gatignon and Robertson (1989) tested their model of technology diffusion in an industrial marketing setting. They found that technological innovations were accepted more readily when industrial buyers were in concentrated industries with limited price sensitivity and when the supplier used incentives and tried to establish vertical links with the buyer. Kosnik and Moriarty (1989) examined differences in marketing high-technology versus low-technology products and concluded that there were more similarities than differences. They recommended that both high-technology and low-technology entrepreneurial firms employ basic marketing concepts in developing and implementing marketing strategies.

One of the major contributions of the marketing literature to the new product diffusion area has been the development of a number of new product diffusion models. Mahajan, Muller, and Bass (1990) reviewed the available new product diffusion models, characterized their strengths and weaknesses, and developed an agenda to improve these models in the future. Although much work remains to be done, one of the exciting developments in the creation of these models is that many researchers are trying to incorporate the specific effects of marketing mix elements in their formulations.

Price strategies.

Pricing is one of the underresearched areas in the marketing strategy literature. Few studies have examined pricing strategies empirically, and no known studies have addressed the pricing strategies of new ventures or smaller, growth-oriented firms. Tellis (1986) did, however, develop a taxonomy of pricing strategies based on patterns of shared economies. The taxonomy classifies individual price strategies according to the objectives of the firm and the characteristics of consumers. Key objectives for a firm may be to vary prices among customer segments, exploit competitive position, or balance pricing over the product line. Key consumer characteristics include high consumer search costs, low reservation prices, or special transaction costs. The taxonomy suggests that entrepreneurial firms should use different price strategies depending on specific firm objectives and consumer characteristics.

Promotion strategies.

Most of the promotion research in the marketing strategy area that is of interest to entrepreneurial ventures has focused on advertising. No known studies have examined personal selling and sales management from the perspective of new ventures or independent, growth-oriented firms.

One of the critical decisions facing entrepreneurs is how much to spend on advertising. This decision is ideally based on an assessment of the expected results from different levels of advertising. Balasubramanian and Kumar (1990) investigated the advertising/sales ratios for larger companies facing different market growth and market share situations and operating in different industries. New ventures typically have low market share and often face different market growth advantages. They found consistent advertising/sales ratios for firms facing similar market growth and market share situations within the same industry, but different ratios across industries. These results suggest that entrepreneurial firms might use industry guidelines, especially expenditure levels of close competitors, as benchmarks for determining the appropriate amount for them to spend on advertising.

Distribution strategies.

Two of the more difficult problems facing entrepreneurial firms that use distributors is getting distributors to carry their products and then developing relationships with distributors to obtain marketing support for their products.

Rao and McLaughlin (1989) studied the decision criteria used by a grocery supermarket chain to decide whether or not to add a new product. The uniqueness of the product, expected growth of the product category, and the number of competing firms were found to have the most impact on getting the new product added. Interestingly, trade promotions (free cases, slotting allowances, etc.) were not found to have much impact on whether or not to add a new product. These results suggest that entrepreneurial firms are more likely to get distributors to carry their products if their product is unique, if there is high market growth, and if few direct competitors exist.

Anderson and Narus (1990) developed and tested a model of working partnerships between manufacturers and distributors. Relative dependence was found to be an important variable in their model. New ventures and independent, growth-oriented firms are typically the more dependent firms in marketing channel relationships. Study results suggest that the more dependent firm should seek ways to add value or lower costs in the exchange relationship, understand the expectations and alternatives available to their channel partner, develop trust in the relationship, and establish mechanisms for resolving the conflicts that will develop.

Buskirk (1987) notes the need to understand how large competitors use market exclusion tactics (even illegal ones) to attempt to bar the entrepreneur from the market, and how entrepreneurs may circumvent such moves. He also suggests that the use of joint venturing to access major distribution systems, direct marketing, and nonstore retailing is worthy of study.

Integrative conceptualizations.

The integrative strategy conceptualizations presented by Park, Jaworski, and MacInnis (1986), Day and Wensley (1988), and Lambkin and Day (1989) are sufficiently comprehensive to address marketing strategy relationships from the initiation of a new venture to the development of the venture into a large, mature firm. Each conceptualization offers a different perspective on marketing strategy.

Park, Jaworski, and MacInnis (1986) introduce a brand concept management framework for selecting, implementing, and controlling a brand image over time. They categorize the main stages of brand management as brand introduction, brand elaboration, and brand fortification. Different marketing strategies are suggested depending upon whether the firm is trying to maintain a functional, symbolic, or experimental image for the brand. The framework suggests appropriate marketing strategies for new ventures (brand introduction stage), the early stages of growth for the new venture (brand elaboration stage), and the later stages of growth, as the venture develops into a large, mature firm (brand fortification stage).

Day and Wensley (1988) conceptualize the process of achieving competitive advantage as transforming a firm's unique skills and/or resources into positional advantages in the marketplace by providing superior customer value or achieving lower relative cost. Since new ventures and independent, growth-oriented firms may typically have fewer or different skills and re-sources than larger firms, the marketing strategy development process and re-sulting strategies are likely to be different. Determining the appropriate positional advantages for a firm requires a balance between customer and competitor considerations. A number of marketing methods for examining competitors and customers are discussed, and many of these are potentially valuable to entrepreneurial firms.

Lambkin and Day (1989) propose a dynamic theory of market evolution based on concepts of population ecology theory. Their theory addresses the population growth process as markets evolve and the types of marketing strate-gies appropriate for each stage of market evolution. For example, their theory suggests that independent, new ventures are most likely to be successful when entering embryonic markets as market pioneers or mature markets as late en-trants. Niche strategies are the most appropriate in both of these situations. This theoretical framework is one of the few in the marketing strategy litera-ture that addresses marketing strategy considerations from the inception of a new venture and throughout the development of the firm and the market.

None of these integrative conceptualizations were developed specifically to address the marketing strategy situations faced by new ventures or indepen-dent, growth-oriented firms. However, all of the conceptualizations are based on a comprehensive and dynamic perspective on marketing strategy. Thus, they address marketing strategy situations relevant to entrepreneurial firms and have the potential to expand the domain of marketing strategy research to encompass new ventures and smaller, growth-oriented firms.

━━ ━━ ━━ ━━ ━━ ━━ ━━
IMPLEMENTATION AND CONTROL

The entrepreneurship literature has focused more on planning and launching ventures than on controlling the sales growth and success of the enterprise. Also, research and teaching in business colleges have had little to say about im-plementation, despite its critical importance. Implementation and execution under great uncertainty and severe resource constraints probably make this subject even more important in new ventures than in large, mature, and rela-tively stable firms. Although implementation is typically situation specific, a major research challenge is to seek new knowledge regarding this process as conducted by successful entrepreneurs.

Control of marketing function in 20 early growth, technology-based manu-facturing firms was studied by Boag (1987). The study found that, at least in some companies, the development of marketing control systems led to im-provements in market performance. Implementation of such systems often fol-lowed crises that threatened the firm's survival. Despite the general recogni-tion that uncontrolled sales growth is often disastrous, untapped research opportunities abound concerning how to control sales growth and monitor the effectiveness of marketing effort.

DEVELOPMENT OF THEORY : A BACKDROP

The consensus which exists in the philosophy of science literature concerning the essential morphology of a theory was summarized by Rudner (1966): 1) a theory is a systematically related set of statements, including some lawlike generalizations; 2) a theory is empirically testable; and 3) the purpose of a theory is to increase scientific understanding through a systematized structure capable of both explaining and predicting phenomena.

As is frequently stated, there is nothing more practical than a *good* theory. A theory must be able to explain and predict real-world phenomena. One need in the entrepreneurship field is to create an integrated framework within which entrepreneurship knowledge can be analyzed and utilized for the purposes of explanation and prediction (Mohan-Neill, Narayana, and Hills 1989). Ultimately this framework could lead to theory development that would facilitate predictions about the probability of the success or failure of new ventures. This would be exceptionally useful for budding entrepreneurs, and for venture capitalists and public policy makers as well. Although a lofty goal, it is the ultimate goal of all the sciences.

Logical empiricism is the dominant philosophical approach employed in marketing. However, in the marketing/entrepreneurship area, there are some drawbacks in adopting this philosophy. Deshpande (1983) argued that by adopting the strictly logical empiricist route, marketing scholars exclude alternative methodologies and are perhaps unknowingly constraining themselves to a set of only partially appropriate techniques for a limited subset of marketing problems. Reichardt and Cook (1979) suggest that quantitative methodology is more appropriate for theory validation and confirmation, and qualitative methodology more appropriate for theory discovery and generation. Significant effort should be devoted to qualitative theory generation in the marketing/entrepreneurship area. The school of discovery should receive considerable emphasis. Moving prematurely to the hypothesis-testing stage can retard the search for meaningful concepts and important explanatory variables.

FUTURE RESEARCH DIRECTIONS

Research at the marketing/entrepreneurship interface is in its infancy. Very little of the mainstream marketing literature explicitly addresses the area of entrepreneurship, despite the importance of the interface. Some progress has been made through the Research Symposia on Marketing and Entrepreneurship that have been conducted in recent years, but numerous research opportunities still exist.

General Research Directions

Researchers should balance their efforts toward theory discovery/generation and theory validation/confirmation. Theories and propositions that are developed need to be tested empirically using two different approaches. First, cross-sectional studies of firms with different characteristics are needed to establish differences in marketing relationships for new versus existing ventures, and small versus large firms. Most of the current marketing literature is based on large, mature firms, while most of the existing entrepreneurship literature is limited to new (and smaller) firms. Studies that incorporate firms with different characteristics are needed to integrate the entrepreneurship and marketing literatures.

Second, longitudinal studies of firms throughout all stages of development and all stages of market evolution are essential for adequate theory testing. Researchers need to identify new ventures being established at each stage of market evolution and continuously examine marketing practices and strategies as these firms develop and as their markets evolve. The findings of these longitudinal studies would illuminate the marketing/entrepreneurship interface.

Specific Research Propositions

Although more work needs to be done in generating propositions and developing theories, the marketing literature provides sufficient insight to introduce some tentative propositions in some areas.

Entry strategy propositions are presented in Table 7-2. These propositions are largely based on the theoretical work of Lambkin and Day (1989). The propositions suggest the appropriate entry timing for new, independent ventures and for corporate ventures, as well as the type of marketing strategy that should be employed.

Growth strategy propositions are presented in Table 7-3. These propositions are derived from the strategic brand concept introduced by Park, Jaworski, and MacInnis (1986). The propositions indicate the appropriate marketing strategies at different growth stages depending upon whether the firm is trying to maintain a functional, symbolic, or experiential brand concept.

Marketing mix propositions are presented in Table 7-4. These propositions are the result of a comprehensive examination of the marketing literature by Davis, Hills, and LaForge (1985). Specific propositions for each element of the marketing mix are presented.

The propositions offered in this section are admittedly tentative and only address a few of the important areas at the marketing/entrepreneurship inter-

TABLE 7–2 — Entry Strategy Propositions

PROPOSITION 1 :   Independent, new ventures are more likely to be
successful when they enter :

    a.   Embryonic markets as pioneers with a marketing strategy designed to achieve competitive advantage through factors other than economies of scale.

    b.   Maturing markets as late entrants with a marketing strategy that focuses on tailor-made products to market segments not served by market leaders.

PROPOSITION 2 :   Corporate new ventures are more likely to be
successful when they enter :

    a.   Developing markets that are related to markets currently served by the parent with a marketing strategy based on high-quality products, broad market scope, and close brand identification with the parent.

    b.   Maturing markets as late entrants with a marketing strategy based on scale economies and efficiencies.

TABLE 7–3 — Growth Strategy Propositions

PROPOSITION 1 :   New ventures conveying a functional brand
concept should base their growth on :

    a.   Problem-solving specialization and generalization strategies in the brand elaboration stage.

    b.   Image-bundling strategies through developing new concepts in the brand fortification stage.

PROPOSITION 2 :   New ventures conveying a symbolic brand
concept should base their growth on :

    a.   Marketing-shielding strategies in the brand elaboration stage.

    b.   Image-bundling strategies through developing new products with symbolic concepts in the brand fortification stage.

PROPOSITION 3 :   New ventures conveying an experiential brand
concept should base their growth on :

    a.   Brand accessory and brand network strategies in the brand elaboration stage.

    b.   Image-bundling strategies through developing new products with experiential concepts in the brand fortification stage.

TABLE 7–4 — Marketing Mix Propositions

PROPOSITION 1 :	New ventures and smaller, growth-oriented firms are more likely to be successful employing product strategies that emphasize substantial levels of service, unique and customized products, high-quality products, and/or strong brand identification.
PROPOSITION 2 :	New ventures and smaller, growth-oriented firms are more likely to be successful employing price strategies that de-emphasize price as competitive advantage, achieve high margins through high prices, and/or use a flexible approach to establish final price through negotiation.
PROPOSITION 3 :	New ventures and smaller, growth-oriented firms are likely to be successful employing promotion strategies that are different from those of their larger competitors, concentrate on targeted media and specialty advertising, utilize personal selling to gain competitive advantage, and/or are able to attract heavy publicity.
PROPOSITION 4 :	New ventures and small, growth-oriented firms are more likely to be successful employing distribution strategies that are affiliated with cooperative or franchised distribution arrangements and/or are based on using their unique information about customers to manage channel relationships effectively.

face. They do, however, provide a starting point for empirical research in this important area. The results of this research will produce new propositions, because this is the nature of scientific inquiry.

REFERENCES

Aaker, D. A., and K. L. Keller 1990 Consumer evaluations of brand extensions. *Journal of Marketing* 54 (1, January) : 27–41.

Anderson, J. C., and J. A. Narus 1990 A model of distributor firms and manufacturer firm working partnerships. *Journal of Marketing* 54 (1, January) : 42–58.

Andrus, D., D. W. Norvell, P. McIntyre, and L. Milner 1987 Marketing planning in *Inc.* 500 companies. In *Research at the marketing/entrepreneurship interface,* ed. G. E. Hills, 163–171. Chicago : Univ. of Illinois at Chicago.

Balasubramaniam, S. K., and V. Kumar 1990 Analyzing variations in advertising and promotional expenditures : Key correlates in consumer, industrial, and service markets. *Journal of Marketing* 54 (2, April) : 57–68.

Boag, D. A. 1987 Marketing control and performance in the technology-based company. In *Research at the marketing/entrepreneurship interface*, ed. G. E. Hills, 135–149. Chicago : Univ. of Illinois at Chicago.

Buskirk, R. H. 1987 Research opportunities in entrepreneurial marketing. In *Research at the marketing/entrepreneurship interface*, ed. G. E. Hills, 107–110. Chicago : Univ. of Illinois at Chicago.

Cravens, D. W., and G. E. Hills 1989 Examining the marketing strategy/performance relationship for new ventures. In *Research at the marketing/entrepreneurship interface*, eds. G. E. Hills, R. W. LaForge, and B. J. Parker, 33–46. Chicago: Univ. of Illinois at Chicago.

Cravens, D. W., G. E. Hills, R. W. LaForge, and D. A. Lunsford 1989 Toward a theory of marketing strategy for new ventures: Some preliminary propositions. In *Proceedings*, American Marketing Association Winter Educators' Conference.

Cravens, D. W., G. E. Hills, and R. B. Woodruff 1987 *Marketing management.* Homewood, Ill.: Richard D. Irwin.

Christensen, P. S., and R. Peterson 1990 Opportunity identification: Mapping the sources of new venture ideas. Working Paper Institute of Management, University of Aarhus.

Davis, C. D., G. E. Hills, and R. W. LaForge 1985 The marketing/small enterprise paradox: A research agenda. *International Small Business Journal* (Spring): 31–42.

Day, G. S., and R. Wensley 1988 Assessing advantage: A Framework for diagnosing competitive superiority. *Journal of Marketing* 52 (2, April): 1–20.

Dickson, P. R., and J. J. Giglierano 1986 Missing the boat and sinking the boat: A conceptual model of entrepreneurial risk. *Journal of Marketing* 50 (3, July): 58–70.

Drucker, P. F. 1985 *Innovation and entrepreneurship: Practice and principles.* New York: Harper and Row.

Farquhar, P. H. 1989 Competitive strategies in the race to get products to market. In *Research at the marketing/entrepreneurship interface*, eds. G. E. Hills, R. W. LaForge, and B. J. Parker, 247–254. Chicago: Univ. of Illinois at Chicago.

Gardner, D. M. 1983 The marketing concept: Its dimensions for the "big" small firm. In *Marketing and small business/entrepreneurship: Conceptual and research directions*, eds. G. E. Hills, D. J. Barnaby, and L. R. Duffus. Washington, D.C.: International Council for Small Business.

1991 Exploring the marketing/entrepreneurship interface. In *Research at the marketing/entrepreneurship interface*, eds. G. E. Hills and R. W. LaForge. Chicago: Univ. of Illinois at Chicago.

Gatignon, H., and T. S. Robertson 1989 Technology diffusion: An empirical test of competitive effects. *Journal of Marketing* 53 (1, January): 35–49.

Giglierano, J., C. Haughey, and J. Kallis 1989 Research on new product strategy: Implications from research on competitive strategies in new firms. In *Research at the marketing/entrepreneurship interface*, eds. G. E. Hills, R. W. LaForge, and B. J. Parker, 267–278. Chicago: Univ. of Illinois at Chicago.

Giglierano, J., and M. J. Kallis 1990 Critical issues in launching the second product. In *Research at the marketing/entrepreneurship interface*, eds. G. E. Hills, R. W. LaForge, and H. P. Welsch, 212–223. Chicago: Univ. of Illinois at Chicago.

Harwood, E. 1982 The sociology of entrepreneurship. In *Encyclopedia of entrepreneurship*, eds. C. Kent, D. Sexton, and K. Vesper, 92, 98. Englewood Cliffs, N.J.: Prentice-Hall, Inc.

Hills, G. E. 1981 Evaluating new ventures: A concept testing methodology. *Journal of Small Business Management* (October): 29–41.

1984 Market analysis and marketing in new ventures: Venture capitalists' perceptions. In *Frontiers of entrepreneurship research*, ed. K. Vesper, 167–182. Wellesley, Mass.: Babson College.

Hills, G. E., ed. 1987 *Research at the marketing/entrepreneurship interface.* Chicago: Univ. of Illinois at Chicago.

Hills, G. E., D. J. Barnaby, and L. R. Duffus 1983 *Marketing and small business/entrepreneurship: Conceptual and research directions.* Washington, D.C.: International Council for Small Business.

Hills, G. E., and R. W. LaForge, eds. 1991 *Research at the marketing/entrepreneurship interface.* Chicago: Univ. of Illinois at Chicago.

Hills, G. E., R. W. LaForge, and B. J. Parker, eds. 1989 *Research at the marketing/entrepreneurship interface.* Chicago: Univ. of Illinois at Chicago.

Hills, G. E., R. W. LaForge, and H. P. Welsch, eds. 1990 *Research at the marketing/entrepreneurship interface.* Chicago: Univ. of Illinois at Chicago.

Hills, G. E., and C.L. Narayana 1989 Success factors and marketing in highly successful firms. In *Frontiers of entrepreneurship research*, eds. R. H. Brockhaus et al., 69–80. Wellesley, Mass.: Babson College.

Hisrich, R. D. 1989 Marketing and entrepreneurship research interface. In *Research at the marketing/entrepreneurship interface*, eds. G. E. Hills, R. W. LaForge, and B. J. Parker, 3–17. Chicago: Univ. of Illinois at Chicago.

Hoy, F. 1987 Entrepreneurship in the management discipline: Coming of age. In *Research at the marketing/entrepreneurship interface*, ed. G. E. Hills, 283–286. Chicago: Univ. of Illinois at Chicago.

Hunt, K., J. C. Huefner, C. Voegele, and P. B. Robinson 1987 The entrepreneurial consumer. In *Research at the marketing/entrepreneurship interface*, eds. G. E. Hills, R. W. LaForge, and B. J. Parker, 175–184. Chicago: Univ. of Illinois at Chicago.

Jacobson, R., and D. A. Aacker 1987 The strategic role of product quality. *Journal of Marketing* 51 (4, October): 31–44.

Jain, S. C. 1985 *Marketing planning and strategy.* Cincinnati, Ohio: South-Western Publishing Co.

Karakaya, F., and M. J. Stahl 1989 Barriers to entry and market entry decisions in consumer and industrial goods markets. *Journal of Marketing* 53 (2, April): 80–91.

Kent, C. A., Sexton, D. L., and K. H. Vesper 1982 *Encyclopedia of entrepreneurship.* Englewood Cliffs, N.J.: Prentice-Hall, Inc.

Kosnik, T. J., and R. T. Moriarty 1989 High-tech vs. low-tech marketing: What's the difference? In *Research at the marketing/entrepreneurship interface*, eds. G. E. Hills, R. W. LaForge, and B. J. Parker, 321–336. Chicago: Univ. of Illinois at Chicago.

Kotler, P. 1972 A generic concept of marketing. *Journal of Marketing* 36(2): 46–54.

LaForge, R. W., and S. J. Miller 1987 The moderating effects of company size on business level marketing strategies. In *Research at the marketing/entrepreneurship interface*, ed. G. E. Hills, 54–64. Chicago: Univ. of Illinois at Chicago.

Lambkin, M., and G. S. Day 1989 Evolutionary processes in competitive markets: Beyond the product life cycle. *Journal of Marketing* 53 (3, July): 4–20.

Lunsford, D. A. 1990 Differences in product diversification strategy across the business life cycle. In *Research at the marketing/entrepreneurship interface*, eds. G. E. Hills, R. W. LaForge, and H. P. Welsch, 3–16. Chicago: Univ. of Illinois at Chicago.

Lunsford, D. A., and R. W. LaForge 1987 Toward a taxonomy of marketing strategy constructs. In *Proceedings*, American Marketing Association Winter Educators' Conference, 182–186.

Lunsford, D. A., R. W. LaForge, and S. J. Miller 1989 Corporate marketing strategies in emerging growth-oriented firms: An initial investigation. In *Research at the marketing/entrepreneurship interface*, eds. G. E. Hills, R. W. LaForge, and B. J. Parker, 255–266. Chicago: Univ. of Illinois at Chicago.

Mahajan, V. R., E. Muller, and F. M. Bass 1990 New product diffusion models in marketing: A review and directions for research. *Journal of Marketing* 54 (1): 1–26.

McDaniel, S. W., and J. W. Kolari 1987 Marketing strategy implications of the Miles and Snow strategic typology. *Journal of Marketing* 51 (4, October): 19–30.

Mohan-Neill, S., C. Narayana, and G. E. Hills 1989 Strategic amoeboid model for entrepreneurship: A theoretical framework for entrepreneurship. In *Research at the marketing/entrepreneurship interface*, eds. G. E. Hills, R. W. LaForge, and H. P. Welsch, 301–321. Chicago: Univ. of Illinois at Chicago.

Morris, M. H., and G. W. Paul 1987 The relationship between entrepreneurship and marketing in established firms. *Journal of Business Venturing* 2 (3, Summer): 247–259.

Park, C. W., B. J. Jaworski, and D. J. MacInnis 1986 Strategic brand concept-image management. *Journal of Marketing* 50 (4, October): 135–145.

Peterson, R. T. 1989 Small business adoption of the marketing concept vs. other business strategies. *Journal of Small Business Management* (January): 38–47.

Rao, V. R., and E. W. McLaughlin 1989 Modeling the decision to add new products by channel intermediaries. *Journal of Marketing* 53 (1, January): 80–88.

Reichardt, C. S., and T. C. Cook 1979 Beyond qualitative versus quantitative methods. In *Qualitative and quantitative methods in evaluation research*, eds. T. D. Cook and C. S. Reichardt. Beverly Hills, Cal.: Sage Publications.

Robinson, W. T. 1988 Sources of market pioneer advantages: The case of industrial goods industries. *Journal of Marketing Research* 25 (1, February): 87–94.

Robinson, W. T., and C. Fornell 1985 Sources of market pioneer advantages in consumer goods industries. *Journal of Marketing Research* 22 (3, August): 305–317.

Robinson, R. B., Jr., and J. A. Pearce 1984 Research thrusts in small firm strategic planning. *Academy of Management Review* 9: 129–130.

Rudner, R. S. 1966 *Philosophy of social science*. Englewood Cliffs, N.J.: Prentice-Hall, Inc.

Sexton, D. L., and N. Bowman-Upton 1987 A growth model of the firm based on market, owner, and strategic factors. In *Research at the marketing/entrepreneurship interface*, ed. G. E. Hills. Chicago: Univ. of Illinois at Chicago.

Sheth, J. N., D. M. Gardner, and D. E. Garrett 1988 *Marketing theory: Evolution and evaluation*. New York: John Wiley & Sons.

Spitzer, D. M., Jr., G. E. Hills, and P. Alpar 1989 Marketing planning and research among high technology entrepreneurs. In *Research at the marketing/entrepreneurship interface*, eds. G. E. Hills, R. W. LaForge, and B. J. Parker, 411–422. Chicago: Univ. of Illinois at Chicago.

Stevenson, H., and J.-C. Jarillo-Mossi 1986 Preserving entrepreneurship as companies grow. *Journal of Business Strategy* 7: 10–23.

Tauber, E. M. 1977 Forecasting sales prior to test market. *Journal of Marketing* 41(1): 80–84.

Tellis, G. J. 1986 Beyond the many faces of price: An integration of pricing strategies. *Journal of Marketing* 50 (4, October): 146–160.

Varadarajan, P. 1989 Product diversity and firm performance: An empirical investigation. *Journal of Marketing* 50 (3, July): 43–57.

Varadarajan, P., and D. Rajaratnam 1986 Symbiotic marketing revisited. *Journal of Marketing* 50 (1, January): 7–17.

Walker, O. C., Jr., and R. W. Ruekert 1987 Marketing's role in the implementation of business strategies : A critical review and conceptual framework. *Journal of Marketing* 51 (3, July) : 15–33.

Wind, Y., and T. Robertson 1983 Marketing strategy : New directions for theory and research. *Journal of Marketing* 47 (2, Spring) : 12–25.

Woodruff, R. B., and E. R. Cadotte 1987 Analyzing market opportunities for new ventures. *Survey of Business* (Summer) : 10–15.

Wortman, M. S., M. S. Spann, and M. Adams 1989 The interface of entrepreneurship and marketing : Concepts and research perspectives. In *Research at the marketing / entrepreneurship interface*, eds. G. E. Hills, R. W. LaForge, and B. J. Parker, 117–137. Chicago : Univ. of Illinois at Chicago.

Chapter

8

Methods in Our Madness?
Trends in Entrepreneurship
Research

Howard E. Aldrich

●

INTRODUCTION

People who study entrepreneurship exhibit a certain sort of madness in their passion for the subject. This zest for the substance of entrepreneurship is what makes the field so attractive to many of us who are refugees from other, more boring fields. It also, however, occasionally draws stares of disbelief from adherents of older, more established fields, who are suspicious of anyone who is excited about an academic subject. Outsiders scrutinize our research closely, looking for flaws that will confirm their worst suspicions that our madness is certifiable.

In earlier reviews of the state of the art in entrepreneurship research, several authors have confronted this negative stereotype. They have asked, implicitly, is there method in our madness? Are researchers using methods of investigation that enrich our knowledge of entrepreneurship? Have we made progress since the days when no self-respecting business school even offered a course in entrepreneurship, and starting a business was something you did when you failed to make a career out of management? Is this even a fair question to ask?

In this chapter, I first review what authors have said about entrepreneurship research in two previous reviews of the literature, and then assess the state of the art since 1985. Insofar as possible, I have maintained continuity in the methods of investigating the trends in entrepreneurship research by following the lead of my predecessors.

■■ ■■ ■■ ■■ ■■ ■■ ■■ ■■ ■■
WHAT MY PREDECESSORS
HAVE SAID

In preparing my review, I looked back at the chapters in the previous state of the art in entrepreneurship texts. In the earlier chapters, Spaulding (1982) reviewed 81 previous studies, beginning with Schumpeter (1936), Wortman (1986) reviewed 49 papers published between 1981 and 1984, and Churchill and Lewis (1986) reviewed 291 journal abstracts and 150 conference papers, also published between 1981 and 1984.

State of the Art in 1980

Paulin, Coffey, and Spaulding (1982) used a nonrandom sampling of a large number of studies to achieve a broad perspective on methods and topics. They developed an elaborate classification scheme, consisting of five dimensions: research purpose, research strategy, research design, data collection techniques, and data recording and analysis techniques. Within each of these classifications, there were further subcategories. They did not report their results in quantitative form, but instead presented a bibliography, with research studies classified according to topic area, and with a notation after each entry indicating what research strategies were used.

Most of their review is devoted to an elaboration of their classification scheme, with comments on the usefulness or appropriateness of various designs and techniques. Accordingly, we learned a great deal about how the authors felt about various techniques, but not really very much about how these research designs or applications were put into practice. One can glean from the text, however, a number of generalizations. They noted that the literature contained quite a few informal, anecdotal schemes developed from nonsystematic research designs — about a quarter of the studies fell into this category. Approximately 64 percent of the sampled studies used surveys, but no information was given on the size of the samples.

Only a few examples of field studies — typically longitudinal — were found in their review. They found very few field experiments, and no laboratory experiments, experimental simulations, or computer simulations.

Their category of "research design" overlapped somewhat with the category of "research strategy," as well as with "data collection techniques." They found that 52 percent of the studies used a descriptive or case study design. About 15 percent of the studies used what they called a "non-methodological" design. They spotted a trend toward more comparative designs, with researchers identifying dependent and independent variables, and identifying subgroups and control groups.

As for data collection techniques, 35 percent of the studies used questionnaires, and 48 percent used interviews. Another 5 percent used direct observation. The other 12 percent apparently were based upon "contemplation." Paulin, Coffey, and Spaulding distinguished between questionnaires and interviews on the basis that interviews require personal interaction between researchers and subjects, whereas questionnaires do not.

These reviewers noted that both qualitative and quantitative techniques were used frequently in all types of research, but they did not expand on this observation. They mentioned the kinds of statistical techniques that were available to investigators at the time, but did not indicate the frequency with which these techniques were used.

The authors summed up their review of research methods with the following statement:

> We found more formal research on entrepreneurship than we had anticipated. Much of the earlier work tended to use non-methodological, contemplative, or anecdotal methods. But a definite trend to more systematic, empirical methods has begun in recent years. Although more explanatory and correlational designs are being employed, exploratory sample survey approaches, descriptive or case study designs, questionnaires and interviews are still the predominant methodologies in the field. (361–362)

When they turned to future directions for entrepreneurship research, they had some very specific suggestions. They asked that investigators state more precisely their propositions in forms which could be tested. They asked for explicit hypotheses, and fewer normative checklists. They argued that much of the "knowledge" in the field was based on untested or narrowly based anecdotal wisdom.

Their remedy to these problems was a call for more systematic research studies. In addition to sample survey and descriptive research methods, they called for more critical incident techniques, field studies, and even field experiments. They wanted more longitudinal studies, and studies that used a variety of methods to reduce the chance of method-bound conclusions. They also asked for more face-to-face interviews and direct observations. Finally, they wanted more comparative and correlation-based research. By "comparative," they did not mean international, but rather comparison across distinct subgroups. And by "correlational," they were not referring to statistical techniques, but rather to the idea that the form and strength of relationships ought to be established.

They concluded their review by noting that the specific choice of a research design must depend upon the topic chosen and also the state of prior research and theory. They were not making a blanket call for methodological rigor for its own sake. Instead, they were linking improvements in research to improvements in knowledge across a number of distinctive topic areas.

Their paper was followed by a very critical rebuttal, delivered by Peterson and Horvath (1982). These authors argued that we should not be so apologetic about our methods, given the young state of the field, nor should we simply exhort young researchers to do better. They felt that the sample of 81 papers was not terribly representative, and should not really be trusted as an index of the state of the field. They noted that most of the papers were from the United States, but entrepreneurship is strongly value-laden and thus cross-national studies ought to be included when considering the state of the art. They were also critical of the 25 category classification schemes used by the authors, saying that 81 papers could not really be used to test such a complex theoretical structure.

More importantly, they argued that the authors did not indicate the unanswered research issues uncovered in their research. What methodological difficulties were faced by earlier researchers, and how could those be overcome? They felt that rather than focus on "the best method" for doing research, investigators ought to be concerned with defining research questions precisely and meaningfully.

In a second critical commentary, Perryman (1982) was more sympathetic to Paulin and his colleagues, arguing that entrepreneurship research was then in the "pre-science" phase of the Kuhnian scientific structure (Kuhn 1970). This phase is characterized by the absence of a definitive set of precepts and by disagreement on accepted methodological procedures. Perryman argued that we should *not* move toward precise theory and verification at this stage.

Instead, his recommendation was for the chaos of the present to continue, apparently by investigators continuing to use whatever methods they felt appropriate, as long as authors reported their studies in full detail. He quoted with approval Sherlock Holmes' dictum that "It is a capital mistake to theorize before you have all the evidence. It biases the judgment" (Perryman 1982, 378).

State of the Art in 1985

Apparently by 1985 we had made so much progress in research strategies that two chapters were needed to cover the field: Wortman (1986) and Churchill and Lewis (1986).

Wortman (1986) reviewed two streams of literature — one on entrepreneurship and one on small business — by reviewing journals, dissertation abstracts, the Babson College Entrepreneurship Conference proceedings, and the proceedings from three other management conferences. Wortman's paper fulfilled a double function, as it proposed a unified framework which would bring together entrepreneurship research and small business research, and it also reviewed the methods of inquiry used in the two fields. Wortman reviewed the small business and entrepreneurship literatures separately, providing tables for each of these research streams. Although Wortman made reference to several chapters in the *Encyclopedia of Entrepreneurship,* he did not refer to the

Paulin, Coffey, and Spaulding (1982) paper which had critiqued the research efforts in the area prior to 1980.

Wortman examined only survey data-oriented research studies on entrepreneurship, arguing that case studies were not worth reviewing because the field had been overwhelmed by exploratory studies. He also excluded studies with students as subjects, and studies of management assistance programs and agencies. And he included only the United States and Canada in his sample.

He classified the research by type of organization studied, sample size, research methods, statistical methods, issues explored, and the content of the study. As in the Paulin, Coffey, and Spaulding (1982) paper, he did not present this information in the form of frequencies and percentages, but rather had a table of all the articles, giving the actual summary description of each one in the table. For the purposes of my own discussion, I ignore his review of the small business segment and concentrate on the entrepreneurship segment.

Wortman presented the results of his review in three paragraphs. He noted that most of the studies used mailed questionnaires or interviews. He also observed that over the five-year period studied, there was little change in the use of statistics. His most negative comment was:

Strangely enough, entrepreneurship researchers are still using raw data in many of their studies with an emphasis upon percentages. Considering the level of statistical sophistication in the past 25 years, it is surprising that more efforts at explanation of the data in terms of relationships and cause-and-effect have not been attempted. When statistics are used, they generally are at a relatively unsophisticated level such as means, standard deviations, ranking, T-tests, and linear correlation. (298)

Of the 51 studies on entrepreneurship which Wortman reviewed, all but three were based on surveys using either questionnaires or face-to-face interviews. Apparently his definition of "case study" also excluded field methods, and he clearly had a much narrower definition of appropriate methodologies than Paulin, Coffey, and Spaulding (1982). He did not mention laboratory studies, ethnographic field work, modelling and simulation, or the use of more descriptive or anecdotal evidence. Given this rather narrow focus, and the fact that only 51 studies were selected to represent the entrepreneurship field, we might be a bit skeptical about his conclusions.

At a number of points in his chapter, Wortman argued very strongly for a unified, overall framework. He argued that we needed fewer case studies and more studies which are targeted to a specific population or sample and which "utilize appropriate statistical techniques that would lead to the external validity of the studies. Moreover, statistical techniques to check the reliability of the data and of the instruments used should be employed" (325). He felt very strongly that researchers were using statistical techniques that were too simple, and that much more sophisticated techniques were available. He argued that the use of increasingly sophisticated techniques of analysis should be tied to the use of a unified framework.

In contrast to Wortman's paper, Churchill and Lewis (1986) explicitly made reference to the paper by Paulin, Coffey, and Spaulding (1982). They were also much clearer about the framework for their study, and much more eclectic in their inclusion of studies from 10 different journals. They used the ABI/INFORM data base and searched for entries which contained any variation of four key words: entrepreneur, small business, corporate venturing, and intrapreneur. When they narrowed the search to 1981 through 1984, and just looked at the 10 major journals, they obtained 298 abstracts for further investigation. In addition to this journal data base, they also examined articles published in the proceedings of the four Babson conferences between 1981 and 1984, and one at Harvard in 1983. This produced 150 research papers for the conference data base. They then classified each item in the data bases by methodology, topic, research objective, and centrality to the core issues of entrepreneurship. They admitted that some of these classifications were rather difficult to make, and thus the resulting categorizations were ambiguous. In my review, I focus solely on methodology and the authors' critical comments.

Like Paulin and colleagues (1982) before them, Churchill and Lewis emphasized that the field of entrepreneurship research was still in its infancy, that the definition of entrepreneurship itself is neither agreed upon nor static, and that the field is still evolving. Hence, they were prepared to find that research directions were fragmented, creative, and diverse.

To provide a baseline for evaluating the entrepreneurship field, they reviewed the fields of business policy and marketing. From these reviews — and *before* presenting the results of their analysis — they drew a number of implications. They concluded that considerable emphasis on exploratory research is justified because the field is at such an early stage, with little theory to guide it, and we should emphasize substance, not method. Care should be taken not to use techniques which put words in the mouths of the people being studied. The case studies which we are so fond of have considerable use, but they should be carried further by embedding them in an historical context and trying to build on what others have done.

They noted a conflict in business policy and marketing between academicians who want to pursue science for its own sake and others who are more interested in applying their knowledge to the broader problems of society. A heavily practice-oriented discipline has some difficulties which more theory-oriented disciplines do not have. For example, a practice-oriented field may take much from other disciplines and return little to them. A focus on practice may contribute little toward generic understanding and also fail to provide a base upon which theoretical understanding can be built. On the positive side, practice-oriented studies can provide feedback to researchers on the accuracy of their perceptions, and hence contribute to a greater understanding of entrepreneurs and entrepreneurship.

The heart of their paper, for the purposes of my discussion, is the analysis of research methodology used by the 298 studies investigated. In Table 8–1, I show the definitions they used to classify studies into six methodology catego-

TABLE 8–1 — Description of Research Methodologies Used by Churchill and Lewis (1986)

Journalistic (vignette or "reportage") : Refers generally to organizational or personal histories ; case studies without conclusions, generalizations, or hypothesis-building ; journalistic reporting of events or circumstances, or about people and / or organizations ; and to a more or less straightforward setting forth of the facts, particularly with regard to new or proposed legislation, government programs, etc. (in the latter case without bringing forth discussion of broader policy issues).

Armchair (observational and contemplative theory building) : Either anecdotal or formal theory that is based on one or more of the following : contemplation, experiential learning, hypothesized relationships between or among variables, or literature review (general).

Survey : Surveys using for the most part random sampling of larger populations based on questionnaires, tests, interviews, or a combination thereof.

Public data base : Surveys based upon review of data from public or private archival sources, e.g., Dun & Bradstreet credit files, industry data bases ("archival survey" of Paulin, Coffey, and Spaulding 1982).

Ethnography (field study) : Direct observation of phenomena in natural settings, usually longitudinal in nature (see Paulin 361, note 1).

Computer simulation or modeling : Mathematical theory building allowing manipulation of variables in a nonexperimental way (see Paulin 361, note 1).

Source : Churchill and Lewis (1986, 303), as modified by the author.

ries, with new labels in a few cases. (They had a category for laboratory experiments, but found none.) In Table 8–2, columns 1 and 2, I show the distribution of the 298 journal articles and 150 conference papers across the six methodology categories.

As the table shows, the modal methods category is armchair (observational and contemplative) theory building, which is the category that Wortman dismissed. As for the other five categories, which more closely resemble the traditional concept we have of empirical research methodologies, a great majority were based on surveys. Thirty-three percent of the total sample, and almost 60 percent of the noncontemplative theory building articles, used surveys. The next most important category was journalistic vignettes, a category which Wortman probably also would dismiss as "mere case studies." Churchill and Lewis found 25 studies which used public data, such as Dun & Bradstreet credit files, or industry data bases. They found only 15 field studies, confirming the observations of Paulin, Coffey, and Spaulding (1982). Finally, they uncovered only two cases of computer simulation or modelling.

Because of the dominance of survey methods, a cross-tabulation of "methods used" by "topics studied" is not terribly enlightening, and Churchill and Lewis really had little to say about this. The majority of the articles — 63 percent — dealt with improving the *practice* of entrepreneurship. They found only six studies, all presented at conferences, that dealt primarily with method-

TABLE 8–2 — Research Methods Used in Entrepreneurship Articles, 1981–1990

METHODOLOGY	1981–1984		1986	1989	1985–1990	
	Journals	Conferences	Babson	Babson	Journals	
					I	II
	%	%	%	%	%	%
Journalistic	15	11	3	3	12	40
Armchair	54	23	3	0	28	54
Survey	24	53	78	72	43	0
(Mailed)	(NA)	(NA)	(36)	(42)	(21)	(0)
(Other)	(NA)	(NA)	(42)	(30)	(22)	(0)
Public data	4	9	9	16	17	2
Ethnography	3	3	6	9	0	4
Computer simulation	0	1	1	0	0	0
Total percent	100	100	100	100	100	100
Total number	(298)	(150)	(67)	(74)	(124)	(57)

Source : 1981–84 Churchill and Lewis (1986, 345).
1985–1990 Author's tabulations.

ological improvements. They noted that these dealt for the most part with building data bases, such as the Dun & Bradstreet credit files data base.

Churchill and Lewis devoted very little attention to research practices, or how they might be improved. They did not mention which methods they thought needed more work, although they did mention that the microdata studies of David Birch deserve more attention. Their summative critical comment was that most studies still used a combination of questionnaire and interview techniques.

In addition to Wortman, and Churchill and Lewis, Carsrud, Olm, and Eddy (1986) also provided a review of the literature and explored what is wrong with statistical analyses and research methodologies. In keeping with some of the comments we have seen before, they felt that investigators were spending excessive amounts of time on descriptive statistics concerning a particular group and on elaborate case study approaches. They argued that these approaches provided valuable information, but were largely descriptive and did not establish adequate causal connections. Such studies prevented researchers from judging the relative direct, indirect, and interactive causal effects of various micro- and macrolevel variables.

The alternative they proposed was a more extensive use of multivariate regression analyses, with independent and dependent variables measured on ordinal or interval scales. They quoted with approval Wortman's argument that the level of methodological and statistical sophistication in most empirical studies was quite low. They also noted that linear models may not be able to capture the richness of entrepreneurial actions, and that we may need to find more sophisticated techniques.

Following Wortman, they proposed a unified research paradigm, which included psychological, organizational, and environmental variables. In this respect they were more specific than Wortman, who simply lamented the lack of an overarching framework, and they suggested a comprehensive categorization scheme for the variables that might go into such a framework. Churchill and Lewis resisted the temptation to propose a particular framework, and instead simply suggested a set of five broad research categories which needed further attention.

Summary of the State of the Art, 1980–1985

If we believe these authors, things had not changed very much between the first and second conferences. Investigators still relied heavily upon nonsystematic methods of data collection, and when they ventured out to collect data, they depended heavily upon surveys. Few investigators conducted ethnographic field studies, and fewer still used publicly available data sets.

To analyze their data, most investigators used very simple statistical techniques. The feeling conveyed in these reviews is of a very rich, creative, and vibrant field, hampered by lack of investigator imagination when it came to actually collecting data to test ideas.

But what view of *science* did these authors have in mind? A few clearly thought of entrepreneurship as a field which could and should develop a unified theoretical framework. Others, and this includes not only the people writing methods chapters but also those writing the other substantive chapters of the two books in which these reviews were published, clearly had a much more eclectic view of the field.

■■ ■■ ■■ ■■ ■■ ■■ ■■ ■■
WHAT IMPLICIT NORMS GOVERN RESEARCH IN ENTREPRENEURSHIP ?

Have we made *progress* in research on entrepreneurship over the past decade ? One's answer to this question depends upon one's assumptions about the scientific and normative structure of our field. We can consider three possible viewpoints : a unitary, normal science view ; a multiple paradigms view ; and a totally pragmatic, antipositivist view.

First, if one adopts a "normal science" approach to organizational theorizing, what indicators would we seek ? Paulin, Coffey, and Spaulding (1982) ; Wortman (1986) ; and Carsrud, Olm, and Eddy (1986) explicitly made comparisons between the state of the field as they found it and an ideal based upon a model of normal science. After observing the relation between research and theory, they were quite critical. Their ideal was the accumulation of empirically tested hypotheses and well-grounded generalizations.

From this view, we will not be able to take our place with the other social sciences until the field takes a normal science approach to theorizing and research — using rigorous research designs, collecting quantitative data, adopting the latest statistical techniques, conducting replications, publishing negative findings, searching for confirming findings, and so forth.

Second, Perryman (1982), and Churchill and Lewis (1986) took a much more eclectic view of entrepreneurship research, emphasizing the importance of diversity in theories and methods. From this viewpoint, the various subgroups of entrepreneurship researchers — those concerned with personality theories, industrial economics theories, ecological theories, and so forth — have achieved significant standing today because, at their core, they have groups of dedicated researchers working on empirical research to test ideas derived from the perspectives. Multiple perspectives can have an invigorating effect on organizational research, causing investigators to stretch their minds to cope with apparently contradictory views.

If we adopt a multiple paradigms perspective, we would neither expect nor wish for complete convergence in methods of entrepreneurship research. Different subfields would have different standards against which to judge research design and execution.

Third, if one adopts a more pragmatic (dare one say "postmodern"?) approach, and simply asks whether entrepreneurship research is tackling important questions, the issue of research methods assumes secondary importance. Peterson and Horvath (1982) argued that we should focus on the questions asked, not the methods used, and that those questions ought to be meaningful. Giola, Donnellon, and Sims (1989, 524) contrasted an "interpretive" with a "positivist" paradigm and argued that "when one adopts different 'lenses' with which to view ostensibly the same organizational phenomena, one simply 'sees' different things."

From this point of view, methods should be chosen to match researchers' purposes, and these will change as the times change. Topical considerations will govern what issues are researched, and changing social and economic conditions will drive research practice, not abstract methodological concerns.

In looking over the past five years of entrepreneurship research, I tried to keep in mind these three rather different views of the research enterprise.

THE PAST FIVE YEARS

As a strong believer in research continuity, I decided to use the same strategy as my predecessors in organizing and defining the field of entrepreneurship research. The Babson College Entrepreneurship Conference is the premier venue for disseminating unpublished research on entrepreneurship, and I examined all the articles and summaries in the 1986 and 1989 conference volumes. I followed Churchill and Lewis's tactic and chose the same 10 academic journals which have published a large number of entrepreneurship articles, with one addition — the *Journal of Business Venturing,* which began publishing articles on entrepreneurship in 1985.

Preliminary inspection of the types of articles published indicated that the journals fell naturally into two groups: Group I, which published primarily empirical articles, and Group II, which published primarily conceptual or "think" pieces. Thus, results are presented separately for these two groups. The journals are listed in Appendix A, classified into the two groups, along with the number of articles found in each source.

I searched the abstracts in the ABI/INFORM data base, just as Paulin, Coffey, and Spaulding (1982) and Churchill and Lewis (1986) did, to identify a population of articles for further study. Paulin, Coffey, and Spaulding (1982) searched for the key words "entrepreneur" and "research methods," whereas Churchill and Lewis (1986) searched for four key words: entrepreneur, small business, corporate venturing, and intrapreneur. I dropped "small business," because my focus is on entrepreneurship, and searched only for the other three key words. I also dropped "research methods" as a key word, preferring to include *all* types of studies. The search turned up 182 articles, which were coded using the scheme presented in Appendix B. Every article and paper analyzed in this chapter was read from beginning to end. Combined with the 146 Babson papers, the total sample size was 328.

Results : Methods and Scope

Research design and methods of data collection have not changed very much from the early 1980s, as shown in Table 8–2. The Babson Conference's success in demanding only papers based on solid data shows up in the very low acceptance rate for journalistic essays and papers based on "armchair theories." Disregarding the journalistic and "armchair theory" papers, Churchill and Lewis's showed that about three-quarters of the journal articles and conference papers in 1981 through 1984 relied on survey data. A very similar percentage of the 1986 and 1989 Babson Conference papers used surveys, as did the recent articles in Group I journals. By contrast, 94 percent of the Group II journal articles were either journalistic or amateurish. Entrepreneurship research is still very much a mono-method field, in spite of repeated calls for the field to free itself from dependence on mailed surveys and related questionnaire-based methods.

Given the increasing number of publicly available data sets, and the openness of governments and some private firms to make their records available, the low number of articles based on public data sets is somewhat surprising. About one in seven conference papers in 1981 through 1984 were based on such data, a ratio that did not appreciably change at the 1989 Babson Conference or in the Group I journals. Computer simulations and laboratory experiments were not popular before 1980, and they have not come into fashion since then.

Ethnographies — observation-based field studies — have also been slow to catch on. Fewer than 1 in 10 of the data-based journal and conference papers identified by Churchill and Lewis used field methods, and that was still true at the 1989 Babson Conference. None of the articles published in the Group I journals from 1985 to 1990 utilized systematic field observation techniques.

Research design issues involve not only data collection but also the dilemma of selecting the scope of the research : what level of analysis, which populations, what time span, and so forth. Previous state-of-the-art reviews mentioned these issues, but presented no data on how investigators had resolved them. In Table 8–3, I present data on five research scope issues.

Churchill and Lewis (1986) attempted to cover the range of research topics with a 15-category scheme, and I would have needed many more categories to cover the additional themes introduced in the late 1980s. I chose only one topic for detailed investigation : the extent to which articles focused on the traits of entrepreneurs versus other themes. The great majority of articles in the past five years have *not* focused on entrepreneurs' personality traits, as shown in the first row of Table 8–3. Indeed, the percent of Babson Conference papers stressing personal traits actually declined somewhat between 1986 and 1989. However, the "traits" theme is still alive in Group II journals, as one-quarter emphasized an entrepreneur's personality traits.

Implicit in every article on entrepreneurship is a decision about the extent of heterogeneity in the business population, and whether the concepts developed or the results discovered apply to the entire population or only to parts of

TABLE 8–3 — Scope of Research : All 1985–1990 Articles

SCOPE OF RESEARCH	1986 Babson	1989 Babson	1985–1990 Journals I	1985–1990 Journals II
	%	%	%	%
Focus on personality traits	18	13	15	25
Homogeneous business population identified as the focus	24	17	11	14
Explicit longitudinal orientation	10	32	44	56
More than one nation studied	4	9	8	18
Included a non–United States nation	35	28	21	23

Source : Author's tabulations.

it. In another context, McKelvey and Aldrich (1983) described this as the issue of "are all organizations alike, or is each unique, or is there a middle ground ?" Authors who draw illustrations of their ideas indiscriminately from all industries, and investigators who draw samples of businesses from convenient lists, are clearly operating on the principle that all organizations are pretty much alike. Authors who devote entire articles to only one organization and who disdain explicit comparisons with other organizations are operating on the principle that each organization is unique. By contrast, some authors explicitly limit their scope to specific types of organizations, such as gasoline stations, venture capital firms, and semiconductor manufacturers.

Most entrepreneurship researchers study and write about businesses without regard to possible subpopulation limits to generalizations, as shown in the second row of Table 8–3. In 1989, only 17 percent of the Babson Conference papers focused on a specific homogeneous business population, as most chose very heterogeneous groups of organizations for study. This tendency was especially pronounced in the journal articles published in 1985–1990. Only slightly more than 1 in 10 articles — in both journal groups — focused on a particular population to which their concepts or results applied. Indeed, only 6 of the 108 journalistic and "armchair theory" papers from the Babson Conference and the journals identified a homogeneous business population. Instead, most were written as if their principles or generalizations were universal and could be safely applied to any industry.

In previous books, authors decried the scarcity of dynamic and longitudinal studies. The Babson Conference papers changed notably in that regard, as shown in the third row of Table 8–3 — in 1989, almost one-third of the Babson papers were explicitly longitudinal in orientation. About 44 percent of the Group I journals and 56 percent of the Group II journals were longitudinal in orientation, but this figure is deceptive, because many of these were journalistic or "armchair" pieces, rather than empirical.

Peterson and Horvath's (1982) call for more cross-national research was partially answered by 1989, as the percent of Babson papers that included more than one nation jumped from 4 to 9 percent. The percent for journals was similar, at 8 percent for Group I and 18 percent for Group II. I suspect, however, that Peterson and Horvath would not be satisfied with these fairly low totals. More interesting is the fairly high proportion of papers and articles which include a non–United States nation : 28 percent for the 1989 Babson Conference and slightly over 20 percent for the journals.

The difference between these two figures illustrates something about the diffusion of entrepreneurship research cross-culturally. Scholars in other countries, mostly Canada and western Europe, have adopted concepts and methods from their U.S. colleagues and have applied them to local entrepreneurial studies. Few have formed collaborative relationships or research teams with U.S. scholars that would permit them to research entrepreneurship on a truly comparative basis.

TABLE 8–4 — Research Design and Analytic Methods Used for Survey and Public Data Base Studies, 1985–1990

	1986 Babson	1989 Babson	1985–1989 Journals I
Research design	%	%	%
Explicit longitudinal data collection	9	29	26
More than one nation studied	5	6	4
Included a non–United States nation	33	28	18
Identified a homogeneous population	22	16	19
Explicitly sampled from an identifiable sampling frame	50	35	62
Sample : response rate			
0– 24	25	29	(25)
25– 49	35	38	(25)
50– 74	20	17	(19)
75–100	20	17	(31)
Total percent	100	101	100
Total number	(20)	(24)	(16)

Research Design and Analytic Methods

In discussing research methods and scope, I included many articles which some people would not consider "research." Certain research issues are simply not relevant when journalistic and "armchair" theorizing are included in the pool of articles. Accordingly, I turn now to just those papers and articles which used survey or public/archival data. Because almost all of the articles in Group II journals were "armchair" or journalistic, those journals are excluded from Table 8–4. In addition to excluding journalistic and "armchair" theory papers, I also excluded 13 ethnographies and one computer simulation, as these will be discussed separately.

Longitudinal studies climbed into prominence between 1986 and 1989 at the Babson Conference, rising to 29 percent of all survey and archival studies, as shown in row one of Table 8–4. One reason for this jump was a doubling in the number of studies using public or archival data bases — from 6 to 12 — as half of these studies followed entrepreneurs or businesses over time. About 26 percent of the journal articles used data collected over time, and the sharp difference between this figure and the 44 percent for journals in Table 8–3 is a result of the exclusion of journalistic and "armchair" theorizing. As with the Babson papers, about half — 22 out of 40 — of the public or archival-based journal articles followed cases over time.

TABLE 8–4, continued

	1986 Babson	1989 Babson	1985–1990 Journals I
All Studies : Number of Cases	%	%	%
1– 4	2	5	7
5– 24	14	13	9
25– 99	38	24	44
100–249	21	20	23
250–999	12	18	14
1000+	12	20	3
Total percent	99	100	100
Total number	(56)	(55)	(74)
Statistical methods			
None	10	13	1
Simple percents or raw numbers	43	23	38
Chi-square	10	2	3
T-tests, analysis of variance	10	24	24
Correlation, regression, discriminant	27	36	28
Other	0	2	5
Total percent	100	100	100
Total number	(51)	(53)	(74)

A very small percent of the survey and archival studies included more than one nation, even though quite a few were conducted outside the United States, as shown in rows two and three of Table 8–4. About 1 in 4 Group I journal articles examined a non–United States nation, but only about 1 in 20 included more than one nation in its research design. As I speculated previously, cross-national research collaboration is emerging much more slowly than theorizing. If one agrees with Peterson and Horvath that cultural values are critical in accounting for entrepreneurship, then the research community is neglecting an opportunity to expand the frontiers of understanding.

The normal science paradigm emphasizes building powerful empirical generalizations by identifying the scope of conditions under which a principle holds (McKelvey and Aldrich 1983). In the social sciences, this means specifying subpopulations which are homogeneous enough to allow generalizations to apply to most of their units, e.g., populations defined by age, race, sex, or religion. As I noted previously, entrepreneurship researchers have a very inclusive notion of the entrepreneurial and business populations. This generalization is illustrated in row four of Table 8–4.

Few investigators are explicit about the limits to their generalizations — caveats tend to focus on statistical rather than research design issues — and thus samples usually include entrepreneurs who own a wide variety of enterprises. One consequence is that samples are extremely heterogeneous, but in spite of this, investigators place few, if any, limits on the generalizations from their studies.

Most modern statistical techniques are based on the assumption that a representative sample has been drawn from a larger, limited population. Although none of the papers presented at previous conferences explicitly addressed this issue, several implied that sampling techniques were haphazard at best. In the past, many investigators depended upon convenience or quota samples, rather than drawing from clearly identified sampling frames.

In the late 1980s, investigators were paying much more attention to sampling issues. In 1986, about half of the Babson empirical studies were based on a clear sampling frame, but this figure inexplicably dropped to only 35 percent in 1989. Slightly less than two-thirds of the Group I journal articles used a clear frame, a much better showing than the Babson papers. (However, this figure may be slightly inflated, as 16 articles provided insufficient information to classify them on this dimension.) Examples include the Small Business Administration Data Base, Dun & Bradstreet's file, membership lists of national trade associations, and all the graduates of a state university. Curiously enough, there is no relationship between whether an investigator focused on a homogeneous or heterogeneous population and whether that investigator used a clear sampling frame.

Response rates to entrepreneur surveys have not been very high, and that tradition continued in 1985–1990. As shown in Table 8–4, 60 percent of the 1986 and 67 percent of the 1989 Babson papers reported response rates of less than 50 percent. Almost a quarter of the papers in each year were below 25 percent. At this level of response, serious questions arise about possible sample bias. Figures for the Group I journals are similar. (Because of a coding problem, only three of the five Group I journals had coded sampling response rates.) Many articles did not report response rates, and so the figures in Table 8–4 are probably biased upwards.

Prodded, no doubt, by skeptical colleagues and tough journal editors, entrepreneurship researchers have continued to increase the size of their samples. About 58 percent of the Babson papers reported sample sizes of more than 100 entrepreneurs or businesses, compared to 40 percent for Group I journals. Indeed, the availability of large-scale public data bases generated some samples of more than 1,000 units at the Babson Conferences (20 percent at this size at the 1989 conference). One-third of all the *Journal of Business Venturing* papers were based on public or archival data sources.

Previous commentators have been quite critical of entrepreneurship researchers' lack of statistical sophistication. As shown in the last panel of Table 8–4, investigators continue to rely heavily on simple percents, raw numbers, or no numbers at all. However, there was a trend at the Babson Conferences toward greater use of significance tests, as well as greater use of linear models assessing the strength of associations and their significance. The level of statistical sophistication was nearly the same in the Group I journals, suggesting that the Babson Conferences are an accurate reflection of the state of the art.

Ethnographies

Ethnographic or direct field observation methods have long been praised in the anthropological and sociological communities for their ability to uncover the meaning of patterns in social processes (Stewart 1989). Trained observers can detect subtle features of social processes and interpret interactions which participants may be unable to articulate in interviews. Unlike mailed surveys, ethnographic methods allow researchers to pursue interesting lines of data collection they had not considered prior to entering the field. Investigators can choose whether to be participant or nonparticipant observers, and may be overt or covert in their roles.

Only 11 true field studies were discovered in the Babson proceedings, and 2 more were reported in the *Harvard Business Review.* None formally tested hypotheses, and about half were explicitly longitudinal. None were based on a clear sampling frame, and as would be expected, the number of cases observed was quite small in all but one case. None used any statistical techniques, as they all relied on an interpretive presentation of what had been observed.

Some of these field studies were quite insightful, but taken as a group, they do not tap the rich potential of modern ethnographic methods. An extensive literature has grown up on such methods, and some of the techniques are enjoying widespread use in organization studies — for example, among organizational culture researchers. Many of the processes we posit as central to entrepreneurship — organizing, leading, creating — are natural subjects for field-based studies, but investigators have been reluctant to explore such methods.

THE FUTURE

Entrepreneurship researchers may be mad, but they are not stupid. In previous "state-of-the-art" books, authors were highly critical of entrepreneurship research, accusing researchers of dependence on surveys and simple statistics. Some changes were already apparent in 1986, and since then the field has continued to expand its repertoire of research designs and analytic techniques. Mailed surveys are still the mode, but public and archival sources are becoming more popular, and some interest in field studies has developed. A growing minority of investigators are using powerful multivariate statistics (when appropriate), especially when analyzing longitudinal data.

So, what are the emerging research norms, and what model of science do they imply? What standard should one use for judging whether we have made *progress* in research on entrepreneurship over the past decade? As I noted previously, our answer to this question depends upon our assumptions about the scientific and normative structure of our field. In this postmodernist age, we can no longer unabashedly assume that there is one "truth" to which we all owe allegiance. Instead, we need to consider at least three possibilities: a unitary, normal science view; a multiple paradigms view; and a totally pragmatic, antipositivist view.

Toward a Unified Science ?

People with a unified science view hold as their ideal the accumulation of empirically tested hypotheses and well-grounded generalizations, developed through rigorous research designs, quantitative data, and the latest statistical techniques. *If* this were our standard, we have many positive developments from the record of the past five years, but also some grounds for concern. Let me address several issues: replications, negative findings, units and levels of analysis, and sampling.

Entrepreneurship research resembles many other social sciences in the way that it systematically disdains two processes central to normal scientific endeavor: 1) attempted replication and confirmation of previous findings; and 2) publication of negative findings. Instead, we are treated to "new" concepts and "positive" findings, as authors try to differentiate their products from their potential competitors. Presently, we have persons calling themselves theorists who need not take seriously the stream of contradictory research findings pouring out of various research programs (Stinchcombe 1986, 84–85). "Theorizing" is often an activity divorced from "research."

Units and levels of analysis are often chosen by investigators in a nonsystematic fashion, with choices divorced from theoretical considerations. Instead, choices appear driven primarily by the pragmatics of data collection. For example, if investigators wish to generalize about entrepreneurial personalities, then they need to study people. If, however, they wish to generalize about the growth and innovation patterns of firms, then they need to study organizations. And if they wish to generalize about new forms of entrepreneurship, then they need to study populations. I found few statements in the articles reviewed which clearly laid out authors' rationales for the scope of their generalizations.

An investigator's choice of units and levels of analysis is intimately bound up with sampling issues. Currently, researchers are remarkably careless in identifying a population from which to draw a sample. Only about one-third of the 1989 Babson papers explicitly sampled from an identifiable sampling frame — the rest were quota samples, samples of convenience, and other grab-bags. Investigators (and reviewers) are also notably tolerant of low response rates, whatever the frame ultimately chosen.

None of these problems pose an insurmountable barrier to progress, but all require a change in the norms governing research.

Toward Multiple, Conflicting Views ?

Some writers adopt a much more eclectic view of entrepreneurship research, emphasizing the importance of diversity in theories and methods. Rather than suppressing the various subgroups of entrepreneurship researchers — those concerned with personality theories, industrial economics, ecological theories, and so forth — advocates for diversity celebrate the invigorating effect of multiple perspectives on organizational research.

But is there enough diversity today ? Several very promising research strategies have languished while investigators concentrated on survey designs and the mining of archival sources : ethnographic methods, laboratory experiments, and computer simulations are used infrequently. The neglect of ethnographies is particularly troubling in a field whose very raison d'être is the dynamic response of creative individuals to turbulent social and economic conditions. Our textbooks and mass-market paperbacks on entrepreneurship praise the exuberant entrepreneurs who skillfully thread their way through economic chaos on their way to above-average rates of return. But *our* research method of choice is the static, cross-sectional, standardized questionnaire which, at best, asks entrepreneurs to recall — in *our* own words — their triumphs.

Encouraging diversity is fraught with certain perils for our field, for in the process of constructing theory or method-based subgroups, the groups have restricted themselves, and organizational boundaries can be extremely difficult to surmount. Groups work very hard at emphasizing how they differ from one another, and investigators have a stake in stressing their incompatibilities. Investigators might ask themselves what someone from another perspective might do with the same information. Some might even argue that we are intellectually harmed by confining ourselves to one mode of thinking. Although we do not need to convert to every new perspective that comes along, we can at least acknowledge that other perspectives exist.

Toward Total Pragmatism ?

If we adopt a more pragmatic approach, and ask simply, "Is entrepreneurship research tackling important questions ?," the issue of research methods assumes secondary importance. From this point of view, methods are chosen to match researchers' purposes, and these will change as conditions change. Current social, economic, and political considerations will govern what issues are researched, and changing conditions, not abstract methodological concerns, will drive research practice. Paulin, Coffey, and Spaulding (1982) implied that this was the normal state of affairs in classical entrepreneurship research, and Wortman (1986) hinted darkly at this in his critique.

Totally giving ourselves over to topical concerns could further weaken the standing of entrepreneurship research in the academic community, damaging our ability to recruit promising young scholars. Such a development is unlikely, however. Several new entrepreneurship research journals have adopted rigorous reviewing standards and are competing for manuscripts with older, established management journals. There is room for a diversity of approaches and orientations in the field, from the totally pragmatic to the totally normal science mode, as the other chapters in this volume attest. Since we belong to the social science field perhaps most closely in touch with its practitioner constituency, I doubt that we will ever stray far from the pragmatic consciousness that attracted many of us to the field in the first place.

━━ ━━ ━━ ━━ ━━ ━━ ━━ ━━
APPENDIX 8–A :

Journals Used in 1985-1990 Literature Search and Number of Articles Found in Each

Babson College Conference
Babson College Conference Proceedings : 146

Group I : Primarily Empirical Articles
Academy of Management Journal [AMA] : 1
Administrative Science Quarterly [ASQ] : 3
American Journal of Small Business [ASB] (renamed as Entrepreneurship : Theory and Practice) : 30
Journal of Small Business Management [JSB] : 58
Journal of Business Venturing [JBV] : 33[1]

Group II : Primarily Conceptual Articles
Academy of Management Review [AMR] : 5
Business Horizons [BHO] : 14
California Management Review [CMR] : 5
Harvard Business Review [HBR] : 20
Journal of Business Strategy [JST] : 13
Journal of Economics and Business [EBB] : 0

[1](Because of time constraints, only half of the original 66 articles in JBV were coded.)

━━ ━━ ━━ ━━ ━━ ━━ ━━ ━━
APPENDIX 8–B :

TYPE OF ORGANIZATIONS STUDIED
ORGTYPE : Type of organizations studied.
　　1. 　　　Homogeneous : Article identifies a specific industry that was studied or specific type of business (e.g., computers,

	banks, semiconductors, insurance companies); or, a population collectively affected, e.g., businesses owned by venture capital firms.
0.	Heterogeneous: Article does not identify a specific population or industry. Instead, it lists a broad class of organizations or industries, or none at all (e.g., "manufactured," or "high-tech" or "services"). Or the research was conducted on individuals, e.g., at a management education seminar.
SIZE:	Sample size. Number of cases in the sample, ranging from 1 (a pure case study) to N.
METHODS:	Research method.
0.	JOURNALISTIC: *Vignette or "reportage."* Refers generally to organizational or personal histories; unstructured interviews; case studies without conclusions, generalizations, or hypotheses; journalistic reporting of events or circumstances; and to a more or less straightforward setting forth of the facts.
1.	ARMCHAIR: *Observation (but not field work) and contemplative theory building.* Anecdotal or formal theorizing, based on some "empirical" grounds, but not formally research based.
2–4.	SURVEY: Structured interviews; formally designed questionnaires; typically based on sampling from a larger population, using questionnaires, tests, interviews, or a combination. 2. Mailed surveys. 3. Face to face or telephone interviews. 4. Mass-administered pencil & paper questionnaires, given at a class or other site.
5.	PUBLIC DATA BASE: Can be based on surveys. Examples are Dun & Bradstreet, Compustat, PIMS, U.S. Census Bureau, Census of Manufacturing, or archives of a venture capital firm, business association, etc.
6.	ETHNOGRAPHY: *Field study.* Direct observation of the phenomenon in its natural setting, participation or nonparticipant, covert or overt.
7.	COMPUTER SIMULATION/MODELLING.
METHODS:	Statistical methods — degree of sophistication.
0.	None.
1.	Simple percents or raw numbers.
2.	Chi-square significance tests on tables.

3.	T-tests for sign. differences in means; analysis of variance (ANOVA; MANOVA); factor analysis.
4.	Examination of strength or pattern of association: correlation and regression; discriminant analysis.
5.	Other.

LONGIT: Cross-sectional or longitudinal.
0. Cross-sectional only.
1. Explicitly longitudinal; time series; "time" a variable, either explicitly via a statistical technique, or implicitly, via multiple observation periods in a field study.

TRAITS: Traits type approach.
0. Not a traits type approach: firm or company focus; demographic; financial; performance; survival.
1. Uses a "traits" type approach: focus on entrepreneur's personality, motives, psychological profile, attitudes, feelings about risk, intentions, etc. Distinguished by an emphasis on psychological tests and instruments.

CROSSNAT: Cross-national focus.
0. Only 1 country.
1. More than 1 country.

NONUS: Non-United States sample.
0. Only U.S. sample.
1. Non-U.S. sample.

RESPONSE: For categories 2–4 of research methods: response rate, especially if a random sample. Some articles report response rates, even if the "sample" was not drawn from a proper sampling frame. (For example, if all graduates of a particular college are sent mailed questionnaires, and the percent returning them is reported as a "response rate.") Varies from 0 to 100.

SAMPLE: Was an explicit population sampled?
0. Not a sample from a known or defined population: convenience or quota sample. "Samples" drawn from membership organizations are coded here, unless the organization represents an entire industry.
1. Sample: a clear, explicit sampling frame can be identified, even if only imperfectly. Includes the USEEM/Small Business data, and also Dun & Bradstreet, the NFIB national sample, and the Fortune 500. Key idea is that a population exists to which these results might be generalized.

■ ■ ■ ■ ■ ■ ■ ■
REFERENCES

Carsrud, A. L., K. W. Olm, and G. E. Eddy 1986 Entrepreneurship : Research in quest of a paradigm. In *The art and science of entrepreneurship*, eds. D. L. Sexton and R. W. Smilor, 367–378. Cambridge, Mass. : Ballinger.

Churchill, N. C., and V. L. Lewis 1986 Entrepreneurship research : Directions and methods. In *The art and science of entrepreneurship*, eds. D. L. Sexton and R. W. Smilor, 333–365. Cambridge, Mass. : Ballinger.

Giola, D. A., A. Donnellon, and H. P. Sims, Jr. 1989 Communication and cognition in appraisal : A tale of two paradigms. *Organizational Studies* 10 (4) : 503–529.

Kuhn, T. 1970 *The structure of scientific revolution.* Chicago : Univ. of Chicago Press.

McKelvey, B., and H. E. Aldrich 1983 Applied population science. *Administrative Science Quarterly* 28 : 101–128.

Paulin, W. L., R. E. Coffey, and M. E. Spaulding 1982 Entrepreneurship research : Methods and directions. In *Encyclopedia of entrepreneurship*, eds. C. A. Kent, D. L. Sexton, and K. H. Vesper, 353–373. Englewood Cliffs, N.J. : Prentice-Hall, Inc.

Perryman, M. R. 1982 Commentary on research in the field of entrepreneurship. In *Enclyclopedia of entrepreneurship*, eds. C. A. Kent, D. L. Sexton, and K. H. Vesper, 377–378. Englewood Cliffs, N.J. : Prentice-Hall, Inc.

Peterson, R., and D. Horvath 1982 Commentary on research in the field of entrepreneurship. In *Encyclopedia of entrepreneurship*, eds. C. A. Kent, D. L. Sexton, and K. H. Vesper, 374–376. Englewood Cliffs, N.J. : Prentice-Hall, Inc.

Schumpeter, J. A. 1936 *Theory of economic development.* Cambridge, Mass. : Harvard Univ. Press.

Stewart, A. 1989 *Team entrepreneurship.* Newbury Park, Cal. : Sage Publications.

Stinchcombe, A. 1986 *Stratification and organization : Selected papers.* New York : Cambridge University Press.

Wortman, M. S., Jr. 1986 A unified framework, research typologies, and research prospectuses for the interface between entrepreneurship and small business. In *The art and science of entrepreneurship*, eds. D. L. Sexton and R. W. Smilor, 272–332. Cambridge, Mass. : Ballinger.

Chapter

9

Longitudinal Methods for Studying the Process of Entrepreneurship

Andrew H. Van de Ven

●

INTRODUCTION

Scholars have many different views about entrepreneurship, and the views they adopt influence the questions they ask and the research methods they employ. This chapter takes a developmental view of the entrepreneurship process, asks questions about how and why this process unfolds over time, and proposes a set of longitudinal research methods for studying entrepreneurial ventures. After an overview of Joseph Schumpeter's ideas for conceptualizing the entrepreneurship process, this chapter focuses on the longitudinal research methods being used to study this process in various organizational field settings. These methods pertain to the selection of cases and concepts; observing change; coding and analyzing event data to identify process patterns; and developing theories to explain observed entrepreneurship processes. It is proposed that these methods can be usefully applied in other studies to examine a range of temporal processes, including entrepreneurial and organizational development, growth, decline, and adaptation.

━━ ━━ ━━ ━━ ━━ ━━ ━━

THE PROCESS OF
ENTREPRENEURSHIP

Schumpeter's (1942) seminal ideas about entrepreneurship, the source of innovation, and discontinuous cycles of creative destruction are very relevant for assessing alternative approaches to contemporary entrepreneurship scholarship. They also set the stage for proposing a specific set of steps for conducting longitudinal research aimed at understanding the process of entrepreneurship. Schumpeter used entrepreneurship as the engine for his dynamic theory of economic development, and personified this engine in the entrepreneur — a type of ideal theoretical construct. This type of ideal actor possessed the creative labor, vision of a business idea, dislike of noninnovative administrators, investment seduction skills to lure capitalists, and risk-taking abilities to strike out into the unknown, carrying out a wide variety of innovations — whether new products or processes, product differentiation, new markets, diversifications, new raw materials, or new market structures (Hagedoorn 1989, 31).

Unwittingly or erroneously, this type of ideal personification of the entrepreneurship process was subsequently interpreted by many scholars, and in places by Schumpeter himself, as a real-world individual who embodied all these entrepreneurial characteristics. This may explain why, until recently, a search for the traits, personalities, and individual characteristics of entrepreneurs (as distinct from nonentrepreneurs) has been the almost exclusive focus of entrepreneurship theories and research. Mixed results have been obtained from an extensive and exhaustive set of studies on entrepreneurial traits. In their chapter within the present volume, Cooper and Gascon, as well as Roberts (1990), constructively separate "the wheat from the chaff" in this mixed body of research by summarizing the empirically reliable characteristics of entrepreneurs.

Recently, scholars have become more interested in the process of entrepreneurship, and begun to see the exclusive search for entrepreneurial traits "as relatively unproductive from a research standpoint and not very useful to practitioners" — a conclusion drawn by Ronstadt, Peterson, and Vesper (1986, xiv), based on a survey of researchers at the 1986 Babson College Entrepreneurship Research Conference. In addition, in a recent Delphi survey of researchers and practitioners, Gartner (1990) found that the attributes rated most highly in definitions of entrepreneurship focused on processes of organizational creation, innovation, and resource mobilization to support perceived opportunities. Rated much lower were definitions which focused on entrepreneurial traits; profit or nonprofit organizational settings in which entrepreneurship occurs; and desired outcomes (whether the entrepreneurial venture creates value or achieves growth). These survey results have been echoed by others (Gartner 1990; Schoonhoven and Eisenhardt 1987; Stevenson and Harmeling 1990; Van de Ven and Huber 1990) who argue for a dynamic and behavioral focus on the process of entrepreneurship, moving away from a static search for the input factors (such as entrepreneurial traits) that explain variations in outcomes (i.e., innovation success or failure).

An appreciation of the temporal sequence of activities in developing and implementing new ideas is fundamental to the management of entrepreneurship, because entrepreneurs need to know more than the input factors required to achieve desired outcomes. They are centrally responsible for directing the innovating process within the proverbial "black box" between inputs and outcomes. To do this, the entrepreneur needs a "road map" indicating how and why the innovating journey unfolds, and the paths that are likely to lead to success or failure. In short, the entrepreneur needs a *process theory* to explain innovation development.[1] As I will discuss in the next section, the development of such a theory requires a new set of methods for conducting longitudinal research.

Schumpeter proposed a dynamic evolutionary model of economic development, which emphasized that innovations come from within the economic system, and not merely from an external random variation to external changes (Hagedoorn 1989, 41 ; Elliott 1983, 282). This suggests that a macroperspective as opposed to a microfocus on individual entrepreneurs is required to examine many questions involving the role of entrepreneurship.

In the past decade a population ecology approach (Aldrich 1979 ; Hannan and Freeman 1977, 1989) to entrepreneurship scholarship has emerged which uses the population of organizations as its unit of analysis, examining organizational birth and death rates as the workings of evolutionary variation and selection mechanisms. Based on Stinchcombe's (1965) liabilities of newness and small size arguments, Hannan and Freeman (1984) propose that organizational death rates should decline monotonically with age because organizational learning and inertia gradually increase with age. Many subsequent studies have provided empirical evidence for this basic proposition (Carroll and Delacroix 1982 ; Freeman, Carroll, and Hannan 1983 ; Carroll 1983, 1984, 1987 ; Singh, House, and Tucker 1986 ; Halliday, Powell, and Granfors 1987). More recently, Fichman and Levinthal (1988) and Bruderl and Schussler (1990) have proposed and provided evidence for a "liability of adolescence" model which introduces two stages in an organizational life cycle. In the first "adolescent" stage, death rates are low because new start-up companies are not expected to be successful immediately, and venture capital represents an initial stock of assets that entrepreneurs can live on. In the later stage, the "honey-

---

[1]Our developmental view of process should not be confused with two other common usages of the term "process" in the literature, where it refers either to : 1) the underlying logic that explains a causal relationship between independent and dependent variables in a variance theory ; or 2) a category of concepts of organizational actions, such as rates of communications, work flows, decision-making techniques, or methods for strategy making. While these concepts or mechanisms may be at work to explain an organizational result, they do not describe how these variables or mechanisms develop — i.e., how they unfold or change over time.

moon" (Fichman and Levinthal 1988) is over, and organizations are subjected to the usual risks of failure, producing an age-dependent, monotonic decline in organizational hazard rates.

This stream of ecological research is providing valuable insights into the time-dependent patterns of organizational demography, particularly of new small businesses (which represent the organizational population of greatest interest to entrepreneurship scholars, although entrepreneurship in other organizational settings has also received attention). In comparison with the microentrepreneurial "traits" approach, this ecological perspective is stimulating entrepreneurship scholars to examine more macroquestions regarding the factors which influence "rates" of organizational births and deaths. As Aldrich (1990) points out, the ecological perspective emphasizes that new company start-ups are highly dependent upon macroprocesses both within and between organizational populations. Intrapopulation processes (such as prior foundings, dissolutions, and organizational density) structure the environment into which foundings are born. Cooperative and competitive relationships between populations of organizations affect the distribution of resources available to entrepreneurs in the environment. Finally, institutional factors (government policies, political events, cultural norms, and so on) shape the macrocontext within which these population processes occur (Aldrich 1990, 7).

Almost of necessity, the macropopulation perspective eliminates the microscopic details needed to observe the complex process of entrepreneurship. Schumpeter located the source of innovations in the microscopic diversity and abnormal behavior of entrepreneurs (either as independent individuals or as employees of a large company). Population ecology models average over these details when they aggregate data and use differential equations to explain the changing populations inhabiting the system. As a consequence, Allen (1988, 105) argues that it is not possible to observe how the entrepreneurial journey unfolds, and whether innovations emerge as a result of random variations or purposeful entrepreneurial activities.

Schumpeter linked macropopulation dynamics with microentrepreneurial processes. He observed that innovations occur discontinuously, rather than smoothly, at the microlevel and bring qualitative changes or "revolutions" which fundamentally displace old equilibria and create radically new macroeconomic conditions (Elliott 1983, 282). As viewed by Marshallian economists, he allowed for economic growth as a continuous stream of small changes adapting to "demographic data" for the economic system (Awan 1986). But he explicitly distinguished this economic growth from economic development as a difference between convergent equilibrium and discontinuous revolutions. In his own words,

> Development . . . is entirely foreign to what may be observed in the circular flow or in the tendency towards equilibrium. It is spontaneous and discontinuous change in the channels of the flow, disturbance of equilibrium, which forever alters and

displaces the equilibrium state previously existing. . . . Add successively as many mail coaches as you please, and you will never get a railway thereby. (Schumpeter 1950, 64)

In striking parallel with Karl Marx, Schumpeter proposed a dialectical theory that explained why economic development proceeds cyclically rather than evenly because innovations appear discontinuously in groups or swarms (Elliott 1983). Schumpeter's theory more nearly reflects a "punctuated equilibrium" model (Gould 1989; Tushman and Romanelli 1985) or an accumulation model (Van de Ven and Garud 1989) than a continuous evolutionary model used in population ecology.

This theory is exemplified by entrepreneurs, financed by capitalists, who strike out, often in competition with other, like-minded entrepreneurs, to introduce new innovations which, if successful, provide opportunities to reap extraordinary profits for a temporary period of time. Imitators follow, and an avalanche of consumer goods pours onto the market which dampen prices, profit margins, and innovation investments. This, in turn forces reorganizations of production, greater efficiency, lower costs, the elimination of inefficient, noninnovating firms, and the replacement of old products and processes with the new ones. This "perennial gale of creative destruction" (Schumpeter 1950, 85) explains macroeconomic development as cyclical fluctuations produced by discontinuous bursts of microprocesses of entrepreneurship and innovation investment. Since monopoly profits are temporary, the process of "creative destruction" benefits society through the introduction of new products or processes, and because the extraordinary profits realized by the innovative firm will be a source of funds for the next round of innovation in the original industry and elsewhere. However, depressions or recessions are a normal part of this cyclical process and are produced by adaptations to the bunching of innovations during the preceding period of prosperity.

As a theory of economic development, Schumpeter's formulation is an impressive achievement. But it is not a theory of innovation. The *engine* of this theory is innovation, which Schumpeter *uses* to explain how and why economic development evolves cyclically through gales of creative destruction. However, he is remarkably silent about the process of innovation, other than observing that they come from entrepreneurs. As Ruttan (1959, 599) notes, "neither in *Business Cycles* nor in Schumpeter's other works is there anything that can be identified as a theory of innovation."

If Schumpeter did not present a theory of innovation, he did provide entrepreneurship scholars a number of penetrating insights for a process theory. Specifically, his work suggests that such a theory should include statements that explain innovation: 1) as a dynamic evolutionary process, 2) in which many actors (including entrepreneurs) undertake time-dependent sequences of activities and events, 3) which produce cycles of discontinuity (punctuated disequilibria) and continuity (convergent equilibria), and that 4) both create and are constrained by different hierarchical levels of the social system.

Stevenson and Harmeling (1990) usefully capture the paradoxical implications of these suggestions by distinguishing the different research assumptions and practices commonly associated with theories of change and equilibrium (see Table 9–1). Responding pragmatically to the needs of entrepreneurs for a more "chaotic" theory, Stevenson and Harveling propose that scholars shift their research assumptions and practices from a traditional focus on theories of equilibrium (the right column) to a more "messy" theory of change (the left column). However, a closer approximation to Schumpeter's suggestions for a process theory of entrepreneurship would be achieved by somehow incorporating both the characteristics of equilibrium (right column) and change (left column). In other words, the issue is not "either/or." "Both" equilibrium "and" change theory characteristics are necessary if we are to be able to explain temporal cycles of stability as well as change across micro- and macrolevels of the entrepreneurship process.

A range of deductive and inductive approaches could be taken to develop a theory of the entrepreneurship process that incorporates these characteristics of equilibrium and change. At the deductive theorizing end of the pole, one might fruitfully begin by applying the methods that Poole and Van de Ven (1989b) propose for using paradox to build and improve management theories. At the inductive end of the pole, one might immerse him/herself in observing processes of stability and change in a few entrepreneurial ventures as they unfold over time in their natural field settings, and then develop a grounded the-

TABLE 9–1 — Research Assumptions in Theories of Change and Equilibrium

Theory of Change	Theory of Equilibrium
Change is normal.	Equilibrium is normal.
Longitudinal studies are necessary.	Time slices provide valid insight.
Understanding the sequence of events is critical.	Sequence is immaterial.
Reciprocal causality is normal.	Unidirectional causality separates independent from dependent variables.
Idiosyncratic phenomena are the most important.	Repetitive phenomena are the object of study.
Small "n" studies give insight.	Only large "n" studies can be valid.
Functional relationships are shifting.	Functional relationships are stable.
Key relationships are nonlinear.	Linear relationships can explain most observations.
Valid observations may not be replicable.	An observation must be replicable to be valid.

Source : Adapted from Howard Stevenson and Susan Harmeling, "Entrepreneurial Management's Need for a more 'Chaotic' Theory," *Journal of Business Venturing*, 5, 1 (January, 1990) : 1–14.

ory of the entrepreneurship process from the observations. At this embryonic state of understanding organizational processes in general, and entrepreneurship development in particular, inductive theory development efforts grounded in concrete and rich field observations are more likely to lead to significant new insights than deductive armchair theorizing approaches. Researchers can substantially increase the likelihood of developing good grounded theories by paying careful attention to new and existing methods for designing longitudinal research on the entrepreneurship process.

Since 1983, researchers at the University of Minnesota have been engaged in a longitudinal field research program with the objective of developing a process theory of innovation and entrepreneurship. The Minnesota Innovation Research Program (MIRP) consists of longitudinal field studies of 14 different technological, product, process, and administrative innovations in public and private sectors (see Figure 9–1). The 14 studies were undertaken by different interdisciplinary research teams (in total consisting of 15 faculty and 19 doctoral students from eight different academic departments and five schools at the University of Minnesota). While the program accommodates individual requirements of each study, MIRP researchers adopted a common framework and methodology to compare and integrate findings across all innovations. This common framework is based on a definition that the process of innovation is the invention and implementation of new *ideas*, which are developed by *people*, who engage in *transactions* with others over time within an institutional *context*, and who judge the *outcomes* of their efforts and act accordingly.

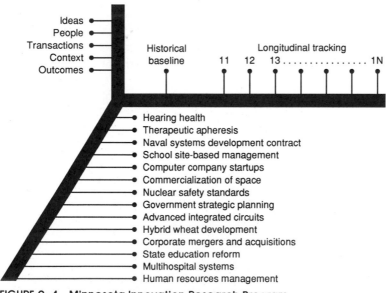

FIGURE 9–1   **Minnesota Innovation Research Program**

Beginning with historical baseline data collected in 1984 when the innovations began in their natural field settings, these core concepts were repeatedly measured over time throughout their developmental period. As of October 1990, most of the innovations were either terminated or implemented, and field work has thus largely concluded. MIRP researchers are presently concentrating on analyzing their longitudinal data in order to determine how and why the innovations developed over time, and what paths lead to successful and unsuccessful outcomes.

The next part of this chapter provides a brief overview of the MIRP research design and longitudinal data collection methods used to track the innovations. Most of these methods are generally well understood, the reader is referred to Van de Ven, Angle, and Poole (1989) for details. They provide a useful background for suggesting some new methods for dealing with problems of tabulating and analyzing data (particularly on qualitative events) collected in the field to develop and test process theories of the process of entrepreneurship.[2] These methods are explored further on in this chapter.

━━━━━━━━━━
OVERVIEW OF LONGITUDINAL FIELD WORK

Five methodological guidelines were adopted to study innovation processes. They pertain to: 1) sample selection, 2) real-time process observation, 3) selecting core concepts for observing innovation processes, 4) identifying and comparing alternative models to explain observed processes, and 5) addressing problems of measurement and sequence analysis to test alternative process models.

Sample a wide variety of innovations in order to enrich the range of insights and enhance generalizability.

Since its inception, MIRP's philosophy involved taking a broad comparative approach to study processes of innovation and entrepreneurship, as opposed to a large sample replication of a narrow set of nearly similar types of innovations, which was typically done in studies of innovation. A broad definition of innovations and their organizational settings was adopted, including both technical innovations (new technologies, products, and services) and administrative innovations (new procedures, policies, and organizational forms) in a wide variety of organizational settings. These settings included new company start-ups, internal corporate ventures, and interorganizational joint

---

[2]A more general application of the longitudinal research methods presented in Parts II and III was presented in A. H. Van de Ven and M. S. Poole, "Methods for Studying Innovation Development in the Minnesota Innovation Research Program," *Organization Science,* 1, 3 (1990): 313–335.

ventures. Through an involved sampling and negotiation process (described in Van de Ven and Angle 1989), access was obtained to conduct longitudinal studies of the innovations listed in Figure 9–1.

Critics have questioned the wisdom of this heterogeneous sampling of innovations, stating it may result in "trying to compare apples with oranges." Our response is that we will never know the limits where valid comparisons end unless we empirically examine the broadest possible range of cases to which our definition of innovation applies. After all, the comparative method is perhaps the most general and basic strategy for generating and evaluating valid scientific knowledge. This strategy involves the selection of comparison groups which differ in the scope of the population and conceptual categories of central interest to the research. As Kaplan (1964, 52) pointed out, scientific knowledge is greatly enhanced when we divide the subject matter into concepts and cases that delineate the problems over the widest possible ranges, types, conditions, and consequences.

This broad sampling scheme also permits us to make empirical links between different specialities or schools of thought that have emerged for different organizational settings in which innovation occurs. For example, because organizational structures for business creation are different in small company start-ups, internal corporate innovation, and interorganizational joint ventures, it is widely believed that the entrepreneurial process in these organizational settings must also be different. Van de Ven et al. (1989, 221–224) question this widespread conventional belief and propose an equally plausible conclusion: namely, that creating a new business entails fundamentally the same process regardless of organizational setting. If empirical evidence is obtained to support this conclusion, then significant benefits and efficiencies can be obtained by applying principles for business creation from new company start-ups to internal corporate venturing and interorganizational joint ventures, and vice versa.

Study the innovation process throughout its entire life, from beginning to end.
Most studies of the process of innovation or entrepreneurship to date have been retrospective case histories, conducted after outcomes were known. However, prior knowledge of the success or failure of an innovation can often bias a study's findings. While historical analysis is necessary for examining many questions, and concerted efforts can be undertaken to minimize bias, it is generally better to initiate an historical study before the final outcomes become known. And it is even better to observe the activities and events that occur as an innovation develops from concept to reality. This approach maximizes the probability of discovering short-lived factors and changes that exert important influences. As Pettigrew (1985) suggests, we are more likely to identify continuities if we spend more time looking at present day events. Appreciating this dilemma requires that investigators carefully design their studies in order to observe changes that are relevant to the purposes and users of their research. Since the purpose of MIRP is to understand the management of innovation, I

decided to frame the research from the entrepreneur's temporal and contextual perspective. This involved gaining access to study innovation projects as early as possible. It also required focusing observations primarily on the actions and perceptions of entrepreneurs over time while they were engaged in developing their innovations, without knowing how the innovation journeys might unfold or even if they would be successes or failures.

Once access was obtained to study specific innovations from fall 1983 to mid-1984, case histories and baseline data were obtained on each innovation. They provided an understanding of the institutional context and the historical events which led to the status of each innovation at the time longitudinal tracking began. A variety of data collection instruments were created to observe the innovations as they developed in the ensuing years, including schedules for on-site observations, interviews, questionnaires, and archival records. These instruments are presented and evaluated in Van de Ven and Chu (1989), and some were initially tested in Van de Ven and Ferry (1980).

Develop a core set of constructs to guide and unify different field studies of innovation, and gather longitudinal data on these concepts.

Implicitly or explicitly, the study of any change or innovation process requires a set of categories or variables to describe innovation development. Because the study of developmental processes is at an embryonic stage, these core concepts are best viewed as "sensitizing categories" for conducting exploratory, grounded theoretical research (Glaser and Strauss 1967).

Based on the MIRP definition of the innovation process, five "sensitizing categories" were adopted to study innovation development: ideas, people, transactions, context, and outcomes (see Figure 9–1). These concepts were selected because they constitute the central factors of concern to innovation managers (Van de Ven 1986). The process of innovation consists of motivating and coordinating *people* to develop and implement new *ideas* by engaging in *transactions* (or relationships) with others and making the adaptations needed to achieve desired *outcomes* within changing institutional and organizational *contexts.*

As is typical in grounded theory research, assumptions and definitions of these concepts changed substantially and became progressively clearer with field observations over time. In particular, Table 9–2 compares the starting assumptions of these concepts drawn from the literature at the time (summarized in the left column), with how we came to view them as a result of their field studies (in the right column). The latter discloses a different reality from the rather orderly and naive conceptions of the former.

According to Van de Ven and Angle (1989), field observations show that innovation is not an orderly process. Innovations result or proliferate into a number of ideas stemming from invention and reinvention. A number of people are involved in the innovation process at different times and at different levels of effort due to other priorities. The "fuzzy set" epitomizes the general environment for innovation as multiple environments are "enacted," accord-

TABLE 9–2 — A Comparison of the Conventional Wisdom and MIRP Observations

	Literature implicitly assumes :	But we see this :
Ideas :	One invention, operationalized.	Reinvention, proliferation, reimplementation, discarding, and termination.
People :	An entrepreneur with fixed set of full-time people over time.	Many entrepreneurs, distracted, fluidly engaging, and disengaging over time in a variety of organizational roles.
Transactions :	Fixed network of people / firms working out details of an idea.	Expanding and contracting network of partisan stakeholders diverging and converging on ideas.
Context :	Environment provides opportunities and constraints on innovation process.	Innovation process constrained by and creates multiple enacted environments.
Outcomes :	Final result orientation ; a stable new order comes into being.	Final results may be indeterminate ; multiple in-process assessments and spin-offs ; integration of new orders with old.
Process :	Simple, cumulative sequence of stages or phases.	From simple to multiple progressions of divergent, parallel, and convergent paths, some of which are related and cumulative, others not.

Source : A. H. Van de Ven and H. L. Angle, "An Introduction to the Minnesota Innovation Research Program," Chapter 1 in A. H. Van de Ven, H. L. Angle, and M. S. Poole, *Research on the Management of Innovation : The Minnesota Studies* (New York : Ballinger / Harper & Row, 1989), p. 11.

ing to Weick (1979). There are multiple tracks to innovation. It is not a simple, unitary, progressive path. Thus, the discrete identity of innovation may become blurred. Based on these field observations, the definitions and measures of the core concepts of innovation were refined.

Compare and test alternative process theories and models (as opposed to a single model).

The MIRP field studies quickly demonstrated that innovation processes are exceedingly complex, and far beyond the explanatory capabilities of any single process theory found in the literature. Moreover, it was feared that efforts to develop a single process theory grounded in the data would either produce an untestable theory or a self-fulfilling prophecy. As Mitroff and Emshoff (1979), among others, observed, when scholars and practitioners have only a single perspective or theory, facts are often twisted and rationalized to fit the model. It is generally better to develop and juxtapose alternative theories, and subsequently determine which theory better explains the data.

Thus, a comparative theory development and testing approach was adopted: that is, alternative models to the data were applied and successively evaluated in comparison to one another (see Poole and Van de Ven 1989a). At the least, this reduces complexity, because it is very difficult to analyze a large array of field data without conceptual guidance. This approach emphasizes that testing a process theory should not be based on Platonic criteria for an ideal theory which may never be found; instead, it should be based on the relative explanatory power of alternative theories. Knowledge advances by successive approximations and comparisons of competing alternative theories.

Evaluating alternative process models or theories is not simply a matter of identifying and testing them, any more than evaluating a theory of structure is merely a matter of conceiving types of structures and testing them. Between conception and test lie the intervening tasks of defining constructs, finding indicators, developing propositions about innovation development, and using appropriate methods of sequence analysis. These intervening tasks constitute MIRP's last methodological guideline, which is to *address problems of measurement and sequence methods in order to identify process patterns in temporal data*. As I will now discuss, undertaking this guideline requires a new set of methods to tabulate and analyze longitudinal data.

METHODS FOR MEASUREMENT AND SEQUENCE ANALYSIS

Consider the challenge confronting MIRP researchers who followed these guidelines in tracking the development of an innovation. Over a three- to seven-year period of real-time field study of an innovation, quantitative and qualitative data are collected with a survey questionnaire completed every six months by innovation participants; interviews are conducted with key innovation managers every six months; direct observations are made of regularly scheduled (monthly or bimonthly) innovation team meetings; and a study diary is maintained to record and file frequent informal discussions with innovation managers, organizational memos and reports, and stories about the innovation in trade journals or newspapers. Confronted with such an array of raw data, how do we transform them into a form useful for developing and testing process theories of innovation development?

Primarily, a theory of development should consist of statements about the temporal sequence of events that explain an observed stream of incidents or occurrences as an innovation unfolds. To make such a theory operational, and hence testable, it is important to distinguish between an *incident* (a raw datum) and an *event* (a theoretical construct). Whereas an incident is an empirical observation, an event is not directly observed; it is a conceptual construct in a model that explains the pattern of incidents. For each event one can choose any number of incidents as indicators that that event has happened. *Measurement* deals with the problem of selecting reliable and valid indicators of each event. But a good process model of innovation development does more than simply define its component events; it strings them together in a particular temporal order and sequence to explain how and why innovations unfold over time. *Sequence analysis* deals with methods to evaluate the degree to which event indicators conform with the model.

Specific methods being used and contemplated to deal with the problems of measurement (tasks 1–4) and sequence analysis (tasks 5–7) are discussed below. While these tasks are interrelated, they will be discussed in the following order:

1. Define a qualitative datum, and enter raw data into incidents.
2. Evaluate the validity of incidents.
3. Code incidents into qualitative event constructs.
4. Evaluate the reliability of coded events.
5. Transform qualitative codes into quantitative categories.
6. Analyze temporal relationships in event sequence data.
7. Determine if chaos is present in seemingly random time series.

Defining a Datum : An Incident

In quantitative survey data, it is typically assumed that the datum is sufficiently clear and requires no explicit treatment. However, this is not so with qualitative data, where a *datum* must be defined, because it is the basic element of information that is entered into a data file for analyzing temporal event sequences in the development of innovations.

In survey research, a *quantitative datum* is commonly regarded to be: 1) a numerical response to a question scaled along a distribution 2) about an object (the unit of analysis) 3) at the time of measurement, which is 4) entered as a variable (along with other variables on the object) into a record (or case) of a quantitative data file, and 5) is subsequently recorded and classified as an indicator of a theoretical construct. In comparison, we define a *qualitative datum* as: 1) a bracketed string of words capturing the basic elements of information 2) about a discrete incident or occurrence (the unit of analysis) 3) that happened on a specific date, which is 4) entered as a unique record (or case) in a qualitative data file, and 5) is subsequently coded and classified as an indicator of a theoretical event.

As these definitions indicate, the basic element of information in a qualitative datum is a bracketed string of words about a discrete incident, while in a quantitative datum the element of information is a number scaled along a predetermined distribution of a variable. Raw words, sentences, or stories collected from the field cannot be entered into a qualitative data file until they are bracketed into a datum or set of datums. Obviously, explicit decision rules are needed to bracket raw words, and should reflect the substantive purposes of the research.

In the case of MIRP, the decision rule used to bracket words into a qualitative datum was the definition of an incident that occurred in the development of an innovation. Following the guideline above, an *incident* was defined as a major recurrent activity or change observed to occur in one of the five core concepts in the MIRP framework: innovation ideas, people, transactions, context, and outcomes. When each incident was identified, the bracketed string of words required to describe it included: date of occurrence, the actor(s) or object(s) involved, the action or behavior that occurred, the consequence (if any) of the action, and the source of the information.

With these conventions a chronological listing of all incidents observed in the development of an innovation was entered into a qualitative data file. Each incident represents a datum that is entered as a unique record into a qualitative data file for each innovation. Table 9–3 shows an example of a few incidents in such a data file. (While a variety of data base software programs can be used, we are using Rbase System V software to organize and manage the qualitative data files.)

As with any decision rule, further subjective judgements are involved in defining innovation incidents in an operationally consistent manner. In particular, Van de Ven and Poole (1990) discuss the effect of different temporal laws on the rate of innovation development. As a result, interpretations among MIRP researchers have varied on the the level of specificity and the temporal duration of incidents. Some MIRP investigators used fine-grained definitions of incidents, while others adopted a more coarse-grained approach. A fine-grained perspective of incidents was often associated with short units of time, on the order of days or weeks; course-grained definitions often included incidents of long temporal duration, perhaps months or years. Methods used to track developmental processes must be adapted to be consistent with the temporal laws of development and the corresponding granularity of incident detail appropriate to different types of innovations being examined.

Validity of Transforming Raw Data into Incidents

It is necessary to test empirically whether researchers' classifications of raw data are consistent with practitioners' common perceptions of events. If the evidence indicates inconsistency, then no claims about the meaning of events from the participants' point of view are valid. Researchers can still sustain claims about the meaning of the incident from their theoretical position, but no claims about the "social reality" of the event are appropriate.

Two basic procedures were used to enhance the validity of the incidents entered into the qualitative data file. First, the entry of incidents from raw data sources into a data file was performed by at least two researchers. Consensus was required among these researchers on a consistent interpretation of the de-

TABLE 9–3 — Example of Innovation Incidents in Qualitative Data File for One MIRP Study

INCIDENT NUMBER : 312   INCIDENT DATE : 06 / 01 / 87
INCIDENT : Firm 1 executive states he will not support TAP beyond 1988. His firm has been investing about $4M per year in TAP, and Firm 2 is only spending between $1 and 1.5M. The Firm 1 executive thinks Firm 2 firm should contribute more. Firm 1 and 2 SBU (Strategic Business Unit) managers meet and offer several options such as donating modules, writing a check for $1M, or taking less royalties. Firm 2 SBU manager will see if Firm 2 executive is still interested.
DATA SOURCE : Phone calls with Firm 1 and 2 SBU managers, 6/ 1/ 87.
CORE MIRP CODES : Outcome-negative / Context-internal / Context-external / Transaction / Contraction

INCIDENT NUMBER : 313   INCIDENT DATE : 06 / 01 / 87
INCIDENT : June SBU meeting canceled.
DATA SOURCE : Phone call with SBU manager 6/ 1/ 87.
CORE MIRP CODES : Context-internal / Contraction

INCIDENT NUMBER : 314   INCIDENT DATE : 06/ 18/ 87
INCIDENT : Emergency meeting conducted of Firm 1 core TAP team to discuss restructuring finances as a result of recent internal management review. Items for discussion included 10–15 percent across the board budget reductions, omission of diagnostics, assumption of improved electronics by 1/ 1/ 88, 70 percent of sales by 1995 will come from tubesets manufactured outside of the firm, and no significant research beyond present diseases being studied.
DATA SOURCE : Internal memo of 6/ 10/ 87 and 6/ 18/ 87 meeting notes.
CORE MIRP CODES : Transaction / Idea-core / Context-internal

INCIDENT NUMBER : 315   INCIDENT DATE : 06 / 25 / 87
INCIDENT : Joint administrative review of TAP by Firm 1 and 2 executives. Firm 1 executive suggests bringing in a third partner to reduce financial burden. He suggests that TAP be spun off into a joint venture with a third partner. No conclusion reached. Firm 2 executive asks, "Why has my partner blinked ?" He questions if Firm 1 is really committed to TAP. The Firm 1 executive states that it is just an issue of financing and additional opportunities for investment.
DATA SOURCE : Research notes of 6/ 25/ 87 administrative review meeting.
CORE MIRP CODES : Transaction / Context-internal / Context-external / Outcome-negative

cision rules used to identify incidents. Second, the resulting list of incidents was reviewed by the innovation's key managers. They were asked to indicate if any incidents that occurred in the development of their innovations were missing or incorrectly described. Based on this feedback, revisions in the incident listings were made if they conformed to the decision rules for defining each incident.

It is important to recognize that the resulting list of incidents does not represent the population of occurrences in the development of an innovation. Even with real-time field observations, it is not humanly possible to observe and record all possible incidents that happened over long periods of time. Thus, as is well established in classical test theory of item sampling (Lord and Novick 1968), incidents should depict a representative sample of indicators describing what happened as an innovation developed over time.

Coding Incidents into Event Constructs

As they stand, the incident listings are not particularly useful for analysis, because each incident is merely a qualitative indicator of what happened in the development of an innovation over time. The next step in representing the data is to code the incidents into theoretically meaningful events. A common problem with many coding systems is that they reduce rich qualitative data to a single dimension of meaning. For example, a failure to get renewed funding for an innovation may influence the development of the idea behind the project, it may also result in layoffs of innovation personnel, and it may signal a change in the relationship of the innovation to external resource controllers. If this incident is coded as an event of the termination of an idea, other dimensions of meaning are omitted. To avoid this problem, incidents should be coded on several dimensions of an event if necessary. For example, we might code the incident on four event dimensions: a negative outcome (resource cut); a change in the core innovation idea; people leaving; and a change in transactions (relations with resource controllers).

The procedure of coding incidents along several conceptually meaningful categories evolved from Poole's (1983a, 1983b) studies of decision development in small groups. Poole argued that previous models of group decision development — which commonly posited a rational decision process of three to five stages — were too simple. He was interested in testing the hypothesis that decisions did not follow a fixed sequence of phases but instead could follow several different paths. He also believed that the previous practice of coding only one dimension of group behavior, such as task process, was responsible for previous findings supporting the single sequence models. To examine a richer model of group development, he developed a three-track coding system: one track coded the impact an incident had on the process by which the group does its work (in this case, an incident was a member's statement), a second coded the same incident in terms of its effect on group relationships, and a third indexed the several topics the incident referred to. By coding an incident on several conceptually relevant dimensions simultaneously, Poole was able to derive a richer description of group processes than had previous studies.

Consistent with the MIRP definition of innovation process, an incident coding scheme was adopted to capture the key dimensions of change in innovation development: ideas, people, transactions, contexts, and outcomes. Definitions and decision rules for coding innovation incidents on each of these core constructs are described in Van de Ven, Angle, and Poole (1989). Table 9–4 summarizes this coding scheme. Of course, the actual conceptual categories used in this coding scheme would differ with the particular questions and interests of other researchers.

Assessing the Reliability of a Coding Scheme

A number of steps were taken to enhance the reliability of coding schemes into indicators of event constructs. First, operational definitions and coding conventions were drafted for event constructs. Periodically, meetings were con-

TABLE 9–4 — Illustration of Coding Tracks on Core MIRP Dimensions

People track	_____
Ideas track	_____
Transactions track	_____
Context track	_____
Outcomes track	_____
TIME	: ____ : ____ : ____ : ____ : ____ : ____ : ____ : ____ : ____ : ____ :

People track : a coding of the people / groups involved in an incident, the roles and activities they perform at a given point in time.

Ideas track : a coding of the substantive ideas or strategies that innovation group members use to describe the content of their innovation at a given point in time.

Transactions track : the informal and formal relationships among innovation group members, other firms, and groups involved in the incident.

Context track : a coding of the exogenous events outside of the innovation unit in the larger organization and industry / community which are perceived by innovation group members to affect the innovation.

Outcomes track : the positive (good news or successful accomplishment), negative (bad news or instances of failure or mistakes), or mixed (neutral or ambiguous news indicating elements of both success and failure) evidence of results of an incident.

ducted with researchers and other colleagues to evaluate the construct validity of these definitions — i.e., the extent to which operational definitions appeared to be logical and understandable indicators of the constructs under consideration.

In prior research Van de Ven and Ferry (1980) found that a useful way to conduct these meetings is to begin with an overall presentation of the conceptual model being studied. Then give participants a paper that defines each construct in the model and the suggested indicators to be used in measuring each construct. Participants are then asked to "suggest better indicators for measuring this construct as defined previously." Often working within a Nominal Group Technique format (Delbecq, Van de Ven, and Gustafson 1975), reviewers are provided a brief period to think and respond to the questions in writing. Then a general discussion ensues to obtain group opinions. The qualitative written comments from these review sessions are especially helpful in sharpening the norms of correspondence (Kaplan 1964) between definitions of constructs and event indicators, and in clarifying ambiguities in decision rules for coding event indicators.

An operating norm of MIRP is that the actual coding of incidents into event constructs is performed independently by two or more MIRP researchers. This permits researchers to compute inter-rater reliability as a basic criterion to evaluate the reliability of the coding procedures. Following these procedures, 85 percent, 91 percent, and 93 percent agreement between coders has been obtained thus far in coding event indicators for three of the MIRP innovations being studied.

In addition to obtaining comments from other researchers and theorists, it is also useful to assess whether the researchers' dimensions of events correspond to those of innovation participants. (For methods of doing this, see Folger, Hewes, and Poole 1984.) Although not necessary for purposes of testing theories, it is useful to determine the interpretive adequacy of our theoretical classifications. If categories map events in ways that correspond to how participants see them, findings can support claims about the social phenomenological processes of innovation.

Transforming Coded Incidents into Bit-Maps for Time Series Analysis

As Abbott (1990) suggests, new analytical methods are needed to identify the sequence, order, and causal relationships among coded innovation events. This requires transforming an innovation's chronological listing of coded incidents into dichotomous indicators of event constructs. Such a transformation of qualitative codes into quantitative dichotomous variables allows us to apply various statistical methods to examine time-dependent patterns of relations among the event constructs.

Theoretically, it is possible to exhaust the information contained in a text with binary oppositions. A dichotomous indicator uses "1" to represent the presence of, and "0" the absence of, a certain code in the qualitative incident. The choice of a particular set of indicators depends on the substantive problem of interest. With the indicators chosen, each coded construct of an incident is transformed into a dichotomous variable of 1 (change occurred) or 0 (no change occurred) in a separate column of a row (an incident) within the incident data file. Then all the rows (incidents) in the file are mapped into a matrix of 1's and 0's, which we call a *bit-map*.

Table 9–5 illustrates a partial bit-map data file for the first 30 of 253 incidents in the development of one MIRP innovation (a new company start-up). In such a bit-map, the chronological listing of qualitative events is time-dependent, meaning that although the columns are interchangeable, the sequential order of the rows is crucial and should be taken into account when information is to be extracted. A method which returns the same results when the rows of an event sequence bit-map are interchanged is not appropriate for identifying dynamic patterns because the information contained in the temporal order of the incidents is not used.

Analysis of Temporal Relationships in Bit-Map Data

The above transformation of qualitative codes into quantitative bit-map data files sets the stage for examining temporal relationships and patterns among dimensions in the development of innovations. *Sequence analysis* is the family of methods concerned with the problem of determining the temporal order among events (Abbott 1984). Analogous to an analysis of variance which de-

TABLE 9–5 — Partial Bit-Map of Innovation Incidents in One MIRP Study

Variables (number in ( ) represents the frequency of 1's) in entire file :

num :	Incident Number
date :	Incident Date
days :	Number of Days from 01/01/68 (the first incident)
ic :	Idea-core (68)
ir :	Idea-related (4)
pe :	People (49)
tr :	Transaction (165)
ci :	Context-internal (8)
ce :	Context-external (22)
op :	Outcome-positive (58)
on :	Outcome-negative (59)
om :	Outcome-mixed (7)

Incident :

num	date	days	ic	ir	pe	tr	ci	ce	op	on	om
1	01/01/68	1	1	0	0	0	1	0	0	0	0
2	01/01/68	1	0	0	0	1	0	0	0	0	0
3	01/01/68	1	0	0	0	0	0	1	0	0	0
4	01/01/68	1	0	0	0	0	0	1	0	0	0
5	01/01/68	1	1	0	0	1	0	0	0	0	0
6	01/01/68	1	1	0	0	1	0	0	0	1	0
7	01/01/74	2193	1	0	1	0	0	0	0	0	0
8	01/01/74	2193	0	0	1	0	0	0	0	0	0
9	12/01/78	3988	0	0	1	0	0	0	0	0	0
10	10/01/79	4292	1	0	1	1	0	0	0	0	0
11	10/07/79	4298	1	0	0	1	0	0	0	0	0
12	01/01/80	4384	0	0	0	0	0	1	0	0	0
13	01/04/80	4387	1	0	0	0	0	0	0	0	0
14	01/08/80	4391	0	0	0	1	0	0	0	1	0
15	01/12/80	4395	1	0	0	0	0	0	1	0	0
16	04/01/80	4475	1	0	0	0	0	0	0	0	0
17	04/07/80	4481	0	0	0	1	0	0	1	0	0
18	05/01/80	4505	0	0	0	1	0	0	0	0	0
19	10/01/80	4658	1	0	0	0	0	0	0	1	0
20	10/07/80	4664	0	0	0	1	0	0	1	0	0
21	11/01/80	4689	0	0	1	1	0	0	0	1	0
22	11/07/80	4695	1	0	0	0	0	0	0	0	0
23	11/15/80	4703	0	0	0	1	0	0	0	1	0
24	11/21/80	4709	0	0	0	1	0	0	0	1	0
25	12/01/80	4719	1	0	1	1	0	0	0	0	0
26	12/11/80	4729	0	0	0	1	0	0	0	1	0
27	12/15/80	4733	0	0	0	1	0	0	1	0	0
28	12/21/80	4739	1	0	0	0	0	0	1	0	0
29	01/01/81	4750	0	0	1	1	0	0	0	0	0
30	03/01/81	4809	0	0	0	1	0	0	1	0	0

termines differences or correlations between spatial orders (variables), sequence analysis examines similarities and differences between temporal orders (discrete events).

The bit-map data files can be analyzed with a variety of statistical methods to identify interpretable time-dependent patterns (or lack thereof) of relationships among innovation dimensions that are coded as 1's and 0's. They include the use of: 1) chi-square tests and log-linear models to examine probable relationships between categorically independent and dependent variables; 2) Granger causality and vector autoregression to identify possible causal relationships between bit-map variables; and 3) time series regression analyses on incidents aggregated into fixed temporal intervals to test specific process models. Other statistical methods are also being explored to examine the temporal duration and sequence among coded events. For example, *renewal theory* can be used to examine whether the duration between two consecutive events in the development of an innovation are distributed according to some known probable distribution, such as the exponential or the more general Weibull distribution. In addition, a "hazard rate" can be computed for each variable of a bit-map if the occurrence of a change on the variable, represented by the value 1, is considered as the occurrence of an event itself.

In an experimental effort, we are currently analyzing bit-map data of several MIRP studies to investigate possible causal relationships among dichotomous indicators of changes in the five MIRP constructs as innovations develop over time. A preliminary cross-correlation analysis, conceptually based on the notion of Granger causality and vector autoregression (Freeman 1983), shows that changes in ideas and, to a lesser degree, in people are significantly associated with later changes in transactions; the reverse, however, is not true. While statements like these are in themselves substantively interesting, other models, such as the lagged log-linear model, are also being explored. Relationships identified in an innovation are being compared with those in other innovations in order to determine if the findings can be replicated in other innovations and settings.

The use of sequential information implies that the values (1 or 0) of some variables at a certain time period may have an impact on the values of the same or other variables at a later time period. For example, changes in an innovation idea may lead to changes in people (a layoff of employees) and transactions (reduced business relationships). Since both causes and effects may take more than the varying time lapse between the occurrence of individual incidents, a researcher may be interested in the aggregate relationships between variables; for instance, between the monthly counts of 1's (changes) in innovation ideas, people, and transactions. Regression analysis of a time series provides systematic methods for going beyond subjective "eye-balling" to an examination of causal relationships in the coded event sequence data.

In order to apply regular time series regression analysis, it is necessary to aggregate the event sequence data into fixed temporal intervals.

("SELAGGR," a computer software program developed by Lin (1989) which performs selection and aggregation operations for raw event sequence data files, was used by MIRP.) Two considerations are involved in aggregating the coded events into fixed temporal intervals: 1) determining the most appropriate interval, and 2) weighting the importance of events.

First, the major substantive consideration is the expected time duration for relationships between variables to take effect. For example, if the time needed for an action or event to take effect is a matter of weeks, aggregation of sequential data into monthly counts could result in the true (weekly) causal links being overlooked or misspecified. On the other hand, other events (such as administrative reviews by resource controllers) often occur in semiannual cycles, and detecting empirical consequences of such events with weekly-count data may produce too much "noise" (extraneous data) and not be possible. In general, the interval chosen should be guided by the substantive theory being examined and the developmental time clock of the innovations being analyzed.

A second consideration in aggregating event sequence data is the assumption that each occurrence has the same weight of importance. This is certainly a strong assumption, but any weighting scheme is arbitrary in some sense. We chose not to weight the importance of events because doing so could bias the results before statistical analysis has demonstrated the importance of certain temporal relationships. Instead, we relied on a qualitative interpretation of the importance of events after quantitative data analysis has established relationships among coded events.

A learning model example.

As an example of the findings produced by time series regression analysis, we are now examining a model of experiential learning to explain the process of business creation in three different organizational settings: 1) a new company start-up, 2) an internal corporate innovation, and 3) an interorganizational joint venture (see Van de Ven et al. 1989; Van de Ven and Polley 1990). The model reveals that actions and outcomes are reciprocally connected: people do more of what is believed to lead to success and less of what leads to failure. Based on this model, incidents were coded in the development of each of the three MIRP innovations in terms of: 1) whether the actions of entrepreneurs expanded or contracted from the previous incident; and 2) whether the actions were judged by entrepreneurs to produce positive or negative outcomes. Figure 9–2 presents graphical profiles of the monthly frequencies of the number of expanding minus contracting actions and the number of positive minus negative outcomes for all incidents throughout the development of the new company start-up, interorganizational joint venture, and internal corporate venture (9–2a, b, and c, respectively).

Three temporal periods are reflected in graphs 9–2b and 9–2c, while no such periods were clearly evident for the new company start-up in graph 9–2a. The three periods include: 1) an initial gestation period, where incidents

FIGURE 9–2a   New Software Company Start-up

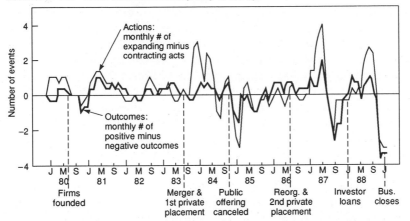

FIGURE 9–2b   Therapeutic Apheresis (TAP) Interorganizational Joint Venture

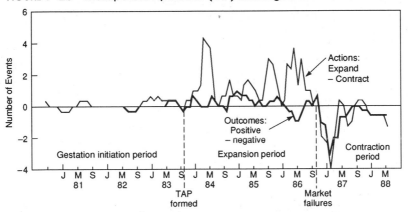

FIGURE 9–2c   Cochlear Implant (CIP) Internal Corporate Venture

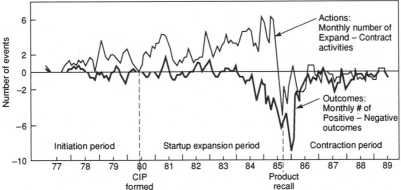

Note: plots are three-month moving averages.

FIGURE 9–2   Three-month moving averages of the number of monthly events in which actions expanded minus contracted and in which outcomes were positive minus negative during the development of three innovations.

occurred that set the stage for entrepreneurs to decide to start a new business; 2) a start-up period of mostly expanding activities that were undertaken to develop a new business with corporate venture capital support; followed by 3) a concluding period of mostly contracting activities and negative outcomes at the time the two business creation ventures were each terminated for different reasons. Very different patterns of associations were found through regression analysis between the actions and outcomes event time series over these three periods. These associations were replicated in the internal corporate venture and interorganizational joint venture cases: 1) actions and outcomes were unrelated in the gestation period, suggesting that no trial-and-error learning occurred; 2) during the expansion period, negative outcomes significantly predicted subsequent expansions of actions, while actions had no effect on subsequent outcomes. This suggests a faulty learning process of escalating commitments to failing courses of action during the expansion period; 3) actions and outcomes were strongly positively correlated during the contraction period, mutually predicting each other over time as the trial-and-error learning model predicted. Unfortunately, in these cases, evidence for trial-and-error learning did not occur until it was too late, as resource controllers terminated the innovations before they could be implemented.

Actions and outcomes were positively related and reflected a greater degree of experiential learning throughout the development of the new company start-up (Figure 9–2a) than in the other two organizational settings. One explanation for these findings is that new products from the business creation process in the new company start-up were more immediately and directly subjected to the "acid test" of the market, whereas new products were withheld from the market for longer times in the business creation efforts within the corporation and the interorganizational joint ventures. In the latter two cases, periodic administrative reviews within or between corporate hierarchies were used to evaluate developmental progress. From these findings we tentatively conclude that administrative reviews are poor substitutes for the "acid" test of the market to judge the economic viability of new business creation efforts.

Pragmatically, this conclusion may be moot since the new company start-up also went out of business in December 1988. These results call into question the basic proposition that the process of learning is related to new business creation success. Evidence of trial-and-error learning was observed to occur (at least for a period) in all the three cases, and all three cases of business creation were terminated or aborted. While the new business creation efforts were terminated for various reasons, the data suggest it was not for a lack of learning.

Analyzing Patterns of Turbulence and Chaos in Temporal Data

The above coding of incidents into event constructs also sets the stage for examining turbulent nonlinear patterns in temporal sequence data. As the previous section suggests, thus far MIRP has had only limited success with efforts to explain innovation development by testing specific theories (such as experiential learning) with general linear models. In particular, the error terms in time series regression models typically account for the major sources of explained variance in the dependent variables, and the time series data have been partitioned into specific temporal periods to capture the shifting relationships among variables over time. This indicates that over the course of innovation development, the relationships among variables are not linear, and that the error terms in our general linear models may contain important signals (e.g., bifurcations, time dependencies, butterfly effects) that are masquerading as "noise." To address these complexities, we are now beginning to explore whether the process of innovation development may be characterized by chaos. While many definitions of chaos theory already exist, even in its short history (Mandelbrot 1982; Prigogine and Stengers 1984; Polkinghorne 1989), we view it as a methodology for examining if the seemingly random behavior observed in the development of innovations contains a pattern of regularity that can result from an underlying deterministic system.

The traditional linear methods used in the previous section assume that a system can produce chaotic behavior only when subjected to random inputs. In other words, an entrepreneurial unit is viewed as an open system subject to random inputs from the environment. The seemingly random component of behavior is then treated as nonmeaningful noise when testing a model of behavior (such as the experiential model of learning examined above). Chaos theory explores whether the random component of behavior might arise endogenously. For example, the time series data graphed in Figures 9–2a, b, and c contain some signal and some "noise." Standard linear techniques focus on analyzing the signal while discarding the "noise" as random. Chaos theory takes the opposite approach. It focuses on the "noise," with the objective of determining to what extent that "noise" can be partitioned into two parts: 1) a truly random component that should continue to be left alone because it remains unmanageable "white noise," and 2) a seemingly random component that may contain meaningful information about system dynamics previously unexaminable without chaos theory and fractal geometry (Mandelbrot 1986, 157).

As applied to entrepreneurship research, the meaningful information that we have not been able to examine systematically before may deal with the inherently open and dynamic processes of innovation development. To say that the process of innovation is open and dynamic implies that the timing and magnitude of perturbations make the dynamic system inherently unpredictable, genuinely novel, and genuinely a "process of becoming" (Polkinghorne 1989). Consequently, one will never know how a system will behave until after it has been developed. However, if the seemingly random behavior of an open system is found to exhibit some regularity (i.e., behaves in a chaotic fashion), then one can identify the permissible boundaries in which entrepreneurial choice and action can occur.

A methodology currently being explored to determine if the innovation process exhibits dynamic properties of chaos was suggested by Koput (1990) for organizational analysis. This methodology consists of both geometrical and numerical procedures. First, a time series of the innovation bit-map data is plotted after removing the autocorrelation and trends from the time series in order to identify the stable or periodic (not random) component of the time series. What remains is the seemingly random portion, to be analyzed for chaos properties. Koput (1990) proposes several procedures for detecting the presence of chaos, including constructing a phase portrait (wherein one plots the values of several states through time), and a power spectrum analysis to examine various fractal/correlational dimensions that would exhibit the presence of chaos. Although these procedures appear promising, it is premature at this writing to go much further, since at present we have no results of these preliminary efforts to determine if innovations exhibit properties of chaos.

CONCLUSION

With the growing interest in understanding how innovation unfolds over time, scholars are searching for conceptual frameworks and systematic methods for studying the process of entrepreneurship. The first part of this chapter summarized some of Schumpeter's (1942) seminal ideas that are very relevant for conceptualizing alternative approaches to contemporary entrepreneurship scholarship in general, and longitudinal research methods for studying the process of entrepreneurship in particular. A set of longitudinal field research methods for studying the process of entrepreneurship, which is centrally concerned with the questions of how and why innovations develop over time, was then proposed. Based on experiences in the Minnesota Innovation Research Program (MIRP), five methodological issues were discussed pertaining to: 1) sample selection; 2) real-time process observation; 3) selecting core concepts for observing innovation processes; 4) identifying and comparing alternative models to explain observed processes; and 5) addressing problems of measurement and sequence analysis to test alternative process models. To deal with this fifth issue, the latter part of this chapter examined the basic operational question of how to represent longitudinal data in a fashion that permits systematic and rigorous analysis of event sequence data. To answer this question, four steps (1–4) dealing with measurement and three steps (5–7) for sequence analysis were suggested:

1. Define the qualitative datum as an incident, bracket raw data collected from the field into these incidents, and enter this information into a qualitative incident data file.
2. Evaluate the validity of classifying raw data into incidents by a) achieving consensus and arriving at consistent interpretations of decision rules among at least two researchers performing this task; and b) asking organizational participants to review the chronological list of incidents that occurred in their innovation or change effort.
3. Code each incident in terms of the presence or absence of theoretical event constructs, and add these codes to the incident data file.

4. Evaluate the reliability of the event coding scheme by following conventional procedures for establishing construct validity and inter-rater reliability of measures.
5. Transform the qualitative codes into dichotomous variables, or a bit-map event sequence data file, which permits time series analysis of process theories of organizational change or development.
6. Analyze temporal relationships between variables in the event sequence data file using a variety of statistical time series procedures appropriate to the theoretical question at hand. Enrich the interpretation of statistical results by reading and content analyzing the relevant sequence of incidents in the qualitative data file (developed in steps 1 through 3 above).
7. Analyze the error component of general linear models to determine if seemingly random behavior exhibits properties of chaos. Procedures and results for undertaking this step remain embryonic and exploratory.

These steps and methods are the children of necessity, in the sense that they are evolving as MIRP struggles with longitudinal field data. Of course, researchers will need to modify and extend these methods to meet the particular circumstances of their own studies; however, they have wide applicability and can also serve a heuristic function by encouraging researchers to think differently about qualitative longitudinal data.

One might draw the conclusion that the methods proposed here may overquantify qualitative data. This conclusion may be the inadvertent result of the objective of this chapter to introduce some systematic new methods which overcome the limitation in most research reports of relying exclusively on subjective "eye-balling" and anecdotal information in qualitative data. However, in practice the objective is to combine the special information that quantitative and qualitative data provide to understand organizational change processes. After all, quantitative data by themselves only provide a skeletal configuration of structural regularities, often devoid of life, flesh, and soul. Qualitative data, by themselves, are like amoebas, which while rich with life are squishy, soft, and absent of apparent structure. Only by combining quantitative and qualitative data in a balanced way can one come to understand the richness of life in its many forms.

REFERENCES

Abbott, A. 1984 Event sequence and event duration: Colligation and measurement. *Historical Methods* 17: 192–204.

1990 A primer on sequence methods. *Organization Science* 1 (4). (Forthcoming).

Aldrich, H. 1979 *Organizations and environments.* New York: McGraw Hill.

1990 Using an ecological perspective to study organizational founding rates. *Entrepreneurship Theory and Practice* 14 (3): 7–24.

Allen, P. M. 1988 Evolution, innovation, and economics. In *Technical change and economic theory,* eds. G. Dosi, C. Freeman, R. Nelson, G. Silverberg, and L. Soete, 95–119.

Awan, A. A. 1986 Marshallian and Schumpeterian theories of economic evolution : Gradualism versus punctualism. *Atlantic Economic Journal* 14 (4) : 37–49.

Bruderl, J., and R. Schussler 1990 Organizational mortality : The liabilities of newness and adolescence. *Administrative Science Quarterly* 35 : 530–547.

Carroll, G. R. 1983 A stochastic model of organizational mortality. *Social Science Research* 12 : 303–329.

1984 Dynamics of publisher succession in newspaper organizations. *Administrative Science Quarterly* 29 : 93–113.

1987 *Publish and perish.* Greenwich, Conn. : JAI Press.

Carroll, G. R., and J. Delacroix 1982 Organizational mortality in the newspaper industries of Argentina and Ireland : An ecological approach. *Administrative Science Quarterly* 27 : 169–198.

Delbecq, A. L., A. Van de Ven, and D. Gustafson 1975 *Group techniques for program planning : A guide to nominal group and Delphi processes.* Glenview, Ill. : Scott Foresman.

Elliott, J. E. 1980 Marx and Schumpeter on capitalism's creative destruction : A comparative restatement. *Quarterly Journal of Economics* 95 (1) : 45–68.

1983 Schumpeter and the theory of capitalist economic development. *Journal of Economic Behavior and Organization* 4 : 277–308.

Fichman, M. A., and D. A. Levinthal 1988 Honeymoons and the liability of adolescence : A new perspective on duration dependence in social and organizational relationships. Working paper, Carnegie Mellon Univ.

Folger, J. P., D. E. Hewes, and M. S. Poole 1984 Coding social interaction. In *Progress in communication sciences,* eds. B. Dervin and M. Voight, Vol. 5. Norwood, N.J. : Ablex.

Freeman, J. 1983 Granger causality and the time series analysis of political relationships. *American Journal of Political Science* 27 : 337–358.

Freeman, J., G. Carroll, and M. T. Hennan 1983 The liability of newness : Age dependence in organizational death rates. *American Sociological Review* 48 : 692–710.

Gartner, W. B. 1990 What are we talking about when we talk about entrepreneurship ? *Journal of Business Venturing* 5 : 15–28.

Glaser, B. G., and A. L. Strauss 1967 *The discovery of grounded theory : Strategies for qualitative research.* Chicago : Aldine.

Gould, S. J. 1989 Punctuated equilibrium in fact and theory. *Journal of Social Biological Structure* 12 : 117–136.

Hagedoorn, J. 1989 *The dynamic analysis of innovation and diffusion : A study in process control.* London : Pinter Publishers.

Halliday, T. C., M. J. Powell, and M. W. Granfors 1987 Minimalist organizations : Vital events in State Bar Associations, 1870–1930. *American Sociological Review* 52 : 456–471.

Hannan, M. T., and J. Freeman 1977 The population ecology of organizations. *American Journal of Sociology* 82 : 929–964.

1984 Structural inertia and organizational change. *American Sociological Review* 49 : 149–164.

1989 *Organizational ecology.* Cambridge, Mass. : Harvard Univ. Press.

Kaplan, A. 1964 *The conduct of inquiry: Methodology for behavioral science.* New York: Chandler.

Koput, K. 1990 Chaos in the evolution of an organizational population: Theoretical speculations and empirical evidence from the U.S. brewing industry. Working paper, Univ. of California at Berkeley.

Lin, T. 1989 SELAGGR: A selection and aggregation program for bit-map data. Technical Report, Strategic Management Research Center, Univ. of Minnesota.

Lord, F. M., and M. R. Novick 1968 *Statistical theories of mental test scores.* Reading, Mass.: Addison-Wesley.

Mandelbrot, B. B. 1982 *The fractal geometry of nature.* San Francisco: Freeman.

1986 Fractals and the rebirth of iteration theory. In *The beauty of fractals,* by H. O. Peitgen and P. H. Richter, 151–160. Berlin: Springer-Verlag.

Miles, M. B., and A. M. Huberman 1984 *Qualitative data analysis: A sourcebook of new methods.* Beverly Hills, Cal.: Sage Publications.

Mitroff, I., and J. Emshoff 1979 On strategic assumption making: A dialectical approach to policy and planning. *Academy of Management Review* 4 (1): 1–12.

Pelz, D. C. 1985 Innovation complexity and the sequence of innovating stages. *Knowledge: Creation, Diffusion, and Utilization* 6: 261–291.

Pettigrew, A. 1985 *The awakening giant: Continuity and change in ICI.* Oxford: Basil Blackwell.

Polkinghorne, J. 1989 *Science and creation: The search for understanding.* Boston: Shambhala New Science Library.

Polley, D., and A. H. Van de Ven 1989 Therapeutic apheresis program joint-venture case. In *Research on the management of innovation,* eds. A. H. Van de Ven, H. L. Angle, and M. S. Poole, 261–276. New York: Harper & Row.

Poole, M. S. 1983a Decision development in small groups II: A study of multiple sequences in decision making. *Communication Monographs* 50: 206–232.

1983b Decision development in small groups III: A multiple sequence model of group decision development. *Communication Monographs* 50: 321–341.

Poole, M. S., and A. H. Van de Ven 1989a Toward a general theory of innovation. In *Research on the management of innovation: The Minnesota Studies,* eds. A. H. Van de Ven, H. L. Angle, and M. S. Poole, 637–662. New York: Harper & Row.

1989b Using paradox to build management and organization theories. *Academy of Management Review* 14 (4): 562–578.

Prigogine, I., and S. Stengers 1984 *Order out of chaos.* New York: Heinemann.

Roberts, E. B. 1990 *Entrepreneurs and high-technology: Lessons from M.I.T. and beyond.* Cambridge, Mass.: MIT Sloan School. Forthcoming

Ronstadt, R., J. A. Hornaday, R. Peterson, and K. H. Vesper 1986 Introduction, in *Frontiers of entrepreneurship research,* eds. R. Ronstadt, et al., xii–xviii. Wellesley, Mass.: Babson College.

Ruttan, V. W. 1959 Usher and Schumpeter on invention, innovation, and technological change. *Quarterly Journal of Economics* 73 (November): 596–606.

Schoonhoven, C. B., and K. M. Eisenhardt 1987 *A study of the influence of organizational, entrepreneurial, and environmental factors on the growth and development of technology-based startup firms.* Washington, D.C.: U.S. Department of Commerce, National Technical Information Service.

Schumpeter, J. A. 1942 *Capitalism, socialism, and democracy.* New York: Harper & Row.

Singh, J. V., R. J. House, and D. J. Tucker 1986 Organizational change and organizational mortality. *Administrative Science Quarterly* 31 : 587–611.

Stevenson, H., and S. Harmeling 1990 Entrepreneurial management's need for a more "chaotic" theory. *Journal of Business Venturing* 5 : 1–14.

Stinchcombe, A. L. 1965 Social structures and organizations. In *Handbook of organizations,* ed. J. G. March, 142–193. Chicago : Rand McNally.

Strauss, A. L. 1987 *Qualitative analysis for social scientists.* New York : Cambridge Univ. Press.

Tushman, M., and E. Romanelli 1985 Organizational evolution : A metamorphosis model of convergence and reorientation. In *Research in organizational behavior,* eds. L. Cummings and B. Staw, 7, 171–222. Greenwich, Conn. : JAI Press.

Van de Ven, A. H. 1980 Early planning, implementation, and performance of new organizations. In *The organizational life cycle,* eds. J. R. Kimberly and R. H. Miles, 83–134. San Francisco : Jossey-Bass.

Van de Ven, A. H., and H. L. Angle 1989 An introduction to the Minnesota Innovation Research Program. In *Research on the management of innovation,* eds. A. H. Van de Ven, H. L. Angle, and M. S. Poole, 3–30. New York : Harper & Row.

Van de Ven, A. H., H. L. Angle, and M. S. Poole, eds. 1989 *Research on the management of innovation.* New York : Harper & Row.

Van de Ven, A. H., and Y. Chu 1989 A psychometric assessment of the Minnesota Innovation Survey. In *Research on the management of innovation,* eds. A. H. Van de Ven, H. L. Angle, and M. S. Poole, 55–104. New York : Harper & Row.

Van de Ven, A. H., and D. L. Ferry 1980 *Measuring and assessing organizations.* New York : Wiley.

Van de Ven, A. H., and R. Garud 1989 A framework for studying the emergence of new industries. In *Research on technological+ innovation, management and policy,* eds. R. S. Rosenbloom and R. A. Burgelman, Vol. 4. Greenwich, Conn. : JAI Press.

Van de Ven, A. H., and G. P. Huber 1990 Longitudinal field research methods for studying processes of organizational change. *Organizational Science* 1 (3): 213–219.

Van de Ven, A. H., and D. Polley 1990 Learning while innovating. Strategic Management Research Center, Univ. of Minnesota, Discussion Paper # 146.

Van de Ven, A. H., and M. S. Poole 1990 Methods for studying innovation development in the Minnesota Innovation Research Program. *Organizational Science* 1 (3): 313–335.

Van de Ven, A. H., S. Venkataraman, D. Polley, and R. Garud 1989 Processes of new business creation in different organizational settings. In *Research on the management of innovation,* eds. A. H. Van de Ven, H. L. Angle, and M. S. Poole, 221–297. New York : Harper & Row.

Weick, K. 1979 *The social psychology of organizing.* 2d ed. Reading, Mass. : Addison-Wesley.

Chapter

10

Research Applications of
the Small Business Data
Base of the U.S. Small
Business Administration

Bruce A. Kirchhoff
and
Bruce D. Phillips

●

INTRODUCTION

The most useful source of data for examining the population of small businesses in the United States is unquestionably the data base edited and maintained by the U.S. Small Business Administration. This source of data is often referred to simply as the Small Business Data Base (SBDB). In truth, however, the SBDB consists of more than one data base, although the majority of use focuses on only one.

The data base most often used is the U.S. Establishment and Enterprise Microdata File (USEEM) and its companion, the U.S. Establishment Longitudinal Microdata File (USELM). This is a unique data base within the federal government, because the data originate in a private, for-profit corporation, and the data base includes clear identification of each establishment, including its location, primary business function (SIC code), owning enterprise, and other descriptive data.

In particular, the identification of each establishment makes the SBDB different from other government data sources. Traditionally, U.S. government data bases are surrounded by individual data privacy rules, regulations, and laws which require that the data be collected solely by authorized government agencies. Microlevel (individual reporting unit) data may not be disclosed to anyone except bonded agents of the government who are sworn to secrecy about the data which they see. This tradition of privacy constrains the research methods that can be applied to government data by prohibiting statistical analysis at the individual reporting unit level.

The SBDB is also the only data base which provides enterprise data by firm size on a current basis. Most federal data bases are establishment data bases, so they do not separate establishments which are large firms from those which are small firms. For studying entrepreneurship, it is critical to make this distinction, because an establishment owned by IBM, for example, is obviously quite different from an individually owned and operated enterprise.

Recognition of typical federal data base constraints led to the development of the SBDB and the selection of a private corporation as the data source. This private corporation is Dun & Bradstreet, which operates the world's largest business credit rating and reporting system. A firm supplies information to Dun & Bradstreet (D&B) knowing that the information will be accessed by other businesses to determine the firm's credit rating. The firm gives the data to D&B so that other firms can have easy access to it, and so that the firm can conduct its regular business functions without having to continually justify its existence to suppliers and customers. Firms which provide data to D&B clearly do so with full knowledge that D&B intends to share the data with other firms and government agencies. There are no government-imposed privacy rules or regulations which restrict the availability of this data. However, the Small Business Administration is not allowed to release the names of individual firms in D&B's files without payment of a licensing fee to the Dun & Bradstreet Corporation.

The availability of microdata has opened up a whole range of new research methods which, when applied, have produced a different view of the U.S. economy. These new understandings have radically changed our perceptions of the importance of small firms to U.S. economic growth and development. Without question, the most important research issue has been the job generation contribution of small firms.

We begin our review of research applications of the SBDB with a discussion of job generation research. This is followed by discussions of financial research, macroindicators of the U.S. economy, and studies of specific public policy topics.

JOB CREATION BY SMALL FIRMS

Interestingly, the original work on this subject was not conducted using the SBDB. In fact, the creation of the SBDB emerged from the seminal work of David Birch with the D&B data files (Birch 1979). It can be honestly said that Birch's work was the impetus for the creation of the Small Business Data Base, and that the SBA file development efforts were designed specifically to replicate and improve upon his methods. Therefore, although somewhat tangential to the strict definition of our topic, it is essential to summarize Birch's work at the outset of our review.

Birch's Research with the MIT Data Base

Birch's seminal contribution exists in the form of an unpublished research report produced for the Economic Development Administration, U.S. Department of Commerce (1979). Entitled "The Job Generation Process," this report noted that 80 percent of the new jobs created in the United States from 1969 through 1976 were created by firms with fewer than 100 employees. Birch came to this conclusion by applying a unique methodology to the D&B data. He identified each firm based upon its size in 1969 or at the time it entered the D&B files. He then examined the net change in employment for each firm and summed up the net new jobs for small firms and large firms separately.

Birch's findings led to quite different conclusions than those widely believed to be irrefutable by labor economists at the time. His methodology stands in sharp contrast with traditional employment analysis methods, which are classified as "comparative static methods." The difference in methodologies is the reason for the difference in conclusions as well as the reason for the emergence of a whole new area of small business economic research. Thus, let us take a moment to contrast the two methodologies.

Comparative Statistics

Labor economists, in general, have applied research methodologies that fit the government's published employment data, which was the only reliable data available. Due to the privacy constraints on government data, as mentioned earlier, such data is published in classified form. Employment within a specific firm is not published, but is accumulated into the sum for the class which it represents — such as total employment counts for all firms within a size class. For example, published data shows total employment for all firms in the United States which have over 5000 employees, 1000 to 4999 employees, 500 to 999 employees, etc.

By comparing the total employment of each size class over many years, economists had unanimously concluded that most growth in employment occurred among firms within the larger size classes (above 1000 employees). Thus, it was assumed that large firms created most of the net new jobs in the United States.

An example of comparative static methodology is shown in the top half of Table 10–1. Note that this method uses the net number of new jobs added to each firm size class. During the 1976–1980 time period, the net change in employment for all firms was 10,983,000. Employment totals for the 1–19 employee size class increased by 918,000 jobs. Employment totals for the other

TABLE 10–1 — A Comparison of Comparative Static and Dynamic Methodologies Net Change in Employment Attributable to Each Size Class : 1976–1980

	Total Employment Change :		Employment Size of Firm :				
	(Thousands)	(Percent)	1–19	20–99	100–499	<500	500+
Comparative static analysis[1]							
Employment change	10,983	14.3%	918	1,379	1,973	4,270	6,622
Percent of employment change	100.0%	N.A.	8.4%	12.6%	18.0%	38.9%	60.3%
Dynamic analysis[2]							
Employment change	10,983	14.3%	3,170	1,460	1,155	5,784	5,108
Percent of employment change	100.0%	N.A.	29.1%	13.4%	10.6%	53.1%	46.9%

[1] Comparative static adapted from Table C–2, page 421 of *The state of small business : A report of the president*, May, 1985. U.S. Government Printing Office, Wash, DC.

[2] Dynamic analysis adapted from Table 1.9, page 22 of *The state of small business : A report of the president*, May, 1985. U.S. Government Printing Office, Wash, DC.

classes are shown in the same row of Table 10–1. Thus, comparative static analysis concludes that firms in the 1–19 size class contributed 8.4 percent of the total increase in employment.

The problem with this type of comparative static analysis is that it assumes that firms in any one size class remain in that size class year after year. Thus, total employment changes are attributable to the growth and/or decline of the firms in the size class. Interclass movement of firms is assumed to be negligible. For example, a firm that grows from 10 employees to 50 employees moves from one class to another and has its total employment added into the 20–99 size class. The net result is the appearance that 50 jobs have been added to that size class while 10 jobs have been lost in the 1–19 size class. Thus, firm growth tends to understate employment changes in small size classes and overstate employment growth in larger size classes.

Another way to view comparative static methodology is to perceive it as defining firm size on the basis of employment at the end of a period, not the beginning. Thus, a small firm (1–19 employees) that grows large (20–99) is defined as a large firm in comparative statics. One might argue that one definition (at the beginning or end of a period) is as good as another, unless one is interested in firm growth rates. As noted above, growth rates cannot be measured accurately if firms are defined by their size at the end of a period.

Dynamic Analysis

What Birch's research revealed is that interclass movements are not negligible; furthermore, they may dominate changes in employment. With a microdata file, firms can now be identified at birth, observed while they grow and decline, and even watched as they terminate operations. Birch's original research (1979) mapped out these dynamics but led the way for further research by the Small Business Administration. Eventually, Birch found that these dynamics — formation, growth, decline, and termination — are the principal causes of employment change. The majority of these dynamics occur among firms that begin small.

Table 10–1 presents a second analysis of the same time period using dynamic methods. Since a different data base (SBDB) was used for the lower half of this table, the change in total employment count is slightly different than the top half. Nonetheless, note that the 1–19 class produces 29.1 percent of the net new employment. And, as we look at the larger size classes, their percentage of net new jobs declines in relation to the comparative static analysis. This result is expected since, in comparative static analysis, firm growth produces a bias which tends to understate the job contribution of smaller size classes and overstate that of larger classes. The true effect of firm growth is apparent in dynamic analysis but is lost in comparative static analysis.

A good discussion of these differences is also found in Armington (1989) in a paper which uses both comparative statics and dynamic analysis to show the differences in growth in the wholesale trade sector in 1982. More recently,

Birch has also published an expansion of his findings in *Job Creation in America* (1987), where his original research is supported by analysis that identifies the role of formation, growth, decline, and termination. Although Birch's first report was subjected to wide criticism, many economists now recognize the bias inherent in comparative static methods and acknowledge the wisdom of Birch's methods and conclusions. But, criticism still appears in the form of traditional comparative static analysis. Recently, Brown, Hamilton, and Medoff (1990) published a book containing a critique of the research which shows that small businesses create most of the new jobs. This critique is actually little more than the application of comparative static methods. The authors do not seem to understand their own methodological process and seem to believe that they have created a new truth.

SBA's Research Findings

SBA's data base development effort was begun in 1979 under Public Law 96–302 with special funding from the Congress and some disagreements over the whole concept of micro data base construction. Because most of the analysts managing and guiding the data base effort today are the same persons who started the data base in 1979, there has been a great deal of continuity in the development of the data base during the past 10 years. Detailed descriptions of the data base are available in the annual *The State of Small Business: A Report of the President* and in publications prepared by the U.S. SBA, particularly the "1976–1986 Linked USEEM User's Guide" (1988), and "The Small Business Data Base: A User's Guide" (1990).

The greatest value of the data base is in longitudinal analysis, because it is such analysis that has revealed the dynamics which drive the U.S. economy. Very early in the development of the data base, there was some effort to replicate Birch's earlier findings from the late 1970s. Thus, "short-run" analyses were and are conducted as each new two-year segment is added to the file. (An insufficient number of small firms are updated each year by Dun & Bradstreet to justify the expense of producing the SBDB on an annual basis, although current files are used as sampling frames.) It was not until 1984, after the 1976 and 1982 data were incorporated into the files, that the SBDB began to be used for meaningful dynamic analysis of longitudinal employment changes.

Short-Run Analyses

No doubt the most significant short-run analysis of the data base has been the biennial (two-year) calculation of the percentage of net new jobs created by small and large firms. The first of these was published in 1982 by the Brookings Institution (Armington and Odle 1982). The authors did not find support for Birch's (1979) conclusions. But by 1988 it was apparent that Brookings had selected the only biennial period which differed from the norm in over 20 years — this is called the "bad luck" of the draw. Since then, the SBA has accumulated net employment shares for six biennial periods, and in all of them, small businesses' job creation share is larger than its share of employment in the economy (consistently about 35 percent). The overall longitudinal series combining Birch's original work with the SBA's subsequent findings is shown in Table 10–2. Unfortunately, Birch discontinued producing two-year employment change shares in 1979, so there is no overlap in the statistical results and no way to do a direct comparison of findings from the two separate data bases. However, consistency of the share percentages over time suggests that small businesses do indeed create the majority of new jobs.

Subsequent research findings also suggest that small businesses' share of net employment growth varies depending upon the overall economic cycle (Gray and Phillips 1983; U.S. SBA 1982–1990: see vols. 1984–1990). Small businesses seem to generate about the same number of jobs in good times and bad, but large firms generate more jobs during the later years of extended economic expansions. So, small businesses' share of total job generation falls during late periods of economic expansion and rises during recessions.

Dynamics and Longitudinal Analysis

Understanding the dynamics of formation, growth, decline, and termination are important research objectives. Although microeconomic analyses have been widely used in understanding the dynamics of growth, the research reported in the first six to eight years' experience with the SBDB suggests that the macroeconomic effects may be far more important than currently realized.

Towards this goal, the SBA carried out a series of job generation studies which are summarized in the form of tables and charts published in the 1985

TABLE 10–2 — Percentage of Jobs Created in the United States by Firms with Fewer than 100 Employees, 1969–1986

Period of Observation	% of Jobs Created by Firms with <100 Employees
1969–1972	82%
1972–1974	53%
1974–1976	65%
1976–1978	57%
1978–1980	37%
1980–1982	92%
1982–1984	65%
1984–1986	44%

Source: 1969–1976: D. L. Birch, "The Job Generation Process," Prepared by the MIT Program on Neighborhood and Regional Change for the Economic Development Administration, 1979; 1976–1986: U.S. Small Business Administration, Office of Advocacy, Small Business Data Base, Linked 1976–1986 USELM file, published in *The state of small business: A report of the president* (Washington, D.C., GPO), 1983–1989 eds., respectively.

edition of *The State of Small Business: A Report of the President.* There is a special appendix that focuses solely on statistical results obtained from the SBDB. For the first time, statistics for longitudinal changes in employment by industry showing the relative contribution of small and large firms appear in this publication. Some statistics are shown for regional changes while others are for national level analysis only.

By early 1987, 10 years of data (including 1986) had been incorporated into the USELM. With this, Kirchhoff and Phillips (1989a) examined the changes in employment due to establishment formation, growth, decline, and termination (exits) for 1976 through 1986. The unique characteristic of this research is that each establishment is classified by the size of its owning firm in 1976 or at the time of its formation. Thus, the changes in employment were attributable to small and large firms based upon their size at the beginning of the period — a truly dynamic analysis.

The results of this analysis are shown in Table 10–3. Most important is to note the surprisingly large "flow" of jobs. In a society where almost 120 million are employed, there were 50.8 million jobs created (37 million entries and 13 million expansions) and 33.8 million jobs lost between 1976 and 1984 to produce a net increase of 17.0 million jobs. This data leads us to the conclusion that labor mobility is the most important characteristic of a dynamic economy.

Table 10–3 also shows that small firms (under 500 employees) have contributed the majority of new jobs due to entries (54.6 percent) and have about the same share of exits (53.6 percent) and expansions (56.8 percent). But small firms also have a disproportionately smaller share of contractions (47.9 percent). Large firms, not surprisingly, have the largest share of job losses due to contractions (52.1 percent). These findings are consistent with the research of Reynolds and Maki (1990) as well as Birch (1987), who show that American labor markets are characterized by large amounts of turmoil and that small firms are vital in providing new jobs.

In 1989, Kirchhoff and Phillips (1989b) published an analysis of job creation in high- and low-technology industries. Comparing high and low job growth with high- and low-technology industry groupings showed that new firms in high-technology industries have a larger percentage of high-growth firms than new firms in low-technology industries. On the other hand, the number of births in low-technology industries so outnumber those in high-technology industries that low-technology industries still dominate job creation by a sizable margin.

Also in 1989, Kirchhoff and McAuliffe used the SBDB to study the growth of new firms during the economic recovery of Massachusetts from 1976 through 1986. Here they found that in the manufacturing sector, large firms showed a net loss of over 51,000 jobs, while small firms added over 52,000 net new jobs. The net effect was that manufacturing employment stayed about the same in Massachusetts for 10 years, because large firms closed plants and reduced work forces in other facilities. Moreover, among the 52,000 net new jobs created by small manufacturing firms, new firms formed between 1976 and

TABLE 10–3 — Employment Dynamics by Firm Size, 1976–1984

FIRM SIZE (Number of Employees)	CHANGES IN ESTABLISHMENT EMPLOYMENT (THOUSANDS)								TOTAL CHANGES	
	Entries		Exits		Expansions		Contractions			
	Number	Percent	Number	Percent	Number	Percent	Number	Percent	Number	Percent
1–499	20,504	54.6%	− 14,312	53.6%	7,490	56.8%	− 3,390	47.9%	10,292	60.5%
500+	17,074	45.4%	− 12,366	46.4%	5,700	43.2%	− 3,692	52.1%	6,716	39.5%
Total	37,578	100.0%	− 26,678	100.0%	13,190	100.0%	− 7,082	100.0%	17,008	100.0%

Source : Adapted from B. A. Kirchhoff and B. D. Phillips, 1989, "The effect of firm formation and growth on job creation in the United States," *Journal of Business Venturing* 3 : 261–272.

1980 created 13,000, or 25 percent, of these new jobs. In other words, new small firms provided a major portion of the net new jobs created by all manufacturing firms.

Across all industries, new small firms created 15 percent of the net new jobs in Massachusetts. Interestingly, during this 10-year period (1976–1986), Massachusetts had a below-average rate of new-firm formations. Thus, Massachusetts' experience with job creation by new firms was atypical. While new small firms are very important to economic growth in their aggregate, their importance in creating new jobs and economic growth has not yet been fully demonstrated in every industry and in every region.

In summary, job generation research is only now beginning to document fully the intricate mechanisms by which small firms account for such a large percentage of net new job formation. David Birch's (1979) original observations were somewhat crude, but subsequent SBA-sponsored research using the SBDB has confirmed his findings and identified the dynamics that underlie his initial observations. Research in other countries using similar microdata sources has confirmed that small business dynamics are also at work in other economies (see OECD 1985; Storey and Johnson 1987), and that a large influx of new jobs and new firms have dominated economic growth from the mid-1970s through the mid-1980s.

Economists have long overlooked the impact of new business formation, growth, decline, and termination, but the SBDB provides a source for continuing research that is changing this traditional view. The concepts of evolutionary economics, scoffed at by many, seem to provide a far better explanation for small business dynamics than classical economic theory. Confirming this perception and uncovering a better theoretical explanation for such dynamics is the challenge which the SBDB and job generation researchers face in the future. In particular, better models must evolve which not only trace the longevity of jobs created by small firms, but which also provide demographic data on job quality as well.

FINANCIAL APPLICATIONS OF THE SMALL BUSINESS DATA BASE

During the past decade, the U.S. SBA Office of Advocacy has also used the SBDB in a number of policy areas to study the sources of financing and the operating characteristics of small firms. These research applications have taken a number of diverse forms. First, the SBDB has served as a *sampling frame* to determine the size and characteristics of the informal capital market, sometimes referred to as "adventure" capital to distinguish it from the better known venture capital market. Second, the SBDB has provided the sampling frame to generate a list of hard-to-identify components of the small business sector — such as minority-owned and women-owned firms — to study their financing characteristics. Finally, the SBDB was also recently used by the Federal Reserve Board to generate the sample for the Study of Small Firm Finances — a very detailed, nationally representative listing of firms used to study changes in the geographic concentration of banking markets resulting from banking deregulation.

In addition to its use as a sampling frame, the Small Business Data Base has been *combined with other unpublished data* to increase the availability of financial information about small firms. For example, the SBDB is now serving as the *control group* in a study of the Small Business Administration's 7a guaranteed loan program. This is the major congressionally authorized program by which small firms receive start-up and expansion financing through a loan from a private bank participating in the SBA program ; up to 75 percent of the loan's value is guaranteed by the government.

Finally, data from the SBDB has also been combined with unpublished IRS information on the characteristics of firms by legal form of organization to derive additional data on the operating characteristics of small firms.

All the major projects mentioned above deserve additional study, discussion, and elaboration.

Informal Investment Capital

During the 1980s, the Office of Advocacy sponsored a number of studies to determine the role of informal equity capital in helping to finance the start-up of new small, entrepreneurial firms. While some regional work had been done prior to the creation of the SBDB (Wetzel and Seymour 1979), the data base provided the first opportunity to conduct a large-scale national survey of informal investors. The work of Aram (1987) and Gaston and Bell (1988) used the SBDB to produce a random, stratified national sample of over 240,000 enterprises to measure the size of the informal investor market.

Probably the most noteworthy finding from these studies is that "business angels" provide the single largest source of external financing for new small businesses in the United States. In particular, the annual increment of new informal capital has been estimated to be $32 billion, compared with about one-quarter of that amount in new venture capital (Gaston 1989 ; Ou 1987). In addition, this finding means that about 1 in 10 new businesses in the United States is started with informal investment capital. These investments average about $40K per investor, and the typical firm financed in this way starts life with about $250K. Some informal investors make two to three investments per year, often within 50 miles of their home, and sit on the boards of the companies in which they invest (Gaston 1989).

Women-Owned and Minority-Owned Firms

As indicated above, the SBDB has also been used as a sampling frame to obtain additional information about the financing of small women-owned and minority-owned firms. But the first problem in obtaining financial information about these business owners is to obtain a representative national sample of the universe of such entrepreneurs. In 1985, a stratified 3 percent random sample of the SBDB was used to derive a national sample of minority-owned and women-owned firms. This was required because there was no other national sample of such firms available to the SBA. A list of women-owned and minority-owned firms is maintained by the Bureau of the Census, U.S. Department of Commerce. This list is used as the sampling frame for the censuses of minority-owned and women-owned business enterprises every five years. But, because of data privacy restrictions, this list is not available to anyone outside of the Bureau of the Census. These efforts were also made more difficult because response rates to such mail surveys are generally low (e.g., in the 15 percent range). The actual response to the SBA survey was 12 percent. To ascertain that no bias existed in the responses, 1000 follow-up telephone calls were also made, with the result that no difference between the mail and telephone surveys was found. Using this derived sample list, the SBA proceeded to conduct a survey to collect financial information on women-owned and minority-owned firms.

The results showed that established women-owned firms faced no disproportionate discrimination in the credit markets. On the other hand, the study did indicate that loans were often unavailable to minority-owned firms. For the first time, baseline data on the assets, liabilities, and sources of start-up capital were also shown for both kinds of firms according to the stage of the firm's development (Ando 1985).

Federal Reserve Study of Small-Firm Finances

As part of its ongoing responsibility to monitor the effects of banking deregulation, the Federal Reserve Board (FRB) needs financial information by firm size. In 1988, the FRB asked the SBA for a nationally representative sample from the USEEM files in order to conduct a study of the changing concentration of financial markets. Using an extremely detailed 35-page questionnaire, 4000 small companies participated in the nation's most comprehensive examination of small firms' funding sources and uses of funds. Detailed information was collected on the borrowing practices of the firms, as well as on major balance sheet and income items. Over 400 women-owned firms were included in the study, as well as a sample of firms that had previously received SBA guaranteed loans. As a result of this study, the FRB will produce publicly available Statistical Analysis System (SAS) files, which should be available in December of 1990.

One accomplishment from the FRB study was that it allowed researchers, for the first time, to estimate the percentage of women-owned firms by legal form of organization in the SBDB. Prior to this survey, there was no *publicly accessible* data on the distribution of firms by gender of owner and legal form of organization. The FRB study revealed, for example, that while women own 31 percent of the nonfarm sole proprietorships in this country, they also own less than 15 percent of the partnerships and corporations, and provide less than 5 percent of the nation's gross receipts (sales).

The Small Business Data Base as a Control Group

Since its inception in 1953, the SBA has had various loan programs designed to assist firms who have difficulty obtaining loans from standard commercial lending sources. The most popular of these has been the SBA 7a guaranteed loan program, in which the government currently guarantees up to 75 percent of the loan, as stated earlier, up to a maximum of $750K.

In light of the significant changes in the banking markets which have occurred since deregulation during the early 1980s, Congress requested the agency evaluate its own guaranteed loan program. For this ongoing study, scheduled to be completed during 1991, the agency chose a control group of non–loan recipients from SBA's USEEM files. Since 25 percent of loan recipients are now start-up companies, the age variable on the Dun's Market Identifier (DMI) data files is particularly useful for this exercise. In choosing a control group, the USEEM files will be sorted by industry, firm size, region, and prior growth. Were it not for the availability of the SBDB, it is not clear what kind of control group could be used, because it is the 1985 and 1986 loan recipients which are being analyzed.

■■■■■■■■■

MACROINDICATORS OF
THE U.S. ECONOMY

The SBDB has frequently been combined with other files to generate a more complete measure of the health of the small business sector within the U.S. economy. Two specific applications of this have been 1) the measurement of employment in "small-business-dominated" industries, and 2) the derivation of a general index of small business health.

There is no current or recent measure of employment change by firm size published by the federal government. Virtually all measures are by establishment size at a particular location, not firm size. Only *Enterprise Statistics,* published by the Bureau of the Census with a three-to-five-year lag, provides employment data by firm size. In order to provide more timely data, the SBA's Office of Economic Research has used the SBDB to classify industries into different subsets based upon the percentage of employees in each industry falling within the small business definition — e.g., employment in firms with fewer than 500 employees. Essentially, the SBDB is used to classify industries as being either small-business-dominated, large-business-dominated, or not dominated by either small or large firms. Using this baseline definition, a small-business-dominated industry is one in which at least 60 percent of the industry's employment is in firms with fewer than 500 employees. Employment change is then calculated on a current basis for both the small- and large-business-dominated subsets of industries by using the current establishment employment data from the Bureau of Labor Statistics (BLS).

In reality, it's a bit more complicated than that. It is possible for small-business-dominated industries to have large firms in them, so long as those firms make up less than 40 percent of that industry. Therefore, using the concept of a small-business-dominated industry to measure employment growth means including a share of large business growth. The opposite is true in the case of large-business-dominated sectors. While this concept tends to confound the measurement problem, it has been used as a proxy for the desired job creation statistics, which are not available on a current basis, as mentioned earlier.

As an example of the use of the SBDB to measure current employment change by firm size, see Table 10-4.

TABLE 10-4 — Small- and Large-Business-Dominated and Indeterminate Industries' Share of Total Employment, 1981–1987 (Percent)

Year	Small-Business-Dominated Industries	Large-Business-Dominated Industries	Indeterminate Industries
1987	53.5	36.4	10.1
1986	53.4	37.0	10.0
1985	53.5	37.0	9.5
1984	52.5	37.8	9.7
1983	51.5	38.7	9.8
1982	50.1	39.5	10.4
1981	50.0	40.0	10.0

Note : Small-business-dominated industries are industries in which a minimum of 60 percent of the industry employment is in firms with fewer than 500 employees in 1986. Similarly, large-business-dominated industries are industries in which a minimum of 60 percent of the industry employment is in firms with more than 500 employees in 1986. In indeterminate industries, the small or large business employment share falls between 40 and 60 percent of industry employment. A few industries (two-digit and three-digit level coverage) were not covered by the BLS in 1981 and 1982. However, from 1983 forward, the BLS expanded its employment coverage and included more detailed industry data. As a result of that survey expansion, adjustments to the post-1983 data were necessary. Some three-digit level industries were condensed to the two-digit level and some industries were deleted due to lack of coverage in the earlier time periods. For further information, see "The Determination of Small Business Industry Dominance Methodology," prepared by the SBA Office of Advocacy, Office of Economic Research, Data Base Development Branch.

Source : Adapted by the Office of Advocacy, U.S. Small Business Administration, from the Bureau of Labor Statistics, U.S. Department of Labor, *Employment and Earnings,* various issues.

The Small Business Health Index (SBHI)

The lack of current or timely measures by firm size has also led to indirect means to create a more effective measure of the overall health of the small business sector. Based upon a study by Archibald and Baker (1985), a more comprehensive index has been used by the SBA to measure the current health of small business. Essentially this index combines three variables on a current basis in order to measure small business health : employment change in small-business-dominated industries, the change in business failures, and the change in new business incorporations. The change in employment in small-business-dominated industries is measured from the SBDB as described earlier. (These three variables are also highly correlated with changes in small business or proprietorship income upon which the index is based.) A fuller, more complete explanation of the SBHI is found in Boden (1990).

Applications

The small-business-dominated industry concept, derived from the SBDB, is used in several ways in *The State of Small Business,* a report prepared annually for the Congress. In addition to displaying the current index of small business health, the small-business-dominated concept is also used to display data on new business start-ups and failures by industry ; this data comes from the Dun & Bradstreet Corporation, and the SBDB is used to classify the component industries. Therefore, in addition to being used as a direct measure of small business health, the small-business-dominated concept is used to place other data series into a small business context, and acts as an anchor to derive macroinformation about the small business sector.

Small Business Share of Manufactured Exports

Recently, for the first time, measurements have been made of the share of manufactured exports contributed by small firms in the economy. This was accomplished by matching data from SBA's USEEM file with the export data from the Port Import-Export Reporting System (PIERS) data base, maintained by the *Journal of Commerce.* This task involved a name and address match because only the exporting firm's name and address were in common between the SBDB and PIERS files (Faucett 1988). What made this data-matching task even more difficult, however, was that an exporting firm was often a freight broker, a wholesaler, or an export trading company, and *not* the manufacturer of the specific product. In this study, the leading industries with significant percentages of small business exports were found to be in the leather, apparel, printing, and lumber industries.

━━ ━━ ━━ ━━ ━━ ━━ ━━ ━━

STUDIES OF SPECIFIC
POLICY AREAS

Geographic Area Studies

In addition to its use in defining aggregate economic indicators and in acting as a sampling frame to study the finances of small firms, the SBDB has also been used in economic development studies of states and regions. Specifically, studies have been conducted to determine the impact of small-firm growth by state, and in both rural and urban areas. In many cases, the state-based studies examined the role of the impact of new births in economic development.

As mentioned earlier, Kirchhoff and McAuliffe (1989) found new-firm formations were an important component of new job creation in Massachusetts. And Reynolds and Maki (1990) have shown that regional growth is dependent upon the degree of formation *and* termination activity. In the case of rural areas, the SBDB was also used to determine the impact of small high-technology firms in bringing jobs to nonmetropolitan counties during the 1980s (Phillips, Kirchhoff, and Brown 1990). The SBDB was also used in studies of the rural Minnesota and Wisconsin economies (Venegas, Evans, and Ripka 1986; Reynolds, West, and Finch 1985). In urban areas, the SBDB has been used to help understand the effect of enterprise zones in helping to revitalize decaying downtown sections (Revzan 1982; Weisbrod et al. 1981).

Some additional applications of the SBDB have cut across specific regions in order to be used for planning purposes. In many of these cases, state and federal agencies have requested tabulations from the SBDB to forecast industrial development by industry, place, and firm size; in such cases, the SBDB products were not research studies per se, but rather data tabulations which served as input into other work. For example, the Port of New York Authority recently requested tabulations from the SBDB to help forecast business growth by firm size class in its 22-county planning region consisting of New York City and its suburbs, including the nearby suburbs of New Jersey and Connecticut (the goal was to forecast traffic flow on bridges and tunnels). The Tennessee Valley Authority also requested tabulations from the SBDB to forecast growth in the Appalachian counties within its planning purview. And the Economic Research Service of the U.S. Department of Agriculture used the SBDB to compare the growth and survival of different types of rural and urban firms (Miller 1990).

In almost all of these cases, the SBDB was used to demonstrate that new small-firm births, and expansions of existing small firms, either made disproportionate contributions to area growth, or acted countercyclically to offset losses in larger firms.

Employee Benefits, Federal Procurement, and Regulations

In addition to studies of specific kinds of regions, the SBDB has also been used for three important policy applications. First, the SBDB has been used to provide samples to study the provision of employee benefits by firm size. These have included both health benefits (Rubin 1987; Lichtenstein 1987) and leave policies (Trzcinski and Alpert 1990).

Second, the SBDB has been used to determine whether small firms are receiving their fair share of federal procurement. In particular, the share of sales in each industry contributed by small firms was compared with the small-firm share of federal procurement in each industry (Faucett, Skulnik, and Chemelynski 1986).

Third, the distribution of employment by firm size and industry has been used to analyze the impact of federal and state regulations on detailed manufacturing industries (Evans 1985).

Because of the recent debates in Congress on family leave and on the mandating of health benefits, the use of the SBDB in these types of studies has been crucial to help inform policy. In particular, the studies have shown that many workers do not receive health benefits in small firms because many of the firms' workers are covered by another family member or because the firms cannot afford it. Health insurance premiums cost at least 10 percent more for small firms (Rubin 1987).

The SBDB is therefore an important resource in policy debates because it is the only available source of information by firm size that can be used fairly rapidly to analyze small-firm data.

In the case of federal procurement, the SBDB has been used to demonstrate that in many industries, small firms do not receive their fair share of federal procurement dollars. In particular, small firms receive the smallest shares of federal dollars in research and development awards, and the largest shares in construction (Faucett, Skulnik, and Chemelynski 1986). This determination was in fact made possible because all federal contractors must now have nine-digit D&B identification numbers. Because of that requirement, industry data from the federal procurement data base can now be matched with the employer and firm size information from the SBDB using the D&B number as a common unit. This kind of research will better permit the SBA to target key industries in an effort to increase their purchases from small business.

▬ ▬ ▬ ▬ ▬ ▬ ▬ ▬
STUDIES OF INDUSTRY RESTRUCTURING

One of the major uses of the SBDB during the past decade has been to study the restructuring of American industry. These applications have included the effect of deregulation of the transportation and financial sectors on new-firm formation and growth, as well as examinations of the increasing importance of small firms in high-technology industries. The SBDB has also been used to study how the retail trade and manufacturing sectors have been restructured. Finally, there has been a series of studies examining the effect of regulations by firm size. These are described in greater detail below.

Industry Deregulation

The deregulation of the transportation and financial services sectors created many new opportunities for small firms. In transportation, entrepreneurs began new regional airlines, taxi services, charter bus companies, and touring firms not permitted before deregulation. The SBDB was used to measure the places in which these new firms began, and their rates of initial expansion. Deregulation also initially caused significant price competition in some sectors, particularly in interstate trucking, and air transportation, as well as in long-distance telecommunications markets following the breakup of the Bell system. Through the SBDB, we have been able to observe some region-specific effects of deregulation; firms in highly dense urban areas obtained greater benefits in some cases (e.g., in the air transportation sector) than smaller firms in more rural areas. In most instances, however, deregulation had overwhelmingly positive price effects for the majority of small firms (Phillips 1985,1986).

It is widely believed that deregulation expanded competition in the commercial lending markets so that more funds became available as the number of new firms began to accelerate during the 1980s. These new firms greatly increased the small-firm share of employment in many deregulated sectors. For example, the employment share of small firms with fewer than 100 employees in deregulated subindustries of the transportation and financial services sector rose from 23 to 28 percent from 1976 to 1982 (Phillips 1985).

While deregulation did not lower the cost of funds, on average, it did make the financial markets increasingly competitive and helped stimulate the flow of funds to the small business sector. Often working from home with their computers, new entrepreneurs took advantage of simultaneous declines in the price of technology, accompanied by easing entry standards in previously closed or tightly regulated markets. Today it seems that much of the deregulation legislation during the early 1980s is responsible for continuing the annual increase of 0.7–1.0 million new firms each year.

Growing Importance of Small High-Technology Firms

As alluded to above, the SBDB has also been used to demonstrate the restructuring which has been occurring in high-technology industries. Once the exclusive domain of large manufacturing corporations, the SBDB has been used to show that the employment share of small high-technology firms with fewer than 500 employees rose from 18.7 percent in 1976 to 24.3 percent in 1986. Small high-technology firms now contribute a quarter of high-tech jobs nationwide, and they contributed almost 40 percent of the job growth during the 1976–1986 decade (Phillips 1990).

On a regional basis, the SBDB has been used to show that high-tech firms have grown in both rural and urban areas. This finding somewhat undermines the product life cycle theory which argues that new products are developed and produced in urban areas and then, as products mature, firms move production into rural areas. In particular, it appears that the declining average size of plants and increased reliance on telecommunications technology during the 1980s served to make many new firms more footloose.

Using the SBDB for high-technology firm analysis, Phillips, Kirchhoff, and Brown (1990) have been able to trace the exact location of new branch plants of existing firms. Because the SBDB allows separate identification of a firm's headquarters from its branch plants, these researchers were able to observe why many rural-headquartered firms begin new branches in urban areas but retain most of their employment growth in rural locations. Meanwhile, urban firms continue to locate branches in rural areas but do not contribute as much employment to rural areas as to urban areas. In addition, the SBDB allows the calculation of birth and death rates separately for these components of the firm, rather than for the firm in its entirety.

This ability to trace particular establishments, branches, and subsidiaries of a firm is a particularly useful aspect of the SBDB, because larger firms frequently open and close company branches much faster than smaller firms, and this cannot be understood without treating a firm's headquarters and component establishments separately (Phillips 1988).

Another application of the high-tech analysis was requested by the National Science Foundation (NSF). It asked the SBA to investigate changes in the structure of high-technology industries between 1980 and 1986. Specifically, the NSF wanted to know how many single-establishment high-tech small firms became multi-establishment high-tech large firms during this period, and vice versa. Although the numbers involved were less than 5 percent of the base population in each case, there were several industries in which concentration had increased, and vice versa. This application was a unique one, and it enabled the SBDB to contribute to a greater understanding of the structural makeup of the high-technology sector (U.S. SBA 1988).

The Changing Nature of Retail Trade and Manufacturing

On some occasions, the SBDB has been useful to illustrate losses that have occurred within the small-firm sector. Retail trade, unfortunately, is such an area. Using the USELM files of the SBDB, Ed Starr (1991) has shown that small firms with fewer than 100 employees lost 6.8 percent of their overall employment share in retail trade between 1976 and 1986; firms with 1000 or more employees picked up most of the gain. In some industries, such as retail building supply stores, employment declines have been as large as 10 percent of the base during this period. Starr attributes much of this shift to increases in productivity and economies of scale in the retail sector. These, in turn, are associated with the use of centralized computers and bar coding systems for cash register checkout and inventory control. Such systems have very large fixed costs, and are not feasible for smaller retailers. There have been large increases of small firms in franchised operations as strategies to counteract some of the overall trends in retailing. Exact measurements, however, of franchises are difficult because of the many different forms of ownership.

Manufacturing

Contrary to the decline of small firms in retail trade during the 1980s, the opposite has occurred in manufacturing. The SBDB has been used to illustrate the gains made by small firms in manufacturing during the 1976–1986 period. While large firms were shedding jobs, the employment share of small firms (fewer than 500 employees) increased in 16 of 20 major manufacturing industries. Among the factors contributing to this gain were flexible manufacturing systems, shorter product life cycles, historically high increases in the cost of capital, and an easing of regulatory burdens (Starr 1988).

Acs and Audretsch (1989) have used the Small Business Data Base to study the entry behavior of new manufacturing firms. In particular, they showed that small-firm births are inhibited in markets which use large amounts of human capital and are highly innovative. While the latter factor is surprising, it is possibly the result of including a major recessionary period in the data set.

The SBDB has also been used to show that both small and large manufacturing firms diversified during the 1980s by creating jobs in other industries, principally services. This was accomplished by firms which bought establishments in industries other than their principal field of activity. Because it has separate SIC codes for each establishment, headquarters, and branch/subsidiary, establishments can be coded differently. Thus, it was possible to use the SBDB to demonstrate that during the 1976–1986 period, manufacturing firms created almost a million new jobs in nonmanufacturing industries. Firms that are typically identified as manufacturing operations started or acquired many nonmanufacturing establishments. For example, RJR-Nabisco and Philip Morris were able to diversify into services while still retaining their corporate identity as manufacturers. The effect of this diversification on the manufacturing industry was to make employment losses in the industry appear less than they actually were (Brown and Phillips 1989).

Regulatory Policy

As discussed earlier, the lack of data to study the impact of regulations by firm size was one of the original justifications for the funding of the Small Business Data Base under Public Law 96–302 (The Small Business Economic Policy Act), passed in 1980. Prior to the creation of the SBDB, there was no current microdata available by firm size at the four-digit SIC level to study the structure of industries.

The SBDB has been used in a variety of ways during the past decade to study and identify regulatory impacts. Some of these uses have been as simple descriptive statistics, for example, identifying the small-firm share of sales or employment in an industry to be affected by a rule under consideration by a federal regulatory agency. Other uses of the SBDB have been more specific, focusing on the impact of a specific regulation, or group of regulations, on small firms.

The impact of regulations issued by the Environmental Protection Agency (EPA), the Occupational Safety and Health Administration (OSHA), the Securities and Exchange Commission (SEC), and the Office of Federal Contract Compliance (OFFCP) has been assessed using the SBDB. In some cases, the SBDB has been used indirectly, as a control group, to compare firms affected by a regulation with those not affected ; in other cases, it has served directly as a sampling frame to help estimate the quantitative impact of a regulation by firm size, based upon a stratified sample.

David Evans (1985 ; Brock and Evans 1986) performed a variety of studies for the Office of Advocacy during the 1980s analyzing the impact of EPA and OSHA regulations by firm size. In particular, he extensively studied the manufacturing sector in an effort to determine whether firms have become larger or smaller than they otherwise would have been in the absence of regulation. In other words, have economies of scale in regulatory compliance affected average business size, and business formation rates ?

While the evidence has been inconclusive, varying by specific regulation, Evans used the SBDB as a model to demonstrate the proper method to assess regulatory impacts — i.e., to build models based upon longitudinal microdata to analyze regulatory impacts by firm size. He also found that in the case of OSHA regulations, small firms have historically been more likely to be fined than their larger-firm counterparts, although somewhat less likely to comply, depending upon the business' understanding of the specific regulation.

Two other analyses of EPA regulations used the Financial Statistics (FINSTAT) file edited and managed by the SBA during most of the 1980s. Based upon Dun & Bradstreet financial statements, the FINSTAT file was used in aggregate form to determine the financial impact of regulations by firm size. In particular, the aim was to determine whether small firms could afford to comply with various kinds of government regulations without being driven out of business. Charles Marshall (1981, 1984) used the FINSTAT file extensively to estimate the financial impacts of EPA pesticide regulations by firm size. In many cases, this work was responsible for the tiering of regulations, offering a different compliance standard to smaller firms than to larger firms.

----- ----- ----- ----- ----- -----
SUMMARY AND
DIRECTIONS FOR FUTURE
RESEARCH

During the past 11 years, the Small Business Data Base of the U.S. Small Business Administration has dramatically helped to alter the course of business research in the United States. Without the ability to identify individual businesses, researchers previously could not trace dynamic movements of firms, nor could they determine whether any individual business location was really a small firm or part of a larger enterprise. Therefore, the legal inability of the SBA to access the data of other federal agencies was actually a blessing in disguise for small business researchers, because it led to the use of edited longitudinal Dun & Bradstreet microdata for business research.

Spurred on by the pioneering work of David Birch, the SBA refined and improved measures of job creation to determine that small firms always create more than their share of new jobs, although the exact share varies with the business cycle. In addition, the SBDB has gone on to be used for other dynamically based studies showing the important role of small firms in new business formation in specific regions and industries. For example, the literature reviewed in this chapter discussed the role of the SBDB in obtaining a better understanding of small-firm contributions in high-technology sectors, as well as in the state of Massachusetts.

As a sampling frame, the SBDB has been combined with other sources to obtain more information about women-owned, minority-owned, and export firms. It has been used for planning purposes by such agencies as the Tennessee Valley Authority. And it has been useful in helping to understand the declining share of small business in retail trade.

Future research is still required to better relate the dynamics of job creation to macroeconomic phenomena, particularly business cycles. And we need more information about job duration and job quality, and its relationship to aggregate job creation statistics. New economic indices are also required so that the long-term health of the economy can be better judged in the short run. And perhaps most importantly, a microbusiness survey is needed in the United States, much like the U.S. Census' Current Population Survey. Such a proposed *Current Business Survey (CBS)* would include data for each relevant business subgroup. In our ideal world, this data would also be publicly available and could be used to expand the variables in the Small Business Data Base.

■■ ■■ ■■ ■■ ■■ ■■ ■■ ■■
REFERENCES

Acs, Z. J., and D. B. Audretsch 1989 Births and firm size. *Southern Economic Journal* 56 (2, October): 467–475.

Ando, F. 1985 *Access to capital by subcategories of small business.* Prepared under contract by the JACA Corporation for the Office of Advocacy, U.S. Small Business Administration.

Aram, J. D. 1987 *Informal risk capital in the eastern Great Lakes region.* Prepared under contract by Aram Research Associates for the Office of Advocacy, U.S. Small Business Administration.

Archibald, R., and S. L. Baker 1985 *Economic signals of business activity.* Prepared under contract by the College of William and Mary for the Office of Advocacy, U.S. Small Business Administration.

Armington, C. 1989 *Differences in business and employment data : Alternative measures of the U.S. wholesale trade sector in 1982.* Prepared under contract by Applied Systems Institute for the Office of Advocacy, U.S. Small Business Administration.

Armington, C., and M. Odle 1982 Small business : How many jobs ? *Brookings Review* 20 (Winter) : 14–17.

Birch, D. 1979 *The job generation process.* A report prepared for the Economic Development Administration, U.S. Department of Commerce.

1987 *Job creation in America.* N.Y. : Free Press.

Boden, R. 1990 *The small business health index.* Washington, D.C. : Office of Advocacy, U.S. Small Business Administration.

Brock, W. A., and D. S. Evans 1986 *The economics of small business.* Herfordshire, Eng. : Holmes and Meier.

Brown, C., J. Hamilton, and J. Medoff 1990 *Employers large and small.* Cambridge, Mass. : Harvard Univ. Press.

Brown, H. S., and B. D. Phillips 1989 Comparisons between small business data base (USEEM) and Bureau of Labor Statistics (BLS) employment data : 1978–1986. *Small Business Economics* 1 (4, Winter) : 273–284.

Evans, D. S. 1985 *An analysis of the differential impact of EPA and OSHA regulations across firm and establishment sizes in manufacturing industries.* Prepared under contract by CERA Economics Consultants for the Office of Advocacy, U.S. Small Business Administration.

Faucett, J. G. 1988 *Small business exports of manufactured products.* Prepared under contract by Jack Faucett Associates for the Office of Advocacy, U.S. Small Business Administration.

Faucett, J. G., J. Skulnik, and H. J. Chemelynski 1986 *Procurement share vs. industry share.* Prepared under contract by Jack Faucett Associates for the Office of Advocacy, U.S. Small Business Administration.

Gaston, R. J. 1989 *Finding private venture capital for your firm.* N.Y. : John Wiley & Sons.

Gaston, R. J., and S. Bell 1988 *The informal supply of capital.* Prepared under contract by Applied Economics Group for the Office of Advocacy, U.S. Small Business Administration.

Gray, T. A., and B. D. Phillips 1983 The role of small firms in understanding the magnitude of fluctuations in the U.S. economy. Paper prepared for the meeting of the Atlantic Economic Society, Philadelphia.

Kirchhoff, B. A., and R. E. McAuliffe 1989 *Economic redevelopment of mature industrial areas.* A report prepared for the Economic Development Administration, U.S. Department of Commerce.

Kirchhoff, B. A., and B. D. Phillips 1989a Innovation and growth among new firms in the U.S. economy. *Frontiers of entrepreneurship research, 1989,* eds. R. Brockhaus, Sr., N. Churchill, J. Katz, B. Kirchhoff, K. Vesper, and W. Wetzel, Jr., 173–188. Wellesley, Mass. : Babson College.

1989b The effect of firm formation and growth on job creation in the United States. *Journal of Business Venturing* 3 : 261–272.

Lichtenstein, J. 1987 Health care coverage and costs in small and large businesses. In *The state of small business : A report of the president,* 133–184. Washington, D.C. : GPO.

Marshall, C. 1981 *Comments on EPA's effluent limitations guidelines for the pesticide chemical industry.* Prepared under contract by the JACA Corporation for the Office of Advocacy, U.S. Small Business Administration.

1984 *Improving economic impact analyses of government regulations on small business.* Prepared under contract by the JACA Corporation for the Office of Advocacy, U.S. Small Business Administration.

Miller, J. P. 1990 *Survival and growth of independent firms and corporate affiliates in metro and nonmetro America.* Economic Research Service, U.S. Department of Agriculture. Report no. 74, August.

Organization for Economic Cooperation and Development 1985 *OECD employment outlook.* Paris : OECD.

Ou, C. 1987 Financing patterns of small firms. In *The state of small business : A report of the president,* 65–104. Washington, D.C. : GPO.

Phillips, B. D. 1985 *The effect of industry deregulation on the small business sector.* Business Economics 20 (1, January) : 28–39.

1986 Deregulation and the growth of small business. *Economic Impact* 53 (1, January) : 70–75.

1988 Birth and death rates in small and large firms, 1976–1986. Paper presented at the meeting of the American Economic Association, New York, N.Y., December 28–30.

1990 The importance of small firms in high-technology sectors. Paper presented at the Babson Entrepreneurship Research Conference, Boston, April 4–6.

Phillips, B. D., B. A. Kirchhoff, and H. S. Brown 1991 Formation, growth and mobility of technology-based firms in the U.S. economy. *Entrepreneurship and Regional Development* 3 : 129–144.

Revzan, L. 1982 *The impact of enterprise zone tax incentives on small business.* Prepared under contract by Coopers & Lybrand, Inc., for the Office of Advocacy, U.S. Small Business Administration.

Reynolds, P. D., and W. Maki 1990 *Business volatility and economic growth.* Prepared under contract for the Office of Advocacy, U.S. Small Business Administration, May.

Reynolds, P. D., S. West, and M. Finch 1986 Estimating new firms and new jobs : considerations in using the Dun and Bradstreet files. In *Frontiers of entrepreneurship research, 1985,* eds. R. Ronstadt, J. Hornaday, R. Peterson, and K. Vesper, 384–399. Wellesley, Mass. : Babson College.

Rubin, P. J. 1987 *Health care coverage and costs in small and large businesses.* Prepared under contract by ICF, Inc., for the Office of Advocacy, U.S. Small Business Administration.

Starr, E. 1988 The growth of small manufacturers, 1976–1984. *Business Economics* 23 (2, April) : 41–45.

1991 The declining importance of small business in retailing. Unpublished manuscript, Office of Advocacy, U.S. Small Business Administration.

Storey, D., and S. Johnson 1987 *Job generation and labor market change.* London : Macmillan.

Trzcinski, E., and W. T. Alpert 1990 *Leave policies in small business : Findings from the U.S. Small Business Administration employee leave survey.* Prepared under contract by the Univ. of Connecticut for the U.S. Small Business Administration, October.

U.S. Small Business Administration 1982–1990 *The state of small business : A report of the president.* Washington, D.C. : GPO.

1988a Unpublished tabulations prepared by the Office of Advocacy under contract for the Science Indicators Division, National Science Foundation.

1988b *User's guide to the 1976–1986 linked USEEM.* Office of Advocacy, Washington D.C., May.

1990 *The small business data base : A user's guide.* Office of Advocacy, Washington, D.C., revised June.

Venegas, E. C., C. Evans, and R. Ripka 1986 Understanding job growth in Minnesota. Prepared by the Policy Analysis Division, Minnesota Department of Energy and Economic Development for the Conference of State and Local Officials, September.

Weisbrod, G. E., H. Pollakowski, M. Laube, H. Hazard, and B. Rittenhouse 1981 *Impacts of downtown revitalization programs on small business.* Prepared under contract by Cambridge Systematics for the Office of Advocacy, U.S. Small Business Administration.

Wetzel, W. W., Jr., and C. R. Seymour 1979 *Informal risk capital in New England.* Prepared by the Univ. of New Hampshire School of Business Administration for the Office of Advocacy, U.S. Small Business Administration.

Chapter

11

Predicting New-Firm Births: Interactions of Organizational and Human Populations[1]

Paul D. Reynolds

●

INTRODUCTION

Every day the number of business organizations increases. This trend has been prevalent for centuries, even millennia. What is known about the growth of organizational populations? In particular, what is known about the role of new-firm births in the growth of such populations? Firm births are, of course, the result of the efforts of entrepreneurs.

Attention to the interrelationship between entrepreneurial activity and the greater context was given indirect treatment in an earlier "state-of-the-art" review (Kent, Sexton, and Vesper 1982). Kent (1982) considered the role of entrepreneurial activity in economic development. Bruno and Tyebjee (1982) and Pennings (1982a) attended to the economic context that fosters entrepreneurial activity. There were no reviews related to this topic in a second review

[1] Original research on the United States discussed in this paper are from projects conducted with Professor Wilbur Maki of the University of Minnesota, sponsored by the U.S. Small Business Administration (SBA contract 3067–0A–88) and the Rural Poverty and Resources Program of the Ford Foundation.

(Sexton and Smilor 1986), although Aldrich and Zimmer (1986) reviewed the significance of one contextual factor affecting entrepreneurial activity : integration into interpersonal networks. Hence, this is the first of these three efforts where the relationship between entrepreneurial activity and the broader population of organizations has received explicit attention.

This chapter will begin with a review of the ideal research setting. If it was feasible to construct a human community for the study of organizational populations, what would be the key variables to control in order to ensure a stable organizational population ? Such an exercise helps to illustrate the problems associated with different approaches to aspects of the central problem — organizational population dynamics. This is followed by a discussion of the existing research related to four types of populations : 1) all firms in all industries in a single nation ; 2) analysis of all firms of one type or in a single industry ; 3) analysis of firms within a single subnational region (state, labor market area) ; and 4) the human population that is the source of entrepreneurs. That such a wide range of research activity focuses on new-firm births and the growth of organizational populations is a testimony to its broad significance. It illustrates the general importance of our expanding knowledge of entrepreneurship.

■ ■ ■ ■ ■ ■ ■ ■ ■
IDEAL RESEARCH
SITUATION

One research strategy for studying the factors that affect populations of biological entities is to create a completely controlled environment, observe the steady-state characteristics of the biological population (birth rates, death rates, etc.), and then systematically vary the characteristics of the context (e.g., the amount of food available) to see how this affects population dynamics and basic characteristics (e.g., size). The short life span of the fruit fly and the low cost of maintaining a population (or community) of fruit flies is one reason they are so popular in such research. Such a strategy could be used with almost any species that reproduced and maintained a self-sustaining population.

While it is inconceivable that a human community could be maintained in a controlled context just to study the organizations that might develop, it is a useful "thought experiment." For it requires attention to those factors that would need to be held constant in order to maintain a stable population of organizations ; that is, those factors expected to affect the number or type of organizations that would emerge in a human population. The measure of successful stabilization of this imaginary population would be no variation, over time, in the size or mixture of the organizational population.

What features of the organizational context, or environment, should be held constant to ensure that the number or types of organizations is invariant over time ? First on the list would be the size and composition of the human population. As human populations grow, there is more opportunity for additional organizations to emerge. Further, it would be critical to maintain stability in the age, gender, and ethnic diversity of the population. Changes in the proportions of youth, mothers, or the elderly could change the demand for different types and numbers of organizations. Second, it would be important that the human population have stable tastes and interests. Changes in their preferences for food, clothing, recreation, and the like could not be allowed. Third, stability in the technology and organizational techniques used to produce the goods and services would be necessary; no innovations in productive process or output could be permitted. Fourth, it would be important to have a stable legal, political, and cultural context. There should be no incentive for the human population to create additional political or special interest groups. This would lead to a fifth requirement: an absence of any external influences from other human populations. This may be done in two ways, either by having fixed and invariant political and economic relations with other "nations," or by ensuring that the human community is entirely self-sufficient and no external contacts are required.

In order to track the presence of organizations, it may be desirable to impose several constraints on the research participants. First, individuals might be required to report all their organizational affiliations including business, religious, educational, recreational, and political affiliations. Second, it would be convenient if all organizations were required to register their existence and, to further facilitate research, were prevented from developing a multiestablishment form. That is, each organization would be restricted to one site, location, or group of participants. Comparing the organizational registry with individuals' organizational affiliations would allow one to distinguish between self-employment and multiperson productive entities — business organizations.

If such an experimental human community could be developed, the number and type of organizations could be systematically tracked. If there was no change in the number or types of organizations over a reasonable period of time, say several years, research could begin. The first analysis, of course, would be to determine the changes within the organizational population. Just because the total number of organizations remains constant is no reason to expect an absence of organizational births or deaths (entrances or exits). These changes may vary for different types of organizations providing different functions for different constituencies.

After the normal turnover is established, then other characteristics of the context or human population could be systematically varied to determine the impact on the character and size of the organizational population. Perhaps most critical to the number of organizations would be to allow the human population to expand. The major issue is how the number of organizations per capita (or per 1000) would change. A larger human population may lead to more organizations, but, as organizations get bigger, to fewer organizations per capita. On the other hand, greater diversity in the human population — a greater variety of tastes and demographic characteristics — may lead to increases in the number of organizations per capita.

Once the impact of changes in the size of the human population and its characteristics is known, then other changes could be instituted — changes in the technology used to produce goods and services, changes in the political context, and changes in external relationships and competition (economic and political). Finally, at some point, it would be necessary to allow multiple-establishment organizations to emerge. To have one organization represented at more than one site is a major shift in administrative technology.

The purpose of this fantasy is to illustrate the complexities of the problem. Virtually the only feature of this ideal situation that is present for the contemporary United States is a reasonably accurate count of the human population. There is, of course, no official mechanism for holding a human population constant in any U.S. community. Most critical for analysis in the United States is the lack of a reliable, complete census of business organizations. This means that neither an accurate count of organizations nor the number of new organizations is available for analysis. Fortunately, some reasonably accurate estimates are available (U.S. SBA 1988a).

These problems do not mean that there is no progress, but that progress is diffuse. A variety of research programs or traditions are emphasizing different facets of the major issues. Each research approach reflects attempts to add to knowledge about some facet of organizational births and, in turn, the organizational population. Each provides a piece of the jigsaw puzzle, some on the borders and some in the center, that helps to clarify the total image.

MAJOR POPULATION ANALYSES

Perspectives or approaches to understanding new-firm births and/or organizational populations can be considered in terms of either: 1) the intellectual structure or theory, or 2) the unit emphasized in the data analysis. These are not mutually exclusive, for it is quite reasonable to assume that effects measured at the most global level of analysis, such as an entire nation, are reflections of an aggregate of regional, industry, firm, or individual processes. Theories developed at the regional, industry, firm, or individual level may contribute to our understanding of national-level phenomena.

For the purposes of this review, discussion will focus on four types of populations, each of which has received research attention: 1) total national population of organizations; 2) total population in one industry or of a specific organizational type; 3) total population in a subnational region; and 4) the population of individuals from which entrepreneurs emerge. Analysis of each type of population has unique advantages and disadvantages for research. Understanding entrepreneurial processes in each population improves comprehension of the entire puzzle.

National-Level Analysis

A major advantage of national-level analysis is the quality and extent of data that is available. For example, data on the size of the human population and status of the economy is most complete and accurate at the national level. The most accurate estimates on the total organizational population are also provided at the national level. Research on three types of issues can be illuminated with national-level analyses: the total number of business organizations, the birth (and death) rates of business organizations, and the effect of national-level characteristics on variations in the national new-firm birth rates.

How many businesses?

For the United States, this question is complicated by several issues. The first is distinguishing between a business activity, business entity, business location (or establishment), and business firm (legal organization or enterprise). An estimate of the total count for 1986 is provided in Table 11–1. The 2,212,000 farms present in 1986 are treated separately, but businesses providing services to farms (equipment, seed, etc.) are included in the table. Franchises, a special form of establishments, are not shown in Table 11–1. They numbered about 462,000 in 1986 or about 9 percent of all establishments. About 20 percent of all franchises are owned by the parent company, and the remainder are classified as "independent" (U.S. Bureau of the Census 1989, Table 1338).

    Examination of Table 11–1 reveals the difficult definitional issues at hand. What is to be considered a "firm"? The count of firms can vary from 4 to 21 million, depending upon the definition. Who is to be considered an "entrepreneur"? Are those with full-time jobs who begin to pursue part-time self-

TABLE 11–1 — Estimate of Number of U.S. Businesses: 1986

(FIGURES IN 1000)	Business Activity	Business Entity	Business Location	Business Organization
Part-time self-employment	4,366			
Full-time self-employment	9,328	9,328		
Branch / subsidiaries	1,216	1,216	1,216	
Business organization	3,805	3,805	3,805	3,805
Total nonfarm	18,715	14,349	5,021	3,805
Farms	2,212			
Total all businesses	20,927			

Estimated from Small Business Administration 1988a, 7 ; Small Business Administration 1989, Tables A19, A20 ; U.S. Bureau of the Census 1989, Tables 627, 1074.

employment to be included ? These issues are critical when the more complex issues of birth and death rates of businesses are pursued.

Because this discussion captures the major focus of much analysis, the emphasis here will be on firms or enterprises with employees. This is the most conservative definition possible, minimizing the count of businesses, ensuring a minimum of confusion. Firms in agricultural production are excluded, as is research treating reported self-employment (Evans and Leighton 1989) as a surrogate for a new business organization.

The capacity of the United States to support a population of businesses can be considered by attending to the density of businesses, measured by firms per 1,000 population, shown in Table 11–2. This data, taken from a special analysis of the Dun & Bradstreet Dun's Market Identifier (DMI) files prepared by the Small Business Administration (U.S. SBA 1988b, 1988c), is the only source of data that provides a count of all business firms (or enterprises) for all industries (except agriculture production) over recent years.

Table 11–2 indicates that for the 1976–1986 period in the United States the number of firms, establishments, and employees has been increasing. During the same period, human population (not shown), grew from 218 to 242 million. The changes in the ratios shown in the three right-hand columns have been less dramatic. The average number of establishments per firm has been about 1.3, with a recent increase. Firms are developing slightly more branches and subsidiaries. The number of firms per 1,000 employees has been about 45, or one firm for each 22 workers. The recent decline indicates that the typical establishment may be getting larger. This evidence is, however, more complex than suggested by this gross pattern. The proportion of extremely large firms (over 10,000 employees) and very small firms (1–19 employees) has been declining, at the same time that intermediate-sized firms (100–500 employees)

TABLE 11–2 — U.S. Business / Population Ratios : 1976–1986[1]

(FIGURES IN 1000)	Firms	Establish-ments	Employ-ment	Estab's per Firm	Firms per 1,000 Employees	Firms per 1,000 Population
1976	3,334	4,151	68,911	1.245	48.38	15.29
1978	3,610	4,503	74,878	1.247	48.21	16.21
1980	3,585	4,566	82,070	1.274	43.65	15.74
1982	3,663	4,667	82,656	1.274	44.31	15.75
1984	3,810	4,855	85,378	1.274	44.62	16.08
1986	3,806	5,020	91,180	1.319	41.74	15.75
Average				1.272	45.15	15.80

[1] Employment (third column) includes owners, partners, managers, as well as paid employees. Total population (not shown) taken from U.S. Bureau of the Census 1989, Table 2.
From Small Business Administration 1988a, Tables 6.4, 6.5, 6.6.

has been increasing. This reflects changes in industry structure and as well as shifts within various industries — manufacturing firms are getting smaller, retail firms larger (U.S. SBA 1988b, Tables 6–10). There have been about 16 firms for each 1,000 of the total human population, or one for every 22 persons; there is no clear, recent temporal trend in this measure.

Despite substantial growth in the numbers of establishments, firms, workers, and the human population, these ratios show only small year-to-year changes over this 10-year period. This would suggest that processes underlying the relationship between a human population and the business organizations it supports change very slowly.

However, despite the evidence of some underlying stability in the support for business organizations, there has been substantial change in the 1976–1986 period. The number of firms has increased by about 14 percent (more than 1 percent per year), and the number of establishments by about 21 percent (more than 2 percent per year). This is somewhat more than the 11 percent increase in the total human population, but somewhat less than the 32 percent increase in the total number of employees.

This draws our attention to the underlying dynamics associated with these changes: the births and deaths of businesses that are behind these net increases. These are presented, for establishments, not firms, in Table 11–3. Both birth and death rates are computed as the number of establishments that entered (or were born), and exited (or were deceased), per 100 establishments at the beginning of the time period. Data for the two-year periods have been adjusted to an annual basis. Data on the births and deaths of small firms — single or multiple establishments with fewer than 500 employees — are provided for comparison. Although the original source of the data is the same for the two analyses (DMI file as edited by the SBA), the procedures for tabulation are slightly different.

The critical feature illustrated in Table 11–3 is the relatively high volatility or turbulence occurring in the organizational population. Despite the rather low annual rate of change, approximately *one in five* establishments or small firms is either created or discontinued *each year.* Just as a slowly growing human population may have high human birth and death rates, the U.S. organizational population growth is the net result of a substantial level of turbulence and volatility. Without the current level of new business births — entrepreneurial activity or new-firm start-ups — the business population would decline at about 10 percent per year.

What then, accounts for the formation and implementation of new firms? One analysis strategy focuses on time series models using the entire national economy as the unit of analysis. Such an analysis was completed for the United States, focusing on rates of incorporation from 1948 to 1984 (Highfield and Smiley 1986). Rates of incorporation were considered as indicators of new-firm births or entrepreneurial activity. This was necessary because of the absence of any other long-term data series that could serve as an indicator of new organizational foundings.

TABLE 11-3 — U.S. Establishment and Small-Firm Birth and Death Rates : 1976–1986

TIME PERIOD	Establishments[1]			Small Firms <500 Emp[2]		
	Birth Rates	Death Rates	Net Change	Birth Rates	Death Rates	Net Change
1976–1978	12.42	9.79	2.63	12.1	9.0	3.1
1978–1980	9.70	10.16	−.46	8.9	10.4	− 1.5
1980–1982	9.87	8.83	1.05	9.4	9.1	0.3
1982–1984	10.55	8.40	2.14	10.2	8.9	1.3
1984–1986	10.81	9.33	1.46	9.0	9.9	−0.9
Averages	10.67	9.30	1.36	9.9	9.5	0.4

[1] From Exhibit 2.10 of Reynolds and Maki, 1990a. Computed as the annual averages for 382 U.S. Labor Market Areas from special tabulations prepared from the Small Business Administration Small Business Data Base.

[2] Annual rates from Table 1 of Phillips, 1988. Special tabulation of the Small Business Administration Small Business Data Base. Data aggregated across industries for national tabulations.

The major focus was on aggregate economic factors, measured for the nation as a whole, affecting changes in entrepreneurial activity (e.g., incorporations). This was done by dividing 1948–1984 into 118 three-month periods (quarters). Five factors were considered to have influenced, or been influenced by, changes in incorporation rates : real gross national product (GNP) growth, real plant and equipment expenditures growth, unemployment rate changes, the real interest rate, and inflation. The procedure used considered the correlations between these variables and changes in incorporation for subsequent time periods.

It is quite possible that the changes in the five aggregate characteristics are not independent. Attempts to explore this possibility through multivariate analysis found that only the inflation rate appeared to have a causal role affecting entrepreneurial activity. As inflation declined, entrepreneurial activity increased. There was some small additional contribution to explain variance if real GNP growth and unemployment were also included.

Overall, the authors concluded that :

> . . . sluggish economic growth seems more likely to spur creation of new firms. . . . however, . . . none of the macro variables appears to be strongly causal . . . Policy implications are not strong in this setting. (Highfield and Smiley 1986, 57)

This analysis, restricted to the United States, is presented as an example of the type of time series multivariate analysis of the role of entrepreneurship in economic change that may fruitfully be pursued at the national level. An analysis of recent time series studies of the United Kingdom suggests a somewhat stronger relationship between unemployment rates and subsequent self-employment than found in the United States (Storey 1990). The low ability to predict new-firm births at the national level masks significant changes occurring in local regions, changes that may be used to predict new-firm birth rates with considerable accuracy.

Markets (Industry) or Organizational Type

The number and diversity of organizations in advanced societies is substantial. Attempts to study the formation of all types of organizations for a large, diverse society can be quite complex. A particular problem is assembling data regarding specific types of organizations. One strategy for simplifying the problem is to focus on one type or subset of organizations. This may be done by considering the nature of the organizational output (all firms producing shoes or breakfast cereal) or type of organization (labor unions or newspapers).

Examination of specific markets by industrial economists usually results in the analysis of specific industry sectors, emphasizing organizational output. Among organizational scholars, attention has been given to specific types of organizations in different social systems. Because they generally deal with an entire population of one type of organization in a single "ecological" context, this approach is referred to as *organizational ecology*. As the conceptualizations and intellectual objectives of these two approaches are distinct, they will be treated separately.

Industry sectors (markets).

It appears to be convenient, at least for most economic analyses, to consider a given society or political system as a set of markets: a labor market, a housing market, a market for steel, food, clothing, and the like. A "perfect market" is one in which there is full information, an open auction, no dominant seller or buyer, identical commodities, and accepted mediums of exchange, and one in which both the demand and supply are very sensitive to prices. Each market is considered as an independent, self-contained competitive system. This is analogous to the observation that different species of wildlife may coexist with other species in the same area, while competing with their own kind over territorial rights, (such as when foxes compete with foxes, rabbits compete with rabbits, and grasses compete with grasses). The interdependence of such species competition, such as when foxes eat rabbits and rabbits eat the grasses, is a separate issue.

When a perfect market clears at the end of a trading period, all purchases and sales are completed, and the resulting price and quantity is considered to reflect an equitable solution. This equilibrium maximizes the utility for all buyers and sellers participating in the market. All who participate are equally responsible for the outcome; no individual actor is culpable. In such a situation the profits gained by sellers and the utility achieved by buyers are considered appropriate because — as long as the rules are "fair" — it is not possible for any specific participant to achieve an unfair advantage (excess profits among producers or excess utility among consumers).

The capacity of new buyers and sellers to enter the market is a key element in providing an appropriate level of profit. That is, no seller is able to develop an advantage that leads to excessive profits if new sellers can enter the market. Attention to the behavior of specific markets has the advantage of allowing careful examination of specific mechanisms that may affect the addition of new producers (including firm births) or the exit of existing producers (including firm deaths). The characteristics of the market that may affect entrepreneurial activity may then be considered, as well as the effects of differing levels of entrepreneurial activity on characteristics of the market, such as relative profitability, presence of innovation, or product changes.

If a set of independent markets are identified, the extent to which market-related phenomena are universal and the magnitude of the effects may be explored empirically. Markets with different characteristics may be compared. A surrogate for a well-defined market is the "industry" or, in some analyses, the "industry group" (a subset of the industry identified by a unique feature of the product — Caves and Porter 1977). By considering each industry that makes up a national economy as a separate market, it is possible to test hypotheses and models regarding market behavior on a sample of markets (Bain 1962).

A number of issues regarding the role of entrepreneurship in markets are of interest, including: 1) What is the effect of high levels of entrepreneurship on industry profitability, process/product innovation, and adaptability? 2) To what extent do market or industry characteristics (average profits as well as barriers to entry and exit) affect the level of entrepreneurship? 3) Can market- or industry-specific features that may have an impact on entrepreneurial activity be controlled by public policy? Must of the research appears to have focused on the sellers or producers, but many similar issues could be pursued regarding the buyers (Schmalensee 1988).

The capacity of buyers and sellers to enter or exit a market is considered a key element affecting the average profit in a given market. Average industry profits are expected to be relatively low if buyers can easily shift to other products (or markets), if there are few barriers to entry, and if a large pool of potential producers are interested in entering the market. Conversely, average industry profits are expected to be high if there are substantial barriers to the entry of new producers, and if the buyers are unable to shift to new products (or markets).

Attention can also be given to market characteristics that affect new entry. Ease of entry and comparatively high average industry profits may lead to relatively high rates of new producers found in the market (Orr 1974a, 1974b). Conversely, high entry costs and low average profits would be associated with relatively low rates of new producers entering the market (see, for example, Acs and Audretsch 1989a, 1989b).

A summary of six such national comparisons (for Belgium, the Federal Republic of Germany, Korea, Norway, Portugal, and the United Kingdom) helps demonstrate the value of such research (Cable and Schwalbach, 1991). Regression models were developed to predict the entry of new producers into selected industries (markets). While the major factor presumed to have an impact on entry rates was the expected (predicted) profitability after entry into the market, a number of other market or production characteristics (industry size, industry growth, and scale economies) were included in some models.

The research strategy was to develop regression models using industry entry rates as the dependent variable. From 62 to 140 industries were used in the six analyses; explained variance ranged from 10 percent to 78 percent. The most important features are the different variables found to have a statistically significant contribution to explaining the variance in entry rates. The general pattern of relationships is quite mixed. A summary of the number of positive and negative standardized beta weights for factors included in four or more of the six analyses reflects this diversity:

	Number Positive	Number Negative
Expected profits	5	1
Industry growth	5	1
Product differentiation, advertising	1	4
Scale economies	2	3
Industry size	3	1
Capital requirements	—	4

The only factor with the same impact in all analyses was capital requirements: higher capital requirements were found to depress entrants in four countries. Four factors had the same effect in all but one analysis; greater expected profits, industry growth, industry size, and less product differentiation and advertising tended to be positively related to the number of new entrants. The effect of scale economies in the industry was mixed, with greater scale economies depressing entrants in three analyses and encouraging entrants in two.

For the study of entrepreneurship, the major disadvantage of this research tradition is the focus on the entrants and exits from existing markets (or industries). For the purpose of a market analysis, it is irrelevant whether or not the business entity is a subsidiary of a larger firm, which may operate in several markets, or a single firm operating in only one market. Entrance into a new market by an existing multimarket firm is an expansion; entrance by a new firm started for only that market would reflect entrepreneurial behavior. Different models may be required for these different types of "market entrants."

Population ecology.

There is a substantial literature on organizational ecology. In addition to the initial overview by Hannan and Freeman (1977), there are useful overviews prepared by Carroll (1984, 1988) and a recent summary of the current status of the research program (Hannan and Freeman 1989). Young (1988) has provided an inventory of the unresolved issues associated with this perspective and the associated research. Explicit attention to the conceptual value of this perspective to the study of entrepreneurial phenomena has been provided by Aldrich (1990).

This alternative perspective on the formation of new organizations starts with a different conception of a social system. Rather than assume a market where buyers and sellers meet for an economic exchange, the alternative is to consider a "host societal-organizational" exchange relationship. Organizations are major providers for the "needs" of society — education, justice, health care, housing, food, transportation, and the like. These organizations receive, in exchange, the resources needed for survival — participants, money, physical facilities, legitimation. Assuming that the demand for any particular type of organizational output is limited, there is a limit on the resources that the society will make available to organizations providing that type of output.

Based on this conception, the focus is on the patterns associated with both the founding of organizations and the total size of the organizational population. It is assumed that organizational birth or founding rates will be quite high when there is a large unmet demand for the organizational output. It is expected that the founding of the organizational community (or industry) will be marked by high rates of organizational births and a substantial growth in the total population. The "life cycle" of the organizational community may be conceptualized as that of a single biological species, with rapid early growth, a plateau, and an eventual decline in the total number of organizations. Birth and death rates would, in this analysis, be either inversely related or unrelated in the following ways: 1) an inverse relationship, with high birth rates and low death rates in the period of organizational community growth; 2) parity or no relationship during a period of population stability; and 3) an inverse relationship, with low birth and high death rates when the organizational population begins to decline.

Most of the research effort has been devoted to assembling longitudinal data sets on specific types of organizations, which may be considered a single organizational population or community. Research is then devoted to predicting the form of the curves that represent temporal changes in the total population including birth and death rates. Because the "total population" in a given host society is the unit of analysis, there is little choice but to use variations of time series or event history analysis for this research. Analysis of organizational populations over long periods of time, and "density conceptualized as the number of organizations in the population" (Hannan and Freeman 1989, 332) leads to some paradoxical inferences. For example, there were about 175 active unions identified for the United States in 1910 and about 175 in 1980 (Hannan and Freeman 1989, 208), implying little change in the societal support for unions over this 70 years. However, in 1910 there was one union for every 520,000 people, but in 1980 about one union for every 1,300,000 people, implying a substantial decrease in the societal support for this type of organization.

In both graphic presentations (Carroll 1984) and the models that represent population change, there is substantial regularity in the empirical patterns. That is to say, formal models predicting the birth, death, and patterns of organizational population growth are found to have a statistically significant fit when applied to the data. This is true for a wide range of organizational communities (or types of industries), including labor unions, semiconductor firms, newspapers, and restaurants (Hannan and Freeman 1989).

Several issues are unresolved in these analyses. First, it is not clear if these regularities would be present if the concept of density were adjusted to reflect changes in the resources available in the host society. The example of the labor unions, mentioned earlier, illustrates this point. Second, there is no discussion of the amount of variation in birth and death rates explained by the models tested with these data sets. The basic strategy has been to demonstrate that some processes affecting births may have been identified and explicated. The possibility that other processes may be present and may affect the birth of organizations cannot be excluded without further information. A modest level of explained variance in the birth rates would imply that other processes may be present. For example, societal support of labor unions may have declined as federal and government agencies began to adopt many of the functions of labor unions — setting minimum wages, regulating worker safety, imposing due process requirements for discharges, and the like.

While retaining a focus on long-term historical changes in organizational populations, we can also pursue new issues. For example, the conditions that will lead to the creation of an entirely new type of community of organizations (or a new industry) is of considerable significance. Major societal upheavals, such as wars or revolutions, may lead to a wide range of new organizational opportunities (Carroll, Delacroix, and Goodstein 1988). For example, the death rates of U.S. business organizations appeared to drop dramatically during and immediately after World War II. Dramatic changes in a national political and economic structure may provide substantial new opportunities (niches) for new organizations, as is expected in the eastern European nations as they shift from centralized to market economies. The presence of reliable data on the organizational populations before, during, and after such changes would greatly facilitate such research.

It is possible to attend to the relative success of organizations that pursue different strategies for survival in different environments (Aldrich 1990). Adopting the biological model on which organizational population ecology was based leads to the use of the same topology of strategies. Two are explained in the following discussion. The first are organizations that emphasize a simple structure, low fixed investments, and speed of reaction to changes in the environmental context. Referred to as the "r-strategy" in the organizational ecology literature, they are remarkably like Dave Birch's description of "gazelles" — fast-growth new firms. The alternative strategy emphasizes large fixed investment, complex, interdependent organizational structures, and efficiency or predictability of performance, referred to as the "k-strategy." The term "elephants" has been used by Dave Birch, Roseabeth Kanter, and others to describe organizations using this approach. This simple dichotomy leads to considering the type of environments most suited for gazelles and elephants. This would, presumably, lead to more accurate predictions regarding the birth and death rates of organizations in different competitive environments. Of particular interest is the extent to which firms can change strategy as the nature of the environment, or their host industry, changes. Can elephants learn to dance? Can gazelles learn to carry heavy loads?

Another extension of the population ecology conceptualization is to consider the nature of the life cycle of an entirely new type of organizational community (new industry) and the implications of different industry life cycle stages for the emergence of entrepreneurs (Romanelli 1988). For example, it is possible that the very first firms in a completely new industry are initiated by entrepreneurs with substantial experience in similar organizational communities (or similar industries). When the organizational community begins to grow, or as density (the total population of organizations) goes up, these entrepreneurs may be expected to come from the industry pioneers. As the industry matures, new firms moving in smaller and more specialized market niches may be created by those leaving the established industry leaders.

In conclusion, the study of economic markets or a single type of organization provides additional knowledge about the broader context of entrepreneurial activity. The basic conceptualization assumes that the industry characteristics or extant organizational population may affect the births and deaths, or entrances and exits of organizations or producers. There is also evidence of the effects of major societal shifts — wars, technical breakthroughs, political revolutions, dramatic changes in government policies — on the organizational populations and births and deaths. Entrepreneurial processes may differ at different states of an industry (or organizational population) life cycle.

However, analyses that focus on a single industry or type of organization distract attention from several critical issues. First, the interdependence among different organizational types (or communities or populations) is not considered. Second, issues of major changes in technology or the structure of organizations (the total number and range of organizational types) are not incorporated into the conceptual framework. Indeed, major changes in technology and administration may make some types of organizations obsolete and open opportunities for entirely different types of organizations. Third, the focus on a single industry or single type of organization does not encourage attention to the alternatives perceived by potential entrepreneurs, the ones that start new firms. Entrepreneurs may consider starting a new business organization as their best career option, compared to *their* alternatives, even if the context is not optimal from the perspective of an industry or population analysis.

Subnational Regions

Another strategy for exploring an organizational population is to consider all those in a given subnational region. In a complex, diverse economy, the national patterns are — in a sense — the aggregate of the economic activity in the subnational regions. Research would proceed by considering the basic pattern of activity found in a given subnational region. Comparison, the basis of all research, is done among regions. This can be either a cross-sectional design, where independent and dependent variables are measured for the same point in time, or a panel, where the independent variables are measured prior to the dependent variables. While there has been analysis by multistate region (dividing the United States into six or eight giant regions) and by counties (Bluestone, Long, and Porterfield 1989; Howland 1985), the most popular basis for analysis has been states or labor market areas. These will be discussed separately.

States.

A variety of analyses have utilized states as the unit of analysis, taking advantage of the vast amount of state-level data.

It has been suggested that regional economies go through a "long-wave" cycle. Rapid economic growth, marked by a high number of new-firm births, is followed by periods of stability or decline, accompanied by a reduction in new-firm births (Booth 1986). Such a period of decline is followed by a regional "rebirth" as new industries grow and replace those in decline. The use of incorporation rates (incorporations per 1,000 population) from 1950 to 1982 allowed a comparison of the trends for eastern rustbelt states (Conn., Mass., N.J., N.Y., R.I., Pa.) with western rustbelt states (Ill., Ind., Mich., Ohio, Wis.). A regression analysis including a dummy variable for eastern and western rustbelt locations indicated significant differences in the effect of geographical position. Recent incorporation rates are higher for the eastern rustbelt states; they are considered to be in the "rebuilding" phase of their long-wave cycle. Western rustbelt states are assumed, for 1950 to 1982, to still be in the decline phase of their long-wave cycle and have lower new incorporation rates. Multiple regression models predicting incorporation rates indicated that population changes were the most significant predictive factor, followed by a measure of status in the long-wave cycle; about 50 percent of the variation in incorporation rates was explained by these regression models.

Several analyses have attempted to explore the effects of variations in tax rates on new-firm starts. Analysis of the absolute number of manufacturing starts was completed using data for 1976–1978 to predict up to 1980–1982 (Bartik 1989). A statistically significant negative effect of higher property taxes was present, although higher corporate taxes had a statistically significant positive effect. Higher personal income taxes had a nonsignificant positive impact; higher sales taxes had a nonsignificant negative effect. Expenditures on public services indicated a mixed pattern, with positive effects of higher educational and fire protection spending, and a negative impact from police, higher educational, and welfare spending. Even though a complete multiple regression model is estimated, no information is provided on the explained variance; it is not possible to determine the relative impact of these various state characteristics.

Another effort explored state characteristics as they affected the absolute number of new-firm entries in all industries for three time periods: 1978–1980, 1980–1982, and 1982–1984 (Kirchhoff and McAuliffe 1989). Eleven independent variables were incorporated in the models. Six were significant in one or more of the three models: federal defense department expenditures, long-term growth in state personal income (1948–1980), state population, percentage of labor force unionized, public school expenditures, and median age. Five were not significant: hourly wages in manufacturing, percentage of college graduates, number of doctoral scientists and engineers, total state tax revenue, and total state taxes per capita. Explained variance exceeded 95 percent for all predictive equations. This suggests that the "nonsignificant" variables had little to contribute. For example, measures of tax burden, as an indicator of "business climate," were relatively insignificant.

Similar types of analysis have been completed for the United Kingdom. From 11 to 12 major geographic regions are utilized in various analyses (Keeble 1989, 1990; Storey and Johnson 1987). A major focus has been to determine the extent to which there is regional variation in new-firm foundings. Analysis is devoted to determining the proportion of regional variation related to various processes that may affect new-firm formation: enforced entrepreneurship through unemployment; large-firm externalization of subcontracting and business services; regional growth in market demand, customization, and specialization; technological change; and government small-firm politics promoting entrepreneurial activities (Keeble 1989, Table 1). However, as these processes may have different effects in different industries and with a small number of geographic regions, it is difficult to sort out the relative influence of the different mechanisms.

One of the most general trends in developed countries — the relatively higher rate of new-firm formation and economic growth in major urban areas — is clearly present in the United Kingdom, often described as the north-south difference. The London area, in the south of England, has experienced substantial economic growth and new-firm birth rates three times that of Scotland and other northern regions in economic stagnation. Ironically, government policies that help new firms are applied where new firms are being created. As new firms tend to emerge in the high-growth regions, these government policies thus contribute to regional variation in economic growth (Storey and Johnson 1987).

Labor market areas.

There are a number of problems with using states as geographic units of analysis for the United States. States are, of course, major political and administrative governing units. But as there is no formal effort to regulate trade between states, there is no reason to expect that state boundaries will be consistent with the naturally occurring socioeconomic communities that may emerge. An alternative unit of analysis is to use socioeconomic regions that develop in the normal course of economic and social life — the geographic patterns that result from decisions regarding where one should live, work, and play.

One such geographic division is major metropolitan areas, formally recognized as the Standard Metropolitan Statistical Areas (SMSAs). As defined, and decennially redefined, by the U.S. Census, many SMSAs include counties from more than one state (for example, New York City may include counties from New Jersey and Connecticut). Because of the long-term interest in SMSAs and their formal recognition by the U.S. Census, there is a large amount of descriptive data available on SMSAs. This substantially facilitates analysis of their characteristics that may affect new-firm foundings.

Three such analyses were completed using the same data set (Carlton 1979, 1983; Pennings 1982b, 1982c). Both used the same data from the Dun & Bradstreet DMI file on new-firm births in three industries: fabricated plastic products (SIC 3079), communications transmitting equipment (SIC 3662), and electronic components (SIC 3679). These were chosen as export-oriented industries not dependent on local demand, with low transportation costs, and with varying levels of technical sophistication. In short, industries that presumably would be most responsive to small differences in the input costs. The dependent variables were the total number of births in about 40 SMSAs for two time periods: July 1967 to November 1971, and January 1972 to December 1975. The earliest analysis attempted to test the fit of a model that would predict new-firm births based on nine SMSA characteristics (Carlton 1979). The resulting regression models fit rather well, explaining about 90 percent of the variance in new-firm births. Business climate and tax rates did not have much effect; but lower wages were associated with more births, existing industry activity seemed to have a positive influence, and so did technical expertise in the area. Energy costs seemed to have a depressive effect for two industries.

The same data was reanalyzed for 70 SMSAs with a wider range of variables (Pennings 1982b). Again, the emphasis was on the absolute number of new-firm births and on SMSA characteristics that would encourage firm foundings. Explained variances for the regression models for the three industries averaged 89 percent. The five predictors that were statistically significant were occupational differentiation, industrial differentiation, industry size, capital availability, and domestic immigration. Thirteen variables had little statistically significant impact, including urban centrality, population size, presence of engineers, foreign immigrants, volatility of recent job growth, firm size distribution, wages rates, energy costs, unemployment, bank concentration, venture capital sources, engineers, and academic influence (Pennings 1982b, 135).

A test of the role of quality of life in entrepreneurial activity was pursued in a third analysis (Pennings 1982c). It is argued that a "good" quality of life will attract entrepreneurs, who will then start new firms. Multiple indicators were used to create five quality of life dimensions. They were incorporated into regression models along with population and urban size to predict births in the three industries; 71–84 percent of the variance in births were explained by the model. The largest quality of life impact was from the environmental dimension, but the better the environment, the lower the new-firm births. Almost as important was the economic variable: a positive economic quality of life promoted firm births. A positive health and educational environment also promoted births. The effects of political and social quality of life were quite small, with the political dimension having a negative influence, and the social dimension a positive one. The patterns suggest that founding new firms is an indigenous response to a favorable economic quality of life, which tend to be in locations with a poor environmental quality of life.

A major disadvantage of focusing analysis on urban areas is their lack of variation. Major urban areas in the United States are similar on a wide range of dimensions, leading to a lack of variation in the independent variables. An alternative is to consider, for the United States, *all* labor market areas — urban and rural alike. Using the 1980 population census data on work locations, labor market areas have been identified for the United States (Tolbert and Killian 1987). Each area represents a cluster of counties in which the majority of the population live and work. Maintaining a minimum size of 100,000 residents led to consolidating the 3,124 counties into 382 labor market areas for the United States. One third of the labor market areas involved counties in two or three states. The 1980 human population ranges from 12 million in New York City and Los Angeles to 100,000 (northeast corner of Arizona).

An ongoing project is utilizing the labor market areas as the regional unit of analysis; preliminary results are now available (Reynolds and Maki 1990b). The purpose is to determine those regional characteristics that are systematically related to variation in new-firm birth *rates*. The birth rates are the number of autonomous establishments that appear per 100 existing establishments. An autonomous establishment is either a single-establishment new firm or one that has a headquarters in the same county such as a local branch of a larger firm. These local branches, a small proportion of total establishment births, are technically expansions. About 80 percent of all establishments are autonomous — they account for about 50 percent of all U.S. business employment. Data related to autonomous establishment births was developed from the Small Business Data Base maintained by the SBA.

Characteristics of the regions are selected to represent six different perspectives or processes that affect new-firm births: 1) longer-term or long-wave processes, with the assumption that population growth and in-migration may offset decline in a stable economy; 2) the factors of production or business climate argument, which assumes that lower costs will encourage new firms by the increased potential for profit; 3) incubator region process, with the assumption that a diverse, expanding economy will provide opportunities for new firms, thereby encouraging entrepreneurial behavior; 4) the assumption that if there is a limit on the carrying capacity of a region, such limits will depress new-firm births; 5) the assumption that higher unemployment will drive the jobless to found new firms; and 6) that those likely to be seeking new career opportunities — the well-educated in mid-career — will create new firms.

The dependent variable in this case is the birth rate of new autonomous establishments (foundings per 100 existing establishments) across the 382 labor market areas for 1982–1984. This is a normal distribution. The 38 indicators for these six processes are presented in Table 11–4. The year of measurement is shown for each indicator. All precede 1982, most by at least several years. The availability of independent variables is somewhat limited by the need to assemble data at the county level for aggregation to the labor market areas.

TABLE 11–4 — Regression Model Prediction of New-Firm Births : 1982–1984[1]

PERSPECTIVE	Variable Description	Yr. Measured	Std. Beta
Long waves	Percent population change	1940–1980	0.17
	Percent living in same county five years	1980	−.20
Factors of production	Local taxes per capita	1972	—
	Local government debt per capita	1972	—
	Infrastructure		
	Local educational spending per capita	1972	—
	Local highway spending per capita	1972	—
	Local welfare expenditures per capita	1972	—
	Local health expenditures per capita	1972	—
	Bank checking deposits per capita	1976	—
	Bank savings deposits per capita	1976	—
	Earned (labor) income per worker	1980	0.15
	Percent 18+ with HS or more education	1980	−.09
	Labor force participation	1980	—
	Occupational emphasis : percent work force in :		
	Sales positions	1980	0.11
	Clerical positions	1980	—
	Service positions	1980	—
	Skilled crafts positions	1980	—
	Machine operator positions	1980	0.22
	Transportation operator positions	1980	—
	Handler, helper, laborer positions	1980	0.06

The right-hand column in Table 11–4 indicates the standardized beta weights for indicators retained in the regression analysis as having a statistically significant impact on the explained variance, which is 85 percent for this set of variables. Of these 38 indicators, only 14 had a statistically significant impact on the explained variance. Most important was the number of business

TABLE 11–4, continued

PERSPECTIVE	Variable Description	Yr. Measured	Std. Beta
Incubator regions	Business establishments per worker	1980	0.60
	Workers per establishment - extractive	1980/82	—
	Workers per establishment - manufacturing	1980/82	—
	Workers per establishment - bus. dist. service	1980/82	—
	Workers per establishment - local market ind.	1980/82	—
	Industry diversity	1980	—
	Occupational diversity	1980	—
	Income per household	1979	−.09
Regional carrying capacity	Population per square mile	1980	−.09
	Establishments per square mile	1980	
Unemployment	Unemployment rate	1980	−.19
Career opportunities	Percent population 25–44 years old	1980	0.16
	Percent 18+ with post-HS, not college	1980	—
	Percent 18+ with college degrees	1980	—
	Percent 18+ with post-college education	1980	—
	Occupational emphasis: percent work force in:		
	Management positions	1980	0.17
	Professional positions	1980	—
	Technical positions	1980	0.12
Explained Variance (R^2)			0.85

[1] Note : Based on SPSS–PC V 3.0 stepwise regression, standard defaults, only statistically significant variables retained in the equation. Unit of analysis was 382 U.S. labor market areas.

establishments per worker, a high standardized beta weight of 0.60. Regions with many small firms tend to be a source of new-firm births ; thus the incubator hypothesis is given considerable support. The importance of long-term growth patterns is strongly supported. Both measures relate to long-term economic change, population growth, and an increase of new domestic immigrants (leading to a lower percentage of residence in the county for five years), both have a positive contribution. There is strong support for the career opportunity hypothesis : those regions with higher proportions of mid-career adults in management and technical positions tend to have more new-firm births. In contrast, high unemployment in a region is associated with lower new-firm birth rates ; there is no support for the "jobless driven to start new firms" hypothesis. Finally, there is mixed support for elements of the factors of production argument. There is no evidence that tax rates or government expenditures have any effect. However, this data was for a period 10 years prior to the measure of birth rates ; perhaps with a shorter time lag the variation in taxes would be significant. The other variables have a mixed pattern that is not easily interpreted.

The preliminary analysis is promising, for the model appears to have a good fit, as reflected in the high explained variance. The preliminary interpretations suggest that improvements in understanding will be possible when analysis is developed for specific industries. Different processes may have different impacts for different industries.

A similar analysis was completed in the United Kingdom, using 57 independent variables and 63 counties as the regional unit of analysis (Moyes and Westhead 1990). While not identical to the travel-to-work areas used in the previous study, it was the lowest geographic unit for which data on the independent variables was available. The dependent variable was the rate of new-firm formation in "production" (mostly manufacturing) per employment in production for 1980–1983. New-firm formation counts were based on new Value Added Tax (VAT) registrations, required when annual sales exceed a modest level. The dates represented by the independent variables tended to be quite close to the 1980–1983 period, with some overlap. Hence this should be considered more of a cross-sectional analysis than a predictive model.

The resultant regression model accounted for 94 percent of the variance in these new production-firm birth rates. Statistically significant independent variables included in the regression equation included the higher death rates of manufacturing firms, higher levels of population growth, larger concentrations of manufacturing employment in small firms, and a larger proportion of locally owned dwellings (considered to indicate higher household wealth).

Sixteen of the characteristics with statistically significant correlations with new-firm birth rates were then incorporated in a factor analysis, with five significant dimensions results. These five dimensions were then used in a cluster analysis to determine those counties with quite different birth rates. The 63 counties could be classified into eight types. The most "fertile" type had new-firm birth rates over three times that of the least "fertile." The most fertile tended to have high proportions of smaller manufacturing firms, more self-employment, higher educational attainment, more household wealth, and higher firm death rates. The least fertile tended to have less household wealth, more mining, fewer service firms, and lower firm death rates. This elaborate and careful analysis indicates the potential payoff from careful attention to the factors affecting regional differences in new-firm formation.

A number of patterns related to the context in which new foundings occur in organizational populations have been discussed in the literature. Regardless of the regional unit of analysis, long-term growth in the host population and a diverse and active economic environment (the incubator hypothesis) appear as quite important. There is little support for the unemployment hypothesis in U.S. data. There is evidence that the presence of a pool of potential entrepreneurs (well-educated, mid-career adults) is important. The contribution of a "good" business climate or low production costs seems modest or mixed. Low taxes are clearly not a major factor affecting births, but there is some evidence that the presence of a public infrastructure (schools, etc.) has an impact. Overall, this seems to be a promising avenue for understanding the context that encourages entrepreneurial behavior.

Two persistent findings are in direct opposition to the basic patterns that emerge from the analysis of a single type of organization. First, in cross-sectional comparisons higher organizational densities in a region have a positive contribution to subsequent birth rates. In longitudinal studies of organizational populations, higher "densities" are found to depress new foundings. Second, regional analyses suggest that birth and death rates are positively correlated. This is true for both the United States and Japan (Reynolds 1990b, Table 6). The organizational ecology perspective leads to predictions of negative or no correlations between births and deaths.

Both sets of findings are probably accurate reflections of organizational phenomena. Considerable conceptual work may be required to reconcile these differences. Regardless of the findings from longitudinal studies of single types of organizations, one fact is clear: when economic regions are the focus of analysis — organizations beget organizations.

Human Populations and Entrepreneurial Behavior

Organizations do not, of course, just "appear." No matter how fertile the context, new organizations occur only when individuals decide to associate for some mutual advantage. The intervening variable between a fertile context and a new firm is the decision of one or more individuals to initiate a new organization. What can be said about the tendency of those in a human population to differentiate themselves through entrepreneurial behavior — participating in a new-firm start-up?

As seen earlier in Table 11–3, each year about 1 new firm is created for every 10 establishments. For 1986, when there were 5 million establishments, this would be about 500,000 new firms. The typical new firm is initiated by a start-up team of two people (Reynolds and Freeman 1986; Reynolds and Miller 1987). Hence, we can assume that about 1,000,000 individuals were engaged in new-firm start-ups each year. In 1986, the U.S. population over 16 years old was approximately 182 million, of which 97 million had jobs, 9 million were self-employed, and about 8 million were unemployed (civilian, nonagricultural only; U.S. Bureau of the Census 1989, Tables 620, 627). Hence, approximately 1 percent of the 114 million in the labor force were engaged in a new-firm start-up in 1986.

This is an annual participation rate. It might be that the same 1 percent are participating in new-firm starts each year — habitual entrepreneurs. It may be a "fresh cohort" each year. How might one resolve this issue — that is, the extent to which entrepreneurial behavior is confined to a distinct subpopulation or a widely pursued career alternative? Two statewide studies of new firms indicate that two-thirds of those starting new firms are doing so for the first time; approximately one-sixth are involved in their second new-firm start-up (Reynolds and Miller 1990). Stated differently, about one-sixth of the members of new-firm start-up teams are on their third or more new firm. Hence, the proportion of the adult population involved in new-firm start-ups each year for the first time — novice entrepreneurs — would be slightly less than the 1 percent estimated above. This is still a substantial number of individuals. As an additional cohort of first-time entrepreneurs develops every year, the cumulative effect could be significant.

Surveys of the adult population would provide evidence of the cumulative effect of the interest in entrepreneurial behavior. Such a survey was completed with a representative sample of Minnesota adults in 1987 (Knudson and McTavish 1988a, 1988b, 1989). In phone interviews, 1,204 adults were asked "How many businesses have you started by yourself and with someone else?" and, "Are you thinking *seriously* about starting a new business, either alone or with someone else?" One in three (34 percent) of the respondents reported that they had been involved in a new-firm start-up some time in their lives. Another one in seven (13 percent) reported they were currently "thinking *seriously*" about starting a new business. A follow-up nine months later indicated that about one-fourth (24 percent) of those "thinking *seriously*" had taken some action to initiate a new business. This was, then, 3 percent of the initial representative sample of typical adults, somewhat higher than the 1 percent estimated from the new-firm start-up team analysis, but in the same order of magnitude. The attrition from the 3 percent "taking steps to start a business" and the 1 percent estimated from the new-firms surveys may be due to attrition in the gestation process.

The dynamic feature of "serious interest" in entrepreneurial activity is reflected in the loss of interest among one-fifth (21.5 percent) of those initially seriously interested. In addition, 7 percent of those who had not shown an interest during the initial interview were now "thinking seriously" about starting a new firm. It would seem that moves toward or away from entrepreneurial behavior are affected by the changes in the individual's context — either their personal situation or their perception of market opportunities. While there may be a predisposition toward entrepreneurship, it is clear from this pattern that contextual factors also have a major effect.

The two questions — past experience with starting, and seriously thinking about starting a new firm — show the same pattern of variation when related to sociodemographic characteristics. Men indicated more past experience with starting new firms than women (34 percent versus 25 percent) and more "thinking seriously" (18 percent versus 9 percent). The age of the respondent did not have a major effect on start-ups, but it did have a considerable impact on "seriously thinking" about starting a business. About 20 percent of those 18–44 were seriously thinking about starting a new firm, compared to 5 percent of those over 44. Those with experience in the work force were more likely to report past experience with starting a new firm, when compared to students or homemakers. Those engaged in part-time work were most likely to be "seriously interested" in starting a new firm (23 percent), followed by those with full-time work (15 percent), and the unemployed (13 percent). Educational attainment had little effect on reports of participating in new-firm start-ups, but a major effect on "serious interest." Those with post–high school education or college degrees were twice as likely (17 percent) to report "seriously thinking" about a new-firm start-up when compared to those with no education beyond high school (9 percent). Hence, those most likely to report that they were "seriously thinking" about starting a new firm were males, 25–44 years old, engaged in part-time work and with education beyond high school.

Exactly the same patterns are found among those participating in the start-up of new firms in Minnesota and Pennsylvania (Reynolds and Miller 1990). Estimates of the participation rates (the proportion of the general population participating in new-firm start-ups) for the two states were almost identical. Men had three times the participation rates as women; the rates peaked for the ages 25–44; and the participation rates rose with educational attainment. Participation in new-firm start-ups, when controlled for educational attainment, were the same for minorities. Entrepreneurial participation rates, however, tended to drop for men with graduate degrees, compared to those with college degrees. This was not the case for women or minorities.

One of the most common findings is that those starting new firms do so in a familiar location. Not only do they do so in a familiar geographical community, but they tend to do so in the same industry in which they have developed knowledge and contacts. These are reflected in the development of a network, now being considered as an important factor in entrepreneurial behavior (Aldrich and Zimmer 1986).

The lack of successful entrepreneurial trait analysis for predictions of entrepreneurial behavior or success has begun to receive substantial attention (Gartner 1989). Three factors may affect an individual's decision to start a new firm: 1) characteristics of the economic context; 2) characteristics of the individual's life or career context; and 3) underlying personal disposition. While individual disposition or traits may have an effect, if the major factors are related to context and stage of life, there will be little variance left for "entrepreneurial traits" to explain.

SUMMARY AND
COMMENTARY

The joint occurrence of two events is critical for the creation of a new firm. The first is the presence of a market or economic opportunity suited for a new firm. The second is a person who is predisposed to take advantage of an entrepreneurial opportunity. When predisposition and opportunity coincide, entrepreneurial behavior may take place, and a new firm is founded.

The societal conditions or context may reflect : changes in technology or products that provide opportunities for new markets or even a new industry ; growth in the total market ; changes in industry mix ; and the availability of resources (employees, facilities, capital) required to start a new firm. The individual predisposition may be affected by a number of factors, including the respect and importance attached to entrepreneurship in the society, career activities of parents and other role models, as well as individual aptitudes and personality characteristics. It may also be affected by the current situation of the individual, such as their age, physical health, and perceived employment or career opportunities.

What is critical for a new-firm birth is the interaction or intersection of these two processes. A person predisposed to start a new firm, finds himself or herself in a situation where a new-firm start-up is seen as a relatively attractive, feasible career option — at that time. Working with others, they initiate a new firm and adopt a new work role. Once in the new work role they confront new responsibilities, new challenges, and new associates. They may lead, in turn, to a shift in their attitudes as well as an emphasis on new facets of their personality.

Most of the current research is consistent with this general model of the start-up process. What is absent is precise information on the relative importance of the different processes, or different factors affecting the two processes.

What do we know ?

The information on national-level analysis suggests that new and small firms are an important feature of the U.S. economy, with a relatively constant ratio of firms to the working population and relatively high turbulence (births and deaths). Recent trends suggest a restructuring of the economy leading to more firms per capita and, perhaps, greater firm interdependence between small and large firms. Contemporary analyses of industries and historical analyses of single populations of organizations indicate that new-firm births are related to ease of start-up (low start-up costs) and demand for the new organization's product (indicated by high average industry profits or a rapid increase in the "density" of the organizations).

Analysis based on geographic regions makes it clear that population growth and turbulence in the organizational community lead to higher firm birth rates. In contrast to a major finding from the study of narrowly defined organizational communities, the density of organizations is found to be positively correlated with firm birth rates. This is due in part to the higher densities (firms per employee) associated with smaller firms and more volatile industries. Most evidence suggests that growing markets and an appropriate infrastructure (education, transportation, efficient government) tend to encourage new-firm births. Reduced cost of government (lower taxes) does not seem to have much effect.

Research on the unique characteristics of those involved in new-firm start-ups suggests experience and situational variables and conditions may be as important as the attitudes and personality in affecting the decision to be "entrepreneurial." Of particular importance are educational attainment, age, and gender — all useful in predicting the decision to be involved in a new-firm start-up. Attitudes and personality variables may help predict who — among those contemplating career changes — elects to start a new firm or chooses to remain employed. However, by the time the nature of the context and aspects of the individual's life course are taken into account, much of the variation related to entrepreneurial behavior may be accounted for. There may be very little unexplained variation in entrepreneurial behavior for personality and attitude differences.

What should we know ?

How can knowledge of the entrepreneurial process — the mechanisms that lead to new firms — be improved ? A distinction may be made between what might be known and what is likely to be known.

It would be useful to have more precise censuses of the total number of establishments and firms *and* birth and death rates. It is, however, expensive and complicated to change ongoing data collection systems at the federal level. Fortunately, the Small Business Data Base as maintained by the SBA appears to provide substantial opportunity for analysis. Although it retains some of the disadvantages of the original Dun & Bradstreet procedures, this a national resource that should be maintained. More complete and detailed data are likely to become available for smaller geographic units, counties, and labor market areas. This will greatly facilitate the study of regional characteristics affecting new-firm births. Equally important is the dramatic increase in size of data sets that may be analyzed with personal computers. This makes it possible to study rather large data sets on a modest research budget.

Data is sparse on a critical feature of the newly emerging economy — the interdependence of new or small firms and large firms. Very little evidence has been assembled that would allow systematic study of this interdependence and how it affects the opportunities for new firms. This may require substantial projects possible only with massive government funding.

What can we know ?

A number of issues may be explored with relatively small-scale projects: the birth of new industries, the decisions of adults to pursue entrepreneurial career options, and the gestation process that follows the adults' decisions.

It is clear that there are major structural changes occurring in the economies of all countries. These structural changes lead to the creation of new industries. Such industries provide major entrepreneurial opportunities and make it attractive to start a new firm. Very little seems to be known about industry births. One complication is the major lag in the revisions of the Standard Industrial Codes (SIC), which reflect the division of economic activity. The codes are currently so gross (only 500 categories), and change so slowly, that it may be several decades before new industries are recognized in official statistics. New industry births, or market niches for new products or services, are better recognized through systematic examination of trade journals or interviews with industry experts.

The actual processes that lead to the birth of new firms clearly demand further study. Such an effort could be considered in two parts. The first would be careful attention to the decision of typical adults to become involved in a new-firm start-up. By incorporating a few questions in omnibus population surveys, it would be easy to identify the adults currently involved in different stages of the entrepreneurial process. The effects of the economic context, their current life situation, as well as distinctive personality traits could be explored as factors affecting the decision to commit to an entrepreneurial behavior.

Complementing this approach would be careful attention to the gestation process — the events between a firm's conception and "live birth." Only recently has attention been given to the events involved in a new-firm start-up (Birley 1984; Katz and Gartner 1988; Reynolds 1990a). Conception may be considered as the moment when the principals elect to initiate a new firm — perhaps at a meeting in somebody's home or office. From that point until the new firm participates in the economy may be considered the gestation period. Major gestation events may include commitment of the principals' time to the new firm, commitment of the principals' money, hiring employees, obtaining loans, and sale of the product or service. There is evidence of substantial variation in the sequencing of these gestation events as well as in the gestation period as a whole. Integrating the analysis of decisions to pursue an entrepreneurial career with an explication of the gestation process would make a substantial contribution to the understanding of new-firm foundings. We have found the tunnel; now we need to find the light.

▬ ▬ ▬ ▬ ▬ ▬ ▬ ▬

REFERENCES

Acs, Z. J., and D. B. Audretsch 1989a Births and firm size. *Southern Economic Journal* 56 (2): 467–475.

1989b Small-firm entry in U.S. manufacturing. *Economica* (May): 255–266.

Aldrich, H. E. 1990 Using an ecological perspective to study organizational founding rates. *Entrepreneurship : Theory and Practice* 14 (3): 7–24.

Aldrich, H. E., and C. Zimmer 1986 Entrepreneurship through social networks. In *The art and science of entrepreneurship*, eds. D. L. Sexton and R. W. Smilor, 3–24. Cambridge, Mass. : Ballinger.

Bain, J. S. 1962 *Barriers to new competition : Their character and consequences in manufacturing industries.* Cambridge, Mass. : Harvard Univ. Press.

Bartik, T. J. 1986 Effects of state and local government policies on the start-up of small business. In *Proceedings*, National Tax Association, 25–33.

Birley, S. 1984 Finding the new firm. In *Proceedings* of the Academy of Management Meetings 47 : 64–68.

Bluestone, H., C. A. Long, and S. L. Porterfield 1989 Small business activity : Does it make a difference at the county level ? Paper presented at the meeting of the Southern Regional Science Association. Presented April 27–29, 1989.

Booth, D. E. 1986 Long waves and uneven regional growth. *Southern Economic Journal* 53 : 448–460.

Bruno, A. V., and T. T. Tyebjee 1982 The environment for entrepreneurship. In *Encyclopedia of entrepreneurship*, eds. C. A. Kent, D. L. Sexton, and K. H. Vesper, 288–307. Englewood Cliffs, N.J. : Prentice-Hall, Inc.

Cable, J., and J. Schwalbach 1991 International comparisons of entry and exit. In *Entry and market contestability : An international comparison*, eds. P. A. Geroski and J. Schwalbach. London : Basil Blackwell.

Carlton, D. W. 1979 Why new firms locate where they do : An econometric model. In *Interregional movement and regional growth*, ed. W. Wheaton, 13–50. Washington, D.C. : Urban Institute.

1983 The location and employment choices of new firms : An econometric model with discrete and continuous endogenous variables. *Review of Economics and Statistics* 65 : 440–449.

Carroll, G. R. 1984 Organizational ecology. *Annual Review of Sociology* 10 : 71–93.

Carroll, G. R., ed. 1988 *Ecological models of organizations.* Cambridge, Mass. : Ballinger.

Carroll, G. R., J. Delacroix, and J. Goodstein 1988 The political environment of organizations : An ecological view. *Research in Organizational Behavior* 10 : 359–392.

Caves, R. E., and M. E. Porter 1977 From entry barriers to mobility barriers : Conjectural decisions and contrived deterrence to new competition. *Quarterly Journal of Economics* 91 (2): 241–261.

Evans, D. S., and L. S. Leighton 1989 *Small-business formation by unemployed workers.* Final report prepared under contract for the Office of Advocacy, U.S. Small Business Administration, SBA–2102–AER–87.

Gartner, W. B. 1989 "Who is an entrepreneur ?" is the wrong question. *Entrepreneurship Theory and Practice* 13 (4): 47–68.

Hannan, M. T., and J. Freeman 1977 The population ecology of organizations. *American Journal of Sociology* 82 : 929–964.

Highfield, R., and R. Smiley 1986 New business starts and economic activity : An empirical investigation. *International Journal of Industrial Organization* 5 : 51–66.

Howland, M. 1985 Property taxes and the birth and intraregional location of new firms. *Journal of Planning Education and Research* 4 (3): 148–156.

Katz, J., and W. B. Gartner 1988 Properties of emerging organizations. *Academy of Management Review* 13 (3): 429–441.

Keeble, D. 1989 Small firms, new firms, and uneven regional development. Working paper. Cambridge, Eng. : Cambridge Univ., Department of Geography.

1990 New firms and regional economic development : Experience and impacts in the 1980s. *Cambridge Regional Review* 1 : In press.

Kent, C. A. 1982 Entrepreneurship and economic development. In *Encyclopedia of entrepreneurship*, eds. C. A. Kent, D. L. Sexton, and K. H. Vesper, 237–256. Englewood Cliffs, N.J. : Prentice-Hall, Inc.

Kent, C. A., D. L. Sexton, and K. H. Vesper, eds. 1982 *Encyclopedia of entrepreneurship.* Englewood Cliffs, N.J. : Prentice-Hall, Inc.

Kirchhoff, B. A., and R. E. McAuliffe 1989 *Economic development of mature industrial areas.* Final report to the Technical Assistance Program, Economic Development Administration, U.S. Department of Commerce. October.

Knudsen, K. R., and D. G. McTavish 1988a Interest in venturing in Minnesota. Bureau of Business and Economic Research, University of Minnesota-Duluth. Working paper No. 88–19.

1988b Venturing : Searching for the high-potential entrepreneur. Bureau of Business and Economic Research, University of Minnesota-Duluth. Working paper No. 88–21.

1989 Modelling interest in entrepreneurship : Implications for small business development. Paper presented at the Babson Entrepreneurship Research Conference, St. Louis, Mo. April 26–29.

Moyes, A., and P. Westhead 1990 Environments for new firm formation in Great Britain. *Regional Studies* 24 (2) : 123–126.

Orr, D. 1974a The determinants of entry : A study of the Canadian manufacturing industries. *Review of Economics and Statistics* 5 : 58–66.

1974b An index of entry barriers and its application to the market structure performance relationship. *Journal of Industrial Economics* 23 (1) : 39–49.

Pennings, J. M. 1982a Elaboration on the entrepreneur and his environment. In *Encyclopedia of entrepreneurship*, eds. C. A. Kent, D. L. Sexton, and K. H. Vesper, 307–315. Englewood Cliffs, N.J. : Prentice-Hall, Inc.

1982b Organizational birth frequencies : An empirical investigation. *Administrative Science Quarterly* 27 : 120–144.

1982c The urban quality of life and entrepreneurship. *Academy of Management Journal* 25 (1) : 63–79.

Phillips, B. D. 1988 Birth and death rates of small and large firms : 1976–86. Paper presented at the meeting of the American Economic Association, New York City. December 28–30, 1988.

Reynolds, P. D. 1990a New firm gestation : Conception, birth, and implications for research. Working paper.

1990b *Small Business Economics.* In press.

Reynolds, P. D., and S. Freeman 1986 *New firm contributions to Pennsylvania.* Vol. 2 of *1986 Pennsylvania new firm survey.* Washington, D.C. : Appalachian Regional Commission.

Reynolds, P. D., and W. R. Maki 1990a Business volatility and economic growth. Final project report prepared under contract for the U.S. Small Business Administration, SBA–3067–OA–88.

1990b U.S. regional characteristics, new firms, and economic growth. Paper presented at the Univ. of Warwick Cross-National Workshop on the Role of the Small, Medium Enterprises in Regional Economic Growth. Coventry, England.

Reynolds, P. D., and B. Miller 1990 Race, gender, and entrepreneurship : Participation in new firm start-ups. Paper presented at the annual meeting of the Academy of Management, San Francisco.

Romanelli, E. 1989 Organizational birth and variety : A community perspective on origins. *Research in Organizational Behavior* 11 : 211–246.

Schmalensee, R. 1988 Industrial economics : An overview. *The Economic Journal* 98 : 643–681.

Sexton, D. L., and R. W. Smilor, eds. 1986 *The art and science of entrepreneurship.* Cambridge, Mass. : Ballinger.

Storey, D. J. 1990 The birth of new firms — does unemployment matter ? A review of the evidence. Paper presented at the Wissenschaftszentrum Berlin fur Sozialforschung (WZB) Conference on the Role of Small Firms and Entrepreneurship : A Comparison between East and West Countries, Berlin.

Storey, D. J., and S. Johnson 1987 Regional variations in entrepreneurship in the U.K. *Scottish Journal of Political Economy* 34 (2) : 161–173.

Tolbert, C. M., and M. Sizer Killian 1987 Labor market areas for the United States. Economic Research Service, Agriculture and Rural Economy Division, U.S. Department of Agriculture. Staff Report No. AGE870721.

U.S. Bureau of the Census 1989 *Statistical abstracts of the United States : 1989.* Washington, D.C. : U.S. Government, Superintendent of Documents.

U.S. Small Business Administration 1988a *Handbook of small business data : 1988.* Washington, D.C. : U.S. Government, Superintendent of Documents.

1988b *Linked 1976–1986 USEEM user's guide.* Office of Advocacy, Washington, D.C.

1988c Uses and limitations of USEEM / USELM data. Office of Advocacy, Washington, D.C.

1989 *The state of small business : 1989.* Washington, D.C. : U.S. Government, Superintendent of Documents.

Young, R. C. 1988 Is population ecology a useful paradigm for the study of organizations ? *American Journal of Sociology* 94 (1) : 1–24.

Part

4

ENTREPRENEURIAL FIRM GROWTH AND FINANCING

Chapter

12

Entrepreneurs, Processes of Founding, and New-Firm Performance

Arnold C. Cooper
and
F. Javier Gimeno Gascón
●

INTRODUCTION

One of the central questions in the study of entrepreneurship is concerned with why some new ventures succeed and others do not. This chapter reviews the relevant literature which bears upon this question, with primary attention devoted to empirical studies.

There are a number of kinds of writings which will not be considered. Books and articles which report upon the experience of individual entrepreneurs or the accumulated wisdom of well-informed observers can be both interesting and valuable. Conceptual papers, which alert us to particular pitfalls and then propose approaches for dealing with those problems, can be of significant value, both to academicians and to entrepreneurs. There is also a growing body of research on corporate entrepreneurship, including the starting of new ventures within established corporations. All these kinds of literature are important, but they are not the focus of this chapter. Here, our concern is with formal, empirical research which considers independent start-ups and the factors bearing upon their performance.

If we can achieve a better understanding of what influences new venture performance, this will have implications for prospective entrepreneurs, as well as their advisors and investors. If certain factors (such as industry experience or education) increase the odds for success, then entrepreneurs can appraise their own prospects with this in mind. If particular founding characteristics (such as having partners or professional advisors) are associated with better performance, then founders can modify their plans to make it more likely that they will succeed.

A Framework for Examining Entrepreneurial Performance

It would be misleading to imply that we have well-developed theories for thinking about factors which bear upon new venture success. We do have general models or frameworks, which are reflective of the research done to date in this young field. In Appendix 12–A, we see five frameworks for factors bearing upon new enterprise formulation and success.

There is considerable similarity in these models, with a lot of attention being devoted to the characteristics of individual entrepreneurs, including their experience, their education, and their psychological makeup. Less universally considered, but important in the schemes of VanderWerf, Gartner, and Stevenson and Jarillo, is how decisions are made and how the entrepreneur goes about starting and managing the firm. Environmental and industry conditions shape the opportunities and are central to the respective frameworks of Gartner, Vesper, and Cooper. Finally, the nature of the new venture, particularly its strategy, is important in the structures of VanderWerf, Vesper, and Gartner.

Our review here of factors bearing upon success could easily lead to consideration of the extensive literature on the management of new and small firms. There would be a logic in this, in that the background of the entrepreneur or the processes of starting do not automatically predetermine the future of every venture. It is in the subsequent unfolding of events, including the key decisions, the strategies developed, and the management practices of the entrepreneur, that success is determined. However, to attempt to encompass all of this would make this chapter unwieldy, and would lead us into some topic areas covered by other contributors to this book. Therefore, the structure for the review of the literature presented here will focus primarily upon variables which can be observed or studied at the time of start-up. This framework examines characteristics of the entrepreneur, the processes of starting, and environmental characteristics. The specific variables considered are described in Appendix 12–B.

Some Characteristics of the Literature

It is striking to note how young the field of entrepreneurial studies is. Systematic research on factors related to new venture success are primarily a product of the 1980s. (There were some important antecedents, notably the longitudinal studies by Hoad and Rosko 1964; Mayer and Goldstein 1961; Roberts 1972; and Cooper and Bruno 1977.) However, as we shall note, both the number and sophistication of studies have been increasing in recent years.

There are at least four major problems in studying and interpreting the literature. Most notable is the lack of well-developed theories of causal relationships (VanderWerf 1989; Hisrich 1988). There are many correlation studies, but it is not clear what is driving the relationships. For instance, VanderWerf (1989) noted that there may be alternative models relating experienced management, aggressiveness of entry strategy, sophistication of planning, and market share and performance. This uncertainty about causal relationships makes it difficult to interpret the spotty and sometimes inconsistent findings to date. Many of the published articles do not have much of a core of theory to motivate the variables that are considered.

A second problem relates to variations in samples. Such variations are to be expected, because there is, in fact, great diversity among the 1.3 million ventures started in the United States each year. As Gartner (1985) noted, differences among entrepreneurs and among their ventures are as great as the variation between entrepreneurs and nonentrepreneurs and between new firms and established firms. These differences may be due to definitional differences. Furthermore, at this stage in the development of the field, we do not know whether there are contingent relationships. For instance, are founding teams and previous management experience more important for high-growth potential firms than for "mom and pop" businesses? Are particular entrepreneurial characteristics, e.g., tolerance for ambiguity, more important in some environments, such as industries in the early growth stage? We should also note that samples vary in the age of the firms examined. Many samples involve cross-sectional studies of young (and not so young) firms. New firms which died quickly are not easy to study and are often not included in samples. We should bear in mind the diversity of samples as we consider the temptation and the risks of generalizing from particular studies.

A third problem involves the variety of performance measures that have been used. Market-based indicators, frequently used in finance and corporate strategy research, are usually not available for new ventures, most of which are privately held. Accounting-based measures, such as return on equity or return on sales, have sometimes been utilized; however, these data can be difficult to obtain and can be heavily influenced by decisions about the owner-manager's compensation as well as by industry margins. Growth measures, considering sales or employee growth, have often been used. However, growth potential varies widely across new enterprises, encompassing what Liles (1974) termed high-potential ventures, attractive small companies, and traditional small businesses. Some studies have used absolute size as a measure of success, without necessarily measuring growth rate. Survival versus discontinuance is another measure, but this often requires longitudinal studies and does not consider whether some "survive" with higher performance than others. Subjective assessments of performance or indices of performances have sometimes been used; they are, of course, dependent upon the expectations of the entrepreneur or upon how the index is weighted. Sapienza et al. (1988) examined whether subjective assessments of sales growth and return on sales were related to objective measures; they found no significant correlations. The upshot of this variety of measures is that comparability across studies is difficult. There is also the question of whether the major influences upon performance are dependent, in part, upon the measure used. For instance, are the variables that are important for growth the same as those having primary influence upon survival?

A fourth problem relates to the analytical methods used. Earlier studies often utilized cross-tabulations only. Many inquiries have used univariate analysis. It is only recently that an increasing number of studies have utilized the multivariate methods so common in other branches of management research. We know that many variables thought to be related to success are correlated. For instance, larger ventures have better survival rates. Larger ventures involve more initial capital and are also more likely to be started by partners, by founders with more education, and by founders with more industry experience. All of these variables have sometimes been found to be correlated with performance (Cooper, Woo, and Dunkelberg 1989). In this, as in many other cases, multivariate analysis is needed to determine the relative influence of each variable upon performance.

We need to be alert to these problems as we review the research that has been done. It is easy to be critical about a developing field, implicitly applying the standards of more mature fields which represent the fruits of decades of scholarship. As we shall note, interesting questions have been posed, and a growing body of research is developing.

The research studies examined are summarized in Appendix 12–C. Included are summary data on the nature of each sample, the variables which are related to performance, the performance measures utilized, and the methods of analysis.

■■ ■■ ■■ ■■ ■■
THE ENTREPRENEUR

We shall first review research on relationships between characteristics of the entrepreneur and performance, considering these roughly in the order in which they may have influenced the entrepreneur. Thus, we examine race and gender, occupation of parents, education, experience, psychological characteristics, entrepreneur's age, and goals.

Race and Gender

We know that there has been a rapid growth in the number of new ventures founded by minorities and by women. This undoubtedly reflects societal changes which influence the expectations and experience of people in all segments of our society.

Four recent studies have examined relationships between these demographic characteristics of entrepreneurs and the subsequent performance of their firms. Minority entrepreneurs started firms which were less likely to survive (Cooper, Dunkelberg, and Woo 1988), more likely to generate lower earnings (Sexton and Robinson 1989), and less likely to grow (Woo et al. 1989). Female entrepreneurs founded firms which demonstrated poorer performance in three studies (Denison and Alexander 1986; Cooper, Dunkelberg, and Woo 1988; Sexton and Robinson 1989). At this time, white males seem to be more likely to be successful, possibly because of the resources they can assemble and the experience they can bring to bear. This may be changing, but much remains to be done to help minorities and women be more successful as entrepreneurs.

Occupation of Parents

A number of studies have noted that entrepreneurs are more likely to be from families in which the parents owned a business. For instance, 50 percent of a sample of 1,805 entrepreneurs and 50 percent to 58 percent of company founders in a variety of surveys in the United States had this family background (Cooper and Dunkelberg 1987; Shapero and Sokol 1982). It has been reasoned that children growing up in such families see the parents as role models, so that, regardless of whether the parents have been successful, entrepreneurship is perceived as a feasible career (Shapero and Sokol 1982). Furthermore, growing up in such families, young people develop knowledge of what is involved in running a business — a valuable background for future entrepreneurs.

There has been little speculation about how this background is likely to influence performance, although presumably the knowledge gained makes success more likely. Two studies have examined this factor. A longitudinal study involving a broad cross-section of entrepreneurs disclosed no significant relation between this background and new venture survival (Cooper, Dunkelberg, and Woo 1988), but a study of founders in an emerging industry found that having had entrepreneurial parents was associated with greater sales (Duchesneau and Gartner 1988). At this time, we would have to say that the evidence on this point is inconclusive.

Education

Education is one of the most widely studied entrepreneurial variables. There have been mixed indications as to whether level of education is associated with becoming an entrepreneur. The early studies by Collins and Moore (1970) examining entrepreneurs who had started machine shops and related businesses in Michigan, found that many had a psychological makeup which made it difficult for them to relate to authority. They tended to leave school at a relatively early age. However, high-technology entrepreneurs, as might be expected, had much more education — an average of a master's degree, in studies of M.I.T. spin-offs (Roberts 1972). A cross-sectional study of 1,805 entrepreneurs reported a mean educational level of 13 to 15 years of schooling, somewhat higher than the general population (Cooper and Dunkelberg 1987).

Theoretically, it is uncertain how level of education might affect performance. Viewing the entrepreneur as the primary resource of a new firm, we might expect that more education would lead to greater success. However, it is not clear whether the things which are learned in school are enough to achieve success. Commitment and determination, obsession with opportunities, and tolerance for ambiguity may be critical for success with some ventures, yet these may not be the product of formal education (Timmons 1990).

In considering level of education (that is, the highest level achieved by the entrepreneur), we see a mosaic of findings. For 17 studies in which there were explicit tests of performance, there were 10 in which there was a positive relationship between educational level and performance. In 6 studies, the results were not significant, and in 1 there was a negative relationship. In the study in which there was a negative relationship, that by Stuart and Abetti (1988), the focus was upon founders of high-technology firms. They found that entrepreneurs with Ph.D. degrees did less well than those with master's degrees. These findings are consistent with those of Roberts (1972), who studied high-technology entrepreneurs in Boston almost 20 years earlier and who also found that those with master's degrees did better than those with more or less education.

A variety of measures of performance and methods of analysis were used in these previous studies. The patterns did not differ significantly, whether multivariate or univariate analysis was performed. There were also no major differences whether survival, growth, profitability, or a composite or scaled performance measure was used.

Another dimension of educational background relates to what kinds of education characterized the entrepreneur or the entrepreneurial team. Four studies have considered this, with three of these finding some evidence that particular kinds of study were associated with higher performance. Bailey (1986) found that a certificate of education or trade qualification went with a higher index of success for his sample of 67 Australian founders. Brush and Hisrich (1988), in studying 172 women entrepreneurs, found that field of graduate study was associated with higher growth, but not better chances of survival. Teach, Tarpley, and Schwartz (1986), looking at founding teams of software firms, found that, if at least one member of the team had a business degree or an engineering degree, then the firm was likely to have grown to greater size. Woo et al. (1989) found that the number of business courses taken was negatively associated with growth for larger start-ups.

There has been no examination of whether relationships are nonlinear or whether there are systematic variations by industry. We know that average educational levels of founders vary by kind of business, with, for example, high technology being relatively high. It appears that for high-technology firms, education to the master's degree level tends, on the average, to be better than both lower and higher levels of education. We cannot say whether there are similar relationships for other kinds of firms. It does appear that level of education has an impact on growth, but not on survival prospects.

Experience

A variety of dimensions of experience have been examined in previous research. Collins and Moore (1970) concluded that their sample of entrepreneurs, with their low tolerance for authority, tended to move frequently from job to job, but that has not necessarily been found in other studies (Cooper and Dunkelberg 1987). Familiarity with product or market has often been examined; entrepreneurs have often been found to start businesses closely related to what they did before (Roberts 1972; Cooper 1985). Breadth of experience, functional experience, and highest level of management experience have also been the focus of research. We do know that there are variations by industry and by kind and size of firm; for instance, larger start-ups tend to be founded by entrepreneurs with higher levels of management experience (Cooper, Woo, and Dunkelberg 1989).

We might expect that greater breadth of experience would lead to higher performance because of the wide range of problems which entrepreneurs confront. (However, excessive job hopping may be associated with shallow experience and a lesser tendency to see problems through to solutions.) Higher levels of previous management experience should make the entrepreneur better prepared and lead to greater success. Familiarity with the field should enable the founder to use product and market knowledge, as well as contacts, to make better decisions. Start-up or small business experience should permit the entrepreneur to anticipate problems encountered by young firms, and to use appropriate management methods.

We review here 25 studies which have examined different dimensions of entrepreneurial experience. Number of previous jobs, which might bear upon breadth of experience, was examined in two studies, with one finding a negative relationship to survival and the other no significant association.

Experience within the field — familiarity — showed a positive relationship to both survival and growth in a study by Brush and Hisrich (1988) and was also seen to be related to success by Neiswander and Drollinger (1986). In research which looked at the influence of this variable within the context of different strategies, Dubini and MacMillan (1988) found no relationships between industry experience and performance for two of four strategies examined, but some positive relationships for the other two strategies. Another study found that experience increased the likelihood of being profitable, but experience plus education was associated with the greatest success (Hoad and Rosko 1964). Three other studies (MacMillan, Zemann, and Subbanarasimha 1987; Van de Ven, Hudson, and Schroeder 1984; Mayer and Goldstein 1961) found no significant relationships between performance and industry experience. Surprisingly, the evidence on the relationship between industry experience and performance seems to be mixed.

Management experience, including the highest level of management previously achieved, has been a focal point for research in seven studies. Here again we find mixed support, with four studies finding positive relationships between performance and management experience. One of these (Teach, Tarpley, and Schwartz 1986) noted that if at least one member of the team had middle management experience (but not top management experience), the business had higher sales. However, two other studies (Cooper, Dunkelberg, and Woo 1988; Sandberg and Hofer 1986) found no relationship to survival. Another study (Dunkelberg et al. 1987) found that surviving firms which grew were *less* likely to have founders with management experience. However, a later study using the same data base found that, controlling for initial size of firm, there was no significant relation between level of managerial experience and growth (Woo et al. 1989).

Functional experience, including breadth of experience within the team, has also been examined. Doutriaux and Simyar (1987) found that marketing experience (but not financial experience) led to higher sales. However, one broad cross-sectional study (Dunkelberg and Cooper 1982) found no relationship between marketing, financial, production, or engineering experience and growth. Eisenhardt and Schoonhoven (1989) examined heterogeneity of industry experience within the team and the team's joint experience, and found no significant relationships.

Experience in prior start-ups or in small businesses was researched in seven studies. One study found no relationship to sales level (Doutriaux and Simyar 1987), another no relationship to "success categories" (Sandberg and Hofer 1987), and another no relation to survival (Reynolds and Miller 1989). Two found positive relationships, both using composite or subjective assessments of performance (Stuart and Abetti 1988; Chambers, Hart, and Denison 1988). Surprisingly, two other research projects reported negative relationships, one referring to previous small business experience and the other to whether the entrepreneur had previously owned or managed a business (Van de Ven, Hudson, and Schroeder 1984; Dunkelberg et al. 1987). Looking across the research to date, it would be difficult to make the case that prior entrepreneurial experience is associated consistently with success.

Psychological Characteristics

The literature on the psychological characteristics of entrepreneurs demonstrates the diversity of approaches used by different researchers. Some 31 different attributes have been investigated for their relation to performance, with several of those having multiple variations. Most have received attention by only a single researcher, but three variables — need for achievement, internal locus of control, and risk taking — have received the most attention.

There is a long tradition of examining need for achievement and its relation to entrepreneurial behavior (Brockhaus 1982). We might expect that this kind of goal-setting activity would be related to success after a venture is started. Need for achievement was examined in four studies, three of which found that positive scores were related to higher performance.

It has often been reported that entrepreneurs have high internal-locus-of-control scores; they believe they can control their own destiny (Brockhaus 1982). It might seem reasonable to assume that a belief that one can make a difference would lead to proactive behavior and higher performance. Surprisingly, the four studies to date show either mixed or nonsignificant results on the relationship between internal locus of control and performance (Bailey 1986; Begley and Boyd 1986; Brockhaus 1980; Duchesneau and Gartner 1988).

Risk-taking behavior or efforts to control risk have been investigated more extensively than any other variable. It is not clear, a priori, how risk-taking behavior might influence venture performance. Findings were mixed, with four showing nonsignificant results. Four studies examined effort to avoid risk or number of ways mentioned to reduce risk and did find correlation between these efforts and performance. In another study, Dubini and MacMillan (1988) examined whether relationships varied within the context of different strategies. They found that the ability to evaluate and deal with risk was important within two of the four strategies they examined.

The rest of the extensive list of psychological variables which have been examined has received attention in single studies only. A number of psychological constructs have shown at least some relation to performance, and, accordingly, seem deserving of further research.

On balance, it appears that need for achievement and ability to manage risk are both related to performance.

Entrepreneur's Age

Most surveys of entrepreneurs have included data on age at time of founding. One question sometimes considered is whether there is a window of opportunity, a time when entrepreneurs are most likely to start firms (Liles 1974).

The results from the nine studies relating age to performance have been mixed, although differences may depend, in part, upon whether the focus is upon survival or growth. Three found that older entrepreneurs were more likely to survive or have higher income (Brockhaus 1980; Cooper, Dunkelberg, and Woo 1988; Denison and Alexander 1986). Three other studies found that older entrepreneurs were less likely to grow (Begley and Boyd 1985; Cragg and King 1988; Dunkelberg and Cooper 1982).

As with almost all of the research reviewed, there has been little consideration of whether there might be nonlinear relationships, with, for instance, very young and very old entrepreneurs doing less well. Likewise, as with almost all of the entrepreneurial variables that have been examined, we do not know much about contextual relationships. For instance, do younger entrepreneurs do better in some kinds of firms or industry settings?

Entrepreneur's Goals

The entrepreneurs' goals have been studied, often with an eye toward determining whether membership in particular entrepreneurial typologies, in turn, is related to performance. Earlier studies suggested that opportunistic entrepreneurs were more likely to grow (Smith 1967; Filley and Aldag 1978). Five recent studies have classified entrepreneurs as opportunistic vs. craftsman type. Two found no significant relationships, using multiple measures of performance (Stuart and Abetti 1988; Smith, Bracker, and Miner 1987), but three other studies found that opportunistic founders were more likely to grow (Stuart and Abetti 1986; Peterson 1985; Peterson and Smith 1986).

Five recent studies which sought to relate emphasis upon particular goals to subsequent growth have largely found no significant relationships. One study did find that the goal of "avoiding working for others" was positively related to survival, but not related to growth (Cooper, Dunkelberg, and Woo 1988; Woo et al. 1989). This raises the question whether these founders were willing to accept marginal returns in order to continue on their own. However, on balance, emphasis upon particular goals does not seem to show consistent relationships to performance.

— — — — — — — —

PROCESSES OF FOUNDING

There are a number of processes of founding — ways in which the entrepreneur goes about starting — which may be related to subsequent performance. These activities, or factors which influence them, include: getting the idea, planning, the role of the incubator organization, negative pushes, seeking information and forming networks, forming teams, starting vs. purchasing, and raising capital.

Idea Sources

The source of the idea for a business is probably related to a number of characteristics of the new venture and a number of aspects of the founding process. For instance, businesses based upon a hobby or interest are usually smaller-scale firms, which would be less likely to utilize information sources connected with the entrepreneur's previous jobs.

Two studies have related idea source to performance, with one finding that businesses based upon ideas from the entrepreneur's previous job were more likely to grow (Dunkelberg et al. 1987). The other found that an "external idea source" was not significantly related to performance (Van de Ven et al. 1984).

Planning Process

Starting a business clearly involves a lot of planning, which may be done quite informally or with varying degrees of formality. Two research projects have investigated whether following a formal planning model leads to greater success. One found that emphasis upon a number of aspects of planning, including assessing the market, considering a number of functional areas, and devoting more time to planning, were all related to success (Duchesneau and Gartner 1988). The other, which considered many of the same dimensions, found only that following a program planning model was associated with higher performance (Van de Ven, Hudson, and Schroeder 1984). Two other studies examined dimensions of planning for technology-oriented forms. Level of detail in planning the development of the technology was positively related to success (Roure and Maidique 1986). The number of people the plan was sent to for feedback was also positively related to performance (Van de Ven, Hudson, and Schroeder 1984). The available evidence suggests that more formal, systematic, and detailed planning does increase the likelihood of success.

Incubator Organization

Entrepreneurs typically leave some organization when they found a firm. This established organization (or incubator) appears to influence the process of founding and the nature of the new firm in a number of ways (Cooper 1985). The characteristics of that organization (including size, growth rate, and type of institution), its relationship to the new venture, and the extent to which the entrepreneur was "pushed out of it" all have been investigated.

Investigation as to whether entrepreneurs who leave certain kinds of organizations are likely to experience more success have produced mixed findings. Incubators may influence subsequent performance both through the product and market knowledge transferred and the management methods learned; large firms may teach different knowledge and methods than small firms. However, nine studies which noted size of incubator have found either mixed results or nonsignificant results. One study did find that those emerging from rapidly growing incubators were more likely to be successful (Roure and Maidique 1986).

The relatedness of the new venture to the incubator organization can be examined through noting how similar the new venture is in products or services offered, in markets served, or in other ways. Eight recent studies have examined relatedness, with considerable consistency in findings. Five out of seven studies have found that, if the new venture is related in products offered, the new business is likely to be more successful. Market relatedness was associated with higher performance in two out of four studies. A study of software entrepreneurs determined that if their previous firm was in the software industry, they were likely to have achieved greater growth (Teach, Tarpley, and Schwartz 1986). However, a study of women entrepreneurs found no relationship between most recent occupation and new venture survival (Brush and Hisrich 1988).

It has been noted that negative displacements or "pushes" may play a role in an entrepreneur's deciding to leave an established organization and start a new venture. Four studies have examined whether a negative push or negative feelings (which might serve as a trigger) is related to later success. One study found that those who were fired or quit without plans were less likely to survive, and another found survival to be negatively related to fear of dismissal from previous job (Cooper, Dunkelberg, and Woo 1988; Brockhaus 1980). However, Brockhaus found an inverse relationship between satisfaction with the previous job and performance (Brockhaus 1980). Feeser and Dugan (1989) also found little relationship between negative feelings and subsequent success, except that entrepreneurs who felt that they had been unable to work on their ideas were later less likely to grow. Another earlier study found no relation between reasons for leaving and subsequent growth (Dunkelberg and Cooper 1982).

On balance, it appears that incubator organizations most influence performance through relatedness. If the new venture is closely related to the organization which the entrepreneur left, it is more likely to be successful.

Information Sources and Networking

The process of starting a firm involves interacting with others, including securing information, advice, and assistance. Networks may evolve whose characteristics may impact not only the processes of starting, but also the later practices and performance of the business (Aldrich and Woodward 1986).

Reliance upon different sources of assistance has been investigated in a number of studies. The specific sources examined have varied, but there are some common findings. Three studies have found that the use of accountants was associated with better performance. In one of these investigations, reliance upon books and manuals was associated with poorer performance, possibly because these founders tended to have less managerial experience. The other sources of assistance, including other business owners, attorneys, trade associations, suppliers, boards of directors, and bankers, showed no significant relationships to performance in most studies (Cooper, Dunkelberg, and Woo 1988; Dunkelberg et al. 1987; O'Neill and Duker 1986). There was one study showing the use of bankers to be associated with greater subsequent growth (Dunkelberg et al. 1987), and another which found use of outside advisors to lead to greater success (Hay and Ross 1989).

Duchesneau and Gartner (1988) considered whether professionals were used in developing the business plan; when they were used, performance was better. Involving professionals (and customers) in planning also was found to lead to higher performance (Van de Ven, Hudson, and Schroeder 1984).

The networks developed by entrepreneurs were investigated extensively in two studies. The descriptors and performance measures used were extensive and varied across studies. One found that network density, average strength of ties, and time devoted to maintaining contacts were related to initial profitability. Network size was related to later profitability (Aldrich, Rosen, and Woodward 1987). The other reported that time devoted to noncustomer external contacts, to suppliers, and to trade associations was positively related to at least two measures of performance. This study found that the percentage of the entrepreneur's time devoted to customer contacts was negatively related to performance (Dollinger 1985).

Forming Teams

Entrepreneurs often join with partners as they form new ventures. Team formation permits the assembly of greater resources and can add to the breadth of skills available to the firm. This, in turn, can give confidence to investors, customers, and the entrepreneurs themselves. We know that the propensity to form teams can vary by industry; for instance, high-technology firms are much more likely to be built around teams than retail firms. However, a firm started by a team must be able to support more than one entrepreneur, and the team must be able to work together.

Both the presence or absence of a team and the number of members of the team have been examined. Four out of five studies have found that firms started by teams did better than those started by single founders. Of the eight studies that examined the number of principals, six found evidence that larger teams did better. There are, of course, questions of causal relationships. More promising ventures may be able to attract and support larger founding teams.

Characteristics of the team have also been considered by some researchers. If partners were involved in determining goals and strategy, the venture did better (Duchesneau and Gartner 1988). If the team members had prior joint experience in working together, and if a higher percentage of essential functions were performed by founders, the firm did better (Roure and Maidique 1986; Keeley and Roure 1989). Greater educational diversity within the team also was associated with higher performance (Teach, Tarpley, and Schwartz 1986). Most of these studies have focused upon high-technology firms, where team formation is most common.

Starting vs. Purchasing

Research does not always indicate how the entrepreneurs became owners. We do know that purchase is a common route to business ownership.

Two studies have investigated whether this mode of entry is related to subsequent performance. One found purchase to be positively related to survival, but not significantly related to growth if the initial size of the firm is controlled for (Cooper, Dunkelberg, and Woo 1988; Woo et al. 1989). Another found purchase associated with greater "success" (Duchesneau and Gartner 1988).

Financing

There is a long tradition of studying the financing of new firms — a part of the entrepreneurial process which is clearly central to the assembly of resources and which has implications for government policy. The amount of initial capital and the sources of that capital have been the primary focus of research.

The amount of initial capital is related to the initial strategy which might be pursued. For instance, more initial capital permits a retail store to carry a broader inventory, or a high-technology firm to undertake more ambitious projects. More initial capital also buys time, while the entrepreneur learns or overcomes problems. Of the eight papers which have reported upon the relationship between initial capital and performance, six have found that more capital was associated with better performance.

The findings on the initial sources of capital have been more mixed. Two studies which examined reliance upon specific sources, such as personal savings, friends and relatives, banks, etc., found no significant relationships (Dunkelberg and Cooper 1982; Dunkelberg et al. 1987). This is surprising, because external sources of capital, such as banks and individual investors, might be expected to restrict their involvement to the most promising ventures. (The results may be sensitive to the size and growth potential of the firms in the sample. The two studies noted were both heavily weighted toward small firms with limited growth potential.)

A number of research projects have considered the extent to which the entrepreneurs retained ownership. It is important to note that outside ownership often goes with larger-scale ventures which may have higher growth potential. Results were mixed, with five of seven studies finding no relationship between percentage ownership and subsequent performance. Bruno and Tyebjee (1984), with their sample of high-technology firms, found that when outside capital was obtained, their firms were more likely to grow. Dunkelberg et al. (1987) found that, for their broad cross-section of small businesses, those entrepreneurs who retained more ownership were less likely to grow.

As we review the extant literature on the processes of founding, we see, with varying degrees of support, some important relationships; we also see a number of nonsignificant findings. It appears that engaging in planning, that starting businesses which are related to the incubator organization in products offered, that relying upon professional advisors (particularly accountants), that entering through purchase of a business, and that starting with more capital are all likely to increase the odds for success.

━ ━ ━ ━ ━ ━ ━ ━

INDUSTRY AND
ENVIRONMENTAL
CHARACTERISTICS

In the literatures on strategic management and on organization theory, there is considerable evidence that environment influences performance. Furthermore, there appear to be contingency relationships, with the most effective strategies and structures depending upon environmental conditions. In the developing literature on new ventures, there has not been much explicit testing of whether relationships between entrepreneurial characteristics, founding processes, and performance vary by environmental setting. Many studies have drawn their samples from particular industries, but the task of determining whether the resultant findings are contingent upon environmental characteristics has hardly begun.

Industry

Several studies have examined whether average performance of small start-ups varies by industry. Three broad-based studies reported lower survival rates for retail firms (Reynolds 1987; Cooper, Dunkelberg, and Woo 1988; Reynolds and Miller 1989), and one reported higher growth rates for firms in construction, manufacturing, transportation, and wholesale industries (Dunkelberg et al. 1987). Neiswander and Drollinger (1986), focusing upon high-technology firms, reported that those in manufacturing had lower sales, and Hay and Ross (1989) also found manufacturing firms to be less successful.

Industry Characteristics

Industry structural characteristics have been explicitly examined in four recent studies. The presence of entry barriers was considered in three of these, and in all cases higher entry barriers or less expected competition were associated with higher new venture performance (MacMillan, Zemann, and Subba Narasimha 1987; McDougall and Robinson 1988; Sandberg and Hofer 1987). The other industry characteristics examined varied across studies. Higher buyer concentration was associated with better performance (Roure and Maidique 1986). "Demonstrated market acceptance" led to higher sales (MacMillan, Zemann, and Subba Narasimha 1987), but market attractiveness was associated with lower initial market success (Stuart and Abetti 1986). Several studies examined competition, with no significant relations to number of competitors or expected change in number of competitors (Eisenhardt and Schoonhoven 1989; Woo et al. 1989). However, "degree of competition" was related to lower returns for older start-ups (Keeley and Roure 1989). Heterogeneous industry products and industry disequilibrium were also related to greater success for venture-capital-funded firms (Sandberg and Hofer 1987).

Other environmental characteristics have included stage of product life cycle. The specific definitions of stages may have varied across studies. However, five studies reported that entry in emergent or growth stages is associated with higher performance than entry into more mature industries. Another study found growth stage to be better than mature stage, but, contrary to the findings noted above, entry stage was associated with the least success (Covin and Slevin 1990). One research project reported no relationship between performance and environmental dynamism or environmental technological sophistication when those factors were considered by themselves; however, if strategic posture was matched to those characteristics, then performance was higher (Covin and Slevin 1989).

Whether a firm had a rural or urban location was not found to be related to performance in two studies (Reynolds 1986; Reynolds and Miller 1989). However, higher unemployment rates in the area were associated with higher earnings (Sexton and Robinson 1989).

Research on environmental characteristics and new venture performance is clearly in its infancy. For the most part, the direct and contingent effects of environmental characteristics upon new venture performance remain to be explored.

━━ ━━ ━━ ━━ ━━ ━━ ━━ ━━
CONCLUSIONS

At this stage in the development of the field, it is clear that there are few unambiguous findings which could give guidance to entrepreneurs and their advisors.

However, despite the diversity of approaches taken to studying entrepreneurial factors and their relation to performance, there do appear to be some common findings. The strongest evidence suggests that ventures are more likely to be successful if they are started by white males who have a high need for achievement, who take explicit steps to manage risk, and who engage in relatively systematic planning involving the input of others. Furthermore, the ventures should be closely related to the incubator organizations, be started by teams, be purchased rather than started, involve larger amounts of capital, and involve industries in the growth stage. There is some evidence, although less strong than for the factors just noted, that success is also more likely if the entrepreneurs have more education, more management experience, be opportunistic rather than craftsmanlike, and utilize external advisors.

One fundamental problem may be that this entire stream of research assumes that there are strong causal relationships between these variables and new venture performance. This assumption may be unfounded. There may be substantial randomness in the processes influencing performance. The population ecology literature emphasizes that there may be natural selection processes, in which firms which are unsuited for their environment are selected out (Aldrich 1979). In this relatively deterministic view, entrepreneurs are limited in their ability to make choices which improve their survival prospects. External factors, such as the carrying capacity of an industry, may determine how many firms can be successful. This approach, which focuses upon a population level of analysis, notes that entire species of organizations may survive or fail, regardless of the actions of individual firms (Astley and Van de Ven 1983).

A new venture represents a concentration of risk upon a few products, a few markets, and a few people. Events beyond the control of the entrepreneur, such as the decline of a local market, the failure of a major supplier or customer, or the entry of a strong competitor (such as a Walmart across the street), all can lead to the failure of a new venture. Being in the right place at the right time, what Vesper has termed "hard-to-arrange events," can make the difference between success and failure (Vesper 1990). Furthermore, a new business is built around one (or a few) entrepreneurs. Even if they are well prepared, the venture will suffer if there is conflict within the management team, if ill health or accidents impair the effectiveness of key people, or if the entrepreneur discovers that business ownership is less satisfying than anticipated. All of this means that success may be less predictable than the stream of research here has assumed.

A second major problem is that the research to date has tended to focus upon variables which are relatively easy to measure. This may not be the same as focusing upon the variables which are most important. Thus, we have many surveys which consider broad categorical variables, such as age, gender, education, and whether the entrepreneur had experience in the same industry. However, entrepreneurs with similar backgrounds may differ markedly in the specific skills, knowledge, and attitudes they have developed. Future research may need to focus upon more specific attributes — those which relate to the particular skills required for success in certain businesses. Behavioral characteristics, such as commitment and determination and the ability to enlist the assistance of others, may deserve more attention than they have received to date.

Another problem relates to diversity. For the 1.3 million businesses started each year, there are clearly wide differences in potential, in risks, in resources needed, and in the critical skills required for success. In the early stages of entrepreneurial research, there has been a lot of pooling of groups of entrepreneurs and firms to determine whether there are central tendencies which relate particular variables to performance. There has also been considerable generalizing from specific samples. Future research may require that much more attention be devoted to contingent relationships. The relationships between entrepreneurs, processes of founding, and performance may differ not only by industry, but also by strategy or specific environmental conditions.

A major problem in studying performance relationships is the difference in goals across entrepreneurs. The decision to start a business and the decision to stay with a business are both intensely personal decisions. In part, they relate to perceived alternatives. Some of the same factors which may contribute to new venture success, such as good educational credentials and management experience, may also open up alternatives outside the business. Thus, in some cases an entrepreneur with poor preparation may stay with a marginal business, while his better prepared counterparts may close down because they think they can be more successful elsewhere. In such cases, better preparation may be associated with increased likelihood of discontinuance.

In addition, entrepreneurs vary greatly in what they expect to put into a business and what they hope to take out. One might expect to create a successful small business which supports a comfortable life style, and which leaves time and money to pursue other interests. Another may hope to grow a substantial firm which could potentially create great wealth. Thus, nascent businesses, similar in the processes which led to their founding, may develop along very different lines, depending upon the commitment and the evolving goals of the entrepreneur.

Research on relationships between founding characteristics and performance also raises fundamental questions about how businesses and performance are to be defined. Thus, in longitudinal studies, how should a firm be classified if it is sold, if it is transformed (strategy, location, and/or name changed), or if it is closed down and then reopened? Determining whether a *business* is still alive is less straightforward than determining whether a person is still alive. Care should also be used in recognizing how the choice of a sample determines whether certain performance levels are likely to be observed. Thus, cross-sectional samples usually omit discontinued firms, and samples of venture-capital-funded firms are much more likely to include some ventures which achieve very high growth.

Implications

It is customary in any review of the literature to call for further research. In that respect, we shall not disappoint readers, for we believe the systematic study of founding factors and their relationship to subsequent performance to be in its infancy.

In considering the desired characteristics of that future research, we should not work toward an orthodoxy which excludes a variety of approaches. One of the strengths of the field of entrepreneurial research has been its openness to a variety of kinds of research. This has led to a climate in which researchers can proceed in entrepreneurial ways.

With these caveats in mind, the following research needs are proposed:

1. More attention should be devoted to theory. More fully developed theoretical frameworks can help us to focus attention upon promising research questions and to interpret patterns of results.
2. More emphasis should be placed upon contingency relationships. We should seek to learn under what conditions particular relationships apply, and whether there are interactions among variables.

3. Attention should be devoted to whether there are characteristics of entrepreneurs or founding processes which deserve attention, even though they are not easy to operationalize or study. We should not limit our efforts to the things which are easiest to research. This may mean that survey techniques are more difficult to utilize.
4. Careful consideration should be given, of course, to the performance measures chosen and to the implications of particular samples; and there should be utilization of the most appropriate analytical techniques. There are probably also opportunities for replication, examining how performance measures and sample characteristics affect results.

Finally, in communicating the results of our research, more emphasis should be devoted to going beyond conference presentations to published articles. A strength of the field of entrepreneurship has been the large number of conferences which have been held and which have been open to a variety of research approaches. A weakness has been the limited amount of this work which has then been published in refereed journals. As articles go through the peer review process, the thinking behind them is often sharpened and the communications are clarified. As research is published in scholarly journals, it then becomes more visible to the rest of the academic world and more likely to be built upon in systematic ways.

Research on entrepreneurs, on the processes of founding, and on new-firm performance has, we think, progressed greatly in recent years. The mixed patterns of findings from this work, as well as the opportunities to strengthen the approaches used, suggest that much remains to be done.

REFERENCES

Aldrich, H., H. Rosen, and W. Woodward 1987 The impact of social networks on business foundings and profit: A longitudinal study. In *Frontiers of entrepreneurship research*, eds. N. Churchill, J. Hornaday, B. Kirchhoff, O. Krasner, and K. Vesper, 154–168. Wellesley, Mass.: Babson College.

Bailey, J. E. 1986 Learning styles of successful entrepreneurs. In *Frontiers of entrepreneurship research*, eds. R. Ronstadt, J. Hornaday, R. Peterson, and K. Vesper, 199–210. Wellesley, Mass.: Babson College.

Begley, T. M., and D. P. Boyd 1985 Company and chief executive officer characteristics related to financial performance in smaller businesses. In *Frontiers of entrepreneurship research*, eds. J. Hornaday, E. Shils, J. Timmons, K. Vesper, 146–165. Wellesley, Mass.: Babson College.

1987 Psychological characteristics associated with performance in entrepreneurial firms and smaller businesses. *Journal of Business Venturing* 2 (1): 79–93.

Brockhaus, R. H. 1980 Psychological and environmental factors which distinguish the successful from the unsuccessful entrepreneur: A longitudinal study. *Proceedings of the Academy of Management, 1980*: 368–372.

1982 The psychology of the entrepreneur. In *Encyclopedia of entrepreneurship*, eds. C. A. Kent, D. L. Sexton, and K. H. Vesper, 39–56. Englewood Cliffs, N.J.: Prentice-Hall, Inc.

Bruno, A. V., and T. T. Tyebjee 1984 The entrepreneur's search for capital. In *Frontiers of entrepreneurship research*, eds. J. Hornaday, F. Tarpley, Jr., J. Timmons, and K. Vesper, 18–31. Wellesley, Mass.: Babson College.

Brush, C. G., and R. D. Hisrich 1988 Women entrepreneurs: Strategic origins impact on growth. In *Frontiers of entrepreneurship, research* eds. B. Kirchhoff, W. Long, W. E. McMullan, K. Vesper, and W. Wetzel, Jr., 612–625. Wellesley, Mass.: Babson College.

Chambers, B. R., S. L. Hart, and D. R. Denison 1988 Founding team experience and new firm performance. In *Frontiers of entrepreneurship research*, eds. B. Kirchhoff, W. Long, W. E. McMullan, K. Vesper, and W. Wetzel, Jr., 106–118. Wellesley, Mass.: Babson College.

Collins, O., and D. Moore 1970 *The organization makers: A behavioral study of independent entrepreneurs.* Englewood Cliffs, N.J.: Prentice-Hall, Inc.

Cooper, A. C. 1981 Strategic management: New ventures and small business. In *Strategic management: A new view of business policy and planning*, eds. D. Schendel and C. Hofer, 316–327. Boston: Little, Brown.

1985 The role of incubator organizations in the founding of growth-oriented firms. *Journal of Business Venturing* 1 (1): 75–86.

Cooper, A. C., and A. V. Bruno 1977 Success among high-technology firms. *Business Horizons* 20 (2): 16–22.

Cooper, A. C., and W. C. Dunkelberg 1987 Old questions, new answers, and methodological issues. *American Journal of Small Business* 11 (3): 11–23.

Cooper, A. C., W. C. Dunkelberg, and C. Y. Woo 1988 Survival and failure: A longitudinal study. In *Frontiers of entrepreneurship research*, eds. B. Kirchhoff, W. Long, W. E. McMullan, K. Vesper, and W. Wetzel, Jr., 225–237. Wellesley, Mass.: Babson College.

Cooper, A. C., C. Y. Woo, and W. C. Dunkelberg 1989 Entrepreneurship and the initial size of firms. *Journal of Business Venturing* 4 (5): 317–332.

Covin, J. G., and T. J. Covin 1989 The effects of environmental context on the relationship between small firm aggressiveness and performance. Paper presented at the Academy of Management meeting, Washington, D.C.

Covin, J. G., and D. P. Slevin 1989 Empirical relationships among strategic posture, environmental context variables, and new venture performance. In *Frontiers of entrepreneurship research*, eds. R. Brockhaus, N. Churchill, J. Katz, B. Kirchhoff, K. Vesper, and W. Wetzel, Jr., 370–382. Wellesley, Mass.: Babson College.

Cragg, P. B., and M. King 1988 Organizational characteristics and small firms' performance revisited. *Entrepreneurship Theory and Practice* 13 (2): 49–64.

Denison, D. R., and J. M. Alexander 1986 Patterns and profiles of entrepreneurs: Data from entrepreneurship forums. In *Frontiers of entrepreneurship research*, eds. R. Ronstadt, J. Hornaday, R. Peterson, and K. Vesper, 578–593. Wellesley, Mass.: Babson College.

Dollinger, M. J. 1985 Environmental contacts and financial performance of the small firm. *Journal of Small Business Management* 23 (1): 24–30.

Doutriaux, J. 1987 Growth pattern of academic entrepreneurial firms. *Journal of Business Venturing* 2 (4): 285–297.

1988 Government procurement and research contracts at start-up and success of Canadian high-tech entrepreneurial firms. In *Frontiers of entrepreneurship research*, eds. B. Kirchhoff, W. Long, W. E. McMullan, K. Vesper, and W. Wetzel, Jr., 582–594. Wellesley, Mass. : Babson College.

Doutriaux, J., and F. Simyar 1987 Duration of the comparative advantage accruing from some start-up factors in high-tech entrepreneurial firms. In *Frontiers of entrepreneurship research*, eds. N. Churchill, J. Hornaday, B. Kirchhoff, O. Krasner, and K. Vesper, 436–451. Wellesley, Mass. : Babson College.

Dubini, P. 1989 Which venture capital backed entrepreneurs have the best chances of succeeding ? *Journal of Business Venturing* 4 (2) : 123–132.

Dubini, P., and I. C. MacMillan 1988 Entrepreneurial prerequisites in venture capital backed projects. In *Frontiers of entrepreneurship research*, eds. B. Kirchhoff, W. Long, W. E. McMullan, and W. Wetzel, Jr., 46–58. Wellesley, Mass. : Babson College.

Duchesneau, D. A., and W. B. Gartner 1988 A profile of new venture success and failure in an emerging industry. In *Frontiers of entrepreneurship research*, eds. B. Kirchhoff, W. Long, W. E. McMullan, K. Vesper, and W. Wetzel, Jr., 372–386. Wellesley, Mass. : Babson College.

Dunkelberg, W. C., and A. C. Cooper 1982 Patterns of small business growth. In *Proceedings of the Academy of Management, 1982.* : 409–413. (Edited by Kae H. Chung)

Dunkelberg, W. C., A. C. Cooper, C. Y. Woo, and W. Dennis 1987 New firm growth and performance. In *Frontiers of entrepreneurship research*, eds. N. Churchill, J. Hornaday, B. Kirchhoff, O. Krasner, and K. Vesper, 307–321. Wellesley, Mass. : Babson College.

Eisenhardt, K. M., and C. B. Schoonhoven 1989 Organizational growth : Linking founding team, strategy, environment and growth among U.S. semiconductor ventures (1978–1988). Department of Industrial Engineering and Engineering Management, Stanford University. Working paper.

Feeser, H. R., and K. W. Dugan 1989 Entrepreneurial motivation : A comparison of high and low growth high tech founders. In *Frontiers of entrepreneurship research*, eds. R. Brockhaus, N. Churchill, J. Katz, B. Kirchhoff, K. Vesper, and W. Wetzel, Jr., 13–27. Wellesley, Mass. : Babson College.

Feeser, H. R., and G. E. Willard 1988 Incubators and performance : A comparison of high- and low-growth high-tech firms. *Journal of Business Venturing* 4 (6) : 429–442.

Ginn, C. W., and D. L. Sexton 1989 Growth : A vocational choice and psychological preference. In *Frontiers of entrepreneurship research*, eds. R. Brockhaus, N. Churchill, J. Katz, B. Kirchhoff, K. Vesper, and W. Wetzel, Jr., 1–12. Wellesley, Mass. : Babson College.

Hay, R. K., and D. L. Ross 1989 An assessment of success factors of non-urban start-up firms based upon financial characteristics of successful versus failed ventures. In *Frontiers of entrepreneurship research*, eds. R. Brockhaus, N. Churchill, J. Katz, B. Kirchhoff, K. Vesper, and W. Wetzel, Jr., 148–158. Wellesley, Mass. : Babson College.

Hoad, W., and P. Rosko 1964 *Management factors contributing to the success or failure of new small manufacturers.* Ann Arbor : Univ. of Michigan Press.

Keeley, R. H., and J. B. Roure 1989 Determinants of new venture success before 1982 and after : A preliminary look at two eras. In *Frontiers of entrepreneurship research*, eds. R. Brockhaus, N. Churchill, J. Katz, B. Kirchhoff, K. Vesper, and W. Wetzel, Jr., 274–287. Wellesley, Mass. : Babson College.

Kirchhoff, B. A., and B. D. Phillips 1989 Innovation and growth among new firms in the U.S. economy. In *Frontiers of entrepreneurship research*, eds. R. Brockhaus, N. Churchill, J. Katz, B. Kirchhoff, K. Vesper, and W. Wetzel, Jr., 173–188. Wellesley, Mass. : Babson College.

Lorrain, J., and L. Dussault 1988 Relation between psychological characteristics, administrative behaviors, and success of founder entrepreneurs at the start-up stage. In *Frontiers of entrepreneurship research*, eds. B. Kirchhoff, W. Long, W. E. McMullan, K. Vesper, and W. Wetzel, Jr., 150–164. Wellesley, Mass. : Babson College.

Liles, P. R. 1974 *New business ventures and the entrepreneur.* Homewood, Ill. : Richard D. Irwin, Inc.

MacMillan, I. C., L. Zemann, and P. N. Subba Narasimha 1987 Criteria distinguishing successful from unsuccessful ventures in the venture screening process. *Journal of Business Venturing* 2 (2) : 123–137.

Mayer, K., and S. Goldstein 1961 *The first two years : Problems of small firm growth and survival.* Washington, D.C. : GPO.

McDougall, P. P., and R. B. Robinson, Jr. 1987 Modeling new venture performance : An analysis of new venture strategy and venture origin. In *The spirit of entrepreneurship*, eds. R. Wyckham, L. Meredith, and G. Bushe, 125–139. Burnaby, British Columbia : Simon Fraser Univ.

1988 New venture performance : Patterns of strategic behavior in different industries. In *Frontiers of entrepreneurship research*, eds. B. Kirchhoff, W. Long, W. E. McMullan, K. Vesper, and W. Wetzel, Jr., 477–491. Wellesley, Mass. : Babson College.

Neiswander, D. K., and J. M. Drollinger 1986 Origins of successful start-up ventures. In *Frontiers of entrepreneurship research*, eds. R. Ronstadt, J. Hornaday, R. Peterson, and K. Vesper, 328–343. Wellesley, Mass. : Babson College.

O'Neill, H. M., and J. Duker 1986 Survival and failure in small business. *Journal of Small Business Management* 24 (1) : 30–37.

Peacock, P. 1986 The influence of risk-taking as a cognitive judgmental behavior of small business success. In *Frontiers of entrepreneurship research*, eds. R. Ronstadt, J. Hornaday, R. Peterson, and K. Vesper, 110–118. Wellesley, Mass. : Babson College.

Peterson, R. 1985 Creating contexts for new ventures in stagnating environments. In *Frontiers of entrepreneurship research*, eds. J. Hornaday, E. Shils, J. Timmons, and K. Vesper, 258–283. Wellesley, Mass. : Babson College.

Peterson, R., and N. R. Smith 1986 Entrepreneurship : A culturally appropriate combination of craft and opportunity. In *Frontiers of entrepreneurship research*, eds. R. Ronstadt, J. Hornaday, R. Peterson, and K. Vesper, 1–11. Wellesley, Mass. : Babson College.

Reynolds, P. D. 1986 Organization : Predicting contributions and survival. In *Frontiers of entrepreneurship research*, eds. R. Ronstadt, J. Hornaday, R. Peterson, and K. Vesper, 594–609. Wellesley, Mass. : Babson College.

1987 New firms : Social contribution versus survival potential. *Journal of Business Venturing* 2 : 231–246.

Reynolds, P. D., and B. Miller 1989 New firm survival : Analysis of a panel's fourth year. In *Frontiers of entrepreneurship research*, eds. R. Brockhaus, N. Churchill, J. Katz, B. Kirchhoff, K. Vesper, and W. Wetzel, Jr., 159–172. Wellesley, Mass. : Babson College.

Roberts, E. B. 1972 Influences upon performance of new technical enterprises. In *Technical entrepreneurship : A symposium*, eds. A. Cooper and J. Komives, 126–149. Milwaukee : The Center for Venture Management.

Roberts, E. B., and O. Hauptman 1987 The financing threshold effect on success and failure of biomedical and pharmaceutical start-ups. *Management Science* 33 (3) : 381–393.

Romanelli, E. 1987 New venture strategies in the minicomputer industry. *California Management Review* 30 (1) : 160–175.

Roure, J. B., and M. A. Maidique 1986 Linking prefounding factors and high-technology venture success : An exploratory study. *Journal of Business Venturing* 1 (3) : 295–306.

Sandberg, W. R., and C. W. Hofer 1982 A strategic management perspective on the determinants of new venture success. In *Frontiers of entrepreneurship research*, ed. K. Vesper, 204–237. Wellesley, Mass. : Babson College.

1986 The effect of strategy and industry structure on new venture performance. In *Frontiers of entrepreneurship research*, eds. R. Rondstadt, J. Hornaday, R. Peterson, and K. Vesper, 244–266. Wellesley, Mass. : Babson College.

1987 Improving new venture performance : The role of strategy, industry structure, and the entrepreneur. *Journal of Business Venturing* 2 (1) : 5–28.

Sapienza, H. J., K. G. Smith, and M. J. Gannon 1988 Using subjective evaluations of organizational performance in small business research. *American Journal of Small Business* 12 (3) : 45–53.

Sexton, E. A., and P. B. Robinson 1989 The economic and demographic determinants of self-employment. In *Frontiers of entrepreneurship research*, eds. R. Brockhaus, N. Churchill, J. Katz, B. Kirchhoff, K. Vesper, and W. Wetzel, Jr., 28–42. Wellesley, Mass. : Babson College.

Shapero, A., and L. Sokol 1982 The social dimensions of entrepreneurship. In *Encyclopedia of entrepreneurship*, eds. C. A. Kent, D. L. Sexton, and K. H. Vesper, 72–90. Englewood Cliffs, N.J. : Prentice-Hall, Inc.

Smith, N. R., J. S. Bracker, and J. B. Miner 1987 Correlates of firm and entrepreneur success in technologically innovative companies. In *Frontiers of entrepreneurship research*, eds. N. Churchill, J. Hornaday, B. Kirchhoff, O. Krasner, and K. Vesper, 337–353. Wellesley, Mass. : Babson College.

Smith, N. R., and J. B. Miner 1984 Motivational considerations in the success of technologically innovative entrepreneurs. In *Frontiers of entrepreneurship research*, eds. J. Hornaday, F. Tarpley, Jr., J. Timmons, and K. Vesper, 488–495. Wellesley, Mass. : Babson College.

Stevenson, H. H., and C. J. Jarillo 1990 A paradigm of entrepreneurship : Entrepreneurial management. *Strategic Management Journal* 11 (Special Issue) : 17–28.

Stuart, R., and P. A. Abetti 1986 Field study of start-up ventures. Part 2 : Predicting initial success. In *Frontiers of entrepreneurship research*, eds. R. Ronstadt, J. Hornaday, R. Peterson, and K. Vesper, 21–39. Wellesley, Mass. : Babson College.

1987 Start-up ventures : Towards the prediction of initial success. *Journal of Business Venturing* 2 (3) : 215–230.

1988 Field study of technical ventures. Part 3 : The impact of entrepreneurial and management experience on early performance. In *Frontiers of entrepreneurship research*, eds. B. Kirchhoff, W. Long, W. E. McMullan, K. Vesper, and W. Wetzel, Jr., 177–193. Wellesley, Mass. : Babson College.

Teach, R. D., F. A. Tarpley, and R. G. Schwartz 1986 Software venture teams. In *Frontiers of entrepreneurship research*, eds. R. Ronstadt, J. Hornaday, R. Peterson, and K. Vesper, 546–562. Wellesley, Mass. : Babson College.

Timmons, J. A. 1990 *New venture creation.* Homewood, Ill. : Richard D. Irwin.

Tyebjee, T. T., and A. V. Bruno 1982 A comparative analysis of California startups from 1978 to 1980. In *Frontiers of entrepreneurship research*, ed. K. Vesper, 163–176. Wellesley, Mass. : Babson College.

Van de Ven, A. H., R. Hudson, and D. M. Schroeder 1984 Designing new business startups : entrepreneurial, organizational, and ecological considerations. *Journal of Management* 10 (1) : 87–107.

VanderWerf, P. A. 1989 Achieving empirical progress in an undefined field. *Entrepreneurship Theory and Practice* 14 (2) : 45–58.

Vesper, K. H. 1990 *New venture strategies.* Englewood Cliffs, N.J. : Prentice-Hall, Inc.

Wainer, H. A., and I. M. Rubin 1969 Motivation of research and development entrepreneurs : Determinants of company success. *Journal of Applied Psychology* 53 (3) : 178–184.

Woo, C. Y., A. C. Cooper, W. C. Dunkelberg, U. Daellenbach, and W. J. Dennis. 1989 Determinants of growth for small and large entrepreneurial startups. In *Frontiers of entrepreneurship research*, eds. R. Brockhaus, N. Churchill, J. Katz, B. Kirchhoff, K. Vesper, and W. Wetzel, Jr., 134–147. Wellesley, Mass. : Babson College.

▬ ▬▬ ▬▬ ▬▬ ▬▬ ▬▬ ▬

APPENDIX 12–A
FACTORS INFLUENCING
PERFORMANCE[1]

VanderWerf

"Who" factors	—	Characteristics of founder(s), of previous organization, and of new venture
"How" factors	—	Decision-making processes, management style, organization style, founder's time allocation
"What" factors	—	Characteristics of venture entry, strategy, market

Stevenson and Jarillo

What happens	—	Effects of entrepreneurship, particularly the impact on the economy
Why entrepreneurs act	—	Psychological characteristics, social influences
How entrepreneurs act	—	Entrepreneurial actions and their relation to performance

Vesper

Industry	—	Competitive pressures, growth potential, entry barriers, stage of maturity, hard-to-arrange events
Strategy	—	Competitive advantage, balanced functional emphasis
Founder characteristics	—	Education, experience, collaboration, starting capital, management practices, psychological characteristics

Gartner

Individuals	—	Psychological characteristics, experience, age, education
Environment	—	Capital availability, economics of location for particular venture, makeup of population, industry characteristics
Process	—	Opportunity identification, resource assembly, marketing, production, organization building, responding to society
Organization	—	Generic strategy, entry strategy (or "wedge")

Cooper

Founder characteristics	—	Genetic factors, family influence, educational choices, previous experience
Incubator organization	—	Geographic location, skills and knowledge acquired, contact with fellow founders, motivation to leave, small business experience
Environmental factors	—	Economic conditions, capital availability, role models, availability of and accessibility to customers, key personnel and services

[1]Variables relating primarily to new venture development within established corporations have been excluded from this Appendix.

— — — — — — — —

APPENDIX 12–B
FRAMEWORK FOR
EXAMINING INFLUENCES
UPON PERFORMANCE

Characteristics of the Entrepreneur(s)

Race and sex

Occupation of parents

Education
　　Highest level
　　Kind of education

Experience
　　Number of jobs
　　Experience within field
　　Managerial experience
　　Functional experience
　　Start-up experience

Psychological Characteristics
　　Need for achievement
　　Locus of control
　　Risk-taking behavior
　　Efforts to control risk

Entrepreneur's age

Goals
　　Opportunistic vs. craftsman
　　Specific goals

Processes of Starting

Idea sources

Planning process

Incubator organization
　　Size of incubator
　　Relatedness of venture to incubator
　　Negative displacement

Information sources and networking
　　Specific sources of assistance
　　Professionals helped with business plan
　　Network characteristics

Forming teams
　　Presence of team
　　Size and characteristics of team

Starting vs. purchasing

Financing
　　Amount of initial capital
　　Sources of capital
　　Ownership by entrepreneur

Environmental Characteristics

Industry category

Industry characteristics
　　Barriers to entry
　　Stage of life cycle
　　Rural vs. urban location

APPENDIX 12-C
RESEARCH STUDIES EXAMINED

Authors	Sample	Age	Research Method / Instrument	Statistical Methods	Issues Studied	Dependent Variables
Aldrich, Rosen, & Woodward (1987)	165 entrepreneurs — members of the Research Triangle Council for Entrepreneurial Development (high-tech)	Median 3 years	2 questionnaires on Research Triangle area entrepreneurs (9-month LS)	Chi-square	Social networks of entrepreneurs	Initial profitability (making profit vs. not in first 3 years). Later profitability (making profit vs. not after first 3 years).
Bailey (1986)	67 Australian company founders	*	Interviews and questionnaires (C-S)	Discriminant analysis	Learning styles of entrepreneurs	Index of business performance (growth in sales, growth in value, growth in employees, age of business, and perceived success).
Begley & Boyd (1985) (1986/JSBM)	471 CEOs of small businesses in New England (only 57.4% founders)	Median 18 years	Questionnaire to members of SBANE (C-S)	Correlation of multiple regression	Characteristics of the company and CEO	5-year growth rate in sales 1-year ROS 5-year ROS ROI

continued

Authors	Sample	Age	Research Method / Instrument	Statistical Methods	Issues Studied	Dependent Variables
Begley & Boyd (1987)	147 founders of small businesses in New England	Mean 20.98 years	Questionnaires to members of SBANE (C-S)	Pearson correlations	Psychological characteristics of entrepreneurs	Growth rate in sales ROA Liquidity
Brockhaus (1980)	31 founders in St. Louis, Mo.	3 months or less	2 questionnaires to new business licensees (3-yr LS)	Discriminant analysis	Psychological and environmental factors	Survival vs. discontinuance
Bruno & Tyebjee (1984)	86 firms in high-tech SIC codes located in northern California	Less than 5 yrs. old	Dun & Bradstreet credit reports (C-S)	Analysis of variance	Effect of outside vs. inside capital investment	Sales (average 80–81) Sales growth (81–80) Employee growth Productivity
Brush & Hisrich (1988)	172 women entrepreneurs	8 years average	2 questionnaires (5-year LS)	Discriminant analysis	"Strategic origins" and effect on performance	Survival vs. discontinuance Growth vs. no growth
Chambers, Hart, & Denison (1988)	100 manufacturing and retail firms in the technology corridor, "Automation Alley," Michigan	5 years or less	Questionnaires to forms filed in the Michigan Employment Security Commission (C-S)	Categorical regression	Different forms of team's experience	Subjective overall performance

328

Cooper & Bruno (1977)	250 high-tech firms founded in San Francisco Peninsula (electronics-based)	Born from 1960 to 1969	Questionnaires to founders and follow-up studies (7-year LS)	Cross-tabs (not statistically tested)	Incubator firms and founding team	High-growth (sales greater than $5 million) vs. discontinued
Cooper, Dunkelberg, & Woo (1988)	2,994 entrepreneurs in all industries	17 months or less	3 questionnaires to NFIB new members (3-year LS)	T-test and chi-square	Entrepreneur, firms, and processes of starting	Survival vs. discontinuance
Cooper, Woo, & Dunkelberg (1989)	1,402 new ventures from members of NFIB	Median 11 months	2 questionnaires to NFIB new members (2-year LS)	T-test and chi-square	Effects of initial size of venture	% growth in sales, % growth in employees, Increase in number of employees, Distribution (decline, stable, growth) of growth in sales, Distribution of growth in employment
Covin & Covin (1989)	69 established small firms in Georgia (service industries not included)	At least 5 years	Questionnaires to presidents of small firms in Georgia (C-S)	Regression analysis	Environmental dynamism and competitive agressiveness	Subjective evaluation of 5 performance criteria

continued

329

APPENDIX 12–C, continued

Authors	Sample	Age	Research Method/ Instrument	Statistical Methods	Issues Studied	Dependent Variables
Covin & Slevin (1989)	92 manufacturing-based new firms (all industries)	Mean 5.26 years (12 years maximum)	Questionnaires to CEOs of firms associated with 3 Pittsburgh-based economic development organizations	Correlations and Fisher Z transformation	Strategic and environmental interaction — fit	Performance index = weighted sum of responses responses to 9 performance criteria
Covin & Slevin (1990)	90 new ventures in manufacturing and service in Pittsburgh area	10 years or less	Questionnaires to senior executives of firms associated with 3 development agencies (C–S)	Pearson correlations	Strategy and structure within the product life cycle	Subjective evaluation of 9 performance criteria
Cragg & King (1988)	179 metal goods manufacturers in East Midlands, England (small firms)	*	Questionnaire (C-S)	Kendall correlations and multiple regression	Entrepreneur, type of firm, and planning process	Sales change 85–84 Net profit return 85 Net profit change 85–84 Sales
Denison & Alexander (1986)	1,222 participants in entrepreneurship forums (seeking funds)	82% are less than 5 years	Entrepreneurial profile questionnaires (C-S)	Multiple regression	Demographic success profiles	Income of entrepreneur

Dollinger (1985)	82 owner/operators of small businesses in Pennsylvania	Average 29 years	Questionnaire to small businesses from telephone directories (C-S)	Partial correlations	Environmental contacts (frequency)	Sales Net income (3-yr. avg.) Profitability index
Doutriaux (1987)	38 technical service and manufacturing firms created by entrepreneurs while at universities in Canada (high-tech)	Average 6.3 years	2 questionnaires to technically-based academic-entrepreneurial firms (4-year LS)	Comparison of means (not statistically tested)	Academic entrepreneurial firms and university links	Growth in sales Growth in employment Growth in productivity
Doutriaux (1988)	65 manufacturing firms in microelectronics and communication field in Canada (high-tech)	Average 10.84 years	Questionnaire + interviews (C-S)	Spearman correlation	Effect of early government contracts	Annual sales level (for 8 years)
Doutriaux & Simyar (1987)	73 manufacturing firms in microelectronics and communication field in Canada (high-tech)	Average 10.84 years	Questionnaire + interview (C-S)	F-tests (from ANOVA or univariate regression)	Duration of the effects of some start-up factors (first 8 yrs. of operations)	Annual sales level (for first 8 years)
Dubini & MacMillan (1988) Dubini (1989)	151 successful and unsuccessful venture capital firms	*	Questionnaires to 67 venture capitalists (C-S)	Multiple regression	Team characteristics for given strategies	Sales Market share Profits ROI

continued

Authors	Sample	Age	Research Method/ Instrument	Statistical Methods	Issues Studied	Dependent Variables
Duchesneau & Gartner (1988)	26 distributors of orange industry (emergent industry)	7 years or less	Interviews with lead entrepreneur (C-S)	F-test of means	Entrepreneur, founding process, and strategies	Successful (growth) vs. unsuccessful
Dunkelberg & Cooper (1982)	890 entrepreneurs in NFIB (all industries)	UP to 38 years (median ≅ 9 years)	Questionnaire (C-S)	Multiple Regression	Impact of owner's background, objectives, and characteristics of firms	Compound annual growth rate in employment
Dunkelberg, Cooper, Woo, & Dennis (1987)	1,178 new founders members of NFIB	17 months or less	2 questionnaires to NFIB new members (2-year LS)	T-test and chi-square	Characteristics of the entrepreneur, process of starting, and nature of new firms	Growth in employment vs. decline in employment
Eisenhardt & Schoonhoven (1989)	92 semiconductor firms born between 1978 and 1985 (total population = 105)	Founded between 1978 and 1985	Interviews and secondary data (10-year LS)	Regression models and event studies	Founding team, strategy, and environment	Sales revenue for each year of life through 1988

Study	Sample	Time period	Data collection	Analysis	Focus	Comparison
Feeser & Dugan (1989)	42 low- and high-growth high-tech (computing industry) firms (108 founders)	Average of 11 years	Questionnaires to 108 founders of firms, using *Inc.*, S&P, and D&B information	ANOVA, chi-square, Fisher's Exact Test	Motivation of entrepreneurs	High-growth (*Inc.*) vs. low-growth (S&P and D&B)
Feeser & Willard (1988)	108 founders of 42 firms in the electronic computing equipment industry (high-tech)	*	Questionnaire to a matching pairs sample (C-S)	Chi-square	Effect of incubator firms	High-growth vs. low-growth firms (in sales)
Ginn & Sexton (1989)	159 firms from 1987 *Inc.* 500 and 150 mfg. and retailing firms in Texas	*	Questionnaires to founders (C-S)	Selection ratio-type tables	Vocational choice of growth and psychological characteristics	High-growth (*Inc.* sample) vs. moderate-growth (Texas firms)
Hay & Ross (1989)	165 Kansas firms which were clients of The Institute for Economic Development at Pittsburgh State University	*	Files of clients of The Institute for Economic Development (3-year LS)	Cross-tabs (not statistically tested)	Firm and entrepreneur characteristics	Failed (discontinued) firms vs. troubled firms (with problems) vs. potentially successful
Hoad & Rosko (1964)	95 new manufacturing firms	First 3 years	Interviews	Cross-tabs (not statistically tested)	Characteristics of entrepreneur, processes of founding, strategy, and major policies	Survival Wages Whether profitable

continued

APPENDIX 12-C, continued

Authors	Sample	Age	Research Method / Instrument	Statistical Methods	Issues Studied	Dependent Variables
Keeley & Roure (1989)	68 technology-based venture capital firms	Median 1982	Archival data provided by venture capitalists	Multiple regression	Industry and strategy factors	Internal rate of return to all shareholders on all investment funds
Kirchhoff & Phillips (1989)	814,890 firms in high-tech and low-tech industries from USELM data base	8–10 years by follow-up	Data base created by Div. of Economic Research, Office of Advocacy, U.S. Small Business Admin.	Cross-tabs (not statistically tested)	Interaction between initial size and innovation	Average change in number of employees per firm Proportion of survivors
Lorrain & Dussault (1988)	70 founder-managers of manufacturing firms in Quebec	Average 5 months old	Interview + follow-up (2-year LS)	Mann-Whitney U Test and discriminant analysis	Psychological characteristics and administrative behaviors	Survival vs. discontinuance
MacMillan, Zemann, & Subbanarasimha (1987)	150 successful and unsuccessful venture capital firms	*	Questionnaires to 67 venture capitalists (C-S)	Multiple regression	Screening criteria for "success"	Sales Market share Profits ROI
Mayer & Goldstein (1961)	81 new service and retail firms	First 2 years years	Interviews	Cross-tabs (not statistically tested)	Characteristics of entrepreneur, capital, and environment	Survival vs. discontinuance

334

Study	Sample	Time	Data source	Analysis	Variables	Measures
McDougall & Robinson (1987)	247 new ventures in two industries: computer-related and communication-related equipment mfg. (includes a small % of corporate ventures)	8 years or less	Questionnaires to firms in 2 industry groups in Dun & Bradstreet data base (C-S)	Duncan's Multiple Range Test	New venture strategy and origin (independent vs. sponsored)	ROI, Market share growth
McDougall & Robinson (1988)	247 new ventures in two industries: computer-related and communication-related equipment mfg. (includes a small % of corporate ventures)	8 years or less	Questionnaires to firms in 2 industry groups in Dun & Bradstreet data base (C-S)	Multiple regression	New venture strategy and industry	ROI, Market share growth
Neiswander & Drollinger (1986)	62 entrepreneurs of highly successful firms (sales 1985 > $5 million) (all industries)	92% less than 18 years old	Questionnaire (C-S)	Comparison of means (not statistically tested)	Entrepreneur's characteristics	Average annual sales, Average employees, Average productivity
O'Neill & Duker (1986)	43 surviving and failed firms in similar environments	*	Questionnaire to successful & failed firms (C-S)	Spearman correlations and t-test	Strategy and use of advisors	Survival vs. discontinuance

continued

APPENDIX 12-C, continued

Authors	Sample	Age	Research Method/ Instrument	Statistical Methods	Issues Studied	Dependent Variables
Peacock (1986)	40 successful and unsuccessful small firms in New Jersey	Less than 5 years	Questionnaires and phone calls (C-S)	T-test	Influence of risk taking and mental ability	Survival vs. discontinuance
Peterson (1985)	4,034 founders in 11 countries	*	ISBC Data Bank (stratified) (C-S)	Univariate regression	Strategy making in stagnating environments	Firms growing more than 25% vs. firms that did not (2 years)
Peterson & Smith (1986)	2,186 founders in 12 countries	*	ISBC Data Bank (C-S)	Multiple regression	Combinations of craftsmanship and opportunism	Growth in sales by more than 25% (2 years)
Reynolds (1986, 1987)	551 firms founded in Minnesota area (all types of industries)	3 to 5 years	Questionnaires + follow-up interview of firms in Dun & Bradstreet data base (2-year LS)	T-test, chi-square and discriminant analysis	Strategy, industry, and growth patterns	Survival form questionnaire time to follow-up (vs. nonsurvival)
Reynolds & Miller (1989)	550 new firms in a Minnesota panel of representative firms (all industries)	Either 2 or 5 years old	Questionnaire + phone follow-ups (4-year LS)	ANOVA, chi-square, or LOGIT model.	Entrepreneur and firm factors	Survival vs. discontinuance

Study	Sample	Time period	Data source	Analysis	Focus	Performance measure
Roberts (1972)	234 high-technology firms	First 4 to 5 years	Interviews	Not reported	Characteristics of entrepreneur, resources, strategy, managerial behavior	Performance Index based upon sales growth, company age, and profitability
Roberts & Hauptman (1987)	26 biomedical and pharmaceutical firms in Massachusetts	Founded from 1968 to 1975	In-depth structured interviews (C-S)	Multiple regression	Financial threshold effect in start-ups	Average sales between 1980 and 1983
Romanelli (1987)	170 minicomputer producers founded from 1967 to 1981 (high-tech)	6 years	Secondary data (6-year LS)	Cross-tabs (not statistically tested)	Strategies for stages of product life cycle	Survival for 6 years after founding (vs. nonsurvival)
Roure & Maidique (1986)	8 successful and not successful venture capital firms in the electronics industry on west coast	All founded after 1984	Semistructured interviews with venture capitalists (C-S)	Comparison of means (not statistically tested)	Factor of success in high-technology venture firms	Successful (growth + survival) vs. unsuccessful companies
Sandberg & Hofer (1982)	8 venture capital firms in different industries ("with some particular interest")	Maximum 7 years	Initial business plans of ventures picked as "typical" representative ventures (C-S)	Cross-tabs (not statistically tested)	Industry and strategy	Successful (growth and profit) vs. non-successful (break-even, losses, or failure)

continued

Authors	Sample	Age	Research Method/ Instrument	Statistical Methods	Issues Studied	Dependent Variables
Sandberg & Hofer (1986, 1987)	17 venture capital firms (both successful and unsuccessful)	*	Search on venture capitalists' files + secondary data (C-S)	Mann-Whitney U Test and Spearman correlation	Strategy, structure and entrepreneur's characteristics	Success (5 categories)
Sexton & Robinson (1989)	21,352 self-employed individuals in all industries	*	Public-use B sample of 1988 U.S. Census of Population (C-S)	Multiple regression	Economic and demographic factors	Annual self-employment income
Smith, Bracker, & Miner (1987)	118 founders who were awardees or applicants for development grants	*	Questionnaires to awardees and applicants for NSF development grants (C-S)	Correlations (Pearson & Spearman) (Spearman corr. are reported)	Entrepreneur and firm characteristics for innovative companies	Growth in employees Growth in employees/ year Growth in sales Growth in sales/year Net profit/sales Yearly income
Smith & Miner (1984)	51 founder applicants for NSF Small Business Innovation Research Program development grants (high-tech)	Average 8.6 years	Questionnaires to awardees and applicants of NSF development grants (C-S)	T-test	Psychological and motivational characteristics	High growth in employment vs. low growth in employment

Study	Sample	Time period	Data source	Analysis method	Independent variables	Dependent variable
Smith & Miner (1984)	97 entrepreneurs having applied for NSF Small Business Innovation Research Program development grants (high-tech)	*	Questionnaires to awardees and applicants of NSF development grants (C-S)	T-test	Psychological and motivational characteristics	High growth (>1.5 employees/year) vs. low growth in employment
Stuart & Abetti (1986, 1987)	24 new technical ventures on RPI Incubator Program or RPI Tech. Park (high-tech)	Mean 2.6 years; maximum 7 years	Interviews of CEOs of firms (C-S)	Regression	Market, innovation, strategy, structure leadership	Initial financial success: combination of 6 objective performance measures Initial non-financial success: combination of 5 perceived measures
Stuart & Abetti (1988)	52 new technical firms in New York State and New England (high-tech)	1982 or later	Questionnaire to firms in CorpTech data base (C-S)	General linear model	Entrepreneurial and management experience	Composite reflecting: growth in sales growth in employment profitability productivity

continued

APPENDIX 12-C, continued

Authors	Sample	Age	Research Method/Instrument	Statistical Methods	Issues Studied	Dependent Variables
Teach, Tarpley, & Schwartz (1986)	483 founders of 237 software development firms	Median age: 2–3 years	Questionnaires to all members of venture team (C-S)	Chi-square	Composition of venture teams	Firm's size in total sales
Tyebjee & Bruno (1982)	177 firms in electronics and communications industry in California	Founded from 1978 to 1980	Dun & Bradstreet credit information (C-S)	Analysis of variance	Start-up capitalization and ownership	Sales level
Van de Ven, Hudson, & Schroeder (1984)	12 educational software companies	*	Interviews and questionnaires (C-S)	Pearson correlations	Entrepreneurial, organizational, and ecological models	Composite performance measure: growth independence perceived performance
Wainer & Rubin (1969)	51 "spin-offs" from MIT labs or Boston area labs (high-tech)	Between 4 and 10 years	Questionnaires (C-S)	Mann-Whitney U Test	Motivational characteristics	Annual growth = annual increase in the logarithm of sales volume between the 2d and most recent year
Woo, Cooper, Dunkelberg, Daellenbach, & Dennis (1989)	385 new founders members of NFIB	17 months or less	3 questionnaires to NFIB new members (C-S)	Multiple regression	Initial size of firm	Absolute change in employment

C-S = cross-sectional   LS = longitudinal study   * = not reported

Chapter

13

Strategies and Environments of High-Growth Firms

Frank Hoy,
Patricia P. McDougall,
and
Derrick E. Dsouza

●

INTRODUCTION

Richard Cantillon (circa 1730) is usually cited as having introduced the word *entrepreneur* in the economic literature. Over the years, the term has been applied to many different groups : adventurers, capitalists, risk takers, small business owners, and others. More recently, attention has expanded from the entrepreneur as an individual or class to the process of entrepreneurship, typically defined as the creation of a venture. This expansion is significant because it allows us to look beyond the innate characteristics of certain people to sets of behaviors that can be learned and practiced.

In current usage, entrepreneurship is not restricted to a single act — e.g., creation. It is the label we attach to a multidisciplinary field of study. Entrepreneurship encompasses such concepts and activities as venture creation, venture acquisition, venture capital, small business ownership and management, family business, corporate entrepreneurship, founder and owner characteristics, women and minorities in business, international venturing, franchising, innovation, economic development, and growth. It is this last concept, growth, which we examine in this chapter.

■ ■ ■ ■ ■ ■ ■ ■ ■
GROWTH AND
ECONOMIC
DEVELOPMENT

Venture creation and growth have been of interest to economists who:

> ... have usually treated entrepreneurship as part of the general study of economic development, "the process of improving the standard of living and well being of the population of ... countries by raising per capita income. ..." (Crego 1985, 60)

Popular media have focused on growth and creation since Birch's (1979) seminal work was published connecting small businesses to job creation. Although some have refuted Birch's figures (e.g., Armington and Odle 1982), his findings regarding the job creation capacity of the small business sector have received support from Kirchhoff and Phillips (1987) in the United States, Doyle and Gallagher (1987) in the United Kingdom, and Williams (1989) in Australia.

Evidence of the importance of entrepreneurship and economic development has instigated numerous activities in the past decade. In academia, new journals have been initiated, such as the *Small Business Forum,* the *Journal of Business Venturing, Entrepreneurship and Regional Development,* and *Small Business Economics.* The Academy of Management authorized an Entrepreneurship Division, and the International Council for Small Business created an Economic Development Committee. There have been two White House Conferences on Small Business, and a survey of representatives of government agencies, congressional staffs, and small business associations revealed that the seventh highest priority issue regarding small business related to job creation (Heller International Corp. 1984).

The Ecology of Job Creation and Growth

Economic development strategies that encompass job creation and venture growth often address the broader environments in which these phenomena occur. Research has shown that environments, both general and competitive, impact on organizations (Hofer and Schendel 1978; Aldrich 1979; Duncan 1972; Bourgeois 1980; Hambrick 1983; Dess and Beard 1984). Lenz and Engledow (1986) summarized five approaches found in the literature for modelling the environments which impact on firms, labeling them the *organizational field model* (Dill 1958); the *industry structure model* (Porter 1980); the *cognitive model* (Weick 1979); the *era model* (Naisbitt 1982); and the *ecological and resource dependency model* (Aldrich 1979). Of these, the last model appears to be garnering the greatest attention in the entrepreneurship literature as a paradigm for explaining venture creation and growth (Low and MacMillan 1988).

Much of the economic development research has roots in population ecology models (Aldrich 1990). This derives from evidence that organizational births in and of themselves are healthy for an economy (Birley 1987; Doyle and Gallagher 1987; Kirchhoff and Phillips 1987). There are two obvious implications for public policy formulation and implementation. The first is that legal and regulatory structures are likely to either encourage or discourage firm creation (see Hendrickson and Woodland 1985, for an investigation of the effects of local and state taxes, high school graduation rates, and welfare payments on organizations' births). The second is the development of public sector programs to advocate and support venture creation and growth (Hoy 1983a, 1983b; Chrisman, Hoy, and Robinson 1987).

Another result of the ecological approach may be public policies targeting growth industries. If international market conditions are conducive to the development of certain industries, support mechanisms and incentives could be structured for the nurturing of companies within those industries. Porter (1990), for example, contended that nations can be more or less desirable as home bases for companies competing within various industries. A nation is effective as a home base if it allows and supports a company in the rapid accumulation of specialized assets and skills for competition within a particular industry. Alternatively, Kirchhoff and Phillips (1989) expressed concern that Americans are enamored of high technology and may inappropriately target industries for development. They found that high-technology firms represent only 7 percent of new ventures created, generating only 12 percent of the jobs created by new firms. They called for public sector encouragement of low-technology enterprises. Mokry (1989) ties industry targeting into broader economic development programs at the community level. Using case study analysis, he described how industry structure issues affect community development efforts that seek to increase the rate of organizational births.

Thus, the population ecology perspective directs us to examine growth in two ways. The first is the growth in the number of firms being created. The second is the growth of industries relative to one another. Since there is some evidence that industry growth and small-firm growth are independent of one another (Acs and Audretsch 1990), companies with growth objectives must devise appropriate strategies even when they are competing within growth industries. Using market growth to classify whether industries were growing, mature, or declining, Chaganti (1987) proposed four strategies associated with more profitable companies: low manufacturing costs, low frequency of product innovation, low use of process patents, and high percentage of local market sales. Bracker, Keats, and Pearson (1988) chose to look only at the electronics industry in order to examine relationships among industry-specific variables. They found that firms employing structured strategic planning procedures outperformed those that did not, both in growth of net income and CEO cash compensation. Structured strategic planning included such activities as writing long-range plans, analyzing the environment, and determining firm strengths and weaknesses. It is evident that understanding how firms plot their own courses for growth within their broader environments requires studying venture strategy formulation and implementation.

The Growth Firm

Among firms within the same industries, growth is not equal. Some firms grow even in declining environments or industries. Others exceed the growth rate of their competitors within expanding areas and industries. The growth of the individual firm has been a topic of research in the entrepreneurship literature.

Although Schumpeter (1934, 1950) described pure entrepreneurship as a single act at a single point in time, he recognized the role of the entrepreneur in managing growth, building up an organization, and defending strategic interests. Penrose (1959) also described the impact of the entrepreneur on growth, emphasizing the activities leading to innovation. Later, Carland, Hoy, Boulton, and Carland (1984) proposed and subsequently empirically derived (Carland, Carland, Hoy, and Boulton 1988) a differentiation between small business owners and entrepreneurs based on growth and innovation. Their research was partially replicated and confirmed by Ginn and Sexton (1990), who contrasted a sample of *Inc.* 500 founders with a sample of owners of moderate-growth firms. Perry, Meredith, and Cunnington (1988) were unable to differentiate in a study of Australian owner/managers, but they did not include any measures of propensity toward growth in their research design.

In analyzing data subsequent to his initial research, Birch (1987) described two groups of small firms: income substitutors and entrepreneurs. Birch observed that the entrepreneurs intended to grow their organizations significantly, and he concluded that these organizations were responsible for a major proportion of job creation over the 1969–1976 and 1981–1985 periods during which he studied them. He also found that, with the exception of manufacturers, older firms in the entrepreneur group grew more rapidly than younger firms.

Some authors have examined limitations on growth. Although this present chapter addresses the strategies and environments of firms that sustain high growth over a number of years, it is not expected that high growth can be maintained permanently. Interestingly, the literature on growth constraints can be traced to Schumpeter (1942), who contributed so much to present-day research and conceptualizations of entrepreneurship. Schumpeter also introduced the theory of "creating destruction." He predicted that the entrepreneurial roles of reforming production patterns, exploiting inventions and technologies, opening up new sources of materials and new outlets for products, and reorganizing industry would, over time, be reduced to routine operations. The entrepreneur would be replaced by bureaus and committees. The notion of entropy that Schumpeter applied to the entrepreneurial function implies both age and size as constraints on growth. This runs counter to Gibrat's Law that firm growth is independent of firm size (Lucas 1978). This law has been tested and rejected in studies that have supported the concept of an organizational life cycle in which newer, smaller firms are found to grow more rapidly than older, larger organizations (Evans 1987; Hall 1987). It should be pointed out that these studies do not necessarily contradict Birch's findings that older firms grow faster. He reported that manufacturers were exceptions, and the studies cited here are a sample of manufacturing companies. Kumar (1985), however, observed a mild tendency for firm growth to be negatively related to age for both manufacturers and nonmanufacturers. Kumar acknowledged that the latter was in disagreement with prior research.

The organizational life cycle literature is beyond the scope of this chapter. An assumption of life cycle models is that growth is one stage through which organizations typically pass. Alternatively, one may be interested in firms that adopt growth strategies and/or take advantage of environmental factors that support growth. Thus, rather than viewing growth as a rite of passage, this chapter addresses growth as a sustainable entrepreneurial activity. Reviews of the life cycle literature as it applies to entrepreneurship can be found in Kazanjian (1983) and Sexton and Bowman-Upton (1991). Sexton and Bowman-Upton go beyond organizational life cycle models and examine product and market life cycles to further explain growth limits. They also introduce limits self-imposed by the business owner. They emphasize that growth is a conscious decision and that the owner/founder/CEO can determine the venture's life cycle.

Using the firm as the unit of analysis, we find growth to be a discretionary variable and that it impacts positively on economic development. The strategic management literature typically treats growth at the firm level as an objective (Baysinger, Meiners, and Zeithaml 1982), or as an element of organizational effectiveness or performance (Steers 1975; Chakravarthy 1986). When looking at the subgroup of high-growth firms, however, it is also possible to consider growth as an organizational strategy (Sexton and Bowman-Upton 1991). Thus, both the environment and strategies must be considered in investigating growth firms.

RESEARCH ON HIGH-GROWTH FIRMS

What do we mean when we use the term "high growth"? Is it synonymous with Timmons' (1986) "high-potential" firms? Although Timmons did not provide a definition, he appeared to be referring to companies that receive venture capital financing. This is an appealing group to study, because the firms must have growth potential to earn the funding, and because the failure rate of these firms is substantially lower than the business population in general.

This subset of high-growth companies receives attention in the entrepreneurship literature. It is accessible via venture capital firms, and the criteria for investment decisions can be ascertained (Sandberg 1986; Bygrave 1988;

Hall 1989; MacMillan, Siegel, and Subbaarasimha 1985). Timmons describes the venture capitalist's perspective on assessing a firm's potential. Funding is a factor of the founding team, the opportunity they are attempting to seize, and their ability to exploit resources.

The receipt of venture capital is one proxy for high growth. There are other measures available. Hall (1977) suggested the use of a *size-based* measure of growth because it is "interchangeable for research and operational purposes." Strong correlations have been found to exist between different size-based measures of growth (Baysinger, Meiners, and Zeithaml 1982). Haire (1959), Starbuck (1965), and Evans (1987) operationalized growth as number of employees in studies of organizational development. Researchers using the PIMS data base have market share as a growth measure variable (Buzzell, Gale, and Sultan 1975; Schoeffler, Buzzell, and Heany 1974). Surveying the strategic management literature, Woo and Willard (1983) identified four growth-related measures of performance: growth in market share, growth in revenues, change in ROI, and change in cash flow/investment. Other measures have included growth in assets (Kumar 1985), in present value (book value, patents, goodwill) (Bracker, Keats, and Pearson 1988), and in number of customers (Woo, Cooper, Dunkelberg, Daellenbach, and Dennis 1989).

Corporate growth has been thoroughly discussed in the finance literature. Financial theory suggests that a major corporate goal is to maximize shareholder wealth. Fisher and Lerro (1971) defined corporate growth as "the profitable increase in total flow of real resources through the structure, in the form of production and sale of output" (27). Singhvi (1974) described corporate growth as the increase in earnings at a rate higher than the average growth rate for the economy as well as the industry. Other measures found in the finance literature include growth in earnings per share (Higgins 1984; Van Horne 1989), growth in total assets (Branch and Gale 1983), and growth in net sales or revenues (Higgins 1977; Miedick and Melicker 1985).

Perhaps the model from the finance literature most popular among strategy researchers is the Capital Asset Pricing Model (CAPM) (Sharpe 1964). The CAPM assumes portfolio diversification by a firm in order to reduce the impact of general economic fluctuations. Its central focus is the increase in investor wealth. Oviatt (1989) argued that the assumptions underlying the CAPM are inappropriate for strategy research. From a strategic management perspective, assuming away unsystematic risk is a fatal flaw (Aaker and Jacobson 1987).

We return to the notion of sales growth, which appears to be the dominant measure selected for entrepreneurship research (Ginn and Sexton 1989; Bailey 1984). Feeser (1987) proposed the use of sales growth for research on the growth strategies of firms. He argued that although sales growth figures would tend to reflect the inflationary pressures of the period being measured, they are familiar to business executives (respondents), are easily obtainable, and reflect both long-term and short-term changes in the firm and the environment.

Ozanian, Maher, and Manzano (1988) have also defended the use of sales growth, arguing that it is the figure "least susceptible to manipulation" (36). Neiswander and Fulton (1989) found that CEOs most often measure growth through sales of the firm.

Using sales figures, high-growth firms may be differentiated in two ways. The first is to select those firms whose sales growth exceeds the average growth rate of their industries. A second method is to choose those firms whose sales growth exceeds the average growth rate of the fastest-growing industries in a particular sector (manufacturing, retail, construction, etc.) (Dsouza 1990).

High-Growth Strategy Research

As the literature shows, sustained high levels of growth are not natural consequences of ongoing businesses. Businesses typically place profitability high on their list of goals and objectives. This does not seem to be true for high-growth firms. Research conducted by Shuman and Seeger (1986) and by McCann and Cornelius (1985) on small high-growth firms shows no statistical correlation between firm growth and financial performance. Earlier research on performance-growth relationships suggested the possibility of a negative correlation between growth and performance. For example, Eriksson (1978), building on the works of Weiss (1971), found a negative correlation between growth and performance of a firm. It is evident that high growth puts severe strains on the organization's ability to meet its profitability goal.

Researchers consistently find that rapidly growing firms are more likely to engage in strategic planning than are slower-growing companies (Shuman, Sussman, and Shaw 1985; Bracker, Keats, and Pearson 1988; Woo et al. 1989). Strategic management is iterative in that plans are formulated, implemented, evaluated, and refined through reformulation. In its pure sense, it is a learning process. This suggests an application of Jovanovic's (1982) theory of firm growth. He postulated that entrepreneurs learn about their abilities over time. Managers of high-growth firms may be expected to learn from their experiences and demonstrate strategies that are in some respects different from the strategies of firms emphasizing profit objectives.

Few researchers have comprehensively investigated the competitive strategies of high-growth firms. Research has primarily concentrated on the strategy-making process in high-growth firms. Three of these studies have researched firms that were ranked in *Inc.* magazine's list of the "fastest-growing" small companies. The studies by Shuman, Shaw, and Sussman (1985) and by Shuman and Seeger (1986) identified four key areas that determine the strategic planning process in high-growth firms. The key areas that they identified were: 1) management planning and posture; 2) the type of planning process; 3) the planning areas; and 4) how planning is organized in the firm. The study by McCann and Cornelius (1985) surveyed a similar sample of firms. However, their study attempted to identify factors that moderated the relationships between growth and profitability in small, rapidly growing firms. They concluded that ownership and age of the firm were the variables that correlated best with the growth of these firms.

Cooper, Willard, and Woo (1986) delved into issues relating to the "niche" strategy as a viable alternative strategy for high-performing new and small ventures. These authors did not address the issue from the perspective of *sustaining* high growth. They proposed that small high-growth firms adopt a niching strategy when challenging the dominant firm in their industry. Using a case study approach, Cooper et al. analyzed five successful high-performing small firms that had developed strategies for direct competition with much larger industry leaders. They argued that the key to successful high performance is the firm's ability to exploit changes in the industry by a quicker response to an environmental change or by limiting the ability of the competitors to erode the firm's new competitive advantage. With the "right combination of corporate resources and industry opportunity, [firms] may be able to develop strategies of direct competition which lead to continuing and enviable success" (259).

Research by Hanan (1987) also focused on the content of strategies employed by high-growth firms. In his book, *Fast Growth Strategies,* Hanan used anecdotal evidence to identify nine "basic model" high-growth strategies which he termed: 1) growth niching, 2) growth branding, 3) growth valuing, 4) growth teaming, 5) growth databasing, 6) growth marketcentering, 7) growth consulting, 8) growth partnering, and 9) growth by participation.

Similarly, Storey (1989) relied on anecdotal evidence to derive a set of lessons for achieving rapid growth from which strategies can be inferred. Working from what he labeled a "journalistic, not scientific" (2) methodology, Storey found fast-growing firms characterized by:

- Leaders with a clear vision of the company's future
- A retention of small company traits
- Market-driven behaviors
- A belief in high quality
- A belief in customer service
- A shared focus
- Increasing flexibility

In their study of 30 rapid-growth firms, Hambrick and Crozier (1985) found that high levels of growth severely tax the structural attributes of an organization. They also found that high growth demands high levels of financial resources. As a result, the sample of firms surveyed were found to be starved for cash. Their findings, along with those of Fredriksen, Klofsten, Olofsson, and Wahlbin (1989) and Swift (1989), suggest that to be successful, growing firms must have the capabilities to manage the high level of organizational change that is demanded by high growth.

Hills and Narayana (1989) reviewed success factors in 63 small high-growth firms. A content analysis suggested that the four most important success factors were the quality of the product/service provided by the firm, a good reputation with customers, the ability to respond to a customer's desires/requests, and hard work and devotion to the business. The firms in the Hills and Narayana sample did not display as high an average rate of growth as those in the Hambrick and Crozier sample.

Dsouza (1990) attempted to move beyond the planning process and the reporting of outcomes by examining the content of strategies implemented by high-growth firms. Surveying a sample of 196 companies that sustained sales growth rates in excess of 25 percent compounded over four years, he identified three primary strategic clusters that describe high-growth firms:

Strategy	Characteristics
1. Build strategy.	Emphasis on vertical integration.
2. Expand strategy.	Emphasis on resource allocation and product differentiation.
3. Maintain strategy.	Emphasis on market dominance and/or efficiency.

Based on his analysis, Dsouza derived the conceptual framework shown in Figure 13–1.

Finally, both Gilmore and Kazanjian (1989) and Sexton and Bowman-Upton (1991) raised the issue of planning for leader/manager transition to maintain or achieve high growth. Gilmore and Kazanjian recommended a

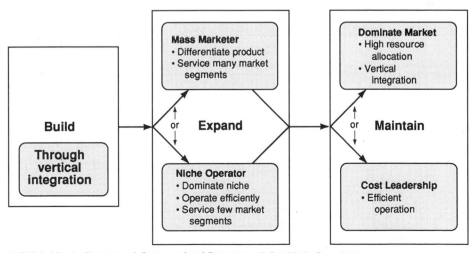

FIGURE 13–1 Proposed Conceptual Framework for High-Growth Strategies

structured decision-making approach to team building that would force information sharing and the delegation of decision making. The purpose is to develop the next generation of leaders to carry on the growth strategy. Sexton and Bowman-Upton raised the long-debated question about whether the entrepreneur can administer the company that he or she created. If not, regardless of choice or capacity, plans should be formulated for transition to ensure growth continuity.

From this review, we conclude that founders and CEOs can consciously choose high-growth strategies for their firms. Strategic planning is important to the achievement of growth goals, particularly if it addresses resource acquisition to sustain growth. Research is incomplete regarding how the strategies of high-growth companies differ from those with slower growth. Recent testable frameworks have been advanced that appear to hold promise.

The review further indicates that growth can be planned and achieved regardless of stage of organizational life cycle and despite other constraints. Nevertheless, firms aspiring to rapid growth must succeed in competitive environments. Environmental variables associated with high growth are examined in the following section of this chapter.

■ ■■ ■■ ■■ ■■ ■■ ■■ ■
RESEARCH ON THE
ENVIRONMENTS OF
HIGH-GROWTH FIRMS

The population ecology literature calls our attention to the environments in which firms attain high-growth status. Most research into the impact of the environment on strategy has not specifically investigated high-growth firms. It is not clear, therefore, that the common wisdom that the competitive environment has a greater impact on business-level strategy than does the general environment (Dess and Beard 1984), is applicable to high-growth companies. In fact, Jauch and Osborn (1981) argued that the growth orientation of a firm makes executives look beyond the boundaries of the industry in which they compete. The relevant variables affecting the firm's strategy are likely to be forged from a combination of the general and competitive environments.

The few research studies that directly address growth issues highlight two environmental factors: market growth and environmental velocity. Hanan (1987) argued that firm growth is related to the growth of the market in which the firm competes. A rapidly growing firm is likely to operate in a rapidly growing market. Cooper, Willard, and Woo (1986) supported this view by finding that markets must change and/or present new opportunities in order for firms to maintain high growth. They went on to say, "The real question is whether the firm can exploit the opportunity presented by market growth to gain a competitive advantage" (409). Measuring industry growth by value of shipments, Acs and Audretsch (1990) found no significant relationship between industry growth and small-firm growth. They concluded that the conditions under which small firms grow are different from those that affect industry growth. They did not investigate the effects of local marketing. They were studying United States manufacturers, which are less dependent on local markets than other industry classifications, such as retailers.

High-velocity environments are those in which changes take place at very fast rates. For example, urban environments are considered to be more volatile and, therefore, more essential for growth than rural environments (Leahy and McKee 1976). Using a case study approach on four companies, Bourgeois and Eisenhardt (1988) developed five hypotheses for organizational decision making in high-velocity environments: effective firms 1) use rational decision-making processes; 2) try new techniques (are willing to take risks); 3) make strategic decisions quickly; 4) build in decision execution triggers; and 5) vest power in the top management team to implement strategies.

In one of the more comprehensive studies to date, Dsouza (1990) identified six dimensions of the environments in which firms achieve high growth. We find in his analysis the recurrent themes of market growth and environmental velocity extended to include the bargaining power of buyers and suppliers and the actions of competitors. Dsouza acknowledged the similarities between these dimensions and the five forces in Porter's (1980, 1985) industry structure model. The six environmental dimensions that have been identified are:

Dimension	*Characteristics*
1. Technology drive.	Recent technological changes, investment in research and development, value added in the industry, technological sophistication, and industry exports.
2. Power of buyers and suppliers.	Product is a major expenditure for the customer, a demand for after-sale service, and the number of raw materials suppliers.
3. Environmental heterogeneity.	Number of new product introductions and number of competitors.
4. Environmental dynamics.	Ability to predict industry sales and ability to predict competitor behavior.
5. Threat from substitute products and services.	Price differential between industry product and substitutes, and availability of close substitute products.
6. Global activity.	Imports into the U.S. market, industry exports, and growth in industry sales.

To summarize, in order to sustain high growth, companies should ensure that they are quickly acquiring and using relevant data about market growth and the velocity within their competitive environments. Because of the inordinate demands growth places on organizational resources, companies must also monitor the broader, general environment, which could act both as a constraint on and a source of resources to achieve growth.

■■ ■■ ■■ ■■ ■■ ■■ ■■ ■■ ■■

FITTING STRATEGY AND ENVIRONMENT TO GROWTH: AN ENTREPRENEURIAL INTERPRETATION

One conclusion we can draw from this review is that research on high-growth firms is increasing not only in the quantity of studies but also in their quality. Advances in designs and methodologies are enhancing the results of case studies, while new technologies improve the ability to analyze data. Researchers are also benefitting from more comprehensive and more accurate data bases. Studies cited in this chapter have used *County Business Patterns* and unemployment insurance data (Mokry 1989), National Federation of Independent Businesses surveys (Woo et al. 1989), Compustat files (Hall 1987), the Profit Impact of Marketing Strategy data base (Hambrick and Crozier 1985), and Dun's Market Identifiers (DMI) data base (Hendrickson and Woodland 1985). The DMI data base shows particular promise for high-growth research in its revised form in the U.S. Small Business Administration's Small Business Data Base (SBDB). (See especially Acs and Audretsch 1990.) The U.S. Establishment and Enterprise Microdata File (USEEM) of the SBDB contains, as of this writing, approximately 20 million individual records derived from the DMI data base and corrected by the Brookings Institution. These data are already leading to breakthroughs in analyzing small business data longitudinally.

As we have seen in this chapter, our knowledge of the strategies employed by high-growth firms and of the environments in which they achieve their growth objectives is beginning to take shape. High-growth strategy formulation and implementation are very much within the control of founders, owners, and CEOs. Yet, there are clearly environmental influences. Future research no doubt will examine the strategy-environment linkages.

There will always be firms that attain high-growth status incidentally and/or unintentionally. The conditions under which such growth occurs is of interest to us from a population ecology perspective. Identifying environmental variables is particularly important for setting a public policy agenda that seeks the benefits that accrue to society from high-growth firms.

Alternatively, if entrepreneurship concepts can be taught to business owners/managers or can be developed within organizations, then the strategies that lead to high growth should be identified and communicated. In this chapter, we have introduced some recent insights into the content of these strategies. Advancement of the field calls for further work to establish the contingent linkages between high-growth strategies and critical environmental variables.

━━ ━━ ━━ ━━ ━━ ━━ ━━ ━━

REFERENCES

Aaker, D. A., and G. S. Day 1986 The perils of high-growth markets. *Strategic Management Journal* 7 : 409–421.

Aaker, D. A., and R. Jacobson 1987 The role of risk in explaining differences in probability. *Academy of Management Journal* 30 : 277–296.

Acs, Z. J., and D. B. Audretsch 1990 The determinants of small-firm growth in U.S. manufacturing. *Applied Economics* 22 : 143–153.

Aldrich, H. 1979 *Organizations and environments.* Englewood Cliffs, N.J. : Prentice-Hall, Inc.

1990 Using an ecological perspective to study organizational founding rates. *Entrepreneurship Theory and Practice* 14 : 7–24.

Armington, C., and M. Odle 1982 Small business — How many jobs ? *The Brookings Review* 1 : 7–14.

Bailey, J. E. 1984 Intrapreneurship — Source of high-growth start-ups or passing fad ? In *Frontiers of entrepreneurship research.* eds. J. Hornaday, F. Tarpley, Jr., J. Timmons, and K. Vesper, 358–367. Wellesley, Mass. : Babson College.

Baysinger, B. D., R. E. Meiners, and C. P. Zeithaml 1982 *Barriers to corporate growth.* Lexington, Mass. : Lexington Books.

Birch, D. L. 1979 *The job generation process.* Cambridge, Mass. : MIT Program on Neighborhood and Regional Change.

1987 *Job creation in America.* N.Y. : Free Press.

Birley, S. 1987 New ventures and employment growth. *Journal of Business Venturing* 2 : 155–165.

Bourgeois, L. J. 1980 Strategy and environment : A conceptual integration. *Academy of Management Review* 5 : 25–39.

Bourgeois, L. J., and K. M. Eisenhardt 1988 Strategic decision process and high velocity environments : Four cases in the microcomputer industry. *Management Science* 34 : 816–835.

Bracker, J. S., B. W. Keats, and J. N. Pearson 1988 Planning and financial performance among small firms in a growth industry. *Strategic Management Journal* 9 : 591–603.

Branch, B. T., and B. Gale 1983 Linking stock price performance to strategy formulation. *Journal of Business Strategy* 12 : 40–49.

Buzzell, R. D., B. T. Gale, and R. G. M. Sultan 1975 Market share : A key to profitability. *Harvard Business Review* 53 : 97–106.

Bygrave, W. D. 1988 Venture capital investing : A resource exchange perspective. Ph.D. diss., Boston University.

Cantillon, R. 1959 *An essay on the nature of business in general,* ed. and trans. H. Higgs. London : Frank Cass.

Carland, J. W., J. C. Carland, F. Hoy, and W. R. Boulton 1988 Distinctions between entrepreneurial and small business ventures. *International Journal of Management* 5 : 98–103.

Carland, J. W., F. Hoy, W. R. Boulton, and J. C. Carland 1984 Differentiating entrepreneurs from small business owners : A conceptualization. *Academy of Management Review* 9 : 354–359.

Chaganti, R. 1987 Small business strategies in different industry growth environments. *Journal of Small Business Management* 25 : 61–68.

Chakravarthy, B. S. 1986 Measuring strategic performance. *Strategic Management Journal* 7 : 437–458.

Chrisman, J. J., F. Hoy, and R. B. Robinson, Jr. 1987 New venture development : The costs and benefits of public sector assistance. *Journal of Business Venturing* 2 (4) : 315–328.

Cooper, A. C., G. E. Willard, and C. Y. Woo 1986 Strategies for high-performing new and small firms : A re-examination of the niche concept. *Journal of Business Venturing* 1 : 247–260.

Crego, C. 1985 Entrepreneurship and economic growth : Toward a new conceptual framework. In *Keys to the future of American business*, ed. G. T. Solomon, 59–68. Washington, D.C. : George Washington Univ. Press.

Dess, G. G., and D. W. Beard 1984 Dimensions of organizational task environment. *Administrative Science Quarterly* 29 : 52–73.

Dill, W. 1958 Environment as an influence on managerial autonomy. *Administrative Science Quarterly* 2 : 409–443.

Doyle, J., and C. Gallagher 1987 Size-distribution, growth potential and job-generation contribution of U.S. firms, 1982–84. *International Small Business Journal* 6 : 31–56.

Dsouza, D. 1990 Strategy types and environmental correlates of strategy for high-growth firms : An exploratory study. Ph.D. diss., Georgia State University.

Duncan, R. B. 1972 Characteristics of organizational environments and perceived environmental uncertainty. *Administrative Science Quarterly* 17 : 313–327.

Eriksson, G. 1978 *Growth and finance of the firm.* N.Y. : John Wiley & Sons.

Evans, D. S. 1987 The relationship between firm growth, size, and age : Estimates for 100 manufacturing industries. *Journal of Industrial Economics* 35 : 567–581.

Feeser, H. R. 1987 Incubators, entrepreneurs, strategy and performance : A comparison of high and low growth high tech firms. Ph.D. diss., Purdue University.

Fisher, W. H., and P. W. Lerro 1971 Corporate growth : Why and how ? *Batelle Research Outlook* 1 : 26–29.

Fredriksen, O., M. Klofsten, C. Olofsson, and C. Wahlbin 1989 Growth, performance and financial structure of new technology-based firms. In *Frontiers of entrepreneurship research*, eds. R. Brockhaus et al., 189–199. Wellesley, Mass. : Babson College.

Gilmore, T. N., and R. K. Kazanjian 1989 Clarifying decision making in high-growth ventures : The use of responsibility charting. *Journal of Business Venturing* 4(1) : 69–83.

Ginn, C. W., and D. L. Sexton 1989 Growth : A vocational choice and psychological preference. In *Frontiers of entrepreneurship research*, eds. R. Brockhaus, N. Churchill, J. Katz, B. Kirchhoff, K. Vesper, and W. Wetzel, Jr., 1–12. Wellesley, Mass. : Babson College.

1990 A comparison of the personality type dimensions of the 1987 *Inc.* 500 company founders/CEOs with those of slower growth firms. *Journal of Business Venturing* 5 : 140–150.

Haire, M. 1959 Biological models and empirical histories of the growth of organizations. In ed. M. Haire, *Modern organizational theory*, 272–306. N.Y. : John Wiley & Sons, Inc.

Hall, B. H. 1987 The relationship between firm size and firm growth in the U.S. manufacturing sector. *Journal of Industrial Economics* 35 : 583–606.

Hall, H. J. 1989 Venture capitalists' decision making and the entrepreneur : An exploratory investigation. Ph.D. diss., University of Georgia.

Hall, R. H. 1977 *Organizations : Structure and process.* Englewood Cliffs, N.J. : Prentice-Hall, Inc.

Hambrick, D. C. 1983 An empirical typology of mature industrial-product environments. *Academy of Management Journal* 26 : 213–230.

Hambrick, D. C., and L. M. Crozier 1985 Stumblers and stars in the management of rapid growth. *Journal of Business Venturing* 1 : 31–45.

Hanan, M. 1987 *Fast growth strategies.* N.Y. : McGraw-Hill.

Heller International Corporation 1984 The nine prime issues : A small business agenda for the 1980s. Institute for Small Business (January). Report.

Hendrickson, L. U., and L. Woodland 1985 Applications of the population ecology model to the estimation of corporate births. In *Proceedings*, 65–72. International Council for Small Business, U.S. Affiliate.

Higgins, R. C. 1977 How much growth can a firm afford ? *Financial Management* 6 : 7–16.

1984 *Analysis for financial management.* Homewood, Ill. : Irwin.

Hills, G. E., and Narayana, C. L. 1989 Profile characteristics, success factors and marketing in highly successful firms. In *Frontiers of entrepreneurship research*, eds. R. Brockhaus, N. Churchill, J. Katz, B. Kirchhoff, K. Vesper, and W. Wetzel, Jr., 69–80. Wellesley, Mass. : Babson College.

Hofer, C. W., and D. E. Schendel 1978 *Strategy formulation : Analytical concept.* St. Paul, Minn. : West.

Hoy, F. 1983a A program for rural development from inception through implementation. *Journal of the Community Development Society* 14 : 33–49.

1983b Small business administration. In *Government agencies*, ed. D. R. Whitnah. Westport, Conn. : Greenwood Press.

Jovanovic, B. 1982 Selection and evolution of industry. *Econometrica* 50 : 649–670.

Jauch, L. R., and R. N. Osborn 1981 Towards an integrated theory of strategy. *Academy of Management Review* 6 : 491–498.

Kazanjian, R. K. 1983 The organizational evolution of high technology ventures : Re impact stage of growth on the nature of structure and planning process. Ph.D. diss., The Wharton School, University of Pennsylvania.

Kirchhoff, B. A., and Phillips, B. D. 1987 Examining entrepreneurship's role in economic growth. In *Frontiers of entrepreneurship research*, eds. N. Churchill, J. Hornaday, B. Kirchhoff, and K. Vesper, 57–71. Wellesley, Mass. : Babson College.

1989 Innovation and growth among new firms in the U.S. economy. In *Frontiers of entrepreneurship research*, eds. R. Brockhaus, N. Churchill, J. Katz, B. Kirchhoff, K. Vesper, and W. Wetzel, Jr., 173–188. Wellesley, Mass. : Babson College.

Kumar, M. S. 1985 Growth, acquisition activity and firm size : Evidence from the United Kingdom. *Journal of Industrial Economics.* 33(3) : 327–338.

Leahy, W. H., and D. L. McKee 1976 A note on urbanism and Schumpeter's theory of development. *Growth and Change* 7 : 45–47.

Lenz, R. T., and J. L. Engledow 1986 Environmental analysis : The applicability of current theory. *Strategic Management Journal* 7 : 329–346.

Low, M. B., and I. C. MacMillan 1988 Entrepreneurship : Past research and future challenges. *Journal of Management* 14 : 139–161.

Lucas, R. E. 1978 On the size distribution of business firms. *Bell Journal of Economics* 9 : 508–523.

MacMillan, I. C., R. Siegal, and P. N. SubbaNarasimha 1985 Criteria used by venture capitalists to evaluate new venture proposals. *Journal of Business Venturing* 1 : 119–128.

McCann, J. E., and W. G. Cornelius 1985 Performance characteristics of small, rapidly growing firms : An examination of the *Inc.* 100. *Academy of Management Best Paper Proceedings 1985*, 62–66.

Miedick, S. J., and R. W. Melicker 1985 Corporate sales growth rate and stockholder return. *Review of Business and Economic Research* 20 : 34–44.

Mokry, B. W. 1989 *Entrepreneurship and public policy.* N.Y. : Quorum Books.

Naisbitt, J. 1982 *Megatrends.* N.Y. : Warner Books.

Neiswander, D., and M. E. Fulton 1989 Successful growth management. In *Frontiers of entrepreneurship research*, eds. R. Brockhaus, N. Churchill, J. Katz, B. Kirchhoff, K. Vesper, and W. Wetzel, Jr., 422. Wellesley, Mass. : Babson College.

Oviatt, B. M. 1989 Caveats concerning application of the capital asset pricing model in the strategic management concept. *Academy of Management Best Papers Proceedings 1989*, 37–41.

Ozanian, M. K., T. Maher, and D. Manzano 1988 The 500 fastest growing companies in America. *Financial World* (August 9) : 36–56.

Penrose, E. 1959 *The theory of the growth of the firm.* Oxford, Eng. : Oxford Univ. Press.

Perry, C., G. G. Meredith, and H. J. Cunningham 1988 Relationship between small business growth and personal characteristics of owner/managers in Australia. *Journal of Small Business Management* 26 : 76–79.

Porter, M. E. 1980 *Competitive strategy : Techniques for analyzing industries and competitors.* N.Y. : Free Press.

1985 *Competitive advantage : Creating and sustaining superior performance.* N.Y. : Free Press.

1990 *The competitive advantage of nations.* N.Y. : Free Press.

Sandberg, W. R. 1986 *New venture performance.* Lexington, Mass. : Lexington Books.

Schoeffler, S., R. Buzzell, and D. Heany 1974 Impact of strategic planning on profit performance. *Harvard Business Review* 52 (March-April) : 137–145.

Schumpeter, J. A. 1934 *The theory of economic development.* Cambridge, Mass. : Harvard Univ. Press.

1942 *Capitalism, socialism, and democracy : Can capitalism survive ?* N.Y. : Harper and Brothers.

1950 *Can capitalism survive ?* N.Y. : Harper & Row.

Sexton, D. L., and N. B. Bowman-Upton 1991 *Entrepreneurship : Creativity and growth.* N.Y. : Macmillan.

Sharpe, W. F. 1964 Capital asset prices : A theory of market equilibrium under conditions of risk. *Journal of Finance* 19 : 425–442.

Shuman, J. C., and J. A. Seeger 1986 The theory and practice of strategic management in smaller rapid growth firms. *American Journal of Small Business* 3 : 7–18.

Shuman, J. C., J. J. Shaw, and G. Sussman 1985 Strategic planning in smaller rapid growth companies. *Long Range Planning* 18 : 48–53.

Shuman, J. C., G. Sussman, and J. J. Shaw 1985 Business plans and the start-up of rapid growth companies. In *Frontiers of entrepreneurship research*, eds. J. Hornaday, E. Shils, J. Timmons, and K. Vesper, 294–313. Wellesley, Mass. : Babson College.

Singhvi, S. S. 1974 A model for corporate growth. *Mergers and Acquisitions* 18 : 10–15.

Starbuck, W. 1965 Organizational growth and development. In *Handbook of organizations*, ed. J. March, 451–533. Chicago, Ill. : Rand McNally.

Steers, R. 1975 Problems in the measurements of organizational effectiveness. *Administrative Science Quarterly* 20 : 546–558.

Storey, M. J. 1989 *Inside America's fastest growing companies.* N.Y. : John Wiley & Sons.

Swift, C. 1989 Financing the rapidly growing firm : Recent Canadian experience. In *Frontiers of entrepreneurship research*, eds. R. Brockhaus, N. Churchill, J. Katz, B. Kirchhoff, K. Vesper, and W. Wetzel, Jr., 318–330. Wellesley, Mass. : Babson College.

Timmons, J. S. 1986 Growing up big : Entrepreneurship and the creation of high-potential ventures. In *The art and science of entrepreneurship*, eds. D. L. Sexton and R. W. Smilor, 223–240. Cambridge, Mass. : Ballinger.

Van Horne, J. C. 1989 *Financial management and policy.* Englewood Cliffs, N.J. : Prentice-Hall, Inc.

Weick, K. 1979 *The social psychology of organizing.* Reading, Mass. : Addison-Wesley.

Weiss, L. W. 1971 Case studies in American industry, 2nd ed. N.Y. : John Wiley & Sons, Inc.

Williams, A. J. 1989 The role of small enterprises in job generation in Australia : A longitudinal study from 1973. In *Frontiers of entrepreneurship research*, eds. R. Brockhaus, N. Churchill, J. Katz, B. Kirchhoff, K. Vesper, and W. Wetzel, Jr., 117–133. Wellesley, Mass. : Babson College.

Woo, C. Y., and G. Willard 1983 Performance representation in business policy research : Discussion and recommendation. *Academy of Management Best Paper Proceedings 1983*, 426.

Woo, C. Y., A. C. Cooper, W. C. Dunkelberg, U. Daellenbach, and W. J. Dennis. 1989 Determinants of growth for small and large entrepreneurial start-ups. In *Frontiers of entrepreneurship research*, eds. R. Brockhaus, N. Churchill, J. Katz, B. Kirchhoff, K. Vesper, and W. Wetzel, Jr., 134–147. Wellesley, Mass. : Babson College.

Chapter

14

Creating and Maintaining High-Performance Teams[1]

Dennis P. Slevin
and
Jeffrey G. Covin

●

Work teams are increasingly recognized as an effective means for accomplishing critical organizational tasks (Hackman 1990). This chapter examines the role of teams in the entrepreneurial process. The chapter begins by reviewing some of the reasons why teams are assuming a more prominent role in the functioning of successful organizations. A research model is then presented which outlines some of the key determinants of team creation and performance. Various topics that relate to team processes and effectiveness are discussed, and problems sometimes associated with teams are identified. Finally, the chapter concludes with a listing of key research questions and a discussion of the future of teams as facilitators of the entrepreneurial process.

INTRODUCTION

Firms in the 1990s must become much more entrepreneurial and adaptable to survive and grow in a rapidly changing world. Environmental pressures have altered the basic nature of the business enterprise, and the challenges these pressures bring to business will continue to increase both in diversity and intensity. Reich (1987) argues that the United States economy that formerly encouraged individual entrepreneurial behavior no longer exists. Today's economy is more global, and innovations pioneered by Americans travel quickly to other countries. Process technology, likewise, is quite transferable to other sites around the globe. Workers in other parts of the world are likely to be both cheaper and perhaps more productive than U.S. workers, and new relationships between engineers, managers, production workers, and marketing people do away with many of the distinctions between entrepreneurs and drones.

Consequently, the entire organization must respond adaptively and collectively to environmental change. Organizations can no longer design monolithic internal systems and structures intended to last over periods of years or decades; rather, they must engage in the continual process of organizational learning and renewal (Kiechel 1990; Stata 1989). Waterman (1987), in his book *The Renewal Factor*, suggests that organizations must continually reorganize themselves to break down bureaucratic barriers and avoid inertia. Since products and markets are likely to change rapidly, entrepreneurial behavior must respond to these shorter competitive half-lives at the organizational level.

Entrepreneurial organizations are those which exhibit particular types of behavioral patterns. While firms that practice corporate entrepreneurship may already employ these behavioral patterns in limited functional areas, in entrepreneurial organizations these patterns necessarily pervade the organization at all levels and reflect the top managers' overall strategic philosophy on effective management practice (McKinney and McKinney 1989). According to Miller (1983):

> In general, theorists would not call a firm entrepreneurial if it changed its technology or product-line . . . simply by directly imitating competitors while refusing to take any risks. Some proactiveness would be essential as well. By the same token, risk-taking firms that are highly leveraged financially are not necessarily entrepreneurial. They must also engage in product-market or technological innovation. (780)

In short, firms with entrepreneurial postures are risk taking, innovative, and proactive. They are willing to take on high-risk projects with chances of very high returns, and are bold and aggressive in pursuing opportunities. Entrepreneurial organizations often initiate actions to which competitors then respond, and are frequently first-to-market with new product offerings (Covin and Slevin 1989). In support of this strategic orientation, entrepreneurial firms characteristically emphasize technological leadership and research and development (Khandwalla 1977).

A variety of definitions exist for entrepreneurship/intrapreneurship. Stevenson, Roberts, and Grousbeck (1989) suggest that "entrepreneurship is a process by which individuals — either on their own or inside organizations — pursue opportunities without regard to the resources they currently control"

(7). Beyond these individual efforts to address opportunities creatively, though, entrepreneurs in the 1990s must merge their talents into groups. It has become clear that some form of collective corporate intrapreneurship/ entrepreneurship is essential to long-term firm survival: the greater the emphasis and success in terms of the speed of innovation, the more entrepreneurial the firm. Researchers are increasing their examination of this phenomenon in a variety of ways (Bailey 1984; Stevenson and Jarillo 1990). Most recently, a special issue of *Strategic Management Journal* addressed the topic of corporate entrepreneurship (Guth and Ginsberg 1990).

Team entrepreneurship has come of age, and organizations may succeed in the long run by "running hot" — collective combinations of creative effort and individual skills (Stewart 1989). The new organizational model will consist of collections of teams which are formed with challenging entrepreneurial objectives. Consistent with this point, Cornwall and Perlman (1990) have recently argued that teams are "an integral part of an entrepreneurial organization," as they provide an effective means for reducing "the harmful effects that dysfunctional bureaucracy has on innovation, creativity, opportunities, and risk taking" (109–110). One example of this concept in action is documented by Tracy Kidder in *The Soul of a New Machine* (1981), where he details the fascinating story of how a team (a group of inventors) designed and built a new computer using team processes or collective entrepreneurship.

Successful organizations of the future need to create and maintain high-performance teams for the accomplishment of both process and product innovation. It is important in the development of the field of entrepreneurial research that key issues around the creation and maintenance of high-performance teams be understood. The purpose of this chapter is to address four questions:

1. How do we create high-performance teams?
2. How do we maintain high-performance teams?
3. What do the current research findings tell us about team creation and management?
4. Where should we go with our research in the future?

In answering these questions, some important findings on team entrepreneurship will be presented, the "holes" in the current research on this topic will be identified, and promising themes for future research will be discussed.

BACKGROUND

In virtually every industry, product life cycles are shrinking rapidly. It has become clear that the design of new products and the incremental improvement in old products must occur at an accelerating rate (Takeuchi and Nonaka 1986). While businesses need increased and speedier responses to changing competitive circumstances, the environment has likewise become more complex and challenging. Vaill (1990) has described the situation as an environment of chaotic change, using chaos in its sense of dynamic, unstable, nonlinear systems (Gleick 1988).

One model that has been developed to articulate the difficulties encountered in this fluid business environment focuses on the variables of complexity and dynamism (Miles 1980; Slevin 1989). Complexity refers to the homogeneity/heterogeneity dimension of the environment — i.e., how many heterogeneous elements exist. Dynamism refers to the rate of change over time or movement in the environment. In discussing this model with literally hundreds of managers in diverse industries, the authors experienced almost unanimous agreement that their industry, whether it be telecommunications, auto paint, steel, or glass distribution, has been moving over the last two decades in the direction of increased complexity and increased dynamism. In fact, it is difficult to name an industry which has not experienced dramatic changes in these dimensions.

Environmental change challenges firms, expanding the differentiation and integration needs of the organization. Firms of the 1990s will require increasing numbers of differentiated specialists who, at the same time, must be integrated and controlled towards achieving a coordinated effort. A variety of authors have addressed over several decades this constant tension between innovation and control, differentiation and integration (Thompson 1967; Lawrence and Lorsch 1967; Faas 1985; Shrivastava and Souder 1987; Feldman 1989; Rockart and Short 1989).

While there may be general trends towards increasing dynamism and complexity, it is still possible to find firms embodying each of the four cells in Figure 14–1. It is arguable that different information flows and decision-making procedures may be appropriate at different levels of dynamism and complexity. For example, in cell 3 (low dynamism/low complexity), it might be suggested that "standard operating procedures" represent the appropriate decision-making style. Numerous rules and predictable information flows maximize efficiency in this traditional organization. In cell 2 (low dynamism/high complexity), some sort of response is indicated by the complexities of the environment. Participatory decision making may be the appropriate model for this environment. Groups must get together to exchange information on complex technological issues in order to accomplish high performance. In cell 4 (high dynamism/low complexity), speed of response is absolutely essential. A combat military situation might be an appropriate example where the organization must respond quite quickly to changes in the environment. Hence an autocratic/centralized decision-making approach is appropriate. While the decision quality may not always be high, decision speed is maximized. Finally, cell 1 (high dynamism/high complexity) represents the most challenging position for the organization. Substantial information flows must be absorbed to resolve complex problems, and yet decision making must occur at a very rapid

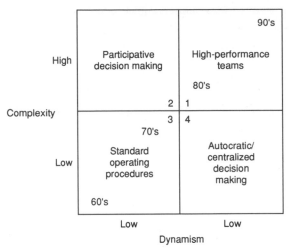

FIGURE 14-1 The Environment is Changing
(*Source*) : Slevin, D. P., *The Whole Manager : How to Increase Your Professional and Personal Effectiveness* (N.Y. : AMACOM, 1989), 225.

pace. Consequently, this cell seems to require the use of high-performance teams. These teams must be able to bring together diverse, differentiated specialists who exchange information creatively to solve problems, developing integrative solutions as a result of these efforts.

A number of good case examples exist demonstrating the effectiveness of high-performance teams in challenging business environments. Increased environmental pressures have demanded that organizations use teams effectively in bringing new products to market :

● The packaging team at a Procter and Gamble soap plant successfully implemented a new manufacturing process due to the suggestion of one team member.
● Shenandoah Life Insurance Company successfully uses self-managed work teams to increase efficiency in customer service.
● Aetna Life uses 12-person teams to handle a variety of jobs that previously were distributed through different departments (Sherwood 1988).

High-performance entrepreneurial teams will be one major tool used by organizations in the future as they attempt to respond quickly and effectively to environmental changes. Kilmann (1989), in his five-track program for organizational renewal, cites team building as one of the essential tracks for organizational change and success. Since team creation and maintenance bring a variety of variables into play, we need to examine further this vehicle for organizational success.

━━ ━━ ━━ ━━ ━━ ━━ ━━
A RESEARCH MODEL

In order to provide a framework for analysis of past research and suggest directions for future research, a general model of project team performance is proposed. This model, shown in Figure 14–2, is by definition general and certainly
tentative at this stage. There are at least four broad categories of variables in
this model that impact both project team creation and project team performance. These variables are discussed below.

Determinants of Project Team Creation

External environmental conditions.
The industry context within which the firm operates can have a major
impact on project team creation. Dynamic, high-technology industries, for
example, often require rapid strategic responses from member firms. The
utilization of structures which employ team-based operations processes is
one means by which firms can meet this challenge. Teams of employees
provide a fluid mechanism for the effective deployment of personnel when
firm objectives and strategies are changing in response to environmental
conditions.

Internal organizational conditions.
The internal environment of an organization is broadly composed of the
firm's structure, culture, and resources. Each of these factors can affect project

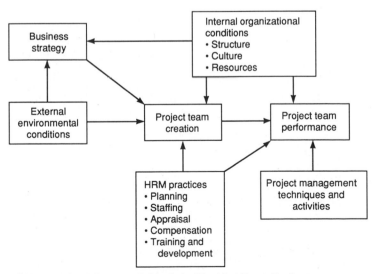

FIGURE 14–2   A Research Model of Project Team Performance

team creation. Teams are an integral and defining part of several structural types, such as the matrix structure and the project management structure. Certain structural forms, like organic organizations (Burns and Stalker 1968), can be particularly amenable to the formation of work teams. Likewise, an organization's culture can either facilitate or impede the formation of work teams. Firms with pro-innovation or entrepreneurial cultures often encourage *ad hoc* assemblages of personnel and foster teamwork among their members. Finally, the formation of teams can be a direct outgrowth of the quality, quantity, and characteristics of an organization's resources, defined as human resources, capital resources, plant and equipment, and any organizational systems and competencies.

Business strategy.

Teams can be used to facilitate the implementation of business strategy and, accordingly, are often created in response to specific strategic choices. For example, if the successful execution of a strategy is dependent upon the firm's developing a distinctive new product, a team of marketing, manufacturing, and R&D personnel might be formed to address the task of product development. Alternatively, a strategy might call for the improvement of product quality. In this case, quality circles composed of personnel from multiple organizational levels and functions could be established to ensure the manufacture of products of the highest possible quality. In short, teams often provide the means by which the tasks demanded by the firm's strategy can be accomplished.

Human resource management practices.

Project team creation is a function of broad-ranging human resource decisions and outcomes, such as whom the organization employs, what their competencies are, and how motivated the individuals are to work together as a team. Clearly the composition of a project team will depend upon staffing decisions and policies as well as job design philosophies. Training and development practices will affect the size of the pool of individuals who could conceivably work together on a project team. The human resource management functions of appraisal and compensation will likewise affect employees' desire to work cooperatively and diligently as team members.

Determinants of Project Team Performance

Project team composition.

The characteristics of the team members will determine to a great extent the effectiveness of the project team. Relevant questions might include: do the members collectively possess the requisite skills and knowledge for the task at hand? How well or poorly do the team members work together? Are those individuals whose firsthand support is necessary for project success adequately represented on the team ? Is project success a top priority for all team members ?

Internal organizational conditions.

The organization's structure, culture, and resources can either thwart or support the project team's efforts. The strength and quality of the structural interface between the project team and other organizational actors will affect the ability of the team to achieve its goals. For example, a project team that does not interact regularly and broadly with other organizational actors upon whose guidance and support the project team depends will probably produce unsatisfactory results. Culture affects the norms for appropriate and inappropriate behavior in an organization, and the project team's group process and consequent performance can easily be affected by solidly entrenched organizational norms which might, for example, strongly encourage the exercise of caution when facing uncertainty. Resources, of course, must be allocated in support of the project team's efforts. Inadequate or inappropriate resource support will result in failure to meet the project team objectives. In short, a project team will not be successful if the organizational context in which it operates is not supportive of the team's efforts.

Human resource management practices.

As with internal organizational conditions, human resource management practices will influence both the creation and performance of project teams. Consider, for example, compensation practices. Group-based incentive systems may result in a higher level of team performance than individual-based systems, particularly if goal suboptimization is a potential problem. As suggested above, the appropriateness of the team personnel to the task at hand will have a major impact on team performance. This is clearly a staffing issue. Likewise, the adequacy and validity of the appraisal criteria will, by definition, affect any evaluation of the project team's performance. Each of these issues is tied to human resource management practice, and each will have an undeniable impact on project team performance.

Project management techniques and activities.

Last but not least, the adequacy with which the project team is managed will affect task performance. In order to achieve the team's objectives, project managers must attend to such issues as planning the sequencing of project activities, assigning specific roles and tasks to individual team members, communicating the significance of the team's efforts to both team members and outside constituents on an ongoing basis, and removing any group process-related or bureaucratic barriers that would preclude the team from functioning at its highest possible level. Successful project team performance can only result when the project team is actively managed toward well-understood and accepted objectives.

The preceding discussion of the research model of project team perform-ance is broadly framed, but should serve as a useful organizing scheme for much of the following material. The material covered in this chapter, however, is not restricted to that which "fits" the model. Rather, topics have been chosen for inclusion when they meet the more relaxed criterion of relevance to the cre-ation and maintenance of high-performance teams.

COLLECTIVE ENTREPRENEURSHIP

Robert Reich (1987) has suggested that collective entrepreneurship is the way firms will succeed in the 90s. Reich argues that it makes no sense to talk in terms of "industries," because boundaries have become so fuzzy both techno-logically and geographically. This ambiguity implies that the rugged individu-alist, the creative entrepreneur of old, can no longer succeed in isolation. The technological challenges are just too great. Instead of the individual as hero, a new culture must develop in which the team is hero. Individuals with diverse backgrounds and fields of expertise must be gathered into cooperative, coordi-nated small groups that are rapidly responsive to environmental challenges. It appears clear that team entrepreneurship will become a primary model for competition in the 90s (Stewart 1989).

CREATING TEAMS

Team creation is a crucial process, because at the very outset mechanisms can be put in place to enhance team success. Kilmann (1989, 114) provides a 10-item checklist to be used during both the start-up and operating phases of teams. Team performance should be given a high priority, and goals and benchmarks should be established at the outset (Nevens, Summe, and Uttal 1990). However the goals need not be overly explicit and may in fact be left de-liberately "fuzzy." Honda, when designing a new automobile, created an au-tonomous team which had the rather vague charge to "create something differ-ent from the existing concept" (Nonaka 1988). The deliberate use of "fuzziness" appears to occur frequently in Japanese firms. Based on a compre-hensive study of the strategy and structure of Japanese enterprises, Toyohiro Kono (1984) concludes, "Japanese organizations are comparable to the natural stone walls that are seen in Japanese castles. The shape of the stones are all dif-ferent but they are combined so as to complement one another. Western orga-nizations are comparable to brick walls, which are composed of standardized square bricks. In Japanese organizations, jobs are ambiguous" (302).

In assembling a team, the technology that is relevant to the innovation must be taken into account (Amara 1990). It is important to ensure that the team is staffed with people having the appropriate and necessary qualities for project success. Thamhain and Wilemon (1987) suggest that both team-related and people-related qualities are important for team success.

It is clear that team members must be selected with both technical and human relation skills in mind. Often people seem to get assigned to teams because they have free time available rather than because they have the qualities and the capabilities required for team success. Things are different in Japan, a country that widely and effectively employs team-based structures. If a Japanese team leader wants a member whose manager does not want to release him, a negotiation occurs between the team leader and manager. This negotiation typically goes in favor of the team leader — i.e., there seems to be a large degree of cross-functional cooperation in the system. This underscores the importance of the team creation process in the ultimate quest for team performance.

CONCURRENCY

The term "concurrent engineering" implies a collective process in which design, engineering, manufacturing, marketing, and other functions work together in the product development and manufacturing processes (Carlyle 1990). Much of the material in this section is adapted from a study by Cleland and Slevin (1989).

Ford Motor Company used concurrent engineering in designing its Taurus and Sable models. Prototypes of these models were built seven months earlier than the traditional design system would have allowed. These models have since become among the company's most successful products (Quinn 1988). General Motors adopted a similar philosophy in its development of a new sports car engine (Stinson 1990). AT&T used to take two years designing a new telephone but, for its 4200 phone, it cut development time to just one year partly through the use of 6- to 12-member product design teams. General Electric reduced its delivery time for custom-made industrial circuit breaker boxes from three weeks to three days, again partly through the use of simultaneous engineering (Dumaine 1989). Hewlett-Packard's Personal Computer Division designed a portable, battery-operated microcomputer and got it to the market in less than 18 months using a team of engineers working in a concurrent fashion (Flint 1984).

Ingersoll Mining Machine Company built a transfer line for machining in-line four-cylinder engine blocks. The project involved 62 customer-initiated changes, which cost about $1.3 million. In 1988, while the firm was using simultaneous engineering, a similar project for the same customer included only seven customer-initiated changes, which cost $436,000 (Stauffer 1988). With examples such as these, simultaneous engineering seems to be an obvious strategy to follow: it encompasses all aspects of a project, from the formation of a product design team and the concurrent evaluation and integration of organizational functions, to consideration of how to manufacture, sell, and service the product once the customer takes ownership. Product design teams connect the functional areas of engineering design, manufacturing process design, marketing, and procurement with representatives from suppliers and even the customer organization. The product design team is organized early in the life cycle of the product, continues its deliberations through the delivery of the product to the customer, and may remain intact to provide after-delivery service of the product for the customer. It provides an organizational focus for simultaneous rather than sequential product and process design.

In the past, product and service design and development were done much like a relay race, with design engineering doing the initial design and then "throwing the product over the wall" to the manufacturing engineers. Manufacturing, in turn, determined how to build the product, usually with extensive back-and-forth discussions and potential redesigns by engineering. The finished product coming out of manufacturing was then "thrown over the wall" to marketing to sell. The result was a protracted product and process design cycle often made more complex through the use of engineering changes responding to what the customer really wanted.

Product design teams operating within the context of simultaneous engineering provide an effective means to reduce the parochial barriers that have traditionally existed among engineering, production, marketing, procurement, and the other organizational functions required to take a product idea through its development cycle to customer delivery. Simultaneous engineering is an idea whose time has come (Berger et al. 1989). Yet the theory and practice of simultaneous engineering is neither fully understood nor accepted as a competitive strategy in global competition (Grossi 1990). The "systems" impact of this evolving method is believed to be significant, yet such impact has neither been studied nor fully understood.

ORGANIZATIONAL STRUCTURE

Teams, by their very nature, represent a more organic, as opposed to mechanistic, organizational structure (Burns and Stalker 1968). Research suggests that an organic structure is crucial to entrepreneurial success (Slevin and Covin 1990). Moreover, successful firms manage to cycle between an organic/entrepreneurial approach for new business development and start-up, and a mechanistic/conservative approach for running the day-to-day operations of the firm. The ability to cycle between these contrasting organizational forms appears crucial to success. The organizational structure must be clearly matched to the entrepreneurial need; the firm must balance the continuous, creative tension between centralization and decentralization, autonomy and control (Feldman 1989). In an attempt to achieve this balance, Campbell Soup broke its organization into 50 independent business units each averaging approximately $50 million in sales (Kotkin 1985). Matching the structure to the need is not an either/or proposition; rather, autonomy and control exist simultaneously. This is one of the secrets of effective entrepreneurial behavior: the organization must have tightly coupled yet flexible processes (Carlyle 1990).

COMMERCIALIZATION PROCESS

A McKinsey and Company study of the commercialization process in the United States, Japan, and Europe found that leading companies:

● Commercialize two or three times the number of new products and processes as do their competitors of comparable size.
● Incorporate two to three times as many technologies in their products.
● Bring their products to market in less than half the time and compete in twice as many product and geographic markets. (Nevens, Summe, and Uttal 1990, 154)

Rapidly changing technology has foisted a commercialization imperative on modern firms. If you cannot commercialize your products efficiently and effectively, you will not sustain a role as a major player in any product or market.

Takeuchi and Nonaka (1986, 138) found through interviews with employees in both Japanese and U.S. companies that six characteristics emerge in the management of the new product development process:

1. Built-in instability.
2. Self-organizing project teams.
3. Overlapping development phases.
4. "Multilearning."
5. Subtle control.
6. Organizational transfer of learning.

Nevens, Summe, and Uttal (1990, 157–159) suggest that the following are good measures of a company's ability to commercialize:

● Time to market
● Range of markets
● Number of products
● Breadth of technologies

They also suggest that building cross-functional skills is a crucial tactic for enhancing the commercialization process. "High performing companies emphasize a set of skills notably different from their less successful counterparts. They value cross-functional skills, while other companies pride themselves on their functional strengths. High-performers boast, 'We've got the best project managers in the world.' Low-performers say, 'We've got the best circuit designers'" (162). One possibility is that a modified Likert linking pin model might be appropriate here. Rather than an individual being a member of two teams, one in which he is a subordinate and one in which he is a superior, an individual could be a member of one or more cross-functional teams linking him/her to individuals widely distributed throughout the organization. Bower and Hout (1988) suggest that, in fast-cycle companies, "the organization chart is more likely to be a set of interlocked circles or a systems flow chart with arrows and feedback loops indicating the actual path of decision and work" (p. 114).

INTERDEPENDENCE

Rockhart and Short (1989, 8) argue that the decreased cost of computers and electronic communications among firms, suppliers, and customers has caused a "disintegration" of the organization. Boundaries are fuzzier, and there is a greater need to manage interdependence due to the following five competitive pressures:

1. Globalization.
2. Time to market.
3. Risk management.
4. Service.
5. Cost.

Interdependence has become a crucial requisite of success in both service (Gosselin 1985) and manufacturing environments, and the need is growing. The Boeing Company, in its manufacturing of each Model 767 aircraft, assembles 3 million parts that are sourced from around the world. Tremendous levels of complexity and interdependence must be managed on a daily basis. Imagine how one product improvement might ripple throughout this complex system.

HRM POLICIES

Human resource management policies serve as the backdrop under which entrepreneurial team behavior can occur. These policies can either facilitate or retard team effectiveness. Consider the underlying elements of an entrepreneurial posture: risk taking, proactiveness, and innovation. Behaviors reflecting each of these entrepreneurial components can be encouraged or discouraged depending upon the characteristics of the organizational reward structure. Senior managers can create "speculative fund" pools for high-risk–high-return projects. R&D, manufacturing, and marketing personnel can be encouraged to think of ways the organization might leverage its core technologies as a means for creating new product/marketing opportunities. Organizational employees at all levels can be rewarded for identifying and suggesting realistic paths for exploiting a competitor's product line deficiencies or other areas of vulnerability. In short, there are numerous and diverse means through which managers can encourage entrepreneurial team behavior (see Schuler 1986; Hisrich and Peters 1989; Rule and Irwin 1988). Human resource management policies are central to such efforts.

The preceding paragraph illustrates how compensation or reward structure policies might affect entrepreneurial team behavior. Likewise, such behavior may be influenced by the other human resource practices and decisions. For example, personnel training and development policies could be geared toward ensuring that employees have the necessary cross-training to be valuable team members. Such training could focus on technical skills, in order to insure that the members bring some critical competence to the team, as well as group process skills, in order to facilitate effective teamwork. Furthermore, cross-training can make better generalists of employees and, accordingly, enable those individuals to potentially contribute to many teams' efforts.

Staffing policies can also have a major impact on entrepreneurial team effectiveness. Flexible staffing policies, for example, allow individuals to work on projects of interest to them. When given such opportunities, employees will often put forth their best efforts. Similarly, flexible job descriptions are particularly valuable in an innovative organization, as they give motivated employees much latitude in applying their talents to diverse entrepreneurial efforts.

Formal human resource planning is a must in the entrepreneurial firm. These organizations must provide for the recruitment, selection, retainment, and development of creative, talented employees who will be the driving force behind any entrepreneurial initiative. Critical human resource planning questions for the entrepreneurial firm would include: what are the implications of anticipated environmental changes for the knowledge and skills employees will need to keep the firm on the cutting edge within the industry? Can our firm maintain its entrepreneurial posture by grooming and developing its current employees, or must we rely on recruitment of outsiders to maintain our innovative capability? How can the employee's job experiences be structured so that hc/she will be capable of contributing to multiple entrepreneurial team initiatives?

Finally, employee appraisal policies can be used to enhance entrepreneurial team effectiveness. Given uncertainty regarding such things as realistic project completion dates and the functional performance capabilities of a development-phase project, superior-established evaluation criteria and standards can be disastrous for the entrepreneurial team. Such criteria and standards can easily be out of line with reality and discouraging to the team members. Accordingly, participative appraisal methods, such as management by objectives (MBO), are often appropriate for the evaluation of individuals who are members of teams performing ill-structured tasks. These methods allow the individuals who are closest to the entrepreneurial effort to have some say in how they are evaluated.

Many of the appropriate human resource practices for a firm relying on entrepreneurial teams can be inferred from the discussion by Schuler and

Jackson (1987) of the human resource management implications of various competitive strategies. These authors examined the needed role behaviors and corresponding human resource policies of firms that pursue three generic strategies — innovation, quality-enhancement, and cost-reduction. The innovation strategy, which places emphasis on the development of new and unique products or services, is the generic strategy that would most likely be used by firms that stress the creation and maintenance of high performing, entrepreneurial teams. According to Schuler and Jackson (1987, 209–210), effective employee role behaviors in firms that have innovation strategies include:

> (1) a high degree of creative behavior, (2) a longer-term focus, (3) a relatively high level of cooperative, interdependent behavior, (4) a moderate degree of concern for quality, (5) a moderate concern for quantity, (6) an equal degree of concern for process and results, (7) a greater degree of risk taking, and (8) a high tolerance for ambiguity and predictability.

Human resource practices argued by Schuler and Jackson to be supportive of such employee behaviors include

> . . . selecting highly skilled individuals, giving employees more discretion, using minimal controls, making a greater investment in human resources, providing more resources for experimentation, allowing and even rewarding occasional failure, and appraising performance for its long-run consequences.

In short, human resource practices can and will have a major impact on the degree to which firms effectively employ entrepreneurial teams. These practices will exert their influence through such wide-ranging factors as team composition, motivation, competencies, satisfaction, performance, and success.

▬ ▬ ▬ ▬ ▬ ▬ ▬ ▬ ▬
PROJECT TEAM
MANAGEMENT

Once formed and charged with its performance goals, the project team must be managed effectively. While the field of small group dynamics is mature (Cartwright and Zander 1960), a growing body of theory is emerging on the specialized field of engineering project teams. Thamhain and Wilemon (1987) have articulated 14 recommendations for effective project team management. These recommendations relate to understanding, communication, team development, project integration, staffing, team building, problem solving, and senior management support.

Concerning general models of project management, Pinto and Slevin have developed the 10-factor Project Implementation Profile (PIP) (Pinto and Slevin 1987a, 1988a, 1988b, 1989; Slevin and Pinto 1986, 1987; Schultz, Slevin, and Pinto 1987).

The 10 critical success factors in the PIP are as follows:

1. Project Mission. Initial clarity of goals and general direction.

2. Top Management Support. Willingness of top management to provide the necessary resources and authority/power for project success.
3. Project Schedule/Plan. Detailed specification of the individual action steps required for project implementation.
4. Client Consultation. Communication, consultation, and active listening to all impacted parties.
5. Personnel. Recruitment, selection, and training of the necessary personnel for the project team.
6. Technical Tasks. Availability of the required technology and expertise to accomplish the specific technical action steps.
7. Client Acceptance. The act of "selling" the final project to its intended users.
8. Monitoring and Feedback. Timely provision of comprehensive control information at each stage in the implementation process.
9. Communication. Provision of an appropriate network and necessary data to all key actors in the project implementation.
10. Trouble Shooting. Ability to handle unexpected crises and deviations from plan. (Pinto and Slevin 1987b, 3–4)

These factors have proven to be effective tools for successful project team management in both research and consulting scenarios. This model provides the project team manager with a broad template for tracking and managing key project factors.

As we move into the interpersonal side of management and into more organic and flexible team structures, it becomes clear that the exercise of control must be accomplished in "softer" ways. Takeuchi and Nonaka (1986, 143) propose seven ways for exercising subtle control in the new product development process:

1. Selecting the right people for the project, based on small group dynamics issues.
2. Creating an open work environment.
3. Encouraging engineers to go out into the field and listen to customers.
4. Establishing an evaluation and reward system based on group performance.
5. Managing the difference in rhythm throughout the development process.
6. Tolerating and anticipating mistakes.
7. Encouraging suppliers to be self-organized and involved early in the design process.

Nonaka (1988, 9) argues for the concept of compressive management, in which "top management creates a vision or dream, and middle management creates and implements concrete concepts to solve and transcend the contradictions arising from gaps between what exists at the moment and what management hopes to create." This process, called "middle-up-down management," places a heavy burden on middle management teams to perform both creative and operating tasks in the new product development process. It essentially implies a more proactive perspective from the standpoint of the project team.

Mohrman and Ledford (1985, 417) have proposed four guidelines to enhance group functioning:

1. Participation groups must include or have access to the necessary skills and knowledge to address problems systematically.
2. Formalized procedures should enhance the effectiveness of the group.
3. Participation groups should be integrated horizontally and vertically with the rest of the organization.
4. The groups should be a regular part of the organization rather than special or extra activities.

In summary, more and more management tools and techniques have been developed for effective team management. The challenge for the organizations of the 1990s is to place priority on team performance in order to ensure organizational effectiveness.

FOLLOWERSHIP

While much has been written about leadership and leadership functions, every good high-performance team requires effective followers. It is arguable that one of the positive aspects of Japanese management is the willingness of individuals to follow and engage in collective efforts. In the United States the appropriate saying may be "the squeaky wheel gets the grease"; in Japan it may be more appropriate to say "the protruding nail gets hammered down." Kelley (1988, 144) proposes four essential qualities of effective followers: 1) they can manage themselves; 2) they are good organizational citizens who subscribe to the organization's purposes and principles; 3) they actively seek to ensure their competence in carrying out the tasks asked of them; and 4) they are honest, credible, and courageous.

He argues that followers' skills could be enhanced through a program of follower training that might include topics such as: improving independent thinking; self-management; improving one's ability to work with others; aligning personal and organizational goals; improving commitment to the organization and peers; and moving between the leader and follower roles.

In the effective team of the future, there will be less difference between leaders and followers. People will easily slide into and out of these roles. Parker (1990) suggests that there are four types of team players: 1) *contributors* are dependable, hard-working persons who furnish the team with useful task-related information; 2) *collaborators* are goal-oriented, "big picture" persons who are willing to work outside of their defined roles in order to enable the team to fulfill its mission ; 3) *communicators* are process-oriented persons who facilitate team functioning through, for example, drawing all team members into group discussions and engaging in effective listening, consensus building, and conflict resolution activities ; 4) *challengers* are persons who often play a devil's advocate role in team functioning through questioning the team's objectives, methods, and ethics. Each of these followership styles has its own strengths and weaknesses, and each may be more appropriate under different circumstances.

CROSS-FUNCTIONAL COOPERATION

As the functional areas of the firm have become more complex and specialized, cross-functional cooperation has emerged as an important area of study. Earlier, many researchers have studied this phenomenon as a dyadic process, usually looking at interactions between two functional areas such as marketing and R&D (Souder 1988), marketing and production (Clare and Sanford 1984), or marketing and finance (Anderson 1981). Temporary task forces that are key to long-term cross-functional cooperation have also been examined (Zmud and McLaughlin 1989). Coalition building across internal constituencies represents a critical element behind the development of cooperative efforts (Kanter 1983, 1988). A number of researchers, using a variety of terms, have studied various aspects of this problem : i.e., coordination (Argote 1982 ; Van De Ven, Delbecq, and Koenig 1976); collaboration (Trist 1977); cooperation (Schermerhorn 1975 ; Sherif and Sherif 1969); and integration (Gupta, Raj, and Wilemon 1986 ; Lawrence and Lorsch 1967).

Pinto, Pinto, and Prescott (1990), in an empirical study on cross-functional cooperation, have proposed the following antecedent, implementation, and consequence variables:

Antecedents :
- Superordinate goals
- Physical proximity
- Accessibility
- Project team rules and procedures
- Organizational rules and procedures

Implementation :
- Cross-functional cooperation

Consequences :
- Task outcomes
- Psychosocial outcomes

They found that superordinate goals, physical proximity of team members to each other, and project team rules and procedures requiring cooperation were significant predictors of cross-functional cooperation. Similarly, cross-functional cooperation was directly and positively related to both task (project team success) and psychosocial (job satisfaction and team cohesion) outcomes. Path analysis also showed positive indirect effects between superordinate goals, project team rules and procedures, and the dependent variables of task and psychosocial outcomes. Clearly, the phenomenon of cross-functional cooperation will receive additional research scrutiny over the next decade, resulting in, we trust, increased understanding by the entrepreneurship research community.

INFORMATION TECHNOLOGY

Information technology will continue to play a larger and larger role in successful high-performance team management. One of the major functions of teams is the fulfillment of the organizational integration function (Lawrence and Lorsch 1967). Rockart and Short (1989) argue that these human integrators of old, people who coordinated the concurrence of effort between adjacent functions of the value-added chain, are being replaced by electronic networks, computers, and data bases performing this integrative function. Boeing, for example, uses a massive computer system with associated data bases to assist its project teams in their integration efforts. As computer power becomes more and more distributed, and networking becomes more routine and less difficult, the high-performance team of the future may be free to spend more time on creative pursuits and less time on information sharing activities. State-of-the-art meeting and conferencing technology will continue to enhance team performance even though members might be distributed widely around the world.

ROLE OF REDUNDANCY

While the U.S. manufacturing organization of the 60s and 70s prided itself on efficiency and the elimination of redundancy, the rapid change of the world today might require the deliberate redundancy of information and task. Japanese organizations have intentionally overlapping functions. There is deliberate ambiguity and overlap across functional areas, circumstances which highlight an explicit need for coordination and information sharing. Nonaka (1990) argues that information redundancy is a factor which is fundamental to the innovation process. He defines information redundancy as "a condition where some types of excess information are shared in addition to the minimal amount of requisite information held by every individual, department (group), or organization in performing a specific function" (28).

He proposes that innovation can be enhanced through the deliberate inclusion of redundancy at the following levels:

● Project team
● Interdepartmental development process
● Interorganizational relations with suppliers
● Potential command (potential to create and suggest a solution to the problem at hand regardless of the individual's status in the corporate hierarchy)

In addition he proposes that mutual investigation should be promoted, and emphasis should be placed on building trust across the organization. On a recent trip to Japan, the authors were struck by the high degree of value placed on information sharing. Where an American manager might be punished for sharing information with a "competitive department," this is a highly valued norm in the Japanese management structure. A tremendous amount of data are continuously gathered and communicated both horizontally and vertically across the organization. The high-performance team of the future will deliberately structure redundancy of information and effort into its processes.

THE TEAM AND PROCESS INNOVATION

In the world of the 1990s, manufacturing organizations must continuously improve their processes in order to stay competitive. The shrinking product life cycle dictates the fundamental need for constantly upgrading the efficiency and effectiveness of manufacturing processes. In fact, some have argued that the ability of organizations to learn (that is, to engage in management innovation) is the only sustainable competitive advantage (Stata 1989). The Japanese have been applauded for their ability to collectively engage in continuous process innovation. They engage in a process of "continuously leveling up": throughout the culture there appears to be a fundamental satisfaction with continuous incremental progress towards goals. This contrasts strikingly with the American approach of setting discontinuous goals and working in an "isolated" fashion towards achieving them. Mitsubishi Electric is in the third year of a campaign which involves 19 product lines and several teams. Awards are given to good team performance, and employees spend substantial amounts of time after hours and on weekends discussing in small groups ways to improve manufacturing processes. Mitsubishi Electric's next campaign will focus on the "flow of information." It will include a review and assessment of:

● Speed of communication
● Timing of information
● Accuracy of information

Even the management processes are continuously being improved. The continuous improvement in process concept of Kaizen (Imai 1986) is integrated throughout the culture. With the increasing interdependency of organizational systems and the increasing complexity of technologies, the entrepreneurial team will be the primary vehicle for continuous process innovation in the 90s.

THE TEAM AND PRODUCT INNOVATION

The team also appears to be central in new product development and commercialization (Nevens, Summe, and Uttal 1990). Takeuchi and Nonaka (1986) use the sports-based metaphor of a team in a rugby match to epitomize a holistic approach to today's new product development. Roberts and Fusfeld (1981) argue that there are five different work roles that are critical to innovation. They are :

- Idea generating
- Entrepreneuring or championing
- Project leading
- Gatekeeping
- Sponsoring or coaching

As one can see, each of these roles is most likely to be accomplished in a team or small group setting. Reich (1987) argues that the secret to competitiveness in the future will be collective entrepreneurship, where individual skills are integrated into a group. This collective capacity to innovate will be a driver of the new product development process.

PROBLEMS WITH TEAMS

Although teams are an effective and essential medium for the implementation of innovation and change in organizations, they are not without their problems. One of the first problems (which relates directly to team processes) is the phenomenon of *groupthink* (Janis 1972). Although this theory is still under empirical testing and verification (Park 1989; Callaway and Esser 1984; Callaway, Marriott, and Esser 1985; Leana 1985; Moorhead and Montanari 1986), it has a validity that seems directly applicable to teams.

Ironically, the more cohesive and creative teams become, the more likely they are to suffer from the dysfunctional consequences of isolation and groupthink. Briefly, *groupthink* denotes a phenomenon whereby the members of highly cohesive groups tend to lose their capacity to make critical evaluative judgements. The desire to maintain group cohesiveness and to avoid unpleasant disagreements often results in too much importance being attached to concurrence and too little to the realistic appraisal of alternative courses of action. The symptoms of groupthink can include the illusion of group invulnerability (which fosters excessive risk taking and unwarranted optimism), belief in the inherent morality of the group's decisions, rationalization of unpleasant or disconfirming data, stereotyping the group's opponents as weak, evil, or stupid, and the illusion of unanimity (whereby silence is interpreted as consent).

Related to the groupthink issue, one of the early and frequently replicated findings concerning small group dynamics concerns pressures towards conformity in the group (Asch 1952). These pressures become especially strong as group cohesiveness grows, and creativity may consequently be reduced. High-performance teams by their very nature must maintain high-level creativity. This can be an ongoing problem.

In addition, although teams can be quite effective in accomplishing complex innovations, they can also be quite inefficient in human terms. Having individuals subsume their separate goals for larger group goals can exact a significant human cost. This cost can be both expensive for the organization, and discouraging or debilitating for its members (Nonaka 1990).

And finally, we should not be complacent in assessing our understanding of the complexity of the phenomenon of team behavior. It is hard to disagree with Rockart and Short (1989, 9) when they say, "Unfortunately, the team-based literature to date is highly speculative. As a general model of organizational structure, it leaves many questions unanswered. Primary among these are the long-term implications of organizing in a manner that moves primary reporting relationships away from the more usual hierarchical, functional, geographic, or product structures."

In summary, although it appears teams are here to stay and will be an essential part of organizations in the 1990s, substantial additional understanding is needed so that we may have a better anticipation of problems that might develop.

▬ ▬ ▬ ▬ ▬ ▬ ▬ ▬
KEY RESEARCH
QUESTIONS

At the risk of sounding overly simplistic, we will propose a general formulation of research questions that attempts to gain further insight into the relation among the variables in the research model. In general, the form of the fundamental research question is: What is the effect of _____ on project team performance?

The blank may be completed by using any of the research variables in the model. For example, what is the effect of the HRM function of staffing on project team performance? For another example, what is the impact of project management techniques on project team performance?

In addition, we suggest the following significant research questions in this area to stimulate discussion and review of the direction the field should be taking:

1. How do organizations encourage creative individuals to work as a team?
2. What types of teams need to be actively led, and what types can be self-managed?
3. What are the attributes of organizational systems (e.g., the MIS system, the decision support system) which effectively support high-performing teams?
4. What are the personnel selection requirements for creating and maintaining high-performance teams?
5. What are the characteristics of effective personnel appraisal systems for teams?
6. What are the major organizational process-related barriers to team effectiveness?
7. In which types of ill-structured situations are teams a generally effective decision-making tool?
8. Through what mechanisms do organizations recognize the need for special purpose teams and provide for their creation?
9. What typically accounts for the success of team-based operations in some organizations and the failure of these operations in others?
10. What policies and procedures ensure the smooth and effective flow of organizational members to and from special purpose teams?

These questions are not intended to be exhaustive in defining key issues for the future, but rather are presented to suggest possible directions for future research.

The accurate assessment of the capacity of an organization to support the creation and maintenance of high-performance teams will be critical to the further accumulation of knowledge on team functioning. Progress has been made by Kuratko, Montagno, and Hornsby (1990) in the development of an intrapreneurial assessment instrument. The purpose of the intrapreneurial assessment instrument (IAI) is to identify the dimensional structure of organizations with respect to their ability to foster intrapreneurial activity. This instrument includes 21 items which load on the following three factors:

● Management support for intrapreneurship
● Organizational structure
● Reward and research availability

Would it not be possible to develop a project team performance assessment instrument (PTPAI)? The purpose of this instrument would be not to measure the dependent variables of project team performance directly, but rather to develop an assessment of the various independent variables listed in the above models so that they might be related to various measures of project team and firm performance. Recently Ahlbrandt and Slevin (1990) have developed a 12-factor model of industrial competitiveness. It appears as though it might be useful at this time in the field's development to propose a project team performance audit of some sort that would be able to assess key variables impacting on project team success. If such an instrument were developed with reasonable reliabilities and validities, it could be used across a variety of organizations in diverse research projects to help us learn more about the creation and maintenance of high-performance teams.

IMPLICATIONS FOR THE FUTURE

It is possible to suggest the direction in which future research and teaching will move concerning high-performance teams. We are prepared to make the following conjectures.

Teams are here to stay.

It appears clear that the global environmental and technological changes which have occurred in the past decade are now providing firms with challenges and problems that can only be overcome through the use of the team structure. Teams will most likely grow in terms of size and complexity as firms attempt to respond to environmental challenges. Employee involvement, both financially and psychologically, will become a more important tactic for successful organizational performance and will increase in the future (Lawler 1986).

Management education must change.

Traditional MBA programs have been criticized for having insufficient focus on issues such as leadership, interpersonal skills, communications skills, and managing people (Porter and McKibbin 1988). An increased emphasis throughout education and business must be placed on managerial competencies in general (Vaill 1990). If managers are to perform effectively in the team-oriented environment of the future, then business schools should attempt to be responsive to this need.

Researchers studying high-performance teams must move more into the field.

While small group research made great progress in the 50s and 60s in laboratory settings, it appears that the complexity and challenges faced by high-performance teams provide a much less clear research environment. Academics studying entrepreneurship must be prepared to move out into the field to talk with team members and to share experiences with them. Only by making contact with real, live organizations and project teams will we be able to better understand how to manage them effectively. The action research model may be appropriate, and the researcher may even serve as a small group facilitator in this context.

To summarize, this chapter has examined the role of teams in the entrepreneurial process. A model of team creation and performance has been presented, and various concepts relevant to team functioning have been discussed. It is clear that the challenge of studying the creation and maintenance of high-performance teams will be an important one for entrepreneurship researchers over the next several decades.

REFERENCES

Ahlbrandt, R., and D. Slevin 1990 *Total competitiveness audit (TCA)*. Pittsburgh, Penn. : Katz Graduate School of Business, Univ. of Pittsburgh.

Amara, R. 1990 New directions for innovation. *Futures* 22 (2, March) : 142–152.

Anderson, P. F. 1981 Marketing investment analysis. In *Research in marketing*, ed. J. M. Sheth, Vol. 4, 1–37. Greenwich, Conn. : JAI Press.

Argote, L. 1982 Input uncertainty and organizational coordination in hospital emergency units. *Administrative Science Quarterly* 27 (3) : 420–434.

Asch, S. E. 1952 *Social psychology*. Englewood Cliffs, N.J. : Prentice-Hall, Inc.

Bailey, J. E. 1984 Intrapraneurship : Source of high growth startups or passing fad ? In *Frontiers of entrepreneurship research*, eds. J. A. Hornaday, F. A. Tarpley, Jr., J. A. Timmons, and K. H. Vesper, 358–367. Wellesley, Mass. : Babson College.

Berger, S., M. L. Dertouzos, R. K. Lester, R. M. Solow, and L. C. Thurow 1989 Toward a new industrial America. *Scientific American* 260 (6) : 39–47.

Bower, J. L., and T. M. Hout 1988 Fast-cycle capability for competitive power. *Harvard Business Review* 66 (6, November-December) : 110–118.

Burns, T., and G. M. Stalker 1968 *The management of innovation*. 2d ed. London : Tavistock.

Callaway, M. R., and J. K. Esser 1984 Groupthink : Effects of cohesiveness and problem-solving on group decision making. *Social Behavior and Personality* 12 (2) : 157–164.

Callaway, M. R., R. G. Marriott, and J. K. Esser 1985 Effects of dominance on group decision making : Toward a stress reduction explanation of groupthink. *Journal of Personality and Social Psychology* 49 (4) : 949–952.

Carlyle, R. 1990 The tomorrow organization. *Datamation* 36 (3, February) : 22–29.

Cartwright, D., and A. Zander, eds. 1960 *Group dynamics : Research and theory*. 2d ed. N.Y. : Harper & Row.

Clare, D. A., and D. G. Sanford 1984 Cooperation and conflict between industrial sales and production. *Industrial Marketing Management* 13 (3, August) : 163–169.

Cleland, D. I., and D. P. Slevin 1989 A strategy for the analysis and enhancement of engineeering and technology management. December. Proposal to the National Science Foundation.

Cornwall, J. R., and B. Perlman 1990 *Organizational entrepreneurship.* Homewood, Ill. : Irwin.

Covin, J. G., and D. P. Slevin 1989 Strategic management of small firms in hostile and benign environments. *Strategic Management Journal* 10 (1) : 75–87.

Dumaine, B. 1989 How managers can succeed through speed. *Fortune* 119 (4, February) : 54–59.

Faas, F. A. M. J. 1985 How to solve communication problems on the R and D interface. *Journal of Management Studies* 22 (1) : 83–102.

Feldman, S. P. 1989 The broken wheel : The inseparability of autonomy and control in innovation within organizations. *Journal of Management Studies* 26 (2, March) : 83–102.

Flint, B. 1984 Design team has a system for getting new microcomputer from drawing board to marketplace in 18 months. *Industrial Engineering* 16 (9, September) : 36–40.

Gleick, J. 1988 *Chaos : Making a new science.* N.Y. : Penguin Books.

Gosselin, R. 1985 Probing into task interdependencies : The case of physicians in a teaching hospital. *Journal of Management Studies* 22 (5, September) : 466–497.

Grossi, G. 1990 Promoting innovation in a big business. *Long Range Planning* 23 (1, February) : 41–52.

Gupta, A., S. P. Raj, and D. Wilemon 1986 A model for studying R&D-marketing interface in the product innovation process. *Journal of Marketing* 50 (2, April) : 7–17.

Guth, W. D., and A. Ginsberg 1990 Guest editors' introduction : Corporate entrepreneurship. *Strategic Management Journal* 11 (Summer 1990 Special Issue) : 5–15.

Hackman, J. R. 1990 *Groups that work (and those that don't).* San Francisco : Jossey-Bass Publishers.

Hisrich, R. D., and M. P. Peters 1989 *Entrepreneurship : Starting, developing, and managing a new enterprise.* Homewood, Ill. : Irwin.

Imai, M. 1986 *Kaizen : The key to Japan's competitive success.* N.Y. : Random House.

Janis, I. L. 1972 *Groupthink : Psychological studies of policy decisions and fiascoes.* Boston : Houghton Mifflin.

Kanter, R. M. 1983 *The change masters.* N.Y. : Simon and Schuster.

1988 When a thousand flowers bloom : Structural, collective, and social conditions for innovation in organization [sic]. In *Research in organizational behavior,* eds. B. M. Staw and L. L. Cummings, Vol. 10, 169–211. Greenwich, Conn. : JAI Press.

Kelley, R. E. 1988 In praise of followers. *Harvard Business Review* 66 (6, November-December) : 142–148.

Khandwalla, P. N. 1977 *The design of organizations.* N.Y. : Harcourt, Brace Jovanovich.

Kidder, Tracy 1981 *The soul of a new machine.* Boston : Little, Brown.

Kiechel, W., III 1990 The organization that learns. *Fortune* 121 (6, March) : 133–136.

Kilmann, R. H. 1989 *Managing beyond the quick fix.* San Francisco : Jossey-Bass Publishers.

Kono, T. 1984 *Strategy and structure of Japanese enterprises.* Houndmills, Basingstoke, and London : Macmillan.

Kotkin, J. 1985 The revenge of the Fortune 500. *Inc.* 7 (8, August) : 38–44.

Kuratko, D. F., R. V. Montagno, and J. S. Hornsby 1990 Developing an intrapraneurial assessment instrument for an effective corporate entrepreneurial environment. *Strategic Management Journal* 11 (Summer, Special Issue) : 49–58.

Lawler, E. E., III 1986 *High-involvement management.* San Francisco: Jossey-Bass Publishers.

Lawrence, P. R., and J. W. Lorsch 1967 *Organization and environment.* Boston: Division of Research, Graduate School of Business Administration, Harvard Univ.

Leana, C. R. 1985 A partial test of Janis' groupthink model: Effects of group cohesiveness and leader behavior on defective decision making. *Journal of Management* 11 (1): 5–17.

McKinney, G., and M. McKinney 1989 Forget the corporate umbrella: Entrepreneurs shine in the rain. *Sloan Management Review* 30 (4, Summer): 77–82.

Miles, R. H. 1980 *Macro organizational behavior.* Santa Monica, Cal.: Goodyear Publishing Co.

Miller, D. 1983 The correlates of entrepreneurship in three types of firms. *Management Science* 29 (7, July): 770–791.

Mohrman, S. A., and G. E. Ledford 1985 The design and use of effective employee participation groups: Implications for human resource management. *Human Resource Management* 24 (4, Winter): 413–428.

Moorhead, G., and J. R. Montanari 1986 An empirical investigation of the groupthink phenomenon. *Human Relations* 39 (5): 399–410.

Nevens, T. M., G. L. Summe, and B. Utal 1990 Commercializing technology: What the best companies do. *Harvard Business Review* 68 (3, May-June): 154–163.

Nonaka, I. 1988 Toward middle-up-down management: Accelerating information creation. *Sloan Management Review* 29 (3, Spring): 9–18.

1990 Redundant, overlapping organization: A Japanese approach to managing the innovation process. *California Management Review* 32 (3, Spring): 27–38.

Park, W.-W. 1989 A comprehensive study of Janis' groupthink model: Questionnaire development and empirical tests. Ph.D. diss., Katz Graduate School of Business, University of Pittsburgh.

Parker, G. M. 1990 *Team players and teamwork: The new competitive business strategy.* San Francisco: Jossey-Bass Publishers.

Pinto, J. K., and D. P. Slevin 1987a Critical factors in successful project implementation. *IEEE Transactions on Engineering Management* 34 (1): 22–27.

1987b *Project implementation profile (PIP).* Pittsburgh, PA: Innodyne, Inc.

1988a Project success: Definitions and measurement techniques. *Project Management Journal* 19 (1, February): 67–71.

1988b Critical success factors across the project life cycle. *Project Management Journal* 19 (3, June): 67–75.

1989 Critical success factors in R&D projects. *Research — Technology Management* 32 (1, January): 31–35.

Pinto, M. B., J. K. Pinto, and J. E. Prescott 1990 Antecedents and consequences of project team cross-functional cooperation. College of Business Administration, University of Maine. Working paper.

Porter, L. W., and L. E. McKibbin 1988 *Management education and development: Drift or thrust into the 21st century?* N.Y.: McGraw-Hill.

Quinn, J. B. 1988 Ford: Team Taurus. Amos Tuck School, Dartmouth College, Hanover, New Hampshire. Case study.

Reich, R. B. 1987 Entrepreneurship reconsidered: The team as hero. *Harvard Business Review* 65 (3, May-June): 77–83.

Roberts, E. B., and A. R. Fusfeld 1981 Staffing the innovative technology-based organization. *Sloan Management Review* 22 (3, Spring): 19–33.

Rockart, J. F., and J. E. Short 1989 IT in the 1990s: Managing organizational interdependence. *Sloan Management Review* 30 (2, Winter): 7–17.

Rule, E. G., and D. W. Irwin 1988 Fostering intrapreneurship: The new competitive edge. *Journal of Business Strategy* 9 (3, May-June): 44–47.

Schermerhorn, J. R. 1975 Determinants of interorganizational cooperation. *Academy of Management Journal* 18 (4, December): 846–856.

Schuler, R. S. 1986 Fostering and facilitating entrepreneurship in organizations: Implications for organization structure and human resource management practices. *Human Resource Management* 25 (4, Winter): 607–629.

Schuler, R. S., and S. E. Jackson 1987 Linking competitive strategies with human resource management practices. *Academy of Management Executive* 1 (13, August): 207–219.

Schultz, R. L., D. P. Slevin, and J. K. Pinto 1987 Strategy and tactics in a process model of project implementation. *Interfaces* 17 (3, May-June): 34–46.

Sherif, M., and C. W. Sherif 1969 *Social psychology.* N.Y.: Harper & Row.

Sherwood, J. J. 1988 Creating work cultures with competitive advantage. *Organizational Dynamics* 16 (3, Winter): 4–27.

Shrivastava, P., and W. E. Souder 1987 The strategic management of technological innovations: A review and a model. *Journal of Management Studies* 24 (1, January): 25–41.

Slevin, D. P. 1989 *The whole manager.* N.Y.: AMACOM.

Slevin, D. P., and J. G. Covin 1990 Juggling entrepreneurial style and organizational structure: How to get your act together. *Sloan Management Review* 31 (2, Winter): 43–53.

Slevin, D. P., and J. K. Pinto 1986 The project implementation profile: New tool for project managers. *Project Management Journal* 17 (4, September): 57–70.

1987 Balancing strategy and tactics in project implementation. *Sloan Management Review* 29 (1, Fall): 33–41.

Souder, W. E. 1988 Managing relations between R&D and marketing in new product development projects. *Journal of Product Innovation Management* 5: 6–19.

Stata, R. 1989 Organizational learning: The key to management innovation. *Sloan Management Review* 30 (3): 63–74.

Stauffer, R. N. 1988 Converting customers to partners at Ingersoll. *Manufacturing Engineering* 101 (3, September): 41–44.

Stevenson, H. H., and J. C. Jarillo 1990 A paradigm of entrepreneurship: Entrepreneurial management. *Strategic Management Journal* 11 (Summer, Special Issue): 17–27.

Stevenson, H. H., M. J. Roberts, and H. I. Grousbeck 1989 *New business ventures and the entrepreneur.* 3d ed. Homewood, Ill.: Irwin.

Stewart, A. 1989 *Team entrepreneurship.* Newbury Park, Cal.: Sage Publications.

Stinson, T. 1990 *Teamwork in real engineering.* Machine Design 62 (March 22): 99–104.

Takeuchi, H., and I. Nonaka 1986 The new new product development game. *Harvard Business Review* 64 (1, January-February): 137–146.

Thamhain, H. J., and D. L. Wilemon 1987 Building high performing engineering project teams. *IEEE Transactions on Engineering Management* 34 (3): 130–137.

Thompson, J. D. 1967 *Organizations in action.* N.Y.: McGraw-Hill.

Trist, E. 1977 Collaboration in work settings: A personal perspective. *Journal of Applied Behavioral Science* 13 (3, July-August-September): 268–278.

Vaill, P. B. 1990 *Managing as a performing art: New ideas for a world of chaotic change.* San Francisco: Jossey-Bass Publishers.

Van de Ven, A. H., A. L. Delbecq, and R. Koenig, Jr. 1976 Determinants of coordination modes within organizations. *American Sociological Review* 41 (2, April): 322–338.

Waterman, R. M. 1987 *The renewal factor.* Toronto and New York: Bantam Books.

Zmud, R. W., and C. P. McLaughlin 1989 "That's not my job": Managing secondary tasks effectively. *Sloan Management Review* 30 (2, Winter): 29–36.

15

Financing the New Venture: A Report on Recent Research

David J. Brophy

●

Entrepreneurship researchers have begun to part the veil of mystery which has been considered to surround the funding of new ventures. In the process, we are participating in a broader scholarly advancement: the gradual reconciliation of the positions of the founder/manager and the venture capital investor in project structuring, valuation, and development over time. The purpose of this chapter is to illustrate the progress made in this respect in recent years and to suggest directions in which continued efforts may yield further results.

PREVIOUS RESEARCH REVIEWS

In preparing this chapter, reference was made to three earlier survey efforts of this type: two chapters titled "Venture Capital Research" (Brophy 1982, 1986), the first published in the *Encyclopedia of Entrepreneurship* and the second published in *The Art and Science of Entrepreneurship*; and an article titled "Venture Capital Research: Past, Present and Future" (Fried and Hisrich 1988), published in *Entrepreneurship Theory and Practice.*

The first two of these chapters reported on work published largely through the *Frontiers of Entrepreneurship Research* and several other journals. The Fried and Hisrich article documents venture capital research published between 1981 and 1987. It reflects the major changes over the period, including the increasing importance of the Babson Conference, the appearance of the *Journal of Business Venturing*, and the growing interest of a broad base of scholars in the issue of entrepreneurial finance, venture capital in general, and issues and problems involved in financing the new venture.

An important point made in the Fried and Hisrich article is that concepts, points of departure, and methodology which will help us to understand the venture capital finance and investment process are likely to emanate from a variety of disciplines and fields of theory as well as from the field of finance. The widely accepted purpose of venture capital is, after all, to "build businesses," and no single discipline should claim to possess the one true faith in developing an understanding of that process. In the research results reviewed for this chapter, it is clear that a considerable amount of progress has been made through application of this multidisciplinary approach over the past 10 years.

▬ ▬ ▬ ▬ ▬ ▬ ▬ ▬
METHODOLOGICAL
ADVANCES

An important part of the progress made over the past 10 years is reflected in the advances which have been made in methodology employed. These advances have occurred along three tracks: the generation of studies based on surveys and in-depth personal interviews; studies based on commercially maintained data bases; and studies based upon applications of theoretical constructs from various fields of study such as finance. Comments on each of these are presented in the following discussion.

Empirical Studies from Surveys and Personal Interviews

Until recently, it has been very difficult for researchers to obtain relevant data and information with which to conduct scholarly research on financing new ventures. Because new ventures and, for the most part, the venture capital investment entities which fund them, are private concerns, the venture capital finance and investment process was virtually secret and protected from view by the private nature of the entities involved.

From the research aspect, much of what we believed in those early days about the process of funding new ventures was based on evidence drawn from small samples, sometimes based on personal acquaintance. This often produced information which was incomplete, typically partial and anecdotal, and usually unsuited to verification, comparison, replication, and extension. Not only did this lengthen the life of the new venture financing puzzle, it also proved to be a discouraging barrier to academic scholarship, particularly to those facing a university clock for contract renewal, promotion, or tenure.

Fortunately, this condition has gradually improved. The job of information development by survey and in-person and telephone interview has been costly and time-consuming both for researcher and subject, but the results are invaluable. Motivations running from a need for understanding at congressional hearings to a willingness to cooperate with legitimate scholarship have gradually impelled venture capitalists and founder/managers of new ventures to disclose certain information publicly, and to "stand still" for scholarly examination. As the wealth of published research regarding new ventures attests, the scholarly community has responded energetically to the opportunity presented by this openness.

Empirical Studies from Established Data Bases

Through work based on access to data bases which provide information on new venture finance, researchers have been able to extend the generality of their findings across cases and across time. Several of these data bases are identified by their ownership and are concisely described below.

Venture Economics, Inc.

Venture Economics gathers data from venture capital investment companies concerning their funding and investment activities. Compilations and analyses of this information are published monthly in the the *Venture Capital Journal* and in special regular and occasional studies derived from the same flow of data. The *Journal* represents a major source of data and information on the activities of venture capital investment firms and their portfolio companies.

I.D.D. Corporation.

I.D.D. Corporation, publisher of the *Investment Dealers' Digest*, obtains information from the SEC on initial public offerings of securities and on aftermarket levels of price and volume as well as capitalization changes in these securities. This information is published twice monthly in *Going Public: The IPO Reporter*, with related information also available through the *Investment Dealers' Digest* corporate data base. I.D.D. also gathers detailed information on privately placed securities — including venture capital investments — and publishes this information twice monthly in *Private Placements.* Both IPO and private placements data are available on a current basis through on-line facilities.

The Center for Research in Securities Prices (CRSP) at the University of Chicago.

The CRSP tapes provide daily return information on securities traded publicly on the New York and American Stock Exchanges and on the Over-The-Counter market. The information is kept current, adjustments for changes in capitalization are made, and the integrity of the information is very well maintained. The tapes are available to academic institutions by subscription.

Venture Capital Network, Inc.

Professor William Wetzel of the University of New Hampshire has created an information and contact network consisting of new venture founder/ managers and individual investor "angels." Initially confined to the New England region, the network data base has been expanded to include participants from other parts of the country.

By gaining access to these data sets, researchers have been able to perform cross-sectional and longitudinal quantitative analysis using "hard data" previously unavailable. This has greatly expanded the opportunities available for research and proven attractive to scholars interested in this field.

The increase in precision, consistency, and continuity through the kinds of research mentioned here provides promise for those who have worked for years with only "hearsay" evidence on certain aspects of new venture finance. It may also expand our understanding of the longer-term development and growth patterns of entrepreneurially-generated firms. Because the data are readily available, albeit at a fee, scholarly use of it is likely to grow.

Application of Theoretical Constructs from Finance and Strategic Management

Scholars have begun to recognize that the market process through which private finance is negotiated between investors and entrepreneurially-driven emerging growth companies offers fertile ground in which to test and apply theories from a variety of fields, among them finance, psychology, organization theory and strategic management. As the ability to identify and track the structural and operating characteristics and performance results of specific firms is increased, the payoff from multidisciplinary research stands to be enriched. An associated benefit is that research on entrepreneurial themes will thereby find its way increasingly into mainstream journals in the various traditional functional fields.

━━ ━━ ━━ ━━ ━━ ━━ ━━
REVIEW OF PUBLISHED RESEARCH

The review of research presented below is organized according to the following topics:

1. Characteristics of new venture investors (the founder/manager team, informal venture investors or "angels," and formally organized venture capital funds).

2. Characteristic new venture factors found to be used by investors as *ex ante* criteria for investment decisions, and factors found to be associated *ex post* with the success or failure of new ventures either to obtain financing or to succeed operationally over time.
3. The investment process, including the negotiation, structuring, and valuation of new venturing financing deals.
4. Monitoring the new venture and making later round investments in the company.
5. Transitions and exits, including the sale of all or part of the new venture by strategic alliance, merger, outright sale, leveraged buyout, or initial public offering.

This set of topics forms a progression which tracks the sequence of financing-related events that occur over the life cycle of the new venture as it moves through its "emerging growth company" stages toward maturity. This approach shows which aspects of the new venture financing process have so far attracted our research efforts, the areas in which we are generating some understanding, and those in which research potential exists.

Characteristics of New Venture Investors

An early example of this type of research was a Babson Conference paper based on the original investment surveys of National Venture Capital Association member firms over the years 1977–1980 (Brophy 1981). This study showed the dramatic increase in the volume of venture capital invested during each year of the study period by these firms, along with information on its distribution by type of investment and life cycle stage of investee company.

At about the same time, Timmons and Bygrave in cooperation with Venture Economics, Inc. produced a number of papers which have been very important to our understanding of the new venture funding process. These papers demonstrated differences by degree of innovativeness in the ways in which venture capital investment firms dealt with investment opportunities and the sensitivity of the investment process to macro- and microeconomic factors. The importance of the Venture Economics, Inc. data is further reflected in the breakthrough work done by Bygrave, Fast, Khoylian, Vincent, and Yue (1988) on measuring returns on venture capital funds. The compilation and analyses of this analytically appropriate information has permitted institutional investors, venture capital fund managers, and the founders and managers of emerging growth companies to have a common view of the economic performance of the venture capital investment market since 1978. Continued analysis of these data promises to provide the ability to track venture capital costs and rate of return performance over time, perhaps making more efficient the acquisition of growth capital by emerging firms at all stages of their lives.

Through survey and interview studies, researchers have provided an increasingly well-ordered understanding of the structural arrangements and processes through which venture capital investors, both full-time professionals and "angels," go about finding, evaluating, choosing, and managing their investments. A leading example of this type of research is the body of work by Bruno and Tyebjee (1981, 1983, 1984, 1985, 1986a, 1986b).

The pioneering work of Wetzel (1987) has provided insight regarding the role of informal investors ("angels") in the venture capital market. Further studies by Freear and Wetzel (1990) and Aram (1989) have added to our understanding of this important source of new venture finance.

These empirical studies filled an information void by clarifying the processes involved in financing the new venture from the viewpoints of both the venture capitalist and the fund-seeking entrepreneur. An important addition to this body of knowledge was provided by Bygrave (1987). This article demonstrated and explained the nature of inter-firm investment arrangements among venture capital firms across functional and geographic areas.

New Venture Factors as Predictors of Success

Perhaps encouraged by the success of this earlier work, MacMillan and Subbanarasimha, along with co-authors Siegel and Zemann, investigated the venture capital investment decision-making process in a set of two papers (1985, 1987). Their contribution added depth to the findings cited above and showed which specific factors in venture capital proposals were considered most important by professional investors at time of funding. Bridging between individual and institutional sources of capital for young companies, an article by Rea (1989) provides insight concerning the negotiation process at this stage of development.

Other significant studies confirmed and supported these findings. Stuart and Abetti (1987) studied start-up firms in an incubator setting. Buttner and Rosen (1989) provided a useful definition and analysis of the bank loan decision process in testing for bias in this type of new venture financing decision.

An important continuing source of research findings in this area has been generated through articles by Roure and Maidique (1986) and by Roure and Keeley (1990). This research is based on analyses of new venture financing projects drawn from the portfolios of several venture capital investment firms. Despite an acknowledged selection bias in this type of information, the study extends, in a significant way, the research link between scholar and practitioner. This development is critically important to any progress which we hope to make in understanding the operational processes at work in the building of new companies. These two studies provide useful evidence regarding the factors associated with success and failure in new venture development. Such research is potentially very useful in helping entrepreneurs organize their companies and prepare the business plans which they will present to venture capitalist investors.

Another source of information on the providers of new venture funding is a study by Q.E.D. Research Corporation. This study was based on a one-time (i.e., 1986) survey of venture capitalists, and it extracted information from investors on a wide range of pricing, structuring, and rate of return questions, all organized by characteristics of investee firms. For the time period in which the survey was made, the information is insightful and valuable. It would be very useful to have this type of study repeated periodically.

A unique article by Amit, Glosten, and Muller (1990) is related to most of the issues raised in the studies discussed in this section. The article uses several well-established arguments from finance theory to suggest that astute entrepreneurs assess probable results of the new venture as a precondition to accepting a financing partner. Following an argument similar to the well-known "lemons/plums, informed/uninformed investor" notion from the finance literature, the authors suggest that entrepreneurs with inferior deals may be the ones who accept venture capital to finance their new ventures while the ones with superior deals find ways to self-finance with their own funds or debt (as opposed to equity). This is a provocative paper, based upon both observed behavior with respect to new ventures and also the body of well-developed finance theory regarding information, efficient contracts, and capital structure.

The Investment Process, Including Negotiation, Structuring, and Valuation

Several pieces of work which promise to enhance our understanding of how information-signalling, conflict-resolving, and risk-adjusting techniques are factored into the structuring and pricing of new venture finance are discussed in this section.

The treatment of information asymmetries, stakeholder conflict, and uncertainty and risk in investment decisions is an important issue in finance. These issues are particularly important in new venture finance, since such finance generally utilizes securities which are (in the short run) illiquid, and which are exposed to most, if not all, of the agency problems associated with financing contracts in general. New venture finance is typically the result of private negotiation, without regulatory intervention or requirements. While deals tend to be tailored to the circumstances of the project involved, a growing set of identifiable principles and practices has come to be associated with the structuring and pricing of new venture financing. These elements affect the availability and cost of such finance and also define the nature of the formal relationship between the investor and the investee firm. Knowledge of the processes involved is vitally important to an understanding of new venture financing.

Investment analysis typically involves the estimation of a project's cash inflows and outflows projected across time and the determination of the net value of those flows, usually at the time of initial or subsequent investment. The time value of money is recognized by the use of a "risk-free" rate with which to discount the future cash flows to "present value" equivalence, for purposes of comparison with competing projects or with a return on investment target or standard. Integration of risk considerations into this framework is achieved through addition of a "risk premium" to the discount rate.

This relationship is commonly represented in the following general form :

Present Value = Periodic Cash Flow/(1 + i)exp n
$$+$$
Terminal Value/(1 + i)exp n

This approach to economic evaluation of projects is by now well accepted and widely used in business. It contains at least two contentious issues, however, causing many to be skeptical about valuations derived through its use. These are : the accuracy of the estimated future cash flows, and the appropriateness of the discount used to adjust for the time value of money and risk. Even when two or more negotiating parties accept the logic of the methodology, they may differ significantly on estimates of projected cash flow and choice of discount rate.

A solution to this problem is offered by the Capital Asset Pricing Model, which provides an objective, market-based method for determining the "risk premium" appropriate to projects with variability of cash flow or stock return characteristics similar to those of the project involved. CAPM has well-known limitations, and is not easily transferable into the private market setting of new venture finance.

Several publications have addressed these and related issues as they relate to the new venture investment decision-making process. Brophy (1982b) demonstrated how investment risk in a venture project could be assessed by entrepreneur and venture capitalist, managed and partitioned by means of covenants and the structuring characteristics of the venture capital deal, and reflected in the pricing of the securities used in the deal. The approach involves probabilistic simulation of the elements of the business plan as reflected in the financial projections, and offers the advantage of producing multiparameter results (means, variance, other statistical distribution characteristics) for investment returns and other pertinent variables. This type of output permits estimates of uncertainty and risk from the point of view of the investment participants to be quantified.

Khan (1987) designed and compared the results of multiattribute actuarial models with the results of judgements by venture capitalists. Khan used survey data and environmental information in showing the potential benefits of formal decision support systems to venture capital investors. He demonstrated that such decision aids provide useful filtering devices for the large number of proposals processed annually by venture capitalists. A potentially useful extension of this type of approach is presented by Myers (1988).

Mechner (1989) sets forth an alternative approach to the incorporation of risk in venture capital investments. Scenarios weighted by the analyst's estimate of their probability are determined, and their weighted sum is then discounted at the risk-free rate to provide an estimated, risk-adjusted valuation. This approach may be intuitively more appealing to practitioners than probabilistic simulation, even though it also requires estimates of likely outcome scenarios (discrete rather than continuous). Both of these approaches show the importance of the type of analysis done by Khan and by Roure, Keeley, and others cited above — that is, the assessment of key new venture operational factors and their association with success or failure in receipt of funding and on subsequent operating success.

Management decision makers, as well as scholars who argue from a strategic planning perspective, have expressed dissatisfaction with the discounted cash flow approach to risk-adjusted investment analysis (Hayes and Abernathy 1980; Hayes and Garvin 1982). The major source of dissatisfaction cited has been the inability of discounted cash flow (DCF) analysis to incorporate managerial flexibility in the value of the project. With respect to financing the new venture, the "plain vanilla" DCF approach does not easily incorporate managerial flexibility — that is, the ability of management and the new venture investor to react to conditions as they unfold. As a result, strategic planners have argued that DCF must be supplemented with strategic value arguments in order to make sensible decisions. The argument turns on how to quantify managerial flexibility so that integration rather than separation of the two approaches is achieved.

While simulation, "best/worst/most likely" scenario approaches, and "what if" analyses are helpful in this respect, application of contingent claims analysis (CCA), a variant of option theory, holds out the promise of the reconciliation of the two positions. An important set of recent papers by Myers (1988), Kensinger (1988), and Trigeorgis and Mason (1988) has demonstrated how contingent claims analysis can be used to incorporate the partitioning of uncertainty, risk, and expected return in investment decisions. Reduced to its simplest elements, CCA recognizes the value of choices, or options, in the hands of management or investors. Examples of these options are: the right to abandon the investment, to expand the investment, and to "tranche" the investment in various stages at different prices. The value of such an option is calculated as the difference between the net present value of the project without the option and the net present value of the project with the option. The value of the flexibility option is additive with respect to the general DCF analysis output, and it provides a route to reconciliation of the two positions.

Sahlman (1988) has provided a useful transference of these arguments to the problem faced by the venture capitalist and entrepreneur as they negotiate the structuring and pricing of the new venture financing contract. His article provides a helpful guide to those concerned with partitioning prospective uncertainty, risk, and expected returns in venture capital projects among the stakeholder parties involved in the transaction.

Some practitioners believe that academic researchers, in their zeal to find and understand underlying processes, may ascribe to new venture financing an analytical construct predicated on an overestimated degree of economic rationality. They fear that the combination of (what is to them) arcane financial economic theory with the power of the microcomputer and programs like

Lotus 1-2-3 will produce a misguided and distracting epidemic of "spread-sheet-itis" — raised, indeed, to new heights of academic folly by the introduction of probability theory! New ventures by definition have no history and often provide an inadequate basis for making accurate predictions. "Gut feel" and the netting of a lot of variables and complex relationships play vital roles in new venture financing decisions. A bridge must be built between the "gut feel" and the "paralysis by analysis" positions so that we can get on with learning how good deals are put together and made to work. An example of a start in this direction is a study by Hisrich and Jankowitz (1990).

The importance of this academic research interest in the assessment and partitioning of expected return and risk may best be reflected by the appearance in a recent issue of *The Venture Capital Journal* of an article titled "Industry Struggling to Forge Tools for Measuring Risk," by Jesse Reyes, research manager of Venture Economics, Inc. It appears that the interests of the entrepreneurship research community and the practitioners in the venture capital industry are rapidly coming to share a deeper understanding of the financing of new ventures. More formal research linkages between the two communities would probably improve the flow and quality of new ventures through dissemination of firm-building principles by means of our business, engineering, and scientific educational facilities.

Monitoring Performance and Later Round Investments

The key element in structuring the new venture financing contract is the partitioning of risk and return through, among other things, the distribution of control through voting power and restrictive covenants. This process reflects the illiquidity of the investment new venture's securities and the likelihood that the typical new venture is a "cash calf" for most of its emerging growth period, often several years.

This area of new venture research holds great potential for scholars in management and finance. In publicly traded companies, it is argued in the literature of finance, shortcomings in internal control mechanisms will be offset by external, market-generated control (e.g., the threat of takeover). New ventures are typically private, closely held companies; as such, they are virtually immune to the threat of takeover usually associated with public companies (that is, the threat that a "raider" can skirt the board of directors and management and make an offer directly to the array of public stockholders). Nonetheless, depending upon the structural characteristics of the deal, a disciplinary tension may exist within the emerging growth company, with the threat of takeover by either the investor or the founder/management group. An article by Walsh and Seward (1990) provides a useful review of the points of contention between organizational theory and financial economics and provides a path to reconciliation of the two views.

Two recent papers provide helpful contextual insight regarding monitoring and control. While scholars have long appreciated the notion of the life cycle stages of the emerging growth company, Ruhnka and Young (1987) provide a sharper image of the processes involved as well as the implications for estimating progress and exerting influence and control. Rosenstein (1988) analyzes the role of the board of directors (for the most part the *de facto* repository of voting control in new venture companies) and strikingly contrasts the role of the board in venture-capital-backed companies with its role in conventional small firms and large corporations.

Another recent paper, by Miller, Wilson, and Adams (1988), argues for the use of a novel summary measure of progress toward the financial goals of new venture projects. This is part of the search for good summary measures for the purposes of monitoring and ongoing evaluation of venture performance. The need for such measures is reflected in the controversy within the venture capital industry concerning appropriate measures of interim performance of portfolio companies used by venture capital funds when reporting to their limited partners.

These papers, and the broader background of issues suggested earlier in this section, take on particular importance when subsequent rounds of financing are implied in the initial investment decision, or when they appear by surprise due to unanticipated developments, either good or bad. Investigation of the linked interdependence of financing decisions across time in the type of setting suggested here represents an area of great research potential for entrepreneurship scholars, with important payoff implications for entrepreneurs and venture capital investors.

Transitions and Exits, Including Sale of the New Venture

Researchers have recently begun to examine the comparative performance at initial public offering and beyond of venture-capital-backed firms and companies which were not backed by professional venture capital firms. These studies have been done by combining three sets of data, described below by source :

1. I.D.D. Corporation : identification, date of issue, opening price, and other information on all initial public offerings. (*Standard and Poor's Daily Stock Guide: Over the Counter* has also been used in this connection.)
2. Venture Economics, Inc. : identification of initial public offerings which were venture-capital-backed — that is, which received capital infusions from established venture capital firms.
3. Center for Research in Securities Prices : daily return data on IPO issues after they have become publicly traded securities.

These papers represent one channel through which the study of financing new ventures is gaining the interest of a broad audience within the field of finance. The research tests the relationship between the characteristic ways in which new ventures are funded and organized and their reception (as measured by degree of underpricing or overpricing at offering and performance in the aftermarket) when they make the transition from private to public company status through the initial public offering market.

Studies by Brophy and Verga (1989), Barry et al. (1989), and Megginson and Weiss (1990) have tested whether firms which had professional venture capital firms participate in their new venture finance experienced significantly lower underpricing at the time of IPO than did firms which did not involve professional venture capitalists. Ongoing research in this area promises to extend and deepen the insights obtained on this very important relationship.

Great research potential also exists in the analysis of the special place of leveraged buyouts (LBO), particularly those which represent either new venture creation vehicles and those which represent transitions between management groups in the life of a venture firm. Two studies contribute to our understanding in this area. The first of these is by Bull (1989), in which the expected positive returns post-LBO are ascribed to the entrepreneurial characteristics of the new, equity-endowed, management group. The second of these is by Malone (1989), who built on an earlier paper by Kelley, Pitts, and Shin (1986) in a study of companies with sales of $50 million and less. The buyout strategy is universal and has had a long and noble history (and a future which will survive the decline of the junk bond market!). Its role in turnarounds and the merging of enterprises is an essential aspect of new venture finance and offers great potential for research and understanding by practitioners and public policy makers.

Perhaps the most important and, to date, the most neglected aspect of this area of research is the increasingly important role of the strategic alliance, especially between firms of vastly different size and different nationality. While there is ample evidence of joint ventures, alliances, and direct investment in new venture companies across their development cycles, little if any scholarly research has been done on the implications of this activity. An example of this research potential is found in the work by Mathews and Harvey (1988). It might be noted that evidence of international activity (especially between very large Japanese firms and young, growing U.S. firms) is much more in evidence than is activity between large U.S. firms and young, growing U.S. firms. The implications of these patterns for global economic power and influence are at least impressive, and they should capture the research attention of our best scholars and of the practitioners who are being directly affected by these developments.

■■ ■■ ■■ ■■ ■■ ■■ ■■
CONCLUSION

This review may have inadvertently omitted some important papers, and apologies are in order to their authors. The overall conclusion of this review, however, is one of significant progress in the new venture finance aspect of entrepreneurship research over the past 10 years. The compilation of relevant information on many aspects of the venture capital market has been achieved, along with the development of analytical constructs which will be useful as we try to better understand the financing of new ventures.

The need for continued scholarly research activity in this field may be more important and potentially more rewarding now to scholars, practitioners, and to public policy makers than ever before. With the declining relative economic position of the United States, and the growing importance of the transfer of technology-based and other forms of innovation through the new venture-emerging growth company channel, we must continue to learn about the forces, factors, and arrangements which make this process work.

■■ ■■ ■■ ■■ ■■

REFERENCES

Amit, R., L. R. Glosten, and E. Muller 1990 Does venture capital foster the most promising entrepreneurial firms? *California Management Review* 32 (3): 102–111.

Aram, J. D. 1989 Attitudes and behaviors of informal investors toward early-stage investments, technology-based ventures, and coinvestors. *Journal of Business Venturing* 4 (5): 333–349.

Barry, C., C. Muscarella, J. Feavy, and M. Vetsuypens 1989 Venture capital and initial public offerings. Working paper 1–24. Dallas, Tx.: Southern Methodist University.

Brophy, D. J. 1981 Venture capital investment. In *Frontiers of entrepreneurship research*, ed. K. Vesper, 246–280. Wellesley, Mass.: Babson College.

1982a Venture capital research. *Encyclopedia of entrepreneurship*, eds. C. A. Kent, D. L. Sexton, and K. H. Vesper, 165–192. Englewood Cliffs, N.J.: Prentice-Hall, Inc.

1982b Analysis of structuring and pricing of venture capital investment proposals. In *Frontiers of entrepreneurship research*, ed. K. Vesper, 140–158. Wellesley, Mass.: Babson College.

1986 Venture capital research. In *The art and science of entrepreneurship*, eds. D. L. Sexton and R. W. Smilor, 119–143. Cambridge, Mass.: Ballinger.

Brophy, D. J., and J. Verga 1989 More than money? The effect of venture capital backing on the returns of initial public offerings. In *Frontiers of entrepreneurship research*, eds. R. Brockhaus, Sr., N. Churchill, J. Katz, B. Kirchhoff, K. Vesper, and W. Wetzel, Jr., 192–198. Wellesley, Mass.: Babson College.

Bruno, A. V., and T. T. Tyebjee 1983 The one that got away: A study of ventures rejected by venture capitalists. In *Frontiers of entrepreneurship research*, eds. J. Hornaday, J. Timmons, and K. Vesper, 289–306. Wellesley, Mass.: Babson College.

1985 The entrepreneur's search for capital. *Journal of Business Venturing* 1 (1): 61–74.

1986a The destinies of rejected venture capital deals. *Sloan Management Review* 27 (2): 43–53.

1986b Negotiating venture capital financing. *California Management Review* 28 (1): 45–59.

Bull, I. 1989 Financial performance of leveraged buyouts: An empirical analysis. *Journal of Business Venturing* 4 (4): 263–280.

Buttner, E. H., and B. Rosen 1989 Funding new business ventures: Are decision makers biased against women entrepreneurs? *Journal of Business Venturing* 4 (4): 249–262.

Bygrave, W. D. 1987 Syndicated investments by venture capital firms: A networking perspective. *Journal of Business Venturing* 2 (2): 138–154.

Bygrave, W., N. Fast, R. Khoylian, L. Vincent, and W. Yue 1989 Early rates of return of 131 venture capital funds started 1978–1984. *Journal of Business Venturing* 4 (2): 93–105.

Chiampou, G. F., and J. L. Kallett 1989 Risk/return profile of venture capital. *Journal of Business Venturing* 4 (1): 1–10.

Chrisman, J. J., F. Hoy, and R. Robinson, Jr. 1987 New venture development: The costs and benefits of public sector assistance. *Journal of Business Venturing* 2 (4): 315–328.

Cooper, A. C., W. C. Dunkelberg, and C. Y. Woo 1988 Entrepreneur's perceived chances of success. *Journal of Business Venturing* 3 (2): 110–120.

Covin, J. G., and D. P. Slevin 1990 New venture strategic posture, structure and performance: An industry life cycle analysis. *Journal of Business Venturing* 5 (2): 123–135.

Daily Stock Price Record, Over-the-Counter. New York: Standard and Poor's Corporation. (Quarterly Journal).

Dubini, P. 1989 Which venture capital backed entrepreneurs have the best chance of succeeding? *Journal of Business Venturing* 4 (2): 123–132.

Freear, J., and W. E. Wetzel, Jr. 1990 Who bankrolls high-tech entrepreneurs? *Journal of Business Venturing* 5 (2): 77–90.

Fried, V. H., and R. D. Hisrich 1988 Venture capital research: Past, present and future. *Entrepreneurship theory and practice*, 15–28. Waco, Tex.: Baylor Univ.

Hayes, R., and W. Abernathy 1980 Managing our way to economic decline. *Harvard Business Review*: 58 (4, July-August): 67–77.

Hayes, R., and D. Garvin 1982 Managing as if tomorrow mattered. *Harvard Business Review*: 60 (3, May-June): 70–79.

Hisrich, R. D., and A. D. Jankowitz 1990 Intuition in venture capital decisions: An exploratory study using a new technique. *Journal of Business Venturing* 5 (1): 49–62.

Kelley, J. M., R. A. Pitts, and B. Shin 1986 Entrepreneurship by leveraged buyout: Some preliminary hypotheses. In *Frontiers of entrepreneurship research*, eds. R. Ronstadt, J. Hornaday, R. Peterson, and K. Vesper, 281–292. Wellesley, Mass.: Babson College.

Kensinger, J. W. 1988 Adding the value of active management into the capital budgeting equation. *Midland Corporate Finance Journal* 5 (1): 31–42.

Khan, A. M. 1987 Assessing venture capital investments with noncompensatory behavioral decision models. *Journal of Business Venturing* 2 (3): 193–206.

MacMillan, I. C., R. Siegel, and P. N. Subba Narasimha 1985 Criteria used by venture capitalists to evaluate new venture proposals. *Journal of Business Venturing* 1 (1): 119–128.

MacMillan, I. C., L. Zemann, and P. N. Subba Narasimha 1987 Criteria distinguishing successful from unsuccessful ventures in the venture screening process. *Journal of Business Venturing* 2 (2): 123–138.

Mathews, H. L., and T. W. Harvey 1988 Strategic alliances and venture capital: Growth tactics for the 1990s. College of Business, The Ohio State University, Columbus, Ohio. Working paper #88–60: 1–12.

Mechner, F. 1989 Present certainty equivalents and weighted scenario valuations. *Journal of Business Venturing* 4 (2): 85–92.

Megginson, W., and K. Weiss 1990 The certification role of venture capitalists in bringing new issues to market. Working paper #1–21. Ann Arbor, MI: University of Michigan.

Miller, A., B. Wilson, and M. Adams 1988 Financial performance patterns of new corporate ventures: An alternative to traditional measures. *Journal of Business Venturing* 3 (4): 287–300.

Malone, S. C. 1989 Characteristics of smaller company leveraged buyouts. *Journal of Business Venturing* 4 (5): 349–359.

Myers, S. C. 1987 Finance theory and financial strategy. *Midland Corporate Finance Journal* 5 (1): 6–13.

1988 Notes on an expert system for capital budgeting. *Financial Management* 17(3): 23–31.

Plummer, J. L. 1986 *QED report on venture capital financial analysis*. Palo Alto, CA: QED Research, Inc.

Rea, R. H. 1989 Factors affecting success and failure of seed capital startup negotiations. *Journal of Business Venturing* 4 (2): 149–158.

Rosenstein, J. 1988 The board and strategy: Venture capital and high technology. *Journal of Business Venturing* 3 (2): 159–170.

Roure, J. B., and M. A. Maidique 1986 Linking prefunding factors and high-technology venture success. *Journal of Business Venturing* 1 (3): 295–306.

Roure, J. B., and R. H. Keeley 1990 Predictors of success in new technology based ventures. *Journal of Business Venturing* 5 (4): 201–220.

Ruhnka, J. C., and J. E. Young 1987 A venture capital model of the development process for new ventures. *Journal of Business Venturing* 2 (2): 167–184.

Sahlman, W. A. 1988 Aspects of financial contracting in venture capital. *Journal of Applied Corporate Finance* 1 (2): 23–36.

Stuart, R., and P. Abetti 1987 Start-up ventures: Toward the prediction of initial success. *Journal of Business Venturing* 2 (3): 215–230.

Timmons, J. A. 1981 Venture capital investors in the U.S.: A survey of the most active investors. In *Frontiers of entrepreneurship research*, ed. K. Vesper, 199–216. Wellesley, Mass.: Babson College.

Timmons, J. A., and William D. Bygrave 1986 Venture capital's role in financing innovation for economic growth. *Journal of Business Venturing* 1 (2): 161–176.

Trigeorgis, L., and S. P. Mason 1987 Valuing managerial flexibility. *Midland Corporate Finance Journal* 5 (1): 14–21.

Tyebjee, T. T., and Bruno, A. V. 1984 A model of venture capitalist investment activity. *Management Science* 30: 1051–1066.

Tyebjee, T. T., and A. V. Bruno 1981 Venture capital decision making: Preliminary results from three empirical studies. In *Frontiers of entrepreneurship research*, ed. K. Vesper, 281–320. Wellesley, Mass.: Babson College.

Walsh, J. P., and J. K. Seward 1990 On the efficiency of internal and external corporate control mechanisms. *Academy of Management Review* 15 (3): 421–458.

Wetzel, W. E., Jr. 1987 The informal venture capital market: Aspects of scale and market efficiency. *Journal of Business Venturing* 2 (4): 299–314.

Chapter

16

Venture Capital: The Decade Ahead[1]

Jeffry A. Timmons
and
Harry J. Sapienza

●

INTRODUCTION

This chapter examines the evolution of the venture capital industry over the last decade, identifies key issues facing the industry in the 1990s, reviews recent streams in research on the venture capital industry, and identifies research opportunities for the decade ahead. As a final note, we offer some cautions to researchers of venture capital in the 1990s.

The 1980s witnessed explosive growth in the venture capital industry at home, and more dramatically, abroad. The growth and internationalization of venture capital resulted in fundamental changes in the structure and functions of the industry. Growth in the number and size of venture capital firms (VC firms) resulted in more heterogeneity across firms and greater specialization by investment stage, industry, and region. The movement of the venture capital industry to later and larger investments reflected a changing strategy and

[1]Adapted in part from Chapters 2, 3, and 5 from a forthcoming book by William D. Bygrave and Jeffry A. Timmons: *Venture and Risk Capital: Practice and Performance, Promises and Policy* (Boston: Harvard Business School, 1991). The authors also thank Tom Soja for his helpful input.

focus. As the number of domestic VC firms grew, the "old boy" network of VC firms began to erode, competition intensified, and a "shakeout" of marginal VC firms was inevitable.

Changes in domestic tax laws made early stage investing less attractive for U.S. VC firms and helped open the door for foreign competition unburdened by these costs. Suppliers of capital demanded more rapid and less risky returns from venture capital investments, driving VC firms to later and later stage investments. As the availability of seed and start-up funding through venture capital began to evaporate and VC firms demanded greater returns on later stage investments, entrepreneurs sought alternative means of financing. The establishment of viable alternatives to venture capital in the form of individual investors or "angels," successful entrepreneurs, domestic and foreign corporate investors, and strategic alliances with other firms served only to exacerbate the already intense competition in the venture capital industry.

Clearly, the 1990s hold great challenges for the venture capital industry. The structural changes mentioned above will continue to intensify competition in the industry. VC firms will be challenged to earn attractive returns while seeking ways of differentiating themselves from the growing pack of U.S. and foreign-based competitors. Successful VC firms will be those which counter the growing threat of substitutes by learning how to add value to the entrepreneurial process and to communicate that value to the increasingly wary and sophisticated set of suppliers and users of capital. Further, domestic VC firms will have to contend with federal and state policies which dampen their incentive to provide early stage investments and put them at a competitive disadvantage relative to foreign competitors. Finally, VC firms will be faced with an increasingly complex legal environment.

Research in the mid- to late 1980s forged new trails in the investigation of the venture capital industry and its impact on the entrepreneurial process. Key streams included: investigations of venture capital flows, investment criteria of venture capitalists, venture capital rates of return, VC firm strategies, the roles and activities of venture capitalists, and the value added by venture capital firms.

The array of research opportunities in the 1990s is vast. Four sets of stakeholders in the industry may provide the focus for research efforts: 1) the suppliers of capital (i.e., limited partners), 2) the users of capital (i.e., entrepreneurs), 3) the investors (i.e., the venture capitalists themselves), and 4) public policy makers. Among topics likely to be of interest to one or more of these groups are further insights on: rates of return; methods of measuring and monitoring VC firm portfolio performance; value-added investing know-how; the effects of global capital markets; deal flow patterns; effective/creative deal structuring and negotiation; deal evaluation; opportunity evaluation; management team evaluation; relative bargaining power; general partnership dissolution; effects and timing of CEO succession; whether, when, and how venture capitalists add value to the entrepreneurial process; board of director and other investor roles in ventures; fiscal policy; the long-term effects of tax policy; the role of venture capitalists and public institutions in economic development; and the privatization of capital markets.

The above list is by no means exhaustive but highlights the richness of research opportunity in the venture capital arena. These opportunities will be realized only if researchers seek methods and issues which bring them in close contact with the industry in the pursuit of an intellectual collision with the real world.

▬ ▬ ▬ ▬ ▬ ▬ ▬ ▬ ▬
VENTURE CAPITAL IN THE 1980S

The venture capital industry received significant attention in the early 1980s with regard to its place in the process of economic growth and development, and this attention appears to be growing. Brophy (1986, 135–136) had this to say about the practical and research importance of the VC market:

> The venture capital market and the process central to it are becoming part of the economic fabric of this country and, to an increasing extent, of other countries as well. The development of this field has been broad, and it has moved ratchet-like to a permanently higher level of significance in our economic and in our research interests.

The Explosive Growth of Venture Capital

The growth of the venture capital industry in the United States is dramatically illustrated in Figure 16–1, which shows that the number of VC firms in the United States (top half of the figure) has tripled from 225 in 1979 to 674 in 1989, and that the average size of VC firms as measured by capital under management (bottom half of the figure) has also increased dramatically from $18 million to $49.5 million during the same period. The combination of these two factors means that the total pool of venture capital in the United States has mushroomed from $2.9 billion in 1979 to $33.4 billion in 1989.

Figure 16–2 shows that the annual commitments of funds to the U.S. venture capital industry (top portion of Figure 16–2) has also grown dramatically from under $700 million in 1980 to $2.4 billion in 1989, peaking at $4.2 billion in 1987. Similarly, annual disbursements of venture capital to the portfolio companies (bottom portion) have grown from $600 million in 1980 to $3.3 billion in 1989; disbursements also peaked in 1987 for domestic VC firms at $3.9 billion.

The mushrooming of the size and number of VC firms in the United States has been triggered to some extent by the influx of institutional money. In 1978, nearly one-third of the money in the industry was supplied by private individuals; in 1989, only 6 percent of venture capital funds were supplied by this group (see Figure 16–3). Bygrave and Shulman (1988) concluded that the 1986 change in the capital gains tax failed to have a significant impact on the money flowing into venture capital because two-thirds of the money was supplied by

USA Venture Capital
Number of Venture Capital Firms
(*Source : Venture Capital Journal.*)

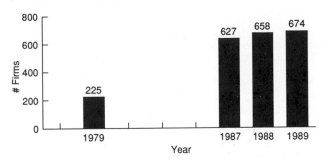

USA Venture Capital
Average Size of Firm
(*Source : Venture Capital Journal.*)

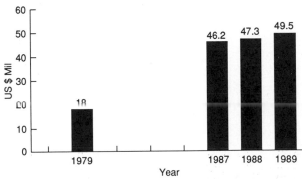

FIGURE 16–1   USA Venture Capital : Number of Venture Capital Firms
and Average Size of Firm, 1980–1989

nontaxable sources (such as pension funds, endowments, and foreign investors); the group most hurt by the law (individuals and wealthy families) supplied only 6 percent of the capital in 1989. Now, institutional investors, led by pension funds at 36 percent, more fully dominate the set of suppliers of venture capital in the United States. However, Soja and Reyes (1990) point out that independently funded investments are key to providing a source of venture capital deal flow, so that policies such as the Tax Reform Act may result in fewer attractive new venture deals in the longer run.

The Globalization of Venture Capital

While impressive, the growth of venture capital in the United States has not been nearly as spectacular as its growth worldwide. The upper half of Figure 16–4 shows that while the pool of venture capital has grown just under 40 per-

USA Venture Capital
Annual Capital Commitments
(*Source : Venture Capital Journal.*)

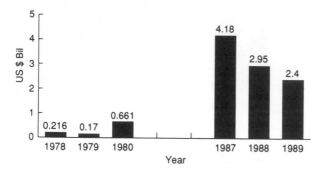

USA Venture Capital
Annual Disbursements
(*Source :* Venture Economics, Inc.)

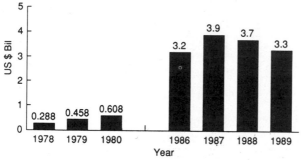

FIGURE 16-2   USA Venture Capital : Annual Capital Commitments
and Annual Disbursements, 1980-1989

cent in the United States from 1986 to 1989, it has grown over 100 percent during the same period in Europe, Japan, and elsewhere. In 1986, Europe's pool
was less than half the size of the U.S. pool ; now, it is over 75 percent as large.
Even more dramatic, however, is the pattern of capital committed to U.S. and
European VC firms in the last few years. As can be seen in the bottom half of
Figure 16-4, the capital committed to European VC firms exceeded commitments to the United States by $1.1 and $3.9 billion in 1988 and 1989 respectively! Britain dominates the European market, but virtually all of the countries of western Europe (including, in diminishing order of size of their venture
capital industries, France, the Netherlands, Italy, Germany, Belgium, Spain,
Sweden, Switzerland, Ireland, Denmark, Finland, Norway, Austria, Iceland,
and Portugal) now boast flourishing venture capital trade.

USA Venture Capital
Source Distribution — 1978
(New Funds : $216 Mil)
(*Source : Venture Capital Journal.*)

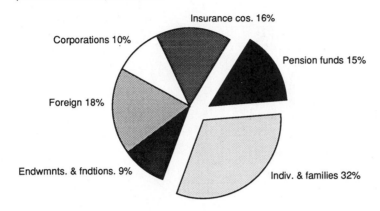

USA Venture Capital
Source Distribution — 1989
(New Funds : $2.40 Bil)
(*Source : Venture Capital Journal.*)

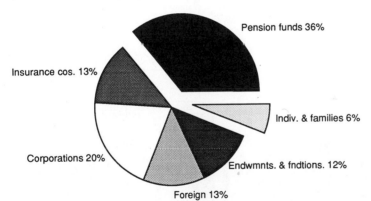

FIGURE 16–3 USA Venture Capital Source Distribution, 1978 and 1989

Figure 16–5 compares the number and average size of VC firms globally. While the United States still dominates in the number of VC firms, the average European VC firm manages about 14 percent more capital than the average U.S. firm ($56.3 vs. $49.5 million in 1989); indeed, in 1989 the median U.S. VC firm had less than $25 million in capital under management. Although the average size of Asian VC firms was about $38 million in 1988, the average firm in Japan manages $67 million (the Asian market also includes significant VC presence in Australia, Hong Kong, Korea, Singapore, Taiwan, and Thailand).

Worldwide Venture Capital
Growth in VC Pool
(*Source : Asian Venture Capital Journal, European Venture Capital Associations Yearbook, Venture Capital Journal.*)

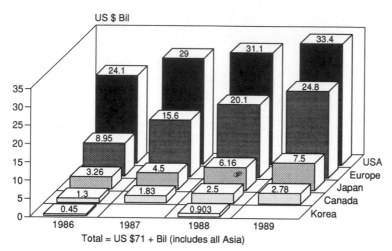

Total = US $71 + Bil (includes all Asia)

Worldwide Venture Capital
Growth in VC Pool
(*Source : Asian Venture Capital Journal, European Venture Capital Associations Yearbook, Venture Capital Journal.*)

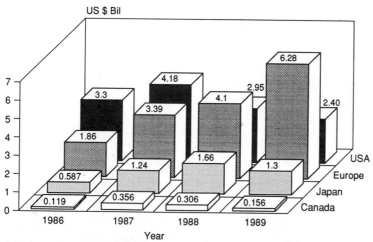

FIGURE 16–4 Worldwide Venture Capital : Growth in VC Pool and Annual Capital Commitments

Worldwide Venture Capital
Number of VC Firms
(*Source : Asian Venture Capital Journal,* Venture Economics, Inc.)

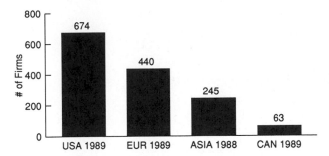

Worldwide Venture Capital
Average Size of VC Firm
(*Source : Asian Venture Capital Journal,* European Venture Capital Associations *Yearbook, Venture Capital Journal.*)

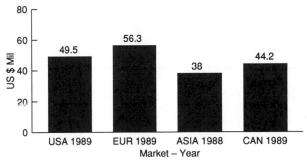

FIGURE 16–5 Worldwide Venture Capital : Number of VC Firms and Average Size of VC Firm

Figure 16–6 shows the sources of venture capital in Europe (top) and Asia (below). This can be compared with U.S. sources (bottom half of Figure 16–3). The strong presence of banks and financial institutions in Europe and Japan is the most striking difference between the sources of venture capital abroad and in the United States; in the United States, these institutions are prohibited from investing in venture capital. In summary, institutional suppliers dominate venture capital worldwide to a much greater extent than ever before.

Structural Changes : Increased Heterogeneity and Specialization

The dramatic growth in venture capital in the United States and abroad is intimately interwoven with fundamental changes in the structure of the industry. Almost as if it were a literal explosion, the growth described above has resulted

Europe Venture Capital
Source Distribution — 1989
(New Funds : $6.283 Bil)
(*Source :* European Venture Capital Associations *Yearbook.*)

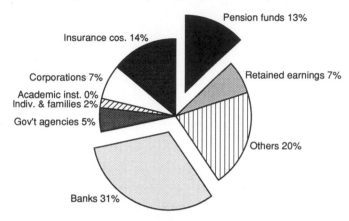

Asia Venture Capital — Japan 1988
Composition of JAFCO's Shareholders
(JAFCO Assets : $2 Bil)
(*Source : Asian Venture Capital Journal.*)

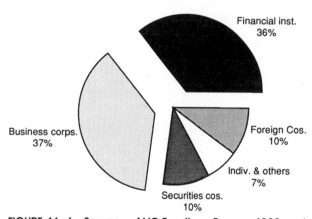

FIGURE 16–6   Sources of VC Funding : Europe 1989 and JAFCO 1988

in a splintering of VC firms into groups of small, medium, and "mega" funds, often specializing by stage, product, technology, region, or customer type.

Figure 16–7 shows that at the end of the 1970s, capital under management in the U.S. venture capital industry was somewhat balanced among private VC firms (45 percent), corporate VC firms (34 percent), and other Small Business Investment Corporations' SBICs (21 percent), whereas by 1989 private VC firms had come to dominate (controlling 81 percent of capital under management), and (SBIC) share had dwindled to under 1 percent. However, this domi-

USA Venture Capital — 1978
Capital under Mgmt. by Type of Firm
($2.9 Bil)
(*Source : Venture Capital Journal.*)

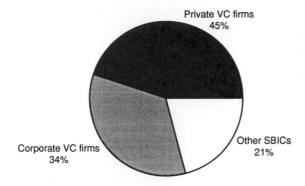

USA Venture Capital — 1989
Capital under Mgmt. by Type of Firm
($33.4 Bil)
(*Source : Venture Capital Journal.*)

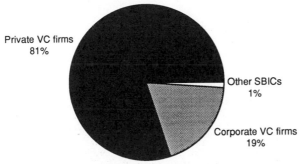

FIGURE 16-7 U.S. Capital under Management by Firm Type, 1978 and 1989

nance by type does not reflect the increasing heterogeneity of the industry along several dimensions.

At one time, only a handful of VC firms were in operation; relatively comparable in size, they focused on providing capital to start-up companies and aiding in the company building process. By the end of the 1980s, vast differences existed in the size, scope, and preference for investment stage among VC firms. Figures 16–8 and 16–9 highlight the vast differences in capital under management in 1989, between the top tier of 95 VC firms (the 14 percent of the firms — of greater than $100 million in size — which control 59 percent of the capital) and the bottom tier of 205 VC firms (the 30 percent of the firms — of less than $10 million in size — which control 2.4 percent of the capital).

USA Venture Capital — 1989
Largest 95 Mega Firms
($100+ Mil under Management) . . .
(*Source* : Venture Economics, Inc.)

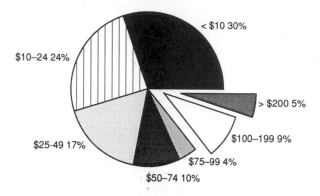

. . . Control 59% of the $ Pool
Average Size : $207 Mil / Firm)
(*Source* : Venture Economics, Inc.)

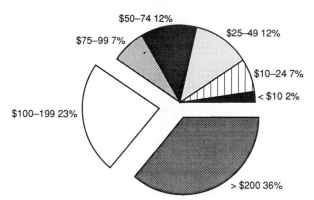

FIGURE 16–8   Largest 95 VC Firms Control the Majority of Capital

Figure 16–10 illustrates investment preferences among U.S. VC firms at the outset and at the conclusion of the 1980s. Despite the press which the biotechnology industry has received, this figure illustrates that investment in biotechnology was moderate, moving from 6 percent at the beginning to only 8 percent at the end of the period. Significant increases in consumer and health segments are evident: the two segments comprise 14 percent of investment dollars at the beginning and 25 percent at the end of the decade. Another noteworthy change was that the relatively heavy investing in energy and natural resources (9 percent) witnessed in 1980 has virtually disappeared (although continued evidence of the instability of the Middle East could once again spur investment). The general trend has been toward lower technology investments

USA Venture Capital — 1989
The Very Smallest 205 Firms
(< $10 Mil under Management) . . .
(*Source :* Venture Economics, Inc.)

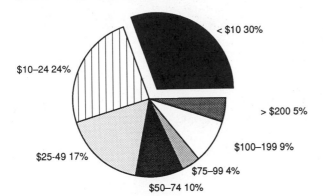

< $10 30%

$10–24 24%

> $200 5%

$100–199 9%

$25-49 17%

$75–99 4%

$50–74 10%

. . . Control 59% of the $ Pool
(Average Size : $207 Mil / Firm)
(*Source :* Venture Economics, Inc.)

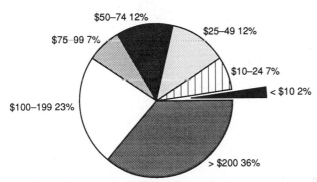

$50–74 12%

$25–49 12%

$75–99 7%

$10–24 7%

< $10 2%

$100–199 23%

> $200 36%

FIGURE 16–9   Smallest 205 VC Firms Control Less than 3 Percent of Capital

in an increasing variety of industries. Figure 16–11 shows that these trends are currently even stronger in Europe (31 percent consumer-related investments and 39 percent "other") and Canada (17 percent consumer-related investments and 46 percent "other").

Indicative of the diversity of venture capital investing today, over 70 industry segments are listed as possible preferences of VC firms in Pratt's *Guide to Venture Capital Sources.* Specialization, however, is not limited to industry preference. VC firms such as Zero Stage Capital and First Stage Capital also specialize by stage of investment. Still, many of the "mega" firms invest wherever the prospects are good, across industries, stages, and regions. It has become an industry of "boutiques" and "department stores," with a vast array of choices in between.

USA Venture Capital 1978–1980
Industry Sector Investment
($1.354 Bil Invested)
(*Source :* Venture Economics, Inc.)

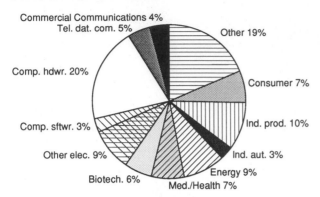

USA Venture Capital 1987–1989
Industry Sector Investment
($10.855 Bil Invested)
(*Source :* Venture Economics, Inc.)

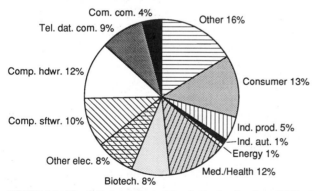

FIGURE 16–10   U.S. Investment by Industry Sector, 1978–1980 and 1987–1989

Intensified Competition

In a presentation to the National Venture Capital Association in May 1990, Porter, Sahlman, and Stevenson illustrated how the structure of the venture capital industry has served to create fierce competition within the industry and to drive down its profitability (see Figure 16–12). The attractive returns of the late 1970s and early 1980s and the low barriers to entry combined to help fuel the rapid expansion of the industry as described above.

This fragmentation and expansion decreased VC firms' relative bargaining power with suppliers (limited partners) and users (entrepreneurs) of capital. Suppliers also experienced an increase in relative power by virtue of

Europe Venture Capital — 1989
Industry Sector Investment
(U.S. $4.617 Bil Invested)
(*Source :* European Venture Capital Associations *Yearbook.*)

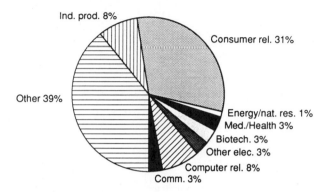

Ind. prod. 8%

Consumer rel. 31%

Other 39%

Energy/nat. res. 1%
Med./Health 3%
Biotech. 3%
Other elec. 3%
Computer rel. 8%
Comm. 3%

Canada Venture Capital — 1989
Industry Sector Investment
(U.S. $289.7 Mil Invested)
(*Source :* Canadian Venture Capital.)

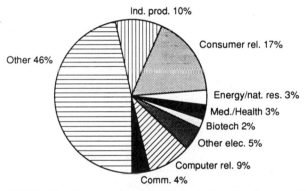

Ind. prod. 10%

Consumer rel. 17%

Other 46%

Energy/nat. res. 3%
Med./Health 3%
Biotech 2%
Other elec. 5%
Computer rel. 9%
Comm. 4%

FIGURE 16–11 Investment by Industry Sector, Europe 1989 and Canada 1989

1) their increased concentration (e.g., pension funds and other key institutions), and 2) their improved information and sophistication. Entrepreneurs' power has also swelled. They have had more VC firms to choose from, more money available within the industry, and an expanding array of alternative methods for financing their ventures, including more active individual investors (Sahlman 1990), direct investment by corporations, and the growing availability of strategic alliances with foreign and domestic firms.

Together, these forces have exerted tremendous pressure on VC firms, squeezing their profitability and resulting in a breakdown of the deal sharing and cooperation characteristic of the industry earlier in the decade.

**Determinants of Venture
Capital Industry Profitability**

(*Source :* M. Porter, W. Sahlman, and H. Stevenson, presentation to the National Venture Capital
Association, May 1989.)

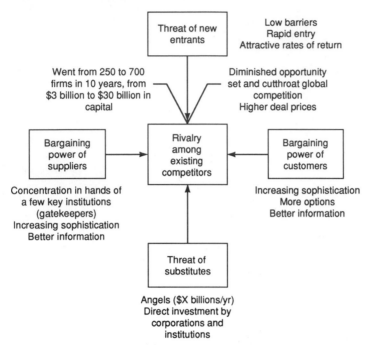

FIGURE 16-12 Determinants of Venture Capital Industry Profitability

Strategy Shifts : Later Stages, Greater Focus

As the power of limited partners increased, they began to demand safer investments with more rapid returns. Institutional investors themselves were facing
pressure to show quick returns in financial statements to vindicate their entry
into the venture capital fast lanes. The change in federal tax laws also increased
individual and family investors' propensity to seek short-term gains. As
Stanley Pratt (1987, 9) put it, "The Tax Reform Act of 1986 eliminated the differential between long term capital gains and ordinary income taxation and
sent a clear signal that government policy would not reward long term building
over short term trading." VC funds formed in the early 1980s when valuations
were extremely high were hit hard when valuations dropped ; here again, pressure built to create quick turnaround to boost track records that might win
back investors. The response of VC firms to all of the above has been to invest
greater and greater amounts in later stage ventures.

Heavier investing and reinvesting in later stage ventures addresses several
risk and efficiency issues for VC firms simultaneously : fewer deals must be

evaluated, risk is lower, returns are quicker, and less managerial assistance is required of the VC firm. Figure 16–13 shows, for example, that the average LBO/acquisition stage investment is on the magnitude of four times the size of early stage investments in America and Europe, and over six times in Canada. The growth of substitutes for venture capital has also depleted the set of attractive investment opportunities, making it difficult for VC firms to efficiently and effectively invest their larger pools of capital.

Figure 16–14 illustrates the shift which has occurred in the United States in terms of stage of investment. In 1980, 44 percent of venture capital investments in the United States were in seed, start-up, or other early stage ventures; by 1989, this amount had dwindled to 28 percent (seed stage investing, however, has increased by 12 times in absolute dollar terms, from $12 million in 1980 to $144 million in 1989). Figure 16–15 shows that in Europe the pattern

Worldwide Venture Capital
Avg. Size of Early Stage Investment 1989
(*Source :* Venture Economics, Inc., *Canadian Venture Capital,* European Venture Capital Associations Yearbook.)
Note : Canadian average slightly higher than actual, based on number of rounds.

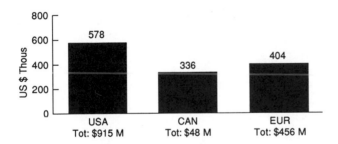

Worldwide Venture Capital
Avg. Size of LBO / Acquisition Investment 1989
(*Source :* Venture Economics, Inc., *Canadian Venture Capital,* European Venture Capital Associations Yearbook.)
Note : Canadian average slightly higher than actual, based on number of rounds.

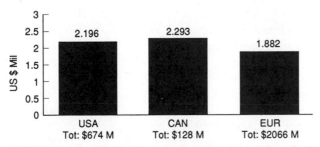

FIGURE 16–13 Worldwide Average Investment Size, Early Stage vs. LBO

USA Venture Capital — 1980
Portion of $ Invested by Stage
($608 Mil)
(*Source :* Venture Economics, Inc.)

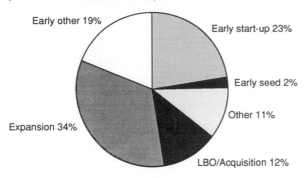

Early other 19%

Early start-up 23%

Early seed 2%

Other 11%

Expansion 34%

LBO/Acquisition 12%

USA Venture Capital — 1989
Portion of $ Invested by Stage
($3.26 Bil)
(*Source :* Venture Economics, Inc.)

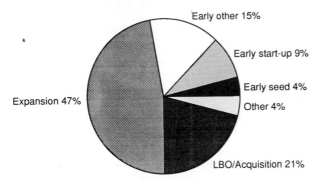

Early other 15%

Early start-up 9%

Early seed 4%

Other 4%

Expansion 47%

LBO/Acquisition 21%

FIGURE 16–14   U.S. Investment by Stage, 1980 and 1989

is more extreme, with early stage ventures receiving only 10 percent of disbursements in 1989; Australia is an anomaly, making 73 percent of its disbursements to early stage investments.

Figure 16–16 illustrates U.S. VC firms' increased propensity to invest money in existing portfolio companies rather than in newly identified opportunities (in 1979, 59 percent were new financings; in 1989, 22 percent were new). In contrast (Figure 16–17), in Europe and Canada, recent investments in new financings are in the range of 70 percent of disbursements.

While the strategic advantages to later stage investing are obvious from the discussion above, two key problems have evolved as a result of this trend. First, the building of larger and larger funds to invest in later stage ventures causes an inherent discrepancy in motivation between limited and general partners.

Europe Venture Capital — 1989
Portion of Disbursement $ by Stage
($4.62 Bil Invested)
(*Source :* European Venture Capital Associations *Yearbook.*)

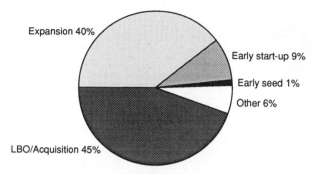

Asia Venture Capital — Australia 1988
Cum. Disbursement $ by Stage
($144 Mil Invested)
(*Source : Asian Venture Capital Journal.*)

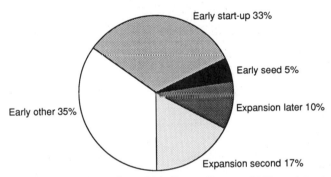

FIGURE 16–15   Investment by Stage, Europe 1989 and Australia 1988

Rick Burnes of Charles River Associates puts it this way : "Many VCs quickly perceive that it is easier and more lucrative to realize 8 percent on a $100 million fund than it is to achieve 100 percent on a $2 million one." Second, as VC firms move toward being pure financial functionaries, their place in the value chain of the entrepreneurial process becomes less critical to the suppliers and users of venture capital.

More Sophisticated Suppliers and Users

Figure 16–12 cited more sophisticated suppliers (limited partners) and users (entrepreneurs) among the forces undermining the structure of the VC industry. In fact, this sophistication is both a cause and a result of the changes in the

USA Venture Capital
Proportion of New vs. Follow-on
Number of Investments in 1979
(*Source :* Venture Economics, Inc.)

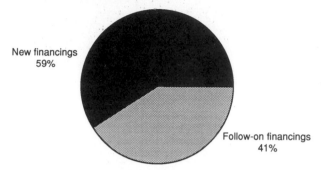

New financings
59%

Follow-on financings
41%

USA Venture Capital
Proportion of New vs. Follow-on
Number of Investments in 1989
(*Source :* Venture Economics, Inc.)

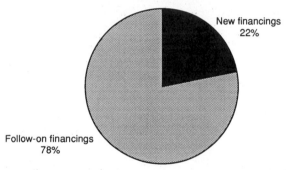

New financings
22%

Follow-on financings
78%

FIGURE 16–16   U.S. Proportion of Number of Investments, New vs. Follow-on, 1979 and 1989

capital markets. Venture capital is now dominated by institutional investors, including pension funds, corporations, and insurance companies in the United States, as well as banking and other financial institutions elsewhere. These investors come to the table with greater resources and greater financial savvy than investors of the past ; they are more apt to place restrictive covenants in agreements and to seek legal solutions to disputes.

Entrepreneurs, too, come armed with more information and more options. The consolidation of venture capital into later stage investing coincides with the emergence of other groups as substitutes for venture capital. Estimates vary, but some experts believe that private individuals or "angels" are playing an increasingly important role in funding entrepreneurial start-ups and technology-based ventures : Wetzel's stream of research (1981, 1982, 1984;

Europe Venture Capital
Proportion of New vs. Follow-on
Number of Investments in 1989
(*Source :* European Venture Capital Associations *Yearbook.*)

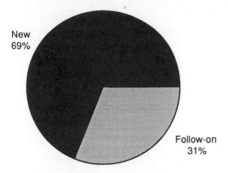

New
69%

Follow-on
31%

Canada Venture Capital
Proportion of New vs. Follow-on
Number of Investments in 1989
(*Source : Canadian Venture Capital.*)

New financings
75%

Follow-on financings
25%

FIGURE 16–17 Europe and Canada Proportion of Number of Investments, New vs. Follow-on, 1989

Wetzel and Wilson 1985) holds that new technology-based firms (for example, in New Hampshire) raise more money from investor angels than from professional VCs, and private individuals are the primary source of capital when the amount raised is under $1 million. Some have estimated that the pool of angels' investments is in the range of $100–300 billion, surpassing that of the professional venture capital industry (Soja and Reyes 1990). This type of investing provides a kind of "farm system of venture portfolios." Often angels are able to provide better terms because of lower ROI requirements or longer time horizons.

Corporate partners can also be attractive alternatives to venture capital for entrepreneurs: 1) they are sometimes less price-sensitive because they are seeking investment for strategic reasons, such as creating synergies with core businesses or gaining a window on technology; 2) for the same reasons, they may be committed for the longer term. As such, they present a fundamentally different type of partnership.

Finally, foreign investors, hungry for high-growth technology companies, enjoy a tax wedge which allows for more attractive offerings to entrepreneurial ventures. These investors, like their domestic counterparts, are seeking strategic advantage through alliance with high-tech U.S. start-ups. Through contact with this array of alternative deal sources, entrepreneurs have become more fully educated about financing options and their own market value.

Some VC firms' push to get in and get out of investments quickly has left a bad taste in the mouths of many entrepreneurs who have frequently generalized this approach to the entire industry. The result of the perception of a "fast buck" approach is a backlash on the part of entrepreneurs who are becoming increasingly wary of professional venture capital and who now have alternative sources from which to obtain capital.

Lagging Performance and Shakeout

The trends described above suggest great pressure on the profitability of the industry. In fact, Bygrave's work (see Chapter 17 in this volume) illustrates that in fact: 1) the rates of return for venture capital have been on the decline since the early 1980s (though they are still outperforming S&P 500 stocks); and 2) VC portfolio companies which went public quickly have been outperformed by those which went more slowly. This latter trend is significant given the increased propensity in the industry to seek quick turnaround for money invested. A dichotomy may be developing between VC firms which are willing to build value patiently in their portfolio companies and those which function primarily as interim financiers.

As industry performance declines and the number of VC firms and the pool of venture capital swells, a shakeout is inevitable. The venture capital industry has expanded at a rate which appears to outpace its capacity to productively invest funds. The increasingly apparent movement away from a heavy reliance on glitzy high-tech investments may indicate that VC firms are now more content to swing for singles and doubles rather than to follow the "home run strategy" popular in the past.

A Lull in Technology Advances

The great wave of technology advances which marked the 1970s and early 1980s (e.g., in communications, personal computers, microwaves, VCRs, compact discs, etc.) seems to have reached a lull. Increasingly, VC firms, especially those outside the United States, are finding investments in low-technology areas attractive avenues to pursue (e.g., see Figure 16–11). This trend, while evident in the United States, is even more apparent in the ever-expanding venture capital market in Europe. Given the rapid growth of venture capital in Europe and the impending changes of 1992 with the potential development of eastern Europe, this trend may prove very significant.

In summary, the VC industry has undergone dramatic transformation in the 1980s. Its explosive growth has been accompanied by more critical scrutiny by suppliers, users, and policy makers. New firms have formed, and foreign competitors have rushed in to try to reap some of the legendary (or mythical?) returns of the late 1970s and early 1980s. A plethora of substitute financing avenues have opened for entrepreneurs. The VC firms themselves have at times dashed, like lemmings, after opportunities in high-tech investments, only to retreat to more cautious approaches. VC "boutiques" have been spawned to specialize along a variety of dimensions. And there has been a retreat from early stage investments; VC firms are now "in" later and "out" more quickly.

▬▬▬▬▬▬▬▬
ISSUES FACING VENTURE CAPITAL FIRMS IN THE 1990S

The trends discussed above raise the question of whether venture capital in the United States needs to be redefined. The 1987 *Guide to Venture Capital Sources* noted that venture capital "is often thought of as 'the early-stage financing of new and young companies seeking to grow rapidly'" (Pratt and Morris 1987, 9). As Bygrave and Timmons (1991) have put it, "where is the venture in venture capital" today? If VC firms are assuming less risk in investing, spending less time evaluating deals for the purposes of funding the ventures with the brightest potential, and spending less time in assisting and monitoring the progress of new businesses, how much value are they adding to the entrepreneurial process?

Much of the industry appears bent on attempting to achieve the paradoxical: specifically, VC firms are aiming at low-risk investments to achieve high returns and investing more money with less actual involvement, while at the same time trying to achieve economies of scale. If the venture capital industry is to reverse the downward spiral of falling rates of return, it will have to come up with effective ways of improving industry structure with regard to rivalry within the industry, suppliers (limited partners), users (entrepreneurs), and potential competitors (entry threats and substitutes for venture capital). All of this must be accomplished within the framework of federal and state policies and an increasingly complex legal environment.

Rivalry: Competitive Strategy, Differentiation, and Value Added

A key issue for VC firms is how to achieve superior rates of return globally and domestically in the intensely competitive environment which has developed. At the same time, such improvements by individual VC firms are best if they do not further undermine the structure of the industry and harm long-term profitability. The choice of competitive strategy by VC firms is thus a key issue to be faced in the near future. Returns may be improved by differentiating in a way that increases the attractiveness of the firm to suppliers and users or by cutting costs.

The problem with attempting to achieve lower costs is that it may require VC firms to put more money in fewer deals and to cut corners on due diligence, monitoring and assisting portfolio companies, or staffing the VC firm itself. These strategies have been tried to some extent, but they contain the seeds of their own destruction, for they reduce the provision of venture capital to something more akin to financial brokerage, and they erode the reputation of the industry.

The issue then becomes, how does a VC firm differentiate itself from the nearly 700 other U.S. firms? Further, how should it add value to limited partners and entrepreneurs in a cost-effective manner? How should firms which add value through utilizing their professional know-how in ongoing efforts communicate this to suppliers and users? How can they distinguish themselves from those which are little more than "financial engineers" looking to push through deals for quick returns with little effort? While evidence suggests that returns are bimodal and that the short-term financial group enjoys much lower returns, the behavior of this subgroup has a highly negative impact on the industry's reputation with suppliers, users, and even policy makers.

Suppliers : Increasing Wariness, Increasing Power

The changing demographics of the typical supplier of capital, the long presence of venture capital in the limelight of financial markets for emerging technologically innovative companies, and the shift of venture capital from providers of early stage assistance to later stage financiers have all worked together to create more sophisticated and wary limited partners. These changes are manifested in these partners' demands for better measures of rates of return for investments and threshold rate provisions, for more immediate transfers of wealth, and for stricter terms and incentive structures for their investments.

The consolidation of supplier power in the hands of fewer institutional investors and the growth of venture capital sources have meant that suppliers have greater power than ever before. Therefore, the issues facing VC firms regarding suppliers are: what can be done to improve the limited partner–general partner climate for deal making? Is there a way to select limited partners who have less relative bargaining power? What creative ways exist to structure deals to provide risk protection for suppliers and not deter or punish venture capital investors who are willing to take some risks? How can partnerships be structured to significantly reward superior performance of 20 percent annual rate of return (ROR), or over 35 percent? Is there a need for and can any consensus be reached in the industry about common valuation methodologies used in determining portfolio valuation and ROR? How can the structure, terms, and conditions of such partnerships be radically simplified to eliminate the "ticking time bombs for future litigation" contained in the detailed provisions of so many agreements? Is there too much money chasing too few deals, or merely too few entrepreneurs who will live with the often supplier-biased terms and conditions of the deal?

Users: More Information, More Options

As the number of VC firms has grown globally, entrepreneurs and companies have grown more savvy and wary about the venture financing process. Increasingly, these users raise questions in their decision processes that pose further challenges for venture investors. These questions include: What do venture capitalists supply beyond the money? How, when, and in what manner will the investor truly add value to our company-building process? Is the set of know-how, skills, and expertise of the funds' managers going to make a difference in value creation in my venture? Is this set of venture capitalists interested only in financial engineering and transaction fee generation? How can I protect myself and my company from the inevitable conflicts with venture capitalists and other investors over control, goals, priorities, and timing of exit? What are the real implications for the instruments, terms, and conditions in the investment agreement proposed by investors? How can I better assess my relative bargaining power while I still have the time and cash on hand to do so? What alternatives should my firm consider other than venture capital?

Threats and Substitutes: "Little Pig, Little Pig, Let Me Come In"

The explosion in the availability of venture capital has been accompanied by an explosion in new entrants, creative alternative financing sources, and substitutes. It seems that the potential suppliers who "want in" on the action are endless: foreign banks and corporations, investment banks for their own and their clients' accounts, and many new players as venture capitalists. Where will the deal flow come from for all these competitors? How can rates of return be sustained? How long will the current industry shakeout continue, and what will be its aftermath? What will be the exit strategies for the 1990s? How lasting and robust will the current uptick in the IPO market be? Is it inevitable that Europe will surpass the United States as the new world center of gravity for venture capital?

Policy Issues: The Paradox of Prosperity

Little sympathy has been voiced in political or academic circles for the industry's fervent cry for a capital gains reduction. The reasoning seems to be: so many venture capitalists have become outrageously wealthy, and others are merely crying in their soup over the painful adjustments from an "old boys' network" to a fiercely competitive industry globally, so why should we worry about them?

Yet, Bygrave and Timmons (1991) provide evidence that venture capital has played an important part in the U.S. entrepreneurial process in fostering innovation, the birth of industries, and regional economic development. Further, these authors argue that policies — or lack thereof — directed toward the venture capital industry, and thus the entrepreneurial process, will alter the "genetic code" of that process in ways that will be felt well into and throughout the 21st century. If classic venture capital has been one of several "geese laying golden eggs" for the U.S. economy during the past four decades, then a number of important policy issues arise: which eggs do state and federal policy makers prefer to have laid? How can this process be encouraged (or discouraged)? Are current federal policies endangering the goose, or ensuring its longevity? What factors and infrastructures are vital at the state and federal level to enhance the value creation and enhancement process? How sensitive is this process to state and federal tax and regulatory policy, especially banking and securities, in the short and long term? Is the U.S. VC industry at a serious competitive disadvantage in the global marketplace because of U.S. tax, banking, and securities regulations?

▬ ▬ ▬ ▬ ▬ ▬ ▬ ▬

VENTURE CAPITAL RESEARCH IN THE LATE 1980S

Brophy's (1986) review of venture capital provides a useful overview of the venture capital industry and the flows of capital from 1969 to 1983, and of the major streams in venture capital research in the '60s, '70s, and early '80s. Brophy noted these key areas of research: in the 1960s, the role of finance in entrepreneurially-driven, emerging growth companies; in the 1970s, the processes of venture capital, their link to modern finance theories, and the efficiencies of capital markets; in the early 1980s, the characteristics of venture capital portfolios, the investment decision processes, and flows of venture capital. Brophy called for more comprehensive information in future research, in-depth case studies, and greater application of modern financial and economic theories.

The second half of the 1980s witnessed a broadening and deepening of academic research on venture capital. The following overview reports on the key streams taken up during this period.

Venture Capital Flows and Industry Structure

One stream of research focuses on venture capital at the macrolevel. Its concerns are with factors which influence the industry as a whole and with the role of venture capital in economic growth. Bygrave and Timmons (1985, 1986) continued their investigations into the flows of venture capital. The 1985 study identified how various exogenous factors such as stock market conditions, long-term interest rates, and public policies (specifically the 1978 change in the capital gains tax) were related to inflows and outflows of venture capital. Using a resource exchange framework, the 1986 study examined the nature of inter-connectedness and deal sharing among venture capital firms. Bygrave (1987) found that 1) the more uncertain the investment, the greater is the co-investing, and 2) firms more highly interconnected to the network control a dispropor-tionate share of venture capital.

The first of these studies had predicted that if the proposed elimination of the favorable capital gains treatment were to go into law, there would be a se-vere loss of capital to the industry. Bygrave and Shulman (1988) examined whether, in fact, this was happening after the Tax Reform Act of 1986 was es-tablished; they concluded that inflows were not hurt severely, because only a small proportion of suppliers of capital to the industry were significantly im-pacted by the policy change.

Timmons and Bygrave (1986) examined the role of venture capital in the development of high-innovation-technology companies. A surprising conclu-sion of this study was that the provision of capital itself by VC firms was one of their least important contributions in fostering technological innovation. In-stead, these authors found that significant contributions from venture capital involved early, active involvement which was highly managerially rather than financially intensive. In his study, Sahlman (1989) concluded that forces had been building to undermine the structure of the venture capital industry; the upshot was that returns were eroding, and the discrepancy between high-performing and low-performing VC firms was widening.

Investment Decision Processes and Criteria

The manner and criteria for selecting among alternative investment opportun-ities continued to interest researchers. In a follow-up of an earlier study, MacMillan, Siegel, and Subba Narasimha (1985) found that venture capitalists systematically assess ventures in terms of several categories of risk posed by potential investments, with the greatest weight being given to characteristics of the founding entrepreneur or the entrepreneurial team. MacMillan et al. were able to categorize venture capitalists into those who carefully assess competi-tive and implementation risks, those who seek easy exit, and those who at-tempt to keep open as many options as possible. In a related study, MacMillan, Zemann, and Subba Narasimha (1987) discovered that business plans which were accepted by venture capitalists differed from those rejected, in that per-formance projections for those rejected tended to be either above (too optimis-tic) or below (too naive) the projection ranges in the set of accepted proposals.

Goslin and Barge (1986) found that venture capitalists surveyed cited the quality of the management team and the attractiveness of the product as the two most critical factors in their decision. Sandberg, Schweiger, and Hofer

(1987) examined the decision process and found that venture capitalists tend to look first at the strategic context and the finances of the venture, and then at the references of the entrepreneur. Hisrich and Jankowicz (1990) examined venture capitalists' intuition in the decision process and determined that decision constructs center around the management team, the opportunity, and the expected return; the importance and application of these constructs vary from individual to individual.

Timmons et al. (1987) noted that studies of criteria rarely linked the criteria to ultimate success or failure; these authors used extensive interviews with venture capitalists to derive a set of propositions regarding factors which were likely to distinguish successful from unsuccessful start-up attempts. Roure and Maidique (1986) examined prefunding factors against early performance and concluded that successful ventures had teams which were larger and more complete, had prior experience working together, and had members with more experience in the function they were performing in the venture.

Venture Capital Rates of Return

The recent work of William Bygrave is the most comprehensive on VC industry performance. His major findings (Bygrave 1989; Bygrave and Timmons 1991) have shown the decline in rates of return in the venture capital industry from a peak of 32 percent in 1980 to under 10 percent by the end of 1985. This area of inquiry will take on even greater importance in the 1990s on a global scale, with its methodological sand traps and political minefields. During the past year alone, major industry debates have erupted over appropriate evaluation methods.

VC Firm Strategies

An area which has received only a smattering of research is VC firm strategies. In fact, Sahlman and Stevenson's (1985) study is notable in that it points up the alarming lack of strategic outlook of an entire set of VC firms and other investors which ignored industry signals and overinvested in the computer disc industry in the early 1980s. Sahlman and Stevenson claim that the behavior observed in this study is merely one example of the myopic tendencies which have at times beset the industry. They claim that the disaster which befell these firms could have easily been foreseen had the VC firms attended to conditions at the industry level, refused to blindly follow the strategy of others, and realized some basic economic concepts such as the fact that growth does not necessarily equal profitability.

Robinson (1987) examined the basic strategies and assumptions of VC firms through questionnaire data. He observed that VC firms appear to be increasingly heterogeneous with regard to their strategies. He noted that strategic groups are forming along four dimensions: 1) the sources of capital sought; 2) the extent of assistance offered to investees; 3) the preferred stage of investing;

and 4) their use of financial resources. Gupta and Sapienza (1988) examined the extent of geographic and industry diversification of 169 VC firms in Texas, Massachusetts, and California. They observed that type of VC firm (private, corporate, or SBIC), preferred stage of investing, and the amount of capital under management all played significant roles in the extent of VC firms' diversification; interestingly, VC firms focusing on early stage, and hence riskier, investments tend to be *less* rather than more diversified. This implies an approach of great involvement to reduce rather than spread risk.

Using data provided by Venture Economics, Inc., Soja and Reyes (1990) note that smaller (i.e., < $25 million) and larger (> $50 million) VC firms appear to be outperforming the average-sized firms. They speculate that the trends at the conclusion of the 1980s will be integrated into the strategies of the early 1990s: institutional investors will seek follow-on funds of VC teams with proven track records; competition for high-quality deals will be greatest; horizons will expand for global capital sourcing, investment opportunities, and strategic partnering; and equity will be the instrument of choice.

Finally, Roure, Keeley, and van der Heyden (1990) examined questionnaire data from 34 European VC firms to examine their perceptions of the growing VC industry in Europe and of the strategies they expect to use to exploit emerging opportunities. Among the most interesting of the findings are: 1) a much broader investment pattern in Europe than in the United States, with no industries dominating in Europe; 2) a strategy of backing a "national champion" venture (regardless of the industry) that (it is hoped) will become a market leader after 1992 when the market opens up; and 3) the intention of most VC firms to become active investors in the closest neighboring country.

The Roles and Activities of Venture Capitalists

An area of research with a long tradition is the area of venture capitalist activities; considerable additional work in this area was published in the late 1980s. Gorman and Sahlman (1986) found that senior partners in VC firms are the ones most actively involved in the portfolio companies; further, early stage investments receive the highest level of involvement. MacMillan, Kulow, and Khoylian (1989) found that the most critical activities of lead investors were acting as sounding boards, locating alternative financing sources, communicating with limited partners, and monitoring financial and operating performance of the ventures. Rosenstein (1988) compared the boards of venture-capital-backed companies to others, finding that boards with venture capitalists tend to be more active and that the venture capitalists' key role tends to be providing strategic advice and perspective.

Sapienza and Timmons (1989b) found that the most important roles played by lead investors with regard to the entrepreneur-CEO of the portfolio company were not only as sounding boards, business advisors, and financiers but as mentors and confidants as well; the importance of these roles to both parties was influenced by such factors as the relative ownership, the geographic distance between the two parties, and the level of innovation pursued in the venture. In a related study, Sapienza and Timmons (1989a) found that the effectiveness of the interaction between lead investor-CEO pairs was positively related to the level of innovation pursued in the venture and the openness or informality of the relationship between the venture capitalist and the entrepreneur. A recent study conducted in Sweden also found that in addition to the traditional functions of financier and industry contact, entrepreneurs find receiving "support" from venture capitalists as important (Fredriksen et al. 1990).

The nature and variations of venture capitalist-entrepreneur relations is an emerging area of study, one in which the entrepreneur's perspective of the venture capital process is for the first time being taken into account. Sapienza (1989) and Sapienza and Gupta (1989) examined factors related to the level of venture capitalist involvement, the openness of exchange of information, and the level of conflict in the relations: the first study examined the impact of market conditions, venture characteristics, and ownership on VC-investee relations; the second noted that VC-entrepreneur relations are influenced by the degrees of marketing and technology innovation pursued in the venture.

Venture Capitalist Value Added

The area of venture capital research currently providing the greatest controversy is the issue of whether or not VC firms add value beyond the capital supplied. This question has been examined at both the macro- and micro-organizational levels, and the issue remains unresolved for the time being. Brophy and Verga (1988) and Cherin and Hergert (1988) addressed the issue by examining stock prices of VC-backed vs. non-VC-backed ventures; the former study found evidence of venture capital value added, while the latter study found no such evidence. Examining the return of high-tech IPOs with VC firm members on the board of directors, Stein and Bygrave (1990) concluded that ventures benefit from the presence of VC firm members on the board only if the VC firms are among the "top 20" in the industry.

MacMillan, Kulow, and Khoylian (1989) identified low-, moderate-, and high-involvement lead investors. They found that for the low-involvement group, providing professional support was positively correlated with performance; for the moderate group, monitoring operations was positively correlated, while strategic involvement and management recruiting was negatively correlated with performance; for the high-involvement group, negotiating employment terms was positively correlated and management recruiting was negatively related to performance.

Rosenstein (1988) found that ventures with a higher percentage of venture capitalists on their boards performed no better than those with a lower percentage. In follow-up studies, Rosenstein et al. (1989, 1990) found that venture capitalists were rated as contributing more to the venture than other board members only for the set of ventures which had board members from the "top

20" VC firms. They concluded that in general VC firms add value only if they are one of the elite.

Sapienza and Timmons (1989a) found that both entrepreneurs and venture capitalists tended to give high ratings to both the importance and the effectiveness of lead investor involvement in the venture in a variety of roles beyond the purely financial; they also found venture capitalist effectiveness positively related to venture performance. They concluded that venture capitalists provide value beyond the money supplied.

Topics other than those covered above have also begun to emerge. For example, suppliers to the venture capital industry (such as pension funds and corporate investors) have recently been gaining some deserved attention (e.g., Brophy and Guthner 1988; Winters and Murfin 1988; Florida and Kenney 1988; Fried and Hisrich 1989). The interest in the venture capital industry as a topic for research has been expanding almost as rapidly as the industry itself; and the quality of the research is ever improving. It was announced, for example, at the 1990 Babson College Entrepreneurship Conference that submissions of venture capital research had grown more rapidly than any other topic area in the last five years. Nonetheless, opportunities for meaningful research on venture capital remain quite abundant.

━━ ━━ ━━ ━━ ━━

**VENTURE CAPITAL
RESEARCH IN THE
DECADE AHEAD**

Opportunities for Researchers

We have just begun to plow the incredibly rich and deep soil of research opportunities in the venture capital industry. It offers a microcosm of the entrepreneurial process — innovation, company formation, building and renewal, the birth of industries, and regional economic progress. Yet, still in its infancy, the venture capital industry has just experienced a decade of explosive growth globally and a subsequent shakeout. Its intricate and vital contributions to the core molecules of economic growth and its dynamic nature make it a fertile and compelling subject of our inquiries. The key question for researchers is: What do we need to know that is of relevance for the various stakeholders, rather than just an academic curiosity?

What follows is not intended to be exhaustive but is a limited set of suggestions for research questions potentially of interest to stakeholders in venture capital.

Suppliers of capital:
● What is the nature and impact of ongoing structural and competitive changes in the global venture capital industry in the 1990s?
● What are the rates of return in the 1990s?

What portfolio and ROR valuation methods are used ? What are the consequences, and which are appropriate ?

How sensitive is fund performance to valuation methods, and why ?

What should institutional investors look for and look out for in selecting a venture fund to invest in ?

What options exist in the structuring of partnerships, and what are the requirements of different stakeholders and limited partners ?

What has to happen for venture capital to become an attractive investment in the 1990s ?

How do these issues contrast and compare globally ?

Users of venture capital :

What is the value-added (or detracted) role of venture capital investors for ventures at different stages ?

How can one assess and utilize the relative bargaining position of suppliers, users, and investors of venture capital ?

What methodologies and decision processes are used to identify and evaluate market opportunities and asymmetries ?

What are the different deal structures, and what difference do specific terms and conditions make for the various stakeholders ?

● What creative deal structures have emerged ?

What is the process of negotiating, valuing, and structuring deals, and what makes a difference to the various stakeholders ?

What has to happen for venture capital to become an attractive source of capital for seed, start-up, and growing young companies ?

What creative financing alternatives and substitutes exist, and how can entrepreneurs evaluate, compare, and select among these ? What are the critical dimensions ?

How do the above issues compare from country to country and globally ?

Venture capital firms :

What competitive strategies exist in the 1990s ? How do firms differentiate themselves ? How are these related to fund RORs; e.g., what strategies make a difference ?

What value-added opportunities exist domestically and globally ?

Given the radically different structure and definition of venture capital in the 1990s, what are the implications for firms ?

Is "capital market myopia" endemic to the industry ? If so, how can it be anticipated, managed, or avoided ?

What exit strategies are viable in the illiquid early 90s ? How have these changed, and to which stakeholders does it matter ?

What deal structures and portfolio valuation methods are appropriate; what do fund managers need to know ?

What has been the pattern of dissolution of funds and partnerships ? What has worked and not worked ? What lessons are emerging ?

- What is the role of outside advisors to venture funds? How has this changed? What are the minefields and sand traps?
- What is the difference between effective and ineffective board members in venture-capital-backed firms?
- What are the "50,000 chunks" of relevant know-how, experience, and networks that are necessary for successful venture capital investing in companies at different stages? What differentiates the effective and the ineffective?
- What are effective and ineffective methods and approaches to conducting "due diligence" and "monitoring and tracking" venture capital investments? What are the value-added investing strategies? What does it really involve and take to be a value-added investor?
- How do the above issues compare from country to country and globally?

Policy issues:
- What fiscal, tax, and regulatory issues can have a positive or negative impact on venture capital and the entrepreneurial process?
- What is venture capital's role in innovation, technological competitiveness, the birth of new industries, and global competitiveness?
- What are the opportunities, risks, and dangers for state and federal government initiatives in this arena?

Cautions for Researchers

Venture capital research, like the industry itself, has experienced explosive growth, so that the developments in the 1980s represent a significant addition to the body of literature. But such growth involves serious perils along with the potential rewards.

A major challenge for academic researchers in any field is to make sure they have practiced "Timmons' Law of Research No. 1": One must engage in "an intellectual collision with the real world" in shaping research ideas, questions, and strategies. This field is no exception. As the botanist, the biologist, and the bioengineer immerse themselves in the garden, the species, and the genetic codes to gain a better understanding and build knowledge, so should entrepreneurship researchers. It is critical to *test the appropriateness and relevance of research questions, the usefulness of variables chosen, the precision of definitions, and the validity of measures used.* Ignorance of the realities and nuances of an industry and an unwillingness to engage in "an intellectual collision" can lead to voluminous but meaningless research. Secondly, methodology is no substitute for relevance. *Researchers cannot allow methodology to override relevance.* They must ask themselves, does it matter? Do my findings make a difference to any of the stakeholders that care? Who will read this, and how can it be used? Finally, *does the research add to the intellectual capital in the field,* or merely fatten one's vita? Can it enhance both theory and practice and be used in the classroom in ways that enhance curriculum and learning?

The risks of failing to heed such cautions are worth considering. First, we risk thoroughly alienating the subjects of our inquiries and cutting off our access to data and interviews. Second, we risk ridicule by those who are knowledgeable and informed about the industry. Third, we risk ridicule by researchers in other fields, and the dismissal of our work. One result of these risks would be a crippling of efforts to build the base of intellectual capital, and a resulting default of this topic to others.

In summary, this chapter examined the causes and implications of the explosive growth in the 1980s in the venture capital industry at home and abroad. Competitive pressures which squeezed the industry also resulted in some benefits for entrepreneurs : knowledge of and access to alternative sources of financing expanded for entrepreneurs. Entrepreneurs with high-potential ventures were particularly well positioned to take advantage of the opportunities. While some evidence emerged that venture capitalists had become less focused on early stage investments, in absolute terms the capital base was growing even for this sector. The venture capital industry enters the 1990s as a fiercely competitive one in which surviving firms will be searching for effective ways to differentiate themselves.

This chapter also focused on the research done in the venture capital arena. It was found that much of this research is beginning to branch out well beyond purely financial aspects of the venture capital process. Research about venture capital has progressed, but ample opportunities exist for more in-depth studies which can help practitioners build on the growing body of knowledge, and which can contribute to the development of a theory of entrepreneurship. These goals are best accomplished by researchers willing to immerse themselves in the venture capital process and gain the expertise necessary to integrate the ideas of theory with the demands of practice.

━━ ━━ ━━ ━━ ━━

REFERENCES

Brophy, D. J. 1986 Venture capital research. In *The art and science of entrepreneurship*, eds. D. L. Sexton and R. W. Smilor, 119–143. Cambridge, Mass. : Ballinger.

Brophy, D. J., and M. W. Guthner 1988 Publicly traded venture capital funds : Implications for institutional "fund of funds" investors. *Journal of Business Venturing* 3 : 187–206.

Brophy, D. J., and J. A. Verga 1988 More than money ? The influence of venture capitalists on initial public offerings. Paper presented at the Babson Entrepreneurship Conference, Calgary, Canada.

Bygrave, W. D. 1987 The structure of the investment network of venture capital firms. Summary in *Frontiers of entrepreneurship research*, eds. N. Churchill, J. Hornaday, B. Kirchhoff, and K. Vesper, 429–431. Wellesley, Mass. : Babson College.

1989 Venture capital industry : A resource exchange perspective. Ph.D. diss., Boston University.

Bygrave, W. D., and J. M. Shulman 1988 Capital gains tax : Bane or boon for venture capital ? In *Frontiers of entrepreneurship research*, eds. B. A. Kirchhoff, W. A. Long,

W. E. McMullan, K. H. Vesper, and W. E. Wetzel, Jr., 324–338. Wellesley, Mass.: Babson College.

Bygrave, W. D., and J. A. Timmons 1985 An empirical model for the flows of venture capital. In *Frontiers of entrepreneurship research*, eds. J. A. Hornaday, E. B. Shils, J. A. Timmons, and K. H. Vesper, 105–125. Wellesley, Mass.: Babson College.

1986 Networking among venture capital firms. In *Frontiers of entrepreneurship research*, eds. R. Ronstadt, J. A. Hornaday, R. Peterson, and K. H. Vesper, 437–456. Wellesley, Mass.: Babson College.

1991 *Venture and risk capital: Practice and performance, promises and policy.* Boston: Harvard Business School. Forthcoming.

Cherin, A., and M. Hergert 1988 Do venture capitalists create value? A test from the computer industry. Paper presented at the Babson Entrepreneurship Conference, Calgary, Canada.

Florida, R., and M. Kenney 1988 Venture capital and high technology entrepreneurship. *Journal of Business Venturing* 3: 301–319.

Fredriksen, O., M. Klofsten, H. Landstrom, C. Olofsson, and C. Wahlbin 1990 Entrepreneur-venture capitalist relations: The entrepreneur's view. In *Frontiers of entrepreneurship research*, eds. W. Bygrave, N. Churchill, J. Hornaday, D. Muzyka, K. Vesper, and W. Wetzel, Jr., 251–265. Wellesley, Mass.: Babson College.

Fried, V. H., and R. D. Hisrich 1989 Venture capital from the investors' perspective. In *Frontiers of entrepreneurship research*, eds. R. H. Brockhaus, Sr., N. C. Churchill, J. A. Katz, B. A. Kirchhoff, K. H. Vesper, and W. E. Wetzel, Jr., 258–273. Wellesley, Mass.: Babson College.

Gorman, M., and W. A. Sahlman 1986 What do venture capitalists do? In *Frontiers of entrepreneurship research*, eds. R. Ronstadt, J. A. Hornaday, R. Peterson, and K. H. Vesper, 414–436. Wellesley, Mass.: Babson College.

Goslin, L. N., and B. Barge 1986 Entrepreneurial qualities considered in venture capital support. In *Frontiers of entrepreneurship research*, eds. R. Ronstadt, J. A. Hornaday, R. Peterson, and K. H. Vesper, 366–379. Wellesley, Mass.: Babson College.

Gupta, A. K., and H. J. Sapienza 1988 The pursuit of diversity by venture capital firms: Antecedents and implications. In *Frontiers of entrepreneurship research*, eds. B. A. Kirchhoff, W. A. Long, W. E. McMullan, K. H. Vesper, and W. E. Wetzel, Jr., 290–302. Wellesley, Mass.: Babson College.

Hisrich, R. D., and A. D. Jankowicz 1990 Intuition in venture capital decisions: An exploratory study using a new technique. *Journal of Business Venturing* 5: 49–62.

MacMillan, I. C., D. M. Kulow, and R. Khoylian 1989 Venture capitalists' involvement in their investments: Extent and performance. *Journal of Business Venturing* 4: 27–47.

MacMillan, I. C., R. Siegel, and P. N. Subba Narasimha 1985 Criteria used by venture capitalists to evaluate new venture proposals. *Journal of Business Venturing* 1: 119–128.

MacMillan, I. C., L. Zemann, and P. N. Subba Narasimha 1987 Criteria distinguishing successful from unsuccessful ventures in the venture screening process. *Journal of Business Venturing* 2: 123–137.

Porter, M., W. Sahlman, and H. Stevenson 1990 The changing structure of the American venture capital industry. Presentation to the National Venture Capital Association, May 11, 1989, Washington, D.C.

Pratt, S. E. 1987 Overview and introduction to the venture capital industry. In *Guide to venture capital sources*, eds. S. E. Pratt and J. K. Morris, 7–9. Wellesley, Mass.: Venture Economics.

Pratt, S. E., and J. K. Morris, eds. 1987 *Guide to venture capital sources*. Wellesley, Mass.: Venture Economics.

Robinson, R. B., Jr. 1987 Emerging strategies in the venture capital industry. *Journal of Business Venturing* 2: 53–77.

Rosenstein, J. 1988 The board and strategy: Venture capital and high technology. *Journal of Business Venturing* 3: 159–170.

Rosenstein, J., A. V. Bruno, W. D. Bygrave, and N. T. Taylor 1989 Do venture capitalists on boards of portfolio companies add value besides money? In *Frontiers of entrepreneurship research*, eds. R. H. Brockhaus, Sr., N. C. Churchill, J. A. Katz, B. A. Kirchhoff, K. H. Vesper, and W. E. Wetzel, Jr., 216–229. Wellesley, Mass.: Babson College.

1990 How much do CEOs value the advice of venture capitalists on their boards? In *Frontiers of entrepreneurship research*, eds. W. Bygrave, N. Churchill, J. Hornaday, D. Muzyka, K. Vesper, and W. Wetzel, Jr., 238–250. Wellesley, Mass.: Babson College.

Roure, J. B., R. H. Keeley, and T. van der Heyden 1990 European venture capital: Strategies and challenges in the '90s. Working paper, Universidad de Navarra, Barcelona, Spain.

Roure, J. B., and M. A. Maidique 1986 Linking prefunding factors and high-technology venture success: An exploratory study. *Journal of Business Venturing* 1: 109–123.

Sahlman, W. A. 1989 The changing structure of the American venture capital industry. Paper presented at the Babson Entrepreneurship Conference, St. Louis.

1990 Venture capital dims for start-ups, but not to worry. *Wall Street Journal*, January 24, B2.

Sahlman, W. A., and H. H. Stevenson 1985 Capital market myopia. In *Frontiers of entrepreneurship research*, eds. J. A. Hornaday, E. B. Shils, J. A. Timmons, and K. H. Vesper, 80–104. Wellesley, Mass.: Babson College.

Sandberg, S., D. Schweiger, and C. Hofer 1987 Determining venture capitalists' decision criteria: The use of verbal protocols. In *Frontiers of entrepreneurship research*, eds. N. C. Churchill, J. A. Hornaday, O. J. Krasner, and K. H. Vesper, 392–407. Wellesley, Mass.: Babson College.

Sapienza, H. J. 1989 Variations in venture capitalist-entrepreneur relations: Antecedents and consequences. Ph.D. diss., University of Maryland.

Sapienza, H. J., and A. K. Gupta 1989 Pursuit of innovation by new ventures and its effects on venture capitalist-entrepreneur relations. In *Frontiers of entrepreneurship research*, eds. R. H. Brockhaus, Sr., N. C. Churchill, J. A. Katz, B. A. Kirchhoff, K. H. Vesper, and W. E. Wetzel, Jr., 304–317. Wellesley, Mass.: Babson College.

Sapienza, H. J., and J. A. Timmons 1989a Launching and building entrepreneurial companies: Do the venture capitalists add value? In *Frontiers of entrepreneurship research*, R. H. Brockhaus, Sr., N. C. Churchill, J. A. Katz, B. A. Kirchhoff, K. H. Vesper, and W. E. Wetzel, Jr., 245–257. Wellesley, Mass.: Babson College.

1989b The roles of venture capitalists in new ventures: What determines their importance? *Proceedings of the Academy of Management*: 74–78.

Soja, T. A., and J. E. Reyes 1990 *Investment benchmarks: Venture capital*. Research report. Needham, Mass.: Venture Economics.

Stein, M., and W. D. Bygrave 1990 The anatomy of high-tech IPOs. Do their venture capitalists, underwriters, accountants, and lawyers make a difference ? In *Frontiers of entrepreneurship research*, eds. W. Bygrave, N. Churchill, J. Hornaday, D. Muzyka, K. Vesper, and W. Wetzel, Jr., 394–407. Wellesley, Mass. : Babson College.

Timmons, J. A., and W. D. Bygrave 1986 Venture capital's role in financing innovation for economic growth. *Journal of Business Venturing* 1 : 161–176.

Timmons, J. A., D. F. Muzyka, W. D. Bygrave, and H. H. Stevenson 1987 Opportunity recognition : The core of entrepreneurship. In *Frontiers of entrepreneurship research*, eds. N. C. Churchill, J. A. Hornaday, O. J. Krasner, and K. H. Vesper, 281–320. Wellesley, Mass. : Babson College.

Wetzel, William E., Jr. 1981 Informal risk capital in New England. In *Frontiers of entrepreneurship research*, ed. K. Vesper, 217–245. Wellesley, Mass. : Babson College.

1982 Project I-C-E : An experiment in capital formation. In *Frontiers of entrepreneurship research*, ed. K. Vesper, 335–357. Wellesley, Mass. : Babson College.

1984 Venture capital network, inc. : An experiment in capital formation. In *Frontiers of entrepreneurship research*, eds. J. Hornaday, F. Tarpley, Jr., J. Timmons, and K. Vesper, 111–125. Wellesley, Mass. : Babson College.

Wetzel, William E., Jr., and I. G. Wilson 1985 Seed capital gaps : Evidence from high-growth ventures. In *Frontiers of entrepreneurship research*, eds. J. Hornaday, E. Shils, J. Timmons, and K. Vesper, 221–240. Wellesley, Mass. : Babson College.

Winters, T. E., and D. L. Murfin 1988 Venture capital investing for corporate development objectives. *Journal of Business Venturing* 3 : 207–220.

Chapter

17

Venture Capital Returns in the 1980s

William D. Bygrave

●

INTRODUCTION

In general, investment fund portfolio managers have an abundance of information on rates of return when they invest in stocks, bonds, and debt instruments. That situation is reversed when they invest in venture capital partnerships where there is — relatively speaking — a dearth of reliable information on rates of return. As one pension fund manager at a major institution remarked in 1984 (Bygrave 1989): "Depending on whose numbers we believe, we should have as little as 5 percent or as much as 50 percent of our portfolio in venture capital partnerships." The need for reliable rates of return on venture capital was noted by Brophy (1986). He observed that although the period 1978–1984 saw a strong surge of funding enter the venture capital business, there had been no analysis of the performance results of this investment, and no evaluation of the benefits accruing to the investors.

Even though reliable numbers were hard to come by, there was certainly no shortage of anecdotal accounts and hearsay. According to venture capital folklore, the rates of return of venture capital funds were 30 percent or better (e.g., U.S. Congress 1984; Kozmetsky, Gill, and Smilor 1984). Stevenson, Muzyka, and Timmons (1986) reported that some pension fund managers were hoping for 75 percent returns on long-term funds. They commented that it was a very optimistic expectation in light of the 25 percent annual returns on venture capital that were experienced in the 1970s. Stevenson, Muzyka, and Timmons noted that if the 1985 pool of venture capital grew at a rate of 75 percent per annum, it would represent 13 percent of the total equity of the Fortune 1,000 firms in seven years — a scenario that was scarcely believable. What's more, it was hard to believe that the industry's folklore return was attainable, for, as Sahlman's (1989) simple model showed, a 35 percent gross return required the creation of 390 "big hits" with an average market value of $349 million in 1988. (A "big hit" is a very successful venture-capital-backed company such as Lotus, Compaq, Federal Express, and Microsoft). Again, it was a most unlikely scenario, since there were only 976 public companies with a market value greater than $349 million in the United States. Also, the average total valuation of venture-capital-backed IPOs and acquisitions was under $100 million.

Clearly, by the mid-1980s expectations were not consistent with realistic predictions. Simply put : either the folklore returns were a myth, or the returns in the late 1980s had to decline due to changes in the environment. The torrent of money that cascaded into venture capital firms in the 1980s and the poor market for initial public offerings had to take its toll.

This review will first look at the historical rates of return from the venture capital industry's beginnings in 1946. Then it will look at the actual returns from 1975 through 1988. A model will be proposed for the factors that influence the returns. Next we will examine a critical factor in that model : venture-capital-backed IPOs. We will end with a look at the research issues that need to be addressed in the 1990s.

HISTORICAL RATES OF RETURN

Probably the most famous venture-capital-backed start-up of all time is Digital Equipment Corporation (DEC). It seems as if everyone knows about American Research and Development's (ARD) investment in DEC. It is part of the folklore of the industry. And deservedly so. Even if the amount invested varies from $60,000 to $70,000 and the amount returned in about 12 years varies from $500 million to $600 million depending on who recounts the tale (e.g., Wells 1974 ; Kozmetsky, Gill, and Smilor 1984), the rate of return of 130 percent or thereabout is the stuff that legends are made of. But what is the reality ? Even with as spectacular an investment as DEC in its portfolio, ARD's rate of return for the 20 years from 1946 to 1966 was only 14 percent, according to Rotch in 1968. True, in 1966, its investment in DEC had yet to come to full fruition, but it was blossoming very nicely. By the late 1970s, after DEC had been harvested and ARD had become part of Textron, ARD's rate of return fell into the single digits (Gervitz 1985).

Since so many of the venture capital firms are private, data on rates of return are hard to find. Two of the most respected private venture capital firms are Bessemer Securities and Hambrecht and Quist. According to Poindexter (1976), Bessemer reported a 17 percent rate of return for the period 1967–1974, and Hambrecht and Quist a 15 percent rate of return over several years through 1972.

Table 17–1 presents a summary of published scholarly research on rates of return of venture capital. Most studies of venture capital returns have used small samples of publicly held firms, primarily small business investment companies (SBICs). A study of 14 public venture capital firms found the rate of return to be 11 percent on average (Faucett 1971). Hoban (1976) constructed a portfolio composed of 110 actual venture capital investments made by four different venture capital firms in 50 different companies during the period 1960–1968. The four venture capital firms were a publicly held SBIC, a private partnership, a private corporation owned by a wealthy family, and a subsidiary of a large bank holding company. He found the gross (before management fees and income taxes) rate of return of the portfolio to be 22.9 percent for the per-

TABLE 17–1 — Venture Capital : Compound Annual Rates of Return

14%	American Research and Development (1946–1966)	Rotch 1968
14%	92 funds	Poindexter 1976
	13% 59 VC firms managing 1/3 of VC pool (rate of return from firm's birth through 1974)	
	12% 29 public VCs (mainly SBICs, 1961–1973)	
	17% Bessemer Securities (1967–1974)	
	15% Hambrecht and Quist (late 1960s through 1972)	
11%	14 public VCs (primarily SBICs)	Faucett 1971
23%	110 actual investments in portfolio companies (gross return before annual management fee)	Hoban 1976
27%	Public VCs (based on stock prices, 1974–1979)	Martin and Petty 1983
30%	267 firms (SBICs, independent-private and corporate)	U.S. Congress 1984
	19% SBICs (based on capital appreciation, 1982–1984)	
	31% independent firms (based on capital appreciation, 1982–1984)	
	4% corporate (based on capital appreciation, 1982–1984)	
16%	Public VCs (based on stock prices, 1959–1985)	Ibbotson and Brinson 1987
24%	Simulation of hypothetical VC investments	Wells 1974
15%	Simulation of 100 funds	Stevenson, Muzyka, and Timmons 1986

iod through the end of 1975. If Hoban's rate of return is adjusted for the typical annual management fee of 3 percent, the rate of return is about 19.9 percent.

Poindexter (1976) gathered data from 29 publicly held firms consisting of 26 SBICs and 3 corporations investing in venture capital. The geometric mean of the annual rate of return for the 29 firms over the period 1961–1973 was 11.6 percent. That compared with the 7.1 percent rate of return for the Standard and Poor's 500 over the same period. The rates of return for Poindexter's sample of venture capital firms varied considerably with the calendar period over which it was computed. For example, it was 10.7 percent for the period 1961–1966, 31 percent for 1967–1971, and 1.2 percent for 1972–1973.

Martin and Petty (1983) analyzed the performance of 11 publicly traded venture capital firms, of which all but two were in Poindexter's sample. They computed the rate of return on the publicly traded stock for each of the six years from 1974 to 1979. The average rate of return on the publicly traded stock of the 11 venture capital firms over that period was 27 percent. Unfortunately, Martin and Petty's rate of return on publicly traded stock is not the actual rate of return on the firm's venture capital investments, and the two should not be compared, because there may be little or no relationship between their values at any one time. For example, Arthur D. Little, former chairman of Narragansett Capital Corporation, which was in both Poindexter's and Martin and Petty's samples, stated that in the mid-1970s Narragansett's share price fell to 80 percent below the value of the assets in its portfolio (Wayne 1988).

A study by First Chicago Investment Advisors (Ibbotson and Brinson 1987) used a method similar to Martin and Petty's (1983) to study the rates of return of public venture capital companies from 1959 through 1985. The compound annual rate of return over the 26-year period was 16 percent.

It is not easy to get the data needed to calculate the actual rates of return on venture capital investments — not even for publicly held funds such as Poindexter's sample of 29. Poindexter commented that it was an arduous task. To get the actual rate of return, it is necessary to dig into the financial statements published in annual reports and 10Ks to get operating expenses, interest expenses, income dividends, capital gains dividends, net assets, long-term debt, and net worth. Those numbers must be adjusted to allow for any additional public offerings and stock splits. The reliability of the net asset figure may be questionable because most of its value resides in a fund's portfolio, for which the value is only an estimate as most of the companies in it are private.

Poindexter (1976) surveyed 270 venture capital firms that managed the bulk of the domestic venture capital pool. He estimated that the respondents who supplied rate of return data managed one-third of the domestic pool of venture capital. They were asked to estimate their firm's rate of return since inception. The mean of the estimated rates of return of the 59 firms was 13.3 percent, with a range from 35 percent to minus 40 percent.

The 1983 study by the congressional Joint Economic Committee (U.S. Congress 1984) found that independent private venture capital firms expected a minimum annualized rate of return on individual investments that ranged from 75 percent for seed stage financing to about 35 percent per year for bridge financing. The same study found that independent private venture capital firms experienced a 31 percent annual net capital appreciation rate over the period 1982–1984. The report went on to conclude that the persistence of above average rates of return on venture capital investments suggests that capital markets may be under-allocating funds to risky, entrepreneurial investments.

That study did as much as any to bolster the folklore return of 30 percent because it was conducted under the auspices of the U.S. Congress (1984). Two hundred sixty-seven venture capitalist firms were surveyed in the summer of 1983. It was at the peak of the IPO frenzy, when valuations on venture-capital-backed IPOs were so high that one wag commented : "Investors buying IPOs at those P/E ratios are not discounting the future, they are discounting the hereafter !" Not surprisingly, venture capitalists were ecstatic and expected the high returns of 1983 to continue. Furthermore, according to Bygrave (1989), the study's research method was seriously flawed. Unfortunately, it carried the imprimatur of the Joint Economic Committee of the U.S. Congress, and it reported what the industry wanted to believe, so it perpetuated the 30 percent plus figure.

━━ ━━ ━━ ━━ ━━ ━━ ━━ ━━
ACTUAL RETURNS VERSUS FOLKLORE

In 1985–1986, in response to the need for valid and reliable data on the actual returns from venture capital funds, the author assisted Venture Economics, Inc. in starting its returns data base (Bygrave et al. 1988). By 1989, Venture Economics' data base contained 42 percent of all the funds formed from 1970 through 1987 and 65 percent of the capital under management. That sample of 197 funds represented the universe remarkably well with 3 percent seed stage, 16 percent early stage, 74 percent balanced, and 7 percent late stage.

When Venture Economics first published the actual returns on those funds it caused quite a commotion. The results — to put it mildly — were disappointing. Since 1980, overall returns briefly peaked above 30 percent in 1983 — the year of the IPO frenzy — and then slid relentlessly to the single digits by 1988. The *Wall Street Journal* November 8, 1988, headline said it all : "Recent Venture Funds Perform Poorly as Unrealistic Expectations Wear Off."

Computations of IRRs

There is no industry-wide standard method for computing the financial returns of venture capital funds. Increasingly, limited partners are computing their internal rate of return (IRR) based on their cash-on-cash returns plus their share of the residual value of the venture capital fund's holdings of cash and investments in portfolio companies that have yet to be distributed to the limited partners (*Venture Capital Journal* 1990).

The algorithm for computing the IRRs is fairly simple in principle. The residual, the disbursements, and the takedowns are each reduced to their present value on the date of the first takedown. A disbursement of D dollars has a present value of $D/(1 + IRR/100)^t$. Here, IRR is the annualized internal rate of return, and t is the time in years from the date of the first takedown to the date of the disbursement. The present values of a takedown of T dollars and a residual of R dollars can be computed the same way. Then by iteration, the value of IRR is computed at the end of each calendar period by finding its value when the present value of the takedowns equals the present value of all the disbursements plus the present value of the residual.

Limitations of IRRs

In practice, this computation is not quite so simple. First, there are limitations in some of the data sets. Some limited partners record the actual dates of the transactions, others record them at the end of the month in which they occur. To put them all on the same basis, transactions are computed as if they occurred on the last day of the month.

Second, although it is easy to construct an algorithm that computes the limited partner's share of a residual, it is difficult to compute it reliably without knowing the intricate details of the partnership agreement — specifically, when and how the general partner's share of the profit is recognized. In principle, the general partner does not get any share of the profit until the limited partners have received all the money that they paid into the fund. After that the profit is split, usually on a 20/80 basis. However, once the sum of the residual disbursements exceeds the sum of the takedowns, the fund is making a profit on paper. Most funds then recognize the unrealized profit that is in the residual. After that point is reached, the general partner holds back its anticipated share of future profits from subsequent disbursements to the limited partners.

The following simplifying method is used to compute the limited partner's residual value : 1) When the sum of the distributions is less than the sum of the takedowns (paid-in capital), the total value of the fund's residual is multiplied by the limited partner's percentage ownership of the fund. 2) When the sum of the distributions exceeds the sum of the takedowns, the total value of the fund's residual is multiplied by the limited partner's percentage ownership of the fund, multiplied by the limited partner's percentage of the allocation of the profits.

A third limitation is the reliability of the valuation of the residuals. Most funds have a valuation committee that estimates the value of its portfolio of investments in companies that have no publicly traded stock. Thus, the value of the residual is a somewhat subjective judgement of each fund's valuation committee. This problem is mitigated to some extent because there are different funds, and there is no reason to believe that there is any overall bias, either high or low, by the valuation committees.

Annualized Rates of Return

The annualized rates of return for all the funds in Venture Economics' data base are presented in Figure 17–1 (Venture Economics 1990). It shows the median IRRs by calendar year for all funds formed from 1974 through 1988. The median IRR peaked in 1982 at 27 percent. The top quartile of those funds peaked one year later at 44 percent. Those returns are in line with what we learned from our historical survey of the scholarly literature: overall returns from venture capital are typically below 20 percent with only brief spikes above 30 percent. However, the top-quartile funds performed much better, with returns above 20 percent in 9 out of 16 years, above 30 percent for 4 of those years, and above 40 percent for 1 year.

The information presented in Figure 17–1 must be viewed with caution because it agglomerates the IRRs of all funds at least five years old in a given year regardless of the age of the funds. To do so is potentially misleading, because it is expected that as funds grow older their portfolio companies move closer to being harvested (e.g., initial public offerings, mergers, etc.) or have actually been harvested. Thus, it is likely that the rate of return of a fund will increase with age, all other things being equal. Of course, all other things are not equal. One important factor is the calendar date, which can have a major effect on the IRRs. For example, as Figure 17–1 shows, IRRs peaked in 1982–1983. Hence, there are three temporal factors that have to be separated: 1) the year a fund was started, 2) its age, and 3) the calendar year for which the IRRs were computed.

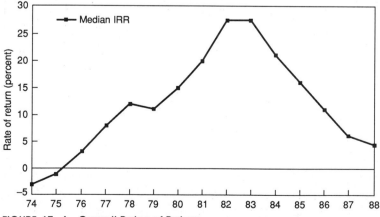

FIGURE 17–1   Overall Rates of Return
(*Source*: Venture Economics, Inc.)

Calendar Date

The funds were grouped in annual vintages according to the year in which they were started. The median IRRs of each group of funds by calendar year are presented in Figure 17–2. The 1977–1979 vintage, which comprises seven funds, performed spectacularly, with a median rate of return peaking at 35 percent in 1983 then gradually declining to 24 percent by 1988. Funds formed after 1979 did not perform as well. For example, at the end of 1985, the average returns of the 1981, 1982, 1983, and 1984 vintages were all lower than 10 percent, with the 1984 vintage being slightly negative. By 1988, every post-1979 vintage was returning less than 10 percent, and what's worse, all post-1980 vintages were below 5 percent.

The median returns in Figure 17–2 demonstrate the dramatic effect of the frenzied IPO market of 1983 when 121 venture-capital-backed companies went public, usually with spectacular offerings. Valuations of venture capital portfolios skyrocketed. Price-to-earnings ratios of 40–60 for venture-capital-backed IPOs (Sahlman 1989) were common. Some were much higher. At the height of the feeding frenzy, for example, Stratus Computer went public with

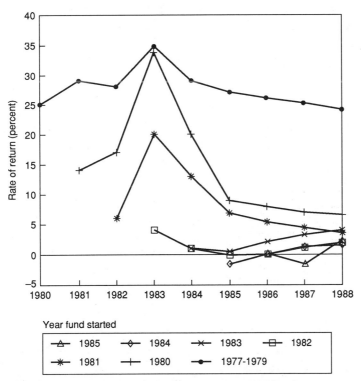

FIGURE 17–2 Median Rates of Return by Calendar Year
(*Source* : Venture Economics, Inc.)

an offering price of almost 200 times its annualized earnings. Other companies had no trouble going public even though they had lost money every quarter since they were founded. It confirmed what others such as Poindexter (1976) had noted: "hot" IPO markets are by far the most important cause of peaks in venture capital returns.

Age of Funds

Next, we will examine the effect of age on the rates of return. The IRRs of the funds grouped according to their starting dates were plotted against the age of the funds (Figure 17–3). It shows that at age five, the earlier a fund was started, the higher its rate of return. As a fund gets older, the value of its portfolio is expected to increase as the companies in which it has invested grow in value. The frequency distribution of each of the groups of three- and five-year-old funds is shown in Figure 17–4. It shows that the median of the distribution is higher for the older funds than the younger ones (25 percent vs. 13 percent). The frequency distributions should be viewed with caution, however, because they are not controlled for the starting date of the funds — which, for this sample, was any time from 1978 to 1982.

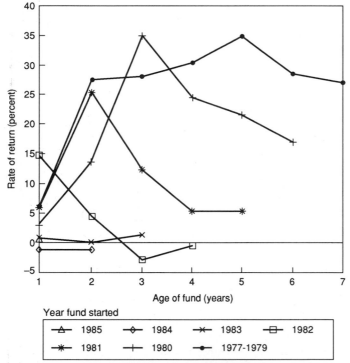

FIGURE 17–3   Median Rates of Return by Age of Fund
(*Source* : Venture Economics, Inc.)

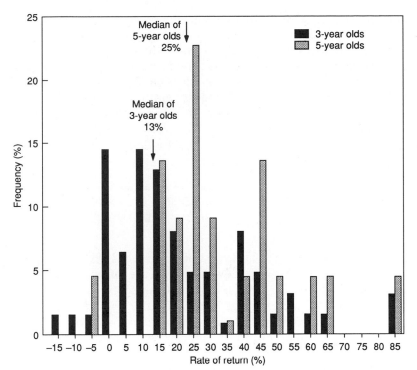

**FIGURE 17–4 Distribution of Returns
All 3- and 5-Year-Old Funds**
Note : Funds started 1978 through 1982.

From Ecstasy to Agony

The early 1980s were glorious days for venture capital. Returns climbed steeply to heights not seen since the late 1960s, which was the previous glory era. But the euphoria was short-lived. After reaching their lofty peak in 1983, returns began a downward slide that continued through the end of the 1980s. When compared to the performance of the stock markets in recent years, venture capital returns have been well below expectations since 1983. *Forbes* (1988) summed it up this way :

> Even the top performers are hurting. Take Boston-based TA Associates, one of the most successful of the large firms, with over $400 million under management. The 41 percent average return it has enjoyed over the past 11 years masks the fact that money invested in 1983 has returned less than a passbook 5.5 percent.
>
> "It used to be hard not to make money," TA Associates general partner P. Andrews McLane says ruefully. "It's definitely not as easy now."

Many factors contributed to the declining returns. Some observers said it was too much money chasing too few deals. Others said it was too much money chasing too many good deals. No question, the United States in the early 1980s was rather suddenly awash with venture capital. There was a shortage of quality deals to invest it in. Complicating that problem was a shortage of experienced venture capitalists to seek out deals, evaluate them, invest in them, and oversee the investments. Then, when it was time to harvest the quality deals that had grown into successful companies, investors had lost their appetites for IPOs. Stock flotations were impossible for most venture-capital-backed companies. Or if they were possible, valuations were down. Let's look at those factors underlying falling returns in more detail. We will examine them within the framework of Bygrave's (1989) resource exchange model.

A RESOURCE EXCHANGE THEORY FOR VENTURE CAPITAL

Acting on Bruno and Tyebjee's (1982) suggestion, Bygrave (1989) developed a theoretical framework to show how the flows of capital are influenced by external and internal factors (Figure 17–5). It is built with concepts from economics and sociology, such as resource exchange theory (Pfeffer and Salancik 1978) and liability of newness (Stinchcombe 1965). Essentially, the model says that venture capitalists operate in an uncertain environment that influences their behavior. Uncertainty comes from capital markets, including the over-the-counter market, the IPO market, and interest rates; government policies, including capital gains tax rates, ERISA pension fund rules, and SEC regulations; technology such as the emergence and commercialization of the microprocessor and recombinant DNA; the stage of the companies in which they invest; and the industries in which they specialize. Those factors influ-

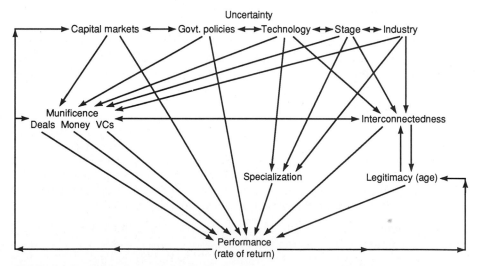

FIGURE 17–5   Venture Capital Industry : A Resource Exchange Model

ence the munificence of the venture capital industry. For example, when the NASDAQ is high, the IPO market is usually "hot." That increases the returns on venture capital investments and stimulates the inflow of new money into venture capital funds. A robust stock market also encourages more entrepreneurs to form companies, thereby increasing the availability of deals, because, according to William Egan (1988) of the venture capital firm Burr, Egan, Deleage, and Company:

> There's a high correlation between company formations and a robust stock market. When things are going great, [people] say, "Hey, I'll take a shot." Now [after the stock market crash of October 19, 1987], people are happy just to have a job. . . . [When stock prices are high] many executives exercise their stock options and use that money to start companies.

For similar reasons, it also increases the number of would-be venture capitalists.

The emergence of new technologies also arouses the venture capitalists. The late 1970s and early 1980s were miraculous years for the commercialization of new technologies. Many new companies, for instance, were launched by the microprocessor and recombinant DNA. Pioneers such as Apple and Genentech, fueled with venture capital, skyrocketed. Other venture-capital-backed companies soon followed, resulting in whole new industries.

To be successful in an environment that is so uncertain, venture capitalists require information and the experience to use it wisely when making decisions. They key to success is both *what* they know and *who* they know. That's where interconnectedness pays off, because venture capitalists share both information and deals with one another. The better connected a venture capital firm, the better informed it is; and if it uses the information wisely, the more successful it is. Interconnectedness and success increases a firm's legitimacy. Of course, success, legitimacy, and interconnectedness boost one another. After all, in venture capital, as in other walks of life, nothing succeeds like success; we all like to be associated with winners. As Bygrave (1988) found, the top venture capital firms form a tight network. At its center are some of the most successful firms.

A venture capital firm has to stay abreast of the information it needs to make wise investment decisions. It's not easy, especially for early stage, high-technology investing where product life cycles get shorter and shorter as technological change gets faster and faster. An average firm has about four professionals who have to gather and disseminate information, watch over portfolio companies, and, from time to time, raise more capital for follow-on funds. Hence, if a firm is to become expert, it must specialize. An outstanding example is Sevin Rosen, which has been one of the most successful venture capital firms of the 1980s — Compaq and Lotus are perhaps the most famous of its "big hits." It specializes in computers and semiconductors. Its two founders, L. J. Sevin and Ben Rosen, are among the most venerated gurus of the semiconductor industry and the personal computer industry, respectively (*Inc.* 1990).

Resource Exchange Model in Practice

Next, we will now see how the resource exchange model for the venture capital industry worked in practice during the 1980s. We will look especially at munificence (availability of capital, availability of deals to invest it in, and availability of venture capitalists to find, evaluate, and monitor investments) and performance, especially as it was affected by specialization, size, and legitimacy.

Availability of Capital

In the 1980s, institutions, especially pension funds, supplied more and more capital to venture capital funds. It caused concern that the flood of money would lower returns. As a 1988 *Business Week* article reported:

> [Pension funds are] "preparing to unleash hundreds of millions of dollars on venture capitalists who already have too much money," frets Don Valentine, a general partner of Sequoia Capital in Menlo Park, Calif. Many other veteran venture capitalists share his worry that the flood of venture capital will force prices of fledgling companies higher while lowering returns for most investors.

Availability of Deals

A good deal flow is the lifeblood of a venture capital firm. At the National Venture Capital Association annual meeting in May 1987, William Hambrecht (1987), one of the leaders of the venture capital industry, commented that what was happening in the industry at that time was "Economics 101." He said there were too many dollars coming into the industry, and competition for deals was pushing returns down. He was not alone in this view. Many veteran venture capitalists were worried that the flood of pension fund money into venture capital funds would force the prices of fledgling companies higher, thereby lowering returns for most investors (*Business Week* 1988).

Availability of Venture Capitalists

In 1978, there was no shortage of applicants who wanted to enter the venture capital profession. What was in short supply, however, was venture capitalists with 10 or more years of experience in the industry. The number of professionals in the industry increased from 597 in 1977 to 1,494 in 1983 — a 150 percent increase. The capital under their management increased from $2.5 billion to $12 billion — a 379 percent increase. And the average capital per professional increased from $4.2 million to $8.1 million — a 93 percent increase (*Venture Capital Journal* 1984).

The rapid growth of the venture capital industry depleted the availability of experienced venture capitalists (Kozmetsky, Gill, and Smilor 1984). For the industry as a whole, venture capitalists were managing more money but were less experienced in 1983 than in 1977. Of 61 new partnerships formed in the period 1977–1982, the level of the general partners' experience was only 5.2 years (*Venture Capital Journal* 1982). The level of experience of general partners in new funds dropped further in 1983. (New partnerships are new venture capital funds raised by new firms. In contrast, follow-on partnerships are new venture capital funds raised by existing firms.)

Harvest

The most decisive determinant of venture capital returns is the health of the IPO market. When the IPO market is buoyant, it's comparatively easy to float new issues of venture-capital-backed companies at high valuations. That causes venture capital returns to rise, because IPOs provide by far the most bountiful harvest of venture capital investments (Venture Economics 1988, 1989, 1990). The average realized gain from an IPO is almost five times greater than from an acquisition, which is the next best harvest.

When we look at the number of venture-capital-backed companies that went public or were acquired during the 1980s, we see that the proportion of acquisitions increased, and conversely, the proportion of IPOs declined (Figure 17–6). It happened because investors lost their appetite for IPOs after the feeding frenzy of 1983. That was not surprising, because anyone who invested in a market basket of venture-capital-backed IPOs from 1978 to 1979 and held on to the stock for four years lost money (Bygrave and Stein 1989). Also, the returns on small company stocks in general, which were above the returns on S&P 500 stocks from 1976 through 1985, fell below S&P 500 stocks from 1986 to the present (Figure 17–7). That also made IPOs less desirable.

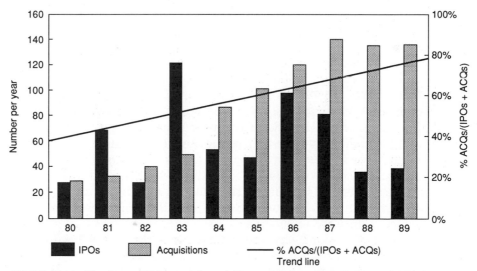

FIGURE 17–6   Number of IPOs and Acquisitions : Venture-Capital-Backed Companies
(*Source* : *Venture Capital Journal.*)

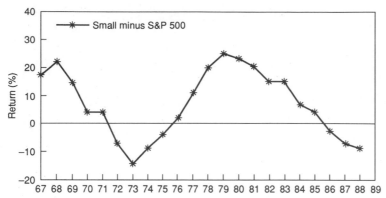

FIGURE 17-7 Difference between 5-Year Returns on Small Company and S&P 500 Stocks
(*Source* : Ibbotson Associates.)

Returns by Type of Fund

According to finance theory, early stage funds should outperform later stage funds and balanced funds because the younger the portfolio company, the riskier is the investment. Clearly, investments in high-technology companies that have yet to develop products and markets are a lot riskier than investments in management buyouts of a low-technology company with mature products and developed markets. That appears to be true in practice ; the average annual return over the five years 1985–1989 was higher for early stage funds (16.2 percent) than either later stage funds (8.1 percent) or balanced funds (11.3 percent).

Returns by Size of Fund

Both small funds (less than $25 million) and big funds (more than $100 million) produced higher returns than mid-size funds ($25 million to $99.9 million). Averaged over the 1985–1989 period, the annual returns by fund size were 13.5 percent for funds less than $25 million, 12.6 percent for funds greater than $100 million, and 8.1 percent for funds between $25 and $99.9 million. The differences in those returns are probably because the key to successful venture capital is *knowledge* — and a fund's knowledge depends on its resources, especially its professionals. Small funds have limited resources, so they take a narrow focus. They tend to specialize in a few niches in which they are experts (e.g., early stage computer companies). Big funds have more abundant resources, so they are able to be successful with a broader focus. Mid-size funds, on the other hand, may have too broad an investment strategy for their resources. The outcome is what Porter's (1980) competitive strategy framework predicts : mid-size funds, which are stuck in the middle, have the lowest returns.

Returns by Experience

The resource exchange model predicts that the greater a fund's legitimacy, the higher its returns should be. Legitimacy is directly related to the experience of the venture capitalists managing a fund. Hence, funds with the most experienced venture capitalists should have the greater returns. As yet no one has measured legitimacy directly. However, a reasonable surrogate is the number of funds that a given venture capital firm has successfully raised. On average, a venture capital firm that is able to raise follow-on funds has more legitimacy than one that has only raised its initial fund, or what we call a new fund. (Of course, a few new funds will have legitimacy because they are started by experienced venture capitalists.) Most of the time, follow-on funds outperformed new funds, which lends credence to the notion that legitimacy goes hand in hand with success. Over the period 1976–1989, the average annual return of follow-on funds was 17.8 percent versus 14.7 percent for new funds; and over the period 1985–1989, the comparable average annual returns were 12.4 percent for follow-on funds versus 8.9 percent for new funds.

Summary of Resource Exchange Theory and Practice

Boylan (1982) commented that venture capital was shrouded in empirical secrecy and an aura of mystical beliefs. Nowhere was that more true than when it came to rates of return. However, during the last eight years, the industry has been studied as never before. By 1990, the shrouds have been lifted — or at least peeked under — and we now have good data on what was perhaps the most guarded secret of independent, private venture capital funds: their actual rate of return — the ultimate dependent variable.

   We can now use rates of return to test theories. What has been presented in this review is a test of a theory rooted in sociology: resource exchange. From the findings presented here, the performance of the venture capital industry from the late 1970s to the present time fits the predictions of resource exchange theory. When these findings are combined with the findings of other work (Bygrave 1987, 1988; Bygrave and Shulman 1988), it seems that Bruno and Tyebjee's (1982) insight was a good one: resource dependency provides useful models for explaining the behavior of the venture capital industry. They are useful in the sense that they have good empirical support.

━━ ━━ ━━ ━━ ━━ ━━ ━━ ━━
IPOS AND BEYOND

Let us hark back to what was writen earlier: the ultimate "big hit" for a venture capitalist is a spectacular IPO. A portfolio needs a few big hits to be an outstanding performer. For instance, according to Ben Rosen, his firm (Sevin Rosen) invested in 36 companies. Eight went public, 8 went bankrupt, and 20 were still in incubation at the beginning of 1988 (Brogan 1988). Its two funds, both specializing in early stage computer and semiconductor companies, have earned several hundred million dollars on an investment of $85 million (Glitman 1987). Among its winners were Lotus, Compaq, and Silicon Graphics; and among its losers were Osborne Computer, Synapse Computer, and Enmasse Computer.

Sevin Rosen's $2.5 million investment in Compaq was worth $40 million at the time of the IPO, and its $2.1 million bet on Lotus was worth $70 million at the IPO. Its $400,000 invested in Osborne was a total loss. Since just two of its investments were worth $110 million at the time of the IPO (and much more, subsequently), it shows that a fund needs a few spectacular winners if it is to make high returns on its entire portfolio.

Because of the importance of IPOs to venture capital returns, and because information on IPOs is public, it's not surprising that they have been getting more and more attention from researchers.

Value Added

There has been a stream of research into returns on stocks on each successive day after their IPO. Those studies found that, overall, returns on IPOs on the days immediately following the offering exceeded market trends (e.g., Ibbotson, Sindelar, and Ritter 1988), which means that the initial offering prices were set too low. One explanation for this underpricing (out of half-a-dozen possibilities) is that the parties involved in setting the price of the IPO have imperfect information. If that is so, then it might be expected that companies with sophisticated investors (such as professional venture capitalists) on their boards would set the price of the IPO closer to what the market is prepared to pay. Hence, the stock price of IPOs with venture capital investors should be underpriced less than those without them. A study by Barry et al. (1988), however, found that venture-capital-backed IPOs were underpriced by approximately the same amount as other IPOs of similar size.

Two recent studies have looked for the effect of venture capital backing on market returns of stocks after IPOs. Brophy and Verga (1989) examined the daily returns of 1,246 IPOs over the period 1978–1985. Of those IPOs, 210 were backed by venture capital. They found that the IPOs of venture-capital-backed companies were valued higher at the IPO than non-venture-capital-backed firms. They also found that the aftermarket performance of venture-capital-backed IPOs was superior. In contrast, however, Cherin and Hergert (1988) found no significant difference between the post-IPO returns of computer companies backed by venture capital and those not backed by venture capital. Thus, the evidence about whether venture capital backing adds value to an IPO and the subsequent performance of a stock after an IPO is inconclusive. But the claim that venture capital backing adds value to the market price of a company's stock appears to be overstated, on average.

Performance of Individual Venture-Capital-Backed Companies

Bygrave and Stein (1989, 1990) mined IPO prospectuses for information on the involvement of venture capitalists. They examined 77 venture-capital-backed companies that had IPOs from 1979 to 1988. These companies were in four industry segments: computer hardware, computer software, biotechnology, and communications. The authors found that the performance of these companies varied significantly accordingly to their venture capital firm, their underwriter, their industry segment, the time from their first round of venture capital to their IPO, and their profitability immediately before their IPO.

A more ambitious attempt to look at the determinants of the performance of venture-capital-backed companies was undertaken by Keeley and Roure (1989). They found that the performance of U.S. companies founded during the period 1978–1981 could be predicted with reasonable accuracy using simple measures of management, strategy, and industry. However, the relationship disappeared for firms started after October 1981. They speculated that it was because the nature of the competition changed. When they extended their study to include European and Japanese venture-capital-backed companies as well as U.S. ones, they found that industry and managerial qualities had the highest correlation with success (Keeley et al. 1990).

━━ ━━ ━━ ━━ ━━ ━━ ━━

A RESEARCH AGENDA
FOR THE 1990S

For the first time in the history of our field we have reliable information on the returns of venture capital funds. This information opens up new realms of research for scholars from many disciplines including entrepreneurship, economics, and finance. After all, as already noted, performance is the ultimate dependent variable. Before discussing the research possibilities, a few words of caution are in order. Although the data on returns are as valid and reliable as can be, there are limitations. Perhaps the most severe is how the returns are computed for funds at an intermediate stage before they have been totally liquidated. The industry is addressing that problem, and, after two years of innumerable discussions, has come up with a set of guidelines in a 10-point statement (*Venture Capital Journal* 1990).

Finance Theory

It's inevitable that the returns will be analyzed with the Capital Asset Pricing Model, CAPM (see Chiampou and Kallet 1989), which has been the leading portfolio tool over the past quarter of a century. Beta is used so extensively by financial analysts that "beta mania" is endemic among portfolio managers. But before we rush in with the CAPM, we should first convince ourselves that it is a valid theory for venture capital funds, especially at intermediate stages.

Above all else, we must remember that private independent venture capital funds are not liquid. They are not traded in a public marketplace where investors have access to the same information if they wish to get it. Hence, it would be foolhardy for theoreticians or practitioners to apply the CAPM to independent private venture capital partnerships as an asset class.

Before we hurry to apply the CAPM, there are other more elementary finance questions that can be answered. For example, do the returns vary with the risks as Venture Economics' preliminary results seem to indicate for early stage funds versus balanced and later stage funds? Are the returns from high-technology funds greater than from low-technology funds? Does the size of a fund make a difference? Do specialists outperform generalists as Bygrave (1989) glimpsed? Do investments in some industry segments outperform others as Bygrave and Stein (1989) and Keeley and Roure (1989) suggest? How does the performance of venture capital funds compare with publicly traded stocks of small companies? We need more data and statistical tests before we can answer those questions.

If we must apply the CAPM, it seems clear that one of the first applications should be to test Brophy and Guthner's (1988) proposition that an investor who diversifies over a set of private venture capital funds should obtain a relatively low-risk, high-return portfolio. That proposition is deduced from Brophy and Guthner's finding that "a fund of funds" of public venture capital firms provides substantial excess returns over the market index. That proposition could be tested on pension funds' portfolios of private venture capital partnerships. If Brophy and Guthner's proposition is true for private venture capital firms as well as public ones, it has important implications for both practitioners and theoreticians.

Economics

Venture capital is seen as a necessary — but not in itself sufficient — ingredient in the birth and growth of new high-technology companies and industries. Hence, it is not surprising that it has received a great deal of attention from economists, none more so than those involved in setting public policy. Until fairly recently some economists fretted that the abnormally high returns indicated that the market for venture capital was inefficient (e.g., U.S. Congress 1984). Those voices seem to have been quieted by the returns since the mid-1980s. Nonetheless, it is an important issue and one that deserves attention from economists. What influences the returns on venture capital? And, in turn, what do the returns influence? Figure 17–8 is an attempt to show the relationships between the returns and the important factors in the venture capital process. It is based on the resource exchange model, and it raises many important research issues. For example, one eternal debate that needs to be resolved is the effect of changes in the capital gains tax. This is an issue that polarizes economists and the politicians they advise. For instance, during the 1988 presidential election, George Bush and his economist Michael Boskin

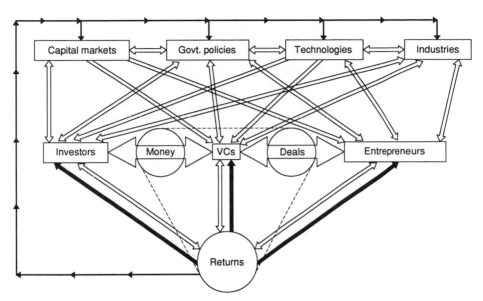

FIGURE 17–8 Factors Influencing the Flows of Venture Capital

were convinced that a reduction in the capital gains tax would stimulate the venture capital industry, while Michael Dukakis and his economist Larry Summers were just as convinced that it would have little effect, if any.

Agency theory (e.g., Jensen and Meckling 1976) and transaction-cost economics (e.g., Williamson 1979) may find venture capital to be a fruitful ground for empirical testing. After all, venture capitalists are agents of the limited partners. Recently, another type of agent has emerged in the venture capital process: investment advisers (such as Abbott) who are intermediaries between limited partners and venture capitalists. Researchers could study whether the agents are "worth their keep." Possible examples are as follows: Are the returns of pension funds that use independent investment advisers to select their venture capital funds greater than those who don't? Are the returns on venture capital invested indirectly in companies by pension funds and corporations through external venture capital firms greater than the returns on venture capital invested directly in companies by pension funds and corporations without a venture capital firm in the middle?

CONCLUSION

There are so many opportunities for entrepreneurship research that it is hard to know which ones to choose. From a theoretical perspective, one of the major debates in our field is the degree to which the environment controls the entrepreneur's fate. In one corner we have the seemingly fatalistic viewpoint of the population ecology model (e.g., Hannan and Freeman 1977), in which success or failure of a start-up is determined by environmental events outside the entrepreneur's control. And in the opposite corner stands the omnipotent strategist model which holds that the entrepreneur determines his or her destiny (e.g., Porter 1980). Somewhere in the middle of the ring stands the resource exchange theory. The venture capital industry provides about as clean a test as could be devised for those theories because venture capital firms have elementary internal structures but make very sophisticated decisions that are influenced almost entirely by external factors (Bygrave 1989). We could get a greater understanding of those theories by looking at the factors that influence the performance of venture capital firms and the portfolio companies they invest in. And what's more, such an endeavor has tremendous practical implications.

A controversial topic for practitioners and academics is the notion of value added (e.g., Sapienza 1989; Rosenstein et al. 1990). Michael Porter (1988) challenged many of the leaders of the venture capital industry when he analyzed the industry with the famous five-force model that bears his name. He suggested that value added was perhaps their most distinct competence, but perhaps it really did not amount to much of a competitive advantage. If it is true, then the value of value added by the VC should be measurable. Funds that vaunt their value-adding ability should produce superior performance for their portfolio companies, and hence their funds. So far the findings are mixed (e.g., Bygrave and Stein 1990; Barry et al. 1988; Brophy and Verga 1989; Cherin and Hergert 1988). As more and more data become available on funds and portfolio companies we will find out whether value adders produce measurable value.

Now that we have a reliable measure of performance for venture capital funds — the financial gatekeepers, so to speak, of knowledge-based new industries — we have the key to systematically understanding their behavior, what influences it, and how those things are related to outcomes. Our discovery has tremendous potential for academics, venture capitalists, investors, entrepreneurs, policy makers, and many others. The 1990s promise an intellectual harvest for those academics who have been laboring in the venture capital fields. Let's enjoy it.

━━ ━━ ━━ ━━ ━━ ━━ ━━

REFERENCES

Barry, C. B., C. J. Muscarella, J. W. Peavy III, and M. R. Vetsuypens 1988 Venture capital and initial public offerings. Working paper, Texas Christian University and Southern Methodist University.

Boylan, M. 1982 What we know and don't know about venture capital. Paper presented at the American Economics Association Meeting, January 19. Washington, D.C.

Brogan, D. 1988 Playing the PC ponies. *PC World* (January): 110–114.

Brophy, D. J. 1986 Venture capital research. In *The art and science of entrepreneurship*, eds. D. L. Sexton and R. W. Smilor, 119–144. Cambridge, Mass.: Ballinger.

Brophy, D. J., and J. Verga 1989 More than money ? The effect of venture capital backing on the returns of initial public offerings. In *Frontiers of entrepreneurship research*, eds. R. Brockhaus, Sr., N. C. Churchill, J. Katz, B. Kirchhoff, K. Vesper, and W. Wetzel, Jr., 192–198, Wellesley, Mass. : Babson College.

Brophy, D. J., and Guthner, M. W. 1988 Publicly traded venture capital funds : Implications for institutional "fund of funds" investors. *Journal of Business Venturing* 3 (3) : 187–206.

Bruno, A. V., and Tyebjee, T. T. 1982 The environment for entrepreneurship. In *Encyclopedia of entrepreneurship*, eds. C. A. Kent, D. L. Sexton, and K. H. Vesper, 288–307. Englewood Cliffs, N.J. : Prentice-Hall, Inc.

Business Week 1988 For venture capitalists, too much of a good thing. June 6, 126.

Bygrave, W. D. 1987 Syndicated investments of venture capital firms : Networking perspective. *Journal of Business Venturing* 2 (2) : 139–154.

1988 The structure of the investment networks of venture capital firms. *Journal of Business Venturing* 3 (2) : 137–157.

1989 Venture capital investing : A resource exchange perspective. Ph.D. diss., Boston University.

Bygrave, W. D., N. A. Fast, R. Khoylian, L. Vincent, and W. Yue 1988 Rates of return of venture capital investing : A study of 131 funds. In *Frontiers of entrepreneurship research*, eds. B. A. Kirchhoff, W. A. Long, W. E. McMullan, K. H. Vesper, and W. E. Wetzel, Jr., 275–289. Wellesley, Mass. : Babson College.

Bygrave, W. D., and J. Shulman 1988 Capital gains tax : Bane or boon for venture capital. In *Frontiers of entrepreneurship research*, eds. B. A. Kirchhoff, W. A. Long, W. E. McMullan, K. H. Vesper, and W. E. Wetzel, Jr., 324–338. Wellesley, Mass. : Babson College.

Bygrave, W. D., and M. Stein 1989 A time to buy and a time to sell : A study of venture capital investments in 77 companies that went public. In *Frontiers of entrepreneurship research*, eds. R. Brockhaus, Sr., N. C. Churchill, J. Katz, B. Kirchhoff, K. Vesper, and W. Wetzel, Jr., 288–303. Wellesley, Mass. : Babson College.

1990 The anatomy of high-tech IPOs : Do their venture capitalists, underwriters, accountants, and lawyers make a difference ? In *Frontiers of entrepreneurship research*, eds. W. Bygrave, N. Churchill, J. Hornaday, D. Muzyka, K. Vesper, and W. Wetzel, Jr., 394–407. Wellesley, Mass. : Babson College.

Cherin, A., and M. Hergert 1988 Do venture capitalists create value ? A test from the computer industry. In *Frontiers of entrepreneurship research*, eds. B. A. Kirchhoff, W. A. Long, W. E. McMullan, K. H. Vesper, and W. E. Wetzel, Jr., 341–344. Wellesley, Mass. : Babson College.

Chiampou, G. F., and J. J. Kallet 1989 Risk/return profile of venture capital. *Journal of Business Venturing* 4 (1) : 1–10.

Egan, W. P. 1988 Quoted in Where venture capital is investing now. *High Technology Business* 8(3) : 19.

Faucett, R. B. 1971 The management of venture capital investment companies. Master's thesis, Massachusetts Institute of Technology.

Forbes 1988 Too much money, too few deals. March 7, 144.

Gevirtz, D. 1985 *The new entrepreneurs : Innovation in American business.* N.Y. : Penguin Books.

Glitman, R. 1987 Sevin Rosen, venture capitalists to call it a career. *PC Week.* July 21, 125–132.

Hambrecht, W. 1987 Quoted in New records set at NVCA meeting. *Venture Capital Journal.* 27(5) : 2 (May).

Hannan, M. T., and J. Freeman 1984 The population ecology of organizations. *American Journal of Sociology* 88 : 1116–1145.

Hoban, J. P. 1976 Characteristics of venture capital investing. Ph.D. diss., University of Utah.

Ibbotson, R. G., and G. P. Brinson 1987 *Investment markets.* N.Y. : McGraw-Hill.

Ibbotson, R. G., J. L. Sindelar, and J. R. Ritter 1988 Initial public offerings. *Journal of Applied Corporate Finance* 1 (2) : 37–45.

Inc. 1990 Risky business. March, 29–36.

Jensen, M. C., and W. H. Meckling 1976 Theory of the firm : Managerial behavior, agency costs, and ownership structure. *Journal of Financial Economics* 3 (4) : 305–360.

Keeley, R. H., and J. B. Roure 1989 Determinants of new venture success before and after 1982 : A preliminary look at two eras. In *Frontiers of entrepreneurship research*, eds. R. Brockhaus, Sr., N. Churchill, J. Katz, B. Kirchhoff, K. Vesper, and W. Wetzel, Jr., 247–287. Wellesley, Mass. : Babson College.

Keeley, R. H., J. B. Roure, J. B. Goto, and K. Yoshimura 1990 An international comparison of new ventures. In *Frontiers of entrepreneurship research*, eds. W. Bygrave, N. Churchill, J. Hornaday, D. Muzyka, K. Vesper, and W. Wetzel, Jr., 472–486. Wellesley, Mass. : Babson College.

Kozmetsky, G., M. D. Gill, Jr., and R. W. Smilor 1984 *Financing and managing fast-growth companies : The venture capital process.* Lexington, Mass. : Lexington Books.

Martin, J. D., and W. P. Petty 1983 An analysis of the performance of publicly traded venture capital companies. *Journal of Financial and Quantitative Analysis* 18 (3) : 401–410.

Penrose, R. 1989 *The emperor's new mind.* N.Y. : Oxford Univ. Press.

Pfeffer, J., and G. R. Salancik 1978 *The external control of organizations : A resource dependent perspective.* N.Y. : Harper & Row.

Poindexter, J. B. 1976 The efficiency of financial markets : The venture capital case. Ph.D. diss., New York University.

Porter, M. 1980 *Competitive strategy.* N.Y. : Free Press.

1988 Paper presented by Michael Porter at the Harvard Business School Conference on Venture Capital, September 22–24.

Rosenstein, J., A. Bruno, W. Bygrave, and N. Taylor 1990 How much do CEOs value the advice of venture capitalists on their boards ? In *Frontiers of entrepreneurship research*, eds. W. Bygrave, N. Churchill, J. Hornaday, D. Muzyka, K. Vesper, and W. Wetzel, Jr., 238–250. Wellesley, Mass. : Babson College.

Rotch, W. 1968 The pattern of success in venture capital financing. *Financial Analysis Journal* 24 (September-October) : 141–147.

Sahlman, W. 1989 The changing structure of the American venture capital industry. Paper presented at the National Venture Capital Association Meeting, May 10–12. Washington, D.C.

Sapienza, H. 1989 Variations in venture capitalist-entrepreneur relations : Antecedents and consequences. Ph.D. diss., University of Maryland.

Stevenson, H. H., D. F. Muzyka, and J. A. Timmons 1986 Venture capital in a new era :

A simulation of the impact of the changes in investment patterns. In *Frontiers of entrepreneurship research*, eds. R. Ronstadt, J. A. Hornaday, R. Peterson, and K. H. Vesper, 343–380. Wellesley, Mass. : Babson College.

Stinchcombe, A. S. 1965 Social structure and organizations. In *Handbook of organizations*, ed. J. G. March, 153–193. Chicago : Rand McNally.

U.S. Congress 1984 *Venture capital and innovation.* A report prepared by the Joint Economic Committee. Washington, D.C. : GPO.

Venture Capital Journal 1982 *The growth of an industry venture capital* 1977–1982. 22(10) (October) : 6–11.

1984 Venture capital industry resources. 24(7) (July) : 6.

1990 Committee issues portfolio valuation guidelines. (June) 30(6) : 1–2.

Venture Economics, Inc. 1988 *Venture capital performance.* Needham, Mass.

1989 *Venture capital performance.* Needham, Mass.

1990 *Investment benchmarks : Venture capital investing.* Needham, Mass.

Wall Street Journal 1988 Recent venture funds perform poorly as unrealistic expectations wear off. November 8, 1988 : B2.

Wayne, L. 1988 Management's tale. *New York Times Magazine*, January 17, 42.

Wells, W. A. 1974 Venture capital decision-making. Ph.D. diss., Carnegie Mellon University.

Williamson, O. E. 1979 Transaction-cost economics : The governance of contractual relations. *Journal of Law and Economics* 22 : 233–261.

Chapter

18

The Informal Venture
Capital Market in the 1990s

John Freear
and
William E. Wetzel, Jr.

●

------- INTRODUCTION

The informal venture capital market in the United States comprises a diverse and dispersed population of high net worth people, many of whom have founded their own successful ventures. The market is a virtually invisible and demonstrably inefficient segment of the total market for capital. There are no directories of individual investors, no public records of their investment transactions, and few vehicles by which potential investors and ventures seeking funds may be brought together.

Perceptions that gaps exist in the equity markets serving entrepreneurs led to the Small Business Investment Act of 1958. The Act created the Small Business Investment Company (SBIC) program. Though capital gaps have never been documented convincingly, perceptions of gaps endure. Perceived capital shortages include product development financing for technology-based inventors; start-up and early stage financing for ventures that fail to meet the size, stage, and potential growth criteria of venture capital funds; and equity financing for closely held firms that are growing faster than internally generated cash flows can support.

The capital gap debate is based upon the observable behavior of financial institutions, including SBICs and venture capital funds. However, the debate over capital gaps overlooks the record of individual venture investors — "business angels." Angels not only exist, they tend to invest in precisely the areas perceived as gaps in the capital markets for entrepreneurs (Wetzel 1983b, 1987).

Despite the apparent size of the informal capital pool, the effect of capital gaps can be created when markets fail to function efficiently. Modern financial theory rests upon assumptions of efficient markets — markets in which information about sources of funds and about investment opportunities is fully and freely available in a timely fashion to market participants. The evidence suggests that this necessary condition is far from fulfilled in the informal segment of the venture capital markets. Capital flows from less productive to more productive investment opportunities are impeded by capital market inefficiencies. In such an inefficient market, the rewards for expertise are higher and the penalties for inexperience or incompetence greater.

■■ ■■ ■■ ■■ ■■
THE RESEARCH AGENDA
IN 1985

In a review of the state of the art in 1985, Wetzel (1986) surveyed the principal studies that had been undertaken to date. These studies included Baty (1964), Hoffman (1972), Charles River Associates (1976), Seymour and Wetzel (1981), Brophy (1982), Neiswander (1982), Shapero (1983), Obermayer (1983), Tymes and Krasner (1983), Wilson (1984), and Tyebjee and Bruno (1984a, 1984b). Based on these studies, Wetzel proposed an agenda for future research into the informal venture capital market. He suggested four principal areas of further study:

1. *Scale.* What is the scale of informal risk capital investing — both in numbers of investors and in dollars invested?
2. *Investor characteristics.* What are the personal characteristics of informal investors? Are there subsets of investors that can be distinguished by investment behavior? Can we model these investors' decision processes, and do these processes differ from those for venture capital funds? To what extent are individual investors motivated by non-financial factors in their investment decisions? Do clusters of individual investors tend to be characterized by the presence of one or more lead investors who influence the other investors' propensity to invest?
3. *Information channels.* What are the characteristics of the information networks that link individual investors? Are there geographic differences in the nature or effectiveness of these networks? To what extent do financial intermediaries influence the effective availability of informal risk capital in a community? What are the most effective methods of locating individual investors and entrepreneurs looking for risk capital?

4. *Venture capital funds.* What are the relationships between individual investors and venture capital funds? To what extent do individual investors and venture capital funds compete with or complement each other? Are there types of entrepreneurial venture or stages in the venture's life cycle that tend to fit the investment objectives of one class of investor better than another? Is informal risk capital more or less expensive than professional venture capital?

This chapter assesses the extent to which the research undertaken since 1985 has answered these questions, and identifies additional questions raised by that research.

SCALE: HOW LARGE IS THE INFORMAL VENTURE CAPITAL MARKET?

Supply Side

There is a lack of hard data on the scale of informal venture investing. However, it is possible to give some indication of the probable numbers involved by looking at three data sources.

Charles Ou (1987), using data from the 1983 Consumer Finance Survey, estimated the investment in privately held businesses by American families. The survey data included a base sample of 3,665 families in all income groups and a subsample of 438 high-income families.

Ou defined informal investment as equity investments in businesses by investors with no management involvement in the businesses. He estimated that 2 million families in the United States (2.5 percent of all U.S. households) have made informal equity investments in privately held businesses totalling $300 billion, an average of about $150,000 per household. By comparison, the 1983 portfolios of venture capital funds amounted to about $20 billion.

Gaston and Bell (1988) examined the annual rate of informal venture investing based upon a sample of 435 individual investors. The individual investors were identified through a sample of business enterprises stratified by employment size and region, drawn from Dun's Market Identifier (DMI) file. They estimated that 720,000 investors annually made 489,000 informal venture investments with a mean dollar value per investment of $66,700. These numbers imply an annual flow of informal equity capital of $32.7 billion. During the same period, venture capital funds were investing about $3 billion annually, with an average investment per business of about $1 million.

Avery and Elliehausen (1986), using 1983 data, found that the net worth of 1.3 million U.S. families (about 2 percent of all households) was at least $1 million. Their data suggested that most of the wealth was saved from accumulated earnings, not inherited. The wealth, income, and asset distribution of the top

1 percent of U.S. households (840,000 families) indicated that 37 percent of the top 1 percent of U.S. households (311,000 families) had invested $151 billion in nonpublic businesses in which they had no management interest.

Demand Side

The demand side of the informal venture capital market is as elusive as the supply side. The ventures funded by individual investors fall into two broad categories.

The first includes start-up ventures requiring more capital (commonly exceeding $50,000) than the founders and their friends and relatives can provide, but less than $1 million in total. A few of these ventures grow fast enough to become substantial companies within about five years. High-growth ventures often attract later rounds of financing from venture capital funds before being acquired by a larger company or undertaking a public stock offering. In 1988, the Center for Venture Research at the University of New Hampshire undertook a study (Freear and Wetzel 1989) for the National Venture Capital Association and found that over 35 percent of a sample of 236 firms financed by venture capital funds had obtained earlier rounds of financing from nonmanagement individual investors. In other words, individual investors generate a substantial fraction of the deal flow for venture capital funds.

The second category comprises privately held firms that outgrow their ability to generate funds from their operations. Even the most profitable firms may not be able to rely exclusively on retained earnings to sustain long-term growth exceeding 25 percent per year. The most dynamic small firms are growing at annual rates exceeding 100 percent. Sales growth for the *Inc.* 500 Fastest-Growing Private Companies (1988) averaged 97 percent per year from 1983 to 1987. The 500th firm on the list grew at an average annual rate of 65 percent over that period.

According to Cognetics, Inc., entrepreneurial ventures include about 50,000 high-potential start-ups each year, and 500,000 private companies growing at rates above 20 percent, including 80,000 with annual growth rates above 50 percent. The equity financing needs of these high-growth ventures exceed $50 billion per year.

▬ ▬ ▬ ▬ ▬ ▬ ▬ ▬
INVESTOR
CHARACTERISTICS,
ACTIVITIES, AND
DECISION PROCESSES

Overview

In 1988, according to *Time* magazine, about two million U.S. men and women were millionaires, and nearly 90 percent of them earned their fortune by starting their own firm. Fifty-four percent of the Forbes (1987) 400 built their fortunes without significant inheritances. Individual investors often contribute know-how as well as capital to the ventures they finance. They are active investors, generally playing an informal consulting role or serving on a working board of directors (Wetzel 1983b). Seymour and Wetzel's (1981) sample of 133 New England investors was a well-educated group with experience in the management of start-up ventures. Ninety-four percent held four-year college degrees, and 51 percent had graduate degrees. Three-quarters of the sample had been involved in the start-up of a new firm. Eighty-four percent expected to play an active role in the ventures they financed.

Freear and Wetzel (1989) shed further light on the characteristics, attitudes, and behavior of individual investors. Most of what follows refers to the Venture Economics, Inc. (VE) sample. A questionnaire was sent to 926 firms in the VE data base that had received venture capital fund financing during the years 1985 to 1988. The firms were spread across all regions of the United States, and all principal industry types were represented. Two hundred thirty-six firms responded to the VE questionnaire, a 26 percent response rate. The investor questionnaire was sent through the responding firms to their individual investors. Thirty-eight responses (a 12 percent response rate) were received from individual investors. A questionnaire was also sent to firms filing equity or convertible issues under SEC Regulation D, Rule 504. The results of this questionnaire are summarized later in this section.

Biographical Profiles

The biographical profiles in this section are drawn from Freear and Wetzel (1989) unless otherwise stated.

Age and educational background.
The average age of the investors was 47.7 years, with a median of 48 years, and a range of 30 to 80 years. Generally, the investors were educated to, or beyond, baccalaureate level. Thirty-three (87 percent) of the 38 investors had studied for four years, with 26 percent of this group holding a master's degree and 24 percent a doctoral degree. Gaston and Bell (1988) reported a median age of 47 years, with 72 percent of their sample having had a college education. These characteristics were in broad accord with the findings of Tymes and Krasner (1984), and Aram (1987). The Harr, Starr, and MacMillan (1988) study found that 56.2 percent of their investors held a master's degree. However, 39 percent of their sample was drawn from the MBA alumni lists of New York University and the Wharton School.

General business experience.
Thirty-three (87 percent) of the 38 investors reported that their general business experience was moderate to substantial, with only 13 percent reporting "limited" general business experience. The experience was somewhat concentrated in sales, marketing, finance, and research and development.

Full-time entrepreneurial experience.

The investors were equally divided between those who had full-time managerial experience in entrepreneurial ventures (medians of 10 years in two ventures) and those who had not. Postma and Sullivan (1990) reported that most of the investors in their sample had start-up business experience. Eighty-three percent of Gaston and Bell's (1988) investors had entrepreneurial experience as owners or managers. Aram's (1989) study, based upon mail questionnaire responses from 55 individual investors, suggested that personal characteristics were a key to persons making a strong commitment to very early stage financing. Aram found that earlier experience in starting a firm was strongly associated with a greater commitment to financing start-up ventures.

Annual household income.

Thirty-two (84 percent) of the 38 investors reported annual household income in the $50,000 to $299,000 range, with the biggest number of responses (32 percent) in the $100,000 to $199,000 range, which was also the median range. Gaston and Bell reported that almost two-thirds of their sample had an annual income of below $100,000. Over half of the Harr, Starr, and MacMillan sample had annual incomes in the $100,000 to $249,000 range.

Household net worth.

Sixteen (42 percent) of the 38 investors reported a household net worth of below $1 million, 32 percent reported a net worth of between $1 million and $2.49 million, and 26 percent a net worth of $2.5 million or more. The median net worth range for investors was $1 million to $1.49 million. Almost 64 percent of Gaston and Bell's investors had a net worth of under $1 million.

Reported Activity in the Market

The 38 investors in the Freear and Wetzel study had made a total of 162 investments (including multiple rounds in the same venture) over the preceding five years. Early stage financing, at the seed or start-up stages, accounted for 72 percent of the investments reported. Fifty-eight percent were for less than $50,000, and 66 percent were for less than $100,000. The median investment was in the $25,000 to $49,999 range. Two hundred fifteen of Postma and Sullivan's respondents had made 525 investments over the preceding five years, a mean of 2.45. The total sum invested was estimated to be between $24 and $35 million. Half of the investments were for less than $25,000, with 21 percent being over $100,000. Gaston and Bell reported that the investors in their sample often extended loans and guarantees (median $21,400) in addition to their equity investment (median $37,500). One hundred sixteen of Harr, Starr, and MacMillan's respondents had invested $38 million in 286 ventures over the preceding three years, with a median investment of $50,000.

For 58 percent of the 38 investors in the Freear and Wetzel study, direct equity investments in entrepreneurial ventures represented less than 10 percent of their total personal assets (excluding their principal residence). Only 8 percent committed over half of their portfolio to venture investing. Informal venture investing represented less than 25 percent of the investment portfolios of three-quarters of the investors.

Investor Expectations

Twenty-two (58 percent) of the 38 investors in the Freear and Wetzel study reported that they expected to add to their portfolios of venture investments over the next two years. Recent investment behavior suggests that individual investor interest in venture investments extended to all financing stages. Eighty-three percent of Postma and Sullivan's investors invested within the first two years of the firm's life. Fifty-six percent of Gaston and Bell's investors invested at the "start-up/idea" stage, about the same percentage as that reported by Harr, Starr, and MacMillan. About two-thirds of the investors expected to invest sums below $50,000, and 86 percent expected to invest amounts below $100,000. Just over half (51 percent) of the Freear and Wetzel respondents stated that they would generally or definitely make no liquidation provision in the initial investment agreement.

Some investors in the Freear and Wetzel study limited their participation to particular industries. High-technology and computer-related and medical technology were the most common among those who expressed a preference. Sixty-one percent of the investors placed no geographical limitation on their investment activity, but 26 percent preferred to invest in ventures located within 50 miles of the investor's residence. Forty-one percent of Harr, Starr, and MacMillan's investors preferred to invest in manufacturing businesses, with the greatest interest in high-technology businesses. In this sample, geographical proximity appeared to be one of the least important criteria in the investment decision process. In the Postma and Sullivan survey, 42 percent of the investments were in service firms, 23 percent in manufacturing, and 21 percent in high-technology firms. Their investors kept closer to home : 75 percent of the investments were located within 100 miles. Gaston and Bell also found that their investors invested close to home, with about 70 percent investing within 50 miles.

Investor Expectations : The Entrepreneurs' Viewpoint

Freear, Sohl, and Wetzel (1990) asked new technology-based firms (NTBFs) for their opinions about the expectations of their investors regarding rates of return, and time and method of liquidation. It should be emphasized that what follows summarizes the perceptions of the entrepreneurs about the firm's individual investors.

The NTBFs reported that the median annual rate of return expected by individual investors was 32.5 percent over the life of the investment. The NTBFs reported that venture capital fund managers expected a median annual rate of return of 40 percent. Perhaps individual investors placed a higher value on "nonfinancial" factors and so expected a lower financial return. Although individual investors and venture capital fund managers concentrated their expectations between 20 and 50 percent, five individual investors expected returns exceeding 100 percent, whereas the highest venture capital fund expectation was 71 percent.

Freear and Wetzel (1990) identified a complementary relationship between individual investors and venture capital funds in the venture capital market. Individual investors tended to invest at an earlier stage, and thus might be expected to have longer exit horizons. However, the responses (Freear, Sohl, and Wetzel 1990) showed a very narrow reverse difference — medians of 4.75 years for individual investors and 5 years for venture capital funds. Individual investors commonly expected to liquidate their investment within 3.5 to 5 years, and venture capital fund managers in 3.5 to 6 years.

Individual investors were more inclined to leave undefined the method of liquidation than were managers of venture capital funds. For both groups, the most common methods, especially for NTBFs financed by venture capital funds, were public stock offerings and acquisition by larger firms.

Working Relationships : The Investors' Viewpoint

Investors reported different degrees of involvement with the ventures in the period following the investment (Freear and Wetzel 1989). Thirty percent were inactive, 23 percent were represented on the board of directors, 25 percent provided informal consulting services, and the remainder worked full- or part-time for the venture. Investors generally did not seem to be strongly in favor of voting control. Postma and Sullivan reported similar numbers : 65 percent of their investors participated "moderately" in the ventures ; 25 percent held full- or part-time jobs with the ventures, and 37 percent were on the venture's board of directors. Gaston and Bell reported that 27 percent of their investors had a consulting role, 15.1 percent were on the board of directors, 19 percent were inactive, and 39 percent worked part- or full-time for the ventures in which they had invested.

Seventy-nine percent of the investors in the Freear and Wetzel survey usually or always participated with other individual investors in financing ventures. Nevertheless, 84 percent of the investors relied upon their own evaluation of investment opportunities, and 16 percent relied on evaluations done by others. This response is in line with that from the Postma and Sullivan study and the Gaston and Bell study.

Working Relationships : The Entrepreneurs' Viewpoint

Seventy-one percent of the 63 firms responding to this question (Freear, Sohl, and Wetzel 1990) stated that there was at least one individual investor on the board of directors. In over 90 percent of the 54 firms receiving venture capital fund financing, venture capital funds were represented on the board. For both groups, this was the most common role, followed in frequency by a consulting relationship — 65 percent for individual investors and 57 percent for venture capital funds. Individual investors also participated in the firms in which they had invested in ways not open to venture capital funds, by way of employment on a full-time or part-time basis.

In almost half of the 57 firms in which there was more than one individual investor, a "lead" investor was present. As one of the respondents stated, the lead investor was not always the first investor, but was "usually the most aggressive and provides other investors with a sense of security." Over two-thirds of the 36 firms financed by venture capital funds reported the presence of a "lead" fund. One firm noted that in each financing round, two venture capital funds "took the lead in negotiating the deal and preparing the closing papers." Another stated that "we were financed by a seed VC firm who led and participated in all three rounds."

The firms were asked to rate their working relationships with individual investors and with venture capital funds on a five-point scale that ranged from very productive to very counterproductive. Fifty-five firms had a working relationship with their individual investors, of which almost three-quarters found the relationship to be either very productive or moderately productive. Three-quarters of the 52 firms that had a working relationship with their venture capital funds found it moderately or very productive. These data suggest that NTBFs derived a benefit from their individual investors that was above and beyond the provision of equity funding.

Attitudes to Risk, Return, and Liquidity

The Avery and Elliehausen (1986) study provided insights into the risk and liquidity attitudes of high-income households. Compared with all U.S. families, high-income households displayed a significantly higher propensity to assume above-average financial risks in order to earn above-average returns. High-income families also displayed a significantly higher propensity to tie up funds for long periods of time in order to earn substantial returns.

The investors in the Freear and Wetzel (1989) study reported that they expected, on average, a minimum annual return of 85 percent on seed stage investments. Thereafter, presumably because of a decline in perceived risk, the expected annual rate declined with each stage. At start-up, they expected an average of 51 percent, with 41 percent at the first stage, 30 percent at the second stage, and 27 percent at the third stage. These figures are substantially higher than those reported by Postma and Sullivan, 47 percent of whose respondents expected an annual return of 15 percent or less; 90 percent would have been satisfied with 25 percent or less. More than half of Harr, Starr, and MacMillan's (1988) respondents expected to multiply their investment 1 to 4 times over as a minimum; and 20 percent expected a multiple of 10 times. Three-quarters expected to achieve these multiples within five years.

Over 75 percent (29) of the 38 investors in the Freear and Wetzel (1989) study expected to hold their investments for between 4 and 9 years, with some clustering in the 4-to-7-year range. Eighty percent of Postma and Sullivan's investors expected a holding period of at least 3 years, and 60 percent expected to hold the investment for at least 6 years. Gaston and Bell's investors expected to liquidate their investments within about 4 years, but the time period was not of major concern to them. The average holding period for the sample was 5.1 years.

Nonfinancial Factors

Nonfinancial factors were an element in the investment decisions made by 53 percent of the 38 investors in the Freear and Wetzel (1989) study. It should be noted that some of the so-called nonfinancial factors — such as the quality and expertise of the management and the character and record of entrepreneurs — have had a considerable direct bearing on the success or failure of the investment.

The Postma and Sullivan (1990) and the Sullivan and Miller (1990) studies offered important insights into the nonfinancial motives of individual investors. The researchers postulated three types of motives: financial, altruistic, and self-oriented. They found that respondents were, on average, willing to accept a reduction of 5 percent from a guaranteed return of 20 percent, in exchange for various nonfinancial benefits. Only 46 percent were willing to make any return trade-off for "an exciting investment." However, for the group of investors as a whole, only two motives ranked above the middle of a five-point scale of importance, and these were both decidedly financial: a potential for high capital appreciation and current or future income. Harr, Starr, and MacMillan (1988) discovered that 86 percent of those investors who had found other forms of investment more profitable than early stage venture investing would make such investments again. Sixty-eight percent of the investors whose earlier venture investment had failed would invest in early stage ventures again. The authors concluded that once an "angel" had made informal investments, there appeared to be a very strong commitment to continuing to do so.

Comparisons Between VE and SEC Investors

The Freear and Wetzel (1989) study drew on two distinct samples. The VE sample was of firms that had raised funds from venture capital companies, and may or may not have raised money also from individual investors. The SEC sample was drawn from firms filing an equity or convertible issue of less than $500,000 under SEC Regulation D, Rule 504, with no presumption of financing by venture capital funds.

The VE investors made more investments in early stage entrepreneurial ventures and in larger dollar amounts than did the SEC investors. The VE investors also committed a larger proportion of their assets to venture investing, and had perhaps more realistic expectations of the outcome of these investments. The VE investors were more inclined actively to search for opportunities, although both groups relied substantially on friends and business associates for information on investment opportunities. The VE investors had a much larger potential deal flow than the SEC investors.

The VE investors expressed more interest in investing more dollars in common stock, at more stages, more often, and in more ventures than did the SEC investors. In contrast with some other studies, neither group viewed geographical location as an important investment criterion. Both groups tended to participate with other investors, but the VE investors relied more on their own judgement than that of others in making an investment decision. The VE investors took more account of "nonfinancial" factors than did the SEC investors. Voting control did not seem to be a big issue with either group, but VE investors tended to participate more actively in the running of the ventures in which they had invested.

VE investors expected higher returns from their investments, and these expected rates declined through the stage at which the investment took place. The SEC investors expected lower rates from seed investments than from start-up investments, but thereafter exhibited the same decline in expectations throughout the stages. Both groups had similar exit time horizons.

━━ ━━ ━━ ━━ ━━ ━━ ━━ ━━
INFORMATION CHANNELS

Finding Entrepreneurs

Data describing the channels through which information about investment opportunities in new/small companies is transmitted can be found in several studies. Without exception, these studies cite the dominant role of informal networks of trusted friends and business associates in the referral/search process.

The Panel on Venture Capital of the U.S. Department of Commerce Technical Advisory Board (U.S. Department of Commerce 1970) cited the importance of such informal networks. The panel reported that it had become increasingly aware of an informal network of people, institutions, and relationships that are significant in the process of financing new enterprises. It also noted that the network does not operate with the same degree of effectiveness in every geographic region of the country.

Early in the development of the venture capital industry in the United States, Rubenstein (1958) found that private investors were even more dependent on informal networks than were venture capital funds. He identified a close-knit "fraternity" of informal investors, among whom much information about possible ventures was passed by word of mouth. He also observed the existence of "lead" investors, whose recommendations were accepted and acted upon by other investors.

The significance of a respected lead investor in attracting the participation of associates was evident in a case study of the Taplin and Montle Development Fund, an informal association of individual investors in the Boston area (Wetzel 1983a). The work of Baty (1964), Shapero (1983), and Freear, Sohl, and Wetzel (1990) also provide evidence of the role played by respected lead investors.

Other studies, notably by Hoffman (1972), Seymour and Wetzel (1981), and Tymes and Krasner (1983), have documented the significance of both informal networks and regional differences in the effectiveness of these networks. The investors in the Gaston and Bell (1988) study claimed that their venture investments would have increased by about 35 percent if acceptable opportunities had been available. This untapped supply of informal venture capital suggests that the cost to investors and entrepreneurs of locating each other, communicating, and coming to terms is a measure of an important inefficiency in the informal venture capital market.

The Freear and Wetzel (1989) study identified the principal sources of information about investment opportunities used by individual investors. Business associates and friends provided over 41 percent of the opportunities and 77 percent of the deals. Friends proved to be the most efficient source, with the highest percentage of deals closed to opportunities presented. Active personal searches produced many opportunities but few deals and thus a low efficiency ratio that was, nevertheless, higher than that of commercial and investment bankers and other professionals. Attorneys and accountants were little used; however, attorneys had the second highest efficiency ratio, and accountants (with commercial bankers) the lowest — zero. The total ratio of deals closed to discovered opportunities was 7.7 percent. Nevertheless, the investors seemed reasonably satisfied with the effectiveness of channels of communication between entrepreneurs and investors.

Postma and Sullivan (1990) reported that 49 percent of the investments made by the investors in their sample had been referred by close friends or family, 24 percent by business associates, and 18 percent by accountants and lawyers, with only 6 percent being brought to them directly by an entrepreneur. Harr, Starr, and MacMillan (1988) provided strong evidence of a referral network among informal investors that consisted primarily of friends and business associates. To this network they referred as much as 60 percent of the proposals that they received and in which they themselves eventually invested. The authors found that informal investors tended to approach mainly close contacts, who were inclined both to be supportive and to rely mainly on the recommendation of the referring investor. Although the study showed that professional advisors were more effective in selecting successful ventures, only a small proportion of professionals was approached by the informal investors in the sample. The authors concluded that investors should use a mixed strategy: they should use mainly trusting referees to ensure full capitalization and a limited number of professional referees to screen the proposals.

Finding Investors

The names and addresses of venture capital funds are publicly available, and so the NTBFs in the Freear, Sohl, and Wetzel (1990) study were asked only about finding individual investors.

As in the Freear and Wetzel (1989) study of investors, entrepreneurs found business associates and friends to be the most widely used sources (91 and 86 percent, respectively) and the most helpful sources (83 percent in both cases) used to find investors. Other sources were much less helpful. Attorneys were used almost as often as friends and found to be more helpful than accountants, commercial bankers, and investment bankers, but less helpful than other entrepreneurs. Commercial and investment bankers received strongly negative ratings from the sample. Other entrepreneurs were the fourth most used source, and were found to be helpful by 31 percent of the respondents. Aram (1989) in his study of entrepreneurs in the eastern Great Lakes region, observed that the probability of gaining start-up financing may be greater from a person with direct experience as an entrepreneur in a related business.

There was a general consensus among the NTBFs in the study that they should have raised more external equity funding earlier; that they should have presented their case for the funding more effectively; that they should have sought more investors and a broader mix of investors, each investing smaller amounts; and finally, that they should have defined their relationships with individual investors more carefully before they made a deal.

Sixty-one of the 63 NTBFs that had raised funds from individual investors reported on their attempts to raise funds from other sources. Thirty-five had sought funding from venture capital funds, of whom 37 percent had been successful. The responses from 53 of the 54 NTBFs that had raised funding from venture capital funds indicated that only 17 had attempted to raise funding from individual investors, but with a much higher success rate of 82 percent. The NTBFs were asked why they had tried to raise funds from individual investors. Cost was an important factor, as was the need for small amounts of money that were below the normal range of venture capital funds. One firm mentioned the wish to keep control over the quality of the investor, and another observed that financing could be raised more quickly from individual investors than from venture capital funds and would require less management time to negotiate.

For the NTBFs in the sample, the median time between the decision to seek funding and the receipt of funds was 4 months for individual investor financing and 6 months for venture capital fund financing. The median lapse of time between the decision to seek funds and the first meeting with a potential investor was 1 month for individuals and 1.75 months for venture capital funds. This outcome seems to be contrary to what might have been expected, given the relative obscurity of individual investors and the public availability of information about venture capital funds. However, although venture capital funds are easier to locate, it may take longer to arrange an appointment with a venture capital fund principal than with an individual investor. The median time between the first meeting and the receipt of funds was 2.5 months for individuals and 4.5 months for venture capital funds. The longer time span for venture capital funds may be explained by the relatively greater number of people involved in the process and by a more protracted or more thorough "due diligence" process.

— — — — — — — —
INDIVIDUAL INVESTORS AND VENTURE CAPITAL FUNDS

Individual investor financing has a particular significance for NTBFs. First, compared to venture capital funds, individual investors are more likely to provide the relatively small amounts of very-high-risk seed financing required to launch new ventures, including those that subsequently attract funding from venture capital sources. Second, individual investors are the primary source of later stage funding when the capital needs are under $1 million.

Freear and Wetzel (1990) and the Center for Venture Research at the University of New Hampshire conducted a study in 1987 into the financing of NTBFs. The study collected the financial histories of 284 NTBFs that had been founded in New England between 1975 and 1986. One hundred seven firms (38 percent) had received no outside equity financing. One hundred seventy-seven (62 percent) raised $671 million in 445 rounds of external equity financing. Individual investors (excluding the founding management team and their relatives) were the most common source of funding, providing 177 rounds of equity financing for 124 firms. Ninety firms raised equity from venture capital funds in 173 rounds.

The total dollar amounts raised show a startling disparity — $76 million from individual investors but almost five times that amount, $370 million, from venture capital funds. Nevertheless, as Table 18–1 shows, individual investors are much more heavily represented in early stage rounds of less than $1 million, which is further evidence of the importance of this source to new firms, and of the complementary relationship between the informal capital market and venture capital funds.

The Freear and Wetzel (1990) study showed that more NTBFs raised equity capital from unaffiliated individual investors than from any other outside source. Individual investors were the primary source of outside funds when the size of the round was under $1 million, and they tended to invest earlier in the life of NTBFs than other sources of outside equity capital.

Freear and Wetzel (1989) provided evidence of a complementary relationship between nonmanagement private individual investors and venture capital funds. Individual investors were particularly active at an earlier stage and in smaller dollar amounts than were venture capital funds. Of the 226 responding firms in the VE sample, 35 percent had raised equity capital from individual

TABLE 18–1 — Rounds Invested in NTBFs

	Private Individuals	Venture Capital Funds
By size of round ($s)		
< $250,000	102 (58%)	8 (5%)
$250,000–$499,999	43 (24%)	14 (8%)
$500,000–$999,999	15 (8%)	31 (18%)
> $1,000,000	17 (10%)	120 (69%)
Total	177 (100%)	173 (100%)
By stage		
Seed	52 (29%)	11 (6%)
Start-up	55 (31%)	38 (22%)
First	29 (16%)	56 (32%)
Second	26 (15%)	46 (27%)
Third	10 (6%)	19 (11%)
Bridge	5 (3%)	3 (2%)
Total	177 (100%)	173 (100%)

Source : Freear and Wetzel (1990).

investors prior to receiving financing from venture capital funds. In 11 percent of the firms, individual investors participated alongside venture capital funds in some financing rounds, or in rounds following venture capital fund financing.

Table 18–2 gives data on dollars, rounds, and stages for the firms that did raise equity from individual investors prior to financing from venture capital funds. Seventy-seven percent of the 108 rounds financed by individual investors were at the seed or start-up stages. One-third of these early stage rounds were for under $250,000, 47 percent were for under $500,000, and 65 percent were for under $1 million, with a median investment per early stage round of $350,000.

TABLE 18–2 — Total Private Investments Raised per Stage of Financing

	Total Investment	Total Firms / Rounds	Median Investment	Mean Investment
Seed	$16,268,000	50	$225,000	$ 325,000
Start-up	28,225,000	33	500,000	855,300
First	20,400,000	14	650,000	1,457,100
Second	8,925,000	11	550,000	811,400
Third	0	0	0	0
Totals	$73,818,000	108 rounds		

Source : Freear and Wetzel (1989).

━━ ━━ ━━ ━━ ━━ ━━ ━━ ━━
EXTERNAL ECONOMIES
AND PUBLIC POLICY

The absence of market imperfections does not imply that the flow of funds to entrepreneurial ventures is ideal. The innovation process, of which venture investing is a part, generates significant social benefits. The nature of the marketplace precludes an innovator from capturing all the benefits of an innovation. Social returns that cannot be captured by investors include the creation of more new jobs, the diffusion of new technology, and increased tax revenues. Indeed, the *Economic Report of the President* (1989) credits innovation and its diffusion with about half the historical increase in the U.S. standard of living. The report estimated the social rate of return at about twice the private rate of return.

Mansfield (1983) measured the external economies associated with technological innovation in a sample of 17 industrial innovations. He estimated the median private rate of return at 25 percent and the median social rate of return at 56 percent. Romeo and Rappaport (1984) tested the hypothesis that innovations carried out by small firms (under 500 employees) tend to involve larger gaps between private and social rates of return than innovations carried out by larger firms. While cautioning that their results were suggestive rather than definitive, Romeo and Rappaport concluded that the gap between private and social returns was related to firm size. Small firms, they argued, were less able than large firms to appropriate the economic gain from their innovations. Thus, governmental encouragement of innovative activity by small firms would yield a greater social payoff than the encouragement of large firms.

During the past 10 years, federal legislation establishing programs to support the formation and growth of entrepreneurial ventures includes:

Omnibus Trade and Competitiveness Act (1988)

Small Business Innovation Development Act (1982)

Small Business Investment Incentive Act (1980)

Stevenson-Wylder Technology Innovation Act (1980)

University and Small Business Patent Procedure Act (1980)

In their discussion of externalities and information, Charles River Associates (1976) noted that too few resources will be invested in small technology-based firms and in generating information about their investment opportunities relative to their ability to produce external economies from these investments.

The research on private versus social rates of return from innovation, coupled with the inefficiency of the informal venture capital market, suggest that efforts to facilitate the flow of information between entrepreneurs and individual investors is an appropriate public policy tool for promoting innovation.

━━ ━━ ━━ ━━ ━━ ━━ ━━ ━━ ━━
DEVELOPING THEORIES
ABOUT THE MARKET

The development of a subject often goes through several overlapping stages. In the first, researchers establish the possible existence of an area worthy of study. In the second, researchers collect, assimilate, disseminate, and interpret empirical evidence about the subject and its context and relationship with other subjects. This stage continues indefinitely as a means of testing and refining the theories developed in the third stage. Researchers in this stage seek to transform interpretation of evidence into explanatory and predictive theories, drawing on their knowledge base in related subjects.

The study of the informal venture capital market in the United States has moved through the first stage and is well into the second. To some extent, researchers have relied upon some basic assumed theoretical relationships. For example, it has been assumed that participants in the informal venture capital market are averse to risk, requiring additional rewards for bearing increased risk. Studies by Avery and Elliehausen (1986), Freear and Wetzel (1989), and Sullivan and Miller (1990) confirmed this positive relationship between risk and return. Thus, as early stage financing is regarded generally as being riskier than later stage financing, early stage return expectations, other things being equal, tend to be higher. At an even more basic level, it is assumed that the market mechanisms of supply, demand, and price would apply to the informal venture capital segment of the finance market, being constrained only by the degree of efficiency in the informal market and the extent of market segmentation. A key element here is the extent of the market's ability to channel information to and from actual and potential market participants.

Nevertheless, although researchers have brought their own theoretical and empirical knowledge to their studies of the informal venture capital market, little attention has yet been paid to the development of explanatory and predictive theories about the venture capital market and its participants. This is in contrast to developments in the field of finance generally, and reflects the "early stage" status of informal venture capital market research. What seems to be happening is a very slow "trickle-down" of theory from general finance theory through to theories about the behavior of professional venture capital funds. This "trickle-down" is only now beginning to seep through to the informal venture capital market.

An unpublished paper by Norton (1990) provides an excellent overview of the state of theoretical knowledge about the behavior of entrepreneurs and professional venture capitalists. What follows draws substantially on Norton's paper. He examined the possible application of theories such as portfolio theory, agency costs, signalling, transactions costs, information asymmetries, static trade-off theory, and option pricing theory. He concluded that although overall financial theory does a satisfactory job of explaining observed behavior in venture capital, its application to venture capital is a neglected area of empirical and theoretical research.

It may prove possible to extend at least some of Norton's analysis to the informal venture capital market. Venture capitalists are financial intermediaries, and as such are principals in their relationship with entrepreneurs, and agents in their relationship with their own investors. Individual investors, in contrast, are essentially principals in the investing relationship with entrepreneurs. Especially in early stage financing where individual investors are particularly prominent, the investor is investing more in ideas and people than in marketable, nonspecific, tangible assets. Brophy (1986) noted that researchers have begun to study the use of complex securities and monitoring systems as substitutes for the "discipline of the marketplace" in situations where agency risk exists and in which no trading in the firm's securities occurs. Individual investors are in situations in which the agency risks are at least as great.

Norton also examined theories surrounding asymmetric information. He identified two asymmetries: 1) between the venture capital fund and the entrepreneur, in which the entrepreneur is assumed to be better informed than the capital markets about the value of the firm and its investment opportunities (see, for example, Giammarino and Lewis 1988); and 2) between the entrepreneur and reality, which the research cited uniformly failed to study. Venture capital funds have attempted to deal with the first by using the "due diligence" process to differentiate between attractive and unattractive investments. The study of both asymmetries would seem to be a potentially valuable research framework to apply to the informal venture capital market.

Methods of attempting to deal with the first type of asymmetry might involve portfolio diversification, networking, and/or syndication, in an attempt both to share information (Bygrave 1987, 1988) and to spread risk. However, far from being well diversified, as general finance theory might predict, many venture capital funds are specialized in both geography and technology (Tyebjee and Bruno 1984b), because funds provide more than just financing. They also provide management guidance and technical expertise (Gorman and Sahlman 1989; MacMillan, Kulow, and Khoylian 1989). Further, Sapienza and Gupta (1989) found that venture capital funds specializing in early stage financing were less diversified than those funds that were more active in later stage financing. They also found that venture capital funds became more diversified the larger the amount of funds they had to invest. Such considerations apply even more strongly to the individual investor, and suggest a need to modify portfolio theory for application to the informal venture capital market.

Norton (1990) observed that since the venture capital investor is investing in an idea and in people more than in tangible assets, option pricing theory has several applications in the valuation of venture capital deals. The typical deal goes through several financing stages. At each stage, more information relevant to risk and return assessment is available for evaluation by the venture capital fund and the firm. By staging financing commitments over time, the venture capital fund is investing in options to abandon or revalue the firm. The value of the option to abandon is the difference between the expected net present value of a deal with staged financing commitments compared to a deal without staged financing commitments. By maintaining the option to revalue the deal, flexible investment pricing can occur in future capital commitments to the benefit of both parties (Sahlman 1988). Whether, how, and to what extent individual investors structure deals in this way are questions requiring further research.

━━ ━━ ━━ ━━ ━━
INTERNATIONAL DIMENSIONS

Most of the research into the informal venture capital market has been conducted in the United States. However, it is clear that in the past few years there has been an upsurge of interest in several other countries, particularly in Europe and Canada. As a means of stimulating further researcher and practitioner interest, a group called the International Informal Venture Capital Research Network was formed in mid-1990, and is based at the University of New Hampshire's Center for Venture Research.

Several countries, such as Germany, Sweden, and the United Kingdom, have noted the existence of gaps in the finance markets, particularly for emerging ventures. Venture capital funds were established in Sweden in the early 1980s, with a strong interest in early stage and high-technology ventures. By the mid-1980s, many of the venture capital funds had disappeared, leaving the remainder larger, but more cautious, in their attitudes towards early stage and high-technology financing. Thus, many ventures are undercapitalized and heavily dependent upon short-term debt. There is anecdotal evidence that suggests that individual investors are beginning to re-emerge (Landstrom 1990).

Germany has engaged in an experimental federal program of grants and other support at the seed stage, particularly for high-technology ventures (Mayer, Heinzel, and Muller n.d.). The apparent desire of several former Communist countries in eastern Europe to encourage the development of entrepreneurial ventures implies the need for venture financing (see, for example, Hisrich and Vecsenyi 1990). It is likely, given the history of those countries over the last 50 years, that government schemes, banks, and professional venture capital organizations are likely to be the principal financing vehicles, at least initially.

In Canada, research into the informal venture capital market has been continuing for several years. Riding and Short (1987, 1988) investigated informal investors in the Ontario region and have reported findings that are broadly consistent with those of Wetzel (1983b), Wetzel and Wilson (1985), and Tymes and Krasner (1983). Riding and Short found evidence of a significant pool of informal venture capital, and personal investor characteristics that were similar to those reported by studies in the United States. However, they noted that Canadian investors seemed to be more active in investing, with a higher rejection rate, but to have a less active working relationship with the ventures in which they had invested. Their risk/return expectations were similar to those reported by Tymes and Krasner, but they perceived less risk than did the New England investors investigated by Wetzel, and Wetzel and Wilson. They also found that although individual investors were content with the channels of information about investment opportunities, entrepreneurs were generally dissatisfied.

In the United Kingdom, the Macmillan Committee drew attention in 1931 to a capital gap that became known as the "Macmillan Gap" (Macmillan Committee 1931). Later government reports, on through the Wilson Committee in 1979, have discussed the existence of such a gap. To date, researchers have focused on the role of government support schemes (such as the Business Expansion Scheme), banks, and bank-related investment groups in dealing with this gap. Venture capital funds are a relatively recent phenomenon, and the existence and importance of an informal venture capital market is only now being acknowledged, appreciated, and researched (Mason and Harrison 1988, 1989, 1990).

CONCLUSION : THE MARKET IN THE YEAR 2000

The 1985 Research Agenda Revisited

The Wetzel (1986) research agenda had four main components : scale, investor characteristics, information channels, and relationships with venture capital funds.

1. *Scale.* All the evidence supports the view that the informal venture capital market is a major component of the finance market as a whole. From both the supply and demand perspectives, it is clear that its size is many times greater than that of the formal venture capital market. It is also probable that there are so-called "virgin angels" — high net worth individuals who have not, for whatever reasons, entered the informal venture capital market as individual investors. Considerable research effort needs to be concentrated on learning more about them, and perhaps from a public policy perspective, seeking ways of mobilizing their investment potential.

2. *Investor characteristics.* Much more information has become available over the past five years about the personal characteristics of individual investors. In particular, their investment attitudes, expectations, and behavior, and personal, educational, and business background are better known. Individual investors display substantial differences in their working relationships with the ventures in which they invest. More is now known about how investors find entrepreneurs (and vice versa), but much more work is still needed on the processes of deal origination,

screening, evaluation, and structuring. Recent studies have confirmed the importance of nonfinancial factors in the individual investor's investment decision. Some regional variations in investor behavior, expectations, and attitudes appear to exist, and several studies have unearthed evidence of the existence of "lead" investors.

3. *Information channels.* As noted in the previous paragraph, much more is known about how investors find entrepreneurs and vice versa. Although there is some variation among the studies, friends and business associates are by far the most used and most efficient channels of information between investors and entrepreneurs, ranking far above all others. In general, it seems that investors rely heavily on their networks, stick to what they know in terms of product, process, or market, and place much emphasis on the quality and personality of the entrepreneur or venture management team. One study found that entrepreneurs themselves believe that they should seek external equity in greater amounts and earlier; they should make more professional presentations to prospective investors; they should seek more and more varied investors; and they should find out more about the prospective individual investors before the deal is struck. These findings should also remind researchers of the direct practical implications of much of their work.

4. *Venture capital funds.* There is strong evidence of a complementary relationship between individual investors and venture capital funds. Individual investors tend to invest smaller amounts at an earlier stage, to have generally slightly lower return expectations in relation to risk, and often, but not in all studies, to be a little more patient than venture capital funds. As the amounts of finance sought by the entrepreneur increase, especially beyond $1 million, and as financing advances through the stages, venture capital funds become more dominant both in dollars and number of financing rounds. Individual investors tend to be less concerned with seeking voting control or setting clear liquidation provisions at the time of the deal, but in some cases work full-time or part-time with the ventures after the investment is made. In common with venture capital funds, they frequently have an informal consulting role and/or a seat on the board of directors.

Current research

The Center for Venture Research at the University of New Hampshire continues to be active in the field of informal venture capital research. Work is continuing on the analysis and interpretation of data from earlier studies, notably Freear and Wetzel (1989, 1990) and Freear, Sohl, and Wetzel (1990). The Center hopes to begin work on a major project to provide statistically reliable estimates of the scale of the informal venture capital market and of the attitudes, behavior, and characteristics of high net worth investors in entrepreneurial ventures, including investors in NTBFs. The work on data collected in Tennessee and referred to earlier (Postma and Sullivan 1990; Sullivan and Miller 1990) is continuing, as is work in Canada (Riding and Short 1987, 1988), and the United Kingdom (Mason and Harrison 1988, 1989, 1990). One of the difficulties faced by researchers in the field has been a lack of awareness of work being done in other countries. It is hoped that the newly formed International Informal Venture Capital Research Network will go some way toward improving the exchange of knowledge on informal venture capital.

Towards the Year 2000: A Research Agenda

1. Research will continue to be needed in all four areas outlined in the preceding section. In particular, more research is needed into investor characteristics, attitudes, behavior, deal processing, and relations with entrepreneurs.
2. Replication of earlier studies will continue, and with it confirmation (or otherwise) of their findings.
3. The reliability and validity of survey instruments and techniques will need to be refined and improved. There will be greater use of longitudinal studies of investor behavior.
4. Practical usefulness will continue to be a central theme in research studies. More precisely, a major aim of research work will be to improve the efficiency of the capital market by identifying ways in which the informal venture market can become more efficient, and in which the degree of market segmentation can be reduced. This would appear to be very much in line with the public policy issues raised in an earlier section.
5. More attention will be given to the need to develop explanatory and predictive theories for empirical testing.
6. Although work on the relationships with venture capital funds remains important, research will be extended to other segments, including commercial and investment banks, and other intermediaries such as accountants and lawyers.
7. The international dimension will gain increasing relevance and importance to researchers. Specifically, researchers will seek to discover the scale, nature, and effectiveness of informal markets in many countries, not least in the eastern European countries as they move towards market economies, and in some Third World countries.
8. Research will continue to be directed towards improving the channels of communication between investors and entrepreneurs, and among different segments of the capital market. An important element in this research is to learn more about the "virgin angels."

REFERENCES

Aram, J. D. 1987 *Informal risk capital in the Eastern Great Lakes Region.* Prepared under contract for the Office of Advocacy, U.S. Small Business Administration.

1989 Attitudes and behaviors of informal investors toward early-stage investments, technology-based ventures, and coinvestors. *Journal of Business Venturing* 4 (5): 333–347.

Avery, R. B., and G. E. Eilliehausen 1986 Financial characteristics of high income families. *Federal Reserve Bulletin* 72 (3): 163–177.

Baty, G. 1964 *Initial financing of the new research-based enterprise in New England.* Boston: Federal Reserve Bank of Boston.

Brophy, D. J. 1982 Venture capital research. In *Encyclopedia of entrepreneurship*, eds. C. A. Kent, D. L. Sexton, and K. H. Vesper, 140–164. Englewood Cliffs, N.J.: Prentice-Hall, Inc.

1986 Venture capital research. In *The art and science of entrepreneurship*, eds. D. L. Sexton and R. W. Smilor, 119–144. Cambridge, Mass.: Ballinger.

Bygrave, W. D. 1987 Syndicated investments by venture capital firms: A networking perspective. *Journal of Business Venturing* 2 (2): 139–154.

1988 The structure of investment networks of venture capital firms. *Journal of Business Venturing* 3 (2): 137–157.

Charles River Associates 1976 *An analysis of capital market imperfections.* A report prepared for the Experimental Technology Incentives Program, National Bureau of Standards. Washington, D.C.

Economic Report of the President 1989 Washington, D.C.: U.S. Government Printing Office.

Forbes 1987 The *Forbes* Four Hundred. (Special Issue.) October 26.

Freear, J., J. A. Sohl, and W. E. Wetzel, Jr. 1990 Raising venture capital: Entrepreneurs' views of the process. Paper presented at the Babson College Entrepreneurship Conference.

Freear, J., and W. E. Wetzel, Jr. 1989 Equity capital for entrepreneurs. In *Frontiers of entrepreneurship research*, eds. R. H. Brockhaus, Sr., N. C. Churchill, J. A. Katz, B. A. Kirchhoff, K. H. Vesper, and W. E. Wetzel, Jr., 230–244. Wellesley, Mass.: Babson College.

1990 Who bankrolls high-tech entrepreneurs? *Journal of Business Venturing* 5 (2): 77–89.

Gaston, R. J., and S. E. Bell 1988 *The informal supply of capital.* A report prepared for the Office of Economic Research, U.S. Small Business Administration.

Giammarino, R., and T. Lewis 1988 A theory of negotiated equity financing. *Review of Financial Studies* 1 (3): 265–288.

Gorman, M., and W. A. Sohlman 1989 What do venture capitalists do? *Journal of Business Venturing* 4 (4): 231–248.

Harr, N. W., J. Starr, and I. C. MacMillan 1988 Informal risk capital investors: Investment patterns on the east coast of the U.S.A. *Journal of Business Venturing* 3 (1): 11–29.

Hisrich, R. D., and J. Vecsenyi 1990 Entrepreneurship and the Hungarian economic transformation: Problems, opportunities, and infrastructure support. Paper presented at the Babson College Entrepreneurship Conference.

Hoffman, C. A. 1972 The venture capital investment process : A particular aspect of regional economic development. Ph.D. diss., University of Texas at Austin.

MacMillan, I. C., D. M. Kulow, and R. Khoylian 1989 venture capitalists' involvement in their investments : Extent and performance. *Journal of Business Venturing* 4 : 27–47.

Macmillan Committee 1931 *Report of the Committee on Finance and Industry.* Cmnd. 3897. London : HMSO.

Mansfield, E. 1983 Entrepreneurship and the management of innovation. In *Entrepreneurship and the outlook for America,* ed. J. Bachman. N.Y. : Free Press.

Mason, C. M., and R. T. Harrison 1988 Small firms policy and the "north-south" divide in the United Kingdom : The case of the business expansion scheme. *Transactions of the Institute of British Geographers* 14 : 37–58.

1989 The role of the business expansion scheme in the United Kingdom. *OMEGA (International Journal of Management Science* 17 (2) : 147–157.

1990 Informal risk capital in the United Kingdom. Paper presented at the Babson College Entrepreneurship Conference.

Mayer, M., W. Heinzel, and R. Muller n.d. Performance of new technology-based firms in the Federal Republic of Germany at the stage of market entry. Working paper, Institute for Systems and Innovation Research of the Fraunhofer Society, Karlsruhe, West Germany.

Neiswander, K. 1982 *Informal seed stage investors : Northeast Ohio angels.* Cleveland, Ohio : Weatherhead School of Management, Case Western Reserve University.

Norton, E. 1990 An overview of venture capital finance. Working paper, Fairleigh Dickinson University.

Obermayer, J. H. 1983 *The capital crunch : Small high-technology companies and national objectives during a period of severe debt and equity shortages.* Cambridge, Mass. : Research and Planning, Inc.

Ou, C. 1987 Holdings of privately-held business assets by American families : Findings from the 1983 Consumer Finance Survey. Unpublished report prepared for the Office of Economic Research, U.S. Small Business Administration.

Postma, P. D., and M. K. Sullivan 1990 Informal risk capital in the Knoxville region. Working paper, University of Tennessee.

Riding, A. L., and D. M. Short 1987 Some investors' and entrepreneurs' perceptions of the informal market for risk capital. *Journal of Small Business and Entrepreneurship* 5 (2) : 19–30.

Riding, A. L., and D. M. Short 1988 On the estimation of the investment potential of informal investors : A capture-recapture approach. *Journal of Small Business and Entrepreneurship* 5 (5) : 26–40.

Romeo, A. A., and J. Rappaport 1984 *Social versus private returns to the innovations by small firms compared to large firms.* Report prepared for the Office of Advocacy, U.S. Small Business Administration.

Rubenstein, A. H. 1958 *Problems of financing and managing new research-based enterprises in New England.* Boston : Federal Reserve Bank of Boston.

Sahlman, W. A. 1988 Aspects of financial contracting in venture capital. *Journal of Applied Corporate Finance* 1 (1) : 23–36.

Sapienza, H., and A. Gupta 1989 The pursuit of discovery by venture capital firms : Antecedents and implications. In *Frontiers of entrepreneurship research,* eds. B. A. Kirchhoff, W. A. Long, W. E. McMullan, K. H. Vesper, and W. E. Wetzel, Jr., 304–317. Wellesley, Mass. : Babson College.

Seymour, C. R., and W. E. Wetzel, Jr. 1981 Informal risk capital in New England. Report prepared for the Office of Advocacy, U.S. Small Business Administration.

Shapero, A. 1983 *The role of the financial institutions of a community in the formation, effectiveness and expansion of innovating companies.* Washington, D.C.: U.S. Small Business Administration.

Sullivan, M. K., and A. Miller 1990 Applying theory of finance to informal risk capital research: Promise and problems. In *Frontiers of entrepreneurship research*, eds. W. Bygrave, N. Churchill, J. Hornaday, D. Muzyka, K. Vesper, and W. Wetzel, Jr., 296–310. Wellesley, Mass.: Babson College.

Tyebjee, T. T., and A. V. Bruno 1984a Venture capital: Investor and investee perspectives. *Technovation* 2 (3): 185–208.

1984b A model of venture capitalist investment activity. *Management Science* 30 (9): 1051–1066.

Tymes, E. R., and O. J. Krasner 1983 Informal risk capital in California. In *Frontiers of entrepreneurship research*, eds. J. Hornaday, J. A. Timmons, and K. H. Vesper, 347–368. Wellesley, Mass.: Babson College.

U.S. Department of Commerce 1970 *Financing new technological enterprise.* Report of the Panel on Venture Capital. Washington, D.C.: Commerce Technical Advisory Board.

Wetzel, W. E., Jr. 1983a The Taplin and Montle development fund: A case study in finance. In *Frontiers of entrepreneurship research*, eds. J. Hornaday, J. A. Timmons, and K. H. Vesper, 335–346. Wellesley, Mass.: Babson College.

1983b Angels and informal risk capital. *Sloan Management Review* 24 (4): 23–34.

1986 Informal risk capital: Knowns and unknowns. In *The art and science of entrepreneurship*, eds. D. L. Sexton and R. W. Smilor, 85–108. Cambridge, Mass.: Ballinger.

1987 The informal venture capital market: Aspects of scale and efficiency. *Journal of Business Venturing* 2 (4): 299–313.

Wetzel, W. E., Jr., and I. G. Wilson 1985 Seed capital gaps: Evidence from high growth ventures. In *Frontiers of entrepreneurship research*, eds. J. A. Hornaday, E. B. Shils, J. A. Timmons, and K. H. Vesper, 221–240. Wellesley, Mass.: Babson College.

Wilson, I. G. 1984 *Financing high growth companies in New Hampshire.* Concord, N.H.: Department of Resources and Economic Development, State of New Hampshire.

Chapter

19

Progress in Research on Corporate Venturing[1]

S. Venkataraman,
Ian C. MacMillan,
and
Rita Gunther McGrath

●

INTRODUCTION

Corporate venturing focuses on the study of new business creations by members of existing firms. Its key concerns are to investigate how market and firm conditions influence the creation of new businesses (Roberts 1968; Hlavacek 1974; von Hippel 1977; Kanter 1983; Burgelman 1983a). Variously described as corporate entrepreneurship, corporate venturing (von Hippel 1977; MacMillan 1986), or intrapreneurship (Pinchot 1985), scholars have approached the study of corporate venturing from different directions. Economists have for the most part studied the underlying market dynamics that foster innovation and entrepreneurship among firms (Scherer 1978; Kamien and Schwartz 1982) while ignoring the organizational and political dynamics within firms. Organization theorists, on the other hand, have studied the organizational dynamics and politics in corporate venturing (Kanter 1983; Burgelman 1983a, 1983b) while ignoring the market dynamics. While this division of labor is understandable, it contributes to our inability to develop a

[1]Funding for this study was provided by the Sol C. Snider Entrepreneurial Center of the Wharton School through a grant from Citibank, N.A.

487

comprehensive understanding of corporate venturing. Indeed, Teece (1987a, 3) states that, "at a time when so much attention is given to innovation and entrepreneurship, it is rather pathetic that a deep understanding of the process is lacking. It is no wonder that firms and governments have difficulty trying to stimulate innovation when its fundamental processes are so poorly understood."

The reason for such lack of knowledge of the process is rooted in good measure on the nature of the venturing process, which is highly complex, uncertain, not very easily modelled, and partly rooted in our own ignorance of the problems facing the economic agent in managing new venture development.

In this chapter we attempt to understand the nature of the challenges facing large organizations in corporate venturing and also to suggest a framework and key research questions for studying the process of corporate venturing. We take the position that a managerial perspective on corporate entrepreneurship is essential — one which highlights the hazards and key challenges confronting managers as they attempt to handle the process of venturing (Lewin and Minton 1986; Van de Ven and Angle 1989). Such a position is warranted, because there is little dispute that the entrepreneurial function is a vital component not only in the competitive potential of a firm but also in the process of economic growth (Schumpeter 1942). But more importantly, it is a *managerial* perspective that distinguishes corporate venturing from other studies of entrepreneurship and innovation in general, and that attempts to open the proverbial "black box" surrounding the process of venturing within organizations.

We attempt to isolate the core processes essential for successful corporate venturing, and sacrifice analytic simplicity for comprehensiveness, in the hope that the promise which the generality of the framework holds for observation and research will make it a worthwhile choice.

■ ■ ■ ■ ■ ■ ■ ■
THE CHANGING NATURE
OF THE VENTURING
PROBLEM

Corporate venturing may be defined as the process by which members of an existing firm bring into existence products and markets which do not currently exist within the repertoire of the firm. This process occurs through transactions (or relationships) with others that take place within different institutional contexts.

Venturing is a highly complex and uncertain process involving numerous actions, events, and decisions during its evolution. But how does one review, let alone study, such a complex, continually changing process? For expositional purposes we will divide the total process into its elemental processes and discuss each of these in turn. In order to break up the total process we first divide all the venturing activities into three distinct challenges faced by managers. We then examine how these challenges change from time to time during the evolution of the new business; in our discussion, we divide the evolutionary dimension into four distinct conditions.

The process of creating new products and markets presents many challenges for large firms. In addition to the hazards confronting the development of any new business, such as the uncertainties of new business start-ups and the liabilities of newness (Stinchcombe 1965), corporate venturing also faces hazards peculiar to its institutional context (Burgelman 1983a; Van de Ven et al. 1989) which manifest themselves in the form of liabilities of size and age (Aldrich and Auster 1986). These liabilities present three distinct challenges for managers.

The first is the challenge of *business founding,* which deals with the issue of creating and developing the functional competencies and infrastructure required to develop, manufacture, market, distribute, and service the product. The focus is upon the transactional environment of a business, and the challenge calls for the creation and development of a primary value chain (Porter 1985) ranging from supplier logistics to distribution and service logistics.

The second is the challenge of *managing the hierarchical process.* Since capital and labor resource allocation decisions and the decision to pursue some businesses and abandon others are taken by managers within firms (whose decision criteria may vary from time to time) rather than through markets, there is the challenge of fostering the new venture initiatives within the firm. The focus here is on gaining political support, currency, and resources for the new economic entity being created.

The third is the challenge of *managing the institutional context* within which founding and fostering take place. This context affects a population of initiatives within the firm and not just a single initiative. The relevant context here is the repertoire of organizational strategies such as incentives, approaches to venturing, and infrastructural support for venturing.

The first two challenges are at the level of an individual venture and are concerned with the questions *why* and *which* new ideas become successful new businesses within a firm, and which new ideas become either failures or are spun off. The third challenge is at the macrolevel of the organization and is concerned with designing the appropriate strategies and structures by top management to produce a vital and innovative organization. The focus is on the effect of such strategies and structures on the population of ventures within a firm, rather than merely on any single venture.

These three challenges do not remain constant over time. They continually change, since business creation is an evolutionary process. Most process studies on innovation or business creation divide up the evolutionary process into some of its elemental stages. Scholars have typically used a variant of the epigenetic or accumulation model (Etzioni 1963) in order to divide the process into these stages. The most common stages that run through these studies on process evolution are idea development, start-up, growth, maturity, and perhaps decline. Consistent with such research, we will divide the total venturing process into four conditions in order to discuss the useful research questions that arise in each context. The basic idea underlying these conditions is that the nature of the venturing problem faced by managers of a firm changes with each of these conditions.

Note that we do not use these conditions to highlight any temporal sequence that may or may not be involved. Rather our motive is to understand the changing nature of the challenges better by simplifying a complex process into some of its significant elementary components.

The four conditions we use are *definition, penetration, contagion,* and *institutionalization.* These conditions were chosen because when taken together they seem to be collectively exhaustive and yet mutually exclusive. In the first condition, definition, managers are concerned with the issue of clarifying and developing the current and expected future positions of a new idea or initiative. The focus of attention is on actions, strategies, and structures that attempt to define the product, market, and the fit between the new business and the corporation. In other words, the question asked is, What is the business?

In the second condition, penetration, managers are concerned with taking an idea from the drawing board to reality or implementation. The focus of attention is on actions, strategies, and structures that attempt to force market entry, break down barriers to start-up, and develop the infrastructure required for successful start-up.

In the third condition, contagion, managers are concerned with coping with growth. The focus of attention is on actions, strategies, and structures that aim to cope with the escalating resource requirements and to cope with the logistical problems thrown up by an exploding bundle of transactions typically associated with growth.

In the fourth condition, institutionalization, managers are concerned with integrating the new initiative with the body corporate or mainstream of the firm. The focus of attention here is on actions, strategies, and structures that aim to develop the next generation of products, to legitimate, to socialize, and to prepare the new business for corporate citizenship.

In the following sections we will discuss the nature of the challenges within each condition, review the research within each condition, and highlight the fruitful areas for further research. The basic framework used is shown in Table 19–1.

THE BUSINESS CHALLENGE OF FOUNDING

Consistent with the four conditions of venturing, we identify four founding challenges: *ideating, forcing, rollercoasting,* and *revitalizing.* We use these labels as illustrative of the dominant challenge and focus of management attention during each relevant condition.

TABLE 19-1 — Framework for the Study of Corporate Venturing

Challenge↓ Condition→	Definition: Attempts to define product, market, and fit with corporation	Penetration: Attempts to force market entry, break down barriers to start-up, and develop infrastructure for start-up	Contagion: Attempts to cope with escalating resource requirements and logistical problems thrown up by exploding bundle of transactions	Institutionalization: Attempts to develop next generation of products, legitimize, socialize, and prepare new business for corporate citizenship
Context-Managing Processes: At population of ventures level: developing the repertoire of routines and styles that foster firm vitality and innovation	Production of variations	Managing selection: pathclearing	Managing selection: autonomy and control	Managing retention: legitimizing
Fostering Processes: At venture level: gaining political support, currency, and resources by managing the hierarchy	Championing ideas	Championing opportunistic behavior	Championing resources	Championing incorporation
Founding processes: At venture level: creating and developing competencies and infrastructure to develop, manufacture, market, distribute, and service the product	Ideating	Forcing	Rollercoasting	Revitalizing

491

Ideating

The process of bringing into existence products and markets which do not currently exist in the firm's repertoire is filled with uncertainties. Much of the information needed by managers to act on many business issues — such as technology, price, quantity, product features, suppliers, distributors, and strategy, among others — is not adequately provided by existing markets. Reliable information will only be provided by future products and markets (Arrow 1974). And yet, the manager has to decide and act on many such issues today in order to bring into existence future products and markets. Hence, market information has to be replaced by expectations : expectations about technological trajectories and standards, customer preferences, regulations, resources, and the environment. Decisions and actions taken on the basis of expectations could turn out to be wrong due to shifts in technology, customer tastes and preferences, and so forth. In short, the manager faces a world of uncertainty when decisions about investing in, creating, and developing a value-chain infrastructure have to be made on the basis of expectations rather than market information (Arrow 1974). Since it is not always possible to know or decide a priori which new products will eventually be "winners" and which "mistakes" (Kimberly 1981), and given that risk preference is a variable across managers and firms (March and Shapira 1987), there is need to understand : *1) how managers develop the concept of a new business ; 2) what is the nature and content of their expectations ; 3) how and why managers choose to pursue a particular set of product attributes (such as technology, features, price, and so on) and markets (suppliers, distributors, and customers) ; 4) how and why such expectations and choices change over time ; and 5) their relation of the choices to success and failure in corporate venturing.*

What do we know about this critical process of ideation ? While many studies have focused on the origins, evolution, and championing of ideas, there are a few which are relevant from a corporate venturing point of view.

Three factors seem to underlie successful ideation. The closer the match between the particular skills of the organization and the market needs, the lower the volatility of the environment, and the greater the rapidity with which learning occurs, the greater seems to be the success of the idea.

Linking technology and market needs.

There is evidence to believe that firms which develop products purely on the basis of technological imperative while ignoring the market imperative have less success (Freeman 1973 ; Utterback 1974 ; Rothwell 1972 ; von Hippel 1977 ; Dougherty 1990a). At the same time, in a competitive market, the closer the technological design of the firm to the market needs, and the greater the technical proficiency and uniqueness of the design, the greater could be the future success (Cooper 1983 ; Roberts 1968 ; von Hippel 1977). Indeed, Kamien and Schwartz (1972) have shown that the uniqueness of the venturing firm's technology combined with demonstrated ability to improve the technology in the event of imitation actually discourages rival entry into the market. This may be especially true in high-technology product markets.

These findings are consistent with the broader argument of the relationship between appropriability regimes and competitive advantages (Teece 1987b). Appropriability regimes are proprietary assets owned by firms that provide protection of future profit streams against erosion due to competition. To the extent that such appropriability is represented by nontrivial entry barriers — such as patents, royalties, highly specialized knowledge, skills, physical assets, information, distribution networks, or service — infrastructure revenue and profit streams can be protected (Teece 1987b). The crucial insight from this argument (in addition to the fact that product concepts which embody some nontrivial appropriability advantage have a greater likelihood of success) is the point that the existence of such appropriability rights and the protection of such rights in society through a legal framework provide powerful incentives to entrepreneurship, risk taking, and economic and technological development (Schumpeter 1942).

How does the market need and technological linking take place ? Available evidence suggests that such linking occurs through a cascading process. At a macrolevel there is evidence to suppose that technology and user linking occurs through an evolutionary process with constant interaction between members of a network or community of researchers and users who, over time, develop a shared understanding or technological paradigm (Dosi 1982, 1984 ; Aitken 1985). Through a process of rich sharing of information, various technological trajectories are invented, developed, tried, tested, abandoned, and diffused. At a microlevel, Burgelman (1983b) discovered that within the firm such linking was accomplished through constant interaction between the business-level managers, who understood customer needs, and the technology managers, who understood the technological constraints. At the interface between the customer and firm, successful linking is found to have been accomplished by those firms which : 1) developed new products with close cooperation between their customers and suppliers (von Hippel 1977 ; Hlavacek 1974 ; Peters and Waterman 1982 ; Kanter 1983 ; Dougherty 1990a) ; 2) had more boundary spanning roles (Tushman 1977) ; and 3) paid particular attention to the education of users (Freeman 1973). Research suggests that irrespective of the origins of the new product — "technology push" (Phillips 1966) or "demand pull" (Schmookler 1966) — the cascading process must flow in both directions between macro- and microlevels for successful integration between technology and user needs.

In a fine-grained analysis of the process of understanding market needs Dougherty (1990a) discovered distinct patterns of "sense making" within firms. The unsuccessful patterns used a "garbage can" model (Cohen, March, and Olsen 1972) of sense making where engineers or planners with prior technological or planning solutions (respectively) went in search of market problems. Consistent with the above findings, the more successful patterns were those that integrated the technology and plans with market needs into a comprehensive approach to business definition.

In summary, it would appear that for successful linking of technology and market need three things have to be accomplished. First, the product engineers and scientists of the firm must be well integrated into the loci of the network of researchers; second, there must be good understanding between the business-level managers and the customers as to the needs of each party; and third, within the firm there must be effective communication between the business-level managers and technical managers.

Volatility of environment.

The process of ideation seems to be hampered in highly volatile markets. Cooper (1983) discovered that markets which were highly competitive or had rapid introductions of new products affected future venture performance. A possible underlying reason could be that in highly fragmented, competitive, rapidly changing markets, there is a lot of "noise" that inhibits learning of any kind. Firms in such environments would have greater difficulty in bringing about a closer match between technical capabilities and market needs, thus affecting successful ideation.

Rapidity of learning.

The rapidity with which learning occurs influences success, because in some industries being an early entrant in the market with a new product yields greater competitive advantages (Schoonhoven, Eisenhardt, and Lyman 1990). There is some evidence (although not very systematic) to believe that in an uncertain, rapidly changing environment, expectations, product market choices, and changes occur primarily through learning (Maidique and Zirger 1984; Van de Ven and Angle 1989). Such learning occurs in a variety of ways, including mimetic learning where others' strategies are imitated; learning by doing, or trial-and-error approach; extrapolation of past experiences in similar situations; and finally, learning by using. These findings suggest that new venture creation often combines conceptualization and implementation where one action influences the other. Firms seem to understand the nature of the technology and the needs of the market only through a process of experimenting, by developing, delivering, and servicing the products to the target markets and making the necessary modifications to the product and market.

Schoonhoven et al. (1990) argued that shipping new products to the markets faster in a competitive environment is important for financial independence, external legitimacy, visibility, and reputation; for cornering market share; and for promoting long-term survival. There is evidence in research work in industrial organization economics literature (Caves and Porter 1977) to suggest that early entry is significant because of market share advantages and the opportunity to erect entry barriers, thus protecting future revenue streams. If indeed early entry is crucial for success, then rapid learning is, in turn, essential for rapid entry into the marketplace.

Forcing

There is another problem born of the uncertainty facing new business start-ups: the problem of engaging in transactions with a whole set of stakeholders required to develop the business. As Arrow pointed out (1974, 8), because of the uncertainty surrounding future markets, neither buyers nor suppliers "are willing to make commitments which completely define future actions." New business creation often implies that many contracts will be fulfilled only in the future. Suppliers may have to make investments in specialized assets today in anticipation of orders from the firm in future when the business does take off. Similarly, customers may have to make changes in their operations and technology because of a proposed new product. Both buyers and suppliers may be loath to share in such risks and make such investments because of the uncertainties regarding future prices, product quality, market sizes, technology, and tastes. This may be called "risk" due to the uncertainty over business growth and success. There is also the ever-present threat of opportunism (Williamson 1975), where even if such investments were made by suppliers and buyers, the entrepreneurial firm might not comply with such contracts or might seek alternative suppliers and customers. This problem due to opportunism is referred to in the insurance and agency theory literatures as the "moral hazard" problem. Even if moral hazard were not a threat (either because of mutual trust or because of efficiently enforceable safeguards), and the firm sincerely intends compliance, it may not be successful in its venture because of unexpected changes in environmental conditions — that is, market risk (Arrow 1974). In such uncertain situations, enforceability of contracts is always a tenuous issue, and there is a failure of markets (Akerlof 1970; Arrow 1974). To overcome this failure of markets, the venturing firm may be required to make significant investments to demonstrate credible commitment (Williamson 1985) to future suppliers and customers. The riskiness of the venture increases if investments in such credible commitments are of the "sunk cost" nature. In a situation where flexibility for adapting to change is of the utmost importance, it is not always feasible or desirable to anticipate and write up all possible contingencies into a contract (Williamson 1975) or make investments which are irreversible. Hence, initial market penetration becomes a vicious circle for new business start-ups. Suppliers and customers wait for other network members to make the initial investments and wait to see how the venture develops before they enter into buyer or supplier relationships with the firm; at the same time, such relationships with the first buyers and suppliers become crucial for the successful commercialization of a new product and development of the business venture. Competitors may wait for other firms in the industry to invest in the development of the infrastructure, thus free riding in the development of the industry. While there are well-established theories from diverse perspectives on managing uncertainty — such as decision theoretic, institutional economic, and interorganizational relations, among others — there are several useful questions to be raised from a managerial view of venturing. Given the vicious circle of initial penetration, there is a need to understand: *1) how managers build the initial transaction set in terms of the first few customers, suppliers, and distributors; 2) how new ventures demonstrate credibility, and what forms such credible commitments take; 3) what is the nature of the contracts with the initial customers, suppliers, and distributors, including the structure, safeguards, and contingencies built in; 4) where resources for the development of product, market, and infrastructure come from; 5) who bears the product and business development risk, and how are these risks shared among the various stakeholders; and 6) how and why contracts, risks, and composition of the set change over time, and their relation to success and failure in corporate venturing.*

Some economists have argued that the innovating firm would have to bear all of the risks of business development at the early stages of evolution. Thus they argue that firms would have to vertically integrate from the production of raw materials to distribution if successful venturing is to occur (Smith 1937; Stigler 1951). Such a claim is made: 1) because of the presence of the moral hazard problem surrounding any activity where information asymmetry is present; and 2) because the market has not yet become large enough to support specializing in the intermediate activities in the value chain. Because division of labor is limited by the size of the market, there is no incentive for other firms to specialize in various functions required to develop the business (Stigler 1951). Therefore, the venturing firm has to bear all the risks of new business creation, ranging from investing in raw material production to final distribution.

However, organization theorists would argue that this is a highly under-socialized (Granovetter 1985; Starr and MacMillan 1990) view of business venturing, one which does not take into account relations of trust developed between network members which mitigate much of the moral hazard problem. Indeed, evidence is slowly collecting to show that firms do engage in a wide variety of cooperative arrangements, including joint ventures with prior network firms and other incumbents in the industry, especially at the early stages of new business development (Kogut, Shan, and Walker 1990; Ring and Van de Ven 1989; Starr and MacMillan 1990). Such cooperative relationships do help reduce the risks due to the moral hazard problem, but they leave the question of market size and incentive to invest in a new business unanswered. The risk due to uncertainty of the market not developing as expected must still be borne by somebody. Hence, a study of the nature of risk bearing by various stakeholders in a new business, and the structure of contracts and safeguards between the venture and its various stakeholders, is still an interesting issue, even if the parties to the contract have developed trustful relations due to prior history. This is an area where not much research has been undertaken; it is a fruitful subject for further investigation. The interesting question here is how contracting parties safeguard themselves against both the moral hazard problem as well as the problem of risk due to uncertainty.

The argument that innovating firms must vertically integrate in all stages from production of raw material to final distribution would seem relevant mainly in a situation of completely radical innovation where no aspect of the existing infrastructure could be employed in the new business development. To the extent that infrastructure is already available to develop the new product and market, the question of market size would not be a major issue. This is an interesting proposition worth testing.

From a process standpoint, how do managers force the transaction set into existence, and how do managers manage this process? This question has not received much attention in the literature, and yet investigation of this question could yield insights into how managers overcome the problem of risks due to moral hazard and uncertainty.

Several studies provide rich descriptions of how early penetration occurs. Ring and Van de Ven (1989) and Ring and Rands (1989) claim that two distinct processes occur as new ventures attempt to engage in transactions with stakeholders in order to create a new business. The first is the formal process, which conforms to the classic stages discussed by Commons (1950) — namely, negotiation, agreement, and administration. Underlying these formal processes is a rich set of informal processes — namely, "sense making," understanding, and committing. Sense making is an enactment process where the parties to a transaction come to appreciate the nature and purpose of their relationships and contributions. Understanding is the process by which the parties to the transaction come to a shared agreement and shared interpretation of their relationships and contributions. Finally, committing is the process of creating the psychological contracts among each other. Ring and Van de Ven (1989) argue that the effective achievement of the informal processes yields successful economic transactions measured in terms of efficiency and norms of equity.

Ring and Van de Ven (1989) make a distinction between risk due to moral hazard and risk due to uncertainty, and argue that trust alone is insufficient to bring about successful relationships. They argue that managers deal with the problem of risk due to uncertainty by making incremental investments in the relationship or new business, so that the risk is kept within manageable proportions by the parties to the relationship. The problem of risk due to moral hazards is mitigated by engaging in relationships with parties with whom they have had prior contact, and by using the rich informal processes to develop trustful relations.

What are the mechanisms used to bring about the social contracting process of sense making, understanding, and committing? Starr and MacMillan (1990) provide some clues to understanding this question. From their study of habitual entrepreneurs they discover that such entrepreneurs use a wide variety of techniques to build social contracts. Thus, credible understanding and credible commitments are promoted by 1) co-opting legitimacy or prior reputation of the organization; 2) co-opting underutilized goods or infrastructure for the benefit of the new venture ; and 3) building an inventory of social assets, including a social network which is deployed when required.

Given the above analyses, successful penetration would seem to be influenced by the novelty of the new product ; the size of the market anticipated ; the availability of existing infrastructure that can be used to develop, produce, and distribute the product ; the level of moral hazard surrounding critical relationships ; the risk due to uncertainty over critical relationships ; the nature of trustful relations between incumbents in the industry and relevant networks ; the diversity and fecundity of such networks ; and finally, the structure and form of the contracts between the parties bearing the risk of investing in the infrastructure for the new product market.

Rollercoasting

With successful penetration there is rapid growth or contagion in the business as the new product gains currency and legitimacy both within and outside the firm. As the market for the product grows rapidly, there is rapid growth in the number of customers to be handled, and a large number of new vendors appear in order to fulfill a wide variety of functional roles and infrastructures in the development of the business. Thus, the hallmark of contagion is the explosion in the bundle of transactions associated with manufacturing, marketing, distributing, and servicing the product of the new business entity.

The explosion in the bundle of transactions brings with it a high degree of complexity and interdependence involved in managing the logistics of numerous linkages with other parties, and proliferating people, roles, functions, skills, and resources (Van de Ven 1986). The logistical problem is exacerbated because much of the timing and trend of the explosion cannot be predicted in any meaningful manner. The environment faced by the manager is like a rollercoaster ride, with sudden explosions in activity followed by lulls. The central issues become managing both attention and logistics (Hambrick and Crozier 1985).

How do managers handle this problem of complexity and interdependence ?

There is a simultaneous demand for efficiency on the one hand and flexibility on the other (Peters and Waterman 1982). Efficiency requires specialists for handling the various functions, stability in relationships, routinization of activities, and specificity in assets and investments. However, flexibility places the opposite demands on the system, with generalists for the various functions, rapid changes in relationships as need arises or disappears, loose structures instead of routines, and general purpose assets instead of specific assets. Thus, simultaneous loose-tight relations are required in the system (Peters and Waterman 1982 ; Hambrick and Crozier 1985) to manage the rollercoaster nature of the problem.

Not much research has gone into operationalizing the concept of loose-tight relations or to suggest where systems need to be tight and where they need to be loose. This is another area for productive and useful investigation. However, the work of Kanter (1983) has provided some evidence as to how the more innovative companies manage this situation. Kanter (1983) and Van de Ven (1986) suggest that the clue to solving the problem lies in the thinking and work design of firms. The research of Peters and Waterman (1982) and Kanter (1983) reveals that less innovative firms emphasize "segmentalist" logic by creating specialist roles and routines to handle the complexity. While this segmentalist thinking makes impeccable sense in handling complexity and often results in superior efficiency, such efficiency is achieved at the cost of flexibility, rapid decision making, and innovativeness (Kanter 1983; Peters and Waterman 1982; Van de Ven 1986). On the other hand, the more innovative firms emphasized "integrative" logic and created autonomous work units to handle diverse tasks. While all the functions were represented within each work unit, the work unit itself was sufficiently general to handle most of the complex task quickly. Such work units sacrificed some measure of efficiency but gained tremendous flexibility through building redundancy but requisite variety in the adapting unit of the organization (Van de Ven 1986).

Another problem facing venture managers in rollercoaster environments is that many strategic decisions have to be made rapidly in an environment of poor information coupled with a lot of "noise" or useless information. As Van de Ven et al. (1989) discovered, there were learning disabilities among decision makers as their "ability to discriminate substantive issues from 'noise' in the system" was impaired. Such noise takes many forms and consists of:

> ... many mixed messages received by decision makers in a seemingly random order over time: Some bear good news, some bad, but most are contradictory; some issues are formulated well, some poorly, but most equivocally; some come from outside, some inside, but most from "nowhere"; some are expressed in meetings, some on expressways, but most are not expressed; some are credible, some incredible, but most are uncredible; some appear once, some disappear, but most reappear; some are stated emphatically, some are whispered, but most are indistinguishable from a din of grumbles, rumors, banter, vendettas, hidden agendas, small talk, and gossip." (Van de Ven et al., 285)

In such a noisy social, political, and economic din, how do managers make decisions rapidly and correctly?

The work of Bourgeois and Eisenhardt (1988), Eisenhardt and Bourgeois (1988), and Eisenhardt (1989) has provided some clues on how fast strategic decisions are made in such turbulent environments. The views emerging from their research are that 1) in turbulent environments executives face a rapidly changing information climate; 2) there are costs to missed opportunities in obtaining and processing information; 3) there is value for real-time information; 4) although information processing is participatory and everyone sees and analyzes data and proposes solutions, decision making is by specialists; 5) the crippling effects of anxiety and fear of failure are mitigated by the use of specialized and experienced "counselors"; 6) multiple solutions are considered for each situation both to boost confidence in making decisions and to cover all bases ; 7) there is a relationship between fast decision making and effective firm performance ; and 8) internal politics slows down decisions. Thus, the research of Bourgeois and Eisenhardt (1988) reveals that a "configuration of cognitive, political, and emotional processes" are associated with rapid closure on strategic decisions in turbulent environments.

The work of March and his associates reveals that such fast decisions may not always yield the "right" decisions. Through a series of experiments, March and his associates have discovered that in situations of highly uncertain technology and diffuse goals, fast learners are apt to settle on inferior technology and leave the superior technology to the slower competitors (Herriot, Levinthal, and March 1985). The results of these experiments have found some support in the empirical literature on corporate venturing. Cooper (1979) found in a sample of high-technology firms that early and fast entry into the market did not yield any significant benefits. Such early entry carried the liability of having to invest in the education of a reluctant market and having to invest in a technology that may become obsolete due to the still-evolving nature of the technology. Followers not only may be able to pursue superior technology but may also benefit from an informed market at no cost, thanks to the investment in the education of the market by early entrants. Early entry may be highly risky, especially if irreversible investment in specialized assets is called for in the growth of the business.

Researchers have also found in other samples of firms that early and aggressive entry yields significant growth in the market share (Biggadike 1979 ; Hobson and Morrison 1983). Thus, the results of the studies on timing of entry and scale of entry (MacMillan and Day 1987) provide support to theories of both early entry and follower strategy. The mixed results of the various studies on the scale and timing of entry suggest that in environments where competition is intense, market segments are not well defined and technology is still evolving a follower strategy. A low scale of irreversible investment in specialized assets and incremental investments over time may be a more flexible and superior strategy. However, in environments where competition is less intense, market segments are well defined, and technology evolution is rather stable and predictable, early and aggressive entry may yield greater market share. These are interesting propositions worthy of development and testing.

In summary, the success of fast or slow decisions and the scale and timing of entry would appear to depend as much on the competitive context and the rate of technological evolution as on the social, political, and cognitive climate within the venturing firm.

Revitalizing

The hallmark of revitalizing is the simultaneous pressure to achieve efficiency and continue innovation in the new venture. Rarely does a new venture achieve lasting success or become successful in reinvigorating a firm with a single product in the marketplace. For continued business and successful incorporation within a firm, it is necessary for a new venture to create synergies and economies of scale across functions (such as R&D, manufacturing, marketing) to bring into existence a family of related products and services over time (Van de Ven et al. 1989). Indeed, one of the main objectives of investing in corporate venturing is to identify new combinations of productive resources in the firm and to extend the frontiers of the corporate capabilities by discovering synergies between resource combinations within the firm (Burgelman 1983a). Creating such synergies implies that the functional competencies and infrastructure must be developed and integrated to exploit a single technology into a family of related proprietary products (Van de Ven et al. 1989).

At the same time, the lasting success of a venture is also determined by the level of efficiency it achieves in its various functions and operations. There is pressure from the larger corporation on the venture managers to begin providing returns on the investment and also to release the cash required for new product and technology development. There is also pressure from competition on the prices in the market (Utterback and Abernathy 1975).

Given the above observation an interesting question arises, which is discussed below.

How do managers achieve and retain the simultaneous requirement of efficiency and innovation ?

The work of Utterback and Abernathy (1975) on the process of product innovation provides some clues as to how the process of efficiency is achieved from the chaotic new venture creation process. The essence of their argument is that efficiency and innovation are related to the stage of the innovation. Their findings suggest that during the early stages of innovation or venture creation the focus of the venturing team is on product innovation and attention, and efforts are expended in making improvements and modifications to the product. At this time, no attention is given to the efficiency of the process of manufacturing and distributing the product. But as the product stabilizes and errors are detected and corrected, and as competitive pressures increase, the need to minimize costs and rationalize operations increases. The focus of attention and efforts shifts to process innovation. At this stage, efforts are cost-stimulated, and routines are introduced to rationalize the various operations and functions in the venture. Thus, from an uncoordinated, chaotic process and a product performance orientation, the management objective shifts to systematic processes with the objective of product cost minimization.

But there is the significant threat that such routinization and cost focus may kill the incentive for further innovation to exploit the technology and develop the second and third generation of products. How do managers handle this dilemma ? Available evidence suggests that managers often handle the problem of fostering innovation and efficiency by spawning new product development teams and providing these teams with protection from the regular operations. Such new teams are often called "skunkworks" in the literature (Peters and Waterman 1982 ; Burgelman 1983a).

In summary, it appears that successful revitalization occurs through simultaneous attention to efficiency and innovation. Efficiency is achieved through attention to process innovations and rationalization. Innovation in second and third generation products is achieved by having autonomous and protected units develop new products.

■■ ■■ ■■ ■■ ■■ ■■ ■■ ■■
THE POLITICAL PROBLEM
OF FOSTERING

For the purpose of simplification, the above challenge of founding can be usefully summarized as problems arising out of the market and the technological imperatives facing a venture team. In addition to the market and technological imperatives, ventures also face what may be called organizational imperatives because of the hierarchical nature of large firms.

The hallmark of a modern-day firm is that many strategic decisions — such as what businesses to pursue, how to pursue them, and how to allocate resources — are made through the use of "visible hand" mechanisms within the firm rather than letting the market decide such choices (Chandler 1977). The venture team members are not free to go outside the firm in order to obtain labor or capital. They have to use the internal labor and capital markets and have to compete with other venture initiatives for these resources allocated by managers of the firm.

By itself this fact does not create any complications, because in a sense the market is simulated within a firm whenever each venture initiative competes with other initiatives within the firm for a fixed or varying pool of resources. But the complication arises because managers lack reliable market criteria, especially at the start-up stages of a venture, to choose between competing ideas or to make resource allocation decisions. In such an environment, other criteria may be used (indeed preferred) as surrogates for a market test.

Often ideas are supported in organizations on the basis of the distribution of political power among various coalitions within the firm (Cyert and March 1963; March 1962). Different coalitions within the firm would prefer different ventures and would use their power to allocate resources and arrange the routines and options within the firm to foster the ventures of their preference. Their goal would be to inhibit the development of other ventures competing for the same scarce resources.

A second heuristic often used for supporting or resisting ideas is to choose old, tested, and reliable ideas and to resist any new ideas (Schon 1971; Aldrich and Auster 1986; Hannan and Freeman 1977; Van de Ven 1986). New ideas are resisted for a variety of reasons. Some ideas are resisted because of the possibility that the new idea may threaten the existing power and resource distribution within the firm, while others are resisted because such ideas may render obsolete the knowledge and skills of powerful members of the organization. Ideas may also be resisted because they require significant investments in retraining personnel and changing the existing routines and the resource base of the firm. Forces of inertia may make these changes a difficult exercise for managers, hence resisting the idea is easier than implementing it. Because of these pressures, the survival of new ideas and products is difficult in ongoing organizations (Aldrich and Auster 1986). Therefore, success in venturing within large firms is a function not only of the external market and the technological imperatives but also of the current routines or political "winds" in the firm.

From a venture team point of view, the critical question is how to ensure the survival of an idea and venture within the hostile firm until a market test can provide the true criteria for retention or divestment. Recently, organization theorists have argued that the role of internal championing is a means of formally managing the sociopolitical process of riding a venture idea into good currency within large organizations (Schon 1971; Galbraith 1982; Peters and Waterman 1982; Burgelman 1983a; Van de Ven 1986). The view that emerges from these studies is that internal championing is a necessary means by which the social and political pressures imposed by an existing organization on a new venture are overcome or converted to the venture's advantage.

If indeed internal championing is a crucial process in the development and success of a new venture, there is a need to understand: *1) what are the roles of a champion and how many such roles are there; 2) which role is appropriate for each condition that a venture faces in its evolution; 3) who in the organization accomplishes each role, and how does the focus of attention vary across levels of the organization; and 4) what are the different mechanisms used by the champions, and how are they related to the development of new venture initiatives?*

While the importance of championing has been acknowledged for some time (Schon 1971; Chakrabarthi 1974; Galbraith 1982), we are only now beginning to understand the role and nature of this process in corporate venturing. There are still more questions than answers about this process. Curiously, we still do not have an acceptable definition of championing or champions, nor has anybody formally attempted one.

Consistent with the four conditions of venturing, four kinds of championing roles emerge as crucial if new venture ideas are to survive the organizational imperative: championing ideas, championing opportunistic behavior, championing resources, and championing incorporation.

Championing Ideas

Because new ideas are resisted within organizations and are often viewed with suspicion, a new venture idea requires one or more powerful agents within the organization who will exercise the required social and political effort to capture currency and galvanize support for the business concept.

Studies by Schon (1971) and Quinn (1980) provide clues as to how ideas evolve and gain or lose currency within organizations. From their description it appears that ideas are championed in two distinct ways. On the one hand, idea championing consists of convincing other coalitions in the organization that the new business concept has value for the firm as well as for the individual coalitions within the firm. On the other hand, championing also consists of ensuring that the new idea is within the limits of the overall institutional goal or charter by cajoling, pressuring, and forcing the venture team to develop, massage, or mold the new idea to conform to the explicit or implicit understanding of what businesses the firm may pursue or not pursue. Sometimes a truly radical idea may require an agent who will champion the cause of modifying current organizational goals if the idea is strongly believed to be powerful and significant for the organization. Burgelman (1983b) discovered that such championing often occurred more easily *ex post,* when the power and success of the idea was self-evident. However, Dougherty (1990b) discovered that such championing tended to occur during the process, rather than *ex post,* in the more successful ventures.

Championing Opportunistic Behavior

A major organizational imperative that fosters or inhibits the development of a new venture initiative is the bundle of routines in the firm. An understanding of the repertoire of routines of a firm may be central to understanding entrepreneurial behavior in the firm because, as Nelson and Winter (1982) point out, the capabilities of an organization are directly affected by the bundle of routines within that organization.

On the one hand, there are strong pressures to conform to the institutionalized "patterns of norms, values, and structures" (Kimberly 1979, 447) and induced strategic behavior (Burgelman 1983a) imposed by the existing organization. On the other hand, the highly uncertain and rapidly changing market and technological conditions require the venture team to break or modify the existing rules and structures and to be more flexible and adaptable.

Routines manifest themselves in many ways which affect the quality and speed of the decisions and actions of venture managers. Such routines include the budgetary process, the capital expenditure process, personnel selections, monitoring and control mechanisms, and resource allocation mechanisms. Organizations develop such routines for a variety of reasons ranging from considerations of bounded rationality (March and Simon 1958; Allison 1971) and operational efficiency, to the hallmark of the modern-day firm — the separation of ownership and control. This separation of ownership and control gives rise to principal agent problems of diverging goals and a propensity to shirk. Control systems, rewards, and sanctions are often designed around such problems in order to ensure that the efforts (or lack of it) of individual agents do not adversely affect the risk-reward structure of other stakeholders (Fama and Jensen 1983; Jensen and Meckling 1976).

Since a great investment of resources and time has been expended in building such repertoires, which are often the basis of the survival advantage of these organizations (Nelson and Winter 1982; Hannan and Freeman 1984), new ideas and initiatives are typically viewed with caution and suspicion within organizations. Thus there is pressure to conform to existing routines and skills. Members trying new initiatives in "an organization might be expected to encounter difficulties in departing from its prevailing routines, but . . . should have no difficulty in conforming to them" (Nelson and Winter 1982, 112). In fact, it is always easier to follow existing routines because of problems of bounded rationality and the wish to avoid upsetting the current distribution of political power within organizations (Cyert and March 1963). Often the pressures to conform to existing routines and to use current skills in an environment of rapidly changing market and technological context adversely affects the development of such initiatives within organizations. As Schumpeter so eloquently pointed out, "carrying out a new plan and acting according to a customary plan are things as different as making a road and walking on it" (1934, 85).

Given this background, it would appear that the development of a new venture initiative within an organization requires one or more powerful agents who will provide the authority to venture managers to break or modify existing routines when so warranted, and who can protect these managers from the hierarchy when they do break such routines. Such champions would also be required to ensure that venture managers act within broad parameters of acceptable norms when breaking existing routines. While this problem of championing what may be called opportunistic behavior within firms is interesting both from a theoretical and empirical point of view, very little research has been undertaken to understand this phenomenon. There is some evidence (although not systematic) that rule bending is often condoned or deliberately ignored in the more innovative firms (Kanter 1983; Peters and Waterman 1982). We do not have a clear understanding of the various strategies used by champions to aid flexibility, experimentation, and rule bending. This is a fruitful area for further research. Interesting questions that arise include : who does the championing, what strategies are used, which routines are allowed to be broken and which are not, and what is the effectiveness of such behaviors within firms ?

Championing Resources

Three facts of organizational life require resource champions for the development of new venture initiatives. First, resource allocation decisions are made by managers whose criteria may vary from time to time. Second, at any point in time a new venture initiative is competing with other such initiatives for resources within the firm. Third, since time and attention span are scarce resources for resource allocators, they do not have sufficient information on all ventures to make informed decisions about resource allocation. In this environment, one or more powerful agents are required to champion the cause of the new venture initiative and to represent the venture to resource allocators within the firm in order to ensure that sufficient resources are released for its development. The hallmark of the contagion condition is the extraordinary re-source needs whose flows cannot be easily predicted (Hambrick and Crozier 1985). Creating such resources is not always within the power of venture man-agers, so they have to look to the budgeting and resource allocation system of the firm for such extraordinary needs. Thus it would appear that resource championing is a necessary condition for the survival and development of a venture within a firm.

From a championing point of view, this is another area where not much re-search has been undertaken; it is a very fruitful subject for further research.

Championing Incorporation

The final role is one of championing incorporation. This involves preparing the new venture for institutional citizenship. Since there are strong pressures within organizations to conform to institutionalized norms, values, and rou-tines, no new venture can continue to break these existing institutions for long and still be part of the body corporate. Successful incorporation requires inte-gration or "fit" between the practices, norms, values, and routines of the new venture and the rest of the organization. One or more powerful agents are re-quired to "educate" and ensure that the new venture is prepared for such insti-tutional citizenship.

Further, as the venture develops over time and stands the test of the mar-ketplace, more and more information is available about the product, market, technology, competencies, and resources that the new venture embodies. With this new and more complete information, more reliable criteria are now avail-able to the various constituents within and stakeholders outside the firm. Such stakeholders can now make a decision as to how the new venture should be structured, including whether the new venture should become part of the body corporate or should be spun off or divested, or future investments abandoned. Given the political nature of organizations and varying preferences, disagree-ments can be expected among stakeholders. In such an environment, a cham-pion is required to settle the differences between conflicting stakeholders and create internal acceptance for the new venture.

Finally, a champion is also required to ensure that the new venture manag-ers are accorded the symbolic gestures and rituals of admittance to the inner circles of the corporate power structure. This may be essential for legitimizing the new venture within the firm and ensuring its retention within the corpora-tion. The process of championing incorporation has also not received much at-tention in the literature and is another fruitful area for inquiry.

We have outlined the critical role of championing and the forms it could take within a firm. With few exceptions (Galbraith 1982; Burgelman 1983a, 1983b), there is very little research on the process of championing. We do not know much about who does the championing in an organization and how it varies across organizational levels. The works of Galbraith (1982) and Burgelman (1983b) suggest the preliminary conclusion that idea championing is often done by the originators of the idea, while opportunistic behavior and resource championing are done by middle managers and incorporation is done by top managers.

We also do not have any research on the relationship between a particular role and the particular condition of a venture. While it would appear that all the roles are important for each condition, some roles would most likely dominate during the definition condition while others would dominate during contagion. Intuitively one could suggest that idea championing is more likely during the definition condition, both opportunistic behavior and resource championing are more likely during penetration and contagion, and incorporation is more likely during institutionalization. This is an interesting proposition that can be tested.

There is hardly any research to indicate how the process of championing takes place within firms, what mechanisms are used by champions to foster new ventures within firms, and which mechanisms are successful and which failures. These are all interesting and fruitful questions for further research.

━━ ━━ ━━ ━━ ━━ ━━ ━━

THE CONTEXT OF
CORPORATE VENTURING

In the previous two sections we discussed the challenges facing an individual venture in its attempt to survive and succeed. In this section we discuss the organizational challenge at a higher level of abstraction — namely, managing the population of ventures within the firm. The major concerns of the top management of a corporation from a corporate venturing point of view are to ensure that a wide variety of new ventures are initiated within the firm and to ensure that as many ventures survive and succeed as possible. The critical focus, then, is on the selection of appropriate strategies and structures to effectively manage the process of producing sufficient variations in the initiatives. This will ensure that as many ventures get selected in and are retained within the firm.

Firms may differ in the styles they adopt to manage the process of variation, selection, and retention. At one end of the spectrum, firms may consciously rely completely on the natural selection mechanisms where individual ventures are allowed to rise and flourish without any direction, support, or interference from top management. With such an approach, only those ideas that are well fitted to the internal and external environment of the firm, and those that survive selection pressures, are retained. At the other extreme is the approach where management selection is substituted for natural selection. Senior management actively imposes its choice on which ideas will be initiated and pursued, which initiatives will be supported and retained within the organization, and which will be selected out. The interesting issues include how firms vary in their relative orientations towards "visible hand" and "invisible hand" approaches to managing the population of ventures, and the relative effectiveness of such approaches for successful corporate venturing programs.

In discussing the sources of variation, selection, and retention, it is important to examine both internal selection pressures and external selection pressures. There are many examples of highly entrepreneurial firms that have completely transformed their product portfolios over time, abandoning their original products for newer products. By the same token, there are also many examples of firms that have not been able to make the required adjustments. In such cases, new products are often attributed to market conditions (Hlavacek 1974) rather than to constraints on entrepreneurial resources or prevailing administrative practices in these firms (Penrose 1959; Kanter 1983). Just as technological and market conditions can limit or foster a venture within any given firm, so can organizational imperatives limit or foster a population of ventures within that firm. But often attention is given only to the economic environment in explaining entrepreneurial behavior or lack of it in firms. There is also the external sociopolitical environment, which plays a crucial role in the nature of activities that a firm may legitimately pursue, thus placing selection pressures on new ventures within a firm (Pfeffer and Salancik 1979).

Given the above discussion, several interesting questions arising from a population perspective require further study: *1) what are the different organizational imperatives that are the sources of variations in new ventures within firms; 2) what are the different selection mechanisms that operate within firms; 3) what are the different retention mechanisms that operate within firms; and 4) what are the effects of the various variation, selection, and retention mechanisms on venturing outcomes at the level of the firm?*

Research over the past several years is beginning to shed light on some of these questions, and a picture is emerging of practices that seem to foster or inhibit innovation. Consistent with the four conditions of venturing, four areas of context-managing processes emerge as crucial for developing an innovative firm. These are: 1) production of variations; 2) managing selection: path-clearing; 3) managing selection: autonomy and control; and 4) managing retention: legitimizing.

Production of Variations

A central issue facing large organizations is how to ensure that members of the organization continually identify new opportunities and create new combinations of resources to pursue such opportunities (Guth and Ginsberg 1990). Such identification and exploration of opportunities are critical because of competitive pressures, because of the need to protect current and future rent streams, and because renewal and rebirth are often carried out through the creation of new businesses from the existing resources and competencies of the firm (Penrose 1959; Rumelt 1987).

Critical questions that arise in this context include: *1) where do new business ideas come from; 2) how do firms manage the process of generating sufficient variations in new products and services within the firm; and 3) what is the relative effectiveness of the various approaches to producing variations?*

Existing studies suggest that there are two extremes to the strategies firms employ to promote variations in new business ideas within their firms. One extreme employs a "visible hand" approach. Here the top management or other such powerful group chooses or dictates which new areas will be explored or which new businesses the firm will enter. The variations generated by such an approach are often characterized as purposeful variations (Aldrich and Auster 1986; McKelvey and Aldrich 1983), or induced strategic behavior (Burgelman 1983a). At the other extreme is the "invisible hand" approach to new venture idea generation where "a thousand flowers" are allowed to bloom (Kanter 1988). New ideas are allowed to surface, encouraged and supported without regard to the rank or position of the originator of the idea or to the potential outcome of the idea. Variations generated by such an approach are characterized as aimless or blind variations (Aldrich and Auster 1986; McKelvey and Aldrich 1983) or autonomous strategic behavior (Burgelman 1983b).

Quinn (1985), Kanter (1983), and Burgelman (1983a) have shown that firms employing invisible hand approaches to venturing have been more successful at producing more variations than those employing visible hand approaches.

The underlying reason offered is that the invisible hand approach is a superior strategy to the visible hand approach given the nature of uncertainty facing new business creations (Kamien and Schwartz 1982). First, letting "a thousand flowers" bloom permits a great deal of blind variations. This then enhances the probability that more ideas will be approved, since the ideas will be better suited to the environment and better able to stand the test of marketplace, firm, and sociopolitical conditions. Second, blind variations are more likely through an invisible hand approach, since such a strategy is not limited by the idiosyncratic vision of top management (Quinn 1985). Indeed, Quinn (1985) discovered that in the more successful firms, vision, preference, and objective statements were deliberately left vague and diffuse so as not to put limits on the creativity of the sources of variations. Third, the likelihood that truly new and radical innovations and resource combinations will occur is higher with blind variations than with purposeful variations (Burgelman 1983a).

If indeed an invisible hand approach is critical to the production of variations in large and varied numbers, then what factors influence the choice or practice of such approaches within organizations? Another way of framing the same question is to ask, why are some large firms more entrepreneurial than others? Existing studies on corporate venturing have emphasized the dominant managerial culture in this context. Kanter (1983), Peters and Waterman (1982), Burgelman (1983a), and Quinn (1985) argue that some firms adopt an invisible hand approach while others adopt a visible hand approach because of the differences in top management vision, top management commitment to venturing, and managerial attitudes towards autonomy and control.

There are other, less thoroughly researched factors that may influence the choice of strategies. Adopting invisible hand approaches places a lot of demand on the resources of the firm. Rather than letting managers allocate scarce resources, the invisible hand approach relies on ideas going in search of resources. This requires resources to be present "between the cracks" (Kanter 1983), thus increasing the likelihood of wastage and of resources being spread too thin. Indeed, an invisible hand approach may already presuppose a highly successful organization, because the requirement of resources is greater under this approach than under a visible hand approach in the first place. The relation between resource constraints or slack availability and the choice of strategies to produce variations is a little researched but essential area for further investigation (Penrose 1959).

The production of variations is also constrained by the existing competencies and assets of the firm (Nelson and Winter 1982; Rumelt 1987; Day 1987; Prahlad and Hamel 1990). New ideas are more likely generated in the areas of one's competencies. The nature of the assets — generic or specific — also influences the nature of new ideas produced within the firm. Firms having diverse competencies and generic assets are more likely to produce broader and unrelated variations in larger numbers. On the other hand, firms with narrow competencies and specific assets are more likely to produce narrower and more closely related variations. Systematic research is required within the area of corporate venturing to see how the existing competency and asset base of the firm influences: 1) the production of ideas and resource combinations within the firm; and 2) the choice of strategy for the production of such variations.

Finally, the relation between compensation and incentives within firms and the production of variations within firms is another fruitful area for research. Economists have long emphasized the relationship between pecuniary incentives and entrepreneurial behavior (Schumpeter 1942). Profit motive is argued to be a powerful incentive for engaging in entrepreneurial behavior (see Kamien and Schwartz 1982 for a survey of such studies). While the relationship between profit motive and innovation has been emphasized, the question of individual differences between firms and how the profit motive is translated at the individual level within the firm has been left unanswered. Given the separation of ownership and control in large firms, most modern-day firms employ fixed wage and income schemes as compensation packages. How does the profit motive get reflected in these compensation packages for individual employees? This is an interesting question which has not received much attention in the corporate venturing literature. More importantly, there is a need to investigate which compensation and incentive schemes are conducive for innovative and entrepreneurial behavior, and which are not.

Psychologists and sociologists have emphasized the nonpecuniary incentives for engaging in entrepreneurial behavior. The desire for such behavior is argued to stem from a need for achievement and job satisfaction rather than profit motive. Indeed, such motives are often invoked as the cause for entrepreneurial behavior in large corporations, given the hostility of such environments for new ideas (von Hippel 1977).

Systematic research exploring the relationship between pecuniary incentives, nonpecuniary incentives, and the production of variations within the firm is both an interesting and critical area for further research.

Managing Selection : Pathclearing

We have talked of the various selection pressures that individual ventures face within the firm, such as the various routines, control systems, budgetary processes, parochial preferences, and behaviors of political actors. In addition to such internal selection pressures, ventures within firms face many external selection pressures from the sociopolitical context in which the firms operate. This environment is distinct from the product market environment faced by individual ventures. There are legal or regulatory restrictions on what a firm may or may not do. Stockholders, unions, consumer protection agencies, local governments, and other such groups place their own conflicting demands on the firm, thus proscribing what new businesses a firm may enter. Such selection pressures systematically affect the viability of the population of ventures within a firm. The bottlenecks and obstacles placed by these institutional actors in the way of the new and evolving ventures have to be removed or influenced by the managers of the firm, in order to maximize the chances that a significant proportion of the ventures survive these selection pressures.

Given that all ventures face such pressures, the interesting issue is the relative orientation of top management to handling such pressures at the individual venture level. Is a visible hand approach used whereby the organizational infrastructure is utilized to remove bottlenecks in the paths of the ventures, or is an invisible hand approach used whereby each venture is left to fend for itself — so that only the fittest survive ? Does top management exercise choice by supporting some ventures while ignoring others ?

Given the above discussion, many interesting questions arise from a corporate venturing point of view, including : *1) how do the various sociopolitical selection pressures manifest themselves ; 2) what is the relative orientation of top management to such selection pressures — are visible hand or invisible hand approaches used to pathclearing ; 3) how do managers perceive and attend to these selection pressures through each approach ; 4) what kind of pathclearing strategies are used by managers to influence their external environment through each approach ; and 5) what is the relative success of each approach in managing such selection pressures ?*

From a corporate venturing point of view, very little research has gone into raising and answering any of these questions.

Managing Selection : Autonomy and Control

As new venture initiatives evolve and grow larger, they require a great deal of attention and numerous resources of the firm. When a firm is faced with a large number of ventures in the contagion condition, severe demands are placed on managers' time, attention, and organizational resources. The simultaneous management of large numbers of exploding ventures becomes a critical issue. Several important questions then arise as to : *1) how resource allocation processes should be managed ; 2) how much autonomy should be provided to these new initiatives ; 3) what should be the nature of control systems to monitor the progress of these new initiatives ; and 4) what decision criteria should be adopted to continue investments in or abandon initiatives.*

Existing studies in the area of autonomy to be provided to new venture initiatives, both for determining their own destiny and for acquiring resources, offer mixed results. The studies of Shapero (1984), Hill and Hlavacek (1974), and Day (1990) strongly support complete autonomy for new venture initiatives. These studies suggest that the more successful venture initiatives are ones which have greater authority and autonomy for defining their own mission, acquiring their own resources from external capital markets without interference from other parts of the organization, and which have freedom from the budgetary deadlines of regular operating units or divisions.

By contrast, Dunn (1977) discovered that failed venture teams did so because of *too much* autonomy. In this study Dunn discovered that these teams had too broad a mission, wasted too many resources, raised senior management expectations too high, and had no incentive or pressure to produce results.

These results, while contradictory, suggest that autonomy is critical for the development of new venture initiatives, but that such autonomy has to be different from that provided to regular operating units (Day 1990). New and novel methods of control and discipline have to be developed which, while not discouraging the use of current corporate competencies or resources, flexibility, and creativity, nonetheless redirect attention and effort towards progress, accountability, and effective use of resources.

Several solutions to the above problem have been proposed in the existing literature. Such solutions include simulating within the firm the monitoring and control systems of venture capitalists (Shapero 1984) ; evaluating progress rather than performance against plans (Quinn 1979 ; Fast 1981) ; and releasing resources and controlling around achievement of key milestone events rather than on the basis of dates (Block 1983 ; Block and MacMillan 1985). Many of these ideas are normative solutions to the prickly problem of monitoring and controlling an inherently uncertain activity. However, not much empirical work has been undertaken to see if such practices are feasible or if firms will indeed follow such precepts. Further work must be done to evaluate the relative efficacy of such solutions.

There is a critical need to compare systematically the resource allocation, resource acquisition, monitoring, and control mechanisms of large firms which have been highly entrepreneurial with those which have failed in their entrepreneurial attempts.

Managing Retention : Legitimizing

The final challenge facing managers of the institutional context is that of influencing the various stakeholders to allow the retention of certain classes of ventures within the firm. For successful retention of ventures within the firm, some collective social acceptability is critical. The fundamental point made in this line of reasoning is that often economic viability is not a sufficient reason for a firm to pursue certain types of businesses or activities. Social and political aspirations of key stakeholders have to be fulfilled in order for a firm to pursue or retain certain businesses (Pfeffer and Salancik 1979). Hence, an important challenge for managers is the challenge of managing the social legitimacy of the ventures within the firm. As Pfeffer and Salancik (1979, 196) have noted:

> While legitimacy is ultimately conferred from outside the organization, the organization itself may take a number of steps to associate itself with the valued social norms. For one thing, the organization may alter or design its actions so that they fit a concept of established legitimacy. That is, the organization may conform to social values. Alternatively, the organization may attempt to change the definition of social legitimacy with respect to its own operations and objectives. Since the broad social norms and values are quite expensive and problematic, what typically occurs is that the organization attempts to have its operations redefined as legitimate by associating them with other generally accepted legitimate objectives, institutions, or individuals.

Thus, managers continually take actions both to influence the values, perceptions, and norms of key stakeholders and to realign the organizational goals and businesses with perceived social norms and values. Such actions range from lobbying the U.S. Congress to redefining the purpose or missions of the firm. Pfeffer and Salancik (1979) suggest that much legitimizing is retrospective in character. After the economic success of an idea is self-evident, managers redefine their goals in order to accommodate the new idea into the firm's repertoire of businesses. Alternatively, it is possible that it is easier to legitimize an economically successful idea with a wider set of stakeholders than an economically unsuccessful idea or venture.

Given the above discussion, from a corporate venturing point of view there is a need to understand: *1) what is the relative orientation of top management to influencing external stakeholders on behalf of the individual ventures — is a visible hand or invisible hand approach used to ensure retention within the firm; 2) what kind of strategies are used by managers to influence their external environment under each approach; and 3) what is the relative success of each approach in managing such retention pressures?*

The relationship between legitimizing strategies and retention of new ventures within firms is poorly understood, and not much research has gone into investigating the relationship. The area of managing the sociopolitical context of corporate venturing is a critical area for fruitful research, both conceptual and empirical.

In this section we have outlined the critical challenges facing top management in fostering new initiatives within the firm and ensuring that the firm remains innovative and vital. The main issue focuses on the type of managerial approach that ought to be used by senior management to produce sufficient variations and to manage selection and retention processes successfully. While we have some understanding of the diverse approaches and their relative efficacy, many questions still remain unanswered. The whole area of context-managing processes is a fertile and fruitful one for further research.

CONCLUSION

Burgelman (1983a, 1354) defined the objective of corporate venturing as providing "the means for extending the frontiers of the corporate capabilities and for the discovery of additional synergies in the large, relatively unique resource combination constituted by such firms." This definition of the objectives of corporate venturing has been widely accepted, but rarely have scholars measured the performance of venturing activities against the yardstick of generating new combinations of productive resources.

Most studies use a financial measure for success or failure, often in terms of revenue growth or return on investments. These measures are important because they make the results of studies in corporate venturing comparable to other studies in organizational performance. However, while financial performance measures do indicate the level of success or failure of a venture, they do not meaningfully indicate performance against the objective of generating new combinations of productive resources for firms.

While firms frequently set out to generate new resource combinations by discovering entirely new products or markets, not all attempts yield such results. Sometimes the firm is successful in achieving this objective, while at other times such activities yield only a marginal product or perhaps a spin-off. As Aldrich and Auster (1986, 191) point out, "many new ideas will be embodied in different forms at different times. . . . a tentative idea at t_1 may be the basis for a new division at t_2, and become a key component in the firm's domain of competence, or a loosely coupled satellite, or fizzle out at t_3."

In addition to defining outcomes in financial terms and examining the factors influencing these outcomes, it is also essential to study discrete outcomes and the relationship between these outcomes and managerial practices. It is possible to distinguish some meaningful and mutually exclusive discrete outcomes of corporate venturing exercises, such as:

1. *A new organizational unit.* This could include a) a marginal product that has met with limited commercial success and does not result in a new division but becomes part of the firm's product portfolio with revenue potential; or b) a new division that reinvigorates the firm.
2. *Vestiges.* This could include a) a major vestige, a venturing exercise that is abandoned after significant investment has been made; or b) a minor vestige, a venturing exercise that is abandoned without significant investment having been made in the development.
3. *Spin-offs.* For example, a) a major spin-off, a product which is a commercial success but is not integrated into the firm and is divested; or b)

a minor spin-off, a product that has met with limited commercial success but is not integrated into the product portfolio of the firm and is sold.

Studies examining the relationship between the above discrete outcomes and the various managerial practices or strategies would be valuable in providing two critical insights into successfully managing the process of corporate venturing. First, at the individual venture level, such studies will tell us *why* and *which* new ideas become successful new businesses or major failures or spin-offs. Second, from a corporate point of view, such studies will also tell us which management styles and approaches will be successful in producing a vital and innovative firm.

In conclusion, the field of corporate venturing promises to be an exciting and fecund area of research in the coming years. We know much about the process through research, and the outlines of the jigsaw puzzle of corporate venturing are slowly becoming clear. While some areas of the puzzle are well populated and fairly clear, much of the puzzle remains to be uncovered, and there are many areas where our knowledge does not go far enough.

In this chapter we have tried to be comprehensive in identifying those areas where we have some understanding of the process and those territories where we do not have much understanding. We have also tried to frame the knowledge base in a way such that it yields interesting propositions that can be tested using imaginative cross-sectional and longitudinal methods.

We have much knowledge of the founding process and factors influencing it. However, most of our information in the area of fostering and context managing comes from rich longitudinal case studies. They have yielded intriguing and often counterintuitive propositions which can now be subjected to rigorous statistical tests. We have a sufficient body of propositions to do cross-sectional work in these areas. The main roadblock facing the field of corporate venturing will continue to remain the challenge of obtaining access to such cross-sectional data from large corporations.

━━ ━━ ━━ ━━ ━━ ━━
REFERENCES

Aitken, H. G. J. 1985 *The continuous wave: Technology and American radio, 1900–1932*. Princeton: Princeton Univ. Press.

Akerlof, G. A. 1970 The market for lemons: Qualitative uncertainty and the market mechanism. *Quarterly Journal of Economics* 84: 488–500.

Aldrich, H., and E. Auster 1986 Even dwarfs started small: Liabilities of age and size and their strategic implications. In *Research in organizational behavior*, eds. L. Cummings and B. Staw, Volume 8, 165–198. San Francisco: JAI Press.

Allison, G. T. 1971 *Essence of decision: Explaining the Cuban missile crisis*. Boston: Little, Brown.

Arrow, K. J. 1974 Limited knowledge and economic analysis. *American Economic Review* 64(1): 1–10.

Biggadike, R. 1979 The risky business of diversification. *Harvard Business Review* 57(3): 103–111.

Block, Z. 1983 Can corporate venturing succeed? *Journal of Business Strategy* 3 (2): 21–33.

Block, Z., and I. C. MacMillan 1985 Milestones for successful venture planning. *Harvard Business Review* 63(5): 4–8.

Bourgeois, L. J., III, and K. M. Eisenhardt 1988 Strategic decision process in high velocity environments: Four cases in microcomputer industry. *Management Science* 34: 816–835.

Burgelman, R. A. 1983a Corporate entrepreneurship and strategic management: Insights from a process study. *Management Science* 29 (12): 1349–1364.

1983b A process model of internal corporate venturing in the major diversified firm. *Administrative Science Quarterly* 28: 223–244.

Caves, R. E., and M. E. Porter 1977 From entry barriers to mobility barriers: Conjectural decisions and contrived deterrence to new competition. *Quarterly Journal of Economics* 91: 241–262.

Chakrabarthi, A. 1974 The role of champion in product innovation. *California Management Review* 17: 58–62.

Chandler, A. D. 1977 *The visible hand: The managerial revolution in American business.* Cambridge, Mass.: Belknap/Harvard Univ. Press.

Cohen, M. D., J. G. March, and J. P. Olsen 1972 A garbage can model of organizational choice. *Administrative Science Quarterly* 17 (1): 1–25.

Commons, J. R. 1950 *The economics of collective action.* Madison: Univ. of Wisconsin Press.

Cooper, R. G. 1979 The dimensions of industrial new product success and failure. *Journal of Marketing* 43 (Summer): 93–103.

1983 Most new products do succeed. *Research Management* (November-December): 20–25.

Cyert, R. M., and J. G. March 1963 *A behavioral theory of the firm.* Englewood Cliffs, N.J.: Prentice-Hall.

Day, D. L. 1987 An empirical test of the synergistic effects from relatedness in corporate venturing. Working paper, Management Department, Wharton School, University of Pennsylvania.

1990 Technological innovation and organization design in internal corporate venturing. Working paper, Management Department, Wharton School, University of Pennsylvania.

Dosi, G. 1982 Technological paradigms and technological trajectories. *Research Policy* 11: 147–162.

1984 *Technical change and industrial transformation.* N.Y.: St. Martin's Press.

Dougherty, D. 1990a Understanding new markets for new products. *Strategic Management Journal* 11: 59–78.

1990b Interpretive barriers to successful product innovation in large firms. Working paper, Management Department, Wharton School, University of Pennsylvania.

Dunn, D. T. 1977 The rise and fall of ten new venture groups. *Business Horizons* 20(5): 32–41.

Eisenhardt, K. J. 1989 Making fast strategic decisions in high velocity environments. *Academy of Management Journal* 32: 543–576.

Eisenhardt, K. J., and L. J. Bourgeois, III 1988 Politics of strategic decision making. *Academy of Management Journal* 31: 737–770.

Etzioni, A. 1963 The epigenesis of political communities at the international level. *American Journal of Sociology* 68 : 407–421.

Fama, E. F., and M. C. Jensen 1983 Separation of ownership and control. *Journal of Law and Economics* 26 : 301–325.

Fast, N. D. 1981 Pitfalls of corporate venturing. *Research Management* 8 : 21–24.

Freeman, C. 1973 A study of success and failure in industrial innovation. In *Science and technology in economic growth*, ed. B. R. Williams, 227–244. N.Y. : John Wiley & Sons.

Galbraith, J. R. 1982 Designing the innovative organization. *Organizational Dynamics* 10(3) : 5–25.

Granovetter, M. 1985 Economic action and social structure : The problem of embeddedness. *American Journal of Sociology* 91 : 481–510.

Guth, W. D., and A. Ginsberg 1990 Corporate entrepreneurship. *Strategic Management Journal* 11 : 5–15.

Hambrick, D. C., and L. M. Crozier 1985 Stumblers and stars in the management of rapid growth. *Journal of Business Venturing* 1 : 31–45.

Hannan, M. T., and J. Freeman 1977 The population ecology of organizations. *American Journal of Sociology* 82 : 929–964.

1984 Structural inertia and organizational change. *American Sociological Review* 49 : 149–164.

Herriot, S. R., D. Levinthal, and J. G. March 1985 Learning from experience in organizations. *American Economic Review* 75 : 298–302.

Hill, R. M., and J. D. Hlavacek 1972 The venture team : A new concept in marketing organization. *Journal of Marketing* 36 : 44–50.

Hlavacek, J. D. 1974 Toward more successful venture management. *Journal of Marketing* 38(4) : 56–60.

Hobson, E. L., and R. M. Morrison 1983 How do corporate start-up ventures fare ? In *Frontiers of entrepreneurship research*, eds. J. Hornaday, J. Timmons, and K. Vesper, 390–410. Wellesley, Mass. : Babson College.

Jensen, M. C., and W. H. Meckling 1976 Theory of the firm : Managerial behavior, agency costs, and ownership structure. *Journal of Financing Economics* 3 : 305–360.

Kamien, M. I., and N. L. Schwartz 1972 Market structure, rival's response, and the firm's rate of product improvement. *Journal of Industrial Economics* 20 : 159–172.

1982 *Market structure and innovation.* Cambridge, Eng. : Cambridge Univ. Press.

Kanter, R. M. 1983 *The change masters.* N.Y. : Simon and Schuster.

1988 When a thousand flowers bloom : Structural, collective, and social conditions for innovation in organizations. In *Research in organizational behavior*, eds. B. Staw and L. Cummings, Volume 10, 169–211. Greenwich, Conn. : JAI Press.

Kimberly, J. R. 1979 Issues in the creation of organization : Initiation, innovation, and institutionalization. *Academy of Management Journal* 22(3) : 437–457.

1981 Managerial innovation. In *Handbook of organizational design*, eds. P. C. Nystrom and W. H. Starbuck, 84–104. Oxford, Eng. : Oxford University Press.

Kogut, B., W. Shan, and G. Walker 1990 The structuring of an industry : Cooperative agreements in the biotechnology industry. Working paper, Reginald H. Jones Center, Wharton School, University of Pennsylvania.

Lewin, A. Y., and J. W. Minton 1986 Organizational effectiveness : Another look and an agenda for research. *Management Science* 32 : 514–538.

MacMillan, I. C. 1986 Progress in research on corporate venturing. In *The art and sci-*

ence of entrepreneurship, eds. D. L. Sexton and R. W. Smilor, 241–264. N.Y.: Ballinger.

MacMillan, I. C., and D. Day 1987 Corporate ventures into industrial markets: Dynamics of aggressive entry. *Journal of Business Venturing* 2: 29–39.

Maidique, M. A., and B. J. Zirger 1984 The new product learning cycle. *Research Policy* 14 (6): 299–313.

March, J. G. 1962 The business firm as a political coalition. *Journal of Politics* 24: 662–678.

March, J. G., and Z. Shapira 1987 Managerial perspectives on risk-taking. *Management Science* 33(11): 1404–1418.

March, J. G., and H. A. Simon 1958 *Organizations.* N.Y.: John Wiley & Sons.

McKelvey, W., and H. Aldrich 1983 Populations, natural selection, and applied organizational science. *Administrative Science Quarterly* 28: 101–128.

Nelson, R. R., and S. J. Winter 1982 *An evolutionary theory of economic change.* Cambridge, Mass.: Belknap/Harvard Univ. Press.

Penrose, E. 1959 *The theory of the growth of the firm.* N.Y.: John Wiley & Sons.

Peters, T. J., and R. H. Waterman 1982 *In search of excellence.* N.Y.: Harper & Row.

Pfeffer, J., and G. Salancik 1979 *The external control of organizations.* N.Y.: Harper & Row.

Phillips, A. 1966 Patents, potential competition, and technical progress. *American Economic Review* 56: 301–310.

Pinchot, G., III 1985 *Intrapreneurship.* N.Y.: Harper & Row.

Porter, M. E. 1985 *Competitive advantage.* N.Y.: Free Press.

Prahlad, C. K., and G. Hamel 1990 *Harvard Business Review* 68(3): 79–91.

Quinn, J. B. 1979 Technological innovation, entrepreneurship, and strategy. *Sloan Management Review* 20 (3): 19–30.

1980 Managing strategic change. *Sloan Management Review* 21 (4) (Summer): 3–20.

1985 Managing innovations: Controlled chaos. *Harvard Business Review* 63(3): 73–84.

Ring, P., and G. Rands 1989 Sensemaking, understanding and committing. In *Research on the management of innovation*, eds. A. H. Van de Ven, H. Angle, and M. S. Poole, 337–366. N.Y.: Harper & Row.

Ring, P., and A. H. Van de Ven 1989 Formal and informal dimensions of transactions. In *Research on the management of innovation*, eds. A. H. Van de Ven, H. Angle, and M. S. Poole, 171–192. N.Y.: Harper & Row.

Roberts, E. B. 1968 A basic study of innovators: How to keep and capitalize on their talents. *Research Management* 11 (4): 249–266.

1980 New ventures for corporate growth. *Harvard Business Review* (July-August): 134–142.

Rothwell, R. 1972 *Factors for success in industrial innovations, from Project SAPPHO.* Brighton, Sussex, Eng.: SPRU.

Rumelt, R. 1987 Theory, strategy, and entrepreneurship. In *The competitive challenge: Strategies for industrial innovation and renewal.* N.Y.: Harper & Row.

Scherer, F. M. 1978 *Industrial market structure and economic performance.* Chicago: Rand McNally.

Schmookler, J. 1966 *Invention and economic growth.* Cambridge, Mass.: Harvard Univ. Press.

Schon, D. A. 1971 *Beyond the stable state.* N.Y.: Norton.

Schoonhoven, C. B., K. J. Eisenhardt, and K. Lyman 1990 Speeding products to market: Waiting time to first product introductions in new firms. *Administrative Science Quarterly* 35: 177–207.

Schumpeter, J. A. 1934 *Theory of economic development.* Cambridge, Mass.: Harvard Univ. Press.

1942 *Capitalism, socialism and democracy.* N.Y.: McGraw-Hill.

Shapero, A. 1984 Intracorporate entrepreneurship: A clash of cultures. Working paper, Ohio State University.

Smith, A. 1937 *The wealth of nations.* N.Y.: Modern Library/Random House.

Starr, J. A., and I. C. MacMillan 1990 Resource cooptation via social contracting: Resource acquisition strategies for new ventures. *Strategic Management Journal* 11 (Summer): 79–92.

Stigler, G. J. 1951 The division of labor is limited by the size of the market. *Journal of Political Economy* 59 (3): 185–193.

Stinchcombe, A. L. 1965 Organizations and social structures. In *Handbook of organizations*, ed. J. G. March, 142–193. Chicago: Rand McNally.

Teece, D. J. 1987a Introduction. In *The competitive challenge: Strategies for industrial innovation and renewal*, ed. D. J. Teece, 1–23. N.Y.: Harper & Row.

1987b Profiting from technological innovation: Implications for integration, collaboration, licensing, and public policy. In *The competitive challenge: Strategies for industrial innovation and renewal*, ed. D. J. Teece. N.Y.: Harper & Row.

Tushman, M. L. 1977 Special boundary roles in the innovation process. *Administrative Science Quarterly* 22: 587–605.

Utterback, J. M. 1974 Innovation in industry and the diffusion of technology. *Science* 183: 620–626.

Utterback, J. M., and W. J. Abernathy 1975 A dynamic model of process and product innovation. *OMEGA, an International Journal of Management and Science* 3 (6): 639–656.

Van de Ven, A. H. 1976 On the nature, formation, and maintenance of relations among organizations. *Academy of Management Review* 1: 24–36.

1986 Central problems in the management of innovation. *Management Science* 32: 590–607.

Van de Ven, A. H., and H. Angle 1989 An introduction to the Minnesota Innovation Research Program. In *Research on the management of innovation*, eds. A. H. Van de Ven, H. Angle, and M. S. Poole, 3–30. N.Y.: Harper & Row.

Van de Ven, A. H., S. Venkataraman, D. Polley, and R. Garud 1989 Processes of new business creations in different organizational settings. In *Research on the management of innovation*, eds. A. H. Van de Ven, H. Angle, and M. S. Poole, 221–297. N.Y.: Harper & Row.

von Hippel, E. 1977 Successful and failing internal corporate ventures: An empirical analysis. *Industrial Marketing Management* 6: 163–174.

Williamson, O. E. 1975 *Markets and hierarchies: Analysis and antitrust implications.* N.Y.: Free Press.

1985 *The economic institutions of capitalism.* N.Y.: Free Press.

Part

5

INTERNATIONAL ENTREPRENEURSHIP AND RESEARCH NEEDS FOR THE 1990s

Chapter

20

Joint Ventures: Research Base and Use in International Markets

Robert D. Hisrich

●

Depending on the business risks, competition, and the volatility and newness of the market situation, joint ventures can be an important strategy option. Through the use of joint ventures, a firm can undertake activities it could not undertake alone. These activities include: acquiring a technology (process or product), diversifying, entering a new market, expanding productive capacity, introducing a new product, or vertically integrating the firm's efforts. Recently there has been a greater awareness of the importance of joint ventures. With this awareness, there has been a corresponding increase in research activity on joint ventures, particularly those having an international dimension. This chapter investigates the past research in the field to provide a basis for a discussion of future research issues and the implications for business strategy and public policy. After looking at strategic options for joint venture formation, we examine research on joint ventures, including general information on joint ventures as well as the specific subjects of domestic, high-technology, and international joint ventures. The chapter concludes by presenting directions for future research.

━━ ━━ ━━ ━━ ━━ ━━ ━━ ━━
STRATEGIC OPTIONS

In terms of two critical dimensions — ownership and control — these are several strategic options available to a company that wishes to grow and diversify. These options are indicated in Table 20–1. Other key issues affecting the choice of corporate strategy include : the time needed to establish the alternative ; the time available to complete the strategic option ; the degree of autonomy needed to compete effectively ; the level of synergy involved ; and the amount of technology transfer involved. The two strategic options indicated that offer total ownership and control are internal ventures, and mergers and acquisitions. Two options — joint ventures and minority investments — involve partial ownership and control ; and three options involve only partial control and no ownership : cooperative agreements, joint activities, and R&D partnerships.

Mergers and acquisitions, an important strategic option, have varied widely in use. During periods of intense merger activity, financial managers spend significant time searching for a firm to acquire and then developing the appropriate deal for the transaction. The final deal should reflect the basic principles of any capital investment decision and should make a net contribution to shareholders' wealth. However, the specific merits of a merger are very difficult to determine. Not only must the benefits and costs of a merger be analyzed, but in addition special accounting, legal, and tax issues must be addressed. These determinations need to be made with an understanding of the complexity of integrating an entire company into a firm's operations.

Any one of five basic types of mergers can be used as a strategic option : horizontal, vertical, product extension, market extension, and diversified activity.

Mergers are the best strategic option when *synergy* is present. Synergy is the qualitative effect upon a firm's rates of return, an effect brought about by complementary characteristics inherent in the firm being acquired.

Some of the largest mergers and acquisitions of 1989 are indicated in Table 20–2. They range from the $12.6 million merger of Bristol-Myers and Squibb to form Bristol-Myers Squibb to the $2.5 million acquisition of five European

TABLE 20–1 — Strategic Alternatives

Total Ownership and Control	Partial Ownership and Control	Partial Control, No Ownership
Internal ventures Mergers and acquisitions	Joint ventures Minority investments	Cooperative agreements Joint activities R&D partnerships

TABLE 20-2 — Significant Mergers and Acquisitions in 1989

DEAL	Value (000) * of Book Value	Transaction	Financial Intermediaries (Client)	Fee (000)	Fee as % of Deal
Bristol-Myers (pharmaceuticals) acquires SQUIBB (pharmaceuticals) and changes name to Bristol-Myers Squibb	$12,656,271 852%	Acquisition for stock, October 1989	Goldman Sachs	$25,000	.20%
			Shearson Lehman Hutton (Bristol-Myers)	$ 3,500	.03%
Beecham Group and SmithKline Beckman (pharmaceutical companies) merge to form SmithKline Beecham	$8,253,000 519%	Merger by exchange of stock, July 1989	Morgan Stanley (Squibb)	$23,900	.19%
			Kleinwort Benson	N.A.	—
			Wasserstein Perella (Beecham Group)	N.A.	—
			Goldman Sachs	$15,000	.18%
			J.P. Morgan (Smithkline Beckman)	$15,000	.18%
Time (broadcasting, publishing) acquires 50.6% of Warner Communications (entertainment, broadcasting, publishing)	$7,000,000 656%	Acquisition for cash, January 1990	Merrill Lynch	$ 1,500	.01%
			Shearson Lehman Hutton	$16,000	.11%
			Wasserstein Perella (Time)	$16,000	.11%
			Alpine Capital Group	$ 6,000	.04%
			Goldman Sachs	$ 1,000	.007%
			Lazard Freres	$20,000	.14%
			Merrill Lynch (Warner Communications)	$ 1,000	.007%
Grand Metropolitan (British beverage company) acquires Pillsbury (restaurants, foods)	$5,757,917 430%	Acquisition for cash, January 1989	Morgan Stanley	$14,200	.25%
			S. G. Warburg (Grand Metropolitan)	$ 7,100	.12%
			Drexel Burnham Lambert	$10,000	.17%
			First Boston	$10,000	.17%
			Kleinwort Benson	$ 1,000	.02%
			Shearson Lehman Hutton	$10,000	.17%
			Wasserstein Perella (Pillsbury)	$10,000	.17%

Acquisition	Amount	Premium	Type	Advisor	Fee	%
Imperial Oil (70% owned by EXXON) acquires Texaco Canada (78% owned by Texaco)	$4,149,595	250%	Acquisition for cash and stock, February 1989	First Boston	$ 100	.002%
				Gordon Capital (Imperial Oil)	$6,672	.16%
				Morgan Stanley	N.A.	—
				Scotia McLeod	N.A.	—
				Wasserstein Perella (Texaco)	N.A.	—
Dow Chemical acquires 67% of Marion Laboratories (pharmaceuticals)	$3,800,000	320%	Cash tender and merger of Marion Laboratories and Merrell Dow Pharmaceuticals to form Marion Merrell Dow, December 1989	Morgan Stanley (Dow Chemical)	$16,000	.42%
				Shearson Lehman Hutton (Marion Laboratories)	$17,000	.45%
Sony (electronic equipment) acquires Columbia Pictures Entertainment (movies, TV production and distribution)	$3,400,000	320%	Acquisition for cash, November 1989	Blackstone Group (Sony)	$ 9,900	.29%
				Allen & Co. (Columbia Pictures Entertainment)	$30,000	.88%
Ford Motor acquires Associates First Capital (finance company) from Paramount Communications (entertainment)	$3,350,000	N.A.	Acquisition for cash, October 31	Goldman Sachs	N.A.	—
				Shearson Lehman Hutton	N.A.	—
				Lazard Freres	N.A.	—
				Morgan Stanley (Paramount Communications)	N.A.	—
Panhandle Eastern (gas, oil) acquires Texas Eastern (gas, oil)	$3,223,799	199%	Acquisition for cash and stock, June 28	Kidder Peabody (Panhandle Eastern)	$14,500	.45%
				Dillard Read	$ 1,750	.05%
				First Boston	$12,900	.40%
				James Capel	$ 1,250	.04%
				Wasserstein Perella (Texas Eastern)	$ 7,500	.23%

continued

TABLE 20–2, continued

DEAL	Value (000) * of Book Value	Transaction	Financial Intermediaries (Client)	Fee (000)	Fee as % of Deal
Black & Decker (power tools, household appliances) acquires Emhart (industrial, consumer products)	$2,670,000 275%	Acquisition for cash, July 18	Salomon Brothers (Black & Decker) Shearson Lehman Hutton Wasserstein Perella (Emhart)	$ 5,000 $ 5,000 $ 5,000	.19% .19% .19%
BSN (French food and beverage company) acquires RJR Nabisco's five European food businesses from RJR Holdings (Kohlberg Kravis Roberts)	$2,500,000 N.A.	Acquisition for cash, June 6	Lazard Freres (BSN) Morgan Stanley Wasserstein Perella (RJR Holdings)	N.A. N.A. N.A.	— — —

Source : This table was adapted from an article in *Fortune*, January 29, 1990, pp. 137–140.

524

food businesses from RJR Holdings by BSN (a French food and beverage company).

Another strategic option that offers the same benefits as mergers and acquisitions in terms of total control and ownership is internal venturing. Internal venturing, or intrapreneurship, recognizes that the dominant culture of the parent company may not be conducive to developing and marketing innovative ideas. The typical corporate culture has a climate and reward system that favors conservative decision making, with the guiding principles being: follow the instructions given; do not take any initiative; do not be creative; do not make any mistakes; stay within your assigned position; and protect your turf. You should just "mind the store" and not do anything creative or independent — particularly if it involves risks. By establishing a quasi-independent internal venture unit apart from the mainstream of corporate activity (and eventually making intrapreneurship the real corporate culture), innovations can be created and marketed on a regular basis.

An organization wanting to establish an intrapreneurial environment must ensure that an appropriate climate for intrapreneurship exists and that there are individuals available in the firm that have entrepreneurial characteristics. In order for success in intrapreneurial ventures, a strong organizational support structure needs to be established. This is particularly important since intrapreneurship is usually a secondary activity in the organization, not a primary one. To be successful, these ventures require flexible, innovative behavior, autonomy, and complete authority over expenditures. When the intrapreneur has to justify expenses on a daily basis, it is really not a new venture but merely an operational extension of the funding source (Peterson and Berger 1971; Miller and Friesen 1982.)

The next strategic alternative — a minority investment — provides only partial ownership and control and does not create a new unit. An investment is made in an ongoing firm to strengthen that firm or to obtain its knowledge or skills. A relationship is established between the two firms without the investing firm being in control and responsible for the operations of the other firm. The minority investment could take the form of venture capital for a firm's growth, or money to fortify a struggling supplier or a pioneering firm without being in control of its operations.

Four other strategic alternatives involve no ownership whatsoever. Cooperative agreements take on a variety of forms depending on the needs of the two or more firms involved. The agreements for exchange of performances usually do not involve jointly owned entities nor do they provide for future joint activities beyond the period of the agreement. Usually, the tasks are performed by the cooperating firms in their own facilities according to the contract specifications without any skills transferred between the partners.

A form of cooperative agreement is a cross-licensing arrangement. This arrangement covers technology developed separately by different firms for the same product or process. By an exchange of licenses, each firm obtains knowledge about the product or process that the other firm has developed.

Other forms of nonownership arrangements can take the form of various joint activities. Perhaps the most frequently used joint activity is a joint bidding activity where a consortium of contractors join together to submit a bid. These occur frequently in offshore oil exploration and large government contract bids.

R&D partnerships are a final nonownership strategic option. An R&D partnership, unlike a corporation, is not a taxable entity. The income (or loss) generated in connection with the business is allocated to the various partners, who in turn report these figures on their individual tax returns. Any losses generated by the operation can be used to offset other income earned by the individuals. As with any limited partnership, there are two primary elements in the organization: the general partner and the limited partners. The general partner, most often the sponsoring company, manages the organization and assumes unlimited liability for the obligations of the operation. The limited partners are the investors in the project that only provide capital and do not actively participate in the management of the operation.

The final type of strategic alternative is a joint venture, which is the focus of this chapter. While the definition of joint ventures has evolved over time, an encompassing definition of a joint venture is *a separate organizational entity composed of two or more active partners.* While offering some interesting possibilities as a strategic option, joint ventures are no panacea. A company should realistically assess their motive for forming a joint venture as well as their future relationship with the newly formed entity in light of the other strategy alternatives available. We will examine motives for joint venture formation later in this chapter, after our review of the literature.

JOINT VENTURES: AN HISTORICAL PERSPECTIVE

In the past, joint ventures were viewed as legal partnerships, often involving a firm whose stock was owned by several other companies. Originally, joint ventures were enterprises used for trading purposes, and as such are one of the oldest ways of transacting business. Merchants of ancient Babylonia, Egypt, and Phoenicia used joint ventures to conduct large trading operations. This use continued through the 15th and 16th centuries, when merchants in Great Britain used joint venturing to trade throughout the world, particularly in the Americas and India.

The use of joint ventures in the United States took a somewhat different form, being used by mining concerns and railroads as early as 1850. The largest, and perhaps best known, joint venture during this period was the formation of ARAMCO by four U.S. oil companies to explore and develop oil reserves. The use of joint ventures increased significantly during the 1950s with more than 350 of the 1,000 largest U.S. corporations having domestic joint ventures in operation. These were often vertical joint ventures which shared the output of the supply facility — the creation of the joint venture. The large volume of output of the joint venture could be absorbed by the two firms where neither one could absorb the total output or afford the diseconomies associated with a smaller plant.

Joint venture activity continued at a rapid pace during the 1960s and 1970s in the United States and even more so in Europe. The use of joint ventures accelerated further in 1980 with the advent of globalization, technological advances, and the need for product innovation. Whereas 63 domestic joint ventures occurred in the United States in 1980, the number exploded in 1983 with 269 joint ventures recorded. This number decreased to 99 in 1984. Since 1984, the activity level of joint ventures has increased radically. As is indicated in Table 20–3, the activity level of all forms of mergers and acquisitions during the period of time we are most interested in (1985–1988) was significant in the United States, with 3,437 occurring in 1985, 4,381 in 1986, 3,920 in 1987, and 3,487 in 1988. In 1988, the activity level was highest in the finance, insurance, and real estate industries (658), followed by services (516), transportation and public utilities (300), retail trade (210), and wholesale trade (206).

RESEARCH ON JOINT VENTURES

In light of the recent opportunities and increased use of joint ventures, what can be learned from the recent joint venture literature? Although there are few direct research findings applicable to entrepreneurs attempting to establish joint ventures, a significant amount of research does shed some light on aspects of joint ventures, particularly the motivations for forming a joint venture and the problems that occur.

However, there are some problems in extracting relevant information on joint ventures from the literature. First, there is the problem of a lack of a theoretical base. There has been little attempt, except in the case of a few articles, to frame the material and the related findings into effective theoretical constructs. In fact, in the general area of joint ventures, there has been very little theory development overall. Most research has utilized a case-specific approach, with little attempt to develop or strengthen a comprehensive theory of joint venture formation.

Second, there has been little or no attempt to establish causal relationships or to use well-defined terms that have been presented in previous studies. And there has been no consistency in the kinds of measurement instruments employed. There is even some interchanging of the phrases "strategic alliances" and "joint ventures." There indeed may not be any real causal relationships in determining the success of joint ventures, since randomness may take over with external factors playing the predominant role.

Third, significant divergence in sample size and composition has occurred. Many articles have focused on one case study, while others have been

TABLE 20-3 — Business Enterprise — Mergers and Acquisitions

ITEM	Unit	1980	1981	1982	1983	1984	1985	1986	1987	1988
All activity: Number	Number	1,560	2,329	2,298	2,391	3,164	3,437	4,381	3,920	3,487
Value	Mil. dol.	32,883	70,064	60,698	52,691	126,074	145,464	204,895	177,203	226,643
Divestitures: Number	Number	104	476	562	661	792	1,037	1,413	1,192	1,090
Value	Mil. dol.	5,090	10,171	8,362	12,949	30,556	43,524	72,320	57,519	80,103
Leveraged buyouts: Number	Number	11	100	164	231	253	254	335	270	318
Value	Mil. dol.	236	3,870	3,452	4,519	18,69ʳ	19,634	45,160	36,069	42,914
Form of payment: All cash	Percent	(NA)	42	55	53	37	40	44	54	59
All stock	Percent	(NA)	22	14	16	12	10	11	11	7
Combination cash, stock debt, other	Percent	(NA)	19	20	25	26	24	20	17	19
Undisclosed[1]	Percent	(NA)	17	11	6	26	26	25	18	15
Ownership status of acquisition targets:										
Public acquired company:										
Number	Number	398	668	687	553	832	817	853	995	874
Value	Mil. dol.	11,948	49,675	46,701	31,891	85,724	91,513	108,894	102,829	125,195
Private acquired company:										
Number	Number	1,059	1,198	1,064	1,192	1,550	1,588	2,123	1,683	1,477
Value	Mil. dol.	15,911	11,215	6,400	8,335	10,007	10,376	24,059	14,853	19,867

ᵃNo. 883. Mergers and Acquisitions — Summary : 1980 to 1988. (Covers transactions valued at $1 million or more. Values based on transactions for which price data revealed. All activity includes mergers, acquisitions, acquisitions of controlling interest, divestitures, and leveraged transactions that result in a change in ownership. Divestiture : sale of a business, division, or subsidiary by corporate owner to another party. Leveraged buyout : acquisition of a business in which buyers use mostly borrowed money to finance purchase price and incorporate debt into capital structure of business after change in ownership.) NA Not available.

¹Price was given but form of payment was not.

No. 884. Mergers and Acquisitions — Number and Value of Transactions, by Industry: 1988.

SIC CODE[1]	Industry	Total Number	Value (mil. dol.)	U.S. Company Acquiring U.S. Company		Foreign Company Acquiring U.S. Company		U.S. Company Acquiring Foreign Company	
				Number	Value (mil. dol.)	Number	Value (mil. dol.)	Number	Value (mil. dol.)
	Total activity[2]	3,487	226,643	2,882	159,326	447	60,818	158	6,500
(A)	Agriculture, forestry, fishing	16	580	12	579	4	(³)	—	(³)
(B)	Mining	141	10,460	112	7,942	17	1,744	12	774
(C)	Construction	33	2,257	30	587	3	1,670	—	(²)
(D)	Manufacturing:								
20	Food and kindred products	136	22,991	100	17,849	24	4,884	12	258
22	Textile mill products	26	2,736	18	2,186	7	501	1	49
23	Apparel, other textile products	34	1,307	28	1,288	3	19	3	(²)
24	Lumber and wood products	28	4,690	24	4,682	1	8	3	(²)
26	Paper and allied products	39	5,438	34	5,329	1	57	4	53
27	Printing and publishing	133	9,625	98	1,523	32	8,102	3	(²)
28	Chemicals and allied products	133	12,318	87	10,849	31	1,245	15	224
30	Rubber and plastic products	53	7,749	43	1,040	5	2,934	5	3,774
32	Stone, clay, glass, and concrete	42	3,545	26	2,379	12	1,143	4	23
33	Primary metals industries	43	3,248	33	3,109	7	118	3	21
34	Fabricated metal products	95	4,666	85	3,500	8	1,165	2	1
35	Industrial machinery, computer equipment	197	11,724	148	8,090	39	3,631	10	3
36	Electrical and electronic equipment	149	9,665	117	5,877	22	3,572	10	217
37	Transportation equipment	56	1,896	44	1,270	7	421	5	204
38	Instruments and related products[4]	189	5,038	139	3,417	42	1,587	8	33
(E)	Transportation and public utilities	300	16,128	276	15,350	17	753	7	26
(F)	Wholesale trade	206	2,896	162	2,529	31	358	13	9
(G)	Retail trade	210	29,481	191	21,308	13	8,097	6	76
(H)	Finance, insurance, real estate	858	32,535	596	21,635	53	10,756	9	134
(I)	Services	516	17,360	436	12,821	59	4,416	21	123

— Represents zero.

[b]No. 884. Mergers and Acquisitions — Number and Value of Transactions, by Industry: 1988.
[1]Standard Industrial Classification   [2]Includes other industries, not shown separately.
[3]Transaction price data not revealed.   [4]Data have been revised since publication release.
Source of tables 883 and 884: MLR Publishing Company, *Mergers and Acquisitions*, 1988 (copyright). Publication contains extract from database, M&A Database.   Source: *Statistical Abstract of the U.S.* (1990, 534).

merely anecdotal with no real data identification whatsoever. There have been few large sample studies or examples of total universe enumeration, and no replication of prior work.

Finally, there have been few hypotheses established and tested. Basically the research question tested in this previous research has been : "What is the effect of blank on blank ?" When data analysis has occurred it has mainly been in the form of percentage counts, categorical comparisons, and, in a few cases, testing linear relationships.

These limitations noted, however, we proceed to our review of recent research. Joint ventures will be discussed in the following four areas : general information on joint ventures, domestic joint ventures, high-technology joint ventures, and international joint ventures. Unless of special interest, only those articles published since 1986 in more academically oriented journals will be discussed here.

General Information on Joint Ventures

The joint venture potential as a strategy for growth is discussed by Schillaci (1987), who explores the advantages and disadvantages of such alliances versus alternative internal or external growth methods. Three strategy options for a joint venture are noted : capacity expansion, vertical integration, or diversification. A joint venture is viewed by the author as the middle ground between internal and external development strategies. Designing a strategic alliance involves a large number of choices including partner selection, legal format of the agreement, time period, division of equity, and management and control mechanisms. Therefore, the author feels that companies must weigh both the pros and cons of using a joint venture, as opposed to other internal or external alternatives.

Based on a survey of four firms with extensive experience in joint ventures, Lyles (1987) classifies the kinds of mistakes uncovered into five categories, each having several different possible causes. Interestingly, Lyles points out that the companies not only did not view these mistakes as possibly having a serious effect on the success or failure of their joint venture, but they usually viewed them as beneficial because of the learning that occurred in the process of overcoming them. This learning in turn led to more effective management of future joint ventures.

Gomes-Casseres (1987) considers joint venture instability by focusing on three different areas. First, evidence is presented for the instability of varying types within a sample of U.S. multinational enterprises. Second, the stability of jointly owned ventures compared to wholly owned ones is discussed. Finally, some reasons that firms have for changing the structure of ownership after entry are explored. The author also notes commonalities between joint venture instability and instability within wholly owned ventures.

For joint ventures to be a success, their properties of self-organization must be fully developed, according to Lorange and Probst (1987). These properties can aid in the implementation of more appropriate organizational forms and more effective processes of management than those learned from the relationship with parents of the ventures. According to the authors, this application will lead to better performance of joint ventures and will increase the rate of long-term success.

Internal as well as external uses of joint ventures are the focus of Part 1 of Harrigan's (1987b) article. Part 2 explains the factors that need to be considered in deciding on the division of ownership, along with human resource and management issues as they affect/pertain to the performance of joint ventures.

Kogut (1988a and b) develops a few theoretical constructs on the creation and termination of joint ventures. Even though joint ventures are formed due to competitive motives, it is these same competitive motivations which are often responsible for their termination. Kogut presents three joint venture theories that are based on three different perspectives: organizational ecology, transaction-cost economics, and strategic behavior. After presenting data on the mortality of joint ventures, Kogut concludes that competitor incentives are important in the formation and termination of joint ventures.

A 1988 article by Devlin and Bleackley expresses concern about the growing number of companies developing too many "bandwagon" consolidations. The aftermath of such joint ventures is that the firms are at a competitive disadvantage in comparison to companies without affiliations. Many sources of these implementation complications are presented such as: management styles, cultures, operational practices, and degrees of control. The authors believe that a success rate of a mere 50 percent will cause businesses to view joint ventures in a strategic context in the future.

Taking a different point of reference, Harrigan (1988b) looks at different relationships within a joint venture and examines how differences between partners in these relationships can affect the success and longevity of the joint venture. The relationships studied are sponsor-to-sponsor and sponsor-to-venture. Harrigan specifically focuses on the effects of sponsor diversification on a joint venture, and whether or not a sponsor was related in product, market, or technology to the venture. In addition, she discusses horizontal and vertical sponsor-to-venture relationships and degrees of unrelatedness. Finally, Harrigan evaluates various factors in partner-to-partner relationships, such as horizontal and vertical relatedness; varying levels of experience in joint venturing; domestic versus international firm locations; and variations in the asset size of the two sponsors.

Another 1988 article focuses on the limitations of joint ventures (*Mergers and Acquisitions* 1988b). A high failure rate was found among those alliances involving a new product and a unique technology. The joint ventures in which partners contributed complementary technologies were found to be generally more successful. The article points out that partners should come to an agreement on a formula whereby one firm has the option to buy out the other at some point in the future. The article concludes by pointing out that although there are some shortcomings, joint ventures provide timely mechanisms for establishing business bases even in remote areas.

Focusing on transaction cost and strategic behavior, Kogut (1988a) looks at the motives for forming a joint venture, and presents a theory of joint ventures as a learning tool. After discussing previously gathered data on joint ventures, Kogut concludes with a discussion of sector distribution and the stability of joint ventures.

Divided into five parts, another study by Kogut (1988b) explores joint venture mortality and then discusses three theories of joint ventures stemming from three different perspectives: transaction-cost economics, strategic behavior, and organizational ecology. Kogut also compares findings of previous studies with these three perspectives. Following a case study analysis including the perspectives of the three theories, Kogut presents conclusions drawn from all the previous discussions.

A general framework for employing joint ventures within numerous competitive contexts is developed in another Harrigan (1988a) article. Industry characteristics and traits are found to determine the form, focus, duration, and degree of autonomy of the firm's cooperative strategies. Competitor traits are found to indicate how firms will react to the need for accord. Harrigan points out that fragmented industries are less attractive settings than are concentrated ones for joint ventures. Harrigan feels that the dynamics of partner interactions must be able to adjust to anticipated changes in the strategic needs, capabilities, and successes of the other parties involved in the joint venture.

Hennart (1988) develops a transaction-cost theory of the decision between contracts, joint ventures, and full ownership. His theory defines *scale* and *link* joint ventures. *Scale* joint ventures are when parents seek to internalize a failing market, where indivisibilities due to scale or scope economies make full ownership of the relevant assets inefficient. *Link* joint ventures result from the simultaneous failure of the markets for the services of two or more assets whenever these assets are firm-specific public goods. Hennart concludes by explaining why joint ventures exchange certain types of know-how and why such ventures have become widely used by many different and diverse firms.

Kohn (1989) develops some basic guidelines for avoiding failures in joint ventures. The author indicates that these failures are frequently caused by: over-optimism about markets, changing objectives within involved organizations, and management style differences. When an alliance is being formed, Kohn argues, there is a need to focus on three areas: the formulation of business objectives and strategy; performance measurement; and management of personnel in order to improve the chance for profitable success.

In a later article, Kohn (1990) describes the benefits and problems with joint ventures, focusing on the strategic opportunity for banks. The three major benefits indicated are: strategic enhancement, market positioning, and cost advantages. Three joint alliances are discussed as an indication of future trends and direction.

Finally, Spalding (1989) looks at the advantages of joint ventures as business start-ups and discusses the accompanying complex accounting procedures. He concludes by commenting on the fact that few entrepreneurs take advantage of this seemingly ideal vehicle for a new company.

Domestic Joint Ventures

In a 1987 article, Weiss focuses on the GM-Toyota negotiations for a joint venture. While creating such an affiliation hinges on the successful negotiations between the prospective partners, the author points out that the process proved to be very complex, both domestically and internationally. Since many aspects of this prominent joint venture negotiation are similar to other such situations, the author feels that many of the challenges will be the same as well.

Otis (1988) describes three different success stories in which the public and private sectors worked together to ensure quality recreational outlets at a reasonable cost and with high payoffs. Otis indicates that by participating in these joint ventures, which enlarged, improved, or created marinas in three cities, both sectors accomplished five major types of success: an increase in tax revenues; an increase in tourists, conventions, and future businesses within the area; the growth of job opportunities; urban renewal; and affordable recreational facilities for the public.

Sramek (1988) examines the use of joint ventures to generate equity and maximize the contributions of real estate assets. According to the author, real estate joint ventures can be employed to the advantage of the corporation, to limit liability and satisfy the facility needs of a firm. This is illustrated in a case study describing the joint ventures of Alco, Inc. Sramek discusses the process used to sell the developer and top management on the idea of financing such a venture, and also describes facility selection.

Using a network analysis approach (much like that used by many sociologists interested in exchange behavior), Walker (1988) examines two aspects of joint ventures: 1) identifying the extent of a firm's cooperative strategy, and 2) evaluating the relative efficiency or strategic value of a cooperative relationship.

Lastly, McClenahen (1990) reviews the current status of the Honeywell, Inc. joint venture with the Japanese firm, Yamatake. While Honeywell has been a major player in global joint venturing, recently, Honeywell has withdrawn a significant amount of funding from the Yamatake-Honeywell Co. While remaining a globally minded and active company, Honeywell is trying to increase returns to shareholders by refocusing on its environmental, industrial, and aviation controls businesses. According to the author, while the two companies have agreed to continue the current relationship, such areas as technology transfer and production have the greatest possibility of creating conflict.

High-Tech Joint Ventures

Doz (1987) summarizes the obstacles that must be overcome if joint ventures between bureaucratic and entrepreneurial companies are to be successful. Although most ventures between large and small companies fail to meet the goals set by both partners, this failure is managerial rather than technological. The author presents three very important issues that should be used as guidelines for the future success of technology partnerships. According to the author, operating interfaces should be established before finalizing any technology joint venture agreement.

After dealing with benefits that can be gained from international R&D joint ventures, Hladik (1988) describes sources of problems for these ventures, as well as an example showing both benefits and problems. The author concludes by listing ways that potential partners can avoid these problems.

Berg and Hoekman (1988) study two aspects of joint ventures : the motives behind them, and the specific patterns of joint venture activity in the Netherlands. Since in the United States the primary motive for joint ventures has been knowledge acquisition, a joint venture allows a U.S. firm either to spend less on R&D or to make better use of money allocated to R&D. The Dutch are interested in risk reduction and innovation (new markets, new uses for old products) as well as knowledge acquisition through participation in joint ventures.

The dangerous risks and costs of strategic alliances are the focus of a 1988 article by Adolph. The author emphasizes dealings with strategic alliances for "technology commercialization" — the transfer of new information from the research and development lab to the current marketplace. Adolph indicates that through a careful blend of technological insight, precognition, business acumen, and some good luck, these alliances can be useful in reducing the risk and sharing the burden of the corporation. The author cites three forces driving companies to form strategic alliances : market emphasis on systems substitution, global competition, and competitive convergence.

Goldbaum (1989) summarizes the advantages of joint ventures within industries and cites numerous examples of partnerships. The idea of joint ventures being used to achieve "critical mass" without consolidating debt is intensifying, allowing companies to benefit from a higher profit potential. "Mega-ventures" allow companies to participate and reap the benefits from synergies in R&D, geographic regions, and marketing without taking on the full financial or strategic obligation. The article indicates that more firms consider joint ventures as assets become more costly and less available, such as in an industry which has already experienced extensive restructuring. The author feels that in the 1990s many enterprises will see joint ventures as a financially appealing way to gain better market positions in sizable businesses.

The results of an exploratory study of three high-tech joint ventures in southeast England are reported by Cartwright and Cooper (1989). Their study indicates that cultural transition is more difficult and problematic for employees who have not self-selected themselves for change. Remnants of the old organizational culture may often linger, causing problems in the new joint venture. The authors feel that the success of any high-tech joint venture can be measured in both financial and human terms.

Shan (1989) points out that many firms involved in high technology choose to commercialize new technology through cooperative relationships. In Shan's study, the motivations of entrepreneurial high-technology companies for establishing such cooperative arrangements were investigated and a theoretical framework established. The theory was tested in the field of biotechnology, and a correlation was found between the tendency to cooperate with the firms' position relative to their competition. A negative correlation was also found between firm size and the use of cooperative arrangements.

Taylor (1989) views the 1990s as an opportune time to use joint ventures to accelerate technological development, enhance productivity, and lower investment risks in the high-risk world of R&D. However, his article points out that joint ventures are not always the correct solution to a problem, as there are other options which a company can use to evaluate compatibility with prospective partners before getting into a joint venture. Ideally, joint venture partners should bring complementary skills and homogeneous corporate structures together. With the emphasis on short-term investment decreasing the amount of R&D efforts, the author feels that joint ventures are the best hope for future developments in research due to their inherent long-term commitment.

Wrubel (1990) discusses the new technology being discovered by both Japanese and U.S. computer-chip firms and the conflict and competition between research and development teams around the globe. The author feels that joint ventures are being formed either to compete against ultra-expensive research projects or to trade technology in manufacturing and processing expertise. Many U.S. companies are using joint ventures as outlets for sharing research and capital spending dollars among themselves, in order to compete effectively with the Japanese. According to the author, the major disadvantage is that U.S. chip makers may be giving away too much information and data.

International Joint Ventures

A "frontier issue" in international marketing — choosing an entry mode into foreign markets — is the subject of Anderson and Gatignon's (1986) article, which offers a framework for investigating this entry mode decision. The literature is reviewed and guidelines given for choosing the most appropriate form of entry depending on the characteristics of the environment, the firm, and its product. Through all these data and information, the authors hope that empirical research will be encouraged. They suggest that data are needed to verify and further improve the management guidelines outlined.

Franko (1987) examines the use of new forms of investment in developing countries by 70 internationally active U.S. corporations. He explores the extent of use of reduced equity and nonequity forms of investment by U.S. firms in the mid-1980s and the motives and patterns of rejection or acceptance. The relationship between the patterns of acceptance or rejection, and the policies for development in the developing country, are also analyzed.

The complexities and challenges of creating a joint venture between the United States and China are explored in an article by Davidson (1987). According to the author, ventures between partners with disparate managerial systems increase the risk of failure by adding more hazardous situations. In addition, all joint ventures in China must endure significant financial, logistic, operational, and political hurdles. Although there are many frustrations and much red tape to overcome, the author feels that joint ventures in China can be highly profitable and are an important form of economic interaction for both the United States and China.

Galuszka and King (1987) discusses a joint venture formed by Combustion Engineering, Inc. and the Soviets to manufacture oil and petrochemical plant controls, and to support the modernization of plants and refineries in the Soviet Union. The author indicates that the management role of western partners and the repatriation of profits are the biggest obstacles to venturing.

Morris and Hergert (1987) comment on the growing use of international collaborative agreements among firms, based on data from the present research program being conducted at the INSEAD Business School (France). The authors feel that these collaborative agreements offer firms the chance to share risks and rewards beyond each firm's individual capability. Only those companies with skill and sensitivity in resolving managerial challenges will benefit from collaborative agreements. According to the authors, research in this important field is lacking because of insufficient systematic data collection and analysis.

Citing two successful international joint ventures in the aerospace industry, Roehl and Truitt (1987) describe the sophisticated and complex business relations required to keep these ventures effective and solvent, as well as the difficulty of developing an appropriate contract because of an uncertain environment. It suggests that companies need to search out a process that protects the interests of both parties and at the same time improves their competitive position.

Using a sample of more than 5,000 subsidiaries wholly or partially owned by 180 multinationals, Gomes-Casseres (1987) examines the evidence for joint venture instability and compares the instability of jointly owned ventures with that of wholly owned ventures. He also discusses the possibility that this instability, when in the ownership structure, sometimes reflects sequential strategies in foreign investment. In his sample, in the instances when ownership changed after entry, the changes represented corrections of mistakes made at the time of venture formation or adaptions to environment shifts. The author suggests that these adaptions may actually be a sign of success, not failure.

Christelow (1987) estimates the importance of joint ventures based on data on ownership patterns compiled by the U.S. Department of Commerce. The data indicates that joint ventures account for about one-fifth of the total foreign affiliated firms that cover two-thirds of the international nonbank enterprises. The author points out that the importance of joint ventures in the United States varies from one industry to another, and that strong diverging industry trends do occur. Christelow observes that in industries such as finance and insurance, firms are moving away from joint ventures, while in manufacturing such alliances are increasing.

Auster (1987) provides an overview of articles focusing on International Corporate Linkages (ICLs). Her review gives definitions, the advantages of ICLs, and the preferred environmental conditions and motives for formation, summarizes the published articles, and explores an ICLs consequences in light of the aforementioned articles.

Joint ventures (as well as other forms of alliances) are being increasingly used by many different types of firms, according to Harrigan (1987c). These ventures are helping to restructure industries, create new product lines, keep abreast of quickly advancing technologies, and ease the problem of worldwide productive capacity surplus. The author feels that since these alliances are being recognized as an important device in global strategy, "savvy managers" must take aggressive, but methodical, procedures to meet the new and challenging task of joint venturing.

Several cooperative ventures that have recently occurred between the United States and Japan are analyzed in Osborn and Baughn's (1987) article, which presents technological, financial, and economic perspectives. Each aspect is discussed using empirical data which isolates key components involved in the formation of cooperative arrangements among nations. It is suggested that standard economic elements will retain an important role in the formation of joint ventures. The article also mentions that although select U.S. and Japanese companies are collaborating in technological advancement, there is no clear evidence of the success of such attempts.

Focusing on 12 joint ventures by multinational enterprises (MNEs), Beamish (1987) examines the performance of these ventures and attempts to delineate the variations that occur. He finds that successful ventures depended on the local partners for local management and local knowledge (for example, being and finding general managers and functional managers, understanding current local business practices, and grappling with the local economy, politics, and customs). According to the author, while companies who were involved with successful joint ventures took the time to find a specific local partner, unsuccessful ventures were satisfied with any local partner as long as he/she was a national of the less developed country. The article concludes that joint ventures were successful or unsuccessful depending on the approach of the MNE and the number of contributions the MNE allowed the local partner to make.

Bruce (1987) describes a joint venture between three computer companies: a state-owned French company, Groupe Bull; a troubled U.S. firm, Honeywell, Inc.; and Japan's NEC Corporation. Bruce indicates that the takeover process and the keys to success for the venture involved reversing Honeywell's bad image and making Groupe Bull both profitable and privately owned. The author feels that the man in charge of Bull, Jacques Stern, is working hard to "privatize" the company and will work just as hard to solve Honeywell's problems. Stern's major challenge will be to create a common culture for this multinational group.

Harrigan (1987a) discusses joint ventures in general and their probable effects on future business competition. The internal, competitive, strategic, and diversification uses of joint ventures are presented as well as the use of control mechanisms within the venture itself. Sidebars within the article give two examples of successful international joint ventures and address the question: "How should joint venture ownership be divided?"

Based on a case study of the J.H. Heinz Company's business approach within newly developed countries, an article by O'Reilly (1988) describes the successful strategy that Heinz adopted and cites examples of Heinz's joint ventures in Thailand, Zimbabwe, and the People's Republic of China. The author feels that a greater understanding of successful joint ventures can be gained by focusing on the "in action" strategy utilized by Heinz.

Afriyie (1988) examines the unique characteristics of production that joint ventures use and the consequences on industrial performance which follow. The focus of the article is on industrial impact rather than corporate profit performance. Included is a discussion of the managerial and public policy implications of the competition between joint ventures and local firms.

An article in *Mergers and Acquisitions* (1988a) is composed of excerpts from the Tokyo Conference on Mergers and Acquisitions on various topics such as: strategy-driven deal making, the Japanese bid for markets, a financial approach to bolstering strategy, the government's outlook on M&As, a management buyout option, M&A regulation in the common market, the advantages of joint venture partnership, language barriers, targets in the Pacific Rim, trends of M&A types in Europe, and the problems and opportunities of acquiring M&As in the United Kingdom.

U.S. News and World Report (1988) summarizes the advantages of using joint ventures in a multinational situation. The article indicates that, overall, firms find that engaging in such alliances raises fewer problems at less cost than other options. The potential benefits presented include: increased market access, greater resource availability, and decreasing risks through sharing and reducing inefficiency in product. While these alliances offer no guarantee of success, the article indicates that the failure rate is declining as more information is obtained and more alliances are developed.

Castro (1988) focuses on the programs of *perestroika* that the Soviet Union is using to obtain American knowledge and thereby increase the pace of their economic development. According to the author, many U.S. firms, encouraged by *perestroika*, are forming joint ventures in the Soviet Union. Even though Soviet and American business interests conflict in several aspects, the author feels that a general loosening of restrictions on ownership has contributed to a growth in U.S. investment in the Soviet Union.

Glinow and Teagarden (1988) concentrate on differences and impediments to the process of modernization of human resource management procedures in Sino-U.S. joint ventures. A normative framework for introducing the use of these modern human resource management practices into such ventures is presented. The article concludes with suggestions focusing on integrating the individual and the enterprise, as well as integrating the enterprise with social and economic goals in both research and practice.

After discussing the criteria for the success or failure of a joint venture between transnational corporations and firms in developing countries, Dymsza (1988) lists factors that contribute to this success or failure. Factors listed for success are: the achievement of major goals; the synergies of combining the partners' contributions; the entry for smaller and medium-sized transnational corporations; the conversion of a licensing arrangement into a successful joint venture; a comprehensive joint venture agreement; joint management responsibilities; the reduction of ownership by a transnational corporation in a joint venture; the resolution of disputes in joint ventures; and financial arrangements as part of joint ventures. The article concludes by listing key factors in failures of joint ventures. Included in this list are: significant differences in the major goals of parties; the perception of unequal benefits and costs; conflicts over decision making, managerial processes, and styles; differences between the partners concerning marketing; and a decline in resource contribution by the transnational corporations.

Kogut and Singh (1988) present the results of a statistical study on the likelihood of a foreign firm entering the U.S. market through a joint venture. The authors based their study on various factors, including: experience (of the firm in joint ventures), size (of the investing firm), industry structural variables, industry R&D intensity, industry growth, and degree of industry concentration.

Focusing on industrial impact, Afriyie (1988) looks at factor use characteristics of joint ventures in a developing economy. Afriyie also explores the impact of factor choice behavior on key industries in which joint ventures and more traditional forms of local investment are allowed. The article discusses the managerial and public policy implications of joint production systems in a structurally polarized manufacturing sector.

A 1988 article by Kirkconnell stresses the importance of Canadian businessmen being competitive (in a global sense) in the free trade deal proposed with the United States. Regardless of whether the proposal succeeds or fails, the author feels that Canadian industries are facing issues that must be dealt with, for these issues will only intensify if Canada does not attain more access to the U.S. market. According to the author, the process of strengthening their position in the competitive market by becoming internationalized has provided needed support for R&D and increased cash flow and growth. This requires the adoption of new corporate strategies that are global in perspective while customized to the local market. Kirkconnell concludes with a summary of the options open to firms who plan to do business outside of Canada, and he presents seven principles that can provide useful guides when developing and implementing worldwide strategies.

Guerin (1988) focuses on three international development strategies within the magazine industry. The first strategy presented is "the wholly owned subsidiary." This is the most expensive and riskiest expansion strategy, yet the one yielding the highest profits. The second strategy presented is a licensing agreement which involves the licensee paying a royalty in exchange for the use of the name and logo. The last strategy is the joint venture, where each partner owns 50 percent of the magazine and shares both the investment and risks involved. The author compares the disadvantages and advantages of joint ventures versus licensing, concluding that the best strategy depends on the company and its philosophy.

The Sino-foreign Contractual Joint Venture (CJV) Law, which gives foreign investors the opportunity to form joint ventures in China without having to commit any equity, is the focus of an article by Salem (1988). A CJV is described as an arrangement by which parties contract to provide certain resources and carry out prescribed jobs under the auspices of a group consisting of representatives from both sides. The author hopes that the new law will encourage those partners with reservations about the venture to move more quickly.

In addition to identifying critical factors that affect the success of joint ventures in third world countries, D'Souza and McDougall (1989) suggest a framework for assessing the "fit" between smaller firms from developed countries and third world firms that enter into such joint ventures. The article links international operations to local operations of the smaller firm from developed countries, and suggests areas for future research.

Eales (1989) presents a survey of 21 joint venture executives, a survey that sought to discover the motivations behind Japanese companies' interest in joint ventures with the United States. The survey results indicate that this type of venture is formed only when certain circumstances occur: adoption — occurring when a U.S. company is in need of capital; rebirth — the restructuring of a dying business to include two parent companies which in turn build a new company; and family ties — stemming from complementary and mutually beneficial business relationships.

Gomes-Casseres (1989) develops a basic structure to help managers who are considering the use of international joint ventures. The author does not recommend the use of joint ventures if potential conflicts of interest exist among prospective partners, or if an existing advantage would simply be exploited. Instead, according to the author, joint ventures should be used as an alternative to total ownership if restrictive policies are employed by the host government. When working with a foreign government, the author argues, the firm is in a better position when it brings advanced technology or capital to the deal.

An article in *U.S. News and World Report* (1989) overviews the many joint venture opportunities in the Soviet Union. The United States is slower than German and Italian companies in engaging in business with the Soviet Union, because U.S. companies are weighing the risks of going into Moscow's ever-changing economy. According to the author, this uncertainty over the Soviet economy is caused by inconvertible exchange, undependable supplies, and red tape in the process of joint venture creation.

"Testing the Water," an article in the *Economist* (1989) summarizes the changes occurring in Hungary and the increase in joint ventures. The article indicates that Hungary entices investors through cheap labor, new legislation (which allows 100 percent foreign ownership), and the formists' zeal of the country; these investors bring working capital, technology, management skills, and basic know-how to the deal and should be aware of possible problems such as government interference in industrial management and the lack of infrastructure.

Langowitz and Wheelwright (1989) present a case study of the formation and operation of a joint venture between a U.S. and a Japanese manufacturer. The authors feel that the principals must manage the joint venture, survive a competitive crisis, and keep the parent corporation satisfied in introducing a unique product to market.

Based on a sample of four European-American alliances, two intra-European alliances, two European-Japanese alliances, and seven American-Japanese alliances, Doz, Hamel, and Prahalad (1989) report the interactions of the partners and the winning and losing aspects of the partnerships. The article focuses on the reasons for collaboration and the methods for building secure defenses. The authors feel that alliances should establish and enforce specific performance requirements.

The various aspects of establishing a joint venture between American companies and Japanese or Chinese companies is the focus of a 1989 article by Webster. According to the author, these important aspects include: a rationale for the international joint venture; the long-term consequences of the venture; structuring the joint venture; and the legal aspects of a joint venture.

Through information gathered in interviews with executives who have entered the Soviet market, Nigh and Smith (1989) present some useful lessons to companies in the United States that are considering investing in the Soviet Union. Within the study, the perception, assessment, and management of risk (both political and economic) by the first companies in America to enter joint ventures with the Soviet Union are examined. A comparison is made between the political risk management of these innovative approaches to firms with another group of novel American firms — those that established joint ventures in the People's Republic of China. The comparison is used as an example, and it provides a useful guide to companies following this same path.

Contractor (1990) lists data from Benchmark Surveys of the U.S. Commerce Department, which indicate a relaxing of government restrictions on foreign equity in the 1980s. The article indicates that this trend was evidenced in small reductions in the share of 50–50 and minority affiliates among U.S. affiliates in a country. The proportional variation from country to country is examined through a cross-sectional regression analysis.

Erickson (1989) discusses the joint cereal venture between General Mills and Nestle as a prototype for companies entering Europe. In this joint venture, the author indicates, the capital investments will be equally split and the venture equally owned, with the companies agreeing that neither will attempt to seek control. The author feels that this is an extraordinary "fit" between two companies, and that it can be an example for other companies to follow in the future.

Concentrating on tributary works in transaction-cost economics, organization theory, and international corporate strategy, Osborn and Baughn (1990) examine governance forms for multinational affiliations. The review of 153 new alliances indicates that the decision to use a joint venture as a form of governance was influenced by the plan to pursue R&D and the technological concentration in the alliances product area. The authors feel that the size of the firms involved, and the parent firms, also contributed to this decision to pursue a merger.

An article in the *Economist* (1990a) indicates that size alone may not help companies meet the challenge of serving so many borderless consumers. One method for obtaining long-term commercial viability is using joint ventures. This also may be the quickest way to expand across Europe, offering the best route to market power (even though these may take three times longer to complete than simple domestic ventures). The article concludes that central efficiency may not be the best strategy for building market share in places where sales are already occurring before the joint venture is established.

Another *Economist* (1990b) article discusses the pros and cons of the rush of West German investors into East Germany. The article indicates that although the quick movement into East Germany may yield high profits and boost the East German economy, there are some disadvantages that must be taken into consideration. These include outdated plant equipment, chronic pollution, poor infrastructure, and a web of legal complications.

After the recent political liberation of eastern Europe, many western businessmen are eager to move in and sign joint ventures, according to Leadbeater (1990). While the prospects for growth are immense due to the size of eastern Europe and the Soviet Union (a market of about 420 million people), there are many problems occurring due to the complexities of different governments within separate countries. The author feels that another drawback to joint ventures within eastern Europe is reflected in the track record of previous deals, as the success rate of the joint ventures that actually get off the ground has not been impressive. Leadbeater mentions other disadvantages such as no established stock market and the problem of repatriating profits making the probability of quick success not good.

Shenkar and Zerras (1990) focus on the problems that joint ventures pose for human resource managers. Some of the more common human resource problems of joint ventures are: staffing friction, blocked promotions, exile syndrome and reentry difficulties, split loyalty, blocked communication, compensation gaps, limited delegation, blurred organizational culture, and unfamiliarity. The article concludes by suggesting a range of possible solutions to these problems.

An article in the *OECD Report* presents the results of a recent study by the Organization for Economic Cooperation and Development (OECD) of more than 5,400 joint ventures between foreign countries in eastern Europe. The article indicates that a significant number of the joint ventures were inactive, especially those in the Soviet Union, and that some countries are in need of re-built legal and economic infrastructures before joint ventures can become fruitful and successful.

Finally, Hisrich, Vecsenyi, and Gross (1990) focus on the joint venture activity of U.S. firms in Hungary. Of the U.S. companies surveyed having other joint ventures in market economies, it was the same or more difficult to establish and operate the Hungarian ventures. However, in comparison with their joint ventures in nonmarket economies, the Hungarian joint venture was found to be easier to operate. Compared to doing business in the People's Republic of China and the Soviet Union, engaging in business in Hungary proved to be easier. The authors indicate that these favorable evaluations occurred even though the joint ventures surveyed were established prior to the two new acts (the Company Act and the Association Act) which eased even further the regulatory aspects of establishing a joint venture in Hungary.

━━ ━━ ━━ ━━ ━━ ━━ ━━ ━━

MOTIVES FOR JOINT VENTURE FORMATION

The area most frequently focused on in previously discussed articles was the increased use of and the motives behind the formation of a joint venture. What has caused this significant increase in usage of joint ventures, particularly in light of the fact that not all joint ventures have worked well?

Probably the most frequent reason for forming a joint venture is to share the costs and risks of an uncertain project. Projects where new technology is involved frequently need resource sharing so that each firm can concentrate on its strengths. Joint ventures can be particularly beneficial to smaller firms who do not have the capital resources to engage in capital-intensive activities. In some cases, these large-scale projects avoid the problems and costs of inefficient, small-scale plants or duplication of facilities.

Another frequent reason for forming a joint venture is the synergy between the firms. This synergy may be in the form of people, inventory, or plant and equipment. The synergy provides leverage for each firm in the market, with the extent of the synergy often being exactly the extent that the joint venture will be beneficial for both companies. This synergy frequently allows a reduction in inventory as neither company has to carry a safety stock. Synergy can also be in the form of information technology that allows each firm to leverage their information without any duplication of efforts.

Another frequent use of joint ventures is to obtain a competitive advantage. A joint venture can preempt competitors, allowing a company to access new customers and expand its market base. It can also result in an entity that is more effective and competitive than either of the original companies. Hybrids of companies tend to possess the strengths of each of the joint venture partners and are therefore stronger than either one alone.

▬ ▬ ▬ ▬ ▬ ▬ ▬ ▬

JOINT VENTURES AS A
METHOD FOR MARKET
ENTRANCE

A simple count of the number of articles discussed here as well as the number of joint ventures being formed indicates that the international arena is one with the greatest amount of joint venture activity. A reason often cited for being involved in a joint venture is that it provides a mechanism for market entrance that would be difficult if not impossible to obtain without the joint venture. Nowhere is this more the case than in eastern Europe. Eastern Europe is not only viewed as a market in itself but as a vehicle for accessing the EC market scheduled for significant consolidation in 1992.

The activity of U.S. imports and exports for the five years indicated in Table 20–4 shows a steady increase in both U.S. imports and exports with eastern Europe since 1986, with imports being $1.58 billion and exports $882 million in 1988. Similar increases have occurred in U.S. trade with the Soviet Union, the People's Republic of China, Taiwan, and Europe during this same time period. Simultaneously the number of Soviet and east European investments in the West has also increased. The number (in 1987) by country is indicated in Table 20–5. Hungary and Poland have the largest numbers of joint ventures in the West compared with other once-CMEA countries, with 86 and 80 respectively. While Hungary's investments are primarily to facilitate trade, those in Poland represent a broader investment strategy, ranging from joint ventures in natural resources and agriculture to trade. The policy of Poland is similar to joint venture investments by the People's Republic of China. A similar variance occurs in the number of joint ventures by western companies in CMEA countries. The number varies greatly, ranging from a high of 685 in the Soviet Union to a low of five in Romania (see Table 20–6).

In spite of being a late starter with its first joint venture in 1972, Hungary has the largest number of joint ventures (628), more than any other eastern bloc country (Yugoslavia has 230, Poland 170, Bulgaria 41, Czechoslovakia 20, and Romania 5). These numbers reflect the number of joint ventures applied for and do not actually indicate operating companies. The joint venture activity level in Hungary reflects the ease of obtaining permission to establish a joint venture in the country versus the other eastern European economies. If the foreign partner's share of the joint venture is 50 percent or less, only a simple registration of the proposed joint venture is needed. When the foreign share exceeds 50 percent, then a permit issued by the Ministry of Commerce needs to be obtained. Even when a permit is needed, it is still usually easier to obtain permission for a joint venture in Hungary than when dealing with the ministry or agency designated in most other eastern European countries. When granting permission to start a joint venture for companies with more than 50 percent foreign ownership, the Hungarian Ministry generally focuses on the impact of the joint venture on the foreign exchange balance of the country.

TABLE 20-4 — U.S. Imports and Exports by Country or Region (In millions of dollars)

| | EXPORTS | | | | | IMPORTS | | | | |
	1980	1985	1986	1987	1988	1980	1985	1986	1987	1988
Europe	67512	56763	61642	69718	87995	46602	79756	89825	95496	100515
Eastern Europe[a]	2347	792	741	720	882	983	1527	1443	1498	1580
U.S.S.R.	1513	2423	1248	1480	2768	454	489	558	425	578
China : Taiwan	4337	4700	5524	7413	12130	6854	16396	19791	24622	24804
Total	220783	213146	217304	252866	320385	244871	345276	369961	405901	441282

[a]Eastern Europe includes Bulgaria, Czechoslovakia, East Germany, Hungary, Poland, Rumania, and other Communist areas in Europe.
[b]Figures in millions.
Source : Statistical Abstract of the U.S. (1990).

TABLE 20-5 — Number of Soviet and East European Investments in the West by Country, October 1987

HOST COUNTRY	Bulgaria	Czechoslovakia	East Germany	Hungary	Poland	Romania	USSR	Total
Austria	2	1	6	26	8	2	4	49
Belgium	2	3	6	1	5	0	13	30
Canada	1	5	0	1	1	1	5	14
Finland	0	0	1	1	1	0	7	10
France	4	3	3	3	8	6	12	39
Italy	5	3	4	5	2	5	8	32
Netherlands	1	1	3	2	3	0	2	12
Spain	1	0	1	3	2	1	5	13
Sweden	0	3	2	2	5	0	3	15
Switzerland	2	2	1	4	2	2	4	17
United Kingdom	6	9	10	6	12	5	13	61
United States	1	2	1	7	12	1	4	28
West Germany	12	3	0	20	15	7	11	68
Other Countries	5	0	4	5	4	2	8	28
TOTAL	42	35	42	86	80	32	99	416

Source : United Nations, Economic Commission for Europe, *East-West Joint Ventures : Economic Business, Financial and Legal Aspects* (1988), 71.

Another factor favoring the establishment of a joint venture in Hungary is the repatriation of profits. While the entire profit in a Hungarian joint venture can be changed to hard currency and taken out of the country, this is not the case in most other eastern European countries. Usually in these countries only the hard currency portion can be repatriated. For example, repatriation in a joint venture in the Soviet Union can only occur for the hard currency portion of the return (see Table 20–6).

In other important areas of consideration in establishing a joint venture in a previously controlled economy (such as percentage tax on dividends and special deals for establishing a joint venture), most eastern European countries are very similar. In terms of the joint venture's tax rate as a percentage of profits, Hungary's is slightly higher, having a 40 percent tax rate on profits up to 30 million forints and a 50 percent tax rate on all profits exceeding this amount. Tax rates in other eastern European countries range from a low of 10 percent in Yugoslavia to a high of 40 percent in Czechoslovakia and Poland.

A Specific Example : Conditions in Hungary

The output of quality agricultural products, the largest area of export for the country, reflects the Hungarian people and their heritage. The population of about 10.6 million mainly reside outside the large metropolitan areas, the largest of which is Budapest, the capital, with a population of about 2.1 million. The present population and country evolved from the time of the Hungarian settlement in 896 A.D., during the period of the great migration of the various tribes. Hungary is known as the "bread basket" of eastern Europe and the Soviet Union. (The joke in Hungary is that if you can find any fresh fruits and vegetables in Moscow, they had to come from Hungary.)

Hungary is a people's republic with the trustees of legislative power being the national assembly (Parliament) whose functions are performed by a council of ministers. Until January 1989 the word "party" would have meant only one political party — the Hungarian Socialist Workers' party (HSWP). However, today the word can mean a multitude of parties, such as the Free Democrats, the Christian Democrats, the Peasant party, or the Social Democrats. Hungary has a free democratic party system, with the first elections held March 25, 1990.

In addition to the new law creating the right to form political parties without permission, other significant reforms occurred in 1989. These reforms have guaranteed freedom of press and trade unions ; guaranteed impartial justice ; and led to the abandonment of the phrase, "the Communist leading role." Reform in the Hungarian political structure is helping to create the environment for economic reform — the movement from a near totally planned to a market-oriented economy.

Until recently, the Hungarian economy since 1949 was more or less planned by the Communist party. The focus and type of planning has varied between a more market-oriented to a more planned approach. Shortly after the

TABLE 20–6 — Rules Governing the Establishment of Joint Ventures in Eastern Europe

	Bulgaria	Czechoslovakia	Yugoslavia	Poland	Romania	Soviet Union	Hungary
Year of first joint venture	1980	1985	1968	1976	1971	1988	1972
Number of joint ventures	41	20	230	170	5	685	628
Permit issuing authority	Council of ministers	Individual ministries, following consultation with other authorities	Varies according to republic ; in special cases — the federal government	Agency dealing with foreign investments	Council of ministers	Council of ministers	Ministry of Commerce and Finance if the foreign share exceeds 50%. Otherwise registration is sufficient
Joint ventures tax rate as a percentage of profits	30	40	10	40	30	30	Up to 3 million forints — 40 ; over 3 million forints —50
Special deals for establishing joint ventures	Special tax-free status can be requested for first 5 years	—	—	First 3 years are tax-free ; an additional 3 can be requested	The first year is tax-free. Second year, 15% tax and 20%	First 2 (3 in the far eastern areas) years are tax-free. Lower taxes	Depends on amount of capital, percentage of foreign capital, type of

			Value of new investments can be deducted from tax base.	reduction if the profit is not taken out of the country	in far East later as well	activity. The special reduction can even be 100% in the first 5 years
Tax on dividends as a percentage	10–15	—	30	10	20 Special reduction possible	20 Private individuals pay personal income tax ; economic organizations do not pay
Repatriation of profits	Only hard currency portion	Only hard currency portion	85% of surplus export	Only hard currency portion	Profit covered by convertible export	The entire profit can be changed to hard currency and taken out of the country with no limitations

549

end of World War II (with Hungary being on the losing side), the forint became the new currency and rapid reconstruction was started. However, this market-oriented era was short-lived, and in 1947 the nationalization of banks, mines, and all forms of business with over 100 employees began heralding the new, centrally controlled economy and society. This less market-oriented, more planned economy continued, until any hope of economic freedom was eliminated with the crushing of the uprising in 1956.

The more market-oriented economic approach introduced in 1968 provided general guidelines for the Hungarian economic and social policy. This policy, supporting to some extent decentralization, along with private initiative and social pluralism, helped Hungary obtain a higher economic level than most other eastern bloc countries. This market-oriented policy was not constant, for significant retrenchment to a more planned approach occurred in both 1974 and 1984.

Two major pieces of market-oriented legislation were enacted and implemented in January 1989: Act VI (the Company Act) and Act XXIV (Investments by Foreigners in Hungary Act). The Company Act regulates the legal corporate structure of foreign firms operating in Hungary while providing guarantees similar to those of the European Community. The Investments Act provides an easy mechanism for foreign investors to change forint profits (soft currency) into original investment currency (hard currency) for repatriation purposes; grants tax benefits for foreign investments; allows 100 percent foreign ownership in certain situations; and allows duty-free importing of production equipment.

Hungarian Joint Ventures

As of June 1989 there were 18 U.S.-Hungarian joint ventures operating (see Table 20–7). Most of these were formed since 1987 and were established because of: lower labor costs, access to Hungarian and other eastern European and Soviet markets, and access to western European markets. For example, due in part to the low labor costs, Levi Strauss is able to operate its Hungarian factories 30–40 percent cheaper than its operations in other European countries. This is aided by the availability of a number of skilled workers in Hungary who are able to work in higher-technology industries. Given the small size of the Hungarian market, few companies can afford to produce for only this market. However, when the Hungarian market is combined with the market potential in other eastern European countries as well as western Europe, there is enough sales potential to warrant locating in Hungary. In certain instances, the Hungarian market alone is of sufficient size. Babalna-McDonald's Restaurant Ltd. in Budapest has little competition for its type of fast food and has become the number one McDonald's in Europe in terms of the number of transactions.

The access to western European markets is another important reason for establishing a joint venture in Hungary. Hungary is the first eastern European country to make a trade agreement with the European Community (EC). This agreement eliminates over 2000 quantitative trade restrictions in three stages and allows Hungary by 1995 to export "very sensitive items" to the EC, which favorably affects any investment in Hungary. By exporting to western markets, a joint venture can obtain a favorable hard currency balance, which is particularly important when the company needs to import raw materials or component parts.

For U.S. companies, not only are the markets more geographically and politically accessible from Hungary, but the understanding gained by dealing in Hungary will facilitate establishing trading relations with other countries in eastern Europe. Given Hungary's present and anticipated status in the European Community in the next few years, joint ventures in Hungary will also allow easier access to these large European markets.

DIRECTIONS FOR FUTURE RESEARCH

The research to date on joint ventures has involved a wide variety of research methodologies and focus. Given the interest in joint ventures and the significant number of studies occurring, there are significant research opportunities available in a wide variety of areas. In order for a comprehensive research base on joint ventures to be established, several areas must be addressed. First, a joint venture research framework is needed. While this framework could emerge in several different forms, given the extent of existing research, two possibilities seem most appropriate. One would be a classification system based on the: 1) motivations for the joint venture (market entrance, competition, synergy, or cost reduction); 2) types of joint ventures (domestic versus international, industry type, or high-technology versus low-technology); or 3) successful joint ventures versus nonsuccessful joint ventures. A second possible framework would employ the basic aspects involved in forming and managing a joint venture. These aspects include: finding the partner, writing the contract, the ownership versus control issue, using joint venture managers effectively, and evaluating joint venture performance. A modified version of either of these alternatives or some other alternative needs to be estimated to provide the conceptual framework needed in future research.

The second area affecting the future research of joint ventures involves several methodological issues and reporting requirements. The first of these is defining terms. In the past, joint venture research has had the problem of a lack of consistency in employing an operational definition of a joint venture. A common definition of a joint venture needs to be used and differentiated from other strategic alternatives, such as mergers and acquisitions, cooperative agreements, and joint activities. All other independent variables also need to be defined and consistently used. Second, the universe of joint ventures from which the sample is drawn needs to be fully specified in

TABLE 20–7 — Hungarian / U.S. Joint Ventures Operating in June, 1989

Name and Address	Year Founded	Share Capital	U.S. Partner	Hungarian Partner	Business Activity
BCR and Lilly Co. Ltd. 1-1364 Budapest, Pf. 72	1982		Eli Lilly USA	BCR Works Babolna	Production, marketing, and sales of medicated premixes for animal husbandry and R&D activity connected with the products
Citibank Budapest Ltd. 1052 Budapest V.	1985	1,000,000,000	Citicorp Overseas Investment Corp.	Kozponti Valto-es Hitelbank Rt. (Central Wehselund Creditbank AG)	Short, medium, and long term credits in convertible currencies and in forints. Collecting deposits. Lease financing. All investment banking services to Hungarian entities
Computerworld Informatics Co. Ltd. H-11536 Budapest, Pf. 386	1986	13,000,000. Ft.	IDG Communications Inc.	Pallas Newspaper and Book Publishing Co., Statistical Publishing Co.	Publishing books and periodicals on computer techniques. Information counselling. Organization of conferences and exhibits
Fotex American-Hungarian Co., Ltd. 1025 Budapest II., Ferenchegyi ut. 20	1984	11,244,000. Ft.	Blackburn International, Inc.	Skala-Coop Ltd., Fenyszov Photographic Cooperative, Forte Photochemical	Photographic service and production for export

Company / Address	Year	Capital	Foreign Partner	Hungarian Partner	Activity
McCann-Erickson Interpress 1021 Budapest 11., Budakeszi ut. 55/D	1988	5,000,000. Ft.	McCann-Erickson Worldwide, Inc.	Interpress Publicity Publishing and Printing House	International Advertising Agency
Babolna-McDonalds Fast Service Restaurant, Ltd. 1054 Budapest, V., Bathony utca. 3	1987	120,000,000. Ft.	McDoncld's Restaurant Operations, Inc.	Agricultural Works of Babolna	McDonald's Fast Food Restaurant
Pangus Rubber Products Corporation 108 Budapest, X jhegyi ut. 25-31	1987	10,000,000. Ft	Pang Rubber Company	Taurus Hungarian Rubber Works	Production and marketing of tire and conveyor belt repair materials
Qualiplastic Co, Ltd.	1982	142,000,000. Ft.	ALM Holding Corp.	PEMU Pest Country Plastic Processing Co., Tejinari Vallalatok Trosztje	Production of thermoplastic basic materials
Radelcor Instrument Sales Ltd. 025 Budapest, II., Zaigmond ter. 8	1975	26,000,000. Ft.	Corning Medical Corp.	Radelkis Electrochemical Instruments. Metrimpex Hungarian Foreign Trading Company for Instruments	Selling and servicing medical instruments manufactured by Corning
Levi Strauss Co., Ltd. 1075 Budapest Vii. Tanacs Krt. 9. VIII 802	1988	90,500,000. Ft.	Levi Strauss (Geneva) S.A.	Tritex Trading Co., Meteor Garment Trading Co., Centrum Dept. Stores; Skala-Tex Clothing Trading Co.	Manufacturing, subcontracting, and marketing of jeans wear under "Levis" brand name
Hemingway Computing International Ltd. 1-1115 Budapest XI., Gzakasits Arpad u. 68	1988	29,000,000. Ft.	Hemingway Unipex Corp.	Szamalk Computer Applications	Systems, software development, and marketing

continued

TABLE 20–7, continued

Name and Address	Year Founded	Share Capital	U.S. Partner	Hungarian Partner	Business Activity
Schwinn (USA) - Csepel Bicycle Manufacturing and Sales Co., Ltd. 1-1751 Budapest, Pf. 113	1988	158,400,000. Ft.	Schwinn Bicycle Company, Willie Bicycle Corp.	Institute for Energetics Csepel Works Machine Factory for the Garment Industry and Bicycles	Design, manufacture, assembly, and marketing of bicycles, including their parts and components
uski-Isis Publisher Ltd. 011 Budapest I., Corvin er 8	1988	14,600,000. Ft.	Puski-Corvin Publishing	ISIS Cultural and Publicity Servicing Small Cooperatix, Hungarian Foreign Trading Co., NEP Book Distribution Co.	Publishing Co.
International Management Center -1775 Budafok 1. Pf. 113	1988	88,000,000. Ft.	Soros Foundation Hungary, Camera di Commecio Industria, Instituto e Agricultura di Milano, Instituto Bancario San	Hungarian Credit Bank, Ltd., Hungarian Chamber of Commerce, Szenzor Company for Organization	Management training and business consulting English language training
TD Printing and Data Processing, Ltd. 145 Budapest XIV. Gyarmat . 52	1988	26,000,000. Ft.	Directory Processing Center, Inc.	Hungarian Credit Bank, Ltd., Reform Newspaper and Book Publishing Co., Skala Publicity Studio, Ribbon Small Cooperative for Publicity and Advertising	Preparation for printing, computerized processing, editing, publication, distribution of all kinds of domestic and foreign publications as well as advertising and publicity work connected with publications

TFC FINANCIAL COMPANIES

UNIC Bank Ltd. H-1364 Budapest, Pf. 173	1986	1,000,000,000. Ft.	Central Wechselund Creditbank AG Deutsche Genossen-schaftsbank Genossen-schaftliche Zentralbank AG, International	National Council of Agricultural Cooperatives, National Council of Industrial Cooperatives, National Council of Consumer's Cooperative Society, National Organization of Artisans National Savings Bank	Full-fledged commercial banking activities in domestic and foreign currencies
Agroferm Hungarian Japanese Fermentation 1113 Budapest XI. Molnar	1968	882,000,000. Ft.	Kyowa Hakko Kogyo, Toyo Menka Kaisha, IFC	Hajdu Region Agrarian Industrial Assn., Commercial and Credit Bank Ltd. Grain Trust	To establish and operate a lysine-plant with a yearly capacity of 5,000 tons in order to supply the feed additive protein
Salgotarjan Glass Wool Ltd. 3104 Salgotarjan, Budapestiut. 31	1987	390,300,000. Ft.	Nitto Boseki Co. Ltd., Paramount Glass Mfg. Co. Ltd., Toyo Menka Kaisha Ltc., International Finance Corp.	Hungarian Glass Works, Skala-Coop Ltd.	Manufacturing and processing, marketing and sales of fiber-glass products for insulating buildings, vehicles, and industrial equipment

terms of size, composition, key characteristics, and relevance to the question at hand. Third, the sampling frame (and size) needs to be indicated. Generally, past research has suffered from use of only case studies or extremely small sample sizes drawn more or less on a convenience basis. Whenever possible (except for those research issues where in-depth case studies are appropriate), statistically valid samples should be drawn using a technique that minimizes type II errors. Fourth, a valid questionnaire that has been pretested should be employed. Whenever possible, questions should be used that have been tested for reliability or have been used in previous research. Fifth, the appropriate data collection technique needs to be employed to ensure that no nonsampling errors occur. Sixth, the appropriate nonparametric and parametric data analysis technique should be used to test the various hypotheses established and determine the nature of any relationships, particularly causal ones.

Finally, more research interest needs to be developed on the part of a wide variety of researchers, and more funds need to be made available. While the latter will help ensure the former, more individuals from a wide variety of business and nonbusiness disciplines need to address joint ventures from different perspectives. This multidisciplinary approach will ensure that the broadest possible research paradigm on joint ventures will be developed.

▬ ▬ ▬ ▬ ▬ ▬ ▬
REFERENCES

Adolph, G. S. 1988 The perils of strategic alliances. *The Corporate Board* 9(50) (May–June): 1–5.

Afriyie, K. 1988 Factor choice characteristics and industrial impact of joint ventures: Lessons from a developing economy. *Columbia Journal of World Business* (Fall): 51–62.

Anderson, E., and H. Gatignon 1986 Modes of foreign entry: A transaction cost analysis and propositions. *Journal of International Business Studies* 17(3) (Fall): 1–25.

Auster, E. R. 1987 International corporate linkages: Dynamic forms in changing environments. *Columbia Journal of World Business* 22(2) (Summer): 3–6.

Beamish, P. 1987 Joint ventures in less developed countries: Partner selection and performance. *Management International Review* 27(1): 23–37.

Berg, S. V., and J. M. Hoekman 1988 Entrepreneurship over the product life cycle: ed. Joint venture strategies in the Netherlands. *Cooperative strategies in international business* 145–167, Lexington, Mass.: Lexington Books.

Bruce, L. 1987 Bull tackles the Yanks. *International Management* 42(12) (December): 30–32.

Cartwright, S., and C. L. Cooper 1989 Predicting success in joint venture organizations in information technology. *Journal of General Management* 15 (1, Autumn): 39–52.

Castro, J. 1988 Perestroika to pizza. *Time*, May 22, 52–53.

Christelow, D. B. 1987 International joint ventures: How important are they? *Columbia Journal of World Business* 22(2): 7–13.

Contractor, F. J. 1990 Ownership patterns of U.S. joint ventures abroad and the liberalization of foreign government regulations in the 1980s: Evidence from the Benchmark Surveys. *Journal of International Business Studies* 21(1): 55–73.

Darrough, M. N., and N. M. Stoughton 1989 A bargaining approach to profit sharing in joint ventures. *Journal of Business* 62 (2): 237–270.

Davidson, W. H. 1987 Creating and managing joint venture in China. *California Management Review* 29 (4): 77–94.

Devlin, G., and M. Bleackley 1988 Strategic alliances — Guidelines for success. *Long Range Planning* Vol. 21/5, No. 111 (October): 18–24.

Doz, Y. L. 1987 Technology partnerships between larger and smaller firms: Some critical issues. *International Studies of Management and Organization* 17 (4): 31–58.

Doz, Y. L., G. Hamel, and C. K. Prahalad 1989 Collaborate with your competitors and win. *Harvard Business Review* 67 (1) (January-February): 133–139.

D'Souza, D. E., and P. P. McDougall 1989 Third world joint venturing: A strategic option for the smaller firm. *Entrepreneurship Theory and Practice* 13 (4): 19–33.

Dymsza, W. A. 1988 Successes and failures of joint ventures in developing countries: Lessons from experience. In *Cooperative strategies in international business*, ed. F. J. Contractor, 403–424. Lexington, Mass.: Lexington Books, D. C. Heath & Co.

Eales, R. 1989 Japanese joint ventures in the USA. *Multinational Business* (Spring): 41–42.

Economist 1989 Testing the water. October 21, 78–79.

1990a Think of the 1992 company. January 20, 16–17.

1990b The art of the blitz-deal. March 31, 71–72.

1990c A shortage of shopkeepers. April 7, 82.

Erickson, J. L. 1989 Euro ventures on the way. *Advertising Age*, December 4, 52.

Franko, L. G. 1987 New forms of investment in developing countries by U.S. companies: A five industry comparison. *Columbia Journal of World Business* (Summer): 39–56.

Galuszka, P., and R. W. King 1987 The twain are meeting and cutting deals. *Business Week*, December 7, 88.

Geringer, J. M. 1988 Partner selection criteria for developed country joint ventures. *Business Quarterly* (Summer): 55–62.

Glinow, M. A. V., and M. B. Teagarden 1988 The transfer of human resource management technology in Sino-U.S. cooperative ventures: Problems and solutions. *Human Resource Management* 27 (2): 201–203.

Goldbaum, E. 1989 Teaming up in search of critical mass. *Chemicalweek*, November 8, 30–34.

Gomes-Casseres, B. 1987 Joint venture instability: Is it a problem? *Columbia Journal of World Business* 22(2) (Summer): 97–102.

1989 Joint ventures in the face of global competition. *Sloan Management Review* 30(3) (Spring): 17–26.

Guerin, D. 1988 Licensing vs. joint ventures. *Folio* 17: 165–166.

Harrigan, K. R. 1987a Managing joint ventures (part 1). *Management Review* 76(2) (February): 24–42.

1987b Managing joint ventures (part 2). *Management Review* 76(3) (March): 52–55.

1987c Strategic alliances: Their new role in global competition. *Columbia Journal of World Business* (Summer): 67–69.

1988a Joint ventures and competitive strategy. *Strategic Management Journal* 9: 319–332.

1988b Strategic alliances and partner assymetries. In *Cooperative strategies in interna-*

tional business, ed. F. J. Contractor, 205–226. Lexington, Mass. : Lexington Books, D. C. Heath & Co.

Hennart, J.-F. 1988 A transaction costs theory of equity joint ventures. *Strategic Management Journal* 9 : 361–374.

Hisrich, R. D., J. Vecsenyi, and A. Gross 1990 Using research in evaluating joint venture activity. In *Proceedings*, 43d European Society for Opinion and Marketing Research Marketing Research Congress : Amsterdam, Netherlands : September (1990) 1–28.

Hladik, K. J. 1988 R&D and international joint ventures. In *Cooperative strategies in international business*, ed. F. J. Contractor, 187–203. Lexington, Mass. : Lexington Books, D. C. Heath & Co.

Kirkconnell, P. A. 1988 Practical thinking about going international. *Business Quarterly* 53(2) (Autumn) : 40–45.

Kogut, B. A. 1988a A study of the life cycle of joint ventures. *Management International Review* 28 : 39–52.

1988b A study of the life cycle of joint ventures. In *Cooperative strategies in international business*, ed. F. J. Contractor, 169–185. Lexington, Mass. : Lexington Books, D. C. Heath & Co.

Kogut, B. A., and H. Singh 1988 Entering the U.S. by joint venture : Competitive rivalry and industry structure. In *Cooperative strategies in international business*, ed. F. J. Contractor 241–251. Lexington, Mass. : Lexington Books, D. C. Heath & Co.

Kohn, S. J. 1989 Averting joint-venture pitfalls. *The American Banker*, September 25, 15–17.

1990 The benefits and pitfalls of joint ventures. *The Bankers' Magazine* (May-June) : 12–18.

Langowitz, N. S., and S. C. Wheelwright 1989 Plus development corporation : Joint venturing a breakthrough product. *Planning Review* (July / August) : 6–20.

Leadbeater, C. 1990 Chipping at the old block. *Management Today* (February) : 23.

Lorange, P., and G. J. B. Probst 1987 Joint ventures as self-organizing systems : A key to successful joint venture design and implementation. *Columbia Journal of World Business* 22(2) : 71–77.

Lyles, M. A. 1987 Common mistakes of joint venture experienced firms. *Columbia Journal of World Business* 22(2) : 79–85.

McClenahen, J. S. 1990 Honeywell resets. *Industry Week*, March 5, 25–26.

Mergers and Acquisitions 1988a M&A in Japan : A new force in a global strategy. 23(1) (July-August) ; 81–84.

1988b All purpose alliances : Joint ventures to cut risks or penetrate tough markets. 23(3) (November-December) ; 23, 73.

Miller, D., and P. Friesen 1982 Innovation in conservative and entrepreneurial firms. *Strategic Management Journal* 3 : 1–25.

Morris, D., and M. Hergert 1987 Trends in international collaborative agreements. *Columbia Journal of World Business* 22(2) (Summer) : 15–21.

Nation's Business 1987 Tapping a growth market. 75(7) (July) : 14.

Nigh, D., and K. D. Smith 1989 The new U.S. joint ventures in the USSR : Assessment and management of political risk. *Columbia Journal of World Business* 24(2) : 39–44.

OECD Report 1990 Joint ventures in eastern Europe. Paris, France : OECD.

O'Reilly, A. J. F. 1988 Establishing successful joint ventures in developing nations : A CEO's perspective. *Columbia Journal of World Business* 23(1) : 65–71.

Osborn, R. N., and C. C. Baughn 1987 New patterns in the formation of U.S./Japanese corporate ventures: The role of technology. *Columbia Journal of World Business* 22(2) (Summer): 57–65.

1990 Forms of interorganizational governance for multinational alliances. *Academy of Management Journal* 33 (3): 503–519.

Otis, S. H. 1988 It's high time for tourists at rejuvenated marinas. *Parks and Recreation* (April): 32–37.

Peterson, R., and D. Berger 1971 Entrepreneurship in organizations. *Administrative Science Quarterly* 16: 97–106.

Roehl, T. W., and J. F. Truitt 1987 Stormy open marriages are better: Evidence from U.S., Japanese, and French cooperative ventures in commercial aircraft. *Columbia Journal of World Business* (Summer): 87–95.

Salem, E. 1988 Legally contracted. *Far Eastern Economic Review*, April 28, 80.

Schillaci, C. E. 1987 Designing successful joint ventures. *The Journal of World Business Strategy* (Fall): 59–63.

Shan, W. 1989 An empirical analysis of organizational strategies by entrepreneurial high-technology firms. *Strategic Management Journal* 11 (May): 129–139.

Shenkar, O., and Y. Zerras 1990 International joint ventures: A tough test for HR. *Personnel* 67(1) (January): 26–31.

Sramek, A. M. 1988 Joint ventures: A vehicle for fixed-asset growth. *Industrial Development* (July-August): 907–909.

Spalding, A. D. 1989 Advantages of joint ventures as business start-up and venture capital vehicles. *The Michigan CPA* 41(1) (Summer): 48–59.

Taylor, G. 1989 The joys of joint ventures. *Business Month* (July): 38–41.

Walker, G. 1988 Network analysis for cooperative interfirm relationships. In *Cooperative strategies in international business*, ed. F. J. Contractor, 227–240. Lexington, Mass.: Lexington Books, D. C. Heath & Co.

Webster, D. R. 1989 International joint ventures with Pacific Rim partners. *Business Horizons* 32 (2) (March-April): 65–71.

Weiss, S. E. 1987 Creating the GM-Toyota joint venture: A case in complex negotiation. *Columbia Journal of World Business* 22(2): 23–27.

Wrubel, R. 1990 Silicon valley squirms. *Financial World*, March 20, 58–61.

Chapter

21

Entrepreneurship Education and Research in Europe

Robert H. Brockhaus, Sr.

●

INTRODUCTION

This chapter describes both academic and nonacademic entrepreneurship programs in Europe. Certainly, the availability of research literature written in English is of great value to North American researchers. Therefore, the work done in the United Kingdom receives considerable attention in this chapter. However, ongoing work in Germany is also a primary focus of this chapter. Entrepreneurship research in Germany, while more difficult to utilize because of the language translation required, promises to become highly important when Europe becomes a more unified entity in 1992. The reunification of Germany will also foster German entrepreneurship efforts and bring them greater visibility. Interesting research is also being done in Austria, Belgium, France, Spain, and Switzerland, and these countries are therefore included in our discussion.

EUROPE

Western Europe has long been a center of entrepreneurial activity. However, many scholars in North America have failed to recognize the major academic research activity in Europe. Recently, more recognition has been forthcoming.

The research has tended to be more oriented toward macroeconomic issues than in North America. But, as more international journals and conferences focus on entrepreneurship, there is a trend toward greater similarities in research efforts.

Until comparatively recently, entrepreneurship research in Europe has remained within national boundaries and has lacked comparative analyses. The European Foundation for Entrepreneurship Research (EFER) was founded in 1987 to fill this gap, to sponsor and publicize collaborative research in the field, and to initiate debate among four interested constituencies: researchers, policy makers, investors, and entrepreneurs themselves. The formation of EFER was a joint initiative by the European Foundation for Management Development (EFMO) and the European Venture Capital Association (EVCA).

Ahead of the EFER forum initiative, the European Institute of Advanced Studies in Management (EIASM) established a European network dedicated to the exchange of entrepreneurial study outcomes. Four workshops on recent research in entrepreneurship have taken place to date. In 1988, the European Council for Small Business (ECSB) was founded as the European affiliate of the International Council for Small Business (ICSB). Since then, ECSB has collaborated with EIASM in organizing and promoting an annual research workshop.

Recently, the European Doctoral Programme in Entrepreneurship and Small Business Management has been initiated by the ECSB in association with 17 universities, and partly financed by the EC Commission (Brussels) under the ERASMUS student exchange scheme.

With the single European market in prospect for the EC by the end of 1992, and with the western hemisphere's concern for successful reconstruction of the economies of the former eastern bloc countries, Europe is facing many fascinating challenges, including previously unimagined opportunities and motivation for the business community.

The 12 EC states will comprise a market greater than the United States, with, on the one hand, enhanced growth potential for the alert exporting firm, and on the other hand, increased competition "from abroad" for the non-progressive enterprise that confines its operations to a localized market.

When one also considers the mega-potential for development that exists in the Soviet Union and its former Warsaw Pact partners, it would be reasonable to expect that the "spirit of enterprise" will be much more evident in Europe, east and west, well into the next century. It would be surprising if business analysts and researchers did not avail themselves of these unique opportunities to study the entrepreneurial environment — opportunities that are occurring at an accelerated pace.

Austria

In Austria, the University of Economics and Business Administration in Vienna offers an extensive list of both graduate and undergraduate courses. Its director is one of the very few European holders of a chair in entrepreneurship.

Research tends to be oriented towards practical topics of value to small businesses and the supporting infrastructure. Recent research studies have included such titles as "Export Behavior of Small Firms," "New Modes of Financing," "Impact of Government Aid on Enterprise Development," "Planning Behavior of Successful and Nonsuccessful Founders of New Ventures," and "The Effects of Subsidies on New Venture Development."

Each year the Vienna International Small Business Forum invites distinguished speakers, normally foreign researchers, to report on developments among small firms in their countries. This activity is oriented towards academics, small business owners, and members of government institutions.

The center is also headquarters for the International Council for Small Business — Europe which sponsors an annual research conference at different European locations.

Belgium

Another major center on the European continent is located in Brussels, Belgium at the KNO-Studiecentrum Small Business Research Institute. The primary function of this center is to conduct entrepreneurial research. It publishes the research in English, German, French, and Dutch. The research is both macroeconomic and practical in its thrusts. Topics include "Women in Small Business," "Multiple Business Starters," and "Multidimensional Modelling of Strategic Behavior in Expansion-Oriented SNE's."

France

Since 1978, a national policy to promote entrepreneurial and new businesses has been launched in France by both public and private organizations. This development is very significant, and a national agency for new business (ANCE) is the main instrument for the conception and the application of this policy. The function of the ANCE is to assist public authorities in promoting the creation of new firms, fostering the growth of start-up enterprises and arranging business takeovers.

As elsewhere, the role of the entrepreneur in society has been rediscovered, but through the firms' activities rather than through the entrepreneurs' behavior. The entrepreneur is thought of as an institution more than a person who runs an institution. This explains why research in the fields where the entrepreneur as a person is a critical determinant is not prevalant (for instance, there has been little work done on characteristics of the successful entrepreneur).

There are several entrepreneurship topics which have received considerable attention in France. Strategic management has been the focus of books by Martinent (1983) and Thietart (1990). Bessis (1988) wrote on venture capital, as did Copin (1987). Small business and its environment was addressed by De Booeck (1986) and Bucaille and de Beauregard (1987). Small business management and strategies were the topic of Julien and Marchesnay (1987), Saporta (1986), and Papin (1986), also discussed start-up issues.

Germany

The topics explored and research methods applied in Germany generally reflect those undertaken in the United States. Thus, the American and German literatures combine to form a fairly well-integrated picture of current state-of-the-art research about entrepreneurial activity.

In the following summary, the most important studies are placed into the context of seven major categories. These generally reflect the areas where the most knowledge has been gained about entrepreneurship, and they are certainly the topics of greatest concern — namely, job generation, the importance of entrepreneurship, the determinants of entrepreneurship, technology, survival and growth, government policies, and activity in East Germany. The last topic, where virtually no studies have been undertaken, reflects an important theme that will surely draw considerable attention from entrepreneurship researchers in the upcoming decade.

Job generation

Studies trying to measure the extent of job generation in West Germany and its relationship to establishment and enterprise size have generally found that, since the mid-1970s there has been either only a very negligible increase in the number of jobs or else an actual decrease, depending upon the time period measured. But, as for other western countries, a clear tendency exists for job generation in smaller-sized plants and firms to exceed job generation in the largest plants (Hull 1986 ; Fritsch and Hull 1987 ; Weimer 1990). For example, Loveman and Sengenberger (1991) found that establishments with fewer than 500 employees experienced an annual increase of employment of 0.2 percent between 1974 and 1981, while firms with at least 500 employees experienced an annual decrease in jobs of 0.5 percent. Acs and Audretsch (1989 and 1990) conclude that, while most new jobs emanate from small firms, the small firms have not served as engines of the job generation process in West Germany to the same extent that they have in the United States.

The importance of entrepreneurship

In 1987, firms with fewer than 500 employees accounted for 65.8 percent of the total employment in West Germany (Fritsch 1991). The small-firm employment share was greater in services (73.0 percent) than in manufacturing (65.8 percent). Fritsch (1991) identifies a reversal of the postwar tendency towards larger firms and plants to have occurred between 1970 and 1987. However, he attributes this statistical finding to the shift in economic activity out of services and into manufacturing. This is consistent with the findings of Schwalbach (1990) and Acs and Audretsch (1990) that during the 1980s there has been no noticeable shift in the West German size distribution towards smaller firms within the manufacturing sector. Rather, as Cramer (1990) shows, the tendency towards smaller firms is more pronounced in services than in manufacturing.

The determinants of entrepreneurship

Hunsdiek and May-Strobl (1986) examined a sample of 200 business start-ups which were established in 1981. They found that most of the entrepreneurial activity (90 percent) occurred outside of the manufacturing sector. Most entrepreneurs in West Germany are apparently more interested in emulating existing businesses than in pursuing innovative activity and developing new products (Albach 1984). Hunsdiek (1987) examined the characteristics of new entrepreneurial start-ups in West German high-technology industries and found that entrepreneurs generally are constrained by financing, red tape, and tax burdens. During the start-up phase, entrepreneurs tend to confront problems such as high interest payments, high debt-equity ratios, and exposure to severe competition by established companies.

Domeyer and Funder (1990) relied on survey data to determine that the threat of unemployment was the primary motivation of about 30 percent of the self-employed in West Germany. However, they also found that the potential for a better work environment and greater responsibility plays an important role in the decision to become self-employed, particularly for women. These results were generally confirmed in a series of interviews with the self-employed by Bogenhold (1990).

Schwalbach (1990) has contributed virtually the only study relating entrepreneurial activity to market structure in industrial markets. He found that entrepreneurial activity is deterred in the presence of high-scale economies, in industries where advertising plays an important role, and in high-R&D industries.

Technology

As Albach (1984) emphasizes, most entrepreneurial activity in West Germany does not involve high technology or rest upon the introduction of new products and innovations. Wudtke (1990) found that in 1987, manufacturing firms with between 100 and 500 employees devoted 2.71 percent of their sales towards R&D, while firms with between 5,000 and 9,999 employees had an R&D/sales ratio of 3.67 percent, and firms with at least 10,000 employees had an R&D intensity of 4.38 percent.

However, direct measures of innovative activity developed and implemented by Oppenlander (1990), Schulenburg and Wagner (1991), and Greif (1989), suggest that smaller firms make a considerable contribution to West German innovative activity. Bruder and Ellwein (1978) found that the innovative activity of small firms has played a key role in regional development.

Sternberg (1990) examined 177 high-technology entrepreneurial start-ups in West Germany and found that the bulk of the entrepreneurs come from private R&D departments in larger companies or else from universities. Oppenlander (1990) identified the sources inhibiting entrepreneurial innovative activity. While large established firms were found to be more deterred from innovative activity because of lack of profitability and a payoff period which is too long, small firms tend to be inhibited by the inability to market the new product.

Survival and growth

Based on a sample of over 100,000 West German firms established between 1980 and 1984, Preisendorfer, Schussler, and Ziegler (1989) found that the mortality rate after five years is about 50 percent. Further, they found that the survival rate is positively related to the size of the entrepreneurial start-up. The ability of a new firm to survive is also found to be positively related to the age of the founding entrepreneur. These results were generally confirmed by Fritsch (1991), using a sample of 3,000 enterprises.

Hunsdiek and May-Strobl (1986) examined 200 new business start-ups in 1981 and found that the failure rate after three years was 17 percent. The ability of entrepreneurs to survive was the lowest in hotels and restaurants, and the greatest in manufacturing. They identified the major factors contributing to firm failure as the lack of a well-defined market for the product, an inadequately formulated and supervised business plan, and an inability to finance the new start-up.

It has also been found that enterprise growth subsequent to start-up is positively related to initial capitalization. Hunsdiek and May-Strobl (1986) found that companies with at least 30,000 German marks of start-up capital grew faster than enterprises with an initial capitalization less than 30,000 German marks. Albach, Bach, and Warnke (1984) and FitzRoy and Kraft (1990) have both identified innovative activity as positively contributing to the growth rates of new and small firms.

Government policies

The craft and handworker system has played a crucial role in entrepreneurial activity in West Germany. There are a series of government laws and rules treating craft firms (defined as those with fewer than 20 employees) differently from larger firms (Audretsch 1989). According to Loveman and Sengenberger (1991): "craft organization has been built on a varying mix of public regulation and self-organization, the latter often being dependent on the former." These regulations and rules are generally implemented by the craft chambers of commerce (*Handwerkskammern*), which are mandated under the statutes of the Federal Republic of Germany.

Since 1983, a number of innovation centers have been introduced with the explicit goal of promoting entrepreneurial start-ups in high-technology industries. Sternberg (1990) carefully analyzed 31 of the 70 innovation centers in existence as of 1989. He found that the innovation centers have, at least to some extent, been successful in overcoming financial constraints, legal assistance, and the lack of business management skills that traditionally have hampered new start-ups in high-tech industries.

Most recently, the government has passed a series of laws in order to better facilitate the relatively small venture capital market in West Germany. Under the *Unternehmensbeteiligungsgesellschaften* Act, venture capital firms will be entitled to special tax status (Hunsdiek 1986).

East Germany

During the postwar period there was virtually no entrepreneurship research undertaken in the German Democratic Republic, or what is now the eastern part of the newly unified Germany. This was at least partially due to the absence of entrepreneurial activity in East Germany during the last four decades. Bannasch (1991) shows how, under the system of centralized economic planning, economic assets were constantly centralized and entrepreneurial activity was effectively prohibited. At the heart of the centralization policy were large corporate-like structures known as combines (*Kombinate*), which controlled numerous establishments. By 1988 there were 224 combines in the economy and about 184 in manufacturing, each one having a virtual monopoly in its main industry. Bannasch (1990) also shows how the number of small manufacturing plants (with fewer than 200 employees) dramatically decreased since 1972, so that the total number of plants in manufacturing decreased from 11,253 in 1971 to 3,449 in 1987.

Audretsch and Wayland (1991) identified at least the start of an entrepreneurial movement in the eastern part of Germany since unification in October 1990. As of November 1990 there were 80,000 registered new start-ups, of which 60 percent were in the service sector and tourism. The process of transformation from a centralized socialist economic system to a democratic capitalist economic system will require a virtual revolution of entrepreneurship. This will undoubtedly be a fertile ground for researchers in entrepreneurship during the decade of the 1990s.

Indeed, these research opportunities will abound throughout old "eastern" Europe. Because entrepreneurship at all levels, except for the informal sector, cooperatives, and a few special circumstances, was forbidden, there is very little research on entrepreneurship prior to 1990.

In summary, one can say that in German-speaking countries, entrepreneurship research concentrates on start-up activities (not on performance), delivers mostly descriptive (not causal) results, and is based on surveys (not on observations) and "reachable" samples (not random samples). One can find only a few longitudinal studies. Almost no research is done under controlled experiments (instead, it is mostly field research). Only a few standardized measurement instruments exist — psychological tests, for example.

In 1989, *Small Business Economics, an International Journal* was established by the Wissenschaftszentrum Berlin fur Sozialforschung in Berlin. This journal has as its purpose "to provide a forum for the economic analysis of the role of small business." It has published articles of a theoretical as well as a quantitative nature from authors throughout the world, on topics of international scope.

Spain

Entrepreneurship research in Spain began in the 1970s with the work of Veciana on entrepreneur and enterprise formation. Veciana (1980) found the characteristics of Spanish entrepreneurs to be similar to those identified by most researchers in other countries, with the exception of internal locus of control, which appears to be lower than in other countries. In regard to vision, Spanish entrepreneurs seem to be less concentrated on the long-term growth goal, which would explain the lack of large Spanish multinational companies.

Lafuente and Salas (1989) also analyzed the personal characteristics of entrepreneurs based on data drawn from new Spanish firms. They constructed a classification of entrepreneurs based on their basic work aspirations. Each type of entrepreneur (craftsman, risk-oriented, family-oriented, and managerial) has then been examined in terms of the origin and personal characteristics of the members of thc class.

The research carried out by Genesca and Veciana (1984) on the attitudes towards entrepreneurship and the start-up of new firms on a sample of students of business administration, engineering, and law and managers from all over Spain showed that a high percentage of the respondents (57 percent of students and 72 percent of managers) consider the possibility of starting a new firm. Among the motives to start a new firm is "personal independence" (in first place), followed by the "possibility of implementing one's own ideas."

The financial structure, profitability, and growth of the Spanish Small and Medium-sized Enterprises (SME) have been analyzed by Lafuente, Salas, and Perez (1985) and by Genesca (1989), whereas Genesca and Veciana (1990) concentrated on the Catalan firms. The work on entrepreneurial dynamics in Catalonia by Genesca and Veciana (1990) identifies the characteristics and the economic and noneconomic factors affecting Catalonian firms. The financial structure of the Catalan firms is compared to firms in the rest of Spain.

The characteristics of the innovative firms in Catalonia have been investigated by Escorsa and Sole (1988). They found that the innovative firms are characterized by:

- A highly motivated management
- The adoption of an "offensive strategy" of differentiation, high quality, and segmentation
- A global orientation (high internationalization)
- An increasing collaboration with universities for joint research

In the field of entrepreneurship and regional development, Cuadrado (1989) analyzed the factors characterizing the geographical distribution of industry in Spain over recent decades. In a recent work on the location of new industries, Cuadrado and Aurioles (1990) come to the conclusion that the existence of an ample entrepreneurial base, and the infrastructures of communications and qualified labor, are of paramount importance.

A comprehensive review of the literature on entrepreneurship in Spain can be found in special issues of the *Revista Economica de Catalunya,* edited by Veciana (1989).

United Kingdom

The United Kingdom has several academic centers of entrepreneurial activity. One is located at the Durham University Business School. The Small Business Centre there is very active in developing research of both a practical and a theoretical nature.

A second center is at the Cranfield Institute of Management. The research efforts there also are both practical and theoretical, with a strong bent toward the individual firm and owner. A third locus of activity is the Scottish Enterprise Foundation at the University of Stirling. In addition to its research efforts, it has an intensive entrepreneurial training program.

The oldest European entrepreneurship journal with wide circulation is the *International Small Business Journal,* which is published in the United Kingdom. It has a worldwide perspective in its articles and a broad scope of topics. An interesting attempt to bridge U.S. and European studies of entrepreneurship has also been undertaken in another journal, *Entrepreneurship and Regional Development* first published by Taylor and Francis (London) in 1989. The establishment of this new quarterly was based on the belief that local or regional, rather than national, factors impact most strongly on economic growth.

Within Europe there are several regional and national SME seminars or conventions held on a regular basis. One of the longest established, the UK National Small Firms Policy and Research Conference, has been held annually since 1978. Increasingly, the conference papers deal with entrepreneurship issues, often involving comparative regional research.

In the United Kingdom, research into small businesses and entrepreneurship is of only recent origin, stemming from the seminal work of the Committee of Inquiry on Small Firms in the late 1960s and early 1970s (Bolton 1971). Not only did the report generate further interest in the small business sector by government and trade associations but also among academics, with the result that in the next decade the body of research expanded with such rapidity as to produce a remarkable period of sustained academic exploration of business activity in Britain (Curran and Stanworth 1982). With the publication of Birch's work (1979) on the role of small firms in the process of job generation, coupled with the advent of both a conservative government committed to the promotion of an enterprise culture within Britain and the onset of massive unemployment and industrial restructuring, the 1980s witnessed a further expansion in the volume of research being conducted. More recently, in 1989, a further fillip has been given to small business research by the Economic and Social Research Council which, has committed £1 million to support research.

Thus, the 1989 edition of the *United Kingdom Enterprise Management Research Association Research Register* (Lynas 1989) lists 483 projects and 126 institutions actively involved in small business and entrepreneurship research.

The main concentrations of research are to be found in the series of publications stemming from the annual National Small Firms Policy and Research Conference. Now in its 13th year, not all of the conference proceedings have been published, but notable editions include Gibb and Webb (1980); Stanworth et al. (1982); Webb, Quince, and Watkins (1982); Scott et al. (1986); Faulkner et al. (1986); and O'Neill et al. (1987). Additionally, the Small Business Research Trust, established in the early 1980s, is an independent research body reporting quarterly on the evolution of small businesses in Britain, and commissioning and publishing research on issues relating to entrepreneurship and small business development in the United Kingdom. Among its many publications is *Bolton Fifteen Years On: A Review and Analysis of Small Business Research in Britain, 1971–1986* (Curran 1986), which provides a comprehensive review of over 200 references under four headings: definition and numbers; entrepreneurs and owner-managers; employment and employment relations; and the small enterprise environment. Additionally, the *International Small Business Journal* (incorporating the *European Small Business Journal*) has, since 1982, provided an important outlet for refereed articles reporting the findings of small business research in the United Kingdom. However, the journal is not confined to research on small businesses and entrepreneurship in Britain; even from an early date it has been fully reporting international research by scholars from the United Kingdom and elsewhere.

From a review of the published proceedings of the annual National Small Firms Policy and Research Conferences and the quarterly publications of the *International Small Business Journal,* it would appear that the main areas of investigation over the past 20 years have been the characteristics of entrepreneurs; ethnic minorities; the founding process; new venture financing; new-firm performance; regional differences; small firms and employment; government policy and support; and entrepreneurial education and training. The literature in each of these fields will be reviewed briefly.

The characteristics of entrepreneurs

Much of the early work on small businesses and entrepreneurship focused on the characteristics of the entrepreneur. Other studies (Bechhofer and Elliott 1976; Scase and Goffee 1982) identified the influence of class or sought to consider the different entrepreneurial types, noting, in particular, the differences between male and female entrepreneurs (Cromie 1987); technical- (Cooper 1986) and service-sector (Kirby 1986) entrepreneurship; and entrepreneurship in large (Cross 1982) and small (Storey 1986) firms. Of particular value is the comprehensive analysis of the statistics generated by the General Household Survey conducted for the Small Business Research Trust by Curran, Burrows, and Evandrou (1987). The 1980 survey, on which this study is based, covered some 12,000 private households or over 31,000 individuals in Britain and reveals valuable insights into the characteristics of small business owners and the self-employed in Britain in terms of gender, age, ethnicity, marital status, educational background, health, social class, economic sector, rewards, personal assets, and hours worked.

Ethnic minorities

Within the field of entrepreneurship and small business development, there is a substantial body of literature reflecting the not inconsiderable amount of research into the ethnic business community in Britain. Perhaps the two most comprehensive reviews are *Ethnic Communities in Business,* edited by Ward and Jenkins (1984), and the 1986 spring edition of the *International Small Business Journal* [4(3)]. As this literature demonstrates, the success of ethnic enterprise in Britain is at best variable and often marginal.

New venture financing

The financing of new small businesses has attracted considerable attention. In a pilot investigation in the mid-1970s, Hutchinson (1980) identified many of the practical problems involved and areas where further research was required. Subsequent studies have focused on investment decision making in small firms (Hankinson 1984); policy issues relating to small-firm financing (Binks, Jennings, and Vale 1986); the relationship between banks and the small-firm sector (Robbie 1986); and the access of small firms to venture capital (NEDO 1986). More recent research has tended to concentrate on the specific schemes introduced in Britain to help overcome the problems experienced by small firms in gaining access to finance. Thus, in *Allowing for Enterprise,* Gray and Stanworth (1986) evaluate the effects of the British Government's Enterprise Allowance Scheme, while *Closing the Equity Gap?* is an examination by Mason, Harrison, and Harrison (1986) of the Business Expansion Scheme. A similar examination of the government's Loan Guarantee Scheme has been published recently by the Department of Employment (Barrett et al. 1990). It reveals that although the LGS may have had some effect in the past, its value is now much reduced, since banks have increased their activities in the small-firms market. One specialist form of small-firm financing — franchising — has received some attention (Curran and Stanworth 1983), but there is opportunity for considerably more detailed investigation, particularly in terms of its role in funding company expansions.

New-firm performance, job creation, and regional variations

Very considerable attention has been paid to the economic contribution of small firms, particularly in areas and times of high unemployment. Initially, however, perhaps more attention was paid to the problems facing small businesses (Donleavy 1980) and to understanding the factors influencing their growth and development (Gibb and Scott 1986; Stanworth and Curran 1986) than occurs currently. Given the radical restructuring of the British economy which has taken place in the 1980s, and the high levels of unemployment, much attention has been paid to the job creation opportunities provided by small firms (Storey and Johnson 1986, 1987; Gallagher and Doyle 1986) and to the potential contribution of the small-business sector to economic regeneration (Storey et al. 1987; Keeble 1990).

As a result of such studies, two important sub-issues have emerged — namely, the identification of fast-growth small firms, and regional variations in small-firm performance. Research by Storey et. al (1989) into 40 small firms in the northeast of England suggests that it is not only possible but also desirable (for policy reasons) to identify fast-growth small businesses. Conversely, Hakim's (1989) work on firms with fewer than 50 employees throughout the United Kingdom would seem to indicate that it is difficult to specify any major distinguishing feature of fast-growth firms compared with no-growth firms. This debate seems particularly relevant given that various studies have revealed that differences exist in the formation (Gudgin and Fothergill 1984; Whittington 1984) and performance (Mason 1985; Stewart and Gallagher 1985) of small firms both regionally and sectorially. Under such circumstances perhaps a case can be made, as Westhead (1989) has argued, for more, rather than less, support being given to those areas and sectors least likely to generate a large number of new, successful small firms.

Government policy and support for small business

The case for a comprehensive policy of support for small business was made in 1971 by the Committee of Inquiry on Small Firms (Bolton 1971), and by 1983 there were in existence some 90 measures designed specifically to assist small firms. Since then, further measures have been introduced, but Curran (1986) has observed that virtually no research on most of the measures introduced since 1979 has occurred. Apart from the work referred to earlier on the Enterprise Allowance Scheme (Gray and Stanworth 1986), the Business Expansion Scheme (Mason et al. 1986), and the Loan Guarantee Scheme (Barrett et al. 1990), it is probably only the creation of enterprise zones which has attracted substantial attention (Roger, Tym and Partners 1982), though Mason et al. (1986) have examined the regional impact of public policy towards small firms. Additional studies of public policy have either reviewed the provision of support both in Britain (Beesley and Wilson 1981) and overseas (Haskins, Gibb, and Hubert 1986), or called for specific types of support (Gill 1988) or support to specific small-business sectors (Kirby 1982).

Entrepreneurial education and training

It has been argued that "the major weakness of small business education is the lack of research" (Curran and Stanworth 1989). Apart from a comprehensive and innovative statement by Gibb (1983) on management education and small businesses, and a similar treatise on enterprise education and training (Gibb 1987), several studies have attempted to identify the training needs of small and medium-sized enterprises (Adams and Walbank 1983) in order to develop programs capable of meeting those needs and to assess their effectiveness (Dyson 1982; Johnson and Thomas 1983; Kirby 1984, 1985; Kirby and Mullen 1990; Lessem 1982). Similarly, more recent work has attempted to monitor the effects of enterprise training (Blythe, Granger, and Stanworth 1989) and of management education on small-business development (Kirby 1990).

This review purports neither to be exhaustive nor to report necessarily the most significant research in the field of entrepreneurship and small-business development in the United Kingdom. Rather, it documents some of the major lines of investigation in the past 20 years and provides insight into some of the most readily accessible published literature and research findings.

Switzerland.

One of the oldest and most respected European centers for the study of small business is at the Swiss Research Institute of Small Business, St. Gallen Graduate School of Economics, Law, Business and Public Administration. It is directed by one of the very few Europeans to hold an academic chair in small business and has a large staff of researchers.

The research covers a wide range of topics and includes research populations beyond the confines of Switzerland. In even-numbered years, the center hosts the Rencontres de St. Gallen which attracts invited entrepreneurship researchers from throughout the world. This conference is the oldest series of entrepreneurship conferences in the world. The best papers presented at the conference are published in German in a book entitled *Internationales Gewerbearchiv.* Topics included primarily have an economic thrust as is typical of most European research in the area of entrepreneurship. In addition to the center at St. Gallen, numerous other research and training centers exist throughout Switzerland.

CONCLUSION

The United States and Europe are not the only places in the world where entrepreneurship is recognized as playing a major role in economic development. Even former Communist countries are focusing a great amount of effort on fostering entrepreneurship. Following governmental initiatives, universities are not only offering courses but are also conducting increasingly extensive practical and theoretical research on entrepreneurship issues. As entrepreneurship and small-business research conferences become even more international in attendance and issues, there will be fewer differences between various regions of the world from an academic research perspective.

The more one learns of the entrepreneurship and small-business assistance programs and research efforts throughout the world, the more apparent it becomes that there are even more activities elsewhere which are still to be discovered by North American researchers. Hence, this chapter represents only the "tip of the iceberg" rather than a complete exploration of entrepreneurship research activities. Hopefully, it will stimulate others to delve more deeply into the international aspects of their research efforts.

REFERENCES

Acs, Z. J., and D. B. Audretsch 1989 Job creation and firm size in the U.S. and West Germany. *International Small Business Journal* 7 (4) : 4–22.

1990 Kleine Unternehmen, Schaffung von Arbeitsplatzen und Technolgie in den USA und der Bundesrepublik Deutschland. In *Kleinbetriebe im wirtschaftlichen Wandel*, eds. J. Berger, V. Domeyer, and M. Funder, 345–360. Frankfurt : Campus Verlag.

Adams, A., and M. Walbank 1983 Research note : Perceived and acted out training needs in small manufacturing firms. *International Small Business Journal* 2 (1) : 46–51.

Albach, H. 1984 Die Rolle des Schumpeter Unternehmers heute. Mit besonderer Boruokoiohtigung der Innovationsdynamik in der mittelstandischen Industrie in Deutschland. In *Schumpeter oder Keynes ? Zur Wirtschaftspolitik der neunziger Jahre*, eds. D. Bos and H. D. Stolper. Berlin : Springer-Verlag.

Albach, H., K. Bach, and T. Warnke 1984 Wachstumskrisen von Unternehman. *Schmalenbach Zeitschrift fur betriebswirtschaftliche Forschung* 36 (10) : 779–793.

Audretsch, D. B. 1989 *The market and the state : Government policies towards business in Europe, Japan and the U.S.* N.Y. : New York Univ. Press.

Audretsch, D. B., and Wayland, H. 1991 Investment opportunities in unified Germany. In *German reunification and the privatization of Czechoslovakia, Hungary, and Poland*, eds. J. Brada and M. Claudon. N.Y. : New York Univ. Press.

Bannasch, H.-G. 1990 Small firms in East Germany. *Small Business Economics* 2 (4).

1991 The evolution of small firms in East Germany. In *Firms and entrepreneurship : An international perspective*, eds. J. Z. Acs and D. B. Audretsch. Cambridge, Eng. : Cambridge Univ. Press.

Barrett, S., D. Colenutt, R. Foster, D. Glynn, S. Jaffer, I. Jones, and D. Ridyard 1990 *An evaluation of the Loan Guarantee Scheme*. London : Department of Employment. Research paper no. 74.

Bechhofer, F., and B. Elliott 1976 Persistence and change : The petite bourgeoisie in industrial society. *European Journal of Sociology* 17.

Beesley, M. E., and P. E. B. Wilson 1981 Government aid to small firms in Britain. In *Small business perspectives*, eds. P. Gorb et al. London : Armstrong.

Binks, A., A. Jennings, and P. Vale 1986 Tripartite funding and the constriction of enterprise. In *Readings in small business*, eds. T. Faulkner et al. Aldershot, Eng.: Gower.

Birch, D. 1979 *The job generation process*. Cambridge, Mass.: MIT Program for Neighborhood and Regional Change.

Blythe, S., B. Granger, and J. Stanworth 1989 *On course for business: Report on a survey of people taking enterprise training in London, 1988–1989*. London: Small Business Research Trust.

Bogenhold, D. 1990 Wage zur eigenen Firma zwischen Anpassungsdruck und Freiwilliget — Ergebnisse einer empirschen Studie uber urbeitslose Werftarbeiter. In *Kleinbetriebe im wirtschaftlichen Wandel*, eds. J. Berger, V. Domeyer, and M. Funder, 159–178. Frankfurt: Campus Verlag.

Bolton, J. 1971 *Small firms: Report of the Committee of Inquiry on Small Firms*. Cmnd. 4811. London: HMSO.

Bruder, W., and T. Ellwein 1978 Forschungs und Technologiefordering als Mittel zur Forderung der Invention und Innovation in Betrieven. *Information zur Ramentwicklung* 7: 515–502.

Cooper, A. C. 1986 Technical entrepreneurship: What do we know? In *The survival of the small firm*, eds. J. Curran et al. Vol. 2, *Employment growth, technology, and politics*. Aldershot, Eng.: Gower.

Cramer, U. 1990 Der trend zu kleineren Betrieven: Ergebnisse einer Auswertung der Beschaftigtenstatistick fur die Bundesrepublic Deutschland. In *Kleinbetriebe im wirtschaftlichen Wandel*, eds. J. Berger, V. Domeyer, and M. Funder, 19–34. Frankfurt: Campus Verlag.

Cromie, S. 1987 Similarities between women and men who choose proprietorship. *International Small Business Journal* 5 (3): 43–60.

Cross, M. 1982 The entrepreneurial base of the large manufacturing company. In *Perspectives on a decade of small business research: Bolten ten years on*, eds. J. Stanworth et al. Aldershot, Eng.: Gower.

Cuadrado, J. R. 1989 Small and medium-sized enterprise and the regional distribution of industry in Spain: A new stage. In *Small and medium-sized enterprises and regional development*, eds. M. Giaoutzi et al. London: Routledge & Kegan Paul.

Cuadrado, J. R., and J. Aurioles 1990 The entrepreneurial decision in the location of new industries. *Entrepreneurship and Regional Development* 2 (2, April-June).

Curran, J. 1986 *Bolton fifteen years on: A review and analysis of small business research in Britain, 1971–1986*. London: Small Business Research Trust.

Curran, J., R. Burrows, and M. Evandrou 1987 *Small business owners and the self-employed in Britain: An analysis of general household data*. London: Small Business Research Trust.

Curran, J., and J. Stanworth 1982 Bolton ten years on: A research inventory and critical review. In *Perspectives on a decade of small business research: Bolton ten years on*, eds. J. Stanworth et al. Aldershot, Eng.: Gower.

1983 Franchising in the modern economy: Towards a theoretical understanding. *International Small Business Journal* 2 (2): 8–26.

1989 Education and training for enterprise: Problems of classification, evaluation, policy and research. *International Small Business Journal* 7 (2): 11–22.

DeBooeck 1986 Les PME dans les systems economiques contemporaire. *Varil auctores*.

Domeyer, V., and M. Funder 1990 Der Kleinbetrieb — Relikt der Vergangenheit oder Modell fur die Zukunft? Ergebnisse einer empirischen Untersuchung uber neugegrundete Kleinbetrieve. In *Kleinbetrieve im wirtschaftlichen Wandel*, eds. J. Berger, V. Domeyer, and M. Funder, 101–128. Frankfurt : Campus Verlag.

Donleavy, D. 1980 Causes of bankruptcy in England. In *Policy issues in small business research*, eds. A. Gibb and T. Webb. Farnborough, Eng. : Saxon House.

Dyson, J. 1982 The position of new enterprise programmes in the process of start-up : An approach to matching enterprise founding programmes to different categories of business founder. In *Small business research*, eds. T. Webb et al. Aldershot, Eng. : Gower.

Escorsa, P., and F. Sole 1988 *La innovacio tecnologica a Catalunya*. Barcelona : Edicions de la Magrana.

Faulkner, T., G. Beaver, J. Lewis, and A. Gibb 1986 *Readings in small business*. Aldershot, Eng. : Gower.

Fitzroy, R. R., and K. Kraft 1990 Innovation, rent-sharing and the organization of labour in the Federal Republic of Germany. *Small Business Economics* 2 (2): 95–104.

Fritsch, M. 1991 The role of small firms in West Germany. In *Small firms and entrepreneurship : An international perspective*, eds. Z. J. Acs and D. B. Audretsch. Cambridge, Eng. : Cambridge Univ. Press.

Fritsch, M., and C. J. Hull 1987 Empirische Befunde zur Arbeitsplatzdynamik in grossen und kleinen Unternehman in der Bundesrepublik Deutschland — Eine Zwischenbilanz. In *Arbeitsplatzdynamik und Regionalentwicklung : Beitrage zur Beschaftigungspolitik*. Berlin : Edition Sigma.

Gallagher, C., and J. Doyle 1986 Job generation research : A reply to Storey and Johnson. *International Small Business Journal* 4 (4): 47–54.

Genesca, E. 1989 Evolucio de l'estructura dels costs i el financement empresarial. *Revista Economica de Catalunya*.

1990 Dinamica empresal en Cataluna. In *Manual de economica de Cataluna*, ed. Espasa-Calpe. Barcelona.

Gibb, A. A. 1983 The small business challenge to management education. *Journal of European Industrial Training* 7 (5): 3–41.

1987 Enterprise culture — its meaning and implications for education and training. *Journal of European Industrial Training* 11 (2): 2–38.

Gibb, A. A., and M. Scott 1986 Understanding small firms' growth. In *Small firms' growth and development*, eds. M. Scott et al. Aldershot, Eng. : Gower.

Gibb, A. A., and T. Webb 1980 *Policy issues in small business research*. Farnborough, Eng. : Saxon House.

Gill, J. 1988 Providing effective help for infant businesses in areas of high unemployment. *International Small Business Journal* 7 (1): 43–51.

Gray, C., and J. Stanworth 1986 *Allowing for enterprise : A qualitative assessment of the enterprise allowance scheme*. London : Small Business Research Trust.

Greif, S. 1989 Zur erfassung von Forschungs — und Entwicklungstatigkeit durch Patente. *Naturwissenschaften* 76 (4, April): 156–159.

Gudgin, G., and S. Fothergill 1984 Geographical variations in the rate of formation of new manufacturing firms. *Regional Studies* 18 : 203–206.

Hakim, C. 1989 Identifying fast growth small firms. *Employment Gazette* (January): 29–41.

Hankinson, A. 1984 Small firms' investment : A search for motivation. *International Small Business Journal* 12 (2): 11–24.

Haskins, G., A. Gibb, and T. Hubert 1986 *A guide to small firms assistance in Europe.* Aldershot, Eng. : Gower.

Hull, C. J. 1986 Job generation in the Federal Republic of Germany : A review. Discussion paper, Wissenschaftszentrum Berlin fur Sozialforschung, Labor Market Research Unit, September.

Hunsdiek, D. 1986 Financing of start-up and growth of new technology-based firms in West Germany. *International Small Business Journal* 4 (2): 10–24.

1987 *Unternehmensgrundung als Folgeinnovation — Struktur, Hemmnise und Erfolgsbedingungen der Grundung industrieller innovativer Unternehmen.* Stuttgart : Verlag C. E. Posechel.

Hunsdiek, D., and E. May-Strobl 1986 *Entwicklungslinien und Entwicklungsrisiken neugegrundeter Unternehman.* Stuttgart : Verlag C. E. Posechel.

Hutchinson, P. 1980 Financing small firms up to flotation : Research issues arising from a pilot study. In *Policy issues in small business research*, eds. A. Gibb and T. Webb. Farnborough, Eng. : Saxon House.

Johnson, P., and B. Thomas 1983 Training means (small) business : An economic evaluation of the new enterprise programme. *Employment Gazette* 91 (January).

Julien, P. A., and M. Marchesnay 1987 *La petite enterprise.* Paris : Vuibert.

Keeble, D. 1990 Small firms, new firms and uneven regional development in the United Kingdom. *Area* 22 (3): 234–245.

Kirby, D. 1982 Training and advisory services for the small retail business — the case for government action. In *Perspectives on a decade of small business research : Bolton ten years on*, eds. J. Stanworth et al. Aldershot, Eng. : Gower.

1984 Training for the small retail business : Results of a British experiment. *International Small Business Journal* 2 (3): 28–41.

1985 Research report : Managing with new technology — the results of a training program for women. *Journal of European Industrial Training* 9 (4): 27–32.

1986 The small retailer. In *The survival of the small firm*, eds. J. Curran et al. Vol. 1, *The economics of survival and entrepreneurship.* Aldershot, Eng. : Gower.

1990 Management education and small business development : An exploratory study of small firms in the U.K. *Journal of Small Business Management* 28(4): 78–87.

Kirby, D. A., and D. C. Mullen 1990 Developing enterprising graduates. *Journal of European Industrial Training* 14 (2): 27–32.

Lafuente, A., and V. Salas 1989 Types of entrepreneurs and firms : The case of new Spanish firms. *Strategic Management Journal* 10 (1): 17–30.

Lafuente, A., V. Salas, and R. Perez 1985 Financiacion rentabilidad y crecimiento de la nueva y pequena empresa espanola. *Economia Industrial* (November-December).

Lessem, R. 1982 Education for capability : Developing the new enterprise. In *Small business research*, eds. T. Webb et al. Aldershot, Eng. : Gower.

Loveman, G., and W. Sengenberger 1991 The re-emergence of small-scale production : An international perspective. *Small Business Economics* 3 (1).

Lynas, M. 1989 *United Kingdom Enterprise Management Research Association research register.* Durham, Eng. : Durham University Business School.

Martinent, A. C. 1983 *Strategie.* Paris : Vuibert.

Mason, C. 1985 The geography of "successful" small firms in the United Kingdom. *Environment and Planning A* 17 (11): 1499–1513.

Mason, C., and R. Harrison 1986 The regional impact of public policy towards small firms in the United Kingdom. In *New firms and regional development in Europe*, eds. D. Keeble and E. Wever. London : Croom Helm.

Mason, C., J. Harrison, and R. Harrison 1986 *Closing the equity gap ? An assessment of the business expansion scheme.* London : Small Business Research Trust.

NEDO 1986 Venture capital in the U.K. and its impact on the small business sector. London : National Economic Development Office.

O'Neill, K., R. Bhambri, T. Faulkner, and T. Cannon 1987 *Small business development : Some current issues.* Aldershot, Eng. : Gower.

Oppenlander, K. H. 1990 Investitionsverhalten und Marktstruktur — Empirische Ergebnisse fur die Bundesrepublik Deutschland. In *Markstruktur und gesamtwirtscheftliche Entwicklung*, ed. B. Gahlen, 253–266. Berlin : Springer-Verlag.

Papin, B. 1986 *Strategie pour la creation d'enterprise.* Paris : Dunod.

Preisendorfer, P., R. Schussler, and R. Ziegler 1989 Bestandschancen neugegrundeter Kleinbetriebe. *Internationales Gewerbearchiv* 37 (4) : 237–248.

Robbie, M. 1986 Small business requests for bank finance : Reasons for decline. In *Small firms' growth and development*, eds. M. Scott et al. Aldershot, Eng. : Gower.

Roger, Tym and Partners 1982 *Monitoring enterprise zones.* 1982, 1983, 1984, Years One, Two, and Three. Aldershot, Eng. : Gower.

Saporta, B. 1986 *Strategies pour la P.M.E.* Paris : Montchrastien.

Scase, R., and R. Goffee 1982 *The entrepreneurial middle class.* London : Croom Helm.

Schulenburg, J. M. G., and J. Wagner 1991 Advertising, innovation, and market structure : A comparison of the United States of America and the Federal Republic of Germany. In *Innovation and technological change*, eds. Z. J. Acs and D. B. Audretsch, 160–182. Ann Arbor : Univ. of Michigan Press.

Schwalbach, J. 1990 Small business in German manufacturing. In *Small business economics : A European challenge*, eds. Z. J. Acs and D. B. Audretsch, 63–73. Boston : Kluwer Academic Publishers.

Scott, M., A. Gibb, J. Lewis, and T. Faulkner, eds. 1986 *Small firms' growth and development.* Aldershot, Eng. : Gower.

Stanworth, J., and J. Curran 1986 Growth and the small firm. In *The survival of the small firm*, eds. J. Curran et al. Vol. 2, *Employment, growth, technology and politics.* Aldershot, Eng. : Gower.

Stanworth, J., A. Westrip, D. Watkins, and J. Lewis, eds. 1982 *Perspectives on a decade of small business research : Bolton ten years on.* Aldershot, Eng. : Gower.

Sternberg, R. 1990 The impact of innovation centres on small technology-based firms : The example of the Federal Republic of Germany. *Small Business Economics* 2 (2) : 105–118.

Stewart, H., and C. Gallagher 1985 Business death and firm size in the U.K. *International Small Business Journal* 4 (1) : 42–56.

Storey, D. 1986 Entrepreneurship and the new firm. In *The survival of the small firm*, eds. J. Curran et al. Vol. 1, *The economics of survival and entrepreneurship.* Aldershot, Eng. : Gower.

Storey, D., and S. Johnson 1986 Job generation in Britain : A review of recent studies. *International Small Business Journal* 4 (4) : 29–46.

1987 *Job generation and labour market change.* London : Macmillan.

Storey, D., K. Keasey, R. Watson, and P. Wynarczyk 1987 *The performance of small firms : Profits, jobs and failures.* London : Croom Helm.

Storey, D., R. Watson, and P. Wynarczyk 1989 *Fast growth small businesses : Case stud-*

ies of 40 small firms in northeast England. London : Department of Employment. Research paper no. 67.

Thietart, R. A. 1990 *La strategie d'enterprise.* N.Y. : McGraw-Hill.

Veciana, J. M. 1980 Un concepto empirico de mepresario. *Revista Economica de Banca Catalana* (56, March).

Veciana, J. M., ed. 1989 Creacio d'empreses. *Revista Economica de Catalunya* Special Issue (8–9).

Ward, R., and R. Jenkins 1984 *Ethnic communities in business : Strategies for survival.* Cambridge, Eng. : Cambridge Univ. Press.

Webb, T., T. Quince, and D. Watkins, eds. 1982 *Small business research.* Aldershot, Eng. : Gower.

Weimer, S. 1990 Arbeitsbedingungen in Kleinbetrieben — Einige Ergebnisse empirischer Forschung und neurer Entwicklungstendenzen. In *Kleinbetriebe im wirtschaftlichen Wandel*, eds. J. Berger, D. Volker, and M. Funder, 87–128. Frankfurt : Campus Verlag.

Westhead, P. 1989 A spatial analysis of new manufacturing firm formation in Wales. *International Small Business Journal* 7 (2) : 44–68.

Whittington, R. C. 1984 Regional bias in new firm formation in the U.K. *Regional Studies* 18 : 253–256.

Chapter

22

Research Issues in Entrepreneurship

Neil C. Churchill

●

In summarizing entrepreneurial research over the last 10 years, the story of the blind men encountering an elephant for the first time comes to mind. In 1980, entrepreneurship researchers, while sighted, were examining the "entreprencurial elephant" in very, very dim light. They were discovering that this animal was different; that it was composed of a number of rather unusual parts; and that there was quite a bit of it. Thus they spent their time describing the beast to one another and to the world at large, relating its similarities and differences to what they knew about animals in general and beasts of burden in particular.

By 1985, the intensity of the light had increased somewhat; the general shape of the elephant had been described; some probes had been made as to the nature of the different parts; and some questions of interest concerning some of these parts had been largely resolved (for example, the psychological characteristics of entrepreneurs and the relationships between entrepreneurship and small businesses). Excitement about the existence of elephants was running high; they were being viewed as a major stimulus to the economy, and the 1980s were being called (so to speak) *the decade of the elephant.*

Unfortunately, the light was still too dim to permit agreement on the overall size of the elephant; on the interrelation of its parts; and on what was going on under the surface of the skin. It was clear to everyone, however, that what was needed was more light and better instrumentation. Indeed, instruments, such as *longitudinal studies of movement and performance*, were called for, and a cry went out for the development and use of a *comprehensive theoretical framework* or, at the least, *causal linkages between the critical elements* of the beast. Additionally, some people were saying that *what we now need to do is to relate what we are studying to the performance of the animal*; and others were saying, *we need to know why some elephants perform better than others* (Kent, Sexton, and Vesper 1982).

By 1990, the intensity of light had increased significantly, and better instruments had been acquired, developed, and applied. Now the beast was seen to be enormous, and the scope of the research had broadened significantly: a number of research studies were examining the inner workings of the animal's different parts; a number were looking at the nature, efficiency, and range of its performance and the consequent effects on the economy; others were examining it and its relation to its environment; and still others were trying to describe its existence by examining the ecological system in which it lived. Most importantly, the elephant research community began to: *1) realize what it did not know; 2) structure its research in a way that permitted it to explore the basic shortcomings in its knowledge in order to build toward a full understanding of the animal; and 3) conduct its explorations in a more careful manner so that the results were extendable and not confounded by uncontrolled and unknown variables.*

In short, in 1980 the atmosphere was one of relatively unguided exploration; in 1985 the attitude was one of excitement, proselytizing, and a few breakthroughs; and in 1990 it was optimism and a maturing awareness of the size and complexity of the subject at hand.

This chapter looks at the research issues that were deemed important in 1985; evaluates the progress that has been made on these and other research fronts; looks at the new issues that have been identified in the years between 1985 and 1990; comments on our progress in understanding the field of entrepreneurship; and highlights some areas of particular challenge for the decade ahead.

■■ ■■ ■■ ■■ ■■ ■■ ■■ ■■

THE STATE OF THE ART
IN 1985

In 1985, although there was very little self-congratulation about how far the field had come, there was considerable excitement about the field's future. Some past developments, however, were specifically highlighted (Sexton and Smilor 1986), and these are briefly discussed below.

Accomplishments since 1980

While there was not total agreement within the research community, most researchers felt that considerable progress had been made in the following areas :

The psychological characteristics of the entrepreneur

A limited number of comparative studies had been studied, and inroads had been made into the development and validation of new test instruments. A few longitudinal studies had been started, and these provided new insights into the relationship between psychological characteristics and sociological factors (Brockhaus and Horwitz 1986).

Venture creation

A great deal had been done with regard to new venture creation, risk capital, and venture capital, and efforts were well underway at Babson College and other academic and business organizations to accumulate the data base necessary for large-scale, systematic longitudinal studies. As Brophy (1986) noted, research activity in new venture creation " . . . has recently moved beyond steps and stages to the development of models depicting interrelationships between the founders, the opportunity, and the necessary resources. Further, the research has moved well beyond the creation stage and into the causal relationships associated with growth." There were even some studies on the sociological aspects of venture initiation from both a specific and a broad policy perspective.

Entrepreneurship and small businesses

There had developed general recognition that the factor of "growth" separates the new venture creation of a small business from the new venture creation of an entrepreneurial firm (Wortman 1986).

The woman entrepreneur

As Hisrich (1986) observed, "The woman entrepreneur, an area open for research a few years ago, has now had her role problems, and motivations more clearly defined. . . ."

Risk capital

In this area, Wetzel (1986) noted that "it is likely that more has been learned about risk capital in the last five years than was discovered in the previous twenty-five years combined."

Corporate venturing

Commenting on a similar high-growth area, MacMillan (1986) remarked, "Corporate venture research has made significant strides."

Future Research Needs

Research methodologies

The majority of the suggestions for future research addressed specific topics that needed studying and areas where there were gaps in our understanding. A number of methodological needs, however, were highlighted by researchers. This is not surprising, for as Sexton and Smilor (1986, xxii) stated:

> The methodology or means by which hypotheses are proven or disproven, leading to the developments of constructs, paradigms, and theories, is an area that requires further development or sophistication as the body of knowledge on entrepreneurship expands. At any point in time in the search for knowledge, the measurement techniques, test instruments, and quantitative methods may range from simple to sophisticated. This occurs because various aspects in the search for knowledge have not progressed at the same rate. Consequently, the need for improved methodological approaches are never completely satisfied. However, this does not mean that researchers should become complacent with current or existing approaches. Rather they should search for more sophisticated techniques as required by a higher level of research effort.

Three methodological approaches were called for by a number of authors:

1. The development of models that illuminate the interrelationships of the various components of entrepreneurship — both internal and external environmental factors — to their ultimate effectiveness, financial success (Churchill and Lewis 1986).
2. The development of a comprehensive theoretical framework or paradigm of entrepreneurship so that research can build upon that of others and also can be replicated (Wortman 1986).
3. The need for longitudinal studies " . . . *to evaluate the impact of decisions or changing dimensions over time. . . .*" (Carsrud, Olm, and Eddy 1986).

Finally, to put these recommendations in perspective, an analysis of publications from 1981 through 1984 showed that just less than 10 percent of the studies involved field research and public data analysis, while surveys involved 33 percent (albeit some of them interview surveys in the field) and theorizing and "reportage" the balance (67 percent).

Almost every author indicated areas in which further research was needed. A number of suggestions were in four major areas: corporate venturing, venture capital, high-tech entrepreneurship, and the process of entrepreneurship. The recommendations for research in these areas, and in a number of additional areas, are described below.

Corporate venturing.

While there had been considerable research on corporate venturing since 1980, a number of fundamental questions were called out for further study

(MacMillan 1986; Hornaday 1986). A key question raised was, *What are the critical factors that aid or hinder the development and success of 'entrepreneurial entities' in large organizations?* Another central concern was the need to explore the causal linkages between corporate venturing variables and firm performance, and the need to conduct *multicase, longitudinal studies, particularly if we wished to tease out causal linkages between venture variables and venture performance.* Finally, the suggestion was made that those who study corporate venturing must *seek comparisons between good and poor performers, rather than study only the attributes of good performers.*

Some authors suggested that we needed, on the one hand, a definition of the nature, scope, and success of corporate ventures and, on the other, an understanding of *what enables the entrepreneur to move quickly and economically* into new opportunities and whether these factors are unique to entrepreneurial organizations or can be installed in large organizations.

Venture and risk capital

With the emergence of better data on the venture capital industry, a significant amount of progress had been made in this field. Considerable optimism was expressed on what studies using the newly developed data bases would reveal, and researchers were looking forward to the efforts then in progress towards *building data bases in this field which will permit large-scale, longitudinal studies.* Other research needs cited were: a determination of the factors critical to success in the venture capital industry; the ethical nature of venture capitalists' social responsibility to society and to the firms they finance; an understanding of when and how the venture capitalists intervene when a portfolio company begins to have problems; and the application and adaptation of modern financial economic theories to the venture capital process. Additional research needs included *case studies which embrace as many of the players (investor, venture capitalist, entrepreneur) as possible and record for analysis the viewpoint and position taken by each over time,* and studies of *the composition and functioning of the entrepreneurial team funded by venture capitalists* (Wetzel 1986; Bruno 1986; Brophy 1986; Kierulff 1986).

Brophy (1986) formulated the research issues around the different participants in the venture capital process:

- *Investor-related questions*: analysis of the performance of venture capitalists and the benefits to investors; analysis of investment strategies; and the effect of regulatory policies, taxes, and tax incentives on the flow of venture capital.
- *Intermediary-related questions*: venture capital management policies; decision-making processes; and incentive systems relative to performance.
- *Investee-related questions*: effects on the entrepreneurial performance of compensation systems; assessment of methods fostering innovation and technological development; the impact of venture capital on firm performance; and effective methods and processes of harvesting or cashing out.

The need for more research into informal risk capital was strongly suggested since so much less was known about this area than about the formal venture capital activities. One general call for research in this area was to develop concepts, theories, and hypotheses, particularly on the importance and role of individual risk capital investors. A third call was more specific, suggesting that:

> We need to learn the following about informal risk capital [IRC]: scale; personal characteristics of IRC investors; decision processes; characteristics of the information nets that link IRC investors; whether IRC is more or less expensive than professional VC; presence and/or role of lead IRC investors; the investing pattern of IRC investors; is it in competition or is it complementary to professional VCs; are financial intermediaries involved in placing IRC; and the effective methods for matching IRC investors and entrepreneurs. (Wetzel 1986)

High-tech entrepreneurship

The need for research into several aspects of high-technology entrepreneurship was noted in a number of papers. The specific research questions mentioned were: a better understanding of the technological transfer process and the innovation process from which high-tech ventures are created; a better understanding of the team formation process and the factors associated with stable and effective teams; the role and impact of incubators and their effects on later performance; and a better understanding of the principles of successful championing of technological innovation (Cooper 1986; Abetti and Stewart 1986; Myers 1986).

One author called for a better understanding of the key success factors in high-technology ventures, stating:

> New work in the field, however, needs to go beyond case studies and descriptive research to rigorous testing of conceptual models by measuring the relationship between the venture's financial success and such variables as the number of founders, the number of disciplines that the founding team includes, the average number of years of related experience, and the quality of their educational experience. (Maidique, 1986)

The process of entrepreneurship

The research needs in the process of entrepreneurship focused on *opportunity, environment*, and *performance*. For opportunity, the suggested research questions were: what enables an entrepreneur to move quickly and economically into new opportunities? How do entrepreneurs solve problems creatively? How do they accumulate information? What are the heuristics they use in "recognizing differences" in what they observe? Do they get personal satisfaction from solving problems or from influencing others to solve problems?

The research focus was toward understanding the environmental factors that shape the climate for entrepreneurship, including networks, sources of assistance, role models, and the actual and perceived risks and rewards. And on performance, the call was for understanding why entrepreneurs succeed or fail, and for determining the critical factors that aid or hinder entrepreneurial development and success.

Other Anticipated Research Needs

The psychology of entrepreneurs

Considerable progress had been made in this area between 1980 (Kent, Sexton, and Vesper) and 1985 (Sexton and Smilor). A number of comments were made indicating that further research in this field should include the context in which the entrepreneur was studied. It was noted that *we lack a generic definition of the psychology of the entrepreneur and the relationship of psychological traits to both the initiation and growth of new enterprises.* Another suggestion was that *it might be beneficial to concentrate our research efforts, not on the psychological characteristics of entrepreneurs, but on determining why they succeed or fail.*

Entrepreneurship and small business

This topic received some attention, with two suggestions as follows:

As the distinction between the two areas [small business and entrepreneurship] becomes more clearly defined and as the interface relationships are identified, the relationships between small business, emerging business (entrepreneurship), and large business (corporate entrepreneurship) should provide fertile ground for research efforts. (Wortman 1986)

The overriding factor for the development of both fields [entrepreneurship and small business] appears to be the need for comprehensive frameworks that provide the impetus for systematic research on all parts of both fields. (Churchill and Lewis 1986)

Other calls for further research.

Additional research areas highlighted were:

● Entrepreneurship and social networks
● More data on women-owned businesses
● The aspects of entrepreneurial organizations that are good for society
● Application and adaptation of modern financial economics theory to the venture capital process

━ ━ ━ ━ ━ ━ ━ ━
THE STATE OF THE ART
IN 1990

The atmosphere in 1990, as reflected by the chapters within this volume, was less one of excitement about what was going to happen than a guarded ebullience about what had been accomplished, an awed perception of the enormity of the entrepreneurial field, a dawning recognition of the breadth and nature of the research methodologies required, and a mature optimism of what work in the next few years would achieve.

Accomplishments since 1985

Considerable progress has been achieved in entrepreneurial research in the last half of the 1980s.

Increased understanding has been gained as to the economic effects of small and growing firms in job creation and innovation ; enough so that, as Acs and Audretsch (Chapter 3) suggest, *Europeans should abandon their cherished but unrealistic faith in economics of scale*, and institute a thoroughgoing reversal of current policy towards large firms, preferably coupled with support for venture capital and new start-up and small firms. This focus on entrepreneurship and economic growth in an international context is echoed in other chapters in this volume, notably the one by Hisrich (Chapter 20).

Increasing consensus has been attained on the concept of entrepreneurship as *the process of uncovering or developing an opportunity to create value through innovation and seizing that opportunity without regard to either resources (human and capital) or the location of the entrepreneur — in a new or existing company.* There is general agreement (with minor variations) on this concept of entrepreneurship among the authors represented in this volume.

Along with increased understanding of the nature and effects of entrepreneurship has come an expansion of entrepreneurial research at both the macro- and microlevels. The *macrofocus* has been on firm start-ups ; survival and growth ; job creation ; industry turbulence ; and firm failure rates. The extent of this research has been made possible by two important developments : the availability of data bases concerned with innovation and small-business growth, and the application of new theoretical tools (such as population ecology models) to the data. This research, in turn, is leading to improved and expanded data bases.

At the *microlevel*, there has been a wealth of information gathered from studies of entrepreneurs, their support groups (incubators, venture capitalists, bankers, family, and the like), and entrepreneurial organizations from pre–start-up, through growth, to death or harvest. These studies have approached the entrepreneurial area from a number of different directions, looked at many different aspects of the entrepreneurial process, and were conducted by examining (or too often surveying) a number of different and nonhomogeneous populations. The result is a number of varied but promising models or frameworks which are based on correlations between variables examined. What is lacking to date are well-developed theories for thinking about entrepreneurship based upon generalizable studies of causal relationships. We are just now beginning to comprehend what we do not know and what we must understand in the future. We are also increasing our use of research methodologies, such as longitudinal studies, which must be utilized if we are to understand the complex problems revealed by previous research.

Future Research Needs

Research methodologies

The methodological needs identified in 1985 were just beginning to be addressed in the late 1980s. Aldrich, discussing methodology in Chapter 8 of this volume, notes that most of the research still relies on survey data ; that longitudinal and other ethnographical studies have been slow to catch on ; that only a small proportion of the studies examined choose homogeneous populations ; and that cross-national research, while increasing, is still a low percentage of the total. Van de Ven, discussing longitudinal research (Chapter 9), notes that the linear research models commonly used may not be capturing important nonlinear aspects of the entrepreneurial phenomena under study, that the error terms may contain important signals, and that *the process of innovation may be characterized by chaos* (in the mathematical sense).

Progress on the research areas deemed important in 1985 is more heartening. Some comments on the changes are provided below.

Corporate venturing

Research in this area in the last five years has directly addressed many of the needs previously identified. Venkataraman, MacMillan, and McGrath (Chapter 19) assert that *we have much knowledge of the founding process (creating and developing the venture initiative and its infrastructure) and the factors influencing it.* However, the authors note that most of our information in the area of fostering and context managing (championing and managing the venturing process) comes from rich longitudinal case studies. These studies have yielded insightful and often counterintuitive propositions which can now be subjected to rigorous statistical tests. The authors state that we have a sufficient body of propositions to do cross-sectional work in these areas. However, the main roadblock facing the field of corporate venturing will remain the challenge of obtaining access to such cross-sectional data from large corporations.

Venture and risk capital

Research since 1985 has dealt directly with the research issues cited at that time. In Chapter 17 of this volume, Bygrave reports on extensive research using a venture capital data base. He cites several areas of work : venture capital flows and industry structure, investment decision processes and criteria, venture capital rates of return, venture capital strategies (fewer studies here), the roles and activities of venture capitalists, and the added value of venture capitalists — the area of most controversy. His quantitative findings on the rate of return to venture capital, the flows of money, and the interconnectedness of the venture capitalists now permit researchers to use this knowledge to test theories in this field.

Brophy (Chapter 15) summarizes the last decade by describing the significant progress in this aspect of entrepreneurship research over a 10-year period. He notes that we have achieved the compilation of relevant information on many aspects of the venture capital market and the development of analytical constructs which will be useful to us as we try to understand more fully the financing of new ventures. Finally, one of the issues in 1985 was the ethical nature of venture capitalists' social responsibility to society and to the firms they finance. While not addressing this venture capital issue directly, the issue of ethics and entrepreneurship are examined explicitly by Dees and Starr (Chapter 5).

Considerable progress has been made in understanding the nature and role of informal risk capital. Freear and Wetzel (Chapter 18) specifically address the four principal areas of further study that were set forth in 1985. These authors state that a great deal has been learned about the scale of the informal venture capital market, the characteristics of these investors, the information channels that are used, and the complementary relationship between investors and entrepreneurs.

High-tech entrepreneurship
This topic was not addressed separately in this volume as the emphasis has moved beyond the basic issues to topics of emerging importance. High-tech entrepreneurship is included in a number of the chapters related to growth. Slevin and Covin (Chapter 14) address high-tech firms in their review of the process of creating and maintaining high-performance teams; the nature and role of corporate champions in high-tech firms is part of the Venkataraman, MacMillan, and McGrath discussion of corporate venturing (Chapter 19); the high rate of job creation in high-tech by small firms is cited by Kirchhoff and Phillips (Chapter 10); the advantages in bringing innovations to market is discussed by Acs and Audretsch (Chapter 3); and funding high-tech ventures is a part of all the chapters on the research relevant to venture and risk capital.

The process of entrepreneurship
The research needs identified in 1985 for this subject area were both *micro* and *macro* in nature (Sexton and Smilor 1986). Research in both these dimensions is currently addressed by examining high-growth firms, since this growth factor seems to be becoming the distinctive factor between *small business* and *entrepreneurship*. Supporting this latter point, the research by Hoy, McDougall, and Dsouza (Chapter 13), looking at entrepreneurial strategies at the microlevel, reveals that *founders and CEOs can consciously choose high-growth strategies for their firms*, and that *growth can be planned and achieved regardless of stage of organizational life cycle and despite other constraints*. In summarizing the state of the art of research in this area, the authors note that *research on high-growth firms is increasing not only in the quantity of studies, but also in their quality.*

Cooper and Gascón (Chapter 12), also looking at research on the entrepreneurial process, find increasing output, considerable diversity in the studies, and considerable promise in the work — but not without some significant limitations. Chief among the latter are 1) a lack of findings related to environmental setting either directly or with regard to contingent effects; 2) the assumption of strong causal relations between the variables studied and the performance of the new ventures without considering external factors and random events; and 3) a focus on variables which are easy to measure but not necessarily the most important.

Research at the macrolevel on the entrepreneurial process has been done by Reynolds (Chapter 11), who examines new-firm births using both national and regional data. His results relate to both the research done on the psychological traits of entrepreneurs and on the work being done using models from population ecology. On the first point he states that three factors may affect an individual's decision to start a new firm: 1) the characteristics of the economic context; 2) the characteristics of the individual's life or career context; and 3) underlying personal disposition. Although individual disposition or traits may have an effect, if the major factors are related to context and life course stage, there will be little variance left to be explained by "entrepreneurial traits."

The second result of Reynolds's work is that birth and death rates on a regional basis seem positively correlated in both the United States and Japan. This finding is striking for, as he notes, the organizational ecology perspective leads to predictions of negative or no correlation between births and deaths. Reynolds shows that both sets of findings are probably accurate reflections of organizational phenomena, and that considerable conceptual work may be required to reconcile these differences. As he puts it, regardless of the findings from longitudinal studies of single types of organizations, when economic regions are the focus of analysis — "organizations beget organizations."

SUMMARY OF THE STATE OF THE ART IN 1990

My general impression of the state of the art in 1990 can be described as the dawning recognition of the breadth and complexity of what we call *entrepreneurship*. To some, entrepreneurship is an engine of social change that produces jobs, increases the effective use of resources, and causes local and even national revitalization. Research, for these individuals, involves studying all the factors that affect the birth of new ventures, their failure (death), and, often to a lesser degree, their growth. In an oversimplistic way, their focus is on the *start-up of a firm* and all the factors that influence this occurrence — such as the characteristics of entrepreneurs, the banking system, and regional development and educational centers — become appropriate objects of study.

A second group views entrepreneurship as being significantly, but not totally, different from the first group above. This group sees entrepreneurship as an engine of change in economic equilibriums. Here, the focus is on the factors that cause *innovations to be developed, recognized, and brought to market rapidly and efficiently*. For these individuals, the births and deaths of small microbusinesses are of little concern; corporate venturing is of considerable interest; high-tech firms are of great importance; and growth-oriented, value-creating companies fall within this purview since growth and successful innovation often go hand in hand. All factors that impinge upon recognizing, developing, and taking innovation to market fall within this research stream. Some of these individuals concentrate on factors that are, or have been, closely related to innovative organizations, such as venture capital firms, university incubators, corporate champions, and the like.

A third set of individuals looks at the entrepreneurial area as a new and fascinating arena in which to both *test and expand the concepts of their base discipline*. The goal of these individuals is to determine a) the applicability of what they know and b) how they might extend these concepts so that they apply to start-up, innovative, and very rapidly growing businesses (or units within a business) until they reach the size and maturity of the companies or other institutions or individuals upon which their disciplines have been developed. Individuals looking at how the disciplines of marketing, strategic management, organizational behavior, social networks, technology transfer, or the philosophy of ethics and the like either apply to or explain the entrepreneurial milieu fall into this category.

While there is considerable overlap in the areas of interest of these three groups — high-growth companies, the process of taking an innovation to market successfully, climates conducive to business start-ups, etc. — there are many aspects of the phenomena being studied that are different : the purpose of the research is different ; the population under study is selected differently ; the "lenses" used to view the problem and the language then used to describe the results are often discipline-specific ; and the research methodology is chosen to be appropriate to the purpose of the study. It is no wonder that it has taken over a decade of entrepreneurial research to recognize the enormity of the problem of understanding "the elephant."

CHALLENGES FOR THE 1990S

The overall challenge to entrepreneurship research is *understanding*. We have mapped the territory, at least domestically ; we have done exploratory studies (most of which are probing in nature) ; and we have begun to understand the breadth of the field. What is now called for is more attention to constructing more fully developed theoretical frameworks for predicting, explaining cause and effect relations, and guiding empirical testing. Aldrich has raised the issue of what research norms should be used in judging the progress in entrepreneurship : those of a unified science, a social science with multiple-conflicting views, or total pragmatism. Elements of each view find proponents among the authors represented in this volume. This could well be due to the diversity of the field and the different research agendas of the authors, as well as to the different stage of development of the particular area being studied.

Educational Issues

The appropriateness of this area has been underscored by Wilson L. Harrell in his foreword to this volume. He has said, "Unfortunately, too many colleges teach *that which was* and *not even that which is*, let alone *what will be.*" John E. Hughes, in his foreword, has echoed the same feeling: "Universities and teachers, if they are to be part of the thrust into the 20th century, must broaden their vision from public corporate America to the rapid-growing emerging private businesses that are the major contributors to growth in jobs and economic development in the United States."

Block and Stumpf (Chapter 2) have raised a number of significant issues regarding *what should be* in entrepreneurship education. Recognizing the breadth of the field, and suggesting that the audience for entrepreneurship education may be composed of students who wish to start a new business, entrepreneurs who wish to grow their businesses, managers of entrepreneurs, support people to the entrepreneurial community, and potential top managers who must provide vision and leadership in large organizations, these authors pose two particularly germane questions for entrepreneurial education:

1. Do sufficient discrete audiences for entrepreneurship education exist? Do they warrant the development of specific courses and course delivery systems tailored to each audience's learning objectives?
2. Are different entrepreneurship education learning objectives best accomplished (as measured by different criteria) through different instructor and student roles?

The implications of these observations are, in their own words, "mind-boggling," for among the "playful propositions" the authors put forth as stemming from these research questions are:

● Do students who have a burning interest in entrepreneurship do less well in school because they are different, because they are less intelligent, because they are less diligent, because they are less analytical, or because they don't fit the educational structure we impose upon them?
● Do they know what is good for them better than we do?(!)

Future Research Needs

Except for the international aspects of entrepreneurship — and expressions of the need to extend our research internationally have appeared in most of the chapters — no one area for future study has been singled out. Rather, the consensus is that the nature of the field calls for us to move forward on a number of fronts but, while doing so, to relate the research to what is going on, what has gone before, and to some relevant measure of entrepreneurial performance.

Broad criteria to guide our research have been suggested by Timmons and Sapienza (Chapter 16); these criteria seem to capture the general feeling: *does the research add to the intellectual capital in the field? Can it enhance both theory and practice, and be used in the classroom in ways that enhance curriculum and learning?* Hence our discussion of educational issues, above, seems especially relevant.

In looking at the ways in which research on entrepreneurship should be conducted, there is considerable agreement in a number of areas. These suggestions and challenges have been summarized in the following categories.

Problems of mind-set, discipline, methodological bias

Researchers bring to their studies a point of view or mind-set that has been formed by training in their discipline and the research questions with which they are concerned. This mind-set can influence both the data that is obtained and the way it is analyzed. The methodology used can also exert similar effects.

Sensitivity to the researcher's point of view is nowhere more important than in research into ethics (see Dees and Starr, Chapter 5), but it is also very relevant when a standardized questionnaire is used which asks entrepreneurs to recall their experiences of triumphs but to do so *in our words*, which can seriously distort the result. Aldrich (Chapter 8) states that the influence of the discipline can cause researchers *not to look at the phenomena being studied from the perspective of other disciplines — or even to avoid acknowledging their existence.* This danger is echoed by Venkataraman, MacMillan, and McGrath (Chapter 19), who observe that scholars from different disciplines approaching the area of corporate venturing too often fail to see the whole process. They assert that economists have for the most part studied the underlying market dynamics that foster innovation and entrepreneurship among firms while ignoring the organizational and political dynamics within firms. Organization theorists, on the other hand, have studied the organizational dynamics and politics in corporate venturing while ignoring the market dynamics.

Bias from the methodology used is also a problem. Van de Ven (Chapter 9) observes that multiple research models are often desirable, for *when scholars and practitioners have only a single perspective or theory, facts are often twisted and rationalized to fit the model.*

Finally, there is the danger that in a new and rapidly changing field, the researcher may not understand enough to ask the relevant questions. As Timmons and Sapienza (Chapter 16) note, ignorance of the realities and nuances of an industry and an unwillingness to engage in an "intellectual collision" with the real world can lead to extensive but meaningless research.

Environmental, cross-sectional, and contingent research

In commenting on the present state of research and on what is needed in the future, nearly half the chapters in this volume call for relating the research to environmental variables. Goodman, Meany, and Pate (Chapter 4) wonder what methods and solutions for the creation of new ventures are needed as cultures and national boundaries and policies change." Cooper and Gascón

(Chapter 12) recommend that more emphasis should be placed on contingency relationships. They note that research on environmental characteristics and new venture performance is clearly in its infancy, and that, for the most part, the direct and contingent effects of environmental characteristics upon new venture performance remain to be explored. They also observe that many studies of new ventures have drawn their samples from particular industries, but that the task of determining whether the resultant findings are contingent upon environmental characteristics has hardly begun. Hoy, McDougall, and Dsouza (Chapter 13) suggest that advancement of the field calls for further work to establish the contingent linkages between high-growth strategies and critical environmental variables.

The lack of research in this area is due in part to the difficulty of obtaining the necessary data. Venkataraman, MacMillan, and McGrath (Chapter 19) discuss the future of corporate venturing research and observe that we have a sufficient body of propositions to do cross-sectional work in these areas. As they put it, the main roadblock facing the field of corporate venturing is still going to be the challenge of gaining access to cross-sectional data from large corporations.

Unit of analysis

Just as there is a need for contingency research in the 1990s, so there is a need for care to be taken in choosing the population studied or surveyed (the unit of analysis) in order to obtain valid conclusions. Two problems arise. One is studying nonhomogenous populations and then writing a report that is, as Aldrich says, written as if the principles or generalizations were universal and could be safely applied to any industry. Aldrich further states that both units and levels of analysis are often chosen in a nonsystematic fashion and that too many surveys report results with low response rates.

The second problem is doing research on a nonrepresentative or too homogeneous subset of the population and then generalizing the findings. Cooper and Gascón (Chapter 12) cite the differing results one would obtain by choosing venture-capital-funded firms on the one hand, as opposed to discontinued firms on the other. Venkataraman, MacMillan, and McGrath (Chapter 19) state the need for research into systems of successful and unsuccessful firms if we are to understand corporate venturing.

Ethnography

Two of the most promising research methodologies for entrepreneurship research in the 1990s are analysis of the increasing number and quality of data bases and *ethnography*, which is described by Aldrich as direct field observation methods that have proven fruitful in anthropological and sociological studies. These methods permit detection of subtle features of social processes and interpretation of interactions which participants may be unable to articulate in an interview, and they enable the pursuit of interesting lines of data collection not considered prior to the field experience.

In his sample of methodologies used in current and past entrepreneurship research, Aldrich cited 11 field research studies, commenting that "some of these field studies were quite insightful, but that taken as a group they do not tap the rich potential of modern ethnographic methods." He further noted that in entrepreneurship research, where diversity in theory and methods is emphasized, no promising research strategy should languish unused. As he says, "the neglect of ethnographies is particularly troubling in a field whose very *raison d'être* is the dynamic response of creative individuals to turbulent social and economic conditions." Why, he asks, do we who "praise the exuberant entrepreneurs who skillfully manage economic chaos . . ." select as our research method of choice "*static, cross-sectional standardized questionnaires?*"

One ethnographic methodology of particular interest is that of longitudinal studies. These are recognized as powerful, demanding, and difficult to conduct given the tenure and promotion criteria of today's universities. But their applicability to entrepreneurship research was unquestioned for as Van de Ven (Chapter 9) notes, *inductive theory development efforts grounded in concrete and rich field observations are more likely to lead to significant new insights than deductive "armchair" theorizing approaches.* Researchers can greatly increase the likelihood of developing good, grounded theories by carefully observing new and existing methods for designing longitudinal research on the entrepreneurial process.

Data bases.

The value of data bases in the entrepreneurial area is unquestioned. The seminal work by Dave Birch on the level of job creation by small businesses sparked an enormous interest in the entrepreneurial field and demonstrated the value of these micro data bases. The rapid expansion of our knowledge in the venture capital area is due in a large part to the existence of the Venture Economics, Inc. data base. Development and improvement in regional and subregional data bases are permitting work on the causes of new business formation as Reynolds (Chapter 11) notes. The improvement of existing data bases and the founding and expansion of new ones is an exciting development for the 1990s.

Macro- and micromodels of entrepreneurship.

The use of population ecology models in the entrepreneurship literature has produced a stream of research that is, to say the least, controversial. While not an explicit topic in this volume, its relevance to entrepreneurship research as opposed to research into small businesses was questioned here. As stated earlier in this chapter, the research reported by Reynolds showing a positive correlation between firm birth and death rates contradicts the expectations of population ecology models. In examining potential reasons for this contradiction, Reynolds calls for a number of adjustments to the population ecology model; with the "density" in the population of different entities being one.

A second limitation of the population ecology model, described by Van de Ven (Chapter 9), is that the macropopulation perspective *eliminates the microscopic details needed to observe the complex process of entrepreneurship.* He further argues that population ecology models average over the varied behaviors of entrepreneurs when data is aggregated and differential equations are used to explain the changing populations inhabiting the system. Thus it is impossible to determine whether innovations emerge as a result of random variation or purposeful entrepreneurial activities.

Bygrave (Chapter 17) suggests that arguments between the population ecology model in which the success or failure of a start-up is determined by environmental events outside the entrepreneur's control, and the omnipotent strategist's model which holds that the entrepreneur determines his or her destiny, research on the venture capital firms themselves could shed a great deal of light and have tremendous practical implications.

Access and relevance.

Entrepreneurship research is a discipline that is close to the hearts of its practitioners. As Aldrich observes, *we will never escape our links to our constituency.* Being so close to the field does carry its own burdens, however, for we are deeply dependent on the entrepreneurial community for the subject matter of our research.

Because of this, Timmons and Sapienza (Chapter 16) make an important point when they call for research that is relevant to the various stakeholders in our efforts. For our results to be relevant, they assert, researchers must understand "the realities and nuances" of an industry. The consequences of ignorance, they warn us, are threefold: first, we risk thoroughly alienating the subjects of our inquiries, thus severing our access to data and interviews; second, we risk ridicule by those who are knowledgeable and informed about the industry; and third, we risk ridicule by researchers in other fields who might dismiss our work out of hand. As a result, we might end up crippling our efforts to build a "base of intellectual capital," causing "a resulting default of this topic to others."

This is a warning we should all heed as we head toward the exciting changes in entrepreneurship education and research in the 1990s.

■■ ■■ ■■ ■■ ■■ ■■ ■■ ■■

REFERENCES

Abetti, P. A., and R. W. Stuart 1986 Entrepreneurship and technology transfer: Key factors in the innovation process. In *The art and science of entrepreneurship*, eds. D. Sexton and R. Smilor, 181–210. Cambridge, Mass.: Ballinger.

Brockhaus, R., Jr., and P. Horwitz 1986 The psychology of the entrepreneur. In *The art and science of entrepreneurship*, eds. D. Sexton and R. Smilor, 25–48. Cambridge, Mass.: Ballinger.

Brophy, D. 1986 Venture capital research. In *The art and science of entrepreneurship*, eds. D. Sexton and R. Smilor, 119–144. Cambridge, Mass. : Ballinger.

Bruno, A. 1986 A structural analysis of the venture capital industry. In *The art and science of entrepreneurship*, eds. D. Sexton and R. Smilor, 109–118. Cambridge, Mass. : Ballinger.

Carsrud, A., K. Olm, and G. Eddy 1986 Entrepreneurship : Research in quest of a paradigm. In *The art and science of entrepreneurship*, eds. D. Sexton and R. Smilor, 367–378. Cambridge, Mass. : Ballinger.

Churchill, N. and V. Lewis 1986 Entrepreneurship research : Directions and methods. In *The art and science of entrepreneurship*, eds. D. Sexton and R. Smilor, 333–366. Cambridge, Mass. : Ballinger.

Cooper, A. 1986 Entrepreneurship and high technology. In *The art and science of entrepreneurship*, eds. D. Sexton and R. Smilor, 153–168. Cambridge, Mass. : Ballinger.

Hisrich, R. 1986 The woman entrepreneur : Characteristics, skills, problems, and prescriptions for success. In *The art and science of entrepreneurship*, eds. D. Sexton and R. Smilor, 61–81. Cambridge, Mass. : Ballinger.

Hornaday, J. 1986 The corporate entrepreneur revisited. In *The art and science of entrepreneurship*, eds. D. Sexton and R. Smilor, 265–269. Cambridge, Mass. : Ballinger.

Kent, C., D. Sexton, and K. Vesper, eds. 1982 *The encyclopedia of entrepreneurship*. Englewood-Cliffs, N.J. : Prentice-Hall, Inc.

Kierulff, H. 1986 Additional directions for research in venture capital. In *The art and science of entrepreneurship*, eds. D. Sexton and R. Smilor, 145–149. Cambridge, Mass. : Ballinger.

MacMillan, I. 1986 Progress in research on corporate venturing. In *The art and science of entrepreneurship*, eds. D. Sexton and R. Smilor, 241–264. Cambridge, Mass. : Ballinger.

Maidique, M. A. 1986 Key success factors in high-technology ventures. In *The art and science of entrepreneurship*, eds. D. Sexton and R. Smilor, 169–180. Cambridge, Mass. : Ballinger.

Myers, D. D. 1986 How many champions will an innovation cycle support ? In *The art and science of entrepreneurship*, eds. D. Sexton and R. Smilor, 211–220. Cambridge, Mass. : Ballinger.

Sexton, D. and R. Smilor, eds. 1986 *The art and science of entrepreneurship*. Cambridge, Mass. : Ballinger.

Wetzel, W., Jr. 1986 Informal risk capital : Knowns and unknowns. In *The art and science of entrepreneurship*, eds. D. Sexton and R. Smilor, 85–108. Cambridge, Mass. : Ballinger.

Wortman, M., Jr. 1986 A unified framework, research typologies, and research prospectuses for the interface between entrepreneurship and small business. In *The art and science of entrepreneurship*, eds. D. Sexton and R. Smilor, 273–332. Cambridge, Mass. : Ballinger.

Index

Note : page numbers followed by *f* denote figures ; those followed by *t* denote tables.

ABI/INFORM data base, 196, 201
Accumulation model, 489
Achieving Society, The, 89
Act VI (the Company Act), 543, 550
Act XXIV (Investments by Foreigners in Hungary Act), 550
Adhocracies, 142
"Adventure" capital, 252–53. *See also* Informal investment capital
Agency theory, 457
Aggressive entry, strategies of, 124–25
Airbus, 72
Allowing for Enterprise, 570
AMA Task Force on Marketing and Entrepreneurship, 168
American Assembly of Collegiate Schools of Business (AACSB), 20
American Marketing Association (AMA), 166
American Research and Development (ARD), 439

ANCE, national agency for assisting new business in France, 562
Angels. *See* Business angels
Annual rate of return (ROR), 424–25
Apple Computer, 147
Architectural innovation, definition of, 122
Association Act, 453
AT&T, breakup of, 79

Babalna-McDonald's Restaurant Ltd., as example of successful Hungarian joint venture, 550
Babson College Entrepreneurship Conference, The, 200
  papers of, 201–07
Bass model, 140
Bessemer Securities, 440
"Beta mania," 455
Birch, David
  and Dun & Bradstreet files, 244

597

Birch, David (*continued*)
  effect of 1979 study, 568
  studies of, 5, 45–46, 198, 280, 594
  summary of research, 245, 247–48, 249*t*, 264
Bit-maps, in time series analysis, 231–34
*Bolton Fifteen Years On : A Review and Analy-
    sis of Small Business Research in
    Britain, 1971–1986*, 569
Borland International, 91
Brophy, David, and research issues in venture
    capital, 583, 585, 587
Business angels, 11, 253, 390, 392, 420, 421,
    463
Business education, general research in, 18–19
"Butec," 62
Byte magazine, 91, 97

Caisse de Depot et Placement, 75
"Can-do" optimism, 97
Capital, availability to venture capitalists, 450
Capital Asset Pricing Model (CAPM), 346,
    455–56
Capital costs, tracking of over time, 10
Capital gains tax, debate over, 456–57
Capital gaps, 462–63, 481
Center for Entrepreneurial Studies, research
    study of, 22–23
Center for Research in Securities Prices
    (CRSP), The, and data base on new
    venture financing, 389–90, 397
Center for Venture Research
  continuing activities of, 482
  1988 study by, 465
Changemasters, 142
Chaos theory, in temporal data, 237–38
Chief technology officer (CTO), 150
Chrysler Corporation, 69, 73
Closing the Equity Gap ?, 570
Collective entrepreneurship, 366
Commercialization, of knowledge, 56
Committee of Inquiry on Small Firms, 568
Communist countries, and entrepreneurship,
    12
Comparative static methodology, 245, 246*t*,
    247
Competitive strategy, 119–27
  entry timing (order of entry), 120–24
  founding conditions, 120
  other, 124–25
  technology/innovation strategy, 126–27
Comprehensive/collaborative, as intervention
    approach, 150
Concept testing, 171, 172

Concurrency, in team creation, 367–68
Conflicts of interest, 99
Constellations, of cooperative relationships,
    131
Contagion, in corporate venturing, 490, 498
Continuous innovations, 172
Cooperative agreements, as strategic alterna-
    tive, 521, 525
Corporate venturing
  challenges faced by, 489
  conditions affecting, 489–90
  definition of, 488
  focus and key concerns of, 11, 488
  objective of defined, 514
  and technology, 492–94
Corporate venturing research, 487–515
  business challenge of founding, 490–502
  changing nature of, 488–90
  conclusions in, 514–15
  context of, 507–14
  framework for study of, 491*t*
  introduction to, 487–88
  political problem of fostering, 502–07
  vestige, 514
County Business patterns, 352
Cranfield Institute of Management, 568
"Creative destruction," process of, 218
Cross-licensing arrangement, as form of coop-
    erative agreement, 525
Current Business Survey (CBS), 264

Decade of the elephant, the, 579
Definition, in corporate venturing, 490
Digital Equipment Corporation (DEC), 439
Discontinuous innovations, 172
Diversification moves, 129
DOKA-Center, 61
Dun & Bradstreet
  data files of, 8, 46
  as data source for SBDB, 244
Dun's Market Identifier (DMI) files
  data use in high-growth research, 352
  data use in informal venture capital market,
    464
  data use in new-firm births, 284
  as prepared by Small Business Administra-
    tion, 273, 274
Durham University Business School, 568

Economic development, and impact of entre-
    preneurship, 45–63
  implications for public policy formulation, 9
  results of empirical research, 80–81
  role of entrepreneurship in, 5

Economic Report of the President (1989), 477
Economics of scale, European attitude toward, 586
Economist, The, 46, 60
Economy, as entrepreneurial-driven, 1
Educational acquisitions, 139
Educational and Psychological Measurement, 27
"Elephants," 280–81
Employers Large and Small, 46
Encyclopedia of Entrepreneurship, 194
Energy Related Inventions Program, 69
Enterprise Allowance Scheme, 570
Enterprise Statistics, 255
Entrepreneur, origin of word, 341
"Entrepreneurial elephant," 579–80, 590
Entrepreneurial euphoria, 97
Entrepreneurial research, 1–5
  areas in need of further research, 3
  factors in, 1
  as legitimate field of study, 4
  practical implications of, 2
  primary objective of, 2
  progress made in last ten years, 2–4
  See also Entrepreneurship research
Entrepreneurial sympathizers, 29–30
Entrepreneurs
  characteristics of, 304–10, 581, 585
  kinds of 28–29
  research suggestions on, 432
  as users of venture capital, 403, 419–22, 425
Entrepreneurship
  as academic discipline, 3
  activities engaged in, 341
  definition of, 586
  as dynamic and creative process, 4
  global reasons for, 2
  micro- and macrolevels of, 219
  main consequences of, 52–53
  study of, 7
Entrepreneurship and Regional Development, 342, 568
Entrepreneurship education research, 17–41
  areas of research, 4, 22–26
  audiences for, 19, 27–30
  history of, 17–22
  issues in, 591
  and new ventures, 18
  objectives of, 4–5, 30–35, 36*t*, 38
  possible studies in, 35–41
  practical application of, 19–20
  and teaching, 18
Entrepreneurship education, European, 560–573

Austria, 561–62
Belgium, 562
France, 562
United Kingdom, 568–69
Switzerland, 572
Entrepreneurship research, 579–95
  audiences for, 4
  change in atmosphere of, 12
  corporate venturing, 581, 582–83, 587
  ethics, 6
  ethnography, 202, 207
  high-growth companies, 9
  high-tech entrepreneurship, 584, 588
  individual entrepreneurs, 8
  longitudinal methods, 204, 214, 221–25
  marketing management, 7
  measurement, 225–36, 238–39
  new-firm population types, 8
  norms governing, 7, 199–207
  overall challenge to, 13
  population ecology approach, 216–17
  potential of international research, 12
  pressures and challenges to firms, 9
  process of entrepreneurship, 584–85, 586, 588–89
  psychological characteristics of the entrepreneur, 581, 585
  research methodology and scope, 201–07, 582, 587
  risk capital, 581, 583–84, 587
  small business, 581, 585, 588
  use by public sector, 4
  venture capital, 583–84
  venture creation, 581
  the woman entrepreneur, 581, 585
Entrepreneurship research, European, 560–73
  East Germany, 566–67
  France, 562–63
  Spain, 567–68
    characteristics of innovative Catalonian firms, 567
  United Kingdom, 568–72
    characteristics of entrepreneurs, 569–70
    entrepreneurial education and training, 571–72
    ethnic minorities, 570
    government support for small business, 571
    new-firm performance, job creation and regional variations, 570–71
    new venture financing, 570
  West Germany, 563–66
    entrepreneurship, 563–564
    government policies, 565–66

Entrepreneurship research, European (*continued*)
   high-technology firms, 564–65
   job generation, 563
   survival and growth, 565
Entrepreneurship research, problems in
  access and relevance, 13, 595
  choice of population, 593
  contingency relationships, 593
  data bases, 594
  environmental variables, 592
  ethnography, 593–594
  macro- and microlevels, 594–95
  mind-set, discipline, methodological bias, 592
Entrepreneurship research, trends in
  challenges for the 1990s, 590–95
  future research, 8–9, 207–210, 587–89, 591–95
  in 1980, 12–13, 192–94
  in 1985, 194–99, 580–85
  in 1990, 585–86
  summary, in 1990, 589–90
  summary, over the last decade, 199, 579–80
Epigenetic model, 489
Equity investments, U.S. venture figures, 11
Ethical virtues and values, 94*t*
"Ethic of change," 102
Ethics, 849–112
  categories of dilemmas, 96t
  definitions of values, 94–95
  entrepreneurial management, 92–93
  Hobbesian state of nature, 94
  implications for education, 112
  implications for practice, 110–11
  and Socrates' question, 93
  and trickster image, 91
Ethics, and ethical dilemmas, 93–103
  of entrepreneurial managers, 95–102
  of innovators, 100–02
  other, 102–03
  of promoters, 96–98
  of relationships, 98–100
Ethics research, 90–91, 103–09
  dimensions of, 103–04, 104*f*
    descriptive 107–08
    normative 103–07
    prescriptive, 108–09
    theory-building, 108
  implications for, 111–12
  need for, 90–95
Ethnic Communities in Business, 570
Ethnographies, 202, 207
"European Challenge," and 1992, 52–53

European Council for Small Business (ECSB), 561
European Community (EC), 551
European Economic Community, 12
European Foundation for Entrepreneurship Research (EFER), 561
European Foundation for Management Development (EFMD), 561
European Institute of Advanced Studies in Management (EIASM), 561
European Small Business Journal, 569
European Venture Capital Association (EVCA), 561
Event constructs, 229

"Farm system of venture portfolios," 421
Federal Reserve Board (FRB) study, and SBDB 254–55
Finance theory, and venture capital funds, 452, 455–56
Financial Statistics File (FINSTAT), 263
"Finders-keepers ethic," 102
Firm growth rate
  research issues in, 128
  trend in, 48–50
Firm survival, related to size, 51
First Chicago Investment Advisors, study by, 441
"First movers," 120, 121, 123. *See also* Innovators ; Pioneers
First Stage Capital, 413
504 loan program, 69
Flexible specialization, requirements and characteristics of, 55
Forcing, as a condition in corporate venturing, 490, 495–98
"Frankenstein's problem," 100
Freear and Wetzel studies
  and informal venture capital market, 11
  1989 study, 467, 468, 469, 470, 471, 473, 474, 475, 476*t*, 478, 484, 588
  1990 study, 468–69, 484, 588

"Garbage can" model, 493–94
Gaston and Bell study, 469
"Gazelles," 280, 281
General management, 146–51
  concerns of, 119
  leadership, 147–48
  succession planning, 150–51
  top management skills and experience, 148–49
  top management teams, 149–50
Gibrat's Law, 49, 344–45

GM-Toyota, as example of joint venture, 533
Golden age of entrepreneurship, 3
Government
  entreprenurial actions of, 5, 68–82
  forms and strategies of entrepreneurial activity, 5–6
  role in industrial development, 68–81
    Brazil, 79
    China, 72
    France, 70, 72, 73, 76, 77, 78, 79
    Germany, 70, 77
    Ireland, 70, 74, 76–77, 78
    Israel, 75
    Japan, 70, 73, 74, 75, 76, 77, 78
    Korea, 74, 75, 76, 78
    Mexico, 79
    Quebec, 72, 75
    Scotland, 70
    South Africa, 71, 73
    Taiwan, 74, 78
    Tanzania, 70, 71
    United States, 68–69, 70, 71, 73, 74, 77–78, 79
  subsidizing activities of, 76–77
  as venture capitalist, 72
Government intervention, reasons for, 81
Governments, and their role in industrial development
  research questions in, 81–82
Government-sponsored research, 77–78
Granger causality, 233
Groupe Bull, 71, 77, 537
Groupthink, 378–79
Growth firms, 344–45
Guerilla tactics, 100
Guide to Venture Capital Sources, 1987, 423

Hambrecht and Quist, 440
Hard currency, 70–71, 550
J. H. Heinz Company, example of successful joint ventures of, 538
Hermes, as patron of merchants, 91
Heuristics, as developed by managers, 134
High-growth firms, 341–53
  research on, 345–53
  strategy and environment of, 352–53
Honeywell, Inc., as example in joint venturing, 533, 537
Human resource managers, and problems posed by joint ventures, 542
Hungary, economic background of, 547–50

I. D. D. Corporation, as data base on new venture financing, 389, 397

Ideating, as a condition in corporate venturing, 490, 492, 494
Impression management, 97
Incident, definition of, 226–27
Incubators, 311–12
Industrial development, strategies in, 69–75
Industrial Market Structure and Economic Performance, 46
Industrial restructuring, in eastern Europe, 57–63
  challenges facing, 62–63
  Czechoslovakia, 58, 58*f*, 59*f*, 62
  East Germany, 57–58, 59, 60, 60*t*
  Federal Republic of Germany, 59–60, 60t
  Hungary, 60, 62
  Poland, 60, 61
  Soviet Union, 60–61, 62
Industry deregulation, and SBDB, 260
Informal investment capital, 253
Informal venture capital market, 462–83
  current research, 482–83
  external economics and public policy, 477
  individual investors and venture capital funds, 475–76
  information channels, 472–75
  international dimensions, 480–81
  introduction to, 462–63
  research agenda, 1985, 463–64
  research agenda, 2000, 483
  scale of, 464–65
  theories about, 478–80
Innovation
  architectural, definition of, 122
  as characterized by chaos, 587
  commitment to by European nations, 79–80
  diffusion of, 7
  key studies of, 57
  methods for tracking, 225–31
  nested, 144
  organizational designs for, 141–45
  as a process, 145–46
  and process theory, 216, 218–21
  of products, 378
  and skunkworks, 141, 142, 501
  and small firms, 50, 53
  strategic management and, 145–46
  strategies and flexibility, 54–57
  and the team, 377–78
Innovativeness, key to, 56
Innovators, 120
  conceptual framework of, 123–24
  See also First movers; Pioneers
INSEAD Business School, 536
Institutional investors, 10

Institutionalization, in corporate venturing, 490, 506, 512
Integrative strategy conceptualizations, in marketing, 181–82
Internal corporate joint ventures (ICJVs), 131, 142, 144
Internal rate of return (IRR), 442–46, 447*f*
  age of funds, 446, 447*f*
  annualized rates of return, 444
  calendar date, 445
  computation of, 442–43
  limitations of, 443–44
Internal venturing, as strategic option, 525
International Council for Small Business — Europe, 562
Internationales Gewerbearchiv, 572
International Informal Venture Capital Research Network, 483
International Small Business Journal, 568, 569, 570
Intrapopulation processes, 217
Intrapreneurial ventures, 525
Investment advisors, as intermediaries, 457
Investment decision processes, 427–28
Investment fund portfolio managers, 10
Investment process, in new venture finance, 393–96
Investor characteristics, 463, 465–72
  attitudes of, 470–71
  biographical profile, 466–67
  expectations of, 468–69
  market activity of, 467–68
  nonfinancial factors, 471
  overview of, 465–66
  VE and SEC investors, 471–72
  working relationships of, 469–70
Investors, individual
  and venture capital funds, 475–76
  See also Venture capitalists
"Invisible hand" approach, 507, 509–10
IPO market, 425, 445–46, 448, 449, 451
IPOs, venture-capital-backed, 10, 439, 442, 451, 453–55
Isolating mechanism, 122

Japanese firms, view of product development, 146
Japanese manufacturing, shifts in, 48
Job creation
  ecology of, 342–45
  and government intervention, 73
Job Creation in America, 248
"Job Generation Process, The," 245
Jobs, Steve, 147

Joint activities, as strategic option, 521, 526
Joint bidding activity, as most used joint activity, 526
Joint Economic Committee, 1988 study, 441–42
Joint venture(s)
  activities of, 11–12, 520
  definition of, 526
  factors promoting, 11
  government role in, 68–82
  historical perspective of, 526–27
  importance of data collection in, 12
  as method of market entrance, 544–47
    example of Hungary, 552*t*–55*t*
  reasons for forming, 12, 543
  as strategic alternative, 526
  strategic options in, 521–26
Joint venture research, domestic, 520–35
  directions for future research, 551, 556
  discussion of, 533
  general information on, 530–32
  high-tech joint ventures, 533–35
Joint venture research, international, 535–51
  in eastern Europe
    rules governing, 548*t*–49*t*
    significance of, 12
  examples of
    U.S. and Canada, 539
    U.S. and China, 535–36, 538–39, 540, 541, 543, 544
    U.S. and France, 537
    U.S. and Hungary, 540–41, 543–44, 547, 550–551, 552*t*–55*t*
    U.S. and Japan, 537, 540, 541
    U.S. and Poland, 544
    U.S. and Soviet Union, 536, 538, 540, 541, 543, 544
    U.S. and Taiwan, 544
    multinational joint ventures, 537–38, 542
Journal of Business Venturing, 201, 342
Journal of Commerce, 257
Journal of Educational Psychology, 26
Journal of Marketing, 168
Journal of Retailing, 168

Kapra, Fritz, 82
Keynesian economic fluctuations, profound challenge to, 54
KNO-Studiecentrum Small Business Research Institute, 562
"K-strategy," 280

Labor market, as analytical tool, 283–89
LBO/acquisition stage investment, 417

"Lead" investors
  existence of, 482
  significance of, 473
Learning cycle model, 139
Liabilities of adolescence, 129
Liability of newness, 129
Limited partners
  and computation of residual value, 443
  research suggestions, 431–32
  as suppliers of capital, 10, 403, 414, 419,
    423, 424–25
  and venture capitalists, 457
Link joint ventures, in transaction-cost the-
    ory, 532
Loan Guarantee Scheme, 570
Longitudinal analysis, and SBDB research,
    248, 249–52
Longitudinal methods, in study of entrepre-
    neurship, 214–39
Longitudinal research
  design issues in, 7–8
  methods in entrepreneurship research, 204,
    214, 221–25
  MIRP field work on innovation, 220–39
  and SBDB, 8
  and USEEM small business data, 352
Longitudinal studies, of organizational popu-
    lations, 289

Macro-population dynamics, 217
Management education, criteria for, 20–22
Management research, survey of cross-
    connections, 6
Managerial perspective, on corporate ventur-
    ing, 488–503, 505–15
Managers
  and autonomy and control, 511–12
  and championing resources, 505
  in context of corporate venturing, 507
  of entrepreneurs, 29
  and forcing, 497
  and fostering, 502–03
  and ideating, 492–94
  and maintaining efficiency and innovation,
    501–02
  and pathclearing, 511
  and production of variations, 509
  and retention of ventures, 512–14
  and rollercoasting, 498–500
Marketing, 164–86
  and company mission, 169–70
  defining the domain, 164–65
  and development of theory, 183
  and entrepreneurship, 166, 168–69

and implementation and control, 182–83
Hills' survey in, 165
issues in, 165–66
managerial perspective, 165–66, 167
and marketing strategies, 7, 174–82
  business, 178
  conceptualization of, 174–76
  corporate, 176–78
  distribution, 180–81
  price, 180
  product, 178–80
  promotion, 180
and market opportunity analysis, 7, 170–74
and venture capitalists, 165
"Marketing concept," first articulated, 169–70
Marketing management, and entrepreneurship
    research, 7
Marketing research, 183–86
  future directions, 183–86
  interface with entrepreneurship, 166–68
  research/plans, and entrepreneurs, 172–74
"Market morality," 91
Market opportunities, in successful business
    creation, 7
Market testing, 171–72
McClelland, David, 89
Measurement, definition of, 226
Mergers and acquisitions (M&As)
  as strategic option, 521, 522*t*–24*t*, 525,
    528*t*–29*t*
  Tokyo Conference on, 538
Microentrepreneurial processes, 217
Ministry of International Trade and Industry
    (MITI), 70, 76, 78
Minnesota Innovation Research Program
    (MIRP), 7, 97, 145
  and longitudinal field work on innovation,
    220–39
  overview of research design, 221–25
Minority investment, as strategic option, 521,
    525
Minority-owned firms, and SBDB, 254
"Missing-the-boat" risk, 176
Moral ambiguity, 95
Moral conflict, 95
"Moral muteness," 110
"Moral point of view," 106

National Institute of Standards and Technol-
    ogy, 69
National Small Firms Policy and Research
    Conference, 569
Nested innovation, 144
Networking, 312–13

Networks, informal, importance of, 472, 473
New corporate ventures, 142–43
New-firm births, 268–94
  factors in founding, 8
  major population analyses of, 271–92
    human populations, 289–92
    industry type, 276–81
    national level, 272–76
    subnational level, 281–89
  summary of, 292–94
New firms, problems in literature, 303–04 *See also* New ventures
New product development, 7
New product teams, 142
Newstreams, of innovation, 141
New technology-based firms (NTBFs), 468, 469, 474, 475, 476*t*, 483
New venture, risk assessment of, 176
New venture creation, 3
New venture financing, 314, 387–99
  conclusions in, 398–99
  methodological advances, 388–90
  performance monitoring, 396–98
New venture investors
  characteristics of, 391–92
New venture research
  conclusions in, 316–18
  implications for, 318–19
  introduction to, 301–02
  predictors of success in, 392–93
  previous research in new venture financing, 387–88
  review of research in new venture financ-ing, 9–10, 390–98
New ventures
  and economic re-structuring, 78–80
  environmental characteristics, 316
  frameworks for examining, 302, 325, 326
  and government, 69, 70–75, 80
  industry characteristics, 315
  market entry strategies, 176–77
  mission of, 169–70
  processes of founding, 310–14
  review of literature, 302–04, 327–39
  study of as a process, 7
  and team formation, 313
  See also New firms

Omnibus Trade and Competitiveness Act (1988), 477
Organizational ecology, 276, 278–79, 280–81, 289
Organization for Economic Cooperation and Development (OECD), 52, 54, 62
  study by, 542–43

"Other-directedness," 91

Penetration, in corporate venturing, 490, 497, 498
"Penrose effects," 128
Personal-social conflict, 95
Pioneers, 120, 122–23. *See also* First movers ; Innovators
Population ecology
  as approach to entrepreneurship scholar-ship, 216–17
  and ecology of job creation and growth, 343–44
  in entrepreneurship research, 458
  and literature on organization ecology, 278–81
Port Import-Export Reporting System (PIERS), 257
Porter and McKibbin study, final conclusions of, 20
Postma and Sullivan study, 469
Pragmatic perspective, 98
Pratt's *Guide to Venture Capital Sources*, 413
Process theory
  of entrepreneurial process, 7–8
  to explain innovation development, 216, 218–21
  and longitudinal field research by MIRP, 220–21
Product diversification strategies, 177–78
Product use testing, 171–72
Prospect theory, 134
Prudential tension, 95
Public Law 96–302 (Small Business Economic Policy Act, The), 262
"Punctuated equilibrium" model, 218

Q.E.D. Research Corporation, and study of new venture funding, 392–93
Qualitative data file, 226, 227, 228*t*
Qualitative datum
  definition of, 226
  use of, 227
Quantitative datum, definition of, 226

R&D partnerships, as strategic option, 521, 526
Rbase System V software, use with qualitative data files, 227
Regression analysis, of a time series, 233, 234–36
Regression models, in prediction of new-firm births, 277–78, 286*t*–87*t*, 287–88
Regulatory policy, and SBDB, 262–63
Renewal Factor, The, 359

Research in Higher Education, 27
Research linkages, framework for, 118*f*
Resource exchange model, 450, 453, 456
Resource exchange theory, 448–49, 458
Retail trade and manufacturing, and SBDB, 261–62
Revista Economica de Catalunya, 568
Revitalizing, as a condition in corporate venturing, 490, 500–01
ROI requirements, 421
Rollercoasting, as a condition in corporate venturing, 490, 498–500
"R-strategy," 280

Sampling frame, and SDBD, 252, 253, 254, 258
Scale joint venture, in transaction-cost theory, 532
Schumpeter, Joseph
early work on innovators, 120, 121
importance of technology to competitive advantage, 126
overview of ideas, 214–19
relation of technological ideas and economic development, 145
Schumpeterian rents, 121, 128
Schumpeterian terms, 93
Science Policy Research Unit (SPRU) Innovation Data Base, 50, 55
Scottish Enterprise Foundation, 568
SEC investors, 471–72
SELAGGR, computer software program for raw event sequence data files, 233–34
Self-renewal process, and innovations, 141
Sematech, 69
"Sense making," 493, 497
Sequence analysis, 231–36, 238–39
7a loan program, 69
and SBDB, 253, 255
Short-run analyses, 248–49
"Sinking-the-boat" risk, 176
Sino-U.S. joint ventures, 538
Skunkworks, use of in innovation, 141, 142, 501
Small- and medium-sized firms (SME), 48, 49*t*
Small business, role in entrepreneurship research, 166
Small Business Data Base (SBDB), 51, 243–64
as control group, 255
as different from other government data bases, 243–44
greatest value in longitudinal analysis, 248, 249–52
and financial applications, 252–59
and job creation research, 244–52

as macroindicator of U.S. economy, 255–59
in new-firm births analysis, 285, 293
in studies of industry restructuring, 259–63
usefulness of, 8, 243
use in employee benefits policy application, 258–59
use in federal and state industry regulations, 259
use in federal procurement, 259
use in regional economic development studies, 258
Small-business-dominated industry concept, 257
Small Business Economic Policy Act, The (Public Law 96–302), 262
Small Business Economics, 342
Small Business Economics, an International Journal, 567
Small business. *See* Small firms
Small Business Forum, 342
Small Business Health Index (SBHI), 257
Small Business Innovation Development Act (1982), 477
Small Business Innovation Research (SBIR) Program, 69
Small Business Investment Act of 1958, 462
Small business investment companies (SBICs), 10, 410, 440, 441
Small Business Investment Company (SBIC) Program, 462
Small Business Investment Incentive Act (1980), 477
Small Business Research Trust, 569
Small firms, 45–63
earnings gap in, 53–54
in eastern Europe, 5
economic role of, 5, 48–52
employment share of, 50–51
high-technology example of, 55
importance in Europe and Japan, 53
importance in job creation, 5, 45–46
critique of job creation, 53
in European job creation, 54
international research on, 52
importance of capital and liquidity constraints, 50
importance of a technology strategy, 55–56
example of Japan, 56
importance to world economy, 12
and innovation, 50, 53
rate of births and deaths, 275*t*
trend toward, 46–48, 49
and turbulence, 63
Small high-technology firms, and SBDB, 260–61

Small manufacturing firms, 47f, 51–52, 53
Socialist governments, and entrepreneurship, 12
Societe Developmente Regionales (SDR), 76
Soul of a New Machine, The, 360
Spin-offs, as area of research in corporate venturing, 514–15
Standard Industrial Classification, 49
 in industry births data, 294
Standard Metropolitan Statistical Areas (SMSAs), 284
State of the Art Conferences, 1981–1985, 7
State of Small Business : A Report of the President, The, 248, 257
Stern School of Business, 22, 37
Stevenson-Wylder Technology Innovation Act (1980), 477
Strategic management, 119–46
 categories of, 119
 definition of, 119
 and entrepreneurial studies, 6
  strategy content, 119–33
   competitive strategy, 119–27
   corporate strategy, 127–33
  strategy implementation, 141–46
   innovation process, 145–46
   organizational designs for innovation, 141–45
  strategic processes, 133–41
   diffusion of innovations, 140–41
   organizational learning, 137
   risk and uncertainty, 136–37
   strategic planning, 134–35
   strategic planning literature, 135
Strategic Management Journal, 146
Strategic windows, 124
Strategies for learning, 138
Strategist model, 458
Levi Strauss, and Hungarian factories, 550
Structural change, in economic development, 78–80
Swiss Research Institute of Small Business, 572
Synergy, qualitative effect of, 521

Tao of Physics, The, 82
Taplin and Montle Development Fund, case study of, 473
Tax incentives, and research spending, 78
Tax Reform Act of 1986, The, 416
Teams, high-performance, 358–82
 background of, 360–62
 concurrency in, 367–68
 creation of, 366–67
 and cross-functional cooperation, 375–76

determinants of team creation, 363–64
determinants of team performance, 364–66
and followership, 374–75
and human resource management policies, 370–72
implications for, 381–82
and information technology, 376
interdependence of, 370
introduction to, 358–60
key research questions in, 379–81
organizational structure, 368–69
problems with, 378–79
and process innovation, 377–78
and product innovation, 378
and project team management, 372–74
research model in, 363t
role in commercialization process, 369–70
and role of redundancy, 376–77
Team members, types of, 374–75
Techno-business management, 127
"Technology commercialization," 534–35
Theory of change, 219, 219t
Theory of equilibrium, 219, 219t
"Third Italy," 55
Timmons and Stevenson survey, 90–91, 109, 111
Transactional ethics, 99–100
Transaction-cost economics, 457
Transaction-cost theory, 532
Turbulence
 analyzing pattterns of in temporal data, 236
 definition of, 51
 in new-firm births, 292, 293
 and small firms, 63

U.K. National Smalls Firms Policy and Research Conference, 568
Unions, and innovation, 53
United kingdom, and economic revival, 53
United Kingdom Enterprise Management Research Association Research Register, 569
University of Economics and Business Administration, 561
University and Small Business Patent Procedure Act (1980), 477
Untermensbeteiligungsgesllschaften Act, 566
U.S. businesses, estimate of number of, 272t
U.S. employment, expansion of, 1
U.S. Establishment and Enterprise Microdata File (USEEM)
 in longitudinal small business data, 352
 as most often used, 243
U.S. Establishment Longitudinal Microdata

File (USELM), as unique data base, 243

U.S. Small Business Innovation Data Base, 50

Value added, notion of in venture capital research, 458
Valued Added Tax (VAT), and new-firm registrations, 288
Vector autoregression, 233
Venture capital, 402–58
  and compound annual rates of return, 440t
  and economics, 456–57
  factors in declining returns, 442, 447–48
  rates of return, 428
    statistical information on
      Asia (Australia), 419*f*
      Asia (Japan), 410*f*
      Canada, 415*f*, 421*f*
      Europe, 410*f*, 415*f*, 419*f*, 421*f*
      USA, 406*f*, 407*f*, 411*f*, 412*f*, 413*f*, 414*f*, 418*f*, 420*f*
      worldwide, 408*f*, 409*f*, 417*f*
Venture capital, informal
  data sources of, 11
  importance of in general venture capital market, 11
Venture capital, policy issues in, 425–26
Venture-capital-backed IPOs, 10, 439, 442, 451, 453–55
Venture capital firms (VC firms)
  and "boutiques," 413, 423
  characteristics of successful, 10
  competition among, 414–15, 416*f*
  and "department stores," 413
  global presence of, 405–09
  growth of, 402–03, 404–11
  investment preferences of, 412–13
  issues facing, 423–26
  "old boy" network of, 403
  performance of, 422
  sophistication in, 419–22
  specialization of, 409–11
  strategies of, 416–19, 428–29
  summary of, 423
Venture capital flows, 426–27
Venture capital fund managers, 10
Venture capital industry
  challenges in the 1990s, 10
  introduction to, 402–04
  issues in the 1980s, 404–23
  issues in the 1990s, 423–26

and resource exchange model, 448*f*
Venture capital investment market, 10
Venture capitalist, government as, 72
Venture capitalists, 10
  availability of, 450–51
  See also Investors, individual
Venture capital market, informal, 11
Venture Capital Network, Inc., as data base on new venture financing, 390
Venture capital partnerships, beginnings of, 10
Venture capital research
  cautions in, 433–34
  issues in 583, 585, 587
  issues in venture capital returns, 455–57
  on roles and activities of venture capitalists, 429–30
  suggestions for VC firms, 432–33
  suggestions for venture capital, 433
  and value added, 430–31
  on venture capital industry, 426–34
Venture capital returns, 438–58
  actual rates *v.* folklore, 442–48
  conclusions in, 457–58
  historical rates of return, 439–42
  introduction to, 438–39
  and IPOs, 453–55
  model for, 10
  and resource exchange theory, 448–53
Venture Economics, Inc.
  as data base, 389
  investors, 471–72
  on new venture financing, 397
  rates of return data base, 442, 444
  sample, 471–475
Venture idea evaluation, 171–72
Venture idea identification, 170–71
Venturing process, conditions of, 11
Ventures, hybrid models of, 131
Vertical integration, argument for, 497
Vestige, in corporate venture research, 514
"Virgin angels," 481, 483
"Visible hand" approach, 502, 507, 509, 510, 511

Women entrepreneurs
  research on, 581, 585
  scholarship on, 3
Women-owned firms, and SBDB, 254

Zero Stage Capital, 413
ZZZZ Best, collapse of, 91